*The Spanish Frontier
in North America*

The Spanish Frontier in North America

DAVID J. WEBER

YALE UNIVERSITY PRESS
NEW HAVEN AND LONDON

Designed by Nancy Ovedovitz and set in Janson
type by The Composing Room of Michigan, Inc.,
Grand Rapids, Michigan. Printed in the United
States of America by Hamilton Printing Company, Castleton, New York.

Library of Congress Cataloging-in-Publication
Data

Weber, David J.
    The Spanish frontier in North America /
    David J. Weber.
        p.   cm. — (Yale Western Americana series)
    Includes bibliographical references and index.
    ISBN 0-300-05198-0 (alk. paper)
    1. Southwest, New—History—To 1848.
2. Southern States—History—Colonial period,
ca. 1600–1775. 3. Spaniards—Southwest, New—
History.   4. Spaniards—Southern States—
History.   I. Title. II. Series.
F799.W42 1922
975′.02—dc20   92-6657
                                              CIP

A catalogue record for this book is available from
the British Library. The paper in this book meets
the guidelines for permanence and durability of
the Committee on Production Guidelines for
Book Longevity of the Council on Library Resources.

10   9   8   7   6   5   4   3   2   1

Publication of this book is supported by grants
from the Program for Cultural Cooperation Between Spain's Ministry of Culture and United
States' Universities, from the Summerlee Foundation, Dallas, Texas, and from Southern Methodist University's ULS Fund for Faculty Excel-
lence.

Compadre, I entreat you to do me the favor of taking my son Antonio among your troops, that when he is old, he may have a tale to tell.
Fulano de Escobedo to Alonso de León,
Coahuila, circa 1690

Contents

Illustrations

Maps

Acknowledgments

In writing this book I have depended indirectly on the research of numerous scholars, whose work is acknowledged in the notes and bibliography, but I have also imposed directly on many colleagues. Some have helped me by reading related manuscripts or by answering my persistent questions—most notably James Axtell of the College of William and Mary; Susan Deeds of Northern Arizona University; Bernard Fontana of the University of Arizona; Ross Frank of American University; Ramón Gutiérrez of the University of California, San Diego; Elizabeth John of Austin, Texas; John Kessell of the University of New Mexico; Jane Landers of the University of Florida; Gene Lyon of Flagler College; Gerald Poyo of Florida International University; William Swagerty of the University of Idaho; and David Hurst Thomas of the American Museum of Natural History. Others generously reviewed portions of my manuscript. All have saved me from mistakes and forced me to think harder, and I hope that each knows the extent of my gratitude even though I have sometimes ignored their counsel.

Peter Onuf, my former colleague at Southern Methodist University and now professor of history at the University of Virginia, asked smart questions, critiqued many of the chapters, and bolstered my flagging confidence. Harry Kelsey of Los Angeles scrutinized the chapter on exploration, teaching me to mistrust translations and to be wary of alleged reproductions of maps. Amy Turner Bushnell of the University of California, Irvine, generously guided me into the bibliography on the southeastern borderlands and read the chapters on the sixteenth and seventeenth centuries. William Coker of the University of West Florida and Light Cummins of Austin College gave me equally generous guidance to sources on the eighteenth-century South and reviewed the relevant chapters. Jack S. Williams, while completing his doctorate at the University of Arizona, afforded me the benefit of his knowledge of Spanish military policy and practice; Iris Engstrand of the University of San Diego examined my treatment of early California; Richard White of the University of Washington reviewed the section on environmental and societal change; and John Chávez of Southern Methodist University critiqued the final chapter.

Several people read the manuscript when it was three-fourths completed and bulky enough to require a substantial investment in time: Donald E. Chipman of North Texas State University and Oakah L. Jones of Purdue University, each with wide-ranging knowledge of the Spanish frontier; my mentor, Donald C. Cutter, professor emeritus at the University of New Mexico, who excited my interest in Spain in North America and launched me into the academy with invaluable advice; and my good friend Marc Simmons, the savant of Cerrillos, New Mexico, who has unflinchingly screened my manuscripts for the last quarter century. Among academics, only Paul Hoffman of Louisiana State University had inflicted upon him the task of critiquing the entire manuscript from end to end—which he did with intelligence, sensitivity, and dispatch.

In addition to acknowledging the remarkably generous help of specialists in the field, I also want to express my appreciation to two experts in hardware and software, William Cronon of Yale and William Rosenthal of Fort Worth, who patiently helped me acquire minimal competence in the processing of words and the construction of databases.

At the Center for Advanced Study in the Behavioral Sciences at Stanford, where I began this book in 1986–87 with financial support from the Andrew W. Mellon Foundation, I am particularly grateful to Gardner Lindzey, Robert Scott, Kathleen Much, and Carol Treanor, and to fellow Fellows, particularly Keith Baker, David Kennedy, and Robert Netting.

In Madrid, where I spent the academic year 1989–90, Pepe Varela and Magdalena Mora provided a quiet and congenial place to work at the Fundación Ortega y Gasset, and Taine Carrozza of Dallas braved the inconveniences of airport security and U.S. customs to shuttle books back and forth across the Atlantic for me.

A welcome fellowship from the National Endowment for the Humanities in 1990–91, gave me priceless time to complete the manuscript, which I acknowledge with gratitude.

Throughout the research and writing of this book, I have received superb support from my own institution and colleagues. Southern Methodist University's generous triennial leaves have enabled me to make maximum use of fellowships; deans Hal Williams, Buddy Gray, and Narayan Bhat, together with Chairman Dan Orlovsky

and my other colleagues in the History Department, have offered warm encouragement and borne the burden that my absences inevitably caused; and the splendid
resources of the DeGolyer and Fondren libraries and the efficiency of Billie Stovall in
our interlibrary loan office, saved me costly and time-consuming travel to other
collections. Finally, the resources of a chair in history at Southern Methodist University, generously endowed by Robert and Nancy Dedman of Dallas, have facilitated my
work beyond measure. Those resources have funded a research assistant, the intrepid
Jane Lenz Elder, who has expeditiously overseen numerous details of research and
manuscript preparation.

At Yale University Press, Executive Editor Charles Grench provided wise counsel
and unflagging enthusiam, and the judicious Jane T. Hedges scoured the manuscript
with a keen eye for detail. Don Bufkin of Tucson, whose maps have graced so many
works of Americana over the last forty years, did me the favor of preparing all the maps
in this volume, and Laura Moss Gottlieb of Madison, Wisconsin, prepared the index.
The Summerlee Foundation in Dallas spearheaded by the veterans of the 1991
Monterey-Saltillo campaign, David Jackson, John Crain, and Ron Tyler, provided a
handsome and much appreciated subsidy to defray the costs of publishing this large
book.

Thanks also to the Smithsonian Institution Press, which published portions of
chapter 4 as "Blood of Martyrs, Blood of Indians: Toward a More Balanced View of
Spanish Missions in Seventeenth-Century North America," in *Columbian Consequences*, vol. 2: *Archaeological and Historical Perspectives on the Spanish Borderlands East*,
ed. David Hurst Thomas (Washington, D.C.: Smithsonian Institution Press, 1990),
and to the *Western Historical Quarterly*, which published portions of chapter 12 as
"The Spanish Legacy in North America and the Historical Imagination," 23 (Feb.
1992): 4–24.

As any parents will appreciate, our children, Scott and Amy, assisted immeasurably
by growing up, leaving home, and turning into resourceful, independent adults. Instead of leaving home while I wrote this book, my wife, Carol Bryant Weber, did the
next best thing. She went to law school. She began and finished a law degree, passed
the bar, and launched a new career while I muddled along with this single project. She
also read each chapter of this book for style and meaning—qualities that she brings to
the lives of all of us who are lucky enough to know her.

Spanish Names and Words

Hispanic surnames usually include the names of one's father and mother, with the father's name preceding the mother's, as in Luis del Río Jiménez. If a person prefers to use only one name, it is usually the name of the father (in this case, Río) rather than the mother's name (Jiménez). Then, as now, however, exceptions were common. Alvar Núñez Cabeza de Vaca, for example, did not inherit his father's name, which was Vera, but rather the name of Núñez, an illustrious ancestor on his mother's side, along with his mother's family name, Cabeza de Vaca. He himself dropped the Núñez in favor of Cabeza de Vaca, an even more illustrious family name, and so modern writers have followed his lead by referring to him as Cabeza de Vaca instead of Núñez.

The irregularities of Spanish usage have been compounded by eccentric Anglo-American practices. The name of Francisco Vázquez de Coronado y Luxán, for example (whose mother's name was Luxán), appears in documents of his day by the name of his father, Vázquez or Vázquez de Coronado, but Americans have come to know him simply as Coronado. The incorrect American usage has become so entrenched that it seems wise to yield to the traditional error rather than jolt readers by making the familiar strange. Similarly, Hernando de Soto would be rendered Soto throughout most of the Spanish-speaking world, but Anglo-Americans know him as De Soto, and that usage seems destined to prevail.

For the convenience of English-speaking readers, I have also used present-day renderings of some place names—using the familiar spelling of St. Augustine, for example, for San Agustín; Apalachee instead of Apalache; and San Antonio for the town known properly in the colonial era as San Fernando de Béxar. Words that should bear an accent, but that have become incorporated into English, appear without diacritical markings. Hence, Santa Barbara, Santa Fe, and Mexico, rather than Santa Bárbara, Santa Fé, or México. This leads to some inevitable inconsistency. Río, or river, carries no accent when used with the familiar Rio Grande, but Río Rojo does.

In Spanish, titles such as *duque* for duke, *marqués* for marquis, *don* for sir, and *fray* for friar, appear in lower case, even when combined with proper names, as in the marqués de Rubí, don Tomás Vélez Cachupín, or fray Junípero Serra. Because their meaning is well known to American readers, I have retained these titles in Spanish and left them in lower case. Titles that may seem strange to American readers, such as viceroy (*virrey*), appear in English.

I have used Spanish words so sparingly that a glossary seems unnecessary, but I define the few exceptions, such as *mestizo* and *encomienda*, when I introduce them for the first time. The index, then, should be your guide to definitions.

The Spanish Frontier
in North America

Introduction

We Americans have yet to really learn our own antecedents. . . .
Thus far, impress'd by New England writers and schoolmasters, we
tacitly abandon ourselves to the notion that our United States have
been fashion'd from the British Islands only . . . which is a very
great mistake.
Walt Whitman, 1883

Across the southern rim of the United States, from the
Atlantic to the Pacific, aged buildings stand as mute re-
minders of an earlier Hispanic America that has vanished.
On Florida's Atlantic coast, some seventy miles south of the
Georgia border, a great symmetrical stone fortress, the
castillo of San Marcos, still occupies the ground where its
bastions once commanded the land and water approaches to
Spanish St. Augustine. Founded in 1565, the town of St.
Augustine itself remains the oldest continuously occupied
European settlement in the continental United States. Farther west, at Pensacola, in the Florida Panhandle, the walls
of the battery of San Antonio of the old Spanish fort of San
Carlos de Barrancas look out over the shallow waters of the
Gulf of Mexico. In New Orleans' vibrant French Quarter,
nearly all of the oldest buildings were constructed in the
city's Spanish era, between 1763 and 1800. Fires of 1788
and 1794 obliterated the earlier French-built New Orleans,
so that even those venerable and much-modified landmarks
on Jackson Square—the Cabildo, the St. Louis Cathedral,
and the Presbytère—date to the era when New Orleans and
all of Louisiana belonged to Spain.

1. The Castillo of San Marcos at St. Augustine. Courtesy, National Park Service, Historic Photographic Collections, Harpers Ferry.

Still farther west, across southwestern America from Texas to California, preserved or reconstructed Spanish forts, public buildings, homes, and missions dot the arid landscape. Today, some of those structures serve as museums—perhaps the best known being the old stone mission in downtown San Antonio, popularly known as the Alamo, and the long, one-story adobe Governor's Palace facing the plaza in Santa Fe. Other buildings continue to serve their original functions. Near Tucson, for example, desert-dwelling Pima Indians still receive the sacraments inside the thick walls of the dazzlingly white mission church of San Xavier del Bac.

Old walls of stone and adobe remain among the most visible reminders that the northern fringes of Spain's vast New World empire once extended well into the area of the present-day United States. Spain's tenure in North America began at least as early as 1513, when Juan Ponce de León stepped ashore on a Florida beach, and did not end until Mexico won independence in 1821. Spain *governed* parts of the continent for well over two centuries—longer than the United States has existed as an independent nation.

The extent of Spanish control over North America shifted with its political fortunes and those of its European and Indian rivals, but Spanish sovereignty extended at one time or another at least as far north as Virginia on the Atlantic and Canada on the Pacific. Between the two coasts, Spain claimed much of the American South and the entire West—at least half of the continental United States.[1] Present-day Spain itself is three-fourths the size of Texas, yet its imperial claims in North America alone embraced an area larger than Western Europe.

Not only did Spain claim much of what is today the United States, but its sons and daughters settled throughout the continent's southern tier, building towns, missions, and fortifications from Virginia through Florida on the Atlantic, from San Diego to San Francisco on the Pacific, and across the states that make up the present American South and Southwest. Spanish subjects also found their way over trails that took them deep into the continent, pursuing treasure in Tennessee, fighting Pawnee and Oto Indians on the Platte River in Nebraska, and exploring the Great Basin.

In the more northerly latitudes of America, no physical remains of Spain's presence have endured, but across the land the names of states, counties, towns, rivers, valleys, mountains, and other natural features, from California to Cape Canaveral, testify to America's Spanish origins. The Spanish derivation of most of these place names is obvious, but for some it is not. The name of Key West, for example, holds no hint that it derives from Cayo Hueso ("Bone Key")—words that Americans would mispronounce and misspell.[2] Indeed, an old story, almost certainly apocryphal, has it that Canada's name resulted from Spanish exploration in the early sixteenth century. When Jacques Cartier met Indians along the coast of Newfoundland they reportedly greeted him with the only European words they knew—"*acá nada*," meaning in Spanish "nothing is here."[3]

Less evident than buildings or place names, but of greater significance, are the human and environmental transformations that accompanied Spain's conquest and

2. The Palace of the Governors at Santa Fe as viewed from the plaza. Photograph by Arthur Taylor, 1977. Courtesy, Museum of New Mexico, neg. no. 70213.

3. The Mission of San Xavier del Bac. Courtesy, Jim Griffith, the Southwest Folklore Center, University of Arizona.

settlement of North America. Spaniards introduced an astonishing array of life forms to the continent, ranging from cattle, sheep, and horses to the grasses those animals ate. At the same time, Spaniards unwittingly introduced alien diseases that ended the lives of countless native Americans and inadvertently created new ecological niches for the peoples, plants, and animals that crossed the Atlantic.

I

Notwithstanding the presence of ancient Spanish structures, the ubiquity of Spanish place names, and the length, range, and influence of Spanish tenure, the Spanish colonial origins of the United States have been dimly understood. The story of Hispanic men and women who changed indelibly the human and natural geography of

North America has only recently begun to be woven into the fabric of American history. Although the United States has always been a multiethnic society, most general histories of the nation have suggested that its colonial origins resided entirely in the thirteen English colonies. In American popular culture, the American past has been understood as the story of the expansion of English America rather than as the stories of the diverse cultures that comprise our national heritage.[4]

Among professional historians, such a teleological and ethnocentric conception of the past has given way to a more inclusive history that considers racial and ethnic minorities, losers as well as winners. Nonetheless, for many historians "colonial America" remains synonymous with English colonial America. Mistaking regional history for national history, most historians have continued to see the nation's "formative years" as a phenomenon of the eastern seaboard.[5] Most overviews of American history, as one historian has recently explained, give "the distinct impression that the English and Americans expanded west and south into vacant lands, except for those held by a few wild aboriginals."[6]

In southwestern America, where continuities with the Spanish colonial past are perhaps most evident, such a view of American history seems myopic at best. Today, the greatest percentage of the nation's Hispanics, some of them descendants of colonial pioneers, live in the Southwest.[7] Throughout the region, and especially in communities that trace their origins to the Spanish colonial era, manifestations of Hispanic culture remain striking. One cannot travel across the Southwest and remain blind to Spanish-Mexican influence on architecture, food, and place names. At the region's greatest natural wonder, the Grand Canyon, a sign at Moran Point on the South Rim explains to visitors that near that spot a group of men dispatched by Coronado in 1540 became the first Europeans to step to the canyon's edge. But the traveler does not need to leave the highway to find reminders of the Southwest's lengthy Spanish heritage. In the mid-1980s, one common billboard alluded to the incredible journey of Cabeza de Vaca by urging visitors to stop in Las Cruces, New Mexico, because it has been a popular place for travelers since 1535!

In southeastern America, where relatively fewer Hispanics live today and where most of the visible remains of the Spanish occupation have disappeared, the region's Hispanic origins have been largely forgotten—buried in historical memory, several levels below magnolias, juleps, and the War Between the States. In Alabama, Florida, Georgia, the Carolinas, Virginia, and Tennessee, nearly all traces of the wooden structures built by Spaniards in the sixteenth or seventeenth centuries have vanished. Initially, Indians or Englishmen destroyed most of those buildings, but nature completed the process and concealed the earliest abandoned Spanish missions and towns of the Southeast even from the prying tools of archaeologists. Until 1979 the ruins of Santa Elena, founded in 1566 and one of the oldest European settlements in North America, lay buried and forgotten near the eighth hole of the Marine Corps golfcourse on South Carolina's Parris Island. The site of the town of San Miguel de

Gualdape, the earliest European settlement in what is now the United States, founded on the Atlantic coast in 1526 and abandoned two months later, continues to elude historians and archaeologists. In addition to the scanty physical remains of its Spanish past, the Southeast lacks an evident population of the descendants of those Spaniards and Hispanized Indians who once inhabited small communities along its coasts and in its forests—people whom some anthropologists have infelicitously termed "human remnants."[8]

That Spain once supported missionaries, soldiers, and settlers in Georgia or Alabama is uncommon knowledge in the South, much less in the nation as a whole. In recalling the dawn of European settlement in Virginia, for example, we readily think of English colonies at Roanoke and Jamestown, but not of the mission that Spanish Jesuits established in Virginia in 1570, fourteen years before the English tragedy at Roanoke began, and thirty-seven years before Englishmen established a permanent colony at Jamestown. And who except local residents knows that a Spanish vessel in the 1520s explored Cape Cod and the Merrimac River and sailed up the Penobscot River to the site of present Bangor, Maine, or that Spaniards in the late 1700s established a military post on Vancouver Island, some 350 miles from present-day Seattle? Conversely, residents of patently Hispanic New Mexico have a wealth of stories about fellow Americans who believe that the state is in a foreign country. Two girls born in New Mexico, for example were denied Social Security numbers on the grounds that they were not born in the United States.[9] In 1990, the state of New Mexico responded by issuing license plates that read: "New Mexico, USA."

II

If we dimly recall America's Spanish colonial origins, it is not for lack of written records. Bundles of documents relating to North America and dating back to Ponce de León's discovery of Florida in 1513, repose in public and private archives in Spain, Mexico, and the present-day United States. The first book devoted entirely to North America, Cabeza de Vaca's account of his stranger-than-fiction journey from Florida to the Pacific slope, appeared in Spain in 1542. From Spain's first contact with North American shores, historians began to fashion the first-hand accounts of explorers into comprehensive narratives, as Francisco López de Gómara did in a work published in 1552. When Spaniards planted permanent settlements in Florida and New Mexico in the latter part of the 1500s, historians retold the stories of those pioneers. Some historians perished before their work was published, but others saw their accounts in print. In 1610, for example, three years after the founding of Jamestown and a decade before Pilgrims first put ashore at Plymouth, a press in Spain printed the *Historia de la Nuevo México* by Gaspar Pérez de Villagrá. Written in blank verse by an eyewitness to the conquest and settlement of New Mexico in 1598, this may represent the first published history of any American state.[10]

From these sixteenth-century beginnings, and continuing to the present day, writers have published widely on Spanish colonial North America. This place in time has come to be known as the *Spanish borderlands* a term that first appeared in the title of a small classic by Herbert Eugene Bolton, *The Spanish Borderlands: A Chronicle of Old Florida and the Southwest*, published by Yale University Press in 1921.[11] Bolton, who taught and wrote at the University of California, Berkeley, from 1911 until his death at age eighty-two in 1953, almost single-handedly shaped the field and gave it identity. One of America's most honored historians, he argued that a balanced view of the nation's past must include an understanding of its Hispanic origins as well as of its French and English backgrounds. The manuscript of one of his textbooks scandalized a reviewer because "nearly, if not quite, one third of the whole is devoted to the period before 1606 . . . before there were any permanent English settlements in America."[12] Bolton lamented the anti-Spanish bias of much American writing, and he bristled at the notion "that the Spaniards did not colonize but merely explored"—a misconception that many textbooks still convey three generations after Bolton voiced this complaint.[13]

Bolton told the Spanish side of American history in a remarkable number of books and scholarly articles, and he also trained disciples in astonishing numbers. He directed the graduate training of 104 Ph.D.'s and 323 M.A.'s, many of whom moved into academic careers, made their own scholarly contributions to the historiography of the borderlands, and trained still more historians.[14] At the same time, scholars who had no connection with Bolton also interested themselves in the new field. One result was an outpouring of hundreds of scholarly articles and books that treat an extraordinary variety of persons, places, and issues in the Spanish borderlands.[15]

In the last two decades alone, scholars of the borderlands have expanded our understanding beyond such important Boltonian concerns as exploration, institutions, and biography, into arenas that earlier generations had slighted—social history, ethnohistory, ecology, historical archaeology, historical geography, demography, and the study of disease. These new approaches have begun to produce fascinating results. Social historians, for example, have enriched our understanding of the past by moving beyond a narrow focus on the public activities of prominent individuals (nearly all of them male) to examine the private and public lives of persons of both sexes and of all classes, even the most marginal. Anthropologists and historians, to cite another example, have begun to unravel the secrets of what one archaeologist has called "the Great Black Hole of Southern History"—the years 1570–1670—and have made stunning identifications of previously unknown native peoples, places, and polities.[16]

Unfortunately for the general reader, scholarly work has increasingly taken the form of specialized monographs and articles that examine discrete subjects with increasingly ingenious methodological sophistication. These studies are of enormous value, but they take us into deep tunnels that often fail to connect with one another and that obscure our view of central themes and larger questions. This problem afflicts all of American history,[17] and in the study of the borderlands the widely lamented fragmentation of historical knowledge has been exacerbated by the tendency of scholars of the so-called western borderlands (the area from California to Texas), to work in isolation from specialists in the eastern borderlands (Louisiana to Florida). Since Bolton's *Spanish Borderlands* appeared in 1921, only John Francis Bannon, in his *Spanish Borderlands Frontier, 1513–1821*, published in 1970, has tried to put the whole story together in a single volume.

III

The Spanish Frontier in North America offers a fresh overview that reflects the concerns of current scholarship as well as the sound conclusions of earlier generations. Simply put, I try to explain Spain's impact on the lives, institutions, and environments of native peoples of North America, and the impact of North America on the lives and institutions of those Spaniards who explored and settled what has now become the United States.

Although the story includes both the traditional eastern and western borderlands, I have chosen to make little use of Bolton's time-honored term, the *Spanish Borderlands*. Its meaning is not clear to the general public, to whom it might suggest the Pyrenees where Spain borders on France. Moreover, scholars no longer agree on the spatial or temporal scope of the Spanish borderlands.[18] Instead, I choose to talk about the *Spanish Frontier in North America*, fully aware of the need for definitions. In this book I use *Spanish* as a political and cultural term, not a racial category. Although Spaniards proudly proclaimed their purity of blood and diligently sought to protect the *limpieza de sangre* of their families, considerable racial mixture had occurred on the Iberian peninsula even before the discovery of America. In North America most of Spain's subjects were either *mestizos* (a term that when used loosely meant racially mixed peoples), mulattos, Indians, or blacks. If these people lived in the manner of Spaniards rather than Indians, I generally refer to them, their institutions, and their society, as Spanish or Hispanic.

For convenience, I employ the term *North America* to mean the continent north of Mexico, as do many geographers, anthropologists, and historians.[19] *America*, in this book, usually means that part of North America that would become the United States, with apologies to Latin Americans who object to the way in which *yanquis* have preempted the term and who have correctly pointed out that the entire hemisphere is America. On both sides of the Rio Grande an *American* is understood to be a citizen of the United States.

By definition, the geographical scope of this book represents a geopolitical anachronism. The United States did not exist during most of the period under consideration. Moreover, it is anachronistic to think of Spaniards occupying a North American frontier, for few would have identified themselves as residents of North America.

Instead, like their counterparts in English America, they thought of themselves as residents of provinces or locales, such as California, New Mexico, or Florida, which existed in isolation from one another.[20] Nonetheless, since my chief purpose is to broaden our understanding of the American past by illuminating its Hispanic origins, I have chosen to frame this study within the boundaries of the present continental United States. This is not to gainsay the fact that America's Spanish past also belongs to the history of colonial Latin America. Although it may discomfit those who yearn for neater categories, it seems clear that the study of the borderlands can add to our appreciation of the varieties of regional experiences within colonial Latin America, while at the same time extending and enriching our understanding of the history of the United States.[21]

In telling the story of America's Spanish origins I try not to cast Spaniards as the villains so often portrayed by hispanophobic writers. At the same time, I do not put a gloss on Spanish behavior, as the pro-Spanish Bolton tradition tended to do. The well-known false dichotomies of the "Black Legend," which portrays Spaniards as uniquely cruel, and the "White Legend," which ennobles them, only distort understanding.[22] Instead, I seek to recreate the past with its own integrity and within its own terms of reference. The behavior of Spaniards toward Indians in the early sixteenth century, for example, often seems cruel and repugnant by present standards. Nonetheless, it fell within the bounds of acceptable behavior for many western European males of the late middle ages, whose behavior toward one another was also cruel and repugnant by our lights. In that time and place the release of aggressive emotions was "open and uninhibited," as one scholar has put it. "Rapine, battle, hunting of men and animals—all these were vital necessities which . . . for the mighty and strong . . . formed part of the pleasures of life."[23]

It is, of course, commonplace to suggest that we should not judge historical figures or events by the standards of our day, but by the standards of their age. This, however, begs the question—what were the standards of an age? In complex societies several standards of conduct can exist side by side. If, for example, "killing and torturing others . . . was a socially permitted pleasure" in late medieval Europe, it was also true that Spanish monarchs, from the time of the discovery of America on, urged humane treatment of Indians.[24] Royal orders to Columbus, issued in 1493, explained that he was to "treat . . . Indians very well and lovingly," and punish severely those who mistreated them.[25] It is also important to remember that standards and practices change over time, even during what we, from a distance, imagine was a single "age" or "era." Spaniards' behavior toward Indians on sixteenth-century frontiers, for example, differed markedly from their more benign treatment of frontier Indians in the late eighteenth century.

Only by understanding the existence of contradictory and competing values and practices, and the changes wrought by time and circumstance, can one move beyond caricatures to full portraits of a society. It seems dangerous, however, to allow understanding to lead to the moral neutrality suggested in the French saying, "to understand is to forgive," for it is too easy a step from there to forgive and forget. History should help us remember that in any age, some men and women have found ingenious ways to rationalize brutality in the name of religion, truth, or the common good. We can understand, but we need not condone their behavior.[26]

One of the themes of this book is that North American natives and Spaniards who met on North American frontiers failed to understand one another, for they came from different worlds. So do we of the late twentieth century inhabit a world remarkably different from *either* of those peoples. A cultural chasm exists, of course, between native Americans and the descendants of European newcomers who constitute the bulk of modern Americans. Although it is less evident, it should also be remembered that a large gap separates the institutions, values, manners, and discourses of Spaniards of early modern Europe and those of present-day Americans. Common cultural roots tie most Americans to the history of Western Europe, but culture is a process of never-ending construction and deconstruction rather than a static condition, and Europeans of a few hundred years ago were not merely "simpler" versions of ourselves. As one historian has recently reminded us, "the past is a foreign country: they do things differently there."[27] For Spaniards of the seventeenth century, for example, love "was considered a subversive sentiment,"[28] and such a basic idea as "choice" held meanings for Spaniards of the early modern era that we might find unrecognizable today. When sixteenth-century Spaniards asked Indians to choose between Christianity and slavery, it may seem in retrospect as though they offered the natives no real choice. Nonetheless, in the prevailing Spanish mentalité, Indians did have a choice, even if they made the wrong one and brought the wrath of Christendom down upon themselves.[29]

Just as the social environment of Spanish North America differed profoundly from ours of the late twentieth century, so did the physical environment. Those who dwelled or traveled in the southern rim of the continent in the 1500s, 1600s, or 1700s, encountered colder and wetter weather than we know today. Spaniards had arrived in North America at the onset of what has come to be called the Little Ice Age, and for the next three centuries, in many areas of the continent, growing seasons were shorter than in the twentieth century, rainfall higher, and rivers that seldom freeze over today could be crossed on ice.[30] The advent of Europeans and their zoological and biological imports changed the natural world beyond recognition. All across the continent, tall native grasses and climax forests have vanished, swiftly flowing streams have slowed, and flora and fauna alien to precolumbian America have established themselves.

IV

To tell of Spanish frontiers in North America in a single volume has required distilling the essence of the story, not compiling inventories. Much as an artist must foreshorten to fit a large scene on a small canvas, I have had to skip over foreground details to bring larger themes clearly into focus.

The main themes of Spain's enterprises in North America can be understood in many ways. Traditionally, Americans and Europeans have explained Spain's early ventures in what is now the United States as episodes in an age of discovery, although we have come more recently to understand that native Americans probably regarded Europe's discoverers as blind—oblivious to meanings, observers of form instead of discoverers of function. Traditionally, Americans and Europeans have categorized Spain's colonizing activities as chapters in the expansion of European institutions,[31] although we now suppose that natives perceived the expansion of Europe as the invasion of America—or, if they understood the impact of European diseases, as the infestation of America.[32] An anthropological model might explain Spain's North American colonies as the domination and transformation of preliterate societies comprised of tribe, band, and other local units by the emerging and literate state societies of Europe.[33] A sociological or economic paradigm might posit Spain's North American colonies as the periphery of an empire that was, itself, part of an emerging world economic system.[34] Still another economic framework might place Spanish North America beyond the periphery of the world economic system, and even beyond the fringes of empire.[35] From local perspectives, where the imperatives of empire paled before the exigencies of daily life for both natives and Spaniards, competition between classes and cultures for control of resources in distinctive environments provides a powerful device for explaining the varieties of Spanish experiences in North America.[36] From another level of abstraction, the story of the activities of Spaniards in North America might be seen as an elaborate fiction, constructed from accounts kept by colonial record-keepers and agreed to by historians, all of whom have created a discourse of colonialism that obscures more than it reveals.[37]

All of these modes of explanation are useful, but no one is fully satisfying. Preferring eclecticism to reductionism, I have sought to incorporate a variety of models into a framework that explains Spain's empire in North America as one side of a many-sided frontier.[38] The notion of the frontier as a line representing the inexorable "advance of civilization into the wilderness" may still hold sway in the popular imagination, but serious students no longer see frontiers in such ethnocentric terms.[39] Frontiers have at least two sides, so that an expanding frontier invariably edges onto someone else's frontier. Rather than see them as lines, frontiers seem best understood as zones of interaction between two different cultures—as places where the cultures of the invader and of the invaded contend with one another and with their physical environment to produce a dynamic that is unique to time and place.[40]

As such, frontiers represent both place and process, linked inextricably. The Spanish frontier in North America, for example, waxed and waned with the fortunes of empire, the expansiveness of Spain's own claims, and the assertiveness of its opponents—both European and native American. This *process* of expansion and contraction gave shape to the *place* that Spain regarded as its North American frontier—or, perhaps more accurately, the distinctive *places* that Spain regarded as its multiple North American frontiers. Expansion and contraction occurred at different rates, of course, so that one Spanish frontier zone might contract even as another expanded.

Within Spain's shifting frontier zones in North America several other processes worked at different rates and exerted different ranges and depths of influence. Perhaps the broadest yet most shallow range of Spain's influence was its claim to much of the continent—a geopolitical frontier of the imagination that existed as an abstraction on Spanish maps and in documents, but that had little actual impact on native Americans or rival European powers. To give substance to its geopolitical claims, Spain occupied territory by planting settlements that became the centers of spheres of Iberian frontier influence. Spain's frontier settlements set into motion several simultaneous frontier processes, including urbanization, agriculture, ranching, and commerce. Each type of frontier exerted different ranges and depths of influence on native peoples. Indians who lived close to Spanish settlers, for example, usually found their lifeways altered substantially, as did Navajos when they began to raise European-introduced sheep and to weave wool into textiles. Natives who lived so far from Spanish settlements that they never saw a Spaniard, still felt the transformative power of European culture, as they obtained European curiosities such as metal tools and coins, clothing, horses, and watermelon and peach seeds through trade with Indian intermediaries. Long before they had commercial relations with Spaniards, Caddos at one village in Texas possessed a number of articles of Spanish origin, including a papal bull exempting residents of New Spain from fasting during the summer.[41]

In contrast to the Anglo-American frontier in North America, which largely excluded natives, Spain sought to include natives within its new world societies. Thus, Spanish missionaries labored to win the hearts and minds of Indians in what might be defined as a spiritual or cultural frontier—a frontier that some natives resisted with a fervor that matched the missionaries' zeal to convert them. Natives who declined to submit passively or who resisted militarily often found themselves caught up in another zone of Spanish frontier influence. Along a wide-ranging military frontier, soldiers and soldier-settlers pounded some natives into submission and tried to hold others at bay through fear and intimidation.

Spaniards, of course, were not alone in contending with natives for control of North America and its peoples. On the North American frontiers of European empires, France, England, the United States, and Russia vied with Spain and with one another as well as with native Americans.

These imbricated zones of political, economic, social, cultural, spiritual, military, and imperial influence constitute the main subjects of the chapters that follow. Most of the chapters are held together by the themes of contention and transformation. Contention for power and resources is, of course, part of an ongoing struggle between classes, cultures, races, and genders *within* established societies. In frontier zones, however, where peoples of different polities, economies, and cultures come into contact, transfrontier contention for hegemony can have powerful transformative effects.[42]

In frontier zones, contention occurs at two interrelated levels. First, frontiersmen from both the societies of the invader and the invaded continue their *intra*mural contention. Along frontiers, new opportunities for spoils often intensify these internal struggles for power and, in the case of state societies, the weak moderating influence of distant central governments also permits intramural contention to escalate unchecked. Second, *inter*mural contention, unique to societies that face one another along frontiers, gives rise to cultural conflict and cultural exchange. Conflict and exchange across frontier societies can take place in a variety of ways that might simultaneously include accommodation, acculturation, assimilation, syncretism, and resistance. But whatever form conflict and exchange might take, be it biculturalism, a new synthesis, or the eradication of one culture by another, the old orders are transformed and new orders arise out of the maelstrom of contention.

It is the power of frontiers to transform cultures that gives them special interest. In the case of the United States, the transformative power of the Anglo-American frontier has been regarded by many historians as so profound that it not only altered the culture of frontier folk, but also transformed America's national character and institutions.[43] In other societies such a broad claim might not be sustained much less suggested. It does appear to be universally true, however, that at those edges where cultures come in contact, friction and cross-fertilization transform local peoples and institutions, giving rise to transfrontier regions with distinctive cultures, politics, economic arrangements, and social networks that set them apart from their respective metropoli.[44] "Human populations," anthropologist Eric Wolf has argued, "construct their cultures in interaction with one another, and not in isolation."[45]

Clearly, then, the Spanish frontier cannot be understood apart from its non-Spanish neighbors who influenced it in countless ways. At the most basic level, for example, the character of indigenous societies determined which Spanish institutions would flourish and which would wither. Where Spaniards encountered sedentary peoples, they could extract labor to support civilian settlements. Where Spaniards encountered resistant nomads, forts with paid soldiers often became the dominant institution.[46] Native peoples, then, must be understood as more than a mere "challenge" to Spaniards, as an earlier generation of historians suggested. Even books like mine, which attempts to illuminate the Spanish experience, must come to terms with Indians, whose societies and cultures Spaniards transformed and who, in turn, transformed the frontier societies and cultures of the Spaniards.[47]

1

Worlds Apart

Give the natives to understand that there is a God in heaven and the Emperor on the earth to command and govern it, to whom all have to be subjected and to serve.
Viceroy Antonio de Mendoza to fray Marcos de Niza, 1538

They wore coats of iron, and warbonnets of metal, and carried for weapons short canes that spit fire and made thunder . . . these black, curl-bearded people drove our ancients about like slave creatures.
Zuni tradition

At no time in history has there been such a significant degree of culture contact between peoples of completely distinct traditions.
George Foster, 1960

Early in the summer of 1540 a group of young Spanish adventurers, mounted on horseback, approached a Zuni village in what is today New Mexico. Led by Francisco Vázquez de Coronado, a thirty-year-old nobleman from the Spanish university town of Salamanca, the Spaniards had traveled for six months to reach this bleak and forbidding land of brilliant skies, broad vistas, red rocks, and sharp-edged mesas. Coronado had moved ahead of the main body of his army with a small group of mounted men, numbering little more than one hundred. Although summer was upon them, some of Coronado's men feared Indian arrows more than heat and wore protective coats of chain mail or thick buckskin. Coronado himself sported a plumed helmet and a suit of gilded armor that dazzled the eyes when it caught the rays of the sun.

The Spaniards had traveled long and hard. They had come through a stretch of uninhabited country and several men had died of hunger and thirst. "I thought we all should die of starvation if we had to wait another day," Coronado later recalled.[1] But as the Spaniards made their way along the narrow plain of the Zuni River, they expected to be rewarded for their troubles by the sight of a splendid city—one of seven cities of a rich province that Indian informants had called "Cíbola." Instead, Coronado saw the sun-baked mud-brick walls of a modest town of multistory apartments, whose inhabitants displayed none of the gold, silver, or jewels that symbolized wealth to the Spaniards.[2]

Unlike the Spaniards, the Zunis were dressed for the season. Coronado noted that "most of them are entirely naked except for the covering of their privy parts."[3] Only able-bodied men remained at Cíbola. Women, youngsters, and the elderly had been sent away, for the Zunis did not intend to allow Coronado's party to enter, much less intend to provide the food and shelter that the Spaniards desperately needed. Coronado's arrival had not surprised the Indians. Their scouts had followed the strangers' movements. Even before Coronado reached the outskirts of their towns, Zunis had attempted an ambush. Now, with the Spaniards on the very edge of Cíbola, the natives sought supernatural assistance. With sacred golden cornmeal, Zuni warriors drew lines on the ground, warning the intruders not to pass beyond them.[4]

While the Zunis waited to see if sacred cornmeal would turn back the unwelcome strangers, the Spaniards also appealed to metaphysical sources for help. Through an interpreter, probably a Pima Indian, Coronado assured the Zunis that he had come on a holy mission. The Spaniards read aloud a statement that summarized Spanish theology, explaining that Spain's monarchs had received temporal powers from a deity through one they called Pope. Spaniards issued this *requerimiento* or notification to natives throughout the New World—on occasion, legalistically reading it in Spanish to Indians who did not speak or understand their tongue. The requerimiento demanded that native peoples accept the dominion of the Spanish Crown and embrace Christianity. If they resisted, their lands would be taken from them and they would be killed or enslaved.[5] Although learned men in Spain had written the requerimiento and a notary probably attested to its reading at Zuni as the law required, the document failed to win the Zunis' obedience.

Instead of submitting, the Zunis fired arrows at the Spaniards. Coronado responded with orders to attack, crying out as an incantation the name of Saint James—*Santiago*! In the bloody battle that followed, the Zunis took several Spanish lives and Coronado himself almost perished. As he explained, "the Indians all directed their attack against me because my armor was gilded and glittering." Struck by rocks and arrows and thrown to the ground, only Coronado's sturdy helmet and the quick action of a companion saved his life. Within an hour, Spaniards armed with guns and steel swords fought their way into the natives' homes. The vanquished defenders fled, leaving behind storehouses of corn, beans, turkeys, and salt, to the delight of their hungry visitors.[6]

Why the Zunis refused to permit Coronado's band to enter their town may never be fully understood, but it seems likely that they already knew enough about the mounted, metal-clad strangers not to welcome them. Like natives throughout northwestern Mexico, Zunis must have heard reports of Spanish slave hunters operating to the south. Then, too, a small Spanish scouting party headed by a black former slave, Esteban, had reached Zuni the year before Coronado arrived. The Zunis killed the black man, they explained to Coronado, because of liberties he had taken with their women. The natives, then, had ample reason to reject the overtures of the bizarrely costumed, bearded interlopers. Their resolve to keep the Spaniards out, however, may have been strengthened by the timing of Coronado's visit. He arrived during the culmination of the Zuni sacred summer ceremonies; his presence threatened to interrupt the return of Zuni pilgrims from the sacred lake and to endanger the prospects for abundant summer rains and a good harvest.[7]

Whatever the reason for Zuni resistance to Coronado's soldiers, one essential fact seems clear. Nothing in either group's previous experience had prepared them to comprehend the other.[8] Coronado's translators could convert words from one language to another, but they could not convey the deepest meaning of the requerimiento

4. The Cíbola that Coronado stormed was one of six Zuni pueblos, probably Hawikuh as depicted here in ruins in 1920. Courtesy, Museum of New Mexico, neg. no. 146086.

to the Zunis. Nor could Zunis convey to the Spaniards the meaning of lines of sacred cornmeal or the significance of their summer ceremonies. The two peoples who met at Zuni in 1540 came from different worlds.

I

The worlds of the sixteenth-century Iberians and their contemporaries in North America differed profoundly, but neither can be easily characterized because neither Iberians nor native North Americans constituted a uniform group. Physically, Amerindians were relatively homogeneous, having descended from waves of hunter-gatherers who had crossed the Bering Strait from Asia, beginning certainly as long as 14,000 years ago. Although they probably came in more than one migration and may have represented different populations, native Americans shared a number of physical, dental, and genetic characteristics that suggest their common ancestry in eastern Asia. Well over 90 percent of native North Americans, for example, have type O blood.[9] As early immigrants from Asia dispersed throughout a hemisphere devoid of previous human occupants, their numbers grew and their cultures and languages became astonishingly diverse and complex. By the time Europeans first encountered them, even those natives who appeared to outsiders as a single "tribe," such as the peoples whom the Spaniards called Pueblos, often differed more than initial impressions suggested.

At Zuni, Coronado met the first of many peoples who lived in compact communities of esplanades, courtyards, and apartment houses, some rising to three and four stories. Spaniards called these prosperous urban-dwelling farmers Pueblos because in contrast to their nomadic neighbors they lived in towns, or *pueblos*. No central government linked the autonomous towns of the Pueblos, but they seemed to the earliest Spanish visitors to be one people. They grew maize, beans, cotton, and gourds in irrigated fields, dressed in cotton blankets and animal skins, and appeared to Coronado's men to have "the same ceremonies and customs."[10] Despite superficial similarities, significant differences in Pueblo religious practices, and in political, social, and family organization probably existed then as they do now. Indeed, Pueblos spoke and still speak several mutually unintelligible languages. For example, Zunis speak Penutian, a language of some California peoples. Hopis, who live in what is today Arizona, speak a Uto-Aztecan language. Neither of these is related to the languages of the many Pueblo towns—numbering perhaps over ninety at the time of Coronado's arrival—that flourished farther east. In the watershed of the Rio Grande, residents of certain pueblos speak at least three mutually unintelligible forms of Tanoan (Tewa, Tiwa, and Towa, all of the Kiowa-Tanoan language family); Indians from still other pueblos speak Keresan, a language apparently unrelated to any other. Still other languages, such as Piro and Tompiro, were spoken by Pueblo groups that have become extinct.[11]

The Pueblos offer only one example of the diversity of native North Americans. In

California alone, with an indigenous population of perhaps 300,000 in the mid-eighteenth century, one linguist has estimated that Indians spoke "no fewer than 64—and perhaps as many as 80—mutually unintelligible tongues, further differentiated into an unknowably large number of dialects."[12] These differences in language suggest differences in culture, but we will never know the full variety of native languages and cultures that existed in North America when Spaniards first arrived. Only two dozen or so of the languages of California natives have survived and many Indian languages, particularly in the Southeast, became extinct without having been recorded.[13]

The variety of languages, religions, and customs of native North Americans in the sixteenth century appears to have been greater than that of their European contemporaries. Some Native Americans lived in large urban centers and others in family homesteads, and their social structures, governments, economies, religious beliefs, technologies, histories, and traditions ranged across a wide spectrum. They engaged in a variety of economic activities, from hunting, fishing, and gathering to irrigating fields and manufacturing tools and wares. Native trading networks ranged from the local level to the transcontinental. Yumas on the Colorado River, for example, knew of Coronado's arrival at Cíbola, nearly four hundred miles to the east, soon after the event, and Coronado's contemporary in the Mississippi Valley, Hernando de Soto, met Indians who owned turquoise that came from the direction of the sunset—from the Pueblos.[14]

Notwithstanding the great variety of their cultures, it appears that many native North Americans held certain attitudes in common, some of which set them apart from Europeans in general and Spaniards in particular. In contrast to Spaniards, for example, most North American Indian people interacted more intimately with the natural world, placed less emphasis on the accumulation of surpluses of food and other goods, and tended to regard the users of land as possessing greater rights than the nominal owners of land.[15]

At the time of Coronado's arrival, natives throughout North America lived in small units, none of which seems to have approached in size what Europeans would come to call a "state." Larger political or economic units existed in Arizona and New Mexico centuries before Coronado's arrival, but we know these so-called Anazasi and Hohokam peoples very imperfectly, largely through physical remains of their great urban centers and cliff dwellings (such as the ruins known today as Mesa Verde, Chaco Canyon, and Casa Grande) and through artifacts unearthed and interpreted by archaeologists.[16] The same may be said of the great chiefdoms of what archaeologists call the Mississippian tradition, which reached its apogee throughout southeastern America between 1200 to 1450 A.D.[17]

The native American bands, tribes, and chiefdoms that the Spaniards encountered were not only smaller than states but lacked some of the institutions of the emerging states of Europe, especially those designed to enforce social order—armies, police, and bureaucracies. As one anthropologist has reminded us, Amerindian communities were not "smaller, backward versions of European villages," but rather unique, non-western cultures "rooted in the obligations of kinship rather than the appeal of political ideology."[18] Beyond this, few generalizations about native Americans at the time of Coronado's visit have value; it is more useful to consider individual tribes than to speak inaccurately of Indians in the aggregate.

II

In contrast to the cultures of native Americans, which had grown increasingly diverse since their ancestors crossed the Bering Strait, the cultures of the various peoples who inhabited the Iberian peninsula had begun to amalgamate by the sixteenth century. Unlike native Americans, who probably had a common group of ancestors, the peoples of Iberia descended from a wide variety of tribes and genetic strains from outside the peninsula, including Phoenicians, Greeks, Romans, Visigoths, Franks, Jews, and Muslims. Indeed, even these broad categories included still smaller tribes and bands, each with its discrete culture. Among the Muslim invaders of Spain, for example, were Arabs, Syrians, and Berbers from North Africa who were themselves splintered into subgroups.

Like North American Indians in the early sixteenth century, Spaniards were not a unified people and did not compose a single nation. The nation state that came to be called Spain had consisted of many tribes organized into kingdoms, such as Castile and Catalonia, which spoke distinct languages. These realms vied with one another for power, and factions within them fought ruinous civil wars.[19]

In 1469, the marriage of Queen Isabel of Castile to Prince Fernando of Aragón brought two powerful kingdoms together in a condominium that laid the foundations of the modern Spanish state. Under these so-called Catholic Monarchs, the realms that would become Spain moved toward greater political and cultural homogeneity, although they never fully achieved it. Isabel and Fernando, for example, sought to insure Christian orthodoxy by establishing the Inquisition and prohibiting Jews and Moslems from living in Spain. Just as Castile came to dominate the other kingdoms, so its language, Castilian, became the most widely used in the peninsula and in America. Because Castile's monarchs took the position that the Spanish pope, Alexander VI, "gave" the New World to Castile in the celebrated papal donations of 1493, its monarchs believed themselves to have exclusive sovereignty over the newly discovered lands (excepting the east coast of South America, which they inadvertently gave to Portugal in the Treaty of Tordesillas in 1494).[20]

Spain remained politically disunited and culturally heterogeneous in the sixteenth century (and in many ways it remains so yet today), but by 1492 its peoples possessed greater organizational unity and common hierarchical and religious values than did the peoples of North America. This relative political and cultural unity worked to Spain's advantage when its seafaring sons discovered another world.[21] In North America, where decision making in most native societies depended on what one anthropologist has described as "a slow process of achieving consensus," Spaniards and other Europeans enjoyed a great advantage.[22] Unencumbered by democratic restraints, Spanish leaders had authority to take quick, concerted action.

So, too, did Spaniards' prior experience with "infidels" from North Africa work to their benefit in the New World. A prolonged struggle to reconquer the Iberian peninsula from Muslim invaders profoundly influenced Spanish values and institutions, making Spaniards uniquely suited among European nations to conquer, plunder, and administer the New World. The reconquest, or *reconquista*, of Iberia began soon after the Muslim invasion of 711; it did not end until 1492, when the combined forces of Isabel and Fernando entered the Alhambra in triumph as the last Moorish kingdom, Granada, capitulated. More than seven centuries of intermittent warfare along a shifting Christian-Muslim frontier had honed Spanish fighting skills and exalted the soldier to a status alongside the lawyer and the priest in Spanish society. Spanish warriors had fought to free their homeland from an alien religion as well as an alien people. Nourished by contention with Moors and Jews, Spanish Catholicism became uniquely vital and intense, its appetite for expansion unsatisfied by the expulsion of Moors and Jews from Spain.

Even before the fall of Granada in 1492, church and state had supported expansion beyond Iberia—into the western Mediterranean, Africa, and far out into the Atlantic. In conquering the Canary Islands (1478–96), which became the starting point for Columbus's venture into the unknown, Spaniards had invoked the values of the reconquest and gained valuable experience in conquering infidels and colonizing overseas territory. With Columbus's return, it seemed only natural for Spaniards to carry their holy war to new frontiers across the sea, and to appeal to Saint James, the Killer of Moors—"Santiago Matamoros!"—against infidels in America, as Coronado did at Zuni. By the time Coronado entered the Pueblo world, Spaniards had refined their fighting skills and modified the institutions of conquest to adapt to new peoples and conditions in Española, Puerto Rico, Jamaica, Cuba, Mexico, and Peru, but the militant values of the reconquista continued to obtain. Indeed, for the next three hundred years, Hispanic soldiers in North America would continue to call upon the patron saint of the reconquest when they went into battle, and some Hispanic frontiersmen would regard Indians as synonymous with "Moors."[23]

The Spanish struggle to control the New World and its peoples became, in effect, an extension of the reconquista—a moral crusade to spread Spanish culture and Catholicism to pagans in all parts of the Americas. Optimism born of religious zeal, ignorance, and intolerance gave Spain's onward-moving Christian soldiers another powerful advantage in their encounters with native Americans. Spaniards believed in a supreme being who favored them, and they often explained their successes as well as their failures as manifestations of their god's will.[24] Was it not providential, for

5. Santiago. Moors retreat before the sword of Santiago in this ornament from the title page of a book apparently used by Franciscans in colonial New Mexico: Propers of the Daily Hours for Spanish Saints *(Antwerp, 1738). Photograph by Blair Clark, 1991. Courtesy, International Folk Art Foundation Collection in the Museum of International Folk Art, a unit of the Museum of New Mexico.*

example, that Spaniards discovered America, with its fresh supply of infidels, in the same year they completed the long struggle against the Muslims in Iberia?

With or without the reconquista, Spaniards of the early sixteenth century would have believed that Providence sided with them. They knew that persons radically unlike themselves, who neither held Christian beliefs nor lived like Christians, were inferior human beings, perhaps even bestial, deserving of slavery or whatever other ills might befall them. Like other Christians, Spaniards understood that their god had given them "dominion" over all creatures on the earth, including these infidels. The god of the Christians, according to their holiest text, had ordered them to "be fruitful and multiply, and replenish the earth and subdue it: and have dominion over the fish of the sea, and over the fowl of the air, and over every living thing that moveth upon the earth."[25] Pope Alexander VI, in a famous decree of 1493, asserted that he had the right, "by the authority of the Almighty God," to "give, grant, and assign" the New World to Isabel and Fernando so that they might convert its inhabitants. In a similar document, an earlier pope had cited biblical justification for such a papal donation of so-called pagan lands: "See, I have this day set thee over the nations and over the kingdoms, to root out, and to pull down, and to destroy, and to throw down, to build, and to plant."[26]

Christianity thus imbued Spaniards with a powerful sense of the righteousness of their aggression against those natives in North America who threatened to block their advance. Nowhere was this clearer than in the requerimiento that Coronado read to the Zunis. Conquistadores had read this summons to countless indigenous Americans since it was drawn up in 1513. The requerimiento commanded Indians to "acknowl-edge the [Catholic] Church as the ruler and superior of the whole world, and the high priest called Pope, and in his name the king and queen [of Spain]." Those natives who did so, the document said, would be treated well. Those who did not were assured that "with the help of God we shall forcefully . . . make war against you . . . take you and your wives and your children and shall make slaves of them . . . and shall do to you all the harm and damage that we can." More zealous than any other European power in its attempt to fulfill what it saw as its legal obligations to the natives, Spain put them on notice that if they failed to obey, "the deaths and losses which shall accrue from this are your fault, and not that of their highnesses, or ours."[27] True to their word, Coronado and his companions invaded Zuni and other recalcitrant pueblos, permitted their animals to eat the natives' crops, appropriated food and clothing as needed (no matter whether Indians went hungry or cold), and destroyed towns that offered armed re-sistance.

Christian belief contrasted sharply with the religious views of many of the natives of North America. Instead of the extraterrestrial god of the Spaniards, who had created nature but was not in nature, the North American natives generally believed in the interconnectedness of god and nature. Natives believed spirits resided in the natural world and not outside of it.[28] The spiritual world of the Zunis, for example, was and is earth-centered. Zunis believe that their ancestors entered this world though a hole in the earth, and that after death a Zuni's spirit continues to reside in the world, in clouds or other natural phenomena depending on the role the deceased played while walking the path of life. Instead of offering prayers and sacrifices to a deity in a distant "heaven" as Christians do, Zunis direct their prayers and offerings toward the natural world. They seek to maintain harmony with earth, sky, animals, and plants, all of which are regarded as living beings capable of taking on several forms.[29] Coronado was close to the mark when he noted that the Zunis "worship water, because they say that it makes the maize grow and sustains their life."[30] Like other native North Americans, Zunis had apparently received no divinely inspired message to subdue the earth. Instead, they sought to live in harmony with it, although in practice they, like other native Americans, contributed to environmental degradation.[31] Similarly, al-though they engaged in warfare, Zunis sought harmony with their neighbors, prefer-ring accommodation and compromise to aggression (by no means a universal trait among North American Indians). The Pueblos, two members of the Coronado expedition correctly noted, seemed "more given to farming than to war."[32]

Spaniards had material as well as spiritual motives to subdue the earth. Like other Europeans, Spaniards placed high value on gold and silver and were willing to suffer extraordinary hardships to obtain these minerals. Cortés exaggerated only slightly when he sent a message to Moctezuma saying that the Spaniards had a disease of the heart that only gold could cure. In contrast, gold and silver held little intrinsic value for most native North Americans until they discovered the value of those metals to Europeans. "These Indians do not covet riches," one seventeenth-century observer wrote of the natives of Florida, "nor do they esteem silver or gold."[33]

For Spaniards, the accumulation of gold and silver was not merely a means to an end, but an end in itself. Thus, men with means to live comfortably gambled all they had in order to acquire more, and the Spanish Crown encouraged their risk taking. Free enterprise had fueled Castile's reconquest of the Muslims and had set precedents that would carry over to the New World. In fighting the Muslims the king of Castile licensed an entrepreneur, or *adelantado* (what the English would later call a proprietor), to push forward the frontiers of Christianity. These military chieftains risked their own capital, knowing that success would bring titles of nobility, land, broad governmental powers over the conquered domain, and the right to part of the spoils of war.[34] Under this arrangement, the rewards for the adelantado could be considerable. So could rewards for those warriors whom he engaged to follow him, many of them villagers whose poverty heightened their ambition and whose experience taught them that honor and wealth could be more easily won through plunder than through manual labor. Since these commissioned bands of warriors enabled Spain's monarchs to add to their realm without risking their own capital, they extended the system to the New World. Typically, then, Coronado financed his own expensive invasion of New Mexico. Since he had no personal fortune, however, he relied upon his patron, the viceroy, and his wealthy wife, Beatriz de Estrada, daughter of the treasurer of New Spain, as Mexico was then called.

Thus, even before the discovery of America, a peculiarly Spanish institution and ethos had developed that would enable the future conquerors of America, most of them predatory young men like those who accompanied Coronado, to serve God, country, and themselves at the same time—with no sense that these goals might be contradictory. To the contrary, if Spaniards served their god well, it seemed only right that he should reward them. One soldier who fought in the conquest of Mexico explained the matter clearly: Spaniards had left Europe "to serve God and his Majesty, to give light to those who were in the darkness and to grow rich as all men desire to do."[35]

In addition to this ethos, hardened in the crucible of the reconquest of Iberia, the conquistadores brought to the New World overheated imaginations, fired by the

popular literature of their day—romantic novels posing as history. Literate and illit-
erate alike knew the stories contained in these widely circulated romances. The novels
extolled knight-errantry in exotic lands, where brave men found wealth and glory.
They exalted courage, stoicism, and heroism, and glorified the warrior as the ideal of
Spanish manhood. Manifestly works of fiction, these romances came to be regarded as
fact by their ordinary readers or listeners. As the line between fantasy and reality
blurred in the popular imagination, it became easy to believe in the existence of the
fabulous places described in these "lying histories," as some critics termed them. Who
could doubt that beyond the horizon there existed enchanted islands, Amazons, and
fountains of youth?[36] Then, too, like many other Europeans of their time, Spaniards
imagined the existence of an earthly paradise in some faraway place, inhabited by
peoples who still lived in an Edenic state of grace.[37] Sophisticated critics might scoff.
One chronicler, for example, noted that it was not the fountain of youth that made
men young, but the search itself, which caused a "reversion to infantile actions and
intelligence."[38] But among most sixteenth-century Spaniards raised in an age of faith,
skepticism remained subordinate to the will to believe.

Reports of the Seven Cities had beguiled Coronado, leading him to abandon the
comforts of home and position to venture into the unexplored interior of North
America. The seven Cities of Antilia, said to have been founded by seven Portuguese
bishops who had fled across the Atlantic during the Muslim invasion of Iberia, existed
so firmly in the popular imagination that fifteenth-century mapmakers drew an imaginary island in the Atlantic called Antilia. At first, Europeans believed that Columbus
had landed on Antilia in 1492, and so the West Indies came to be called the Antilles.
Five years after Columbus, John Cabot landed on the shores of New England and
named that area the "Seven Cities."[39] The cities proved elusive, but that seemed no
reason to doubt their existence. Thus, when reports reached Mexico in the late 1530s
of seven cities to the north, Coronado willingly risked his life and his wife's fortune to
find them. Coronado expected to find seven cities, and he refused to be disappointed.
He reported to the viceroy that seven Zuni towns existed, although archaeological
evidence suggests only six Zuni pueblos in Coronado's day.[40]

Like his Spanish contemporaries, Coronado's view of reality had been shaped by
literature and lore. He projected his fantasies onto an unfamiliar world, where they
became superimposed on the garbled translations of stories that Spaniards heard from
the natives. But the dreams of Coronado and his fellow conquistadores floated over a
bedrock of reality. Coronado knew of the extraordinary discoveries of Cortés and
Pizarro, where fact seemed more fantastic than fiction. In this new world, dreams had
come true. It seemed reasonable to suppose that beyond the horizon a new Mexico
might await discovery.

So it was that fact and fantasy intertwined to shape the minds and motives of those
Iberians who came to the New World in the first decades after its discovery. Today's
conventional wisdom holds that the native Americans lived in a world of myth and

legend while Europeans inhabited a world of rationality and well-grounded religious faith. In truth, each world contained elements of the mythic and the rational, but those worlds did not harmonize well with one another.

III

The coming together of Spaniards and Indians in North America represented more than an encounter of peoples with different values and institutions. Spaniards arrived in the New World with a variety of practical advantages that enabled them to turn many of their dreams into realities. One advantage was technology. Europeans living in an age of iron and steel entered a hemisphere where technology remained in the stone age.

At the time of their first encounter with outsiders from across the sea, native Americans living in the Southeast knew how to build and navigate large, swift dugout canoes that could carry people and goods along coastal waters and from island to island in the Caribbean.[41] Spaniards, however, sailed more sophisticated craft than the natives had ever known. In the century before the discovery of America, the Europeans, with Iberians in the vanguard, had mastered the winds. Innovations in reckoning latitude, shipbuilding, and rigging had made Spanish vessels suitable for blue-water sailing, beyond the continental shelf. No matter how cramped, crowded, filthy, or vermin-infested their vessels and how much the uncomfortable passengers and often-mutinous mariners suffered from spoiled food, acrid water, illness, and monotony, Spaniards could cross the Atlantic void and return again to Spain.[42] The disparity between European and Indian mastery of the seas determined that encounters between the two peoples would take place in the New World, rather than in the Old.

Carried to American shores by the new technologies and navigational know-how, Spaniards found that the technological superiority of their weaponry—steel swords, guns, and explosives—gave them tactical and psychological advantages that helped them defeat overwhelming numbers of natives on their home ground.[43] Weapons, for example, seemed to give Coronado the edge in storming Zuni, where the Pueblos held a defensive position with superior numbers. "God," a Spanish priest in New Mexico later observed, "hath caused among the Indians so great a fear of [Spanish soldiers] and their arquebueses that with only hearing it said that a Spaniard is going to their pueblos they flee." Or, as a Spanish priest in Florida put it, "Gunpowder frightens the most valiant and courageous Indian and renders him slave to the White man's command."[44]

Sixteenth-century Spaniards, some of whom were literate, also enjoyed an advantage in what one writer has called the "technology" of manipulating symbols.[45] "Your Majesty, language is the perfect instrument of empire," the Bishop of Avila reportedly told Queen Isabel upon presenting her with the first grammar of a modern European language.[46] Not only could Spanish leaders read and write, but those skills may have

6. *Explorers used an astrolabe or cross-staff (shown here) to determine latitude by "shooting" the angle of the sun or the north star at its zenith in relation to the horizon, then reading from a table that listed latitude entries for that angle for every day of the year. Juan de Escalante de Mendoza,* Itinerario de navegación de los mares y tierras occidentales *(1575). Courtesy, Jerald Milanich.*

honed their analytic abilities and produced superior modes of gathering intelligence. Spaniards, then, may have been more adroit than certain Indians at interpreting symbols or signs and using them to manipulate the natives. As Hernando de Alarcón made his way up the Colorado River in search of Coronado, for example, an Indian asked "whether we had sprung from the water or the earth or descended from the sky." Alarcón, like other Spaniards who were eager to convince the natives of their extra-worldly powers, answered that he had come as a messenger from the sun, and that he was the son of the sun.[47] North American natives, however, also used symbols to manipulate Spaniards, as Coronado and other explorers soon discovered. Many Spanish explorers in North America came to believe, in the words of one chronicler, that Indians were "born liars and in the habit of always telling falsehoods," even as they themselves lied to Indians.[48]

Europeans gained further advantages from animals, plants, and microbes that were commonplace in the Old World but not previously known in the New. Columbus's voyage marked the beginning of a lengthy and profound biological exchange between the two worlds. Although the exchange went both ways, it initially facilitated the European domination of North America.

North American natives, for example, had only one domestic four-legged animal, the dog. Whatever their virtues as man's best friend, dogs clearly are inferior sources of food and leather and less effective beasts of burden than two European domestic quadrupeds—horses and cattle. Without competitors or predators in the new American environment, some European animals flourished and played a vital role in the military campaigns of their Spanish masters. Herds of pigs and cattle provided a mobile larder for the Spanish invaders. Horses, some of them trained for war, increased the range and speed of the conquistadores' movement on land, just as their vessels increased their mobility on the water, and also gave Spaniards a psychological advantage. "The most essential thing in new lands is horses," one of Coronado's soldiers wrote upon returning to Mexico. "They instill the greatest fear in the enemy and make the Indians respect the leaders of the army."[49] Similarly, greyhounds, unknown in America but long trained by Europeans for hunting and warfare, guarded the Spaniards' camps, tore limbs from Indian adversaries, and frightened others into submission. Although it was a rare occurrence on Coronado's expedition, one of his lieutenants set dogs loose upon an Indian in order to extract information from him.[50]

Invisible organisms, unknown in the western hemisphere before the 1500s, took passage on Spanish ships and committed silent carnage. Native Americans certainly

7. *Pictograph of Spaniards on horseback in Cañón del Muerto, Arizona. Photograph by Helga Teiwes. Courtesy, Arizona State Museum, University of Arizona, neg. no. 28883.*

did not live free of illness before the arrival of Europeans. In Southwestern America, for example, they suffered the ravages of parasites, tuberculosis, and dental pathology.[51] Contagious "crowd" diseases endemic to Europe, however, seem to have been unknown in America—including smallpox, measles, diphtheria, trachoma, whooping cough, chicken pox, bubonic plague, typhoid fever, scarlet fever, amoebic dysentery, and influenza. These became epidemic killers in the New World, where natives had no prior exposure and, therefore, had acquired no immunities against them.[52] In central Mexico alone, some 8 million people, perhaps one-third of the native population, perished within a decade of the Spaniards' arrival. The vast majority of those who died probably succumbed to disease. Pathogens, then, served as valuable if accidental allies of the Spanish conquistadores.

Among Europeans, Spaniards held no monopoly on the introduction of disease to the New World, but far more natives apparently perished from diseases introduced by Spaniards in the first half of the sixteenth century than at any other time. Two common European maladies, smallpox and measles, struck this virgin population with deadly force, producing what one specialist has described as "possibly . . . the greatest demographic disaster in the history of the world."[53] The most extreme estimate suggests that during a great pandemic of 1519–24, smallpox alone took the lives of three of every four Indians who came in contact with it. A more conservative estimate places the death rate at one out of every three.[54] Disease not only took native American lives but demoralized grieving survivors and weakened their resolve to resist if not to live. The same diseases that devastated and dispirited Indians raised the spirits of Europeans and strengthened their faith in a divine providence. One of Cortés's followers put it succinctly when he explained the fall of the Aztec capital of Tenochtitlán: "When the Christians were exhausted from war, God saw fit to send the Indians smallpox."[55]

No one doubts that a large number of native North Americans died from diseases of European origin, but scholars disagree about the rapidity and extent of the disaster. Estimates of the number of natives living in North America when Europeans first arrived vary considerably. The question may be unanswerable, but scholars in the twentieth century have tended to accept increasingly higher figures. Many experts believe the native population of the entire hemisphere in 1492 exceeded 100 million although more conservative estimates put the total at half that number and below.[56] In America north of Mexico, recent estimates range as high as 18 million with 7 million representing a more conservative conjecture (5 million in the area of the present-day conterminous United States).[57] In comparison, the combined kingdoms of Castile and Aragón probably did not exceed 7 million in 1492, and the population of all Europe, eastern and western, may have stood at about 70 million in 1500.[58]

Ironically, then, it may be that disease, the least visible trans-Atlantic baggage, was Spain's most important weapon in the conquest of America. Had diseases worked against them, Spaniards might have found North America as impermeable as sixteenth-century West Africa—a "white man's grave" where indigenous diseases formed a deadly shield against encroaching Europeans and their animals.[59] Instead, disease in North America worked so much in the favor of Europeans in thinning the native population that it is more accurate to think of subsequent generations of "settlers" as re-settlers of the continent.

Although it might be argued that disease was the single most important element in assuring the Spaniards' quick victory over the natives, such an assertion cannot be proved. In practice Spaniards took advantage of a combination of circumstances— institutional, technological, and natural—that they believed their god had presented to them.[60] These circumstances became a potent mixture when blended with the powerful motives of individual Spaniards who journeyed into a new world to pursue particular religious, imperial, and personal goals. This heady mixture of motives and circumstances enabled the sons and daughters of Iberia to penetrate a world that they dimly understood and to make a stunningly rapid series of discoveries and conquests in lands where natives vastly outnumbered them. In the process, Spaniards began to transform that new world, even as it began to transform them.

2

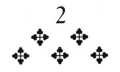

First Encounters

I grant you permission and authority to go to discover and settle. . . .
The Indians who should be in the island aforesaid, shall be allotted
in accordance with the persons [in your expedition].
King Fernando to Ponce de León, 1512

[In Alabama] we dressed our wounds with the fat of the dead
Indians as there was no medicine left.
Luys Hernández de Biedma to the king, 1544

[In Texas] half the natives died from a disease of the bowels and
blamed us.
Alvar Núñez Cabeza de Vaca, 1542

Columbus's accidental encounter with America, as he res-
olutely rode the winds toward the eastern shores of Asia,
represented both the discovery and the rediscovery of America. Asians crossing the Bering Strait had found America
thousands of years before, and Norsemen had established a
colony on what we today call Newfoundland about A.D. 1000.
Indeed, inconclusive but tantalizing evidence points toward
multiple discoveries of America before Columbus, including
an English visit to North America in 1481.[1] America's rediscovery by Columbus, however, represents the first significant meeting of the peoples of the two hemispheres. No
matter that Columbus and his Spanish sponsors did not know
where he had been and believed initially that he had visited
the Indies.[2] In Columbus's wake, white-sailed vessels from
Spain conducted a remarkable reconnaissance of the new-
found lands—a reconnaissance that lasted, in a sense, for

over three centuries, as Spaniards probed ever more deeply to understand the secrets of the American landscape.

From a European perspective, intrepid explorers sailed across the Atlantic to discover a new world. From native American viewpoints, Europeans came as predators rather than discoverers. Both were correct. The western hemisphere had not existed to Europeans until they found it, and it had taken courage and ingenuity to cross the ocean sea. To indigenous peoples, however, it must have seemed inconceivable that Europeans had discovered them or had a right to demand food, take captives, and claim sovereignty over them and their lands.

Whether one understands the first significant encounters between peoples from the two hemispheres as discoveries or as invasions, it is clear that those encounters were remarkably swift and pervasive. Spaniards, who stood in the vanguard of European westward expansion, penetrated some of the most remote corners of the hemisphere within a half century of Columbus's first landing. With few exceptions, the preponderance of those Spanish explorers were males. Gender roles, as all Europeans imagined them, rendered exploration an inappropriate activity for women.

I

Before all else, the geographic contours of the major Caribbean islands became known to Spanish mariners, and Spaniards quickly subjugated the large native populations of the Greater Antilles—Española (1496), Puerto Rico (1508), Cuba (1511), and Jamaica (1509). But within a few decades, Spain controlled empty islands. Caribs and Arawaks died in appalling numbers, their bodies wracked by strange diseases, and some killed outright by Spanish steel. By 1520 only 30 thousand natives remained on Española—apparently a densely populated island when Columbus planted Spain's first New World colony there less than thirty years before.[3] Soon after invading these islands, then, Spaniards needed to find additional lands with fresh sources of Indian laborers for the mines and plantations they had begun to operate in the Caribbean. Even though the Spanish Crown forbade the taking of Indian captives without provocation, Spaniards searched for Indians to enslave and the search led them to make further discoveries. So, too, did their continuing quest for the Asian islands that had eluded Columbus.

The Gulf of Mexico remained "a hidden sea," in the phrase of one historian, until 1508 when Spanish navigators threaded through the Greater Antilles in search of richer Asiatic islands.[4] Beyond Cuba, however, lay neither the Spice Islands nor the Orient. Instead, the contours of another continent gradually emerged. The first part of the North American coast to reveal itself to Spanish mariners was Florida, which they initially regarded as part of Asia. Spaniards may have seen Florida on a forgotten voyage in 1499; an outline of the peninsula, connected to Asia, appears on maps of

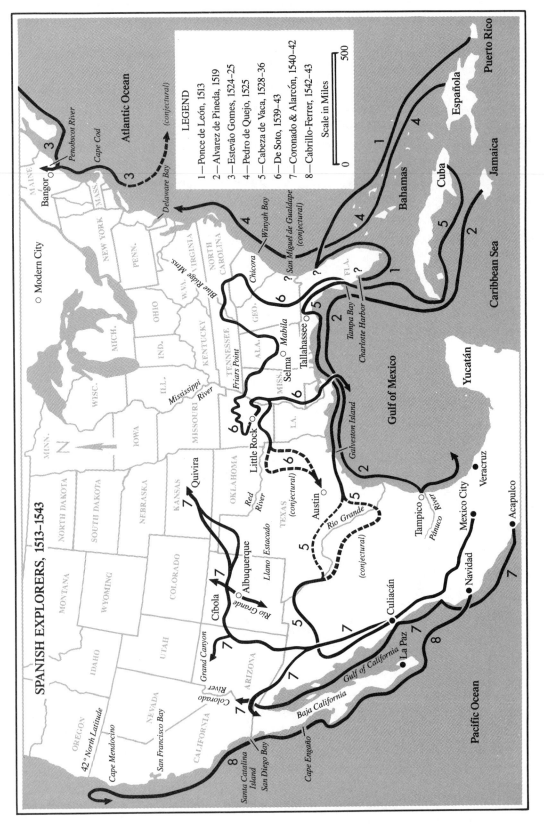

Map 1. Spanish explorers, 1513–43.

1500 and 1502.[5] Spaniards sailing from the Antilles had also landed on the Florida coast while on a surreptitious visit to capture Indian slaves.

The first recorded visit to Florida by a European was that of Juan Ponce de León, a veteran of Columbus's second voyage to America (in 1493), and a former governor of Puerto Rico, whose conquest he had spearheaded in 1508. With its abundant placer gold and native workers, Puerto Rico had made Ponce one of the richest men in the Caribbean and added luster to his reputation; his wealth had not dulled his ambition. When he lost a struggle for political control of the island, he began to look elsewhere for gold and Indian slaves. Intrigued by reports of an island to the north called Bimini, he returned to Spain to seek permission from King Ferdinand "to discover and settle" the island—to become an adelantado in the tradition of the Castilian reconquest of Iberia from the Muslims. No firsthand report supports the often-told story that the thirty-nine-year-old explorer went in search of a "fountain of youth," but it may contain some element of truth. The idea of such a fabulous fountain, located on an enchanted island, was deeply rooted in the lore and imagery of medieval Europe and had strong religious and sexual overtones. One chronicler, who scoffed at the notion of such a fountain, suggested that the search for it did not turn old men into young ones, but did weaken their minds and make them act like children, "with little sense."[6]

Whatever his goal, and gold and slaves seem to have been at least as important as rejuvenating waters, in March 1513 Ponce sailed northwest from Puerto Rico with three vessels and a pilot from the Andalucian port of Palos with long experience in Caribbean waters, Antonio de Alaminos. Making landfall far up the Atlantic coast of Florida, perhaps near present Daytona Beach, Ponce named the "island" of Florida for the day he went ashore—Easter Sunday, or the *Pascua Florida*. Like European explorers who followed him in North America, he took possession of the land for his sovereign in a stylized ceremony. Natives would surely reject such presumption, but until the late eighteenth century most European nations recognized these rituals of possession as establishing legal validity of claims to sovereignty over *terra nullius*— land previously unknown to Europeans.[7] Native rulers, Europeans supposed, lacked legitimate dominion over their lands and subjects for they were neither Christians nor did they live according to what Christians understood as "natural law."[8]

From the area of present Daytona Beach, Ponce's vessels beat their way south, hugging the shore to avoid being swept northward by the Gulf Stream. At their first meeting with natives in Florida, at a village south of Cape Canaveral, the Spaniards suffered an attack by Ais Indians, who may have been incited by earlier visits from Spanish slave hunters. Ponce moved on. The pilot Alaminos guided the little fleet through the dangerous Florida Keys, which the expedition discovered and named the "Martyrs," then sailed up the west coast of Florida, perhaps as far as Charlotte Harbor. No one knows. Once again, Ponce met open hostility from natives—this time Calusas who had had previous contact with Spaniards.[9]

Ponce returned to Puerto Rico by a roundabout route through the Bahamas, then journeyed on to Spain and petitioned the Crown for permission to conquer and settle the "new island" of Florida. The Crown gave its authorization in 1514, but Ponce delayed. As he explained to one royal official, "my wife has died and I have daughters still, and I have not dared leave them unprotected until they marry."[10] But Cortés's amazing discovery of the Aztec empire in 1519 apparently rekindled Ponce's interest in Florida—an interest that proved fatal. In 1521, Ponce landed at or near the place on Florida's Gulf side where Calusas had attacked his party in 1513. When the Spaniards began to construct buildings, they met fierce resistance. Wounded by a Calusa arrow, Ponce retreated to Cuba where he died a few days after his arrival.

Juan Ponce de León went to his painful death still believing that Florida was an island. Word had not reached him that a recent expedition, inspired by Antonio de Alaminos, his former pilot, had proved otherwise. In 1517 and 1518 Alaminos had guided expeditions that revealed the entire western coastline of the Gulf of Mexico, from the Mayan-occupied Yucatán peninsula to the Pánuco River, north of Veracruz near the future site of Tampico. Thus, Alaminos had narrowed the search for a sea lane through the Gulf to Asia to the unexplored coast of the northern Gulf, from the Pánuco River westward to Ponce de León's discoveries in Florida. With this special knowledge, Alaminos apparently had persuaded the governor of Jamaica, Francisco de Garay, to finance a reconnaissance of this last unexplored section of the Gulf. Alaminos could not accompany the expedition himself, but Garay outfitted four ships and put them under the command of one Alonso Alvarez de Pineda. Spain's rapid discoveries of the contours of the Gulf of Mexico apparently owe as much to the skill and experience of Antonio de Alaminos as to the commanders he served.[11]

Setting out from Jamaica in early 1519, Alvarez de Pineda coasted westward along the shallow waters of the unexplored northern shores of the Gulf. Along the way he noted several large rivers, including the Mississippi, which he may have seen on the feast of the Pentecost and named the Espíritu Santo. Whatever name he gave it, it was Alvarez de Pineda who discovered the Mississippi, not the later expeditions of Hernando de Soto or La Salle as is commonly believed. Far to the west of the Mississippi, Alvarez sailed up a river that he called "Las Palmas," where he spent more than forty days repairing his ships. Some historians have identified this Río de las Palmas as the Rio Grande, thus bringing Pineda into the interior of the present-day United States. The discovery in 1974 at the mouth of the Rio Grande of an inscribed clay tablet that appeared to have been left behind by the expedition seemed to strengthen their case, but most scholars doubt its authenticity. Alvarez de Pineda's Río de las Palmas was probably farther south—the river called Soto la Marina. In any event, Alvarez completed the circuit of this last unexplored section of the Gulf coast. He apparently became the first European to see coastal areas of western Florida, Alabama, Mississippi, Louisiana, and Texas—lands that he called "Amichel." Most important, he demonstrated that Florida was a peninsula, not an island, and that no passage to India threaded its way out of the Gulf.[12]

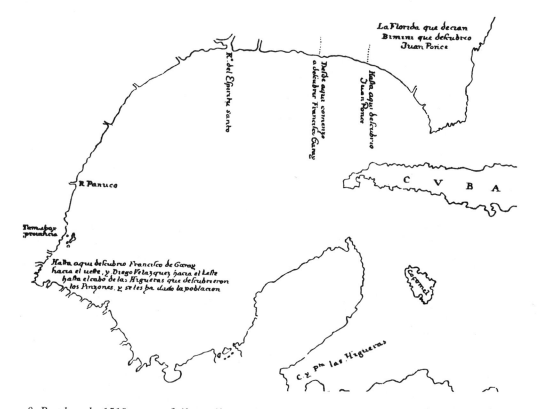

8. Based on the 1519 voyage of Alonso Alvarez de Pineda, and perhaps drawn by Pineda himself, this is the first map to show the entire Gulf of Mexico, with the Mississippi River (the Espíritu Santo) flowing into the Gulf and Florida attached firmly to the mainland. From a tracing of the original in the Archivo General de Indias, relettered for greater legibility. Courtesy, Institute of Texan Cultures, San Antonio.

II

Meanwhile, Spanish mariners had also begun to probe the Atlantic coast of North America. As early as 1500 Spaniards knew the outline of the continent north of present New England as a result of English exploration.[13] It appears, however, that no European visited the coast between Maine and Florida until Spanish slave hunters from the Antilles began to probe the area illegally, beginning in 1514 if not before. That year, one Pedro de Salazar discovered the "Island of the Giants"—apparently one of the barrier islands off the coast of present South Carolina. The "giants," so called because they were taller than the natives of the Caribbean and the Bahamas, seem to have had no prior experience with Spaniards. They treated their visitors graciously until Salazar's men began to seize them.[14] In 1521, Spanish slavers returned to the South Carolina coast, dropping anchor at Winyah Bay north of present Charleston and enslaving more large mainland natives to replace the nearly extinct Indian labor force on the island of Española.[15]

Behind these expeditions stood the money and influence of several prominent residents of Española, who justified enslaving the "giant" Indians on the grounds that they were cannibals and sodomites. One of these well-to-do figures, Lucas Vázquez de Ayllón, a high-ranking government official and sugar planter from a prominent family in Toledo, returned to Spain in 1521 to seek the Crown's permission to explore further the new discoveries and to colonize them. Ayllón, who had not visited the North American coast himself, took with him a remarkable witness, a native captured at Winyah Bay in 1521 whom the Spaniards called Francisco de Chicora. Chicora charmed the Spanish court, telling fabulous stories that may have helped persuade Ayllón that South Carolina, if not a land of milk and honey, was at least a land of almonds, olives, and figs—a new Andalucia. Indeed, to strengthen his case with Carlos V, Ayllón deliberately falsified the location of the "Land of Chicora," as he called the area around Winyah Bay, in order to put it in the same latitude as Andalucia—the classical geography of Ptolemy suggested that similar products would be found along the same lines of latitude.[16] For his pains, Ayllón received a license in 1523 to settle, at his own expense, a vast stretch of the Atlantic coast over which he would have a temporary monopoly. The Crown instructed the new adelantado to search for a strait and to learn about the peoples of the region, what they had of value, and "what must be done to put the said land under our Royal possessions . . . [and] have the incomes, profits and services of the said land." The "principal purpose" of the license, the Crown characteristically reminded Ayllón, was to convert the natives.[17]

Delayed by business and political affairs, Ayllón finally sent an expedition out from Española in 1525, in order to fulfill the requirement of his contract that he explore the coast. Captain Pedro de Quejo made a careful if hurried reconnaissance, taking soundings and bearings of the coast between Ponce de León's Florida and Delaware Bay. At several points he took formal possession, erecting stone crosses inscribed with the name of Carlos V and the date.[18] Although Quejo's reports of barrier islands with sand dunes and pine barrens along a sparsely settled coast failed to suggest a Mediterranean-like new Andalucia, Ayllón mortgaged his fortune to recruit and supply some 600 colonists, including some women and children. When he set out with six vessels from Puerto Plata on Española in 1526, he also brought along some black slaves, and a few Indians seized on previous expeditions to act as interpreters—including Francisco de Chicora. At least three Dominican priests accompanied Ayllón. One was the feisty Antonio de Montesinos, who some years earlier had escaped Española with his life after berating colonists for their cruel treatment of Indians. He is still remembered as the first Catholic priest in the Western hemisphere to speak out publicly against abusing the Indians.[19]

Ayllón's fleet made landfall in the area of Winyah Bay and the South Santee River in present South Carolina. There, Francisco de Chicora and other Indian interpreters soon fled into the swamplands, displaying their lack of appreciation of the benefits of European civilization. This stretch of coast, Ayllón quickly discovered, was too thinly populated to supply Indian labor and its acidic soils uncongenial for pasturage and farming. Ayllón abandoned the land of Chicora and sent his ships down the coast while he and a small party of horsemen rode south along the coastal Indian trails. The two parties reunited on Sapelo Sound in present Georgia, where Ayllón established the town of San Miguel de Gualdape, the first Spanish settlement in what is now the United States.

Ayllón had come to stay. His colonists built houses and a church among Indians whom the Spaniards called Guales, but the delay of moving the colony to this more congenial place proved costly. The Spaniards did not establish the town until October 8, too late to plant, and they began to suffer from cold fronts and, very likely, contaminated water. Sickness spread through the colony, with Ayllón himself among the fatalities. Without firm leadership, the demoralized colonists broke into warring factions and finally decided to return to Española. A freezing winter voyage claimed still more lives; of the 600 or so who set out originally from Española, only 150 returned alive—among them was Father Montesinos, killed by Indians a few years later in Venezuela. Ana Bezerra, Ayllón's widow, had stayed behind in Española and would spend the next years raising her small children alone and paying off a pile of her late husband's debts. Out of this tragedy, however, had come knowledge of the middle latitudes of the Atlantic Coast and the mirage of a new Andalucia, which would rise again on the Atlantic horizon to beguile a later generation of Europeans.[20]

Meanwhile, far to the north of Chicora and Delaware Bay, still more of the Atlantic Coast came into view. In September 1524 Estevâo Gomes, a Portuguese pilot in Spain's employ, sailed directly from Spain to America in search of the elusive passage to Asia. Gomes cruised an enormous stretch of the Atlantic Coast of North America in a single vessel, making an especially close survey of the coast between either Narragansett Bay or Buzzard's Bay and Cape Breton. No narrative or log of the voyage remains and so little information has been preserved that it is not certain whether Gomes sailed from south to north or from north to south, but a map based on his findings testifies to the ambitious scope of his journey. In addition to coasting the shoreline of what would become New England, Gomes sailed up the Penobscot River, in present Maine, to the head of navigation at today's Bangor. He took note of landmarks such as the "Río de San Antonio," which came to be called the Merrimac River, and "Cabo de las Arenas," known today as Cape Cod.

Upon his return to La Coruña, on the north coast of Spain, in August of 1525, Gomes sent a message to the king that he had brought with him Indian slaves, or *esclavos*. The message was garbled along the way and set tongues to wagging: Gomes had returned with *clavos*, or cloves! He must have found the way to the spice-rich Orient. But the truth soon emerged.[21] No strait could be found in that part of the hemisphere. Gomes, having failed to find a strait, had resorted to taking slaves, perhaps Algonquian speakers.[22]

As a contributor to cartography, Gomes achieved little more than revealing Cape

Cod to European mapmakers. The Italian mariner Giovanni da Verrazzano, sailing in the service of Francis I, went out in 1524–25, just ahead of Gomes, and crafted what one historian has termed "the first coherent narratives and maps of the east coast from Florida to Cape Breton."[23] Nonetheless, Gomes and other mariners sailing for Spain strengthened its claim to the Atlantic coast by right of discovery. This was suggested on the exquisite 1529 manuscript map by Diego Ribero, which shows the mid-Atlantic north of Florida as the "Land of Ayllon," with the New England states as the "Land of Estevâ [*sic*] Gomez."[24]

As prospects dimmed of finding a passage to the Indies along the Atlantic coast, Spain's interest in exploring its middle latitudes also diminished. Late in the sixteenth century, Basques from northern Spain near the French border continued to hunt whales and cod off the coasts of Newfoundland and Labrador, where they had established permanent posts.[25] Beyond that, the woodlands and their inhabitants along the cold-watered Atlantic held little attraction for a people who had found the riches of the Aztecs and the Incas. "No hay alla de oro"—there is no gold there—someone scrawled on the map from the Gomes expedition. As Peter Martyr, the Italian humanist in the Spanish court of Carlos V and an acquaintance of Ayllón's, wrote:

> But what need have we of what is found everywhere in Europe? It is towards the south, not towards the frozen north, that those who seek their fortune should bend their way; for everything at the equator is rich.[26]

III

Meanwhile Spaniards had not neglected the Pacific coast of the Americas. Crossing the isthmus in present Panama in 1513, Vasco Núñez de Balboa apparently became the first European to see the Pacific Ocean from the shores of the New World (Asian mariners had almost certainly visited America's Pacific shores before Columbus).[27] Less than a decade after Balboa sighted the Pacific, Spaniards sailed across it—in 1522 Sebastián Elcano completed the epic voyage around the world begun by Ferdinand Magellan, who had been killed by natives in the Philippines. Spain's discovery of the Pacific from American shores opened the way for the Pizarro brothers to conquer the Inca empire in 1531–33, and for less fortunate Spaniards to make new discoveries in northern latitudes.

Along the Pacific coast of North America, Hernán Cortés dominated maritime exploration for nearly two decades. In 1522, within a year after his stunning conquest of the Aztec capital of Tenochtitlán, Cortés sought new Indian kingdoms to conquer. He sent some of his men across Mexico where they began the slow and costly work of constructing ships at the port of Zacatula, north of present Acapulco. In 1523 the project caught the attention of Carlos V, who ordered Cortés to dispatch his ships to search for a strait through North America. With characteristic grandeur of vision, Cortés announced to the king that he would not only explore the Pacific but would

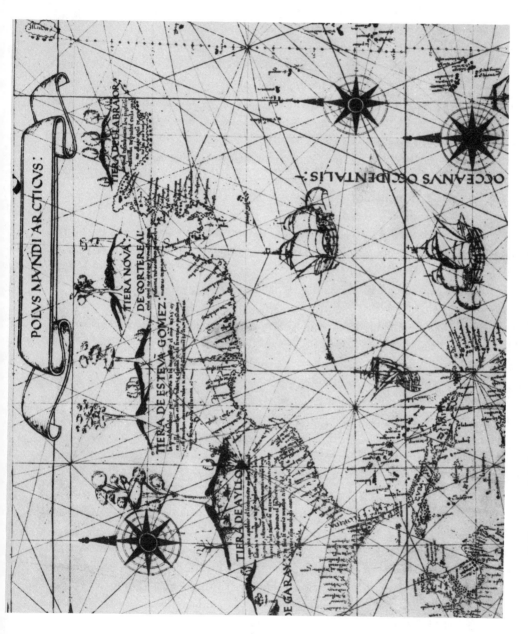

9. *Fragment of the Diego Ribero manuscript map of the world, 1529. Courtesy, the Biblioteca Apostolica Vaticana, which holds the original, and the Newberry Library, Chicago.*

also send a fleet along the coast of the Gulf of Mexico to Florida, and up the Atlantic to Newfoundland. A strait, "if it exists," could not elude this two-pronged quest, Cortés told the king, but at the very least "many great and rich lands must surely be discovered."[28] More pressing business delayed the enterprise and he failed to explore the Atlantic, but in 1532 Cortés finally sent ships northward on the Pacific.

In 1533 one of Cortés's pilots, Fortún Jiménez, sailed into a placid bay, which he named La Paz, on what he believed to be an island.[29] In actuality, he had discovered the tip of the nearly eight-hundred-mile-long Baja California peninsula. Perhaps it was Jiménez who gave California its name, one that soon extended to both upper and lower California, and then to the entire West Coast as far north as Alaska when Spanish mariners reached it in the late eighteenth century. Records do not reveal who named California, or when, but it is clear that by the early 1540s Spanish mariners referred to the land Jiménez had discovered as California. The name derived from a tale of chivalry popular in the early sixteenth century, *Las Sergas de Esplandián* by García Ordóñez de Montalvo, which told of an island called California, located "at the right hand of the Indies." There, the story went, Amazon-like women entertained men only once a year in order to engage in an intimate activity designed to perpetuate the race. Nearly a decade before Jiménez discovered Baja California, Cortés had heard accounts of an island rich in pearls and gold and, as he put it, "inhabited only by women without any men." Jiménez, then, may have known what to look for.[30]

Six years after Jiménez's discovery, another mariner sailing for Cortés, Francisco de Ulloa, proved that California was not an island. In 1539 Ulloa sailed up the west coast of Mexico to the head of the Gulf of California—also known as the Sea of Cortés—then turned south along the coast of Baja California, demonstrating that what had appeared to be an island was actually a peninsula. Ulloa's two vessels continued southward, rounded the tip of Baja California, then clawed their way up the Pacific coast against contrary winds and currents. One ship apparently sailed as far as Cape Engaño, about three quarters of the way up the peninsula. Claims that Ulloa continued north to the present United States appear fraudulent; the first European to reach the Pacific coast of what is today the United States was Juan Rodríguez Cabrillo, who sailed for Cortés's rival, Antonio de Mendoza, the viceroy of New Spain, as Mexico had come to be called, and the highest ranking Spanish official in the New World.[31]

A veteran conquistador from Andalucia, who apparently came to the New World as a teenager, Juan Rodríguez Cabrillo had fought in the conquests of Cuba, Mexico, Guatemala, and Honduras. Cortés had employed him to make pitch to seal the brigantines that he launched to conquer the Aztec's island capital city of Tenochtitlán in 1521—a task that Cabrillo had carried out with grisly efficiency, apparently using the fat of dead Indians for tallow. By the 1530s Cabrillo had become one of the richest men in Guatemala, but a series of financial reverses may have led him to accept

Viceroy Antonio de Mendoza's offer in 1542 to command a small fleet to explore the northwest coast of New Spain and then continue to China.[32] By then, Viceroy Mendoza dominated the exploration of the Pacific coast of New Spain. Cortés, the loser in a power struggle with the viceroy, had departed for Spain in 1540 to present his grievances to the king. He died there in 1546, never to return to Mexico.

In June 1542, Cabrillo sailed north from the Pacific port of Navidad, on a voyage from which he would never return. He led three small ships, whose construction he had overseen, across the Sea of Cortés and up the west coast of Baja California beyond Cape Engaño into waters no European had seen before.

On September 28, 1542, Cabrillo anchored his ships under the protective arm of Point Loma in the magnificent bay of San Diego, which the ship's log laconically described as "closed, and very good."[33] As the Spaniards came ashore, natives fled before them, but a few who remained behind conveyed through signs the remarkable news that people like the Spaniards had passed through the interior of the country. Reports of these Spaniards had alarmed the coastal Ipai, bands of semi-nomadic Yuman-speaking peoples whom Cabrillo's men described as "comely and large" and dressed in animal skins.[34] During that first night in San Diego, Ipai fired arrows at Spaniards who had gone ashore to fish, wounding three of them. The next day, Cabrillo assuaged the Ipais' hostility with presents and elicited more details about the strange men to the east. "In the interior," Cabrillo learned, "men like us were traveling about, bearded, clothed and armed . . . killing many native Indians, and . . . for this reason they were afraid." Cabrillo heard similar reports on three more occasions, as the expedition moved northward.

From San Diego the expedition continued to follow the coast, pausing at such places as Santa Catalina Island and San Pedro, today the principal harbor of Los Angeles. North of Santa Barbara, beyond Point Conception, autumn storms and heavy seas made the going slow. Cabrillo's ships put in on Santa Catalina Island and waited out the winter. When they left again, it was without their commander. Cabrillo had died shortly after the New Year, apparently from an infection that set in when he fell on slippery rocks and shattered a shinbone while trying to rescue some of his men from Indian attack.[35] Leadership of the expedition fell to the chief pilot, Bartolomé Ferrer, who pointed the three ships north beyond Cape Mendocino to the area of the present California-Oregon boundary at 42° latitude. There a shortage of supplies and a tempest, "with a sea so high that [the sailors] became crazed," forced him to abandon plans to continue to China. He turned back to Mexico, having reached the high water mark of Spanish exploration on the Pacific in the sixteenth century.

Although Cabrillo and Ferrer had failed to locate a strait or rich civilizations, they did explore some 1,200 miles of California coastline and established a Spanish claim to the Pacific coast of North America that was not challenged seriously for over two centuries.[36] They also provided evidence to Spanish cartographers that Asia and

North America were two separate continents, made exceptional navigational notes that would be of use to later mariners, and added to the growing doubts that a strait existed through North America.[37]

IV

With Cabrillo's voyage of 1542–43, just three decades after Ponce de León discovered Florida, Spaniards had completed a remarkable reconnaissance of North America's coastlines, up the Atlantic and the Pacific and along the Gulf of Mexico. Meanwhile, Spaniards on land had kept pace with their seafaring countrymen. The reports that Cabrillo had heard of "men like us" in the interior of California were true. Members of the expedition of Francisco Vázquez de Coronado, which had set out from Mexico in 1540, had reached the Colorado River about 150 miles due east of San Diego, and word of their presence had reached Cabrillo. On the other side of the continent, contemporaneous with Coronado's foray into southwestern America, Hernando de Soto cut a swath across the Southeast.

Fortunately for the Spaniards, the interior of North America was penetrable. No deadly diseases, hostile animals, extremes of climate, or geographical barriers stood insurmountably in their path. Coronado and De Soto hoped to find wealthy civilizations in the interior of the continent. "This was understandable on the analogy of both Mexico and Peru," historian David Quinn has reminded us, "where the coasts had offered little, the interior had produced a great deal."[38] Moreover, stories had persisted that the Seven Cities of Antilia existed somewhere in the New World, and by the late 1530s evidence pointed to North America. By then, Spain's relentless explorers had exhausted most other options, and fresh rumors emerged from North America with the dramatic return of Alvar Núñez Cabeza de Vaca, whose unintentional journey gave impetus to the expeditions of both Coronado and De Soto.

In the spring of 1536, Spaniards hunting slaves in what is today the northwestern Mexican state of Sinaloa encountered a black man and a white man, both dressed as Indians, traveling with an Indian retinue. They were, as Cabeza de Vaca put it, "dumbfounded at the sight of me, strangely undressed and in company with Indians. They just stood staring for a long time."[39] So ended an extraordinary odyssey that had begun at Tampa Bay, Florida, eight years before, and had taken Cabeza de Vaca across the continent.

A man of about forty and a native of Jerez de la Frontera in Andalucia, Cabeza de Vaca had come to Florida with the red-bearded Pánfilo de Narváez, a veteran conquistador of Cuba and would-be conquistador of Mexico. Although Cabeza de Vaca had no prior experience in America, his record in a lifelong military career apparently had earned him the position of second-in-command to Narváez. In the spring of 1528, Narváez's party had landed on the coast of Florida near the entrance to Tampa Bay with some 400 men, 80 horses, and a license from the Crown "to explore, conquer, and settle lands from the Río de las Palmas to the Island of Florida"—that is, the northern Gulf coast or what Alvarez de Pineda had called the land of Amichel.[40]

Instead of building a firm base at Tampa Bay, Narváez allowed Timucuan Indians to persuade him to go farther on, toward the northwest. In a province called Apalachen, Cabeza de Vaca later recalled, the Timucuans assured the Spaniards that they would find "gold and plenty of everything we wanted." The expedition had barely begun before Narváez made another fatal choice. He decided, according to Cabeza de Vaca, to "march along the coast while the ships sailed along it till they joined at the same harbor." Unfortunately, the land and sea parties failed to reunite. After a year of fruitless searching, the vessels sailed for New Spain. Ten women who followed their spouses to America remained aboard the ships, never to see their husbands again.[41]

Meanwhile, Narváez and 300 of his men plundered their way northwesterly to "Apalachen"—the chiefdom of Apalachee in the rich hill country near present-day Tallahassee. Initially, the Apalachees received them cordially but turned against the Spaniards after they took a chief as hostage. Then, illness and harrying attacks by Indians began to take a terrible toll on the Spaniards. Cabeza de Vaca remarked on the deadly accuracy and power of Apalachee bowmen, who could sink an arrow six inches into the trunk of a poplar tree or pierce Spanish armor with deadly accuracy. Members of the expedition of Narváez, and those who succeeded him into the Southeast, marveled at the native archers' skill at using the longbow—what one writer has characterized as "the most efficient missile weapon known to [sixteenth-century] man."[42] Spaniards later took Indian archers from Florida back to Spain where they astounded audiences with demonstrations; their accuracy exceeded that of European bowmen. Optimum use of the longbow required specialized muscles, usually acquired only by lifelong hunters. In western Europe and in the Aztec and Inca empires hunting had declined along with wild game, so archers in those places apparently handled the longbow less skillfully than North American sharpshooters. Many members of Narváez's band preferred to suffer raw sores from wearing heavy armor in the tropics rather than make themselves more vulnerable to Apalachee archers. Soon, however, Spaniards began to adapt to local conditions by discarding their disfunctional metal armor in favor of thickly padded cloth, patterned after that used by the Aztecs.[43]

At Apalachee it seemed to the Spaniards that they would leave Florida alive only if they made their way by water along the Gulf coast, back to Mexico. Setting up camp on the salt marshes bordering Apalachee Bay, and living on horsemeat, they made ropes from palmetto fibers and horsehair, turned their shirts into sails, and constructed five barges of horsehides. After hauling these insubstantial vessels through the marshes for several days until they reached the sea, the 242 survivors of the 300 who had started north from Tampa sailed along the coasts of present Florida, Alabama, Mississippi, Louisiana, and Texas. A month and a half later, in November 1528, the dazed occupants of two of these makeshift, overloaded craft washed up on or near Galveston Island, off the Texas coast.[44] They had survived the storms, Indian attacks, thirst, and hunger that had taken the lives of their companions, including Narváez, but the worst was yet to come. In a curious reversal of roles, the coastal Karankawas enslaved the Spaniards, who had arrived without benefit of horses, firepower, or sword. Although Spaniards would later describe Karankawas as cannibals, there is little reason to believe this charge, one that Europeans had long leveled at pagans. Indeed, the Karankawas were "shocked," Cabeza de Vaca remarked, at evidence that the starving Spaniards had eaten the flesh of their dead companions.[45]

Over the next few years most of Cabeza de Vaca's companions died or scattered so that he lost track of them. Resourceful and resilient, Cabeza de Vaca survived as a medicine man and merchant, which earned him a degree of freedom. In his travels among the coastal peoples he located three other survivors, Alonso del Castillo, Andrés Dorantes, and Dorantes's black Moorish slave, Esteban, all of whom joined Cabeza de Vaca in his flight toward Mexico. The foursome set out in September of 1534 and, for nearly two years, journeyed through Indian lands posing as holy men who possessed the power to heal. Adept at the manipulation of symbols, the Spaniards learned Indian languages and lifeways. With Paternosters, Ave Marias, a bit of theater, and at least one surgical operation, they cured Indians' maladies more through the power of suggestion than through the strength of medicine. Cabeza de Vaca, however, regarded these cures as signs of divine intervention. More than a century later, a Spanish jurist cited these "miraculous" cures as evidence that the God of the Christians wished the Spaniards to possess the Americas.[46]

As their fame as healers spread before them, Cabeza de Vaca and his companions received food, lodging, and escorts to lead them along Indian trails. When, dressed like Indians, they stumbled upon fellow Spaniards in July of 1536, their Indian retinue, according to Cabeza de Vaca, numbered six hundred. This Pima-speaking escort refused to leave Cabeza de Vaca and his companions with their fellow Spaniards—people whom Cabeza de Vaca acidly called "Christian slavers." How, the Pimans wondered, could the slave hunters and Cabeza de Vaca's band be of the same people: "We healed the sick, they killed the sound; we came naked and barefoot, they clothed, horsed and lanced; we coveted nothing but gave whatever we were given, while they robbed whomever they found."[47]

The long journey that Cabeza de Vaca and his companions took to return to their people cannot be reconstructed with precision from his confusing account, but the foursome probably moved southwesterly through Texas, crossing the Rio Grande between Brownsville and Laredo, then continued westerly across today's northern Mexico.[48] Lost, Cabeza de Vaca contributed little to cartographical knowledge; his route is of more interest to us today than it was to his contemporaries. "They did not even have any way of knowing in what longitude or latitude they roamed when they were lost," wrote the chronicler Gonzalo Fernández de Oviedo, who spoke with Cabeza de Vaca upon his return.[49] What was significant in the 1530s, however, was that the four wanderers, in the course of becoming the first Europeans to cross the continent north of Mesoamerica, saw more of its inhabitants than any of their countrymen and thus excited further exploration. Cabeza de Vaca made only modest claims about what he had seen, but his published account of his adventures, printed in Spain in 1542, brims with respect for many of the natives he encountered and contains a tantalizing reference to lands to the north where emeralds could be found and "where there were towns of great population and great houses."[50]

V

Despite his apparent reluctance to exaggerate what he saw, or perhaps because of that reluctance, Cabeza de Vaca's reports seemed to substantiate earlier rumors of a wealthy civilization to the north of Mexico. Thus, the return of Cabeza de Vaca stirred the ambitions of the two most powerful men in Mexico, Viceroy Antonio de Mendoza and Hernán Cortés. Both Mendoza and Cortés, Cabeza de Vaca wrote, "gave us clothes and whatever else they had," and presumably pumped him for information.[51]

Inspired in part by Cabeza de Vaca's reports, Cortés sent the expedition of Francisco de Ulloa to investigate the Pacific coast in 1539.[52] A year before Ulloa left, Viceroy Mendoza had launched his own quiet investigation, hoping to stave off rivals such as Cortés and Hernando de Soto. In the autumn of 1538 the viceroy put a peripatetic Franciscan, fray Marcos de Niza, in charge of a reconnaissance, reckoning that a small expedition led by a priest would draw little attention. Mendoza had hoped

10. *Viceroy Antonio de Mendoza. From Manuel Rivera Cambas,* Los gobernantes de México *(Mexico, 1872–73). Courtesy, DeGolyer Library, Southern Methodist University.*

to have Cabeza de Vaca, Alonso del Castillo, or Andrés Dorantes guide the expedition, but when each declined, Mendoza turned to Andrés Dorantes's black slave Esteban.[53]

Within a year fray Marcos returned to Mexico City, stirring up waves of sensational rumors of rich kingdoms with camels, elephants, and animals "with a single horn reaching to their feet, for which reason they must feed sidewise."[54] In a powerful, skillfully composed report, he claimed to have seen a city "bigger than the city of Mexico." The natives, the friar learned, called this place Cíbola, perhaps from an Opata word meaning Zuni (Spaniards later applied the word cíbolo to the curious "cattle" they found on the great plains—the buffalo). Fray Marcos described Cíbola as just one of seven cities in a country that appeared to be "the greatest and best of the discoveries"—an extravagant recommendation from a man who knew firsthand the wealth of Mexico and Peru, and an alluring suggestion that the fabled seven cities stood on the northern horizon.[55] In private conversations, fray Marcos apparently revealed more than he had in his written report. A fellow Franciscan, for example, remembered that fray Marcos "told me . . . that he saw a temple of their idols the walls of which, inside and outside, were covered with precious stones."[56]

Fray Marcos did not, however, claim to have entered the Zuni town that he called Cíbola. He said that he feared that he might meet the same fate as Esteban, whom he had sent ahead to scout. Esteban had reached the Zuni villages, but the Cíbolans had killed him. Fray Marcos decided to view the city from the prudent distance of a nearby hilltop. As he explained to the viceroy, "If I died, I would not be able to make a report of this country." Some historians doubt that fray Marcos saw Cíbola at all, or even came close to it—thus echoing Hernán Cortés, who termed the friar a liar.[57]

On the strength of fray Marcos's seductive reports, Viceroy Mendoza authorized Francisco Vázquez de Coronado to lead one of Spain's most elaborate expeditions into the interior of North America. Mendoza had toyed with leading the expedition himself, before entrusting it to his protégé. The second of four sons, whose father had signed the family estate to his oldest brother, Coronado had left his family home in Salamanca to seek his own fortune. He had come to Mexico in Mendoza's retinue in 1535 and advanced quickly under his patronage to the governorship of Nueva Galicia, the farthest point of Spanish settlement in northwestern Mexico, or New Spain. With funds from a providential marriage and a larger contribution from the viceroy, Coronado assembled and outfitted an enormous party: over three hundred Spanish adventurers (at least three of them women), six Franciscans, more than one thousand Indian "allies," and some fifteen hundred horses and pack animals.[58] Most of the Spaniards who signed up with Coronado had apparently come recently to the New World and, like Coronado himself, were novice conquistadores.[59] At the head of the Franciscans went fray Marcos, whom the viceroy seems to have sent to guide Coronado to the fabulous new lands.

The party traveled over well-worn Indian trails to Cíbola, the end of the road for the unfortunate fray Marcos.[60] The startling contrast between that Zuni village,

11. Zuni, photographed circa 1890 by Ben Wittick. Courtesy, School of American Research Collections in the Museum of New Mexico, neg. no. 16440.

numbering perhaps one hundred families, and the great city of his description, won fray Marcos the curses of the soldiers. Coronado sent him back to Mexico City, telling the viceroy: "He has not told the truth in a single thing that he said, but everything is the opposite of what he related, except the name of the cities and the large stone houses."[61]

For Coronado there would be no turning back. After taking Cíbola by force, Coronado made it his headquarters, then sent scouting parties out in several directions. Pedro de Tovar led a group that headed to the northwest, climbed the Colorado Plateau, and crossed the Painted Desert to investigate the people called Hopi, a Shoshonean-speaking group rumored to dwell in seven cities. Tovar found the Hopis living in splendid isolation in towns that resembled Cíbola, nestled at the bases of windswept mesas. Word of the Spaniards' attack on Cíbola had preceded them, and so the Hopis refused hospitality. As they had at Zuni, the Christian invaders invoked the aid of Santiago and seized a pueblo.[62]

Don Pedro returned to Cíbola bearing reports of a great river still farther west, so Coronado dispatched another scouting party, this led by one of his most trusted lieutenants, García López de Cárdenas, another second son of a Spanish nobleman. Twenty days beyond the Hopi villages, López de Cárdenas stopped short. His Hopi guides had brought him to the edge of the Grand Canyon of the Colorado, near the remarkable vista known today as Moran Point. There was no getting across. Impressed by the immensity of the canyon, the Spaniards saw it as a formidable obstacle, but they appear not to have regarded it as a place of beauty. To the sensibilities of most sixteenth-century Europeans, unbridled wilderness held little aesthetic appeal.[63]

The same September that López de Cárdenas saw the Colorado from the rim of the Grand Canyon, another Spanish party entered the river through its mouth on the Gulf of California. Three vessels sent by Viceroy Mendoza under command of another of his protégés, Hernando de Alarcón, had come to deliver supplies to Coronado and to explore the Pacific coast. In no small part because of the distorted report of fray Marcos, Coronado and Mendoza believed that Cíbola lay close to the coast, so Alarcón searched the lower Colorado River in a vain attempt to rendezvous with Coronado. After he had abandoned the search and returned to Mexico, one of Coronado's lieutenants reached the Colorado and, amazingly, located a tree with the inscription: "Alarcón came this far; there are letters at the foot of this tree." Nearly four centuries passed before another European duplicated Alarcón's feat of sailing into the treacherous shoal-ridden mouth of the Colorado, the greatest river in southwestern America.[64]

While some of his men explored the lands to the west of Cíbola, Coronado sent others to the east. On the Rio Grande and its tributaries, Coronado's emissaries entered the heart of the Pueblo country where irrigated fields produced food and forage in a land of little rain. The Spanish scouting parties explored the Rio Grande, from present Albuquerque north to Taos Pueblo, and eastward beyond the great river to the imposing pueblo of Pecos on the edge of the buffalo plains. Meanwhile, Coronado moved his main army from Zuni to the Rio Grande. There, not far from Albuquerque, he made his headquarters for the winter.

Coronado quickly became an unwelcome guest among the Pueblos. Hundreds of Spaniards and Mexican Indians, together with the ravenous livestock that accompanied them, strained the resources of Pueblo farmers. Shortages of clothing and food became acute in the cold winter of 1540–41. Then Christians alienated Pueblos by literally taking the clothes off their backs and the food from their larders. Tensions mounted in the months that followed, as Pueblos suffered other indignities. One soldier, for example, lured an Indian away from home by asking him to watch his horse, then returned to rape the Indian's wife. Finally, the Pueblos rebelled and Coronado's men fought for their lives. Determined to make an example of one village in order to discourage others from rebelling, García López de Cárdenas destroyed the pueblo of Arenal and its residents. He set fire to the rooms to smoke out resisters, then captured fleeing Indians and burned them alive at the stake. Still the Pueblos refused to submit. The conflict did not end until spring, by which time Coronado's forces had destroyed perhaps as many as thirteen villages. Rather than surrender, some Pueblos had fled to the mountains.[65]

When spring came, Coronado pushed deeper into the continent, now seeking a kingdom called Quivira, described to him by a native of that land whom Coronado's men had encountered at Pecos and whom they called the Turk. The Turk portrayed Quivira as fabulously wealthy: "The lord of that land took his siesta under a large tree from which hung numerous golden jingle bells," and "the common table service of all was generally of wrought silver, and . . . the pitchers, dishes, and bowls were made of gold."[66] Little wonder that a beguiled Coronado followed the Turk on a circuitous search that took him onto the high plains of today's West Texas, then northeast across the panhandles of Texas and Oklahoma before ending in frustration at a Wichita village on the Arkansas River near the present-day town of Lyons, in central Kansas.[67] There, Spaniards garroted the Turk, having learned from him that Pueblos from Pecos had asked him, as Coronado put it, to "take us to a place where we and our horses would starve to death."[68] If the Turk had planned such a strategy, it might have worked. On the trackless sea of grass, men had no other landmarks than moving herds of buffalo, "nothing but cattle and sky" as the expedition's chronicler, Pedro de Castañeda, remembered it. Hunters could not find their way back to camp, and a scouting party had to rely upon "a sea-compass" in order to make its way.[69]

Following their compass, Coronado's discouraged force returned to the Rio Grande for the winter. Notwithstanding their repeated disillusionment, many in Coronado's entourage wished to stay in Tierra Nueva, "the new land," as they called New Mexico, and Coronado himself planned to reenter the plains the next spring to explore beyond central Kansas. In December, however, a riding injury, from which he never fully recovered, awakened Coronado from his dreams of empire. He decided to go home. In the spring of 1542 his expedition returned the way it had come, taking with it nothing more than hard-won knowledge of the new land. In New Mexico, Coronado left behind some Indian allies and Negroes, two Franciscans who soon became martyrs, and embittered Pueblos who would long remember these first Spanish intruders.[70]

In Mexico City Coronado faced an official investigation of his management of the expedition to Cíbola. The court exonerated him of all charges, a decision that may have been influenced by his failing health and changed character. "He is more fit to be governed . . . than to govern," the presiding judge wrote to the king.[71] Coronado died in Mexico City in 1554, a dozen years after returning from his failed quest. Coronado's chief lieutenant, García López de Cárdenas, was less fortunate. Tried in Spain of various crimes against Indians, he died in prison.

VI

During the same years that Coronado explored the southwestern corner of the continent, Hernando de Soto became the first European to penetrate the heart of the Southeast, traveling several thousand miles through ten states in what is today the American South. Like Coronado, De Soto was the second son of prosperous parents whose oldest son would inherit the family's entailed estate in the Extremaduran town of Jerez de los Caballeros. Unlike the novice Coronado, De Soto had had substantial experience in Central America and Peru before launching his extraordinary foray into North America. Great expectations had drawn him to the Indies at age fourteen; he had returned to Spain twenty-one years later, in 1535, with a share of the treasure of the Incas and with unquenched ambition.[72] Convinced that another Peru existed in Florida, De Soto gambled his newly won fortune on the chance that he would find power, glory, and a still greater fortune in the lands that had devoured the expeditions of previous adelantados—Juan Ponce de León, Lucas Vázquez de Ayllón, and Pánfilo de Narváez.

In April 1537, Hernando de Soto received royal authorization to explore and settle Florida. In the Spanish imagination, Florida had come to embrace all of southeastern North America—from the Pánuco River, on the western side of the Gulf of Mexico where Cortés had founded a settlement in 1523, to Delaware Bay, the farthest point of Pedro de Quejo's explorations in 1525 for Ayllón.[73] De Soto hoped to enlist the aid of Cabeza de Vaca, who had returned to Spain too late to obtain Florida for himself. Cabeza de Vaca declined to serve under De Soto, however, and received instead the governorship of Paraguay where further misfortunes, no less remarkable than those he encountered in North America, awaited him. Meanwhile, De Soto assembled and launched an expeditionary force so large and costly that it exceeded even his considerable resources; like many other conquistadores, he had to borrow funds from Genoese merchants based in Seville. De Soto's nine ships landed on the west coast of Florida in late May 1539, probably at Tampa Bay, with a large number of horses, mules, pigs, and dogs, and well over six hundred Europeans. Most were young soldiers, but at least two Spanish women and several priests were on board.[74]

Shortly after landing, Florida's newest adelantado had the good fortune to find Juan Ortiz, a survivor of the Narváez expedition, living among Indians. Until his death in the winter of 1541–42, Ortiz pierced the language barrier that separated De Soto from Apalachees and other Muskoghean peoples whom he encountered across most of the South. "This interpreter puts new life into us," De Soto wrote, "for without him I know not what would become of us." De Soto regarded the appearance of Ortiz as a sign that God "has taken this enterprise in His especial keeping."[75]

If De Soto believed that he enjoyed the favor of his deity, Indians with whom he came into contact must have felt that they had incurred the wrath of theirs. De Soto, who had come to pillage, was a scourge upon the land. He may have been no more ruthless than Coronado, but De Soto traveled through more prosperous and populous country that afforded greater opportunities for mayhem. Along his path, in the densely populated interior of the Southeast, stretched the fertile farmlands and great urban centers of peoples who belonged to the so-called Mississippi tradition, Indians whose distant descendants would be known by such names as Caddos, Cherokees, Chickasaws, Choctaws, and Creeks.

The linguistically diverse but culturally similar Mississippian peoples inhabited most of southeastern America, west to the perimeters of the dry country beyond the Trinity River in Texas and north to the edges of the colder climates of the upper Mississippi and Ohio valleys. They had built the most elaborate civilization north of Mexico, with large secular towns, ceremonial centers with immense temple mounds, sophisticated arts and crafts, and hierarchical political, economic, social, and religious systems. Water, more bountiful in the Southeast than in the arid Southwest, nourished this culture. Across much of the South, rich, well-drained soils of the flood plains of numerous rivers and streams yielded surpluses of corn, beans, and squash to native farmers, and dense woodlands offered abundant game, fish, nuts, fruits, and berries to hunters and harvesters.[76] In the mid-sixteenth century, De Soto found many of these people living in polities larger than tribes, which anthropologists have termed chiefdoms. The largest chiefdoms, Apalachee, Cofitachequi, Coosa, and Tascaloosa, ruled over smaller, dependent chiefdoms, and collected tribute that filled storehouses with agricultural produce and luxury items. Some chiefdoms were in decline in De Soto's day, but others still functioned vigorously; De Soto's men were the only Europeans to see them in full operation before they began to shrivel in the wake of European disease and depopulation.

De Soto had brought an ambulatory larder in the form of hundreds of pigs whose numbers increased along the march, but he regularly plundered the food supplies of the natives, taking dried corn, squash, and beans from storage. He had brought twice the number of Spaniards that Coronado did, but unlike Coronado, who imported Indian allies into North America from central Mexico and treated them reasonably well, De Soto captured slave labor along his route. He had worked out the plan before leaving Spain, for he brought along iron chains and collars to link Indians into human baggage trains. Indian women "who were not old nor the most ugly," De Soto's secretary later explained, the Spaniards "desired both as servants and for their foul uses . . . they had them baptized more on account of carnal intercourse with them than to teach them the faith."[77] Uncooperative Indians might be put to the sword, thrown to the dogs, or burned alive, or might have a hand or nose severed. De Soto killed and mutilated Indians with little provocation, for in the words of one chronicler who knew him in Panama, De Soto was "much given to the sport of hunting Indians on horseback."[78]

The Spaniards' reputation, already established by the Narváez expedition, had preceded them, so that Indians in De Soto's path often resisted his incursions by abandoning their towns and employing guerrilla tactics or, on occasion, executing massive assaults. These tactics weakened De Soto, but did not stop him, and Spanish firepower took a terrible toll. Accordingly, some Indians chose diplomacy, trying to enlist De Soto as an ally against a rival chiefdom or feigning cooperation with De Soto while pointing him toward distant lands. Despite his protestation that "of what these Indians say I believe nothing but what I see," De Soto believed what he wished to believe.[79] Journeying wherever rumors of gold took them, De Soto and his men left a trail of shattered lives, broken bodies, ravaged fields, empty storehouses, and charred villages.

In contrast to the route of Coronado, much of which can be accurately reconstructed because the sites that he visited remained occupied by Indian peoples and because landmarks stand out in sharp relief in the Southwest, the precise route of De Soto's elliptical wanderings in the southern woodlands remains a matter of conjecture. The broad contours, however, seem clear.[80] Cutting a sanguinary path northward from Tampa Bay through the Florida peninsula and the lands of Tocobagans and various Timucuan tribes, De Soto halted for the winter at the site of present Tallahassee in the lands of the prosperous Apalachees—the first of the Mississippian chiefdoms he would encounter. On a ridge east of today's Florida state capitol building, De Soto's men moved into the town of Anhaica, which the Apalachees had abandoned, and spent an uneasy winter as Apalachees twice set fire to their fortified camp.[81] In early March, when spring approached, De Soto resumed his journey. Using Indian guides and following Indian trails, he traveled northeasterly through central Georgia and into South Carolina to a chiefdom called Cofitachequi, which Indians described as rich in gold, silver, and pearls.

At the principal town of Cofitachequi (located perhaps on the Wateree River near Camden, South Carolina, where mounds still testify to an ancient site), Indians carried a young female provincial leader to the river's edge on "a litter covered with delicate white linen," according to De Soto's secretary. This "Lady of Cofitachequi," as the Spaniards called her, crossed the river in a canoe covered with a canopy. She greeted the Spaniards with gifts of clothing and placed a string of pearls around De Soto's neck.[82] The Spaniards found no gold or silver among these impressive people, but fresh-water pearls, inferior to the salt-water variety, abounded. De Soto's men stole pearls wherever they could find them, looting temples and tombs. One grave yielded Spanish axes, a rosary, and some trade beads, leading De Soto to conclude correctly that he was "in the territory where the lawyer Lucas Vázquez de Ayllón came to his ruin."[83]

After pillaging nearby villages, De Soto seized his gracious hostess and moved on toward another people who reportedly enjoyed great wealth. The Lady of Cofitachequi managed to slip away, but the Spaniards pushed northward without her into present North Carolina before turning westward into the Appalachians. Mountains, De Soto knew, had yielded the treasures of the Aztecs and the Incas. Propelled on the wings of avarice, De Soto's men became the first Europeans to cross the Appalachians; they crossed the Blue Ridge Mountains through Swannanoa Gap to the French Broad River, which they followed into the Tennessee Valley. This achievement brought no consolation. When they reached their destination at Chiaha, near present Dandridge, Tennessee, rumor once again fell hard upon reality. No treasure was to be found in the lands of these Muskoghean-speaking peoples.[84]

12. *A Timucuan "queen elect," carried to the king on a litter. Engraving by Theodore de Bry after an original water color by Jacques Le Moyne, 1564. Theodore de Bry,* Historia Americae *(Frankfort, 1634). Courtesy, DeGolyer Library, Southern Methodist University.*

Stories of wealthy kingdoms to the southwest then drew De Soto down the length of the Tennessessee River Valley, into the heart of present Alabama and a devastating setback. Much of the way he traveled through Coosa, a large chiefdom whose principal town of the same name stood in northeastern Alabama or northwestern Georgia, but which extended from Chiaha, in present Tennessee, to Childersburg, on the Coosa River in central Alabama. Below Coosa, De Soto moved into the chiefdom of Tascaloosa, where forces led by the handsome, tall chief Tascaloosa, mauled De Soto's army at the stockaded town of Mabila. Spaniards and Indians suffered heavy casualties. "At night," one participant remembered, "we dressed our wounds with the fat of the dead Indians as there was no medicine left." In addition to men and horses, De Soto lost supplies, clothing, and booty, including a chest of pearls hauled all the way from Cofitachequi.[85]

A less determined leader would have quit, and De Soto had the opportunity. Juan Ortiz, the translator, had brought him the location of supply ships on the Gulf of Mexico that might carry the Spaniards to safety, but De Soto kept this information to himself and turned the tattered remnants of his army away from the Gulf. He led his men northerly through difficult country between the Alabama and Tombigbee rivers, before stopping to winter at "Chicaça" near Tupelo in northeastern Mississippi, some fifty miles below the Tennessee border. Perhaps the same cold weather that prompted Coronado's men to steal blankets from the Pueblos that winter of 1540–41 extended into Mississippi. There, one of De Soto's men remembered, "snows fall more heavily . . . than they do in Castile."[86]

In March, before the Spaniards broke winter camp, ancestors of the modern Chickasaws launched a surprise attack, setting De Soto's winter quarters afire and burning horses and swine as well as Spaniards and their clothing, saddles, and remaining supplies. The Chickasaws inflicted greater losses than the Spaniards had suffered at Mabila. Still De Soto pushed on, following Indian trading trails to the "Rio Grande"—the Mississippi River. De Soto's band became the first land expedition to see the Mississippi, probably near Friars Point in the northwest corner of the present state of Mississippi.

The great river might have carried De Soto's shattered army quickly toward safety on the Gulf. Instead, he ordered his men to build barges and cross the river. On the densely populated alluvial shores of the Mississippi they had seen urban centers with temples atop man-made mounds. Indians, however, reported that cities with gold lie ahead, thus enticing De Soto to continue westward into present Arkansas. The Spaniards apparently made their way to the Arkansas River past the future sites of Pine Bluff and Little Rock, then continued into Caddo country on the edge of the Great Plains. Along the way they asked Indians about the distance to the South Sea—to the Pacific! At one point during De Soto's sojourn in Arkansas, his expedition came within 300 miles of Coronado's, which was then in Kansas. Ironically, a Plains Indian woman bridged the gap between the two parties. One of Coronado's men had "acquired" her among the Pueblos. She escaped from her Spanish captors in the Panhandle of Texas and fled eastward only to fall into the hands of the De Soto party.[87]

Another harsh winter came and went in Arkansas, near present Little Rock. In the spring, apparently aware that he had reached the edge of the same buffalo plains where Cabeza de Vaca had reported impoverished Indians, De Soto led a retreat down the Arkansas River to the Mississippi. As the troops moved slowly downriver through swampland, their numbers and firepower dangerously reduced, De Soto tried a ruse that had worked elsewhere for Spaniards in the New World, including Alarcón on the Colorado. To gain the help of a group of powerful Natchez Indians, De Soto sent word that he was "the son of the sun." He may have known that rulers of the Natchez theocracy claimed to be descended from the sun, and he would gain considerable power over them if they believed his story. But a Natchez chief put De Soto to the test, telling him to "dry up the great river and [then] he would believe him."[88] Even subterfuge now failed De Soto.

In May 1542 Hernando de Soto took ill and died. His diminished party, now led by Luis de Moscoso, started overland for Mexico. They hoped to reach Pánuco, which Narváez and Cabeza de Vaca had also seen as the source of their salvation. For four months they traveled westward, again crossing present-day Arkansas and Louisiana and pushing well into Texas, perhaps to the Colorado River near present Austin, until they found themselves beyond the borders of the Mississippian corn culture and among a people who "neither planted nor gathered anything."[89] With what must have been heavy hearts, they turned back to the Mississippi River. Over the winter of 1542–43 they built seven sturdy boats on the Mississippi, perhaps near today's Natchez, Mississippi, and stocked them with animals, dried meat, fruits, corn, and beans. The first Europeans known to sail on the Mississippi, they managed to navigate it to its mouth despite continual harassment by natives. In September 1543, fifty-three days after entering the Gulf of Mexico, they arrived at the small settlement near the mouth of the Pánuco River. The survivors, some three hundred men and one young woman, a servant named Ana Méndez, represented about half of those who first landed with De Soto on the Florida coast in 1539; in addition, two women from Coosa and perhaps other North American Indians as well, accompanied the survivors to Mexico.[90]

VII

When the remnants of the De Soto expedition entered the harbor at Pánuco, thirty years had passed since Ponce de León had first sighted Florida. During that interval tenacious Spaniards had not only navigated the shores of North America, but had spanned the continent. These remarkable forays failed to yield a strait to Asia, the fabled cities of Antilia, or another Mexico, Peru, or Andalucia, but they did open new geographic vistas. By the 1520s the broad outlines of the North American continent had begun to appear on European maps.

Most of the details uncovered by Spain's explorers, however, did not appear on printed charts. Two explanations seem clear. First, even the most purposeful of those explorers who penetrated the interior of North America, Coronado and De Soto, did not emphasize map-making or the systematic acquisition of geographical knowledge. By responding to stories of treasure, they allowed Indians to set the course of their travels. Second, eager to protect its New World discoveries from European rivals, Spain guarded the reports of its explorers as state secrets. New pilots, for example, took an oath in the name of the Holy Trinity never to relinquish their charts to foreigners. In Seville, Spanish officials recorded the results of discoveries on a master chart, the *padrón real*, but prohibited its publication.[91]

Spain succeeded remarkably well at blocking the dissemination of geographic information. Into the nineteenth century, printed maps failed to portray accurately the North American interior as generations of Spain's explorers understood it (printed foreign maps came closer to the mark than those printed in Spain). But Spain succeeded to a fault. By not publicizing its discoveries, Spain weakened its later claims to ownership by right of prior exploration, and handicapped its own explorers. Expeditions that sailed from Spain seem to have made good use of the geographic information that rested in archives in Seville, but Spanish explorers who set out from bases in North America often lacked knowledge of previous discoveries. That Baja California was a peninsula, that New Mexico existed, and other lesser details of geography uncovered during the initial phases of Spanish exploration, became lost from view.[92] Discoveries were remade as Spaniards continued to search North America for a strait to Asia, wealthy civilizations, and other fabulous places long after the so-called age of exploration had ended. "Unicorns have been seen in this land," a professor at the University of Salamanca wrote a generation after the expeditions of Coronado and De Soto had revealed no signs of unicorns.[93]

Spaniards had covered a vast portion of North America by 1543, but they had failed to find the North Americans themselves.[94] Cabeza de Vaca may be an exception, for he lacked the means to impose his will upon the natives. His very survival required him to learn Indian languages and adopt Indian lifeways, even when it meant eating plants, animals, and insects unfamiliar to European palates. To a remarkable degree, Cabeza

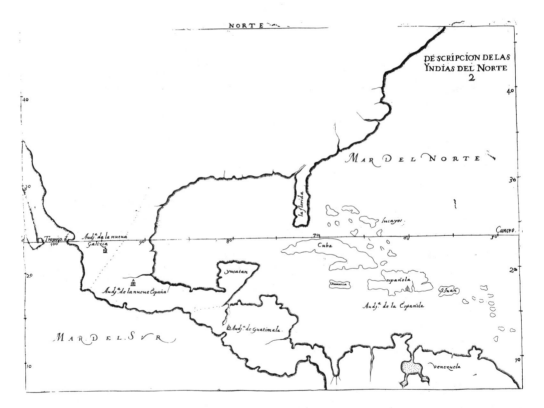

13. *The dearth of information on this map, an illustration in Antonio de Herrera y Tordesillas*, Historia general de los hechos de los Castellanos en las yslas i tierra firme del mar oceano, *8 vols. (Madrid, 1601), may suggest Spanish interest in keeping the geographical information gleaned by Coronado, De Soto, and other explorers from falling into the hands of foreign rivals. Courtesy, DeGolyer Library, Southern Methodist University.*

de Vaca penetrated the worlds of North American natives and came to understand them on their own terms. Coronado and De Soto, on the other hand, had no reason to adapt or to learn. They brought sufficient arms, men, and animals to impose their will. Rather than try to comprehend Indians, who interested them chiefly as a source of wealth, Coronado and De Soto projected their own dreams upon the natives. They exploited Indian labor, food, and know-how in unsuccessful efforts to make their dreams come true. In the nightmares that followed, Spaniards blamed Indians for treacherously deceiving them.[95]

Perhaps it could not have been otherwise. These Christians of the late Middle Ages and the early Renaissance had traveled beyond the horizons of their intellectual experience. They had moved beyond their known geography into worlds that did not fit their conceptions of history, theology, or the nature of man and beast. Attempting to understand a strange new world required mental adjustments that engaged and defied the best European minds. Even as Spanish exploration of North America reached a crescendo in the early 1540s, Spanish scholars had entered into a new round of inquiry about the nature of America and its native peoples. But to incorporate Amerindians into their own schema required that Europeans either question and revise deeply held beliefs in religious traditions such as monogenesis or Noah and his ark, or hold fast to their assumptions and view Indians in what one historian has termed "the half light of [the Europeans'] traditional mental world."[96] Similarly, rather than do violence to traditional categories and discourses, the earliest European explorers and scholars described America's exotic flora and fauna as like their own. In this way, they not only rendered the strange familiar, but managed a cognitive conquest of a world whose profound unfamiliarity might otherwise have overwhelmed them.[97]

If the early exploration of North America opened hazy vistas of a new world to the Spaniards, it began to diminish and alter the worlds of the natives. Over the course of the next several centuries, North American Indians would adopt elements of European culture, many native peoples becoming acculturated over time. In the initial phase of Spanish-Indian contact, however, deculturation rather than acculturation characterized the transformation of Indian cultures.

If natives learned anything of value from their contact with brutal Spanish explorers in the first half of the sixteenth century, it was probably to distrust them. In these first brief encounters, Indians had little opportunity and perhaps little desire to learn European folkways or acquire European material goods—tools, weapons, or other trade items—as they would in subsequent centuries. In pursuit of sexual pleasures, Spaniards in the mid-sixteenth-century had produced the first mestizos or mixed bloods in North America, but their numbers were too small to make a significant impact on Indian communities. Horses, which would dramatically alter the lives of Plains Indians by the eighteenth century, appear not to have remained in North America in the aftermath of these first Spanish *entradas*. Among the animals introduced by the Spaniards in the early sixteenth century, perhaps only pigs escaped in sufficient numbers into the southern forests to reproduce and become a staple of Indian diet.[98]

Pathogens, on the other hand, followed Spain's first explorers everywhere, with devastating and profoundly transformative effects on some Indian communities. Fragments of documentary, archaeological, and circumstantial evidence suggest that the collapse of the North American population began when Spain's explorers introduced new diseases early in the sixteenth century.[99] Cabeza de Vaca reported that after he and his companions arrived ill on an island off the coast of Texas in the fall of 1528, "half the natives died from a disease of the bowels and blamed us."[100] Once on American shores, Old World microbes could, of course, move faster than Spaniards. Infectious diseases traveled with Indian traders and in native canoes along the waterways of the Southeast—a region of North America that, in the words of one specialist, "has been gravely burdened by disease . . . beyond the American norm."[101] In the dry, sparsely populated Southwest, contagion would have spread more slowly than in the humid, densely peopled Southeast with its higher rates of contact. But in the Southwest, too, significant numbers of Indians probably died from these first encounters with previously unknown European diseases, even if they met no Europeans. Indeed, climatic conditions in the Southwest were unusually favorable for the transmission of smallpox, the most virulent of European diseases.[102]

The beginnings of the collapse of native populations must have begun to restructure Indian societies, even before Europeans established permanent settlements. Disease probably caused some natives to flee their communities, and dramatic declines in population must have led to the abandonment of those native towns that lacked enough residents to carry on the specialized functions of urban life. Shortages of skilled persons to make complex societies function probably led to the simplification of political, economic, and social institutions and weakened the control of elites. Survivors, even those from different ethnic groups, probably joined together to form new living arrangements. Nowhere was this process more dramatic than in the Southeast, where the great chiefdoms of the Mississippi tradition began to disintegrate as their population bases began to dwindle.

Still other effects of large-scale demographic disaster seem likely. Among some native peoples, including the Pueblos, motives for intertribal warfare may have lessened as a shrinking population raised the per capita resource base. In other areas, diseases probably tipped the balance of power between tribes. The riverine peoples of the lower Mississippi Valley and its tributaries, for example, enjoyed considerable power at the time of De Soto's arrival but probably declined in influence as diseases, carried swiftly along waterways, weakened their population base. Their decline facilitated the rise in influence of upland peoples, such as Chickasaws and Choctaws, whose relative isolation may have afforded them greater protection from European diseases. The first disease-bearing Spaniards, then, inadvertently set into motion rapid cultural and structural transformations of native societies that would repeat themselves over the next two centuries, whenever Spaniards or other Europeans pushed onto new frontiers in North America.[103] In the mid-1570s one Hernando de Escalante Fontaneda, who knew Florida Indians well because they had held him captive for thirteen years, suggested that the native population was so dense and obdurate that Spaniards could gain access to Indian land only by abducting and selling Indians. "In this way," Fontaneda wrote, "there could be management of them, and their number become diminished."[104] With virulent microbes as allies, the Spaniards had little need for such a strategy. As diseases caused their numbers to diminish, the natives' ability to resist European invaders declined and more land became available for subsequent waves of Europeans and their livestock.

3

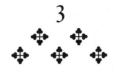

Foundations of Empire:
Florida and New Mexico

*He shall endeavor, in every way possible to carry out the said
discovery in all peace, friendship and Christianity. . . . He must be
given the title of adelantado [of Florida], for himself and for his
heirs in perpetuity.*
Agreement between Felipe II and Pedro Menéndez,
March 15, 1565

*In thé name of the most Christian king, Don Philip . . . I take and
seize tenancy and possession, real and actual, civil and natural, one,
two, and three times . . . and all the times that by right I can and
should . . . without limitations.*
Juan de Oñate at El Paso, April 1598

In the afternoon of September 8, 1565, at a sheltered harbor in a land that he had first seen on the day of San Agustín,
Pedro Menéndez de Avilés took possession of Florida in
the name of his king, Felipe II. Banners unfurled, trumpets
sounded, and the explosions of gunpowder echoed across the
beach as Menéndez stepped ashore from his small boat. Before an assembly of his officers and natives from the nearby
village of Seloy, Florida's newest adelantado knelt to kiss the
cross and to establish the municipality of St. Augustine.[1]

For the previous three days his men had worked unceremo-
niously to dig defensive trenches around Seloy, a palisaded
village of Timucuan-speaking Indians of a group called Saturiba. The Spaniards feared an attack from French Protestants. Just the year before, a group of Huguenots, as French
followers of John Calvin were called, had constructed a fort

60

called Caroline near the mouth of the St. Johns River, some forty miles to the north. Now, instead of waiting for the French to attack, Menéndez launched an offensive. With knapsacks full of biscuits, canteens heavy with wine, and twenty scaling ladders, five hundred Spanish arquebusiers hiked in the rain through soggy marshlands to the French fort. Pedro Menéndez took the lead, but Saturiba Indians showed him the way.

At dawn on September 20, with rain still falling, Menéndez's men surprised the luckless Frenchmen, many still in their nightshirts. The Protestants offered little resistance. As Menéndez knew, most of the Huguenots of fighting age had sailed south in pursuit of two ships from Menéndez's fleet. Victory, then, came easily for the Spaniards who showed the French heretics no mercy. An artist, Jacques Le Moyne, who slipped out of the fort in the confusion, remembered that the Spaniards "searched the soldiers' quarters, killing all whom they found, so that awful outcries and groans arose from those who were being slaughtered."[2] Menéndez had spared women and children, but he reported with pride to his Catholic king that over 130 members of the "evil Lutheran sect" had vanished from the earth.[3] Menéndez's efforts that morning, his chaplain believed, had been guided by the "Holy Spirit."[4]

14. *Plan of Fort Caroline, drawn by a settler in 1564. The deepening of the St. Johns River in 1880 inundated the site of the fort but a replica, Fort Caroline National Memorial, stands on a nearby bluff ten miles east of present Jacksonville. Courtesy, John Carter Brown Library, Brown University.*

Leaving a small garrison at Fort Caroline, which he renamed San Mateo, Menén-dez returned to the marshy embankments and ditches called St. Augustine. There he learned that the French ships that had left Fort Caroline had met disaster farther south, wrecked on the beach by a storm. Survivors had started north along the coast toward the refuge of Fort Caroline, unaware that it had fallen to the Spaniards. Apprised by Indians of the Frenchmen's approach, Menéndez met two groups of them at a broad inlet about eighteen miles south of St. Augustine. There, at a place known to this day as Matanzas—the "slaughters"—the Protestants offered to surrender if Me-néndez would spare their lives. "I answered," Menéndez reported to the king, "that they might give up their arms and place themselves at my mercy; that I should deal with them as Our Lord should command me." The Frenchmen accepted. As they were brought in small groups across the Matanzas inlet, Menéndez had them taken out of sight: "I caused their hands to be tied behind them, and put them to the knife."[5]

Although witnesses disagreed, no fewer than 150 Frenchmen died, and perhaps twice that number. Menéndez spared only the lives of some Catholics, a few teenagers, and some musicians and tradesmen whose services he needed. Officially, Menéndez argued that he killed the Frenchmen because they were pirates and because he lacked

15. Menéndez de Avilés, with the cross of the Order of Santiago on his left breast, in an engraving reportedly based on a portrait by Titian, lost in a fire. From Retratos de los españoles ilustres con un epítome de sus vidas *(Madrid: Imprenta Real, 1791). Courtesy, St. Augustine Historical Society.*

16. Felipe II (1556–98) defending the Church, with the Escorial in the background and the inscription "all reason for religion" (suma ratio pro Religione) under his right arm. From Luis de Cabrera de Córdova, Filipe [sic] Segundo, Rey de España *(Madrid, 1619). Courtesy, DeGolyer Library, Southern Methodist University.*

the facilities to take prisoners. Privately, Menéndez explained his actions as a necessary strike against heresy. He believed that Protestants and American Indians "held similar beliefs, probably Satanic in origin," and that an alliance between these peoples had to be prevented.[6] "It seemed to me," he told Felipe II, "that to chastise them in this way would serve God Our Lord, as well as Your Majesty, and that we should thus be left more free from this wicked sect."[7]

Felipe II approved, as one Spanish scholar who wrote a lengthy account of the episode for the king knew he would: "It was my thought that Your Majesty would derive singular pleasure from reading and savoring the wreaking of a justly deserved punishment upon the Lutheran enemies."[8] After inheriting the throne from his father, Carlos V, in 1556, Felipe II had ordered foreign trespassers in American waters to be hanged, but the most serious crime that the Huguenots had committed in his view was heresy, which he equated with treason. Felipe subscribed to his father's dictum that because Protestants were "guilty of rebellion, they can expect no mercy."[9] Like a cancer, heretics needed to be removed lest they infect the body politic, in America or in Europe.

The austere Felipe II, who ruled Spain from 1556 to 1598, succeeded no better than his father in stopping the tide of the Protestant Reformation that swept over northern Europe. In North America, however, Felipe did stop French Protestants from establishing a beachhead on the Atlantic. During his long reign Spain established the foundations of its own North American empire by planting colonies in Florida and New Mexico, and in laying the groundwork for the settlement of California, where foreigners also seemed to threaten Spanish hegemony. To establish these settlements, the king found men of broad vision—Menéndez for Florida and Juan de Oñate for New Mexico. Each aspired to a transcontinental Spanish frontier in North America, but each would be disappointed. As they contended with natives for territorial control, Menéndez and Oñate managed only to found modest outposts of empire.

I

St. Augustine represented the culmination of a half century of Spanish efforts to settle Florida. Like others before him, Pedro Menéndez de Avilés had come to Florida on what Felipe II termed missions of "discovery and settlement."[10] From the first discoveries in the New World, Spanish monarchs had sought to establish permanent settlements in what is now the United States. "Without settlement there is no good conquest," wrote one sixteenth-century Spanish chronicler.[11] Spaniards were town dwellers and the municipality served as a key institution of conquest and settlement. By 1565, Spaniards had established scores of towns in the western hemisphere, but if St. Augustine was born late in Spain's New World empire, it came early by North American standards.[12]

That Spaniards came to the New World simply to plunder, whereas Englishmen and Frenchmen came to settle or to engage in honest trade, is a popular but false dichotomy.[13] Explorers such as Juan Rodríguez Cabrillo, who discovered the Pacific coast of North America for Spain in 1542, carried clear instructions: "If you find a good country where you can make a settlement . . . you should remain settled there."[14] Similarly, the first adelantados—Juan Ponce de León, Francisco de Garay, Lucas Vázquez de Ayllón, Pánfilo de Narváez, and Hernando de Soto—had orders to establish settlements as well as to explore.[15] Some of those adelantados such as Ponce de León and Vázquez de Ayllón, took seeds, tools, and livestock and made an effort to follow royal orders. Others, most notably Narváez and De Soto, did not attempt to plant settlements. Their expeditions typified what one historian has described as "the traditional Hispanic preference . . . treasure rather than arable land."[16] That individual preference, by no means limited to Spaniards as Englishmen demonstrated at Jamestown and elsewhere, did not, however, reflect royal policy.[17] Spain's monarchs in the sixteenth century saw exploration, conquest, and settlement as nearly inseparable parts of a single process.

For Carlos V, settlement of North America held little interest or urgency. Hernán Cortés conquered the Aztec capital in 1521; in the next decade Spaniards discovered and conquered the Inca empire. In contrast, the great explorations of North America by De Soto, Coronado, and others, carried out later in Carlos's reign (1519–56), failed to reveal valuable minerals in the northern climes. Although explorers extolled the potential of North America for agriculture and ranching, and some survivors of the De Soto and Coronado expeditions wished to return "because of the goodness of the country," Spain had sufficient arable land in or near the mineral-rich areas of the Americas to support farmers and stockmen.[18] There was no reason to settle the northern fringes of the Indies. When Felipe came to power in midcentury, however, new exigencies suggested the wisdom of planting settlements on the southeastern shores of the North American continent.

French pirates or corsairs, a nuisance in times of peace, had become a menace to Spanish shipping and to the Spanish economy as relations between France and Spain deteriorated in the 1550s. In 1556–60, the Crown's revenue from the New World fell to less than half of its levels in the previous years, with much of the treasure stolen by French corsairs who preyed on Spanish vessels along the sea lanes that connected Spain and the Caribbean.[19] For Spain's homeward-bound mariners, one of those sea lanes lay along the Atlantic coast of North America. Spanish ships generally caught the Gulf Stream, which carried them out of the Gulf of Mexico and the Caribbean though the Bahama Channel. Limited by their navigational instruments, Spanish sailors tended to hug the Atlantic shore and use headlands and islands as points of reference as they followed the northeasterly trend of the continent. Off South Carolina, in the latitude of the Bermudas (discovered in 1505 by Juan Bermúdez on a homeward-bound voyage), sailing ships finally left the coast behind as they caught the westerly winds and currents that would take them back to Europe.[20]

A Spanish base on the Florida coast, then, would help protect the homebound silver fleets. This base would also buttress Spanish claims, which France was challenging, provide refuge for survivors of all-too-common wrecks of Spanish ships, and serve as centers for salvaging. Florida's treacherous Keys, and the wide shoals hidden beneath the waters of the east coast as far north as Cape Canaveral, snared so many ships that by the 1550s Indians on both sides of the Florida peninsula—Ais and Calusas in particular—had stored up a substantial amount of treasure and other salvage from Spanish wrecks, and held captive a number of hapless passengers and crewmen. Storms, too, stranded Spanish voyagers along the trade routes. In 1554, three heavily loaded vessels en route to Spain from Veracruz crashed on Padre Island (the site is in present-day Texas but was then within the area Spain defined as Florida). Some 250 survivors of the wreck began walking along the gulf to the nearest Mexican settlement.

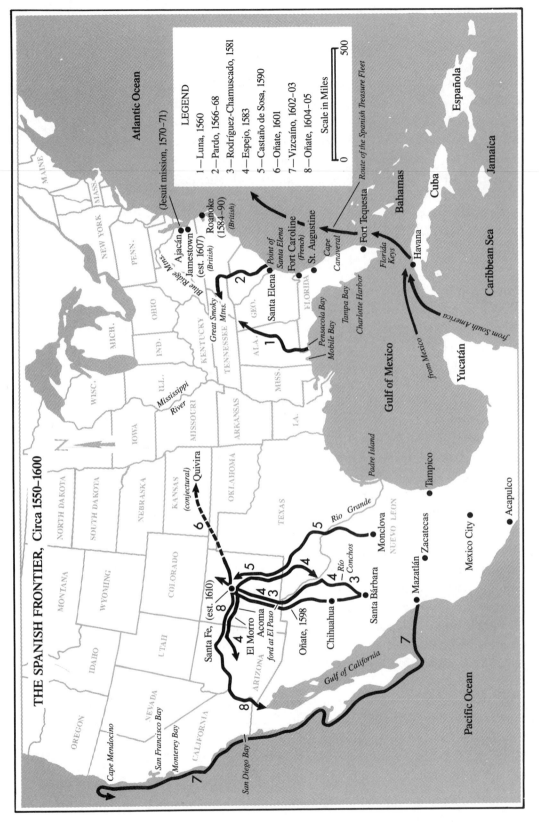

Map 2. *The Spanish frontier, circa 1550–1600.*

THE SPANISH FRONTIER, Circa 1550–1600

LEGEND

1 — Luna, 1560
2 — Pardo, 1566–68
3 — Rodríguez-Chamuscado, 1581
4 — Espejo, 1583
5 — Castaño de Sosa, 1590
6 — Oñate, 1601
7 — Vizcaíno, 1602–03
8 — Oñate, 1604–05

Route of the Spanish Treasure Fleet

Scale in Miles

0   500

Atlantic Ocean

MAINE
N.H.
MASS.
NEW YORK
PENN.
OHIO
MICH.
IND.
ILL.
WISC.
IOWA
MISSOURI
KENTUCKY
TENNESSEE
ALA.   GEO.
MISS.
ARKANSAS
LA.
FLORIDA

Ajacán (Jesuit mission, 1570–71)
Jamestown (est. 1607) (British)
Roanoke (1584–90) (British)

Blue Ridge Mtns.
Great Smoky Mtns.

Santa Elena
Point of Santa Elena
Fort Caroline (French)
St. Augustine
Cape Canaveral

Fort Tequesta
Florida Keys
Havana
Bahamas
Cuba
Española
Jamaica
Caribbean Sea

Gulf of Mexico

Pensacola Bay
Mobile Bay
Tampa Bay
Charlotte Harbor

Route of the Spanish Treasure Fleet
from Mexico
from South America

Yucatán

Mississippi River

NORTH DAKOTA
SOUTH DAKOTA
NEBRASKA
KANSAS
OKLAHOMA
TEXAS

Quivira (conjectural)

N

MONTANA
WYOMING
COLORADO
UTAH
ARIZONA
NEVADA
IDAHO
OREGON
CALIFORNIA

Santa Fe, (est. 1610)
El Morro
Acoma
ford at El Paso
Oñate, 1598
Chihuahua
Santa Bárbara

Rio Grande
Rio Conchos
Monclova
NUEVO LEÓN
Mazatlán
Zacatecas
Tampico
Mexico City
Acapulco

Padre Island

Gulf of California

Pacific Ocean

Cape Mendocino
San Francisco Bay
Monterey Bay
San Diego Bay

Only one priest survived to reach Tampico and tell the story of the party's terrible suffering.[21] Other expeditions vanished without a trace. Indeed, the only son of Pedro Menéndez had disappeared with a Spanish fleet struck by a hurricane in the latitude of the Bermudas in 1563. Two years later, when Menéndez began to colonize Florida, the adelantado must have hoped that he would find his son still alive in an Indian village.[22]

The need for an outpost on the Atlantic seemed especially clear and urgent, but St. Augustine was not the Crown's first choice. In 1557 Felipe II ordered the construction of a base on the Gulf of Mexico and another on the Atlantic at the Point of Santa Elena. Since the 1520s and the voyages of Lucas Vázquez de Ayllón, Spaniards had identified today's Tybee Island, Georgia, as the "the Point of Santa Elena, which is in Florida."[23] To the north of Tybee Island, in present South Carolina, lay Port Royal Sound, one of the finest harbors on the Atlantic coast, but Felipe and his advisors apparently knew nothing of its quality. Rather, they chose the Point of Santa Elena because they mistakenly associated it with Vázquez de Ayllón's legendary Land of Chicora, remembered as rich in treasure and in natives, and close to the pearl-rich kingdom of Cofitachequi visited by De Soto.[24]

Although he was so short of cash that he had suspended payments on all of his debts in a desperate effort to finance a war in Europe, Felipe nonetheless authorized the viceroy of Mexico, Luis de Velasco, to draw on the royal treasury to support an expedition to Santa Elena.[25] To head the enterprise Viceroy Velasco named a close acquaintance, Tristán de Luna y Arellano, a wealthy, middle-aged conquistador who had sought Quivira with Coronado a generation before. Embarking from Mexico with the title of governor of Florida, Luna carried orders to proceed in two stages: first, to build a settlement on the Gulf of Mexico; second, to open an overland route from the Gulf coast to Santa Elena by way of Coosa, a rich province in the Tennessee Valley known to De Soto. This strategy would not only avoid a dangerous voyage around the Florida peninsula, but would give Spain a base on the Gulf to aid wrecked sailors and begin missionary work. In retrospect, the plan seems foolhardy due to the great distance from the Gulf coast to Santa Elena, but difficulties of measuring longitude, and hence of measuring east-west distances, made such errors inevitable throughout the sixteenth-century, and Spaniards usually underestimated distance rather than overestimated it.[26] Indeed, Viceroy Velasco so miscalculated distance that in his more exuberant moments he planned to supply Luna's colony on the Gulf coast with cattle and horses driven from the mining town of Zacatecas, 375 miles north of Mexico City—a trail drive of over 1,600 miles. Only the problem of moving the stock across the Río Espíritu Santo, the name by which Spaniards still knew the Mississippi, seemed to give the viceroy pause.[27]

His optimistic miscalculation notwithstanding, Viceroy Velasco had prepared for the enterprise with his customary attention to detail, furnishing Luna with a written report and perhaps a map from the De Soto entrada. Moreover, at least five veterans of the De Soto expedition signed on, and a woman taken from Coosa to Mexico by the

De Soto party was conscripted to serve as translator.[28] Well-equipped and informed, Luna seemed assured of success when he set sail from Veracruz in June 1559, with a party of restless and idle young men whose departure from New Spain pleased the viceroy. On Pensacola Bay, Luna laid out a classic Spanish city, Santa María de Filipino, the first in North America.[29] A hurricane and a shortage of supplies soon sent most of the party inland in search of an Indian village whose foodstores might sustain them. Few Indians inhabited the sandy shores of Pensacola Bay, but Luna knew of rich native farming communities in the interior from reports of the De Soto expedition. By the winter of 1559, Luna and most of his entourage had established themselves on the Alabama River in the Mobile Indian town of Nanipacana, not far above Mobile Bay, only to have Indians abandon the town and deprive the Spaniards of food.

Meanwhile, Felipe II had learned that Frenchmen planned to build a settlement on the Atlantic, and he sent Luna an urgent message. "I therefore command you notwithstanding whatever other order you may have to the contrary from our viceroy, to make first a town at the Punta de Santa Elena rather than at any other place."[30] Although he had not yet established a solid base on the Gulf, Luna had to look beyond in the summer of 1560. Some of his colonists started overland for Santa Elena but got no farther than the familiar province of Coosa; Coosa'a population had declined somewhat since De Soto's visit, and its chief was interested in an alliance with the Spaniards.[31] Luna also sent a ship to Santa Elena, but it was wrecked in a storm. Plagued by bad luck, deteriorating mental faculties, and dissension among his followers, Tristán de Luna was relieved of his post in 1561 and the city of Santa María de Filipino was abandoned. In a final effort to salvage the enterprise, Viceroy Velasco dispatched an experienced mariner, Angel de Villafañe, to the Atlantic. Villafañe reached Santa Elena, but he, too, failed to establish a colony.

The expeditions of Luna and Villafañe had cost Felipe II dearly, leading him to ask "whether it would be expedient to continue populating . . . Florida, or not."[32] But he had little choice. By the 1560s Frenchmen had come to threaten not only Spanish shipping, but Spanish hegemony over North America as well (the English evinced little enthusiasm for overseas colonies in the sixteenth century). French Huguenots, who had tried and failed to plant colonies in Canada and Brazil, had succeeded in establishing Charlesfort in 1562 on an island in the strategic bay of Santa Elena. Spain launched an expedition from Cuba in 1564 to expel the Huguenots from Charlesfort but discovered only abandoned buildings, which they destroyed. The Huguenots had failed again, but Spain feared that they would return—a realistic concern since French policy aimed at establishing bases near the Caribbean.[33]

Decades of diplomacy had failed to persuade France or England to recognize Spanish claims to much of the New World based on the papal donations of 1493. Francis I summed up the French position in 1540 when he apparently told a Spanish envoy that the Pope lacked authority "to distribute lands among kings." The French king impertinently remarked that "he much desired to see Adam's will to learn how he had partitioned the world."[34] Perhaps more disquieting for Spain, the papacy denied that Spain had an exclusive right to North America since it had not been discovered at the time of the donations of 1493.[35]

For Spain, then, settlement of Florida seemed the best way to establish an effective claim that rival monarchs would respect. This time, the Luna debacle still fresh in his mind, Felipe abandoned the viceroyalty of Mexico as the administrative center for Florida. To thwart further French incursions, Felipe II looked again to Spain itself as the staging ground for new efforts to plant Iberian settlements on the Atlantic. He also turned to private capital, seeking an adelantado who would gamble his own funds rather than the Crown's. His father had abandoned this strategy, for adelantados had proved difficult to control, but Felipe's empty treasury left him little choice. In 1562 he contracted with the son and namesake of Lucas Vázquez de Ayllón to settle Florida as adelantado, but the expedition that the debt-ridden and desperate younger Ayllón patched together made it no farther than Santo Domingo before creditors and deserters forced him to abandon the project.[36]

II

At this discouraging juncture, Felipe turned to Pedro Menéndez de Avilés, and the two, following considerable haggling, signed an adelantado contract on March 20, 1565. Ten days later, the alarming report reached the Spanish court that French Huguenots had established another colony on the Atlantic, at Fort Caroline. The new French threat led Felipe to give Menéndez more than he had bargained for, including direct financial assistance. The settlement of Florida, then, turned into an unusual joint venture, similar to that which the king had arranged with Tristán de Luna. Menéndez set sail from Cádiz with over a thousand persons, including three hundred soldiers on the king's payroll, and the promise that reinforcements would be sent soon.[37] Instead of directing his course toward Santa Elena, Menéndez headed toward Fort Caroline, making landfall nearby at what would become St. Augustine.

Felipe's contract with Menéndez had authorized him to establish settlements and to seek out foreigners and "cast them out by the best means . . . possible."[38] That Menéndez succeeded where his predecessors had failed owed at least as much to the force of his ability, knowledge, dynamism, and family connections as to the royal support that he received. Born in 1519 to a seafaring clan on the north coast of Spain in the Asturian city of Avilés (where his home and a monument to his achievements stands today), Menéndez had years of experience on the sea in both the Old World and the New. His exploits as a privateer had brought him to the attention of the Crown, and he had served his king in several capacities, including as captain-general of the fleet that Spain sent to and from the Indies in 1555–56. A successful businessman, Menéndez had also traded extensively in the Indies. A less successful smuggler, he had been convicted and jailed for introducing contraband from the Indies to Spain.[39]

Due in no small part to the work of his predecessors, Menéndez had a clear if inflated idea of what Florida might become. He also had an ambitious plan and the promise of resources from the Crown. He envisioned nothing less than the economic exploitation of the continent from northwestern Mexico to Newfoundland, all of which Spain claimed, and control of the Grand Banks with its valuable cod fishery. Menéndez moved swiftly. By March of 1567, within a year and a half after he had founded St. Augustine and destroyed Fort Caroline, he had established seven coastal bases designed to hold Florida and the critical Bahama Channel. On the west coast he established two garrisons, one at Tampa Bay among the Tocobaga Indians and another at Charlotte Harbor in the territory of the Calusas, who had dashed Ponce de León's dreams of colonizing Florida. On the strategically more important east coast, Menéndez built a string of five forts. These stretched from Tequesta, near the south end of the peninsula where the Miami River flows into Biscayne Bay (in today's downtown Miami), to Santa Elena in present-day South Carolina. They included what one geographer has termed "the three most eligible harbors of the mainland, convenient to the sailing route that followed the Gulf Stream": St. Augustine, San Mateo at the mouth of the St. Johns River, and Santa Elena. The dangerous Florida Keys hindered communication between Florida's east and west coasts, but Menéndez believed that a waterway across the peninsula awaited discovery and would solve that problem. In Menéndez's eyes, however, Florida's greatest potential lay far to the north of the peninsula.[40]

In the middle of Port Royal Sound, on what is today Parris Island, Menéndez built Fort San Felipe and established the municipality of Santa Elena, not far from the ill-fated settlement of Charlesfort that French Protestants had established in 1562. He pronounced the port of Santa Elena "the best there is in the whole of . . . Florida," and he might have made his initial settlement there had Fort Caroline not diverted him southward.[41] In August of 1566, Menéndez established the capital of his *adelantamiento* at Santa Elena.[42] He saw it as the hub of still further expansion to the north and west. That same year, from Santa Elena, he sent out expeditions in both directions.

Westerly, Menéndez dispatched a party toward New Spain, with instructions to open a road to Mexico, search for precious minerals, and pacify Indians along the way. He hoped to blaze a trail from Santa Elena to Zacatecas—the site of the richest silver mines in New Spain. This represented the reverse of Viceroy Luis de Velasco's plan to open a trail from Zacatecas to Santa Elena via Tristán de Luna's colony on the Gulf of Mexico. Menéndez believed that the distance from Santa Elena to Zacatecas was no more than 300 leagues, or about 780 miles (traveling rather directly, the distance is twice as great—some 1,800 miles) and that 100 leagues to the northwest of Santa Elena he would find the beginnings of the same range of silver mountains in which Zacatecas lies. There, Menéndez hoped to find his own silver mines, and he also planned to open a road that would carry silver directly from Zacatecas to Santa Elena and thereby bypass the pirate-infested Caribbean.[43]

The adelantado entrusted the initial exploration to an energetic captain, Juan Pardo, who led expeditions toward Zacatecas in 1566–67 and again in 1567–68. Pardo headed northwesterly from Santa Elena, following the same route and visiting many of the same towns as Hernando de Soto had before him. Pardo explored the length of South Carolina and western North Carolina, crossed the Blue Ridge Mountains through Swannanoa Gap into the kingdom of Chiaha in eastern Tennessee, and ended his journey in the Tennessee Valley on the western slope of the Great Smoky Mountains. Zacatecas eluded him. Unlike De Soto, Pardo planted settlements along the way. He built a chain of five small fortifications with a detachment assigned to each one. Pardo returned safely to Santa Elena, but his path of garrisons disappeared, their few defenders either killed by Indians or absorbed into Indian tribes.[44]

Meanwhile to the north of Santa Elena, Menéndez tried to plant a settlement on Chesapeake Bay, known to the Spaniards as the Bahía de Santa María. The bay, Menéndez suspected, stood strategically at the entryway to the long-sought passage through the continent to the Orient—a mythical waterway that Spaniards would come to call the Strait of Anián and Englishmen the Northwest Passage. Reports of such a strait had come to Menéndez from a variety of sources. At Havana in January of 1566, however, he talked the matter over with fray Andrés de Urdaneta, a former sailor who was en route to Madrid to report on the successful discovery of a way across the Pacific from the Philippines to Mexico. Like other maritime experts of his day, Urdaneta assumed the strait existed, but he believed it much farther north than Chesapeake Bay.[45] As a result of that conversation, it would appear, Menéndez's enthusiasm for the Chesapeake diminished, but did not disappear. Menéndez stretched his thinning resources and sponsored two feeble attempts at settling the question. The first, which included Dominican missionaries, set out in 1566 but lost its way, apparently near Roanoke Island.[46] Four years later, eight Jesuit missionaries led by the quixotic Father Juan Baptista de Segura, set out from Santa Elena with a remarkable translator and guide.

The Jesuits employed an Indian whom Spaniards had captured on the Chesapeake some years before. This young Algonquian, the son of a chief and apparently the brother of the Powhatan whom the British would come to know, had been taken to Spain on two occasions. He had also lived for a time in Mexico City, where he had acquired the name Luis de Velasco after his patron and godfather, the viceroy of Mexico. The native Luis de Velasco had accompanied the abortive 1566 expedition to the Chesapeake, nearly becoming reunited with his people; in 1570 he inspired Father Segura to take him home to his people.

The Jesuits' single vessel apparently sailed to the mouth of the James River, where the priests stopped to hold a religious ceremony at the future site of Newport News. Entering the James, they landed five miles from the later site of Jamestown in what they called the "land of don Luis."[47] The ship returned to Santa Elena for supplies while the Jesuits apparently crossed the peninsula to the York River. The site has not been found, but it appears that not far from where Englishmen would later find Powhatan's village the Jesuits constructed the mission of Ajacán (or Jacán)—a single wooden building that served as both shelter and chapel. The Spanish clerics hoped to convert the Algonquian-speaking Indians and to find "an entrance into the mountains and on to China."[48] Instead, the inexperienced Jesuits began to starve.

Father Segura's tiny band, which had brought few provisions, arrived in the autumn of 1570 following a time described by the natives as "six years of famine and death."[49] The local Algonquian-speakers had no surplus to share with missionaries and Luis de Velasco offered little assistance. Instead, to the Jesuits' disgust, he returned to his own people and took several wives (much as Francisco of Chicora had abandoned Vázquez de Ayllón on the Carolina coast under similar circumstances some forty-four years before). In February 1571, apparently chafing from Jesuit insults to their religion and culture, a group of natives led by Luis de Velasco put the outsiders to death.[50] The killing proceeded with dispatch, for the Jesuits lacked protection. Father Segura had insisted that no soldiers accompany them; he feared they would provide a bad example for the natives, as they had elsewhere in Florida. Menéndez, who had attempted to discourage the Jesuits' attempt at conversion without military protection, learned the details of the tragedy when he journeyed to the Chesapeake in 1572. A young boy from Santa Elena who had accompanied the priests lived to tell the story.

The Algonquian Luis de Velasco apparently remained among his people and took the name Opechancanough, "he whose soul is white." His special knowledge of the Spaniards might have made him unusually adept at manipulating subsequent Europeans visitors to the James River. It may have been Opechancanough who led a group of natives dressed in the black robes of the Jesuits in an unsuccessful effort to lure a Spanish ship ashore and attack it, and Opechancanough's skillful diplomacy and tactics nearly destroyed the English colony of Jamestown in 1622. At an advanced age, reportedly one hundred, Opechancanough died on a street in Jamestown in 1644, shot in the back by an English settler.[51]

Like the Jesuit outpost on the Chesapeake, most of the missions and garrisons that Menéndez established in Florida had short lives. Fort San Mateo, on the site of the former French Fort Caroline, died as violently as it was born. In 1568 a French privateer, Dominique de Gourgues, destroyed San Mateo and hanged its surviving defenders in revenge for the Spanish massacre of his countrymen. That same year, Indians extinguished Menéndez's garrisons at Tampa and Biscayne bays. Santa Elena and St. Augustine survived Indian assaults, but narrowly. At both places, colonists and soldiers frequently fled or tried to flee, hoping to make their way back to Spain or to one of the Caribbean islands. At one of many low points in troop morale, a nephew of Menéndez begged the defenders of St. Augustine not to desert. Soldiers should not run away from a military post under attack, he explained to his men, and it was even more disgraceful for them to abandon "a fortress which has no enemy whatever

17. *This imaginative engraving by Melchoir Küsell, done for an early Jesuit history by Mathias Tanner, S.J., Societas Iesu Militans . . . (Prague, 1675), shows Father Segura and his three companions, "murdered in Florida for the Faith of Christ." The ax-wielding don Luis personally killed Segura, according to one account. Courtesy, Bridwell Library, Special Collections, Perkins School of Theology, Southern Methodist University.*

attacking it."[52] Even the militant Jesuits, frustrated by Indians, abandoned Florida entirely after the disaster on Chesapeake Bay.[53]

In part, these reverses reflected a scarcity of Spanish resources and will. Having achieved the limited objective of securing the east coast of Florida from the French at considerable cost to the royal treasury, Menéndez had taxed his own capital and credit to the limit. He could not persuade the king to pour still more treasure into a grand but distant vision of what Florida might become. Then, too, Menéndez's vigorous and direct leadership became sporadic after 1567 when he accepted the additional office of governor of Cuba and responsibilities for planning the defense of the Caribbean.[54] The greatest deterrents to Spain's rapid expansion in Florida, however, were the absence of precious metals, which would have justified further investment, and the Florida natives themselves, whose labor proved difficult to exploit and who harassed Spanish farmers and ranchers.

Like adelantados before and after him, Menéndez's instructions required "the good treatment and conversion to our Holy Catholic Faith of the natives."[55] He was supposed to persuade Indians to become vassals of Felipe II, to pay tribute, and to accept missionaries.[56] In practice, however, Menéndez proceeded gingerly, recognizing that his colony's survival depended upon the Florida natives' goodwill. Not only did Florida Indians vastly outnumber the Spaniards, but Menéndez worried that they might ally themselves with the French. Learning from the mistakes of his predecessors, he ordered his followers not to pillage Indian villages. He urged the king to send a year's supply of corn for every horse that he brought, "for in no manner, will it be well to take it from the Indians, that they shall not take up enmity against us."[57] On several occasions, Menéndez took pains not to offend the natives, as in 1566 when he visited the main town of the sophisticated Calusas in southwestern Florida. In Estero Bay near present-day Fort Myers, on a small island dominated by tall, symmetrical temple mounds and bisected by a wide canal, Menéndez met the powerful chief whom the Spaniards called Carlos. When Carlos insisted that Menéndez "marry" his unattractive, middle-aged sister, "doña Antonia," Menéndez obliged. With considerable reluctance, according to his brother-in-law, the already married Menéndez consummated the "marriage" in order to win the friendship of the powerful Calusas. When Menéndez left the Calusas, doña Antonia remained with her people.[58]

Menéndez's self-sacrifice and diplomacy, however, could not overcome the antagonism that soldiers and priests aroused among the Florida natives. Unruly soldiers assaulted the persons and the property of the natives while well-intentioned missionaries insulted their religious beliefs and practices. Little wonder that Calusas, Tequestas, and Ais lost patience with the newcomers, or that Saturiba Timucuas, who had initially aided Menéndez, enthusiastically joined the French privateer Gourgues in destroying Fort San Mateo in 1568.[59] Unable to understand the natives' motives, Menéndez and his compatriots decided that the coastal tribes of Florida were naturally treacherous and deceitful—"warlike" and of "bad disposition," as one Spaniard put it.[60] In 1572 Menéndez urged the Crown to permit "that war be made upon them with all vigor, a war of fire and blood, and that those taken alive shall be sold as slaves, removing them from the country and taking them to the neighboring islands."[61] If Indians remained, Menéndez warned the Crown, the colonists might abandon Florida entirely.

In urging the Crown to fight a war of extermination against Florida Indians, Menéndez recommended a course of action that many colonials endorsed. The morality of a "war of fire and blood" became the subject of debate among the bishops of New Spain a decade later. Although they heard a number of arguments in favor of exterminating rebellious Chichimecas of northern Mexico, and even though members of the religious orders equivocated, the bishops took the unpopular position of condemning total war. They blamed their fellow Spaniards for violating the king's instructions and provoking Indians to retaliate; among the offenders they singled out adelantados who won favors from the king with "false promises of new lands." The bishops recommended peaceful colonization by Spaniards and Christian Indians, presumably indoctrinated by missionaries.[62]

Menéndez personified antithetical impulses in Spanish Indian policy: to convert obedient Indians and to kill or enslave rebellious Indians. In 1573, for example, Menéndez pronounced the coastal Indians of Florida an "infamous people, Sodomites, sacrificers to the devil . . . wherefore it would greatly serve God Our Lord and your majesty if these [Indians] were dead, or given as slaves."[63] The next year, just before he died after the sudden onset of an illness, this same Menéndez wrote: "After the salvation of my soul, there is nothing in this world that I desire more than to see myself in Florida, to end my days saving souls."[64]

When Menéndez died in 1574, at Santander in Spain, Florida had been reduced to two settlements: St. Augustine and Santa Elena. Both towns housed garrisons but Santa Elena, Menéndez's principal settlement where his Spanish wife and family had lived for a time, was wealthier and had more settlers than soldiers. In 1572 Santa Elena's 171 settlers outnumbered its 76 officers and soldiers. A microcosm of Spanish urban life, Santa Elena housed tradespeople as well as farmers and stockmen, women and children as well as men, and social classes ranging from noblemen to servants.[65] Despite the presence of troops, both communities lived on the edge of extinction. Orista Indians forced the abandonment of Santa Elena in 1576. Spaniards reoccupied it, but left permanently after Francis Drake revealed the vulnerability of the Florida outposts. In 1586, on route home to England with a substantial force that had sacked Santo Domingo and Cartagena, Drake stopped on the Florida coast and razed St. Augustine, burning its houses to the ground, cutting down its fruit trees, and carrying away everything of value. The town's inhabitants resisted only briefly before retreating hastily. Only good fortune saved Santa Elena from a similar fate. Drake's attack was prompted in part by reports that Spaniards from Florida planned to attack the fledgling English colony of Roanoke and was justified by the fact that England and Spain were in the throes of a conflict that would last until Queen Elizabeth's death in 1603.[66]

Drake's shattering assault on St. Augustine suggested to Spanish officials the wisdom of consolidating the two sparsely settled and highly exposed Florida communities. Santa Elena was believed to occupy the less defensible position. It disappeared in 1587 almost as violently as if pirates had attacked it. Under orders from the Crown, Spaniards burned the town, dismantled the nearby fort, and destroyed orchards, farms, and gardens lest any other power try to occupy the site. This time Spaniards left Port Royal Sound for good. With their livestock and other transportable possessions, the residents of Santa Elena moved to St. Augustine, which became the sole Spanish settlement in Florida.[67]

By the century's end, only a single garrison remained to sustain Menéndez's vision of an empire that would control the southeastern part of the continent, export hides and sugar, and dominate sea routes to Asia and land routes to the mines of Mexico. Shattered dreams and modest success would also be a by-product of the settlement of New Mexico—the other salient of the Spanish empire to extend into North America during the waning years of the sixteenth century and the reign of Felipe II.

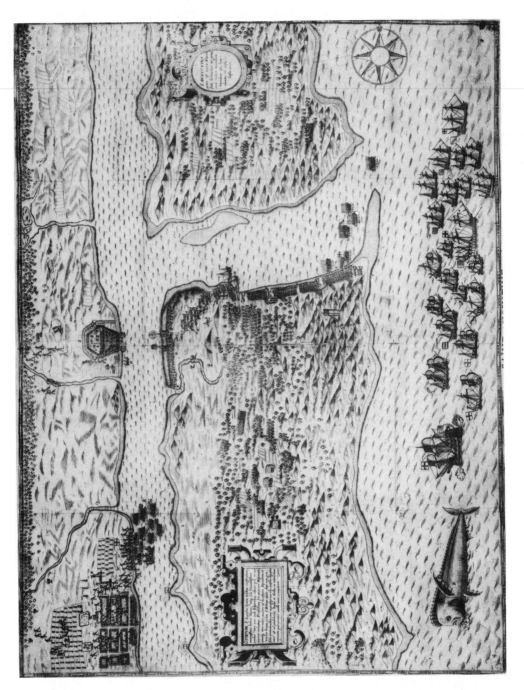

18. *Detail from a drawing of Drake's attack on St. Augustine, attributed to Baptista Boazio, from Walter Bigges, A Summarie and True Discourse of Sir Frances Drakes West Indian Voyage (London 1589). Courtesy, John Carter Brown Library, Brown University.*

III

On the south side of the Rio Grande, not far below the ford in the river where El Paso would be founded nearly a century later, Juan de Oñate, governor, captain general, and soon-to-be adelantado, took possession of New Mexico at the end of April 1598. In a lengthy discourse that echoed the Book of Genesis, he proclaimed Spanish dominion over the new land and its inhabitants, "from the leaves of the trees in the forests to the stones and sands of the river." In addition to the usual solemn High Mass, sermon, trumpets, and banners, the choreography of conquest included a play. Written by one of Oñate's officers, the dramatic production imagined New Mexico Indians happily embracing Christianity.[68]

Several days later, Oñate's armored and heavily armed band forded the river at the site of present-day El Paso and continued north for another two months. Three hundred miles beyond *el paso*, Oñate conducted similar ceremonies at a large town of Keresan-speaking Indians that still stands above present-day Albuquerque. At this town, which the Spaniards called Santo Domingo, he assembled leaders from nearby Pueblo communities. In a large *kiva*—a circular, windowless, semi-subterranean ceremonial room—Oñate addressed the Pueblo leaders. He explained through interpreters that the natives' submission to the rule of Spain would yield peace, justice, protection from enemies, and the benefits of new crops, livestock, and trade. Obedience to the Catholic church would bring them an even greater reward: "an eternal life of great bliss" instead of "cruel and everlasting torment." Upon hearing this, the natives "spontaneously" agreed to become vassals of the Spanish Crown and to render obedience to the Spanish god, or so it seemed to the Spaniards. The Pueblo leaders, the Spaniards noted, submitted "of their own accord," and so it was "recorded and attested for the greater peace and satisfaction of the royal conscience."[69] Oñate and this entourage repeated these ceremonies on six more occasions, with leaders from all of the pueblos ostensibly swearing their fidelity. Although Spaniards no longer read the requerimiento, it remained important to the king that his subjects agree voluntarily to become his vassals and that their submission be recorded.[70]

Oñate established his headquarters at the Tewa-speaking pueblo of *Ohke*, which the Spaniards called San Juan. An oasis in a land of little rain, San Juan occupied a rich alluvial flood plain on the east side of the Rio Grande, near the confluence of the Chama about twenty miles north of present Santa Fe. Just as Pedro Menéndez de Avilés established Florida's first settlement in an Indian village, Juan de Oñate and his colonists crowded into the apartments of the king's new vassals, who were permitted to remain to provide labor, food, and clothing. Within a short time, perhaps because quarters in the pueblo of San Juan had become uncomfortably tight and because the colonists declined to build their own settlement nearby, the Spaniards moved across the Rio Grande to *Yúngé*, another Tewa pueblo. Oñate had persuaded most of the residents of Yúngé to move to San Juan, allowing the Spaniards to occupy their vacated apartments. Oñate declared the pueblo a Spanish town, gave it the Christian name of San Gabriel, and began to remodel the dwellings and to construct a church. San Gabriel would remain the sole Spanish settlement in New Mexico until Oñate began to move some of his colonists south to Santa Fe, a more defensible and less crowded location, perhaps as early as 1608.[71]

So it was that in the last year of the reign of Felipe II another kingdom in North America was added to his realm—a kingdom that, like Florida, had eluded earlier Spanish efforts to settle it. As the king had noted, the settlement of New Mexico "is an important matter and has been sought for some time."[72] Indeed, Spanish efforts to plant a colony among the Pueblos dated back to the reign of Felipe's father and the unsuccessful entrada of Francisco Vázquez de Coronado. Despite New Mexico's relative poverty, some of the Spaniards who had accompanied Coronado to New Mexico in 1540–1542 wished to return and settle there. The land was good, and some believed that close at hand lay the Atlantic Ocean and the Strait of Anián that Menéndez had sought from the east.[73] But within a generation the precise location of Tierra Nueva, as Coronado's men called the lands from Cíbola to Quivira, had been forgotten.[74] Spaniards rediscovered those lands, and Juan de Oñate initiated permanent European settlement there as a result of the northward movement of the mining frontier of New Spain and the initiative of Franciscans.

IV

By the mid-1560s, Mexico's mining frontier had pushed north of Zacatecas into what is today the state of Chihuahua, where silver strikes created several boom towns. Santa Bárbara, in the valley of the Río Conchos, from which Oñate set out in 1598, was the most important. Inevitably, Spaniards who poured into Santa Bárbara and adjacent towns heard rumors of rich lands and important peoples just beyond the northern horizons. At the request, it appears, of a Franciscan, Agustín Rodríguez, who sought a new group of Indians to convert, the viceroy of New Spain authorized a small expedition to probe the far north in 1581. Royal approval was essential. In order to protect Indians and to preserve royal prerogatives, the Spanish Crown had consistently discouraged efforts to explore and settle Indian lands without royal permission. Appalled by the excesses of individuals in the first decades of the conquest of America, Felipe II took stronger measures. Comprehensive Orders for New Discoveries, issued by the Crown in 1573, had emphatically prohibited the entry of unlicensed parties into new lands, under "pain of death and loss of all their property."[75] The regulations prohibited the use of the word *conquest* to describe "pacifications" of new lands, a habit that proved impossible to break, and they made missionaries the primary agents for exploration and pacification. Under these new regulations, Father Rodríguez apparently had no difficulty in securing official approval to investigate the lands to the north.

In 1581 a party of three Franciscans headed by fray Agustín Rodríguez, with an escort of seven soldiers led by Capt. Francisco Sánchez Chamuscado, made their way up the Conchos River to the Rio Grande and continued several hundred miles beyond into the Pueblo world. Members of the Rodríguez party seemed to believe themselves the first to visit the Pueblos. In an apparent reference to Coronado, the expedition's principal chronicler noted that "before this time numerous Spaniards with ample commissions from the viceroys of New Spain had entered the land in an attempt to discover this settlement, and they had not found it. Thus we concluded that our project was directed by the hand of God."[76] The Rodríquez expedition named the area San Felipe del Nuevo México.

Spanish rediscovery of "this populated territory" of New Mexico, where Indians lived in multistory houses, cultivated corn, and wore cotton clothing, excited considerable attention in New Spain.[77] In 1582 Antonio de Espejo, a former member of the powerful Inquisition police who had fled to the north of New Spain after running afoul of the law, received permission to lead a party to New Mexico. Espejo's announced intention was to rescue fray Agustín Rodríguez and a companion who had stayed behind to convert natives. The Franciscans had received the heavenly reward of martyrdom by the time the rescue party arrived, but Espejo, who had come to New Spain in 1571 with the Inquisition, had more earthly treasures in mind for himself. In search of gold and silver, he explored well beyond the Pueblo country, venturing eastward onto the buffalo plains and westward across present Arizona. Espejo's exaggerated report added to the stir caused by the return of the Rodríguez party. "If what they tell me is true," the archbishop of Mexico wrote, "they have indeed discovered . . . another new world."[78]

Encouraged by these reports, in 1583 Felipe II authorized the viceroy of Mexico to find a suitable person to pacify the potentially rich new lands, in conformity with the Orders for New Discoveries of 1573.[79] Slowly, bureaucrats began to review eager applicants, including Antonio de Espejo, for the position that would eventually go to Juan de Oñate. In contrast to Florida, no foreign challenge to Spain's sovereignty and no piratical threat to the transport of Spanish treasure gave urgency to the settlement of New Mexico, although the viceroy and the Crown did see New Mexico as occupying a strategic position close to the yet-to-be discovered Strait of Anián, which connected the Atlantic and Pacific.[80] While officials pondered the applicants, two unauthorized expeditions invaded New Mexico. Both came to grief. One, a group of adventurers led by Capt. Francisco Leyva de Bonilla and Antonio Gutiérrez de Humaña, festered and died of its own corrupt leadership.[81] Another, led by Gaspar Castaño de Sosa, ended when officials in Mexico determined to enforce the royal Orders for New Discoveries.

A seasoned and energetic frontier officer, Castaño de Sosa held the position of lieutenant governor of Nuevo León, the most northeasterly province of New Spain. In 1590, he led a group of over 170 men, women, and children from the failed mining town of Almadén (on the site of present-day Monclova), northward to the Pueblo country. He apparently gambled that successful establishment of a colony in New

Mexico would earn royal forgiveness of any laws that he violated, a time-honored tradition going back to Hernán Cortés. With two-wheeled carts (perhaps the first to roll across the high plains in what is now the United States), and with oxen, goats, and dogs as well as horses, Castaño pioneered a new route into New Mexico. He led his group across the Rio Grande near present-day Del Río, Texas, then up the Pecos River to the great pueblo of Pecos, where the Spaniards fought their way inside. From there, they proceeded into the heartland of the Pueblo country, the Rio Grande Valley, erecting crosses in each Indian town through which they passed.

Castaño and his colonists imposed themselves on the Pueblos, but only briefly. The next spring one Juan Morlete, who held the office of Protector of the Indians, arrived at Santo Domingo pueblo with forty armed men and orders from the viceroy to arrest Castaño. Morlete took the astonished colonists back to Mexico with Castaño himself, as he complained, "laden with a stout pair of leg irons and a chain that is very thick and heavy."[82] Irons were only the first of his troubles. New Spain's highest court, the *audiencia* in Mexico City, found Castaño guilty of invading "lands of peaceable Indians" and sentenced him to six years of exile in the Philippines.[83]

Officials in New Spain seemed determined to enforce the Crown's policy of protecting natives by bridling individuals who bolted onto lands beyond the frontier without royal permission. Juan Morlete had carried orders from the viceroy to explain to the Indians that he had come "to free them and restore them to their own lands, and to punish those who had troubled and injured them."[84] The Pueblos, however, may have learned a different lesson: they would pay a high price if they resisted Spanish demands. Those Pueblo towns that had failed to offer hospitality suffered atrocities at the hands of Espejo and Castaño, just as they had from Coronado two generations before. Perhaps that explains why Pueblo leaders acceded to Juan de Oñate's demands with such apparent docility when he took possession of New Mexico in 1598 and asked them to submit to Spanish rule.[85]

Oñate's establishment of a Spanish base amidst the Pueblos, some eight hundred miles north of the nearest Spanish community at Santa Bárbara, climaxed a half-century of Spanish efforts to settle New Mexico. Thus, as with Menéndez's enterprise along Florida coasts, Oñate's venture represented a culmination as well as a new beginning. In the case of New Mexico, however, the continuity of Spanish efforts at settlement is clearer in retrospect than it was to contemporaries. The geography of New Mexico remained so hazy that four years after Oñate moved into San Gabriel, the viceroy of Mexico remained uncertain if "the seven cities of Cíbola, discovered by fray Marcos de Niza and which Francisco Vázquez de Coronado tells of having visited, are a part of the same area now under Don Juan de Oñate."[86]

V

Perhaps due more to relatively meager resources than to lack of vision, the scope of Oñate's achievements in New Mexico was more modest than that of Menéndez in

Florida, but his motives and methods were similar. Like Menéndez, Oñate had entered North America with a contract from the king that permitted him to settle New Mexico at his own expense. Oñate seemed a wise choice. Nearly fifty years old, this Mexican-born aristocrat from the silver mining town of Zacatecas was an experienced leader from a prestigious family that possessed a substantial fortune, and he had the ear of the viceroy, Luis de Velasco. Don Juan had inherited wealth and prestige from his father, Cristóbal de Oñate, one of the conquerors of New Galicia and a discoverer of the fabled silver mines of Zacatecas—the same mines that Menéndez had sought to reach from Florida in the mid-1560s.[87] Juan de Oñate had acquired additional prestige and wealth through his wife, Isabel Tolosa Cortés Moctezuma, the great granddaughter of the Aztec emperor Moctezuma, and the granddaughter of Hernán Cortés.

The costly conquest of New Mexico taxed the resources of Juan de Oñate. By his own estimate, he poured a half million pesos into New Mexico, much of it spent before he ever reached New Mexico. Bureaucratic formalities and struggles for power, including Oñate's own effort to make himself independent of the viceroy and responsible directly to the king, had delayed his departure for New Mexico by two years. During that time Oñate had to feed his impatient colonists and their livestock.[88] Once he reached New Mexico, the poverty of the land further drained his fortune and left him increasingly dependent on the Crown.

Unlike Menéndez, Oñate initially received little financial support from the king, who had ordered that "this discovery and pacification is to be accomplished without spending or pledging anything from my treasury."[89] For the Crown, the stakes were much lower in New Mexico, which faced no immediate foreign threat. Then, too, such a policy was consistent with the 1573 Orders for New Discoveries. In a reference to earlier adelantados, perhaps including Menéndez, the Orders noted that leaders of previous expeditions had "sought to enrich themselves from the Royal Treasury" and prohibited the use of Crown funds in future efforts at settlement.[90]

When Oñate finally set out for New Mexico in 1598, delays had reduced his army to about 130 men of fighting age—one-sixth the size of the force that Menéndez brought to Florida. Some of Oñate's men traveled north with their wives, children, servants, and slaves; the entire expedition may have numbered over 500 persons.[91] Ten Franciscans went along; the Crown, and not Oñate, bore their expenses, as was usual in such cases. Oñate, then, lacked the manpower and resources to expand beyond San Gabriel and to establish a network of far flung bases as Menéndez had done. New Mexico also lacked seaports or navigable rivers that would facilitate the transport of reinforcements or supplies. Nonetheless, Oñate sent out or led exploring parties that stretched his small band to the limit.

Like Menéndez and other would-be adelantados, Oñate had visions of grandeur. "I shall give your majesty a new world, greater than New Spain," he told the king.[92] At the least, he expected substantial returns from his investment. His official declarations emphasized the saving of souls as his principal mission, but his carefully worded contract with the king makes clear that he also expected to receive broad governmental powers, rich mines, lands, Indian labor, access to a strait through North America, and a seaport on the Pacific or the Atlantic, or both. Like Menéndez, Oñate underestimated the distance across the continent. He believed that New Mexico could be supplied by sea, from either the Atlantic or the Pacific, and he had asked for the right to bring two ships annually to the Pueblo country. His request was granted.

The expeditions of Coronado and Espejo had failed to dispel the notion that the Pacific coast was not far from New Mexico,[93] and Menéndez's failure to bridge the distance from Santa Elena to Zacatecas had done nothing to diminish official ideas of the narrowness of the continent. To the contrary, others took up Menéndez's cause. In 1600, Florida governor Gonzalo Méndez de Canzo revived the idea of a Spanish colony on the Chesapeake and of following the route of Juan Pardo across the Blue Ridge, "until we come upon the people from New Mexico."[94] In Mexico City, Viceroy Velasco believed that New Mexico stood at the same latitude as the recently established English colony at Roanoke, and that the distance between New Mexico and Roanoke, "though not actually known, is not thought to be too great."[95] Even a lengthy trek to the Quivira villages on the Great Plains failed to disabuse Oñate of his belief in the proximity of the Atlantic. In 1601, Oñate led seventy men on a five-month-long foray that took them eastward along the Canadian River, then northeasterly to a point near the Arkansas River in north central Oklahoma or south central Kansas, near Arkansas City. There, in the country of the prosperous Wichitas whom the Spaniards called Quivirans, Oñate reluctantly halted and turned back toward New Mexico. Eight wooden carts pulled by mules and oxen (the first wheeled vehicles on what would become the Santa Fe Trail after 1820), had creaked so steadily over the plains that Oñate reckoned that if the animals had not become exhausted and his men restive they could have proceeded on to the Atlantic Ocean, "which cannot be very far away."[96]

On three occasions, Oñate also tried to find a route to the Pacific. He had hardly established himself at San Juan before setting out in the autumn of 1598 to "discover the South Sea." Forced to turn back, he tried again the next year, sending one of his lieutenants, who also failed to get through. Finally, in 1604–1605, Oñate succeeded in making his way across present Arizona and descending the Colorado River to its mouth on the Gulf of California. On his return, he stopped at El Morro, a great sandstone promontory along the old Indian trail that ran between Acoma and Zuni pueblos, and etched a message in the cliffside over an Indian petroglyph. His inscription still remains visible: "There passed this way the Adelantado Don Juan de Oñate, from the discovery of the South Sea, on the 16th of April, 1605."[97]

VI

As Oñate knew, the establishment of a Spanish settlement on the Pacific coast of North America had taken on strategic importance that recalled Spain's earlier interest

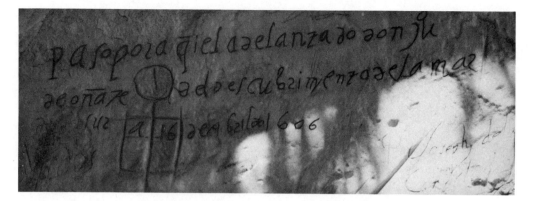

19. Juan de Oñate's inscription at what is today El Morro National Monument. Courtesy, the Vargas Project, University of New Mexico.

in planting a settlement along the Bahama Channel on the continent's Atlantic coast.[98] California's coast gained new significance for Spanish officials in 1565 when fray Andrés de Urdaneta solved the vexing problem of how Spanish vessels engaged in rich trade from Mexico to the Philippines could return again to Mexico against contrary winds and currents. From 1565 on, galleons returned at least annually from Manila by sailing north into Japanese waters, then picking up westerlies that took them to the California coast sometimes as high as Cape Mendocino, and running south with prevailing winds to Acapulco. A haven high on California's outer coast would enable returning galleons to stop for repairs and refresh their crews after four or five months of trans-Pacific sailing.

The idea of a base on the California coast took on special urgency when foreigners found their way into the Pacific—previously a Spanish lake. Foreign intrusion into the Pacific began with Francis Drake, who plundered his way up the Pacific coast in 1579, perhaps as far as present California. His exact whereabouts remain shrouded in the secrecy and contradictions that he and his queen, Elizabeth I, deliberately cultivated. Drake apparently traveled north in search of a strait that would take him through the continent, but when he failed to find one he crossed the Pacific and returned to England. His round-the-world voyage of 1578–80 (the second such journey after that of Magellan and Elcano over a half century before), alarmed Spanish officials who feared that he had found the long-sought Strait of Anián and a short-cut back to England. With or without the fabled passage, pirates could lurk unchallenged in quiet coves on the long California coast and prey on treasure-laden Spanish vessels, as Thomas Cavendish demonstrated when he seized a galleon returning to Mexico from the Philippines off the coast of the California peninsula in 1587.[99]

Spain responded to this new challenge by authorizing exploration for a suitable place to settle. The search culminated with the voyage of Sebastián Vizcaíno, an energetic merchant with long experience in the Pacific trade and in Baja California. In 1602–1603, while Oñate yearned to reach the Pacific from New Mexico, Vizcaíno mapped the California coastline and bestowed new names on it, replacing those left sixty years before by Cabrillo, whose charts had apparently been forgotten. With few exceptions, Vizcaíno's names remain unchanged.[100] Vizcaíno recommended that Spain establish a base on the bay that he named for the conde de Monterrey, the viceroy who sponsored his expedition. In retrospect, it appears to be a curious decision, for California had two manifestly superior bays. San Francisco, however, had eluded Vizcaíno as it would other mariners, and San Diego, Vizcaíno's second choice, was too far south of the landfall of ships returning from Manila and also seemed to lack abundant wood and game.[101]

Vizcaíno's recommendation still remained under consideration when Oñate's exuberant report of his discovery of "a great harbor on the South sea"—actually the mouth of the Colorado River at the head of the Gulf of California—reached Mexico City in 1605.[102] The marqués de Montesclaros, who had succeeded Monterrey as viceroy and who believed that no good would come of the New Mexico venture, sardonically noted that Oñate's discovery was "the greatest benefit that we could hope for" from his entire operation.[103]

VII

In Viceroy Montesclaros's eyes, Oñate's standing as an explorer may have risen when he claimed to have discovered a great harbor on the Pacific, but his reputation as a leader had fallen. Oñate had sent fray Francisco de Escobar to Mexico to report in detail on how the expedition learned of "extraordinary riches and monstrosities never heard of before."[104] Along the route to the Pacific, as Escobar explained to the viceroy in exquisite detail, Oñate's small band learned of, but never actually saw, a variety of curious peoples: one group had ears so large that they hung on the ground; another never ate, but lived only on the odor of their food "because they lacked the natural means of discharging excrement"; and still another "whose men had virile members so long that they wound them four times around the waist, and in the act of copulation the man and woman were far apart."[105] Indians who passed these stories on to the credulous members of the Oñate party must have had a fine time, but the viceroy was not amused. "This conquest is becoming a fairy tale," Montesclaros wrote to the king.[106] He sought authority to remove Oñate from New Mexico and to disband his colony.

Reports of the poverty of the land, the dissatisfaction of the colonists, and abuses of Indians had long before reached Mexico City and weakened the viceroy's confidence in Oñate. Escobar's fanciful report seemed to confirm the viceroy's deepest suspicions and to harden his resolve to end the venture. As with Menéndez's mutinous men in Florida, Oñate's followers had quarreled among themselves from the first. In the summer of 1598, having barely arrived in New Mexico, forty-five disillusioned soldiers and officers, over one-third of his small army, had planned to mutiny and flee the province.[107] As that first winter came on, a familiar scenario began to unfold. Soldier-settlers extorted corn, beans, squash, and clothing from the Pueblos, resorting to torture, murder, and rape. A wide chasm separated the Crown's good intentions, as expressed in the Orders for New Discoveries of 1573, from the practices of its disillusioned and desperate representatives. The Pueblos' wary hospitality soon turned to overt hostility.[108]

Before the first year was out, Indians on the mesa-top pueblo of Acoma retaliated by killing eleven Spanish soldiers, including Oñate's nephew, Juan de Zaldívar, in a surprise attack.[109] After consulting with the Franciscans and determining that Spanish law permitted him to punish the Acomas because they had violated their oath of obedience to the king, Oñate retaliated swiftly and audaciously. He sent Vicente de Zaldívar, the younger brother of the slain Juan, to invite the Acomas to surrender the rebels and submit to Spanish rule, or to face war with no quarter—war by fire and blood. It was a bold challenge to Pueblos who lived atop what one of Coronado's men described as "the greatest stronghold ever seen in the world."[110] Through a diversionary tactic, Zaldívar's band gained the top of the seemingly unassailable mesa. Aided, it was said, by Santiago, who rode a white horse and carried a flaming sword, the small

20. *Acoma pueblo, circa 1940, by Ferenz Fedor. Courtesy, Museum of New Mexico, neg. no. 100364.*

Spanish army of seventy-two men achieved a brillant victory. In three days of hard fighting they destroyed the pueblo, killed some 500 men and 300 women and children, and took no more than 80 men and about 500 women and children captive. These Oñate subjected to a formal trial, providing them with a defense attorney.

Found guilty of murder, the Acomas received a punishment calculated to make them living reminders of the cost of resistance. Oñate sentenced all the captives between the ages of twelve and twenty-five to twenty years of personal servitude, and he condemned males older than twenty-five to have one foot severed. These mutilations, an acceptable punishment for miscreants in Renaissance Europe, were carried out in public. Oñate declared the children under twelve innocent but ordered them taken from their parents or relatives and placed under the care of the Franciscans where, Oñate noted, "they may attain the knowledge of God and the salvation of their souls." Two generations passed before the Acomas rebuilt their pueblo at its present site in the late 1640s.[111]

Oñate's harsh punishment of the Acomas was not unique to Spaniards in America. At the fledgling English colony of Jamestown, Thomas Gates had the hand of an Indian cut off as a warning against spies. Another Jamestown colonist, eager to force the Potomac Indians to trade with him, used "some harshe and Crewell dealings by cutteing of [f] towe of the Salvages heads and other extremetyse." Nor did those early English settlers spare women and children from harsh reprisals. Jamestown colonists punished some Powhatan children, taken captive in 1610, by throwing them off a ship and "shoteinge owtt their Braynes in the water."[112]

Oñate's brilliant and brutal action momentarily ended overt Pueblo resistance, but the problems that caused the revolt remained and provoked a Jumano rebellion the next year. Reinforcements, fewer than one hundred, arrived in 1600 but did not alleviate disillusion or discontent. Meanwhile, eager to find avenues to spectacular wealth, Oñate neglected San Gabriel, failing to build it into a self-sufficient base. In 1601, when he returned from an extended trip to the eastern plains in search of Quivira,[113] he found San Gabriel nearly deserted. Most of his colonists, expressing the fear that they and the Pueblos alike would starve to death, had fled to Mexico. The wheels of bureaucracy ground slowly, but by 1605, when the adelantado returned from the Gulf of California, Viceroy Montesclaros had become convinced that the New Mexico enterprise should be abandoned. The following year, the king ordered that Oñate be replaced and that charges of his mismanagement be investigated. New Mexico had bankrupted Oñate, so that what had begun as a private venture now threatened to drain the royal treasury.[114] Even with new management, it seemed unlikely that returns from what the viceroy termed this "worthless land" would repay the costs of supplying and maintaining a colony hundreds of miles beyond the nearest Spanish settlements.[115]

In 1614, following a lengthy investigation and judicial proceedings, authorities in Mexico City acquitted Oñate of a number of allegations, but found him guilty of a variety of charges, including abuses of Indians; ill-treatment of some of his own officers, colonists, and priests; and adultery.[116] Stripped of all the privileges and titles he had been promised in his initial contract, he was fined and banished permanently from New Mexico. Misfortune seemed to wash over Oñate from every direction. In 1612, his only son, to whom he hoped to leave his New Mexico fiefdom, died. The resilient adelantado did, however, manage to rebuild his fortune through careful management of the family mines at Zacatecas, and he began a persistent series of appeals to rehabilitate his honor. He moved to Spain in 1621, soon after the death of his wife. There, Oñate doggedly employed his wealth and influence to win a partial pardon from the king and to regain his titles, although he remained banished from New Mexico. Like Menéndez, Oñate also gained a coveted knighthood in the Order of Santiago. Vindicated, the vigorous septuagenarian stayed on in Spain, traveling widely as the king's chief mining inspector until he collapsed and died in a mine shaft in 1626.[117]

VIII

As instruments of royal policy, Juan de Oñate and Pedro Menéndez had laid the foundations of what would become Spain's North American empire, but the footings were so precarious that the Crown considered abandoning both enterprises at the outset of the 1600s. Neither England nor France, Spain's principal rivals, had succeeded in establishing a permanent base in North America, and they would not do so until the founding of Jamestown in 1607 and Quebec in 1608. Initially, neither colony posed a significant threat to Spain's interests, but the establishment of Jamestown may have contributed to the Crown's decision not to abandon Florida.

Spanish policymakers feared that colonists from Jamestown (like those from the earlier failed English colony of Roanoke) would succeed in their professed goal of preying on Spanish shipping. Spain had protested the English presence in Ajacán, as Spaniards then called Virginia, and employed agents in England, and perhaps in Jamestown itself, to sabotage the colony. Spain insisted that the Englishmen had settled on "lands that are not theirs and that do not belong to them,"[118] but higher priorities in Europe discouraged Spain from carrying out plans to dislodge the intruders. Moreover, Spanish intelligence revealed that Jamestown was in such disarray that the English could hardly maintain themselves much less go on the offensive against Spanish shipping. Rather than try to destroy Jamestown, Spain adopted the policy of making menacing gestures toward it in order to goad English stockholders into squandering still more resources to shore up what Spain regarded as a losing venture.[119]

Inadvertence and domestic distractions, however, more than Spain's defensive initiatives, explain the failure of France and England to contend successfully for a share of North America in the sixteenth or early seventeenth centuries.[120] Whatever the reason, however, Spain's claims to North America remained secure well after the founding of Jamestown, and the Crown appeared to have met its most pressing strategic goals. On the Atlantic coast, the arena of greatest imperial contention, Spain had dislodged the French from Florida, strengthened its hold on the vital Bahama Channel, and established a base that would provide relief for Spanish victims of shipwrecks.

Securing North America had proved costly. In the Spanish imperial system, the Indies existed largely as a source of revenue to support Spain's European ventures, yet Florida and New Mexico consumed revenue rather than generating it. Little wonder, then, that the Crown considered abandoning each enterprise. Initially, the Crown had relied upon private capital to develop these new North American colonies, promising Menéndez and Oñate that they and their immediate heirs could operate their proprietary colonies for a profit as semi-independent fiefdoms. In both cases, however, the Crown had found the work of its adelantados wanting and had supplanted them. Juan de Oñate's conviction cost his descendants all influence in New Mexico, but the family and associates of Pedro Menéndez, who died without the dishonor that interrupted Oñate's career, managed to hold on to key positions in the Florida treasury even after the colony came under royal control.[121] Florida and New Mexico had been transformed into colonies of the Crown, their governors appointed by royal officials. Until the eighteenth century, Florida's governors answered directly to the Council of the Indies; New Mexico's governors, to the viceroy of New Spain. In both cases, the royal treasury bore much of the cost of maintaining what the adelantados had begun.[122]

Florida proved to be the more expensive of the two enterprises. From the beginning, the Crown's special arrangements with Menéndez had produced deficits. In the first three years of what had begun as a private venture, from 1565–68, the Crown invested four pesos for every one that Menéndez spent.[123] Beginning in 1570, the government agreed to send an annual subsidy, or *situado*, to support the Florida garrisons, and it did so regularly for well over a century, even as it entertained the possibility of retreating from Florida.[124]

Even before Menéndez's death in 1574, the main governing body for Spain's American empire, the Council of the Indies, had debated the merits of shutting down the Florida enterprise—an event that would no doubt have pleased the colony's unhappy soldiers and settlers.[125] In 1600, having sent an annual subsidy to St. Augustine for thirty years, the Crown ordered an investigation into the garrison's continuing viability but decided that the post still had strategic value.[126] Six years later, Felipe III became convinced that foreign danger to the Florida coast had dissipated and that the garrison should be abandoned. Missionaries and their new converts, however, still needed Spanish military protection, a problem the king tried to solve by ordering Florida officials to move Christian Indians to the island of Española. If that could be accomplished, the St. Augustine garrison, which he had already ordered cut in half, could be closed completely. Franciscan missionaries, however, argued that the number of native converts had grown so large that relocating them was unthinkable. Nor

could the Franciscans leave Florida without jeopardizing the spiritual welfare of baptized Indians. What would become of those souls if Indians no longer had access to the
sacraments? The missionaries' plea, directed to "Your Majesty who is a most Christian
King," won the day.[127]

Meanwhile, the Council of the Indies and the Christian king debated the same
issues in regard to the future of New Mexico. New Mexico was not as costly as Florida,
for the Crown maintained no garrison of salaried soldiers there. Nonetheless, it
drained the treasury enough so that the council agreed with Viceroy Montesclaros
that the enterprise should end. As in the case of Florida, however, the council yielded
to Franciscan arguments that it was impractical to remove large numbers of baptized
Indians. In 1608, the same year that it decided not to abandon Florida, the Crown
authorized the Franciscans to remain in New Mexico and minister to the Pueblos. The
royal treasury would continue to subsidize the colony.[128]

California never gained such a royal reprieve. At the same time that Viceroy
Montesclaros moved to end Oñate's venture in New Mexico, he halted plans to build a
Spanish outpost on the California coast. Rather than repel foreign interlopers and
protect the Philippine trade, Montesclaros decided that a Spanish base would attract
English and Dutch smugglers who would come to trade, as they did in the Caribbean
and on the Florida coast. California's security, Montesclaros believed, resided in its
inaccessibility (the passage of time confirmed his judgment). Finally, he did not
believe that the benefits of building a base fifteen to twenty days' sail from Acapulco
would justify its costs. Officials resurrected the project from time to time, some
suggesting that a port far up the Pacific coast would also be useful to supply New
Mexico. Late in the seventeenth century, Spanish soldiers and missionaries began to
occupy the southern portion of the 800-mile-long peninsula of Baja California, but
Spain did not begin permanent occupation of the coast in what is today the American
state of California until 1769, over a century and a half after Viceroy Montesclaros
declared such a plan impractical.[129]

Although plans to plant a colony in California faltered, Florida and New Mexico
endured to become the first permanent European enclaves in territory that has become the United States. Saved from abandonment by Franciscan missionaries, the two
outposts developed in the seventeenth century chiefly as centers for Franciscan proselytizing of Indians. The two colonies differed in important ways, but both were
essentially armed camps, teetering on the northernmost edges of Spain's American
empire.[130]

Neither Florida nor New Mexico grew immediately into full-blown Spanish colonies. To the contrary, both initially skidded into decline as their limited opportunities became evident to the pioneers who founded them. Young, unemployed men
had responded eagerly to Menéndez's and Oñate's promises of wealth, Indian labor,
and the title of *hidalgo*—the lowest rank of minor nobility, literally meaning "son of
someone."[131] From Spain itself, hunger for land among the dispossessed, particularly

those from Galicia, Extremadura, and Andalucia, had driven men and a few women to places like Santa Elena and St. Augustine. As Menéndez and Oñate quickly discovered, however, when promised lands proved unpromising, would-be hidalgos abandoned their adelantado and soldiers deserted their posts. This phenomenon was widespread among Spaniards in America.[132] Although some 440,000 Spaniards emigrated to the New World by 1650, few were drawn to the backwater provinces such as Florida or New Mexico.[133] Unlike English and French voyagers to the New World, for whom North America was the only option, Spaniards had opportunities to make their fortunes in the fabulous mining regions of Mexico, Central America, and in the Andean regions of South America.

From the abandonment of Santa Elena in 1576 until the founding of Pensacola in 1698, St. Augustine was the only Hispanic settlement of consequence in Florida. A muddy garrison town of flammable huts of palmetto, St. Augustine supported a population of just over 500 in 1600, including men, women, children, and 27 slaves. As might be expected at a military base, single men constituted about half of the Spanish population. Of the Hispanic males, all but 5 were on the government payroll. Known for its hurricanes, Indian and pirate attacks, and sterile soil, St. Augustine repelled rather than attracted ambitious Spaniards. "It is hard to get anyone to go to St. Augustine because of the horror with which Florida is painted," the governor of Cuba wrote in 1673. "Only hoodlums and the mischievous go there from Cuba."[134] Initially, some government officials tried to avoid living in Florida by appointing substitutes to take their place. Nonetheless, the population grew modestly through natural increase and because the Crown augmented the troops with exiles and criminals.[135] By 1700, St. Augustine's population had risen to between 1,400 and 1,500 persons, including black slaves and Hispanized Indians. Many of the Hispanic residents of the town actually lived on outlying ranches and farms but maintained their official residence in St. Augustine.[136]

New Mexico, isolated by hundreds of miles from the nearest settlements of northern New Spain, also grew slowly in the seventeenth century. The number of Spaniards in New Mexico in the 1600s probably never exceeded 3,000—twice the size of Florida but still a modest number. Through most of the century, New Mexico had only one formal municipality, the Villa Real de Santa Fe, founded in 1610 under viceregal orders by Oñate's successor, Pedro de Peralta, who moved the capital from San Gabriel to a more defensible site in an unpopulated valley selected earlier by Oñate. In contrast to Florida, no formal presidio existed in New Mexico in the 1600s, but the king expected its leading citizens to serve as soldiers as well as settlers. As in Florida, many of New Mexico's pioneers lived outside of the province's single urban center in clusters of farms and ranches too small to call towns. The Hispanic population had scattered up and down the Rio Grande, from Taos pueblo to below Albuquerque (founded in 1706), in order to be close to the province's most evident source of revenue—the labor of Pueblo Indians. Farther south along the Rio Grande, still within the jurisdiction of New Mexico, a small community of Hispanics and His-panicized Manso Indians also took root at El Paso del Norte, where Franciscans had begun in 1659 to build the mission of Nuestra Señora de Guadalupe at the site of the present-day Ciudad Juárez.[137]

Thus, throughout the seventeenth century the civilian-military populations of Spain's two North American colonies remained modest, and until the century's end Spain found no reason to expand its frontiers into other areas of North America. Measured against the expectations of Pedro Menéndez, Juan de Oñate, and the Crown, the gains made in Florida and New Mexico were very modest. Born in dreams of transcontinental empires in North America, the two colonies hung on through much of the seventeenth century as little more than the precarious towns of Santa Fe and St. Augustine. Begun as entreprenuerial ventures designed to enrich the Crown, the adelantados, and their followers, both enterprises drained the resources of their founders, of the Crown, and especially of those Indian peoples in whose midst Menéndez and Oñate planted these outposts of empire. Built on high-minded sentiments of peaceful persuasion, Spain's enclaves in Florida and New Mexico degenerated into places where natives and colonizers alike lived in profound fear of one another. Unwelcome Europeans maintained themselves with brutality, using gunpowder, fire, and the sword to punish and intimidate natives. In turn, natives resisted the intruders through ambush and other techniques of guerrilla warfare, as in Florida where one contemporary noted that Indians "employed their force and ingenuity so that no Spaniard, neither his crops nor his cattle should remain in this land."[138]

Nonetheless, Spaniards remained and from these modest initial settlements began to transform nearby lands and peoples, just as they themselves would be transformed. In the absence of a significant influx of new colonists or the growth of the military, however, missionaries came to play the most dynamic role in expanding and trans-forming Spain's feeble North American frontiers in the seventeenth century.

4

Conquistadores of the Spirit

If your highness may be pleased to have the Holy Gospel preached to the people in those provinces with the necessary zeal, God our Lord will be served and many idolatries and notable sins which the devil has implanted among the natives will be eradicated. Thus having succeeded in this holy purpose your royal crown will be served by an increase of vassals, tribute, and royal fifths.
Baltasar Obregón to the king, Mexico City, 1584

It has been impossible to correct their concubinage, the abominable crime of idolatry, their accursed superstitions, idolatrous dances, and other faults.
fray Nicolás de Freitas, New Mexico, 1660

On the feast of the Pentecost, June 3, 1629, a day in which Christians commemorate the descent of their Holy Spirit to the initial twelve apostles of the son of their god, fray Estevan de Perea led a group of thirty road-weary Spanish priests into the tiny, adobe town of Santa Fe. They had come to the end of a long and dangerous journey that had begun nine months before in Mexico City. A caravan of thirty-six heavily loaded oxcarts and a small military escort had brought the Spanish priests more than fifteen hundred miles to the dusty plaza of the most northerly Spanish community in the western hemisphere.[1] In New Mexico these holy men planned not only to minister to the fledgling colony that Juan de Oñate had founded in 1598, but to destroy the indigenous religion and replace it with their own.

These Spanish priests believed that Jesus Christ, who had lived some sixteen hundred years before, was the only son of the one true god. In the words of the Christians' creed, Jesus Christ "was crucified, died and was buried. He descended into hell; the third day He rose again from the dead; He ascended into Heaven to sit at the right hand of God." The priests sought to convince the natives of the truth of this credo and of the efficacy of their god. The task must have seemed daunting, for tens of thousands of natives occupied the vastness that Spaniards called New Mexico, and there were few priests to convert them. The thirty new arrivals more than doubled the number already there, bringing the total to fifty.[2] Notwithstanding the odds against them, faith and reason told these conquistadores of the spirit that they would prevail.

Fray Estevan's tiny band wore no armor and carried no weapons. For inspiration, they looked to San Francisco rather than to Santiago, and they gave thanks to St. Francis upon reaching Santa Fe. Members of a religious order of celibate males founded in 1209 by Francis Bernardone of the Italian town of Assisi, Franciscans vowed not to possess private or community property. They lived only on alms, for which they begged or which the king or other patrons bestowed upon them. Like members of other mendicant brotherhoods, the friars, or brothers, wore the simple

21. *St. Francis of Assisi, as depicted in an ornament on the title page of a missal apparently used by Franciscans in colonial New Mexico:* Missae Propriae Sanctorum Trium Ordinum Fratrum Minorum *(Antwerp, 1731). Photograph by Blair Clark, 1991. Courtesy, International Folk Art Foundation Collection in the Museum of International Folk Art, a unit of the Museum of New Mexico.*

robe and cowl of an Italian peasant of St. Francis's day. In theory, if not always in practice, the Franciscans emulated peasants by walking rather than riding on horseback and by wearing sandals rather than shoes.[3] Instead of an isolated and contemplative monastic life, Franciscans ministered among the laity. Popes had sent them to convert pagans in central Asia and China, and in Spain Franciscan friars had sought to convert Muslims and Canary Islanders. The first Franciscans had come to America in 1493, on Columbus's second voyage; they had begun work in New Spain in 1523, on the heels of the Spanish conquest of the Aztec empire. As early as 1526, royal regulations required that at least two priests accompany all exploring parties. More than any other religious order, Franciscans rose to the task of serving as chaplains to explorers in North America. They accompanied expeditions such as those of Pánfilo de Narváez, Hernando de Soto, and Francisco Vázquez de Coronado—"that the conquest be a Christian apostolic one and not a butchery," as Mexico's first bishop explained.[4]

Franciscans had come to America with a militant vision that rivaled the more worldly dreams of the conquistadores. Instead of cities of gold, however, the friars imagined a spiritual Antilia. The discovery of America seemed to provide a heaven-sent opportunity to rescue the spirits or souls of benighted aborigines and send them to the Christians' eternal paradise. Some Spaniards had doubted that Indians were human beings who possessed a soul, but in 1537 in a papal bull, Sublimis Deus, Pope Paul III put the question officially to rest by declaring that "Indians are truly men capable of understanding the catholic faith."[5] In addition to "saving" souls, most Franciscans also hoped to reshape the natives' cultures. At first, many Franciscans paternalistically and optimistically regarded Indians as pliable, childlike innocents, uncorrupted by Europeans—clay to be molded into ideal Christian communities. With communally owned property, communal labor, and representative government, these Indian communities would be heavenly cities of God on earth—utopian Christian republics. In such places, one sixteenth-century Franciscan noted, Indians might live "virtuously and peacefully serving God, as in a terrestrial paradise."[6]

In the decades following the fall of the Aztecs, Franciscans had worked with special urgency to construct an earthly paradise in central Mexico. The discovery of previously unknown pagans seemed to foretell the end of the world, predicted in early Christian writings, and this would be the friars' last opportunity to fulfill their destiny of converting all peoples of all tongues.[7] By their own accounts, the Franciscans achieved a series of stunning successes in saving the souls of the native Mexicans, but within two generations their future in New Spain looked bleak.

Although the apocalypse expected by the friars failed to arrive, the world of the Aztecs crumbled. Opportunities for Franciscans to make further conversions declined as European diseases consumed the natives. At the same time, the colonists' demands for the diminished supply of Indian laborers grew intense and put more pressure on missionaries to relinquish control over Indians. Finally, the Crown itself concluded that the Franciscans had outlived their usefulness in central Mexico. In an effort to cut government costs and to control the powerful and independent friars, the Crown took steps in 1572 to bring them under diocesan control. It began to replace the Franciscans in Mexico with their bitter rivals, the secular or diocesan clergy. *Doctrinas*, or Indian parishes, which had received support from the royal exchequer, were to become self-supporting diocesan parishes. Indian converts were to become tax-paying citizens whose labor could be more easily exploited than when they had been under the paternalistic care of the friars.[8] This so-called secularization of the missions, one historian has explained, left the mendicants with two alternatives: "to abandon their ministry and retire to their convents, or to undertake the conversion of remote pagan regions."[9] The friars chose the latter and discovered that whatever influence they had lost in their tawdry struggle with the diocesan branch of the church in central Mexico, they more than regained on the frontiers of the empire.

The decline of opportunities for mendicant missionaries in central Mexico coincided with issuance of the Royal Orders for New Discoveries of 1573, which gave missionaries the central role in the exploration and pacification of new lands. The Orders of 1573 reiterated the Crown's often expressed intention, that "preaching the holy gospel . . . is the principal purpose for which we order new discoveries and settlements to be made," and established stricter rules to assure that this pious wish would become a reality.[10] The Royal Orders prohibited conquest or violence against Indians for any reason. Pacification rather than conquest would be the new order of the day. Missionaries, their expenses still paid by alms from the Crown, were to enter new lands before all others.[11]

On the frontiers, then, Franciscans could begin anew to build a terrestrial paradise. The fringes of empire beckoned especially to those Franciscans who had not lost their apocalyptic zeal for new conversions or their taste for lives of personal deprivation. Those few moved quickly into North America.[12] In 1573 friars began sustained missionary work in Florida. In 1581 fray Agustín Rodríguez, encouraged by the Royal Orders of 1573, had rediscovered the Pueblos of New Mexico; by 1598 Franciscans had returned to New Mexico with Juan de Oñate and had begun to build missions. Until 1821, when the Spanish empire in North America collapsed, members of the Franciscan Order monopolized the missions along the Spanish rim from California to Florida. Only Jesuits, who had worked briefly in Florida (1566–72) and whose missions among Pimas extended to the northern edge of Pimería Alta into today's southern Arizona (1700–1767), effectively challenged Franciscan control of the vast mission field of Spanish North America.

Franciscans who initially pushed the frontiers of Christianity into Florida and New Mexico enjoyed more favorable conditions than they had previously known in Mexico. In theory, the Royal Orders of 1573 assured them the opportunity to contend for the souls of Indians through friendly persuasion rather than to minister to alienated peoples conquered by force. Then, too, they could depend upon financial support from the government so long as Spain relied upon missionaries to advance and hold its

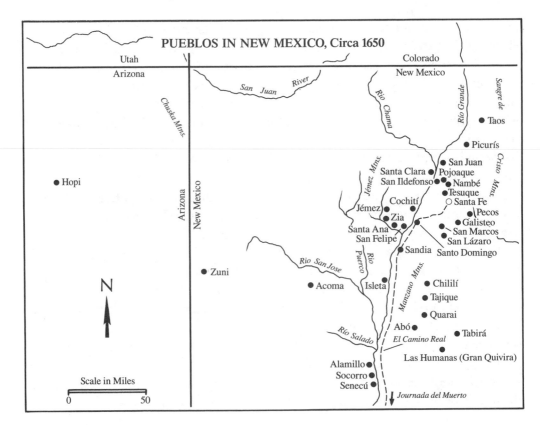

Map 3. Pueblos in New Mexico, circa 1650.

American frontiers. Finally, in North America the padres moved into areas that were so marginal to the economic life of the Spanish empire that they met less competition from civilians, secular priests, or members of other religious orders who had been their chief rivals in core areas of the empire.[13] In this frontier milieu, the missionaries made the most of their opportunities.

I

The Franciscan reinforcements who arrived in New Mexico with fray Estevan de Perea on the feast of the Pentecost in 1629 found their brethren had made rapid progress in building missions among the Pueblo Indians. By that year, according to one count, Franciscans had already overseen the construction of fifty churches and friaries (residences for priests) in New Mexico.[14] Under the friars' supervision, Pueblo women did the actual work of building the walls, just as they constructed those of their own homes, while Pueblo men apparently did much of the carpentry. The Pueblo communities, as one Franciscan noted, spread out across New Mexico in the shape of a huge cross, evocative of the crucified Christ, and the Franciscan missions followed that configuration.[15] The arms of the cross ran up the Rio Grande Valley, from the Piro pueblo of Socorro in the south to the Tiwa pueblo of Taos in the north—over two hundred miles. The top of the cross extended eastward, from the Rio Grande to the pueblos of Pecos, Chililí, and Abó, where Franciscans had also established missions. Work along the long western base of the cross, however, had awaited the arrival of additional Franciscans.[16]

Resting for only three weeks after their 1,500-mile journey to Santa Fe, eight of the friars who arrived in 1629 completed the cross by establishing missions in the pueblos of the Acomas, Zunis, and Hopis—the latter some 250 miles west of the Rio Grande. Sixty-four-year-old Estevan de Perea, who had labored in New Mexico since 1609, led the priests. The governor, Francisco Manuel de Silva Nieto, and a small military escort accompanied them, promoting the friars' work with standard theater rather than force of arms. At Cíbola, for example, the largest of the Zuni pueblos, the governor and soldiers knelt before the Franciscans and kissed their feet, "in order," fray Estevan wrote, "to make these people understand the true veneration that they should show the friars whenever they met them." Through an interpreter, a priest

22. The mission chapel at Zuni, with the friars' quarters attached on the left. Pueblo of Zuñi, New Mexico. *Engraving of a drawing by Seth Eastman, from a sketch by Richard H. Kern, 1851. Henry Schoolcraft,* Indian Tribes, *6 vols. (Washington, D.C., 1851–57), vol. 4.*

announced that he had come to free natives "from the miserable slavery of the demon and from the obscure darkness of their idolatry . . . giving them to understand the coming of the Son of God to the World."[17] The Zunis had heard this message nearly a century before from Coronado's friars. They had rejected it then and the Spaniards had waged war on them. This time, rather than risk a similar fate, they, like the Acomas and the Hopis, tolerated the messengers of the new religion, if not the message, and allowed a Franciscan to remain among them.

The Franciscans' apparent success at Zuni occurred at the high point of Franciscan missionary expansion in New Mexico. In the late 1620s Franciscans basked in a moment of extraordinary optimism, when anything seemed possible. Astonishing events had occurred and the Franciscans' century-long dream of imposing their religion upon the Pueblos seemed within their grasp.

News of the natives' rapid and sometimes astounding conversions in New Mexico soon reached Mexico City and the capitals of Europe, carried by an eye witness, fray Alonso de Benavides. When the supply caravan that had brought fresh Franciscan recruits to Santa Fe in the spring of 1629 turned around that autumn to return to Mexico City, fray Alonso traveled with it. He had served in New Mexico since 1626 as the chief administrator, or *custodio*, of its missions. Leaving fray Estevan de Perea as the new custodio, fray Alonso journeyed to Mexico City and then to Spain, which he reached in 1630. In a report published in Madrid that year (and in French, Latin, Dutch, and German editions between 1631 and 1634), he described the progress of the disciples of St. Francis in a faraway corner of the world.[18]

Over and over again, as fray Alonso de Benavides recounted it, Franciscans had convinced natives to submit to a ritual known to Christians as baptism. They instructed Indians briefly, then used water and formulaic incantations to admit them to the Christian community and to enable their spirits to pass upon death into an eternal and paradisiacal afterlife. The Franciscans, he reported, had baptized 86,000 Indians in New Mexico, Apaches and Navajos as well as Pueblos. Most of the conversions were recent, but it seemed to fray Alonso as though the Pueblos in particular had been Christians for a hundred years. "If we go passing along the roads, and they see us from their pueblos or fields, they all come forth to meet us with very great joy, saying: Praised be our Lord Jesus Christ! Praise be the most holy Sacrament!"[19]

But, fray Alonso lamented, many Indian souls remained unconquered. He urged the Crown to undertake nothing less than the spiritual conquest of all of North America. The geographical scope of the friar's vision rivaled the expansive secular goals of the adelantados Menéndez and Oñate. Alonso de Benavides called for the conversion of Indians all the way to the Atlantic coast. This would not only "save" the souls of new converts, he argued, but it would protect those already converted in New Mexico from the contamination of heresies introduced by the Dutch and English, whom he believed were not far away. He estimated that the Spaniards had pacified over 500,000 Indians in New Mexico and on its vast peripheries, and those natives still needed baptism.[20]

The Franciscans' apparent conquest of the hearts and minds of Indians in New Mexico had occurred in no small part, in fray Alonso's view, as a result of divine intercession. Magical events, of the kind known to Christians as "miracles," had taken place. Baptismal waters, he said, had brought an Acoma infant back to life, a Christian cross had restored the eyesight of a Hopi boy, and a thunderbolt had struck a "sorceress" dead at Taos Pueblo. This powerful magic, fray Alonso reported, suggested to the Pueblos the power of the Christian god and facilitated the Franciscans' work. Although a number of Franciscans had won martyrdom in New Mexico, some enjoyed divine protection. Indians from Picurís Pueblo discovered this, according to fray Alonso, when they entered the room of a priest intending to kill him. The priest became "invisible" and the Indians fled in confusion.[21]

In Spain, Alonso de Benavides learned that one source of the unusual occurrences in New Mexico was a well-known mystic. Reports had it that a Franciscan nun of the order of Poor Clares of St. Francis, María de Jesús de Agreda, had made spiritual journeys to North America.[22] Eager to hear the story from her own lips, in the spring of 1631 fray Alonso journeyed to the nun's convent at Agreda, on the northern edges of Castile near the Ebro River. As he told it, the beautiful twenty-nine-year-old abbess revealed how, for the last decade, she had made flights to New Mexico. Delegations of Plains Indians, known to the Spaniards as Apaches and Jumanos, had told the Franciscans that a woman dressed like a nun had preached to them in their own language, but the friars had not known what to make of such a story. Now Benavides understood. María de Agreda had spoken to the natives, to whom she was visible, and urged them to seek the Franciscans, to whom she remained invisible.[23]

At the urging of fray Alonso, Sister María wrote a letter to the Franciscans in New Mexico. She recounted her numerous trips to New Mexico, "transported by the aid of the angels," and expressed admiration for the friars' work.[24] Fray Alonso forwarded a copy of the letter to New Mexico, along with his own enthusiastic interpretation of his conversation with the nun dressed in the Franciscan robes and blue cloak of her order.[25]

Two decades after Benavides's visit, by which time she had become one of the most eminent women in Spain, María de Agreda repudiated much of what she had told the priest from New Mexico. She burned a copy of her 1631 letter to the friars of New Mexico and claimed that she had been misunderstood and badgered by fray Alonso and the two Franciscans who accompanied him. "I have always doubted that it was my actual body that went," she wrote in 1650. But since fray Alonso had told her that Indians had seen her, she surmised that "it might have been an angel impersonating me."[26]

María de Agreda's repudiation of Alonso de Benavides's account was soon forgotten, but the memory of her miraculous visits to America endured. Across New Spain's far northern frontier, from Texas to Arizona, Franciscans continued until the end of the century to report meeting Indians who remembered a visit from a "Lady in Blue."[27] On at least three occasions in the next century, María de Agreda's 1631 letter was reprinted in New Spain,[28] and in 1769 when Junípero Serra began to build missions in Alta California, the Spanish Franciscans' last frontier in North America, he and his confrères continued to draw inspiration from the story of the Lady in Blue.[29] Today, those interested in explaining María de Agreda's behavior rather than in drawing inspiration from it might regard her visions as induced in part by the disease anorexia mirabilis—a "miraculous" loss of appetite apparently brought on by fasting in search of perfection of the spirit.[30] Its modern manifestation is, of course, anorexia nervosa— excessive fasting seemingly caused by an inordinate desire for perfection of the body.

Fray Alonso de Benavides never returned to New Mexico to implement his plan to convert all of the Indians of North America. Reports of *Grandiosa Conversion* of the Zunis and Hopis, written by fray Estevan de Perea, who died in 1638 after nearly three decades of missionary labor in New Mexico, were published in Seville in 1632 and 1633. After midcentury, in 1659, Franciscans established the mission of Nuestra Señora de Guadalupe de los Mansos in what is today downtown Ciudad Juárez across the river from present-day El Paso (then considered a part of New Mexico), but in the main the friars had reached the limits of their expansion into New Mexico in fray Alonso's day. Their spiritual conquest of the Pueblos had proceeded with remarkable speed, but with a thoroughness that would prove illusory.[31] Meanwhile, using Spain and the Antilles as their bases, Franciscans had begun a similar process of converting natives on the Atlantic coast, long before Benavides urged that strategy on the king.

II

A generation before the Franciscans began to minister to the Pueblos of New Mexico, friars had already established themselves in southeastern America. In the humid, low-lying areas of what is today Florida, Georgia, South Carolina, and Alabama, but what was then known simply as Florida, Franciscans labored without noting the aid of a miraculous nun. They too, however, reported supernatural assistance, including the appearance of the Lady of the Rosary in the form of a bluish light. They also reported rapid success at mission building, and they continued to expand their operations in Florida long after the New Mexico enterprise had reached its peak.[32]

The first Franciscans arrived in Florida in 1573, the year after the Jesuits who came with Menéndez de Avilés had left.[33] Between 1566 and 1572, Florida had been the scene of the first Jesuit proselytizing in Spanish America. Jesuits had built ten missions at sites ranging from Virginia, near present Jamestown, to south Florida at present Miami, and up to Tampa on the Gulf coast, but they met such fierce Indian resistance that they gave up on the area as a lost cause.[34] The Franciscans persisted. Beginning a sustained, large-scale program in 1595, the friars' missions steadily expanded. As in central Mexico and New Mexico, the Franciscans established themselves in existing villages. By 1655, seventy Franciscans served in Florida (the high for that century), and ministered to 26,000 natives, a claim that some historians find exaggerated. Twenty years later, in 1675, the Franciscans reached the high point of their territorial expansion in Florida. Although the number of friars had diminished to forty, and they had retrenched on the Atlantic coast, the Florida missions extended westward over 250 miles beyond St. Augustine.[35]

By 1675, Spanish Florida had come to comprise four mission provinces: Guale, Timucua, Apalachee, and the short-lived Apalachicola.[36] Each province corresponded to the friars' understanding of a distinctive zone of Indian culture. Yet whatever differences the friars perceived, these native peoples seemed to share a great many characteristics common to southeastern Indians, including social organization, culture, and language (all, with the possible exception of the Timucuans, spoke Muskhogean languages, although those languages were mutually unintelligible).[37] Most lived in small, scattered towns with circular public plazas that also served as ball courts. These towns generally held a variety of circular buildings with dome-shaped roofs of palm thatch: communal store houses, large public meeting halls called *buhíos*, and private residences with their own outbuildings for storage.[38] Most cultivated corn, beans, and other crops and supplemented their diet by hunting, fishing, and gathering. The

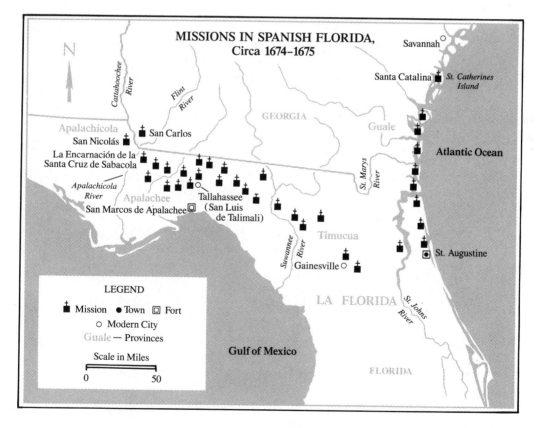

Map 4. Missions in Spanish Florida, circa 1674–75.

Guales, who had lived along the inland waterway and sea islands of the Georgia and South Carolina coasts, and the coastal dwelling Timucuans may have reversed the emphasis, migrating seasonally to fish, hunt, and gather, and supplementing those activities with farming.[39]

In 1674–75, at this zenith of Franciscan expansion, Gabriel Díaz Vara Calderón, the bishop of Cuba under whose jurisdiction Florida fell, inspected Florida's four mission provinces. One leg of his arduous tour took him northward by sea from St. Augustine to the missions that dotted the coastal plain and islands of present-day Georgia—the Province of Guale. Franciscans had begun to evangelize among the Guale-speaking Indians in the 1570s. By the mid-seventeenth century they had expanded their mission chain beyond Guale into present South Carolina, which they called the Province of Orista. By 1660, however, Indians had forced the Franciscans to retreat from Orista to the south of the Savannah River, into Guale.[40] Traveling "among shoals, bars, and rivers," Bishop Díaz visited eight missions in Guale—two were in Timucua villages. European diseases had taken a toll. The largest of the missions, Santa Catalina, held 140 neophytes, but Christian Indians numbered only

23. *A palisaded Timucuan town, with its palm-thatched houses and sentry posts at its narrow entrance.*
Engraving by Theodore de Bry after an original watercolor by Jacques Le Moyne, 1564. Theodore de Bry,
Historia Americae (Frankfort, 1634). Courtesy, DeGolyer Library, Southern Methodist University.

40 in most of these missions.[41] On the surface, life in Guale seemed tranquil, and Spain had only token military force in the area. At the most northerly Guale village, on what is today Saint Catherine's Island, some 150 miles beyond St. Augustine and 25 miles south of present Savannah, Spain maintained a small garrison as well as the mission of Santa Catalina.[42]

Close to St. Augustine, Bishop Díaz toured the Province of Timucua. When Spaniards first encountered them, Timucuans comprised at least fifteen different tribes with communities scattered over a small portion of southeastern Georgia and the northern third of the Florida peninsula, westward nearly to the Gulf coast. Beginning in the 1570s Franciscans established several missions near St. Augustine among coastal-dwelling, or Eastern Timucuans, who had adapted to the coastal marshes, barrier islands, and pinewoods as far inland as the St. Johns River. In the early 1600s, beginning with the work of the vigorous fray Martín Prieto among the Potano peoples near present Gainesville, Franciscans became a permanent presence among the Western Timucuans of the forests and fields of central Florida.[43] By 1674, when Bishop Díaz made his inspection, a trail of eleven Franciscan Timucua missions extended west from St. Augustine along a trail that skirted swamps, crossed savannas, and penetrated forests of live oak drapped with Spanish moss. But epidemics of European diseases had swept away most of the Timucuans. Perhaps as few as 1,330 remained in the missions in 1675.[44]

Beyond the westernmost Timucuan towns, Bishop Díaz pushed across the mosquito-infested peninsula, beyond the Aucilla River into the Florida panhandle and the lands of the Apalachee, known to Spaniards since Pánfilo de Narváez and Hernando de Soto had made themselves unwelcome visitors. An armed escort of Spanish infantry and two companies of Indians kept the bishop secure from Chiscas and Chichimecos—the latter a Mexican name that Spaniards appropriated and applied to maurading barbarians in northern Mexico as well as Florida.[45] These natives, the bishop believed, had little other ambition in life than to roast and eat hapless captives. Some 98 winding leagues (255 miles) from St. Augustine by his reckoning, the bishop arrived at the heartland of Apalachee—a fertile farmland of red clay hills that supported the most intensive native agriculture in Florida and the densest native population.[46] Near what is today Tallahassee, he found the great ceremonial center of the Apalachees—a people who spoke Hitchiti, a Muskhogean language that survives today among some Seminoles.

Franciscans had preached in Apalachee as early as 1608, when the peripatetic Martín Prieto visited this prosperous people, who were reputedly superb warriors. The first Franciscan visitors did little more than erect crosses in the natives' villages, however, and then move on. A shortage of missionaries and the problems of moving supplies across the peninsula from St. Augustine had discouraged the friars from establishing a permanent presence. So, too, had the absence of military support. "Moved by the devil," as Father Prieto put it, the Indians might mistreat the priests or "take away their lives," and the king would be "obliged" to punish them.[47] Not until 1633 did Franciscans take up permanent residence in Apalachee. Then, Spaniards hoped that the natives and the natives' prosperous farms would alleviate the chronic labor and food shortages at St. Augustine and offset the liabilities of such distant operations.

By the 1670s the Apalachee missions seemed the most prosperous and populous of the Florida mission provinces, containing at least eight thousand baptized Indians—perhaps 75 percent of the mission Indian population in the four provinces of Florida.[48] Bishop Díaz inspected all eleven missions in Apalachee in 1674, and he himself founded two more. At the largest of the Apalachee mission towns, San Luis de Talimali, on a hilltop within the limits of present-day Tallahassee, the bishop entered a community of some fourteen hundred residents. At one end of the town a massive circular council house served as a place for public meetings and dances. As a public space, it dwarfed the nearby church—and every other church Spaniards built in Florida. San Luis, the bishop learned, also had a small garrison inhabited by a few soldiers and their families—the only Hispanic outpost west of St. Augustine in Spanish Florida. Nearby, in the late 1670s, Spaniards would build a rude fort, San Marcos de Apalachee, on the Gulf near the mouth of the St. Marks River where, a century and a half before, Cabeza de Vaca and the Narváez expedition had built their horsehide barges to flee the region. The fort of San Marcos de Apalachee was to protect the principal river route into Apalachee from pirates, but pirates soon destroyed it.[49]

Beyond Apalachee, Bishop Díaz traveled still farther west—some twenty-six leagues or sixty-eight miles—to inspect missions in Apalachicola, the most tenuous of the four Franciscan provinces of Florida. Missionary labors had begun there just months before, as Spanish officials sought to build a barrier against Englishmen pushing toward the Gulf of Mexico from their base in South Carolina. In 1674, in what is today southwestern Alabama and southeastern Georgia, above where the Chattahoochee and Flint rivers merge to form the Apalachicola River, Franciscans had built the missions of San Nicolás and San Carlos in two villages of Chacatos (whom Englishmen would call Choctaws). Nearby among the Apalachicolas (later known to the English as the Lower Creeks), Bishop Díaz established a third mission, La Encarnación de la Santa Cruz de Sabacola, in February 1675. Before the year was out, the Chacatos rebelled and abandoned their villages; two years later, Franciscans abandoned the mission that Bishop Díaz had founded.[50]

The Franciscan failure in Apalachicola was not unusual. Attempts to convert Calusas, Tocobagas, and other tribes in the southern two-thirds of the peninsula had also failed—and would continue to fail, and north of the St. Augustine-Apalachee road the Chichimecos and Chiscas resisted conversion.[51] Nonetheless, the bishop must have been impressed that so few Franciscans had cut such a wide swath up the Altantic coast and across Florida. Altogether during his ten-month tour of the four provinces of Florida, he had counted thirty-six churches staffed by some forty Franciscans. By his own reckoning, Bishop Díaz administered the rite of confirmation to 13,152 Indians.[52] He had found the converted Indians "weak and phlegmatic as regards work," but "clever and quick to learn." Like Benavides in New Mexico, he glowingly described the neophytes as devoted Christians who attended the ritual of the Mass on Sundays and all holy days and contributed to the support of the priest: "They are not idolaters, and they embrace with devotion the mysteries of our holy faith."[53] Unmolested by pagan Chiscas and Chichimecos, Bishop Díaz traveled back to St. Augustine the way he had come and then returned to Havana where he soon died. His strenuous journey, it was said, had weakened his health.

III

On the southern fringes of seventeenth-century North America, then, a small number of Spanish preachers—seldom exceeding fifty at a time in either Florida or New Mexico—made rapid inroads into the communal and individual lives of large numbers of natives.[54] Alone, or with the aid of a single companion and a small military escort, a Franciscan moved into an Indian community and persuaded the residents to construct a temple to an alien god. Among the Pueblos of New Mexico and the natives of the four provinces of Florida, whose largest enclosed public spaces had been circular kivas or council houses, the Franciscans oversaw the construction of small, rectangular, fortress-like churches.

These foreign priests persuaded numerous Indians to participate in Christian rituals and, at the least, to take on some of the external attributes of Spanish Christians. At mission schools, adults and children learned the rudiments of Catholic doctrine—set prayers and rote answers to questions in a catechism. Some students reportedly learned so well that they, in turn, taught the catechism. Franciscans also instructed natives in the singing of Christian hymns and playing of European musical instruments in honor of the Christian's single diety. Indians learned to participate in the Catholic ceremony of the Mass, where Indian boys assisted the priests at the altar. In the earliest mission schools, some boys and girls as well as adults of both sexes apparently took instruction in reading and writing. A few became literate in Spanish and others in their own language. Like lower-class Spaniards of the era, however, most natives mastered the recitation of prayers without knowing how to read or write.[55]

Franciscans also altered native societies in ways that had nothing to do with Christianity but everything to do with living in civilized or European fashion—living *políticamente* as fray Alonso de Benavides and his contemporaries would have put it.[56] For many of the Spanish padres, like their English and French counterparts, it seemed plain that a people could not become Christians unless they also lived like Christians. Christian doctrine and social behavior were inextricably linked in the minds of Spaniards, who had also sought to make converts from Islam dress, cook, eat, walk, and talk like Spaniards. Only if natives lived like Spaniards would they move upward on the hierarchical scale of mankind, from barbarism to the apex that Europeans believed they occupied. Given that premise, missionaries concluded that they had "to deal a body-blow at the whole structure of native society," as one Franciscan historian has explained.[57] The Spanish Crown presented the scenario in the Royal Orders for New Discoveries of 1573. Indians who swore obedience to Spain and accepted missionaries were to be taught

> to live in a civilized manner, clothed and wearing shoes . . . given the use of bread and wine and oil and many other essentials of life—bread, silk, linen, horses, cattle, tools, and weapons, and all the rest that Spain has had. Instructed in the trades and skills with which they might live richly.[58]

Depending on climate, soils, and local needs, missionaries in Florida and New Mexico taught native converts to husband European domestic animals—horses, cattle, sheep, goats, pigs, and chickens; cultivate European crops, from watermelon to wheat; raise fruit trees, from peaches to pomegranates; use such iron tools as wheels, saws, chisels, planes, nails, and spikes; and practice those arts and crafts that Spaniards regarded as essential for civilization as they knew it.[59] Variations in native tolerance and the availability of goods from Spain helped determine the level and pace of instruction. A century after Franciscans had begun to preach in Florida, for example, Bishop Díaz counted no fewer than 4,081 neophyte women who still lacked "proper" clothing. They were "naked from the waist up and the knees down" and he ordered them to cover the rest of their bodies in a local fabric made of Spanish moss. The friars lacked not only the silks and linens that the Crown spoke of as "essentials of life," but cotton and weavers as well.[60]

Although the rate of success varied with time and place, it seems remarkable in retrospect that a small number of Franciscans managed to direct changes in the external and internal lives of many Indians. How does one account for the steady expansion of the friars' missionary programs in New Mexico and Florida? Perhaps, as Franciscans believed, divine intervention played a role, but more worldly explanations suggest themselves: the zeal and skill of the Franciscans, the powerful economic and bureaucratic apparatus of church and state that supported them, and the natives themselves, who decided when and how they would cooperate with the Christians.

IV

The Franciscans' work in North America coincided with a general decline in clerical fervor in the Hispanic world, but many of the missionaries who served on the fringes of Spain's empire, whatever their religious order, went prepared to make great sacrifices in the new lands. Some wore hair shirts, walked barefoot, or flagellated themselves. All sacrificed a way of life, "voluntarily depriving ourselves," as one

Franciscan explained, "of our homes and loved ones in the solitude of the forest, destitute, without enjoyment, comforts, medical aid in sickness and accident, and without the company of others like us."[61] "Beyond a doubt they eat their bread in sorrow in these places," wrote one visitor to Florida.[62] Some preachers seemed eager to make the ultimate earthly sacrifice, believing that martrydom would guarantee them a favorable place in an eternal afterlife. "The thought of dying for Jesus burned in his heart like a spark of fire," one Franciscan wrote of a colleague in Florida.[63] Some who sought martrydom had their wish fulfilled.

Along with extraordinary dedication, Franciscans brought to North America a number of shrewd strategies for imposing Christianity upon native peoples. Refined through decades of experience, some of these strategies had proved so effective that the Crown had mandated their use in the Royal Orders for New Discoveries of 1573, and they remained popular with religious orders for over two centuries throughout the Spanish empire.[64]

In the initial entrada or *misión* stage, Franciscans often sought to dazzle natives with showy vestments, music, paintings, statuary of sacred images, and ceremonies. They often won native people over with gifts, such as hawks' bells, glass beads, hatchets, knives, scissors, cloth, and clothing. As a missionary in Florida explained, "this world is the route to the other . . . gifts can break rocks." Gifts of food were especially effective and brought some Indians "like fish to the fish hook," one Franciscan in New Mexico exclaimed.[65] In many Indian societies, as among many Spaniards of that day, the acceptance of gifts established a sense of obligation and reciprocity.[66]

Once they won the confidence of a group of natives, Franciscans attempted to bring about conversions. In Florida and New Mexico in the seventeenth century, the friars concentrated on the time-honored strategy of insinuating themselves into existing communities of sedentary natives. In indigenous towns where they chose to reside, Franciscans persuaded the natives to build friaries or *conventos* for priests, and temples that the Christians called *iglesias* or churches. Urban centers gave Franciscans access to the greatest concentrations of natives, and they extended their influence to nearby towns by employing the *cabecera-visita* system that they used in central Mexico. Towns where friars resided became the head, or *cabecera*, of mission districts. Like later-day circuit riders, but often on foot, friars regularly toured nearby villages, which they termed *visitas*, thus increasing the scope of their native congregations, or *doctrinas*.[67]

The spiritual success of missions required that Indians live in towns, within the sound of the mission bell and the reach of the sacraments, and the "civilization" of Indians required that they follow the Spanish ideal of urban life.[68] In Florida and New Mexico, missionaries found ample Indians already living in towns. On occasion, the friars tried to relocate sedentary natives in order to increase the size of towns, make them more defensible, and minimize travel to distant visitas. In general, however, the Franciscans in Florida and New Mexico did not need to devote energy and resources to congregating or "reducing" dispersed natives into towns, or *reducciones*, as they had done earlier in the Caribbean and in central New Spain, and as they would do again in eighteenth-century Texas, Pimería Alta, or California.[69]

In all stages of a mission's development, gifts, ceremony, and showy display remained important. Although most frontier churches were plain compared to their Gothic counterparts in the Caribbean and central Mexico, Franciscans in Florida and New Mexico adorned the interiors of their modest chapels with as much religious treasure as circumstances allowed. At its dedication in 1668, for example, the church of Nuestra Señora de Guadalupe in El Paso contained several paintings and statues, including one of the Virgin of Guadalupe, "dressed in flowered silk and a silver crown," and silver wine goblets, a silver plate and spoon, and three chalices probably made of precious metal.[70] In the Florida missions, an inventory taken in 1681 reveals an extraordinary quantity of costly solid silver vessels for a poor area and an excessive number of vestments, paintings, and statues by present-day standards. In Apalachee alone, religious articles valued 2,500 pesos per town by the 1680s—"more than a single Indian could earn in a lifetime of work at the king's wages," one historian has calculated.[71]

Extrapolating from their knowledge of European societies, Franciscans made a special effort to win the allegiance of native leaders, assuming that if they won over the "natural lord" of a native group they would also gain the loyalty of the lord's vassals. Thus, friars worked through the existing native power structure, including some women *caciques*, or chiefs, in Timucua and Guale. The friars replaced recalcitrant leaders with more pliant figures as the need arose and sought to put themselves at the apex of Indian political leadership—although they often failed to understand the nature of native politics.[72]

The opportunistic Franciscans also directed their attention to the conversion of children, whom they perceived to be more malleable than adults. Once the celibate missionary fathers had made Indian children their own, they enlisted their aid in converting others and in discrediting the beliefs and undermining the authority of obdurate members of the older generation, including native religious leaders. "Nourished by the milk of the gospel" as one Florida friar put it, young people often ridiculed their elders with enthusiasm.[73] As the elders lost influence and the native social structure began to fracture, the power of the padres and their youthful neophytes grew accordingly.[74]

As they had on earlier frontiers, many Franciscans became linguists and ethnographers in order to facilitate conversion and instruction and perhaps to fulfill the Crown's requirement that all missionaries learn native languages (a regulation that proved impossible to enforce).[75] Throughout Spain's long tenure in North America, some Franciscans recorded native languages and a few published the results. The linguistically talented Francisco de Pareja, for example, prepared a Castilian-Timucuan catechism and a confessional, both published in Mexico City. These imprints, the first of which appeared at least as early as 1612, may constitute "the earliest surviving texts in any North American Indian language" according to one study (Timucuan-speakers spoke different dialects but shared a common language, one that remains poorly understood.)[76] More important, these bilingual texts, which often reveal considerable knowledge of the beliefs and customs of Indian peoples, facilitated the Franciscans' efforts to enter into the private worlds of the natives without the intermediary of a translator—to redefine Indians' values and to alter their rituals and their sexual behavior. A priest using Pareja's *confesionario* could, for example, ask in Timucuan:

"Have you said suggestive words?"

"Have you shown some part of your body to arouse in some person desires of lust or to excite them?"

"Have you desired to . . . do some lewd act with some man or woman or kin?"

"Have you had intercourse with someone contrary to the ordinary manner?"[77]

24. *One of two woodcuts carved in Mexico to illustrate fray Francisco Pareja's* Confesionario en lengua castellana, y timuquana *(Mexico, 1613), this image was probably designed to show Timucuans that the devil would try to prevent them from confessing their sins. Courtesy, the New-York Historical Society, New York City.*

Father Pareja's bilingual catechism and *confesionario* were not unique in Spanish North America. Franciscans in Texas and California continued to produce religious primers in native languages until late in the eighteenth century. Few were printed, for the variety of native languages and the relatively small number of native speakers of any single language made publication impractical.[78] Published or in manuscript, however, these aids must have been highly valued by priests, and perhaps by a few laymen as well. By the 1630s an Indian trader in New Mexico, Nicolás de Aguilar, had acquired a copy of Pareja's Castilian-Timucuan catechism. Given the Spaniards' hazy knowledge of North American geography, it seems likely that Aguilar expected to find the Timucuan vocabulary useful should his business take him beyond the Great Plains into Florida.[79]

Notwithstanding official injunctions to learn native languages, most Franciscans apparently failed to do so. Their enthusiasm for language study seems to have waned from a high point in the first half of the sixteenth century. Some Franciscans simply lacked the talent or energy for learning other languages—a task that may have seemed counterproductive in much of North America where native languages were so numerous and where the difficulty of crossing cultural barriers with language must have become painfully evident.[80] "Words, such as God, Trinity, Person, Blessed Sacrament," as one Franciscan in New Mexico noted, needed to be taught in Castilian because Indian languages did not have "equivalent terms." Those friars who did not know the language of their converts commonly used trained translators to hear confessions and otherwise communicate.[81]

Even as the Crown urged priests to learn native languages for more effective instruction, it also urged friars to teach Castilian to natives. This would not only rescue Indians from their barbarism by making them more like Spaniards but would reduce the babble of Spain's New World domain to a common language. Governor Pedro de Peralta, for example, arrived in New Mexico in 1609 with orders from the viceroy to encourage the padres to instruct the natives in Castilian. Effective administration of New Mexico required a common language, the viceroy told the governor, because "that land is populated by a variety of nations, with very few people in each one of them, who speak various difficult and barbarous languages."[82] The extent to which the friars complied with those instructions became a matter of contention between them and civil officials. Early on, in both Florida and New Mexico, some neophytes learned to use Castilian proficiently, some reading and writing as well as speaking it, but the majority probably used it only for ceremonial occasions and religious instruction. In New Mexico, after a century and a half of exposure, some Pueblos still spoke no Castilian. Most, however, spoke it poorly but well enough that it became a *lingua franca*. The extent to which the Pueblos acquired Spanish due to the teaching of Franciscans, or as a result of exposure to Spanish settlers remains a matter of conjecture.[83]

Paradoxically, the same padres who sought to bring Spanish culture into every corner of native life also tried to insulate Indians from what they saw as the baneful influence of Spanish laymen. Pope Pius V had reminded Pedro Menéndez de Avilés that "there is nothing more important for the conversion of those idolatrous Indians than . . . to keep them from being scandalized by the vices and bad habits of those who go to those lands from Europe,"[84] and his concern was well founded. In New Mexico, one Franciscan reported, a Pueblo Indian had asked "if we who are Christians caused so much harm and violence, why should they become Christians?"[85] In variant forms, this question would echo across the next two centuries, asked by Indians from California to Florida.[86]

To shield Indians from Europeans, missionaries tried to maintain segregated communities. That policy coincided with the Crown's vision of Indians and non-Indians residing in separate spheres or "republics"—a Commonwealth of Indians and a Commonwealth of Spaniards. By law, mission Indians could not leave their village to travel to Hispanic towns such as St. Augustine or Santa Fe without a pass, and Europeans, mestizos, blacks, mulattos, and other non-Indians could not live in Indian villages or spend more than three days in one.[87] In New Mexico, demographic pressure and a shortage of secure, well-watered land, invited Hispanic colonists to encroach on Pueblos' lands, to the annoyance of natives and missionaries. In Florida, with its reduced Hispanic and Indian populations and more abundant grazing lands, it appears that colonists found government regulations easier to honor.[88]

V

The spiritual conquest of North American Indians moved forward on more than Franciscan zeal and technique. Franciscans also had behind them a sizable state apparatus. The Spanish Crown, which enjoyed patronage over the Catholic church in its American colonies and used the church as an instrument of conquest and consolidation, provided the friars with resources and military support that enabled them to impose their will by force upon certain natives.[89]

The mendicants who preached in remote North America received alms chiefly from the king's coffers. Through much of the seventeenth century, for example, government-financed caravans of large iron-tired wagons, each pulled by eight oxen, lumbered north from Mexico City every three years, heavy with supplies bound for New Mexico. That structures in the mission compound might be properly built, government wagons carried metal tools and other hardware—nails, hinges, and hook and eye latches. That Catholic rituals might be properly performed, the Crown sent sacramental wine and oil, candles and candle wax, candlesticks, bells, musical instruments, and other accoutrements. That the padres might live like Europeans, the Crown shipped sackcloth, sandals, stockings, hats, medicines, cooking utensils, and foods such as sweetmeats, raisins, almonds, flour, oysters, sugar, saffron, pepper, and cinnamon.[90] More accessible by sea and by relatively short overland routes, the Florida missions received supplies three times a year rather than every three years, as in New Mexico. In both places, when government support arrived late or inequities seemed to occur, the mendicants plied their trade with vigor. "The missionaries . . . kill me with petitions," one governor of Florida wrote to the king.[91]

Indirectly, the Crown's subsidy of the New Mexico and Florida missions also included maintaining officials and soldiers in provinces that existed primarily for the conversion of Indians. Over the course of the seventeenth century, New Mexico alone cost the Crown nearly 2,390,000 pesos, according to one estimate, with more than half, some 1,340,000 pesos, representing direct costs of maintaining missions and missionaries. Florida, with its permanent paid garrison, cost nearly three times as much as New Mexico where unpaid citizen-soldiers served, or were supposed to serve, the friars.[92]

The Crown supported the Franciscans in North America for reasons both pious and practical. First, the papal bull of May 4, 1493, which was issued by Alexander VI and gave the Spanish monarchy title to the Indies, had obliged Spain's monarchs to convert native Americans. Franciscans, such as Alonso de Benavides, did not fail to remind the Crown of its responsibility.[93] Second, if missionaries succeeded in Hispanicizing natives, they would add to the number of laborers and taxpayers—an important consideration for a nation so small in relation to the size of its empire. Natives themselves, then, would become Hispanic residents of frontiers that might otherwise be neglected for lack of Spaniards.[94] Third, the government regarded support of missions as an investment in war and peace. Missionaries, it appeared, could pacify natives at less cost and with longer-lasting results than could soldiers.[95] "We are the ones who are subduing and conquering the land," fray Francisco Pareja wrote from Florida, where the Crown gave each Franciscan a soldier's annual wage and rations.[96] Indeed, well into the eighteenth century, the royal treasury debited the war fund for the expenses of missions. In general, missions in areas deemed strategically vital received more support than those that failed to serve the Crown's political ends.[97]

Franciscans, however, did not usually attempt a spiritual conquest without the aid of soldiers. The Royal Orders for New Discoveries of 1573 had prohibited military conquest as an instrument for pacifying frontiers, and some missionaries took the extreme view that North American natives were best converted in the complete absence of armed men. By the 1570s, however, most priests recognized the high risks of that strategy. Soldierless proselytizing by Dominican Luis Cáncer de Barbastro on the beaches of Florida in 1549 and the Jesuit Juan Baptista de Segura on the Chesapeake in 1570 had come to tragic ends; an elaborate plan for Franciscans to pacify North America from New Mexico to Florida without the aid of troops was never attempted. It seemed prudent to take minimal military precautions to avoid failure and the senseless deaths of missionaries—especially as Indians obtained firearms and horses.[98]

In North America, soldiers accompanied Franciscans to ensure their safety, but not to impose Christianity by force on unbelievers. Following a brief period of theological dispute over the question, missionaries had rejected forced conversion as bad theology and poor strategy. "With suavity and mildness an obstinate spirit can better be reclaimed than with violence and rigor," fray Estevan de Perea wrote from New Mexico.[99] Once natives consented to receive baptism of their own free will, however, Franciscans commonly relied upon military force to prevent them from slipping back into apostasy. If new converts could leave the missions, they might miss essential sacraments and fall into the company of pagans who would surely lead them further into sin. Franciscans turned to soldiers, then, to compel baptized Indians to remain in mission communities, as Spanish law required, hunt down neophytes who fled, and administer corporal punishment to natives who failed to live up to the canons of their newly adopted faith or who continued religious practices that Spaniards found loathsome.[100]

In the Florida missions, according to Bishop Díaz Vara Calderón, Franciscans appointed certain neophytes as spies, to "report to them all parishioners who live in evil."[101] Indians who failed to receive instruction or attend Mass, or who committed what the padres regarded as sexual transgressions, theft, or acts of idolatry were commonly placed in stocks, incarcerated, or whipped—a punishment "so necessary to their good education and direction," as one Florida missionary put it.[102] Franciscans usually avoided applying the lash personally, delegating the task to a soldier or an Indian assistant (a *fiscal*) toward whom punished Indians could direct their anger.[103] Occasionally, however, as in central Mexico, a few ill-tempered friars took it upon themselves to whip, strike, or verbally abuse neophytes, or smash offensive objects. On rare occasions they administered ghastly punishments. In New Mexico, fray Salvador de Guerra whipped Juan Cuna, a Hopi Indian suspected of idolatry, until he was covered with blood. The priest then smeared burning turpentine over the idolator's body. Juan Cuna died.[104]

Father Guerra's brutality was extraordinary, but whipping seemed an appropriate punishment to Franciscans reared in an era when the lash was commonly applied to Spanish miscreants from schoolchildren to soldiers. Until the end of the Spanish era in North America, the padres defended the practice of flogging disobedient Indians, and to atone for their sins they whipped themselves as well. "You Christians are so crazy . . . flogging yourselves like crazy people in the streets, shedding blood," one Jumano "wizard," or *hechicero*, told Father Benavides. Exclaiming that "he did not want to become crazy" like the Christians, the Jumano fled. The episode heartened Benavides, leaving him "persuaded that it was the Demon, who went fleeing."[105]

To many Franciscans, native religious beliefs seemed to mock Christianity and to represent the work of the devil, whose playground extended to the New World as well as the Old. "They adore the Devil," one Franciscan in Florida exclaimed.[106] Missionaries, then, sought to remove all traces of what they saw as satan-inspired caricatures of the True Faith. Initially, friars in North America fought the devil through persuasion and prayer. Father Benavides, for example, exorcised the churches in an effort "to conjure and banish the devil."[107] When exorcism, and other nonviolent means failed, however, Franciscans reached into their arsenal and made war.

In New Mexico and Florida, as they had done since the earliest stages of the conquest of America, the preachers smashed, burned, or confiscated objects sacred to the natives—what one friar in New Mexico described as "idols, offerings, masks, and other things of the kind which the Indians were accustomed to use in their heathenism."[108] Franciscans also tried to suppress native religious rituals and ceremonial dances because they saw them as expressions of "idolatry and worship of the devil."[109] In Florida, when they belatedly discovered what they perceived to be idolotrous symbolism and magic in a popular ball game, Franciscans banned the game. They ordered ball poles lowered in the plazas of Indian towns and crosses raised in their stead.[110]

Native spiritual leaders came under special attack by the friars.[111] Whatever similarity might have existed between native and Christian priests in their common roles as intercessors between man and the supernatural was disregarded by most Franciscans, who saw the sources of their respective powers as fundamentally at odds. In fact, native religions and Catholicism contained a number of compatible elements. Pueblos and Christians, for example, each believed in sacred places, a religious calendar that regulated community life, and ceremonies that used altars, ritual chants, and sacred utensils. Popular religion in Spain had a long tradition of devotion and prayer to a variety of saints and their images.[112] Like Pueblo deities, Spanish images of saints occupied sacred places and specialized in combating a variety of natural ills, from pestilence to locusts.[113] But the few Franciscans who argued for coexistence and gradual change lost out to those who advocated their rapid and violent eradication.[114]

Franciscans who defended the use of corporal punishment and force, did so on firm philosophical ground. First, as one padre claimed, only through forcible means could a people "of vicious and ferocious habits who know no law but force" be rescued from their own barbarism.[115] Second, schooled in a time and place where the good of the community prevailed over the rights of the individual, some Franciscans regarded it as their duty to punish individuals harshly lest they infect others with their wicked ways. Third, thoughtful Franciscans saw the use of force as essential to saving their own souls, for their theology suggested that "he who could prevent a given sin and failed to do so was actually cooperating in the offense committed against God and therefore shared in the guilt."[116] Finally, in a struggle with Satan, the end surely justified the means.

Even when the friars did not use force or unleash soldiers on the natives, the possibility of force must have persuaded some natives to accept baptism and cooperate. To suppose, for example, that Indians would have voluntarily performed such tasks as building churches because priests and soldiers were too few to compel them to work, misses an essential point. In the process of "pacifying" Florida and New Mexico,

Spaniards had inflicted devastating punishment on Indians. "War by fire and blood" had probably served its intended purpose of breaking the will of some Indian communities to offer further resistance to missionaries accompanied by solders.[117]

As much as Franciscans depended upon soldiers to maintain the new order, their relationship with them remained ambivalent. Until the end of Spain's tenure in North America, friars deplored the scandalous behavior and immoral examples that military men set for neophytes. Many of the soldiers, one California friar wrote in 1772, "deserve to be hanged on account of the continuous outrages which they are committing in seizing and raping the women."[118] Antipathy toward soldiers ran so deeply that friars occasionally sought permission to found new missions without military protection and frequently opposed stationing troops near missions. They argued vigorously against the building of a blockhouse in Apalachee in 1657, for example, even in the face of strong pressure from government officials. "The damned priests," wrote Florida's annoyed governor. On the other hand, when hostile Indians threatened their work, friars pleaded for troops.[119]

VI

Whatever skill, resources, and force the Franciscans brought to their struggle to extend Christianity to North American natives, they did not succeed unless Indians cooperated, and Indians cooperated only when they believed they had something to gain from the new religion and the material benefits that accompanied it, or too much to lose from resisting it.

Some natives welcomed missionaries, calculating that friendly relationships with friars would bring material benefits, such as gifts and access to Spanish trade goods.[120] Other natives saw the Franciscans as a key to defense against predatory Spaniards or predatory Indian neighbors. Natives often regarded priests as useful intermediaries between themselves and the potentially hostile Spanish soldiers. Indians, Viceroy Antonio de Mendoza reported, "welcome the friars, and where they flee from us like deer . . . they come to them."[121] Some natives saw an alliance with the friars as a way to shift the balance of power against enemies from other tribes. In the early stages of Franciscan missionary work in New Mexico, for example, growing pressure from Apaches appears to have driven a number of Pueblos to the friars—just as pressure from Comanches would later drive Apaches to seek missionaries.[122] Thus, natives sought to manipulate missionaries to promote their own security much as the Spanish Crown tried to use missionaries to secure its frontiers from natives and imperial rivals. When conditions were right, the natives' tactics worked and enabled some of their societies to survive.[123]

Initially, at least, submission to the foreign priests also seemed to offer natives access to awesome spiritual power. To some Indians, Franciscans may have appeared to be "powerful witches" who needed to be appeased, or powerful shamans with whom it seemed wise to cooperate.[124] Like Christians, many North American Indians believed that priests and ceremonies had power to mediate between man and nature, and Franciscans claimed such power as they conjured cures, rain, and good harvests.[125] From the first, several signs of the friars' power were readily evident to Indians. Armed Spanish soldiers and splendidly attired government officials prostrated themselves before the unarmed, plain-robed friars. Franciscans introduced and controlled domestic animals, larger than the natives had previously known, and could thereby provide a steady supply of meat without hunting.[126] Strange diseases that took the lives of Indians spared Europeans who followed the Christian god. At first, then, natives had reason to believe that the foreign preachers possessed life-saving powers. The specter of death from mysterious maladies, rather than the apparition of the Lady in Blue, probably persuaded some tribes to request missionaries and some Indian mothers to seek baptism for their children.[127]

The extent to which Indians saw themselves as beneficiaries of relationships with missionaries was, in part, specific to the values of each native society. Franciscan celibacy may have seemed unremarkable to some natives, for example, but probably awed the Pueblos for whom, as one historian has put it, "coitus was the symbol of cosmic harmony."[128] Pueblo males believed that by abstaining from sexual activity for several days they achieved greater strength for the hunt, for curing, or for conjuring rain. What power might accrue to those friars who practiced lifelong sexual abstinence!

Economic and environmental conditions also figured into the natives' calculations of costs and benefits. Nomads and seminomads, such as Apaches and Chiscas, succeeded in retaining their spiritual and physical independence for they could move beyond the Spanish sphere and leave behind little of value at traditional hunting or gathering places—a fact that Franciscans recognized.[129] Conversely, Franciscans in Florida and New Mexico made their earliest conversions among town-dwelling agriculturalists, who had the most to lose if antagonized Spaniards burned their villages and trampled their crops—the more so perhaps in arid New Mexico which offered few ecological niches to which native farmers might escape. Of course, some town-dwellers, protected from reprisal by distance or natural barriers, managed to retain a high degree of spiritual independence and physical freedom. Hopis, for example, submitted to missionaries in 1629, but regained their independence in 1680 and refused thereafter to permit a missionary to remain among them. "The religion of the Moqui [Hopi] today is the same as before they heard about the Gospel," lamented one Franciscan who visited their isolated mesa-top villages in 1775.[130]

Natives who decided to accept missions after weighing their apparent benefits and liabilities also determined which aspects of Christianity and European culture they would embrace and which they would reject. As a rule, those native societies that had not been vitiated by war or disease adopted from the friars what they perceived was both useful and compatible with their essential values and institutions. Ideally, they sought to add the new without discarding the old, or to replace elements in their culture with parallel elements from the new—as they had done long before the arrival of Europeans.[131] In the religious sphere, for example, many natives simply added Jesus, Mary, and Christian saints to their rich pantheons and welcomed the Franciscans into their communities as additional shamans. Guales who had previously carried offerings of food to mortuary temples now brought those offerings on the Day of the Dead; in place of shell gorgets, Guales wore religious medals.[132] Some Pueblos seem to have incorporated Franciscans, and perhaps even Jesus, into their cosmography as kachinas, or representatives of mythological beings.[133] To cite other examples in the area of material culture, neophytes added foods to their diet without discarding the old, added metal to their hoes yet retained their way of farming, and used metal tools for carpentry but did not change radically the method of constructing their own buildings.[134]

However selectively neophytes adopted aspects of Christianity and Spanish culture, these borrowings began to transform their cultures—often in ways that neither they nor the missionaries intended.[135] Indians such as the Guales, for example, who had enjoyed a rich variety of foods from fishing, hunting, and gathering, experienced a decline in nutritional quality on the more restricted mission diet, making them more prone to disease, iron-deficiency anemia, and lower birthrates.[136] On the other hand, by cultivating certain European crops and raising European domestic animals, other natives enriched their diet, lengthened the growing season, deemphasized hunting in favor of agriculture, and made it possible for their villages to support denser populations. Their prosperity also made them more attractive targets for raids by nomads and forced them to devote more resources to defense.[137] To take still another example, the political structures and religious systems of some Indian communities fractured as leaders became bitterly divided between those who converted and those who did not. On occasion, factionalism (presumably a feature of precontact Indian societies, too) became so bitter that it led to bloodshed.[138] Thus, in ways too numerous to enumerate, but that varied greatly among Indian peoples, acceptance of missionaries and European material goods transformed native economies, polities, social structure, and family life. Indians who had previously enjoyed independence found themselves reduced from the status of sovereign peoples to subject populations, occupying one of the lowest rungs on the socioeconomic ladder of the new social order.

The direct and indirect transformations effected by the missionary process notwithstanding, it appears that most natives successfully resisted the friars' efforts to eradicate or significantly transform their religious beliefs or cultural values. One cannot take as disinterested the effusive reports of fray Alonso de Benavides, Bishop Gabriel Díaz, or the optimism of a fray Juan de Prada, who announced from New Mexico in 1638 that "idolatry has been banished."[139] Fray Francisco de Jesús María

Casañas was probably more on the mark when he wrote of the Pueblos in 1696, a century after Franciscans had begun their missionary labors: "They are still drawn more by their idolatry and infidelity than by the Christian doctrine."[140]

It is impossible, of course, to know the depth of change that Franciscans effected in the internal lives of numerous Indians. Some probably underwent profound and complete conversions, and others almost certainly found ways to synthesize old and new religions—much as their Christian contemporaries in Spain blended elements of pagan and Catholic belief and ritual. Then, too, some mission Indians made superficial adjustments to please the friars or to win the favor of the Christian god, such as participating in Catholic rituals or changing burial customs, while also continuing to practice the old religion.[141] Mission Indians did not survive long enough in Spanish Florida to provide testimony to the depth or manner of their conversions, but Pueblos did. Well into the twentieth century they simultaneously practiced Catholicism, through the intermediary of a Catholic priest, and indigenous religious traditions through native priests—"compartmentalizing" the two religions rather than synthesizing them.[142]

One can imagine many reasons why neophytes did not succumb so completely to the blandishments of the new religion that they rejected the old. One reason seems especially evident. The bright future that Franciscans offered at the outset of the courtship quickly lost its luster as the terms of exchange shifted against mission Indians. Along with gifts and access to trade goods had come demands for labor and resources, and those demands on individual neophytes increased as local Indian populations declined. Obedience to the Franciscans and their god did not stop the spread of diseases strange to the natives. The worlds of the natives continued to collapse. By 1680, the Pueblo population had declined by at least half, to some 17,000, since the Franciscans' arrival.[143] In Florida, the Eastern Timucuans had nearly disappeared by 1680; a Spanish census of 1675 reported that only 1,370 Timucuans remained, most of them west of the Suwannee River. Florida, as one historian has put it, "had become a hollow peninsula."[144] The Apalachees had declined from about 25,000, from their first contact with missionaries early in the 1600s, to some 10,000 by about 1680.[145] Enemy raids, desertions, movement into colonists' communities, and forced labor also diminished the numbers of Indians in missions, but epidemics of smallpox, measles, and other difficult-to-identify diseases appear to have been the principal cause of premature Indian deaths.[146]

The prayers of the padres did not shield the natives from European diseases or from other natural or man-made disasters. In the semiarid Southwest, years passed when little rain fell upon the land. Crops failed, hunger increased, and the surviving crops and livestock proved tempting targets for Apache raiders. In the Southeast, a skilled Indian labor force at the Spanish missions proved irresistible to English slave hunters by the late seventeenth century.

In such troubled times it must have seemed to Indian neophytes that Franciscan shamans had lost their magic, or that the Christian god did not have the strength of the old god. A story handed down among the Pueblos, originating perhaps at Zuni, tells of a struggle between the Christians' "God" and Poshaiyanyi, a Pueblo deity to whom the Pueblos would turn when they launched a full-scale offensive against the Spaniards in 1680.

> God and Poshaiyanyi were going to have a contest to see which one had the most power. They were going to shoot at a tree. God shot at it with a gun and cut a gash in the bark. Poshaiyanyi struck it with a bolt of lightning and split the trunk in half. Next they were going to see which one had the best things to eat. God had a table with lots of good things on it. Poshaiyanyi ate on the ground; he had some fat deer meat and some tortillas. God watched Poshaiyanyi eat for a while, then he got down on the ground and ate with him.[147]

To control the forces of the cosmos, which seemed to have deserted them, mission Indians turned more openly to traditional gods, such as Poshaiyanyi, and to prayers, ceremonies, and priests that had proved efficacious in the past.[148] Indians learned to their sorrow, however, that Christianity was incompatible with some of their most cherished values and institutions, and that their decision to accept baptism was irrevocable in the eyes of the friars. Mission Indians heard their traditional religious practices condemned as idolatrous by the padres, who quashed non-Catholic public religious ceremonies and who intruded into the most private aspects of natives' lives. Friars, for example, attempted to end polygamy among those natives who practiced it and to impose upon them indissoluble monogamy. In so doing, the friars often enraged and humiliated native males who lacked the Christian arithmetic that one wife was better than two or three. Timucuans, who explained to one priest that "they enjoyed their vice and therefore it must not be evil but good and just," received an unsympathetic hearing.[149] Among the Pueblos, where sexuality and sanctity were closely linked, the affront to their dignity must have been especially deep, and the hypocrisy of Christians (including some of the friars), who themselves engaged in sexual practices they sought to prohibit, could not have gone unnoticed.[150]

Oppressed in body and in spirit, many mission Indians sought ways to extricate themselves from the loving embrace of the sons of St. Francis. Strategies varied. Some individuals fled, as did entire communities on a few occasions. Others tried to rid themselves of individual priests by murdering them or by making their lives unpleasant (Pueblos at Taos served their padre corn tortillas laced with urine and mice meat).[151] Prior to their successful rebellions of the late 1600s, neophytes rebelled on a large-scale at least once in each of the four mission provinces of Florida, and on a number of occasions in New Mexico. Friars often understood these revolts as the work of the "devil," or as a sign of native ingratitude.[152] The actions of natives, however, who killed Franciscans, mocked their religion, and desecrated the friars' sacred objects and shrines, make it clear, at least in retrospect, that these rebellions represented efforts to achieve freedom of religious and cultural expression.[153] Franciscans met similar displays of resistance when they sought to extend the spiritual conquest to other North American peoples in the eighteenth and nineteenth centuries.[154]

VII

The Spanish Franciscans who contended with native religions on the seventeenth-century frontiers of North America both succeeded and failed, as would those friars who followed them on subsequent Spanish frontiers. By their own count, the friars succeeded when they tallied the numbers of souls saved through baptism and the number of mission communities where natives worshiped as Catholics and lived as Spaniards. From the missionaries' vantage point, and the viewpoints of historians sympathetic to their goals, their enterprises in North America represented a "triumph" and a "success," exemplifying "Spain's frontiering genius."[155] From the missionary perspective, even when native rebellions took the lives of missionaries their missions were not judged as failures. Overlooking the blood shed by Indians, one Jesuit historian has argued that "in mission history every page written with the blood of martyrs is glorious" and "would attract the blessings of heaven for the conversion of natives."[156] Nor could the deaths of neophytes from European diseases inadvertently introduced by the friars be considered a mark of failure. Franciscans not only regarded the deaths of Indians and non-Indians as manifestations of God's will but, as one historian has noted, "missionaries would have philosophically preferred dead Christians to live pagans."[157]

At a less transcendental but more demonstrable level, the friars could also count among their achievements the number of natives saved from extinction at the hands of unscrupulous Spanish settlers and soldiers.[158] The Spanish missions, as one historian has argued, were designed "for the preservation of the Indians, as opposed to their destruction, so characteristic of the Anglo-American frontier."[159] It must be remembered, however, that the friars intended to preserve the lives of Indian individuals and not the individual's Indian life.

Whatever they accomplished, the Franciscans recognized that they fell short of their goal of weakening the indigenous religions and replacing them with their own. After eighty years of missionary efforts among the Pueblos, for example, one Spaniard complained that "most" of them "have never forsaken idolatry, and they appear to be Christians more by force than to be Indians who are reduced to the Holy Faith."[160] A true synthesis of the belief systems of the natives and the Spanish intruders did not occur in seventeenth-century North America any more than it had in sixteenth-century New Spain. Rather, religions and values remained in lively contention with one another. To the extent that the militant Franciscans persecuted native religious leaders and tried to impose religious orthodoxy by force, they drove true believers into secret worship and provoked violent resistance.[161] Critics of the missions have compared them to penal institutions and Indian neophytes to inmates, who suffered from pestilence, oppression, brutality, and "near-slavery."[162] Critics have questioned the right of missionaries "to invade the most sacred inner precincts of another man's being" and have charged the Franciscans with "religious persecution." They have asked: "If the Indian cultures are extinct is that success?"[163]

The friars also failed to achieve fully their goal of Hispanicizing Indians. In retrospect, it seems clear that they could not have done so in an institution that, in practice, isolated Indians from the larger Hispanic community and in which members of the recipient culture, apparently as dedicated to their own values as Spaniards were to theirs, so vastly outnumbered the missionaries who represented the donor culture.[164]

Finally, missions failed to serve the defensive function that the Crown envisioned. In Florida and New Mexico, native rebellions proved especially costly. They destroyed not only the missions but, as we shall see, rolled back the entire Spanish frontier. As one historian has argued, Spain's "fantasy" of relying on missionaries for Indian control had "helped to divert it from establishing realistic defenses."[165] In the late seventeenth century, reality intruded and the Crown began to abandon its excessive dependence on missions for frontier defense and relied more heavily on soldiers to advance and hold subsequent Spanish frontiers in North America. Nonetheless, even though the government sought to deemphasize them, missionaries would remain in the vanguard of Spanish expansion into Texas, Pimería Alta, and California in the eighteenth century.

Whatever their spiritual successes, then, missionaries failed to advance permanently, defend effectively, or Hispanicize deeply North American frontiers in the seventeenth century.[166] Although Franciscans succeeded initially in pushing the edges of Christendom into parts of North America, natives pushed them back. Despite new safeguards that the Spanish Crown had built into the system in the late sixteenth century, friars and natives in seventeenth-century North America repeated a cycle that had played itself out a century before in other regions of Spanish America where natives' initial acceptance of missionaries had turned to disillusion, estrangement, and finally to resistance in its many forms, including rebellion.[167] The reasons for the missions' failures, however, lay only partially with Indians and missionaries, for missions represented but one of the oppressive frontier institutions of the Spanish state.

5

Exploitation, Contention, and Rebellion

*Indians [of New Mexico] do not attend mass and the teaching of the
doctrine . . . because they flee from the excessive work which the
religious make them do under guise of instruction.*
Gov. Bernardo López de Mendizábal to fray Diego de
Santander, New Mexico, 1660

*These natives [of Florida] have not had justice . . . I beg that Your
Majesty will . . . [give] them the relief which they request, in order
that these provinces be not destroyed and made waste.*
Antonio Ponce de León to the king, Havana, 1702

In Florida and New Mexico, Spain's laboriously constructed colonies fell apart with surprising speed. New Mexico's demise took only a matter of days in 1680. In a display of
unity that astonished Spaniards, Pueblos forcibly evicted all
Hispanics and sent them retreating down the Rio Grande to
El Paso. The mission provinces of Florida disintegrated
more slowly. Because the fortifications at St. Augustine held
firm, natives did not oust the Spaniards entirely, but between
1680 and 1706 the Florida missions also collapsed.

In both upheavals, attacks by outside forces served as
catalysts—drought and Apaches in New Mexico, and Englishmen and their Indian allies in Florida. In each case,
however, deep structural weaknesses within Spain's frontier
colonies themselves contributed to the native rebellions.
New Mexico and Florida depended on Indian labor. When

the demands of friars, soldiers, settlers, and government officials became more than the natives wished to bear, they rebelled.

In their dependence on forced labor, these first Spanish colonies in North America typified frontiers in other times and places. Contrary to conventional wisdom, frontier zones with open resources often foster human bondage rather than free labor. Why should people work willingly for others when free land and opportunity beckon? On many frontiers, where only coercion could guarantee a steady supply of cheap workers, compulsory labor took its place alongside racial and ethnic tensions as an important cause of violence and unrest.[1]

I

Franciscans depended almost entirely on native laborers to make missions work. Under Spanish law, Indians paid no tithes to the church, but Indian men, women, and children constructed the buildings of the mission complex, performed the daily mission routines from the ringing of bells to the preparation of food, and raised the stock and tilled the fields that fed neophytes and friars alike. Neophytes also produced surpluses that the friars marketed to raise money to supplement the subventions they received from the Crown. In Florida, Franciscans sold pigs, fowl, maize, beans, grains, vegetables, and tobacco—products of Indian toil that Indian men hauled to markets in St. Augustine or to a port in Apalachee for shipment to Havana. In New Mexico, friars sent surplus livestock from herds tended by Indians south to the markets in New Spain.[2] Less directly, native labor also supported missions when natives served as captive consumers, forced to buy merchandise from the friars at exorbitant prices.[3]

No doubt many natives worked "voluntarily" at missions, "much to their pleasure," as one friar claimed.[4] There is evidence, too, however, that some neophytes worked unwillingly and resentfully. In Apalachee, for example, mission Indians complained bitterly in 1657 to a sympathetic Gov. Diego de Rebolledo that the padres forced them to travel to the lands of pagan Indians to trade for deerskins and to serve as unpaid porters.[5] In New Mexico, when Gov. Bernardo López de Mendizábal prohibited involuntary labor at the missions in 1659, many Pueblos quit, unwilling to work even for wages. So many Pueblos stopped work that the mission livestock suffered heavy losses for lack of herders.[6]

The Franciscans' reliance upon Indian labor brought them into direct competition with soldiers, settlers, and government officials who sought to build a secular society atop a foundation of native workers. Spanish gentlemen, or would-be gentlemen, might operate farms, ranches, or mines, but these *caballeros* had no intention of performing monotonous, back-breaking manual labor if Indians could be made to do it for them. Viceroy Luis de Velasco, in a moment of pique, once complained that "no one comes to the Indies to plow and sow, but only to eat and loaf."[7]

Spaniards, who had a long tradition of extracting wealth and prestige from the work of conquered peoples on the frontiers of Iberia, may have placed less value on their own manual labor than did their European counterparts. In the New World, however, differences in European attitudes toward work were not initially apparent. Neither the Frenchmen whom Menéndez cut down at Fort Caroline in 1564–65, nor the Englishmen who established a short-lived settlement at Roanoke in the 1580s and a more enduring colony at Jamestown in 1607, came to America to "plow and sow." Instead, like Spaniards, they devoted their energies to searching for gold and silver and seeking a strait to the Pacific. They depended on Indians for their survival. Like Spaniards, Englishmen taxed the natives' resources beyond the breaking point. When the colonists' demands for food provoked Indian resistance at Roanoke and Jamestown, English gentlemen retaliated with a brutality that their countrymen believed to be uniquely Spanish.[8] That Englishmen and Frenchmen came to rely less on Indian labor than did Spaniards may have had more to do with American opportunities than with attitudes and institutions that Europeans brought with them.[9]

Like other European colonizers, then, Spaniards initially relied upon natives to feed them. Menéndez and Oñate lived in Indian communities and collected tribute from Indians in the form of maize and other foods. As the colonies of Florida and New Mexico matured, Spaniards continued to depend on Indians for their well being. If they did not exploit Indians to extinction, as they had in the Caribbean, it was in part because they had found no precious metals and because the Crown had taken measures to curb the greatest excesses. Nontheless, Spaniards found a variety of ways to exploit Indians—some of them legal, by Spanish definition, and others illegal.

One legal means of exploitation involved the collection of tribute, which the Crown determined that all subject natives owed. In New Mexico, the Crown transferred its right to collect tribute to a few privileged citizens or *encomenderos*—trustees who held a specified number of natives in trust or in *encomienda*. Rewarded by Oñate and his successors according to their rank and services to the Crown, encomenderos enjoyed the privilege of receiving tribute from one or more pueblos, or fractions of pueblos. Among his encomiendas, for example, Francisco Gómez Robledo held title in 1662 to "all of the pueblo of Pecos, except for twenty-four houses held by Pedro Lucero de Godoy; two and a half parts of the pueblo of Taos; half the Hopi pueblo of Shongopovi; [and] half the pueblo of Acoma, except for twenty houses."[10]

The encomienda represented the survival of a feudal institution through which the king or his representative rewarded subjects who risked their lives in frontier warfare. Accorded the privilege of collecting tribute for a lifetime, encomenderos could often pass their encomienda on to their heirs for two generations. In exchange, encomenderos were obliged to provide military service for the Crown and to assume responsibility for the natives' defense and spiritual welfare. In the initial decades after the conquest of America, encomenderos abused the system infamously. Eager to bring the independent encomenderos under control, Carlos V attempted to abolish the encomienda in 1542. The powerful encomenderos managed to thwart reforms and to maintain most of their privileges, however. Guided by expediency, the Crown continued throughout the sixteenth century to allow the establishment of new encomiendas, even through it disapproved of them in principle. The Orders for New Discoveries of 1573, for example, under which New Mexico was colonized, prohibited the expenditure of royal funds for "pacifications" of new frontiers. Instead, the Crown permitted adelantados such as Oñate to assign encomiendas to their followers so that natives would pay their conquerors' expenses.[11]

Commonly, Indians in New Mexico paid tribute to their encomenderos in goods, set at an annual legal limit per household of a *fanega* of maize (1.6 bushels) and a cotton blanket or deer or buffalo hide. In a province with few Spaniards and many tributary Indians, tribute represented a bonanza for the encomenderos, who formed the local aristocracy (at first, it was understood that anyone who served the Crown at his own expense could, after five years, become a hidalgo and receive an encomienda, but about 1640, the viceroy limited the number of encomenderos in New Mexico to thirty-five).[12] Initially, Pueblo households may not have regarded tribute as excessive, but it seems to have grown more burdensome over the course of the seventeenth century—especially in times of drought and of raids by nomads on Pueblo fields.[13] As with all Spanish systems for extracting labor from natives, the encomienda weighed on women as well as men. To raise crops and produce blankets for their encomendero, Pueblo women cleared irrigation ditches and spun and wove.[14]

However it should have worked in theory, the encomienda continued to be abused in practice. For example, some encomenderos in New Mexico, as in other areas far from royal control, exacted tribute in the form of direct labor or personal service although the Crown prohibited the practice.[15] The burden of this illegal employment fell on men and women alike, but Indian women working in Spanish households often bore the additional anguish of their employers' sexual assaults.[16] Other encomenderos violated royal policy by settling on native land. By law, encomiendas never included land—only Indian tribute—and in general, the Crown prohibited Spaniards from residing on Indian lands. New Mexico officials knew that some encomenderos violated these strictures but justified the practice as a necessity of frontier life. They argued that only by living among their tribute-paying Indians could encomenderos effectively aid in defending them against attacks by nomads.[17] After the Pueblo revolt of 1680, Spanish officials did not reestablish the encomienda in New Mexico. Its demise, however, seems to have come about more as a result of the Crown's interest in collecting tribute from the lapsed encomiendas than from an awakened royal conscience.[18]

The encomienda never took root in southeastern North America. When Pedro Menéndez de Aviles contracted to settle Florida in 1565, the encomienda stood in especially bad repute with the Crown. Instead of creating a class of soldier-citizens dependent upon Indian tributaries as he would in New Mexico, Felipe II maintained a garrison of paid soldiers in Florida. His decision may have been dictated by timing, but Florida's peculiar politics and the Spaniards' perennially weak position relative to the natives may also explain why the encomienda was not established by later governors.[19] Indeed, Indian recalcitrance apparently discouraged officials in Florida from establishing a regular system of collecting tribute for the Crown.[20] What they failed to collect in tribute, however, Florida officials made up for by compelling Indians to labor on public works.

Indians were assigned to public projects through the *repartimiento de indios*, a time-honored institution by which Spanish officials distributed native men to work on a rotating basis at tasks deemed to be for the public good. The infrastructure of Spain's fledgling empire in North America was built with repartimiento labor in both New Mexico and Florida. Levies of Pueblo Indians, for example, constructed Santa Fe from its founding in the 1610s. In Florida, when the successful plundering of St. Augustine by English pirates suggested the wisdom of replacing the nearby wooden fort of San Marcos with a more durable stone structure, waves of Indians hauled, cut, and fitted the coquina building blocks of the new fort—an investment of fifteen years of labor between 1672 and 1687.[21] In the service of the Crown, Indians under the repartimiento also did such everyday work as repairing roads, building bridges, unloading ships, accompanying wagon caravans, and operating ferry services on the St. Johns and Suwanee rivers.[22]

For the natives, participation in the repartimiento was compulsory, but they were to receive wages and the law set limits on the length of their service and the type of work they could be compelled to do. In practice, however, Spanish officials commonly ignored these legal safeguards. On the frontier, as throughout the Spanish empire, Indians were unpaid, underpaid, paid in overvalued merchandise, unfed, underfed, kept for longer periods of time than regulations permitted, and pressed into the personal service of individuals who confused their own good with the public weal. Illegally, soldiers and settlers used the repartimiento to force natives to take turns at tending herds and tilling fields, cutting firewood, serving in non-Indian households, and hauling cargo as human pack animals. The latter was one of the most onerous duties under the repartimiento. Because it took Indian men away from home for long periods, sometimes never to return, an assignment as a cargo carrier also imposed grave hardships on their wives and children. Despite government strictures against using Indians as burden bearers, officials, friars, and private citizens alike continued the practice—especially in Florida where horses and mules were scarce.[23]

Just as the Crown found it impossible to prevent abuses of the repartimiento, it found it difficult to abolish the institution itself. The repartimiento lingered in peripheral areas such as Florida and New Mexico, long after it had disappeared in central New Spain, Peru, and other more settled areas of the Spanish empire.[24]

Still another source of exploitable native labor was trade with Indians, or *rescate*, in which Spaniards paid ransom to free Indians that one tribe or band had captured from another. Christian charity and Spanish law required that these captives be rescued.

Indeed, after a tragic episode in 1694 when Navajos beheaded some children whom Spaniards in New Mexico had refused to ransom, the Crown itself authorized paying such expenses from the royal treasury. Apaches, Navajos, Utes, and other ransomed Indians were often placed with Christian families where they might become Hispanicized and, in exchange, do household work for their keep.[25] The orphaned children of mission Indians sometimes met the same fate.[26] In the seventeenth century, Christian households in New Mexico commonly had one or more of these servants or *criados*, and the number probably rose in the eighteenth century. By the mid-1700s, Indian servants easily averaged one per Hispanic household.[27]

Technically these *indios de depósito* were not slaves, although New Mexicans in the seventeenth century paid the price of a good mule, thirty or forty pesos, for them. In theory these Indian "servants" could be set free after a specified period of time; they could not pass their condition of servitude onto their children. Such legal niceties were probably not appreciated by the captives. Some may have been treated warmly in New Mexico households, but all were demeaned and marginalized, and some were brutalized. Women, in particular, had little defense against sexual abuse by their masters—such as one Alejandro Mora, who raped his servant Juana "to determine if she was a virgin." When Juana resisted, "he hung me from a roof-beam and beat me."[28] Some New Mexicans whose avarice exceeded their scruples apparently sold ransomed Indians into slavery in markets to the south.

In addition to exploiting Indian labor through the legally sanctioned institutions of missions, encomiendas, repartimientos, and rescate, some Spaniards turned directly to the patently illegal enterprise of taking Indian slaves. Spaniards seldom enslaved mission Indians (they had other ways of exploiting their labor), but they did reach beyond the frontiers of Christendom to seize pagans—most of them women and children. Spaniards had bought and sold natives since the earliest stages of the conquest of America (just as Indians had bought and sold one another before the Spaniards' arrival), but by the late 1500s the Crown had made it plain that Indians should not be enslaved for any reason. Most clergy concurred, although some wondered if slavery would not improve the natives' lot.[29] Frontiersmen of all classes, however, ignored royal and religious prohibitions and continued to enslave pagans who committed unprovoked attacks on Spanish settlements. Those unconverted Indians who would not oblige Spaniards with an unwarranted attack were provoked, on occasion, into doing so by Spanish slaving parties.[30]

In Florida and New Mexico, some Spaniards employed Indian slaves in their own households, ranches, and farms. In Spain, aristocrats and would-be aristocrats of that era regarded slaves as status symbols as well as providers of labor; the wealthier frontiersmen followed suit.[31] In Florida, however, the overwhelming majority of domestic slaves were blacks imported legally from nearby markets in the Caribbean, rather than Indians (although the Crown prohibited enslaving Indians, it had long condoned black slavery).[32] New Mexicans, on the other hand, had no need to import costly black slaves for they garnered enough Indian slaves to produce a surplus.

Indeed, New Mexico became a net exporter of Indian slaves in the seventeenth century, sending captives south to be sold to Christian families in the mining regions of New Spain where labor was in great demand. Known by various euphemisms, the illegal trade in Indian slaves was practiced quite openly in New Mexico—in 1714, Gov. Juan Ignacio Flores Mogollón ordered that all Apache captives be baptized before New Mexicans "take them to distant places to sell."[33] Only occasionally did a slave trader run afoul of the law.

Spaniards, then, found a variety of ways to coerce Indians into working for them, either through institutions that Spaniards, if not Indians, regarded as legal, or by violating laws designed to protect Indians. There is special irony in Spaniards' illegal exploitation of Indian labor, for Spain had debated the rights of Indians and developed a more enlightened body of law to protect them from involuntary labor than did any other European colonizing power.[34] The pragmatic Crown, however, often allowed appearances to mask harsh realities and did not look too closely into the ways in which its distant colonials circumvented laws intended to shield natives from compulsory labor. For example, to enforce laws that would prevent Spaniards from wronging natives, the Crown had established the office of Protector of Indians, a position held by the celebrated Dominican priest Bartolomé de las Casas as early as 1516. In seventeenth-century North America, however, this office was filled only on rare occasions—beginning in 1659, if not earlier, in New Mexico and, after several failed attempts, at least by 1695 in Florida. The few people who sporadically held the position of *protectores de indios* in these frontier regions seemed to represent the interests of one of the contending Spanish factions more than the interests of Indians. Natives made some use of the protector, but as one Florida clergyman noted, Indians were reticent to make claims against a Spaniard because "they might suffer some injury or loss" as a result of the Spaniard's "good connections."[35]

In a legal sense, the Protector of Indians was a superfluous office, because all government officials, implicitly or explicitly, had a responsibility to protect Indian rights. In Florida, the Crown offered that argument when it turned down Gov. Marques Cabrera's appointment of Domingo de Leturiondo as protector in 1681, suggesting that the job could be done at less cost by ordinary judges.[36] In peripheral areas, however, officials charged with upholding laws favorable to Indians were most likely to violate them. Governors provide a clear example.

Throughout the Spanish empire in the seventeenth century, governors and other high-ranking officials regarded public office as a way to enrich themselves, legally or illegally. In nearly all cases they had made a substantial investment to acquire their position. Governors commonly bought their office from the Crown and, in addition,paid a tax equivalent to half of a year's salary (a *media anata*).[37] In order to recapture their initial investment and turn a profit, governors went into private business flaunting regulations and direct orders that prohibited them from engaging in commerce in their jurisdictions.[38]

For governors of Florida and New Mexico, Indian labor was their only source of profit. Always outsiders, governors held no encomiendas in the provinces to which they had been assigned. Thus, they turned to repartimiento and slave labor to assemble an unpaid or underpaid work force for a variety of personal ventures.[39] Gov. Bernardo López de Mendizábal of New Mexico (1659–61), who ran a retail shop in the Palace of the Governors in Santa Fe, used Pueblo men and women in a variety of ways: to gather piñon nuts and salt for export; to manufacture goods for export, including stockings, shoes, leather doublets, and leather tents; to prepare hides and tanned and painted leather for export; and to construct wagons and leather bags to ship these products south to markets in New Spain. Moreover, the natives themselves transported the governor's goods to market, just as they did those of the friars—but with less happy results. On one occasion, as one of his officers explained, López de Mendizábal sent some Pueblos to sell salt in Parral, over 600 miles to the south of Santa Fe. Along with the salt, the Indians were required to sell the wagons and oxen that took them to Parral. "The miserable Indians remain there adrift, away from their wives and children, until they are lost completely or until happily they are sent back upon his Majesty's business." López de Mendizábal was apparently not exceptional in putting his interest in immediate profits above the law or above the natives' welfare.[40]

Frontier officials who misbehaved had little to fear from the institution that the Crown established to keep them in check. Royal policy required an incoming governor to conduct an investigation, or *residencia* of his predecessor's conduct in office. These investigations, which occurred every few years as governorships changed hands, became notoriously corrupt. The incoming governor often demanded a bribe to clear the record of the outgoing governor. López de Mendizábal described the custom succinctly: "You will give me so much [money] or [lose] your honor." He boasted that he could extract up to 10,000 pesos from his predecessor. In Florida, Gov. Diego de Rebolledo calculated that 4,000 to 6,000 pesos could make any charge against him evaporate.[41] To pay these predictable bribes, governors had to raise still more money while in office—money often earned by the sweat of native brows. The Crown reformed the procedure for residencias in the eighteenth century, but the investigators and the investigated both had more to gain from collusion than they did from obeying the law. Governors continued to find ways around the system in the remote North American provinces, far from the watchful eye of royal officials.[42] One angry Franciscan in New Mexico lamented that when he accused Gov. Francisco de la Mora of taking Pueblo children from their parents to use them as servants, "the governor laughs . . . because he is so far away."[43]

II

Throughout the Spanish empire the sacred and the profane contended for Indian labor, but in remote areas that lacked powerful mediators and had no other sources of wealth, the struggle became especially intense. New Mexico, more isolated than Florida and less able to depend upon outside resources for support, seems to have been the scene of especially bitter contention over Indian labor.

In both Florida and New Mexico, as on later Spanish frontiers in North America, the invaders' demands for Indian labor exceeded the supply—the more so as native populations and productivity declined.[44] Inevitably, then, at the same time that they struggled to maintain a docile native labor force, Spaniards quarreled among themselves. In ever-shifting alliances, friars, encomenderos, soldiers, settlers, and frontier officials contended with one another for a larger share of native workers, insisting that their own claims on Indian labor were in the natives' best interests.[45]

Franciscans defended their use of Indian labor with the classic rationalization of colonialists, arguing that it improved the natives' naturally indolent character.[46] Conversely, the friars accused settlers, soldiers, and government officials of exploiting natives in ways that were not only illegal but that also weakened the mission Indians' ability to provide for their own livelihood and that obstructed the padres' efforts to evangelize. Excessive demands for labor and tribute from Christian Indians, the friars argued, made pagans wary of missionaries. Perhaps most abhorrent to the priests, some government officials sought to curry favor with the mission neophytes by refusing to enforce strict discipline and undermining the missionaries' work. Governors such as Juan de Eulate (1618–25) and Bernardo López de Mendizábal (1559–61) of New Mexico, and Diego de Rebolledo (1654–1658) of Florida took the Indians' side in the Franciscans' war against the natives' "idolatry," ceremonial dances, polygamy, and concubinage. López de Mendizábal, for example, professed to see no religious significance in Pueblo ceremonies. When he attended a dance at Isleta, one of his companions noted, the Pueblos "sang something which sounded like 'Hu-hu-hu.'" "Look there," the governor said, "this dance contains nothing more than this 'hu-hu-hu,' and these thieving friars say that it is superstitious."[47]

Outraged and determined to exert authority over the neophytes, the padres fought back. Ignoring the exhortation of their order's founder to "neither quarrel nor contend in words," Franciscans marshalled the power of church and state.[48] Over the heads of local governors, Franciscans in Florida appealed directly to the king; friars in New Mexico appealed directly to the viceroy. The men of the cloth usually emerged victorious. As the only religious order in Florida or New Mexico, Franciscans generally spoke with one voice. Because they represented the most sacred values of their culture, at least in theory if not always in practice, they made a persuasive case against local officials. Complaints lodged by Franciscans, for example, led to the arrest and conviction of Gov. Juan de Eulate for exporting slaves from New Mexico; Franciscan charges that Diego de Rebolledo abused Indians led the king to remove him from the governorship of Florida and bring him to Spain to stand trial. Rebollado died before his case was heard.[49]

In addition to enlisting the aid of outside authorities, Franciscans in New Mexico wielded fearsome spiritual weapons to win their way. In remote New Mexico, where they operated independently of episcopal authority and where Indian labor was the only source of wealth (New Mexico had no garrison to receive an annual stipend, or situado), Franciscans used their ecclesiastical arsenal with less restraint and greater fervor than they did in Florida. Friars in New Mexico excommunicated so many of their political opponents that the town council of Santa Fe complained to the viceroy in 1639 that "on the doors of the church are posted more excommunications than bulls."[50] Among the excommunicated were the province's first three governors following Oñate—Pedro de Peralta (1609–14), Bernardino de Ceballos (1614–18), and Juan de Eulate (1618–25). Friars excommunicated Governor Peralta twice![51] If they needed heavier artillery, the friars sent their enemies before the Inquisition (established in New Mexico in 1626)—as they did governors López de Mendizábal and Diego de Peñalosa (1661–64).[52] Tactical weapons, called upon to achieve more limited objectives, included the withholding of spiritual services to an individual or an entire community. Indeed, the friars discovered that the mere threat of deploying any of these weapons often forced their opponents to surrender.

Reliance upon force instead of diplomacy brought mixed results for the Franciscans. In the short run, victory often came their way. In Florida, for example, after the padres denied him the sacrament of confession for a year, Gov. Juan Marques Cabrera (1680–87) suffered a nervous breakdown and abruptly deserted his post.[53] In the long run, however, the Franciscans lost respect. They alienated government officials and settlers alike, just as they alienated Indian neophytes, with unrestrained displays of power over what were often petty issues.[54]

Contention over Indian labor was not the only issue that caused Franciscans to take aim at their secular rivals, but it often lay behind their fusillades. For their part, officials, settlers, and soldiers defended their own use of native labor and attacked the friars for exploiting the natives. Unlike the friars, the secular community spoke with many voices, for its members contended with one another as well as with the priests for native workers. Missionaries, however, who usually controlled the best land and whose neophytes constituted nearly all tributary Indians, were the easiest target. The most outspoken of the governors assailed the friars for failing to pay Indians for their work, for overworking Indians so that they fled the missions, and for enriching themselves at the expense of Indians.[55] Settlers and soldiers coveted the mission lands and labor and criticized the friars. The town council of Santa Fe, for example, contrasted the poverty of New Mexico's settlers with the "all-powerful" Franciscans, who "enjoy rich profits from the labor of the natives." The council members complained to the viceroy in 1639 that the friars received a sufficient subsidy from the Crown and should not be allowed to use native labor to produce surpluses. Instead, their herds should be divided among the poor.[56]

In advancing such an argument, the laymen stood on the side of the Crown. The viceroy of New Spain, for example, had admonished the friars in New Mexico in 1620 not to use native labor "except for things necessary for the church and the convenience of the living-quarters, and in those things with the greatest moderation."[57] In both Florida and New Mexico, however, the friars could and did interpret broadly what was "necessary." In the late 1700s, a Franciscan visitor apparently believed that the problem still existed in New Mexico, for he urged his fellow friars not to force Indians to work "beyond the limit of what is strictly necessary for the maintenance of the minister." Excessive work, he warned, could cause the neophytes "not only to abhor their minister but even to conceive no little repugnance for Christianity."[58]

Not content to limit their charges and countercharges to appeals to higher officials, Spaniards fought openly with one another. In New Mexico, where the struggle over Indian labor was most bitter, insults and blows were exchanged, mail opened, and documents forged. One governor interrupted Mass to call a priest a liar, and friars hurled the pew of another governor into the street in front of the church. Friars used the authority of the Inquisition to arrest and imprison governors, and governors arrested friars. At their most bitter, these conflicts between church and state amounted to civil war. Gov. Luis de Rosas was assassinated by his enemies—Franciscans among them, although the friars did not bloody their own hands. In Florida as well as New Mexico, all sides engaged in character assassination, accusing one another of sexual improprieties and greed—often with good reason.[59]

Natives could not remain blind to these contretemps, and at times they were caught in the middle. In Apalachee, for example, women neophytes who failed to spend their days in the woods gathering nuts to make oil received fifty lashes from one priest. Capt. Francisco de Fuentes, who objected to the missionaries' demands on these women, threatened them with one hundred lashes if they *did* obey the priest. Both the friars and the governors enlisted or coerced natives to testify against the other side.[60]

Through such behavior, Spaniards must have demeaned themselves in the eyes of natives and diminished their own prestige and authority. One priest in New Mexico suggested as much during a period of especially acrimonious feuding between friars and Gov. López de Mendizábal over the question of unpaid Indian labor: "The Indians are totally lost, without faith, without law, and without devotion to the Church; they neither respect nor obey their ministers."[61] Certainly among the Pueblos, where one sign of an effective religious leader was an ability to maintain harmony in the community, the contentious Franciscans must have lost face.[62] At the very least, the Spaniards' failures to cooperate among themselves in Florida and New Mexico weakened the administration of the two colonies and left them more vulnerable in time of crisis.[63]

Conflict between representatives of church and state in seventeenth-century Florida and New Mexico was apparently the norm—interrupted only occasionally by harmonious relations between particularly accommodating personalities. Friction over jurisdiction and privilege often seemed to be the source of the discord, but the deeper issue of who would exploit Indian land and labor stood at the core of the Spaniards' debilitating intramural contention.[64]

III

By squandering their moral authority and dissipating their energies through internal quarrels, Spaniards weakened their hold over their Indian subjects. At the same time, native societies grew increasingly volatile, aggrieved by religious persecution and oppressive demands on their labor and resources. When the natives' resentment reached the boiling point, it shattered the fragile colonial structures of Florida and New Mexico.

Violent eruptions that Spaniards characterized as rebellions but which Indians probably saw as armed struggles for liberation, broke out in Guale in 1597, 1645, and the early 1680s, in Apalachee and Timucua in 1565, in Apalachee in 1647, and in Apalachicola in 1675 and 1681.[65] In New Mexico, in the first half of the sixteenth century alone, Pueblos took the offensive at Zuni in 1632, at Taos in 1639–40, at Jémez in 1644 and 1647, and in a number of Tewa villages in 1650.[66] Indeed, Pueblos and Florida Indians may have rebelled more frequently than Spanish reports indicated.[67] In all of these episodes, Spaniards lost property and lives—especially the lives of missionaries.

Occasionally rebellions brought lasting independence for natives. Isolated groups, such as Hopis and Apalachicolas, revolted and retained their liberty through Spanish inadvertence; Pueblos from Taos, who killed two priests and burned the church down in 1639, retained their freedom by fleeing to western Kansas and remaining for over twenty years at an Apache settlement the Spaniards called El Cuartelejo.[68] In the main, however, rebels won only temporary reprieves from Spanish domination. Although vastly outnumbered, Spaniards crushed most of these rebellions primarily because the linguistically and culturally diverse native communities could not unite. On a few occasions, as in New Mexico in 1650 and 1667, several Indian villages joined in rebellion, but they lacked sufficient strength to prevail. Spaniards hanged their leaders and sold suspected participants into slavery.[69]

Not until 1680 did Pueblos launch a highly unified, full-scale offensive against Spanish intruders. Mission Indians in Florida, scattered in three provinces, never emulated the Pueblos by cooperating with one another to drive Spaniards out, but by the early 1700s they had achieved much the same result. The appearance of outside forces—Apaches and drought in New Mexico and Englishmen in Florida—provided the impetus for the large-scale native resistance that began in both places in the 1680s.

Pueblo society in New Mexico grew increasingly restive during two decades of low rainfall and higher-than-average temperatures, which began in 1660 and lasted until the Pueblo Revolt of 1680.[70] During the worst of it, one priest reported, "a great many Indians perished of hunger, lying dead along the roads, in the ravines, and in their huts."[71]

Pueblos lost herds and crops not only to bad weather, but to raids by Navajos, Apaches, and others. Traditional trade between Pueblos and nomads had probably deteriorated in the seventeenth century as Spanish demands for labor crippled the Pueblos' ability to produce surplus crops for trade.[72] Plains Indians apparently responded by taking by force what they could no longer obtain through commerce. Then, in the 1660s and 1670s the nomads intensified their raids on the Pueblos' fields, flocks, and storehouses. Recently imposed Spanish prohibitions against trade with the Pueblos gave them little choice, and shortages brought on by the great drought must have increased their desperation.[73] Some of the eastern Pueblos on the marginal farming lands on the edge of the high plains could not survive the years of scanty rainfall, much less raids by nomads. Pueblo communities such as Abó, with its great red stone mission complex, were abandoned in the 1670s and refugees moved into the Rio Grande pueblos where they put additional strain on the meager resources of those drought-stricken communities.[74]

To the Pueblos, these years of starvation, disease, and death offered grim testimony to the Christians' inability to intercede with supernatural forces. In search of more efficacious prayers, Pueblos turned to traditional religious leaders and ceremonies. Anxious to halt this Pueblo religious revival and to maintain orthodoxy, Spaniards harshly suppressed native ceremonies and persecuted native priests. In the most notorious case, Spanish officials in 1675 hanged three Pueblo priests (a fourth committed suicide in jail) and lashed forty-three others at the whipping post for crimes of sorcery and sedition.[75]

The escalation of Spanish oppression at a time of unusual stress galvanized Pueblo leaders. They worked out a strategy to regain their religious freedom and, perhaps of equal importance, to free themselves from obligations of labor and tribute.[76] Rather than settle for halfway measures that had failed in the past, they planned to rid New Mexico entirely of Spaniards.[77] In 1680 Pueblo leaders united most of their communities against the European intruders.

It required careful planning to coordinate an offensive involving some 17,000 Pueblos living in more than two dozen independent towns spread out over several hundred miles and further separated by at least six different languages and countless dialects, many of them mutually unintelligible. The magnet that drew these disparate people together seems to have been Popé. A resolute religious leader from San Juan Pueblo, Popé had been among those accused of sorcery and whipped in the witch hunt of 1675.[78] Five years later, concealing himself in a sacred room, or kiva, at Taos, the most northerly and remote pueblo in the province, Popé directed a rebellion against his oppressors. Popé failed to unify all of the Pueblos, however, for mutual suspicions ran deep. Some communities were not invited to join; others refused to join. Within rebel Pueblo communities, some individuals remained staunchly loyal to the Spaniards (dissent created severe rifts within pueblos if the civil strife that swept Pecos may be taken as typical). Nonetheless, Popé did unite most of the Pueblos. Moreover, some neighboring Apaches, who had their own score to settle with Spanish slavers, also joined his cause.[79]

From Popé's headquarters at Taos, runners secretly carried calendars in the form of knotted cords to participating pueblos. Each knot marked a day until the Pueblos would take up arms. The last knot was to be untied on August 11, but rebellion erupted a day early. Tipped off by sympathetic Pueblos, Spaniards had captured two of the rebel messengers on August 9. When Pueblo leaders learned that their plans had been betrayed, they moved the attack up a day. Although the Spaniards had received some warning, they could not have imagined the magnitude of this unprecedented plan. The revolt caught them off guard. Scattered in farms and ranches along the Rio Grande and its tributaries, Spaniards were easy prey.

Spaniards who survived the initial attacks fled to Santa Fe and to Isleta Pueblo, one of the few pueblos that did not follow Popé. Believing themselves the only survivors, 1,500 refugees at Isleta abandoned the Pueblo on September 14 and fled down the Rio Grande toward El Paso. Meanwhile, in Santa Fe, Gov. Antonio de Otermín found himself under siege by Pueblos who were armed not only with bows and arrows, but also with guns, lances, swords, and leather armor that they had seized from unfortunate victims. At the height of the siege, nearly 2,000 Pueblos surrounded Santa Fe. Inside the city, Spaniards numbered about 1,000, but only 100 or so were men capable of bearing arms.

Despite the odds, the Spaniards put up a game struggle. According to their own reports, they inflicted heavy casualties on the Pueblos. Slowly, however, they lost ground, crowding into a few government buildings as the Pueblos sacked and burned their homes. Governor Otermín, who suffered two arrow wounds in the face and a gunshot wound in the chest,[80] finally concluded that they had to flee or be slaughtered. Pueblos had cut off the villa's water supply, and the Spaniards had no prospects for reinforcements. Caught up in the momentum of the revolt, even once-friendly Pueblo leaders had turned against them. On September 21, the Spaniards abandoned the charred remains of Santa Fe. The Pueblo rebels allowed their adversaries, including several hundred Christian Pueblos, to retreat down the Rio Grande some three hundred miles to El Paso.[81]

In a matter of weeks, the Pueblos had eliminated Spaniards from New Mexico above El Paso. The natives had killed over 400 of the province's 2,500 foreigners (nearly all in the initial days of the rebellion), destroyed or sacked every Spanish building, and laid waste to the Spaniards' fields. There could be no mistaking the deep animosity that some natives, men as well as their influential wives and mothers, held toward their former oppressors.[82] "The heathen," wrote one Spanish officer in New Mexico, "have conceived a mortal hatred for our holy faith and enmity for the Spanish nation."[83] Some Pueblo leaders, including Popé, urged an end to all things Spanish as well as Christian. After the fighting subsided, they counselled against speaking Castilian or planting crops introduced by the Europeans.[84] This nativistic resurgence succeeded only partially in reversing the cultural transformation that Spaniards had set in motion. Some reminders of Spanish rule, such as forms and motifs in pottery, seem to have disappeared, but Pueblos continued to raise Spanish-introduced crops and livestock and to make woolen textiles. Just as they had been selective in adapting aspects of Hispanic culture, so too were they selective in rejecting them.[85]

The Pueblos' repudiation of the symbols of Christianity suggested the strong religious impulse behind the rebellion. The natives desecrated churches and sacred objects. They killed twenty-one of the province's thirty-three missionaries, often humiliating, tormenting, and beating them before taking their lives. Under questioning, one Pueblo captive later explained how Popé traveled from pueblo to pueblo ordering that

> they instantly break up and burn the images of the holy Christ, the Virgin Mary and the other saints, the crosses, and everything pertaining to Christianity, and that they burn the temples, break up the bells, and separate from the wives whom God had given them in marriage and take those whom they desired. In order to take away their baptismal names, the water, and the holy oils, they were to plunge into the rivers and wash themselves . . . there would thus be taken from them the character of the holy sacraments.[86]

Spaniards clearly understood the Pueblo Rebellion as a rejection of Christianity. As Governor Otermín watched the church in Santa Fe burn, he listened to "the scoffing and ridicule which the wretched and miserable Indian rebels made of the sacred things, intoning . . . prayers of the church with jeers."[87] Far to the south in Querétaro, witnesses reported that on the day of the revolt, between 1:00 and 3:00 P.M. an ancient and sacred stone cross shook thirty-three times (once for every year that Christians believe Christ walked on the earth).[88]

Spanish survivors of the tragedy, however, were unwilling or unable to acknowledge that they themselves had goaded the natives into rebelling either through religious persecution or through excessive demands on native labor. "This ruin did not originate because either of the repartimientos or of other drudgery which might have aggrieved these Indians," Governor Otermín explained to the viceroy.[89] Instead, Spaniards imagined the revolt as divine retribution for their sins or as the work of the devil—explanations that had helped them understand earlier native rebellions.[90] More on target, a royal attorney in Mexico City who examined the testimony in the case concluded that the Spaniards' "many oppressions . . . have been the chief reason for the rebellion."[91]

The Pueblos had conducted one of the most successful Indian rebellions against Spanish colonizers anywhere in the hemisphere, but they could not maintain their independence.[92] Buffered from the nearest Spaniards at El Paso by three hundred miles of rugged terrain, much of it controlled by Apaches, Pueblos repelled initial Spanish efforts to return. As the Pueblos' unity fractured, however, internal divisions made them increasingly susceptible to the Spanish invaders' tactics of divide and conquer.[93]

Thirteen years passed before Spaniards reestablished a base in the Pueblo country. Meanwhile, many remained in or near El Paso, then located on what is today the Mexican side of the Rio Grande at Ciudad Juárez. Site of a mission since 1659, El Paso's beginnings as a Hispanic civil community date to the Pueblo Revolt, when it became New Mexico's temporary and unhappy capital. There, factious New Mexico exiles found themselves unable to reconstruct their old way of life by exploiting Indian labor and tribute. Many of the refugees fled farther south, in violation of government orders. Those who remained behind in El Paso lived in peril and extreme poverty, lacking resources and manpower to launch an effective counteroffensive against the Pueblos. Most resembled the eleven-person household of one Cristóbal Martín, whose corn crop had failed and left them without food. He and his wife dressed in rags, to the point of being "indecent," and their children went naked.[94]

Instead of reasserting control over the Pueblos, Spanish soldiers, colonists, and missionaries found themselves hard pressed to hold ground in El Paso. Beginning in 1684, the rebellion of the Pueblos had begun to spread beyond the Pueblos' world, like an "epidemic" as one Spanish official put it.[95] The contagion eventually spread as far east as Coahuila and as far west as Sonora, in what some historians have termed the Great Northern Revolt.[96] Throughout the vast lands just below the present United States-Mexican border, exploited natives, many of them mission Indians such as Janos, Sumas, Conchos, Tobosos, Julimes, and Pimas, ravaged missions and settlements and fled from Spanish oppression.[97] Spanish troops dispensed harsh treatment that suppressed individual rebellions temporarily, but for decades thereafter outbreaks of violent resistance continued across New Spain's far northern frontier.

The great rebellions of the 1680s and 1690s might have delayed indefinitely the Spanish reconquest of the Pueblos had it not been for the intrepid Diego de Vargas. In 1691, Vargas arrived at El Paso with the dubious honor of governing lands held by Indian rebels. A forty-eight-year-old Spanish nobleman of middle rank, Diego de Vargas had left his wife and children behind in Madrid and sailed to the Indies in order to increase his family's income. As he put it, "Spain was like a stepmother to me, for she banished me to seek my fortune in strange lands."[98] Twenty years after leaving home, he had acquired debts in two hemispheres rather than a fortune, but New Mexico provided him with another roll of the dice. Victory there might bring more profitable appointments.

Vargas made a preliminary expedition into the Pueblo country in 1692, planning to test the waters before plunging in with an occupying force and colonists. His initial four-month campaign in 1692 seemed to succeed beyond all expectation. With the aid of Pueblo allies who had come with him from El Paso or joined him in

25. This portrait of Diego de Vargas, which hangs in the private chapel of San Isidro in Madrid, was apparently painted in Madrid prior to his departure for New Spain in 1672, at age twenty-nine. Courtesy, J. Manuel Espinosa.

New Mexico, and through skillful diplomacy and intimidation, the steel-nerved Vargas avoided annihilation on several occasions and won the token allegiance of twenty-three Pueblo communities.[99] Like others before him, he could not resist memorializing his achievements on Inscription Rock, as he paused en route to Zuni on November 8. Carved deeply, Vargas's words can still be read:

> Here was the General Don Diego
> de Vargas, who conquered
> for our Holy Faith, and for the Royal
> Crown, all the New
> Mexico, at his expense,
> Year of 1692[100]

Vargas's exploits were not only carved in silent stone, but noisily celebrated in Mexico City with the ringing of the cathedral bells. On orders of the viceroy, New

Spain's most prominent scientist, Carlos de Sigüenza y Góngora, lauded Vargas in a lengthy pamphlet. Vargas, Sigüenza y Góngora wrote somewhat hyperbolically, had restored "an entire realm" to the king "without wasting a single ounce of powder, unsheathing a sword, or (what is most worthy of emphasis and appreciation) without costing the Royal treasury a single maravedi."[101]

But Vargas's claim to victory proved premature, as he discovered the next year. Encouraged by the Pueblos' initial professions of friendship, the viceroy gave Vargas financial support and authorization to recruit colonists, soldiers, and priests to reoccupy New Mexico. For Spain, the province had strategic value in the face of what Spanish officials perceived as growing Indian and French threats to the northern frontier. Moreover, the perennial chimera of mineral wealth—this time in the form of the mythical Sierra Azul—a mountain range of silver and a nearby lake of quicksilver—provided additional incentive for the viceroy to reclaim Spanish hegemony over the Pueblos.[102]

When Vargas returned to New Mexico in late 1693 with some eight hundred persons, including one hundred soldiers and a number of Pueblo allies, many of the Pueblos who had sworn obedience to him the year before now offered staunch resistance. It had cost the Pueblos nothing to humor Vargas on his reconnaissance in 1692, but when he returned to stay the Pueblos were less accommodating. No amount of diplomacy, for example, could persuade Tewas and Tanos to relinquish Santa Fe, which they had occupied since 1680. Spaniards, with Indian allies augmented by volunteers from Pecos Pueblo, stormed their former capital amidst the usual appeals to Santiago. They made special entreaties, however, to a New Mexican image of the Virgin Mary, *Nuestra Señora de la Conquista*, whose wooden statue had been spirited out of New Mexico in 1680, brought back again with the reconquerors in 1693 (this icon, popularly known as *La Conquistadora*, continues to be venerated in Santa Fe for aid rendered to Vargas and also serves as a powerful civil and ethnic symbol).[103] The victorious Spaniards executed seventy natives who had refused to surrender, charging them with treason against church and state. The hard-won victory at Santa Fe gave Vargas a foothold among the Pueblos, but only through determined military campaigns waged throughout 1694 did Vargas subdue most of the remaining Pueblos.

The natives' fealty remained more apparent than real. As Franciscans began to rebuild missions in the pueblos, they met such bitter hostility that many fled back to Santa Fe. They reported that the Pueblos planned another revolt and begged Vargas to assign soldiers to the missions. "Although shedding one's blood in defense of the holy gospel and in the name of Jesus Christ is very pleasing to His Divine Majesty, and martyrdom is pleasing to our souls," one priest explained to Vargas, it is only useful "when some gain is expected."[104] In June of 1696, the predicted rebellion broke out. Although it was not as carefully coordinated as the revolt of 1680, Pueblo rebels killed five Franciscans and burned churches and convents. Many Indians abandoned their pueblos rather than continue to submit to Spanish rule.

26. The three-foot-tall statue of Nuestra Señora del Rosario, best known as La Conquistadora, *still reposes in the north chapel of the parish church of Santa Fe. Photograph by Robert H. Martin, 1948. Courtesy, Museum of New Mexico, neg. no. 41984.*

Better prepared for another rebellion than Governor Otermín had been and more cunning, Vargas launched a methodical war of attrition, striking food supplies as well as rebel positions. After a six-month campaign, Vargas and his Pueblo allies had reasserted Spanish control over all of the rebellious communities except the westernmost—Acoma, Zuni, and Hopi.[105] Acoma and Zuni soon submitted again, but the isolated Hopis, their population swelled by refugees from the Rio Grande pueblos, retained their independence throughout the next century.[106]

The struggle for independence had cost the Pueblos dearly. Their population declined sharply, from about 17,000 in 1680 to 14,000 in 1700. A disproportionate number of Pueblo males had died, and entire families had fled their communities. Many, for example, joined the apostate Hopis, and some Pueblos from Picurís fled to the Apache settlements at El Cuartelejo in western Kansas, just as Pueblos from Taos had done in a time of trouble a few generations earlier. A shrinking population forced Pueblos to abandon some of their smaller communities, never to rebuild them. Zunis, who occupied six villages when Coronado encountered them, consolidated their reduced population into the single village of Halona—still today the principal Zuni community.[107]

Exhausted from war, their property and population diminished, Pueblos did not launch another major rebellion while under Spanish rule. Nor did the Spaniards, fearful of another rebellion, offer as much provocation.[108] After the 1696 revolt the Spaniards lowered the level of exploitation. In the eighteenth century, pragmatic Franciscans displayed less zeal in attempting to stamp out Pueblo religious practices, and colonists and officials eased (but did not cease) their demands on Pueblo laborers. The encomienda system, destroyed by the Pueblos, was never reestablished in New Mexico. The diminution of Spanish provocation, then, diminished tensions and opened the way for an era of peaceful coexistence between Pueblos and Hispanics—an accommodation cemented by their common need for defense against unrelenting attacks by Utes, Apaches, and Navajos.[109]

IV

In Florida as in New Mexico, mission Indians, who harbored deep resentment because of religious persecution and heavy demands on their labor, occasionally erupted in bloody rebellions.[110] In Florida, however, marauding Englishmen rather than Apaches served as the spark that touched off a series of explosions that permanently crippled the Franciscan missions.

English traders had operated on the fringes of Spanish Florida for decades, but not until 1670, when they established a permanent settlement at Charleston, did they threaten Spanish hegemony over southeastern America. Although alarmed by this foreign presence on the northern edge of the Guale missions, Spain failed to dislodge the English from Carolina. Instead, the Charleston settlers, whose royal charter granted them lands claimed by Spain, including the northern Gulf Coast and St. Augustine itself, put Spaniards in Florida on the defensive. Eager to control the sea lanes and expand the fur trade, the Carolinians entered into alliances with neighboring tribes and plotted to eliminate their Spanish rivals. Over the next decades, they attacked Spanish missions, sold mission Indians into slavery, and nearly succeeded in driving Spaniards out of Florida entirely.[111]

Carolinians and their Indian allies launched this offensive in 1680 in Guale, with attacks on missions on Jekyll and St. Catherines islands. Within six years they had shut down nearly all of the Spanish missions in Guale and had begun to chip away at Timucua and Apalachee. Hostilities abated somewhat in the 1690s, in a period of amicable relations between Spain and England (although Carolinians continued to capture Spanish Indians and sell them into slavery) but resumed again with the outbreak of the War of Spanish Succession in 1701—known to English colonists in America as Queen Anne's War.[112]

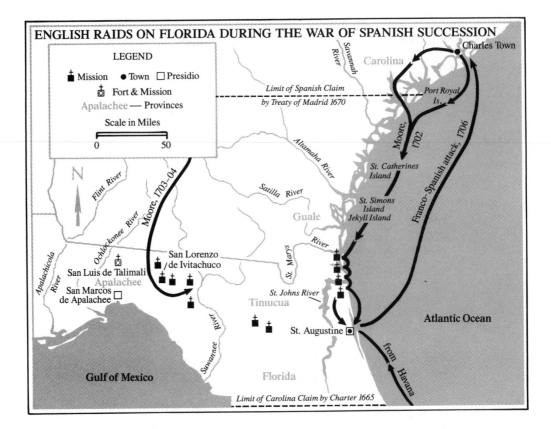

Map 5. English raids on Florida during the War of the Spanish Succession.

In 1702, Carolina Gov. James Moore led simultaneous land and sea attacks on St. Augustine. He devastated the town but failed to take the redoubtable fort of San Marcos. In direct response to the English establishment of Charleston in 1670, Spain had replaced the old wooden fort or *castillo* of San Marcos with a stone structure, completed in 1687. The castillo's massive coquina walls held firm against Moore and provided refuge for townspeople, loyal Indians, and Spanish troops until reinforcements arrived and Moore fled.

Disgraced by his failure to take the castillo of San Marcos, Moore lost his position as governor but not his interest in preying on his Spanish neighbors. With the blessings of the Carolina assembly, he raised a private army of slave hunters who invaded Apalachee twice in 1704. Within a year Moore's forces destroyed Florida's most prosperous and populous mission province, reducing most of its mission towns to ashes and presiding over horrifying carnage. Moore's allies, whom he apparently could not control, roasted some of their captives alive. In the case of one hapless Spaniard, several witnesses reported, they "cut out his tongue and eyes, cut off his ears, slashed him all over, stuck burning splinters in the wounds, and set fire to him while he

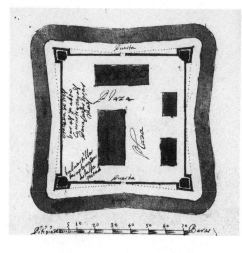

27. In response to English raids, the mission of Santa Catalina de Guale was moved south, from St. Catherine's Island to Amelia Island. There, officials planned to fortify the mission compound with a palisade, moat, and bastions, as shown in this plan of 1691. Englishmen destroyed the mission in 1702 before the new defenses had been completed. Courtesy, Archivo General de Indias, Seville, and P. K. Yonge Library, University of Florida.

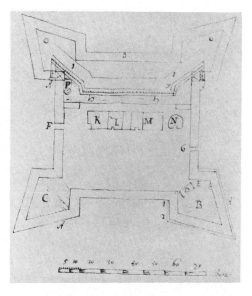

28. The castillo de San Marcos in the midst of reconstruction by Indian laborers in July 1575, as ordered by the king. The west wall (H) had not yet been built, but had been closed by earthworks. Courtesy, Archivo General de Indias, Seville, and Luis Arana, Castillo de San Marcos National Historic Site.

was tied at the foot of a cross."[113] Moore boasted that he had "killed, and taken as slaves 325 men, and have taken slaves 4,000 women and children."[114]

Apalachee could not survive. Later that year Spaniards abandoned the province and put to the torch its one remaining fortification, a blockhouse at San Luis de Talimali, to keep it from falling into English hands. By the end of 1706 Carolina raiders had destroyed most of the remaining missions of Timucua. Only St. Augustine, and villages in its immediate vicinity, survived.

The Carolinians succeeded in large part because they had won Indians to their side. Non-mission Indians such as the Yamasees had joined Englishmen in their raids on Guale, and Moore had supplemented his army of fifty whites with some thousand Creeks when he invaded Apalachee. Englishmen offered powerful incentives in the form of rum, arms, ammunition, booty, and cheap trade goods. Spain, on the other hand, had little more to offer than a foreign religion. Spain officially prohibited its subjects from furnishing Indians with firearms (a prohibition that occasionally went unenforced), and Spanish traders could not match their English counterparts in price or quality of trade goods. Moreover, Spanish demands for labor had alienated non-mission Indians who lived within striking distance of slavers and labor levies.[115] As in New Mexico, non-mission Indians also had before them the example of Spaniards' treatment of Christian Indians. When asked to become Christians, one priest in Florida explained, "the pagans . . . do not want to, saying that, on their becoming Christians the Spaniards treat them as slaves, that they no longer have liberty, nor are they masters of their possessions, [and] that they mistreat them."[116]

Equally important in assuring English success, large numbers of alienated mission Indians deserted the friars and went over to the English side—a process that had begun even before the English attacks began. Repelled by the treatment they received from Spanish missionaries and colonists and lured to the English cause by guns, ammunition, and other trade goods, Indian apostates attacked their former mission homes alongside the Carolinians.[117] Like the Pueblo rebels, some of the Florida mission Indians explicitly repudiated baptism as the symbol of Christianity. Striking themselves on the forehead, some neophytes are said to have exclaimed, "Go away water! I am no Christian!"[118] Church ornaments were hauled away, churches burned, and some of the friars tortured and mutilated. Apostate Indians seem to have joined in this war by fire and blood with an enthusiasm equal to that of Englishmen and their pagan Indian allies.

Many mission Indians, however, remained loyal to the Spaniards in Florida as they did in New Mexico. In Apalachee, the number of neophytes who deserted may have been matched by the number who defended the missions.[119] Nonetheless, few of the loyal mission Indians survived in Spanish territory. Some 300 made their way to St. Augustine, where they sought refuge near the castillo of San Marcos. Most notable among this group were Apalachees from the town of Ivitachuco, whose highly acculturated and literate chief, Patricio de Hinachuba, had warned the Spanish officials several years before that as a result of excessive demands on them "we are most unhappy and the natives are fleeing . . . in disorder. Some have fled to the woods . . . others to Saint George [Charleston] with the English." When Moore's raids began, Patricio de Hinachuba saved his town through skillful diplomacy and then retreated to St. Augustine. It was to no avail. In the spring of 1706, within sight of the fort, Creek and renegade mission Indians massacred the Christian Indians from Ivitachuco, including its resourceful chief.[120] A pitifully small remnant of Apalachees fared better by migrating westward to the shelter of Pensacola and Mobile, posts founded on the Gulf in 1699 and 1702 by Spaniards and Frenchmen respectively. After the diaspora, the adaptable Apalachees, described as prosperous by Cabeza de Vaca and De Soto, became extinct as a people.[121]

By 1706, then, the laboriously constructed chains of Franciscan missions that once ran north from St. Augustine into Guale and west through Timucua and Apalachee had collapsed. As two officials wrote from St. Augustine that year: "In all these extensive dominions and provinces, the law of God and the preaching of the Holy Gospel have now ceased."[122] Although Spaniards saw Englishmen as the sole cause of the destruction of the Florida missions, their demise should also be recognized as a massive rebellion by Indian neophytes.

English raiders and their allies had offered Christian Indians a choice, albeit an unhappy one, and many chose the English.[123] Just as Spaniards enslaved pagans who attacked them in this border warfare, the Carolinians enslaved many of the mission Indians and shipped them off to labor in other English colonies, especially Barbados from which many of the Carolinians had come.[124] Like Spanish imperialists, English-men justified their exploitation of Indian labor as beneficial for Indians. As one Carolina slaver explained, "Some men think . . . it is a more Effectual way of Civiliz-ing and Instructing, then [sic] all the Efforts used by the French Missionaries."[125] Ironically, within a few years, many Creeks and Yamasees would become disaffected with their English allies and seek the protection of Spaniards in Florida.[126]

The devastation of the Florida missions was nearly as complete as the Pueblo Revolt. In Florida, however, there would be no Spanish reconquest of rebel territory, for most of the rebels went over to the English side. Franciscans made an effort to lure Indians to St. Augustine, restore the lost missions, and extend missions to other native groups, but the friars' feeble efforts were wracked by internal dissension and gained little support from the Crown. Their modest achievements were quickly undone as neophytes continued to desert, be taken off by English raiders, or die in epidemics.[127] As if to complete the circle begun in the 1560s, Jesuits returned to Florida to attempt another mission, this one at the mouth of the Miami River in 1743–44. They aban-doned the project when the Indians whom they had come to save refused everything except gifts.[128]

In the 1700s, Spain continued to hold bases in Florida—at St. Augustine, San Marcos de Apalachee, and at Pensacola—but never again converted or exploited significant numbers of natives. Control over Florida's meager Indian population shifted to traders from England and France who had more experience and more abundant trade goods to offer than their Spanish rivals.[129]

V

As profoundly tragic and consequential as rebellions in New Mexico and Florida were for all parties involved, they did not end the cycle of exploitation, contention, and rebellion. As Spaniards expanded into new arenas in North America in the 1700s, missionaries and settlers alike continued to exploit native labor and to provoke violent rebellions as they had in New Mexico and Florida in the 1600s. Sometimes natives won temporary freedom, as did the Pimas, or O'odham, in southern Arizona in 1751. Occasionally, rebellious neophytes permanently blocked the advance of the Spanish frontier, as at San Sabá in central Texas in 1758, and at the strategic ford of the Colorado River in 1781, where Yumans (Quechans) closed the overland route to California for as long as Spain ruled in North America.

In the eighteenth century, however, a new element came increasingly into play. The successful expansion of the Carolinians and a growing French presence in the

Gulf of Mexico in the late 1600s had made it clear that European control of the Southeast and its native laborers would be a three-way contest. As Spaniards had learned to their horror in Florida, foreign arms in the hands of hostile natives could quickly turn the odds against them. If the Spanish Crown wished to maintain its claims to North America, it would have to check the expansion of its imperial rivals—France, England, Russia, and, after 1783, the United States. Friars with crosses, small military escorts, and soldier-citizens lacked muscle. The new challenge required a larger military presence and a more imaginative Indian policy to offset the commercial advantages that natives received from Spain's rivals. North America would prove to be more complex and costly for the Bourbons, who ascended to the Spanish throne in 1700, than it had for their Hapsburg predecessors.

6

Imperial Rivalry and Strategic Expansion: Texas, the Gulf Coast, and the High Plains

If we do not make one kingdom of all of this, nothing is secure.
Gov. Joseph de Zúñiga y Cerda to the king,
St. Augustine, 1704

Your Excellency can see what a condition the French are placing us. They are slipping in behind our backs in silence, but God sees their intentions.
Francisco Hidalgo to the viceroy, San Francisco
de los Tejas, 1716

From their base in Carolina, Englishmen had set in motion the forces that nearly destroyed Spanish Florida, but England was not the only European power to challenge Spain in the late seventeenth century for territory along the southern fringes of North America. In the troubled 1680s, as Carolinians and their Indian allies began to wreak havoc in the missions of Guale and as Pueblos regained autonomy over New Mexico, France established an outpost on the Texas coast. Spanish policymakers correctly regarded the French intruders as a potential threat to the security of Florida, New Mexico, and the mines of northern Mexico, as well as to the strategic sea-lanes of the Gulf of Mexico, over which Spain had enjoyed exclusive control. French interest in the

Gulf coast worried England, too, which had designs on the same region. Thus, by the eighteenth century, the southern rim of the continent, from the Texas coast to St. Augustine, had become the scene of a protracted three-way struggle among Western Europe's most expansive empires. The contest, which inevitably involved native Americans, further transformed the political map of the continent.

I

France's imperial ventures on the Gulf coast of North America began with the disaster-ridden attempt by René Robert Cavelier, Sieur de La Salle, to plant a colony at the mouth of the Mississippi in 1685. Three years earlier, La Salle had explored the Mississippi Valley in an epic journey from Canada to the Gulf of Mexico. At the mouth of the Mississippi, he had claimed for France the region that De Soto had explored for Spain 140 years before, naming it Louisiana for his king. From the comforts of his palace at Versailles, Louis XIV, the expansion-minded Sun King, had hoped that La Salle would locate a harbor for France in the forbidden waters of the Gulf as well as a route by which France could invade New Spain. La Salle had inadvertently obliged.[1] He had not only found his way to the Gulf in 1682, but he had made several miscalculations leading him to conclude that the Mississippi flowed into the Gulf on the very edge of New Spain, not far from the mineral-rich province of Nueva Vizcaya.[2]

La Salle had returned to France in 1683 to promote the idea that a post at the mouth of the Mississippi would serve as a springboard to invade northern New Spain. A small number of Frenchmen, La Salle argued, could carry out a successful invasion with the assistance of 15,000 Indians "who have a deadly hatred for the Spaniards because they enslave them."[3] When Spain declared war on France in October 1683, Louis XIV found La Salle's idea irresistible. As one of the king's ministers put it, La Salle could "spread terror in that part of New Biscay [Nueva Vizcaya] which lies in the vicinity of the river he has discovered."[4]

La Salle was not the first to provide the Sun King with a plan to invade northern Mexico from a colony on the Gulf. A few years earlier a Spanish exile living in France had suggested a similar idea. Peruvian-born Diego de Peñalosa, a former governor of New Mexico who had run afoul of the Inquisition, had fled to England and then to France, offering the monarch of each country his expertise and plans for seizing parts of the Spanish empire. As early as 1678, Peñalosa had volunteered to assist Louis XIV in invading northernmost Mexico, including Quivira, which he described as a remarkably fertile area far to the east of Santa Fe. Peñalosa also proposed that France invade Nueva Vizcaya from the Gulf of Mexico and seize its mines. With La Salle's return to France in 1683, the irrepressible Peñalosa renewed and elaborated on his previous proposals to the king, offering to put himself at the head of an expedition that would march all the way to the Gulf of California and sever Mexico's entire northern frontier from Mexico City. Discontented *criollos* (American-born Spaniards), mestizos, and mulattos would join the French invaders, he assured the king. To bolster his authority, Peñalosa fabricated an account of an expedition that he pretended to have led to Quivira and the "Mischipi" in 1662 and presented it to the king.[5] Taking Peñalosa seriously, French ministers first considered merging Peñalosa's plans with those of La Salle and sending both men to the Gulf, but finally decided to back only La Salle.

La Salle set sail from France with four vessels on August 1, 1684, at an unfortunate moment. Two weeks later, hostilities between France and Spain ended, Louis IV's enthusiasm for invading New Spain faded, and La Salle was on his own, without further government assistance. His small expedition, numbering some 280 persons, entered the western part of the Gulf where his earlier miscalculations of latitude and longitude led him to believe he would find the Mississippi. Unable to locate the mouth of the great river, he supposed that it lay hidden behind one of the many barrier islands that shield the lagoons and sandy brush country along the flat Texas coast. In February 1685, far from the Mississippi, La Salle began to construct a small fort on the Texas mainland. Choosing a site that would conceal his location from Spaniards, he ordered his colonists to construct what he called Fort St. Louis five miles up Garcitas Creek on an extension of what is today called Matagorda Bay.[6] From there, La Salle continued to search by land for the great river that had eluded him from the sea. Some of his men traveled overland as far west as the Rio Grande, questioning Indians about the whereabouts of Spaniards and Spanish mines, offering gifts and friendship, and explaining the virtues of Frenchmen and the evils of Spaniards.[7]

Meanwhile, French officials had taken such pains to keep La Salle's purpose a secret (suggesting Canada as his destination), that a year passed from the time he had left France before Spaniards learned of his mission.[8] Only a serendipitous encounter with a young French peasant who had deserted La Salle in Santo Domingo alerted Spanish officials, in September 1685, to "Monsieur de Salaz" and his intention to establish a base on the "Mischipipi."[9]

The alarming news galvanized Spanish officials, who saw the French colony as a threat to the mines of New Spain and to shipping in the Gulf. Moreover, as one high official warned, the Frenchmen might "settle as far as New Mexico and make themselves Lords of many Kingdoms and Provinces."[10] Although Spain had not protested French settlement in Canada, which began with Quebec in 1608, or French expansion into the region around the Great Lakes beginning in the 1670s,[11] it moved quickly to stop France from establishing a foothold on the strategic Gulf. In the judgment of Carlos II's Council of War, Spain needed swift action "to remove this thorn which has been thrust into the heart of America. The greater the delay the greater the difficulty of attainment."[12]

Nonetheless, considerable delay ensued. Before Spaniards could remove the thorn they had to find it. Not only had La Salle concealed his location, but Spaniards no longer recalled the geography of the Gulf that their countrymen, Alonso Alvarez de Pineda, Hernando de Soto, Tristán de Luna, and others, had revealed over a century

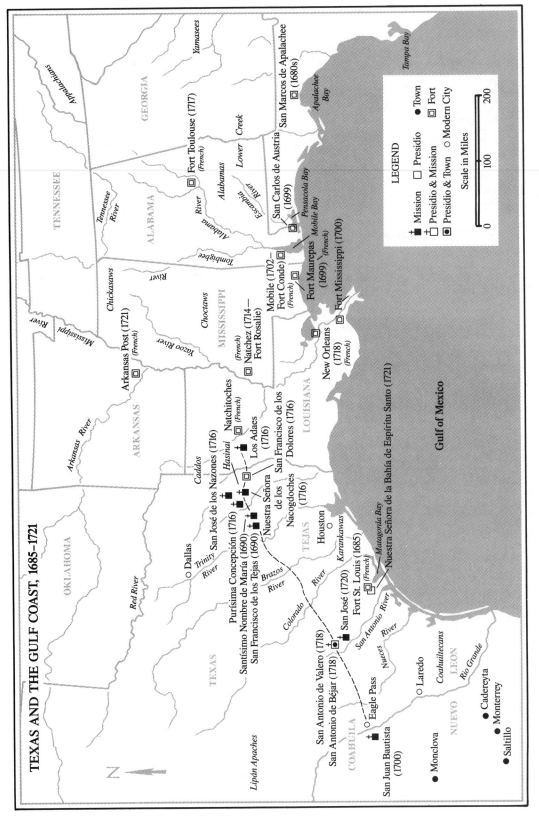

Map 6. *Texas and the Gulf Coast, 1685–1721.*

before. Spaniards had not penetrated the monotonous Gulf coast of present-day Texas or Louisiana since the days of De Soto and Luna, much less attempted to colonize it. La Salle's "Mischipipi," a name that meant nothing to Spanish officials, seemed however to correspond to the River of Espíritu Santo, found by Pineda in 1519.[13]

The Spanish quest for La Salle and the River of Espíritu Santo began in earnest in 1686. Early that year an expedition led by captains Juan Enríquez Barroto and Antonio Romero coasted the Gulf from Apalachee Bay to the Mississippi. Although they rediscovered Pensacola Bay, the scene of Tristán de Luna's nearly forgotten debacle in 1559, the Spanish explorers failed to recognize the terminus of a great river in the labyrinthine channels of the muddy, vegetation-choked Mississippi Delta, which they named Cabo de Lodo—Mud Cape. Bars of mud, that looked from the sea like a palisade, led them to call one of the channels of the Mississippi the Río de la Palizada and discouraged them from venturing too close. Cabo de Lodo also intimidated subsequent mariners; not until 1699 would another European, a Frenchman, accidentally find his way into the river's mouth.[14]

The initial reconnaissance by Barroto and Romero was followed up later in 1686 by two Spanish land expeditions that scoured both the eastern and western reaches of the Gulf. From the most northeastern province in Mexico, Nuevo León, the governor dispatched forty-nine-year-old Sargento Mayor Alonso de León to find the mouth of the great river on the Bay of Espíritu Santo, said to be only six or seven days beyond the provincial capital, the city of Monterrey. León, a frontier-born soldier and veteran explorer, made it from the frontier town of Cadereyta to the Rio Grande in five days, but it took another twelve days of hacking through tangled woods and underbrush to reach the river's mouth.[15] With exhausted men and animals, he returned home without having found either the Bay of Espíritu Santo or firm evidence of Frenchmen, whom Indians claimed to have seen on the Rio Grande. Meanwhile from Florida, Gov. Juan Marques Cabrera had dispatched a native-born presidial officer, Marcos Delgado, to travel overland from San Marcos de Apalachee to La Salle's post, and then to continue to Mexico City and report to the viceroy. Delgado made it through swamp and forest to central Alabama before fever, worn axes, and little prospect of food caused him to turn back prematurely.

By the end of 1686, then, these expeditions had narrowed the search for La Salle to the coastal stretch between the Rio Grande and the Mississippi. There Spain concentrated its operations the following year, sending out four more expeditions, two by land and two by sea. These searches contributed substantially to Spain's understanding of geography. Still, they could not find La Salle or any sign of him, save the wreck of a French ship found by light vessels that Spain constructed especially for exploring the Gulf's shallow coastal waters.[16] Failure heaped upon failure caused the viceroy of New Spain who headed these operations, the conde de Monclova, to suspect that the French settlement no longer existed. Nonetheless, fed by fresh rumors, the quest continued. An encounter with one Jean Géry, who had apparently deserted La Salle and taken up life among Coahuiltecan Indians in southern Texas, prompted two more expeditions by sea and another by land in 1688. The site of La Salle's fort eluded them all.[17]

In the spring of 1689, the indomitable Alonso de León, who had led three previous entradas in search of La Salle finally succeeded. Promoted in 1687 to the rank of general, León also served as the first governor of Coahuila, a province that Spain had carved out of Nuevo León and Nueva Vizcaya in response to the French threat.[18] As his guide and translator, León took along Jean Géry, whom the Spaniards believed demented but who had enough wit to hinder rather than to help them. Despite Géry's efforts to throw him off the track, León found his way to La Salle's fort in late April, but he found it in ruins, as Tonkawa Indians had told him he would. Karankawa Indians, angry at Frenchmen who had seized their canoes without payment, had taken retribution on the post a few months before.[19] Everywhere before him, León saw signs of destruction and death—"books and papers throughout the patios, broken chests and bottle cases, and more than a hundred broken harquebuses."[20] The men also found the remains of three of La Salle's colonists, the flesh gnawed away by animals. By the clothing that clung to the corpse, Spaniards identified one of the three victims as a woman, shot in the back by an arrow. In an effort to explain the terrible scene, the expedition's chronicler, Juan Bautista Chapa, speculated that God had punished the Frenchmen "as an admonition that Christians should not go directly against the bulls and mandates of the pontiffs." Pope Alexander VI, Chapa recalled, had granted the Indies exclusively to the Spanish monarchs.[21]

From two French survivors whom he found tattooed, painted, and living nearby among Indians, León learned of the sequence of events that had ended with the collapse of the French colony: the loss of La Salle's ships; deaths from disease, exposure, and hostile Indians; La Salle's efforts to reach Canada by way of the Mississippi; La Salle's murder by several of his own men; and the assault by Karankawas that had destroyed Fort St. Louis. La Salle had died in March 1687, more than two years before León stepped into the ruined fort. What the French-speaking Spanish officer who interrogated the two survivors did not learn was that one of them, Jean L'Archevêque, had been among La Salle's assassins.[22]

II

The mobilization of six expeditions by land and five by sea in a four-year search for La Salle, epitomized the essentially reactive nature of Spain's policy toward its European rivals in North America. Stretched too thin to initiate settlements throughout the hemisphere, Spain concentrated on vital areas, such as the great natural harbors of the Caribbean that lie along the route of the silver fleets—Porto Bello, Veracruz, Havana, and San Juan. In peripheral areas of the empire, Madrid took no action until foreign powers threatened.[23] If Spain had planted no settlement of its own along the arc of the Gulf from Tampico to the tip of Florida, neither could it allow a European rival to occupy that strategic coast. Thus, as it had done in Florida in the sixteenth century, Spain attempted to forestall further French initiatives by occupying more territory. In the late seventeenth century, spurred on by La Salle's venture, the Crown authorized modest outposts in eastern Texas and at Pensacola.

Spain moved first to secure Texas, blending strategic and religious objectives in a way that achieved neither. Although well-founded reports of continued French activity in the lower Mississippi valley suggested the need to defend Texas militarily, Spain's response was essentially ecclesiastical.[24] Spanish officials hoped to continue the tradition of advancing and defending its frontiers with peaceable and inexpensive missions.

At first, prospects looked bright for the success of missions in Texas. It seemed to Spaniards that the same divine providence that had sealed La Salle's fate had brought them into contact with a remarkably sophisticated and receptive people beyond the Río Grande. On the same expedition in which he had located La Salle's fort, Alonso de León had made contact with a representative of the Caddo-speaking peoples who inhabited the rolling woodlands between the Trinity and Red rivers in what is today eastern Texas and western Louisiana. Although León had not entered the Caddo country in 1689, he and a priest who accompanied him, the Mallorcan-born Franciscan Damián Mazanet, had learned that the Caddos yearned for Christianity since, as they acknowledged, the ubiquitous nun, María de Jesús de Agreda, had visited them long ago.[25]

Culturally similar to other southeastern tribes, such as the Natchez and the Creeks, Caddo farmers inhabited a universe that Spaniards could understand and appreciate. As León told the viceroy, the Caddos lived in "towns with wooden houses, and plant corn, beans, squash, watermelons, and melons . . . they have civilization and government like the Mexican Indians."[26] Caddos made their homes in dispersed communities rather than in compact villages, building their houses near their fields in fertile bottom-lands. They were organized politically into some twenty-five communities, most of which belonged to one of three confederacies: the Hasinai, the Kadohadacho, and the Natchitoches. The reputation of the prosperous Caddos extended below the Rio Grande and as far west as New Mexico, where Franciscans had heard stories about the largest, and westernmost Caddo confederacy, the Hasinai. Early reports referred to the Hasinai confederacy as the "Kingdom of Tejas"—derived from a Caddo word meaning "friends" or "allies" that Hasinai used to address one another; Spaniards and later Americans appropriated the name for themselves—Tejas or Texas.[27]

Pragmatism, piety, and geopolitics combined to persuade officials in New Spain to establish a distant outpost beyond the Trinity River in the land of the congenial Caddos, rather than among the nomadic hunters and gatherers who lived closer to the frontier of New Spain, between the Rio Grande and the Caddo country. In so doing, officials chose to ignore the strategic coast, including the site of La Salle's fort on

Matagorda Bay, where Karankawa Indians had gained a reputation for ferocity.[28] Spaniards also dismissed the Coahuiltecan-speaking peoples who lived comfortably on the grassy prairies on both sides of the lower Rio Grande, and who occupied the interior of Texas well beyond what is today San Antonio. Coahuiltecans had pleaded for missionaries since the 1670s, when southward-moving Apaches began to make their lives miserable. Spaniards knew the Coahuiltecan people well. In the 1670s, Franciscans had established four missions for them below the Rio Grande, and Spanish expeditions from Monclova and El Paso had traveled through the country of the Coahuiltecans in what is today south-central and west-central Texas. Nonetheless, these numerous small bands of scantily clothed, politically unorganized hunters and gatherers failed to interest most Spanish priests or officials.[29] The Caddo farmers did, and so Spain prepared to occupy a site inaccessible by sea and over 600 miles from the Rio Grande over a difficult land route.

In 1690, Alonso de León and Damián Mazanet led a small party of soldiers and four priests across the Rio Grande to begin what they hoped would be the permanent occupation of Texas. The expedition paused at Matagorda Bay while Father Mazanet set fire to Fort St. Louis, apparently so that Frenchmen would not readily reoccupy the place.[30] In a half hour, fray Damián later recalled, only ashes remained. From Matagorda, the Spaniards trudged eastward to receive a friendly reception in the Caddo country. In the Hasinai village of the Nabedaches, surrounded by piney woods and rolling red hills along the upper Neches River, León and Mazanet established San Francisco de los Tejas, the first of two missions; nearby, fray Francisco de Jesús María Casañas founded Santísimo Nombre de María.[31]

The ecclesiastical character of Spain's advance into Texas became even more exaggerated when Father Mazanet refused to tolerate unruly soldiers in the neighborhood of the new missions. León returned to Monclova, the capital of Coahuila, late in 1690 with all but 3 of the 110 soldiers who had come with him.[32] León, who died the following year, had twice recommended extending a line of forts into Texas to protect the remote missions from Indians and Frenchmen, but Spanish officials continued to place their confidence in missionaries.[33] Spain did appoint an military officer as governor of Texas—Gen. Domingo Terán de los Ríos, who marched into Texas in 1691 with more supplies and gifts to placate Indians, then left the following year. Governor Terán, who was subordinate to Father Mazanet, did not come equipped to establish a strong military presence beyond the Rio Grande.[34] When trouble threatened, then, the isolated and poorly supplied missionaries had no effective defense.

The first threat to the fledgling East Texas missions did not come from Frenchmen, whose aggression Spaniards anticipated, but from Hasinais, who had reportedly received the missionaries with "love and affection."[35] Within a few years, however, the Tejas had had their fill of the Spaniards. A fatal smallpox epidemic had arrived with the Spaniards, and the Christian message failed to provide comfort. Father Casañas had explained to the Caddos that the deaths of their friends and neighbors was God's "holy will," and that "when He wishes He will kill the Spaniards as He was now killing them." The natives, Casañas said, "were amazed."[36] In the autumn of 1693, the Tejas warned the Franciscans to leave or die. Choosing to live rather than win a martyr's eternal reward, Father Mazanet ordered the church bells buried and his mission burned, apparently to keep Indians from defiling it. Then he led his fellow friars on a harrowing four-month retreat over the 600 miles back to the Rio Grande. Three years later, fray Francisco Casañas was among five priests slain by Pueblo rebels in New Mexico.[37] Just as the apparent docility of the Tejas had drawn Spaniards into eastern Texas, so had Tejas hostility ended the experiment. Spain could not sustain a modest missionary outpost so far beyond the frontier without the natives' cooperation. Pressed on other fronts, including the effort to reconquer New Mexico from the Pueblos, Spanish officials ignored Texas for the next twenty years, until Frenchmen once again seemed to threaten it.

Meanwhile, La Salle's intrusion also prompted Spain to consider occupying the Gulf coast itself. From the first reports of La Salle's activities, Spanish policymakers had talked of such a project, but years went by before officials agreed on an appropriate site. Spanish mariners had dismissed La Salle's Matagorda Bay as insignificant and had ruled out the muddy delta at the mouth of the Mississippi, with its complicated maze of bars, banks, and shoals. Instead, they had extolled Pensacola. "The best bay I had ever seen in my life," one Spanish mariner enthused, echoing a sentiment expressed by Tristán de Luna over a century before.[38] Known as the Bay of Ochuse to Luna, Pensacola acquired its present name in 1686, when Spanish mariners recorded the name that local Indians gave it—"Panzacola."

Reports of the magnificence of Pensacola Bay excited Capt. Andrés de Pez, an ambitious and opportunistic naval hero and cartographer who had never seen the bay even though he had led three of Spain's maritime searches for La Salle. In 1689, Pez began to press the viceroy to occupy Pensacola. Unless Spain did so, Pez argued, France or England would. Spain's rivals, Pez noted, had already established themselves on unoccupied Caribbean islands. "What wouldn't they do to settle a place which has exceptional facilities?" Once established on the Gulf, France or England would not only threaten Spanish shipping, but northeastern New Spain and New Mexico as well. Anticipating the Crown's objection to occupying Pensacola because of its cost, Pez urged Spain to abandon the "exceedingly inconvenient harbor" of St. Augustine and divert its resources to the Gulf.[39]

In Mexico City, Pez's arguments won the support of the viceroy, who sent him in 1690 to argue the case in Spain. In Madrid, however, Pez met considerable opposition from the king's Council of War, which resisted the idea of abandoning St. Augustine and questioned the strategic value of holding but a single point on the spacious Gulf coast. With neither logic nor prescience, one council member observed that if Spain's enemies had not occupied Pensacola in the past, they were unlikely to do so in the future. He urged that the entrance to the bay be blocked with old hulls to prevent it from becoming a "back door for contraband."[40]

Paralyzed by indecision, the Council of War called for more research. As a result, Capt. Andrés de Pez and Mexico's leading scientist, Carlos de Sigüenza y Góngora, inspected Pensacola in 1693, confirming its magnificence and pronouncing it "the finest jewel possessed by his Majesty . . . not only here in America but in all his kingdom."[41] Meanwhile, an expedition led overland by the governor of Florida revealed that Englishmen from Carolina had begun to trade with Indians to the north and west of Pensacola.[42] This news of foreign intruders, more than a glowing scientific report, convinced Carlos II of the urgency of occupying Pensacola, which he ordered in 1694. Royal funding, however, lagged behind royal enthusiasm. The project waned until the arrival in Spain in 1698 of trustworthy reports of a new French colonizing expedition to the Gulf. Then, prodded into quick action after eight years of procrastination, Spain began to build a small fort of pine logs at Pensacola in mid-November of 1698. The timing was fortuitous. The signing of the Treaty of Ryswick in 1697 had ended a struggle known in the Anglo-American colonies as King William's War and had freed both France and England to pursue their long-standing interests in the Gulf.

In the Treaty of Ryswick, Spain had acknowledged France's undisputed possession of the eastern half of the island of Santo Domingo (today's Haiti), thus strengthening France's position in the Caribbean and giving it a base for further expansion. The next year, France sent five vessels to the Gulf under a naval officer, Pierre LeMoyne, Sieur d'Iberville, who had distinguished himself in Canada. The French minister of marine, Louis de Ponchartrain, had instructed Iberville to find and occupy the mouth of the Mississippi, without antagonizing the Spaniards; the mines of northern New Spain continued to attract French attention.[43] On January 26, 1699, Iberville's vessels entered the fog-bound harbor of Pensacola, which he apparently hoped would be the mouth of the Mississippi. When the fog lifted, he discovered that Spaniards had beaten him. He had arrived two months late. Noting no great river flowing into Pensacola Bay, Iberville continued his quest for the Mississippi, following the coast westward to the Mississippi Delta. Like Spanish mariners before him, he could not find clear passage into the river's channels, but he accidentally discovered an entryway when foul weather chased him to shore. Through serendipity, Iberville became the first European to enter the Mississippi from the sea. He returned to Biloxi Bay, where he established the tiny Fort Maurepas along the coastal approach to the Mississippi, then sailed back to France for reinforcements.[44]

Iberville's mission to the Gulf had been prompted in part by reports of English designs on the same region. Like Spanish officials, French policymakers had long known of Carolinians moving westward across the northern reaches of Florida toward the Gulf. More immediately, as Iberville outfitted his initial expedition to America in

1698, officials in Paris had learned that a celebrated London physician, Dr. Daniel Coxe, had received an enormous tract of land to the west of Carolina, from the Appalachians to the Pacific, and that he planned to establish a colony on the Gulf. One of Coxe's captains, William Bond, managed to guide a vessel into the Mississippi in late 1699, only to meet disappointment much like Iberville's at Pensacola. Sixty miles up the Mississippi, Bond encountered Iberville's brother, Jean-Baptiste LeMoyne de Bienville, who warned him to leave. At a place still called English Turn, Bond turned back. This brief confrontation with Englishmen spurred Iberville to build Fort Mississippi, a small post near the river's mouth, some thirty miles below present-day New Orleans, intended to prevent foreign vessels from entering the river from the Gulf.[45] While Spain might continue to claim the Mississippi by right of prior exploration, France now held the stronger claim of actual occupancy.

Although Spain had won the three-way race for Pensacola, it had captured the wrong prize. Pensacola Bay, and the Escambia River that flows into it, would prove valuable to traders as a gateway to the Creek country, but no river system that might serve as a major highway for commerce emptied into the bay. Englishmen from

29. *The first commander of the presidio of San Carlos de Austria, Andrés de Arriola, made this map of Pensacola Bay in 1698. The presidio, which seemed indefensible to him, stood at the entrance to the bay. Courtesy, J. P. Bryan Map Collection, Eugene C. Barker Texas History Center, University of Texas.*

Carolina continued to have designs on Santa María de Galve, as Spaniards called Pensacola in honor of the viceroy, but the large bay could not be easily defended. As the first commander of its presidio, San Carlos de Austria, gloomily told the king, "This fortification will be able to defend only the single site where we are located."[46] Finally, the sandy pine barrens behind the bay were inhospitable for agriculture. The colony never produced enough to feed itself, failed to attract civilian settlers, or even to become a base for the conversion of nearby tribes. Pensacola, then, remained an isolated military post, without financial assets to offset its liabilities. It devoured an annual subsidy from the Crown; in 1714, for example, the figures came to some 100,000 pesos. Soldiers themselves shunned it as a place of disease, famine, and death—a "land galley" in the striking phrase of one resident. Ironically, the small fort survived its initial decade due to the hospitality of Frenchmen in neighboring Louisiana.[47]

Inadvertently, fin de siècle France had grabbed the gold ring. By seizing the mouth of the Mississippi, it gained access to the great river system that led into the heart of the continent and connected the Gulf with French Canada, and it cracked Spain's monopoly on the north coast of the Gulf by driving a wedge between northern New Spain and Florida.

III

The establishment of French forts on Biloxi Bay and on the Mississippi in 1699 marked the beginning of French hegemony in Louisiana and the end of Spain's claim to exclusive control of the Gulf coast of North America. For another year, the opportunity remained for Spain to dislodge the French from Biloxi, but it lost the moment through indecision if not incompetence.[48] With the death in November 1700 of the last of the Hapsburg monarchs, the deranged Carlos II, Franco-Spanish rivalry in North America took a curious turn. On his deathbed, the childless Carlos II had designated as his heir Phillipe d'Anjou, the grandson of the French king Louis XIV. Thus, a member of the French Bourbon family, the Hapsburgs' long-standing nemesis, ascended to the Spanish throne. That improbable event gave the French colony in Louisiana a measure of protection from Spanish forces during its formative years.

In his new role as Felipe V of Spain, Philippe d'Anjou refused to expel his grandfather's colonists from the Louisiana coast. In 1702, for example, when Iberville transferred the post at Biloxi to Mobile Bay, Felipe V ignored this new trespass on Spanish-claimed territory. Felipe's own War Council disapproved of his magnanimity, and Spain refused to concede France's right to be in Louisiana—a position that it maintained consistently thereafter. Spain took no stronger action, however, than to warn Louis XIV that he could be excommunicated for ignoring the papal donation of America to Spain, over two centuries before. Noting that a more recent pope had given his blessing to French Canada, the Sun King ridiculed the Spanish claim.[49]

French Louisiana, then, took root on the Gulf during an interlude of harmonious relations with Spain. In the years that followed, the French colony continued to grow as the War of the Spanish Succession brought Spain and France closer together. Triggered by the Bourbons' acquisition of the Spanish throne in 1700 and its implications for the balance of power in Europe, the war pitted France and Spain against England, Holland, and Austria. During that war, which began in 1701 and lasted until 1713, Spaniards and Frenchmen, no matter how deep their mutual distrust, cooperated against mutual enemies.

In North America, where English colonists knew it as Queen Anne's War, the War of the Spanish Succession put Spain on the defensive. Carolinians and their Indian allies, led by James Moore, burned the town of St. Augustine and lay unsuccessful siege to its fort in 1702. In 1704, with the assent of the Carolina legislature, Moore rampaged across northern Florida, destroyed the missions in Apalachee, and caused Spaniards to abandon the province.[50] Farther west, Carolinians burned the town of Pensacola in 1707, although there, as in St. Augustine, Spaniards successfully held the fort. Englishmen did not occupy Apalachee, but by the end of the decade English traders had won the loyalty of tribes across northern Florida as far west as Pensacola. It seemed only a matter of time before Pensacola would fall, but dissension among Carolinians spared the post from another attack until 1711 when, once again, the fort held firm against Carolinians and their Indian allies.[51]

With the aid of Alabamas, Creeks, Choctaws, and other tribes whom they had won to their side, the Carolinians also planned to seize Mobile Bay and drive France from the Mississippi Valley. The English colonists might have succeeded in eliminating France as well as Spain had it not been for internal discord and Spanish-French cooperation. Hard-pressed for supplies from the Crown, Spanish officials in St. Augustine and Pensacola sought and received help from their French neighbors in Louisiana. Pensacola, the viceroy later noted, "would have been abandoned had it not been for French aid."[52] With the assistance of French privateers, Spaniards from St. Augustine went on the offensive against their English neighbors; combined Spanish-French forces twice attacked Charleston, although they failed to take the city.[53]

On balance, the War of the Spanish Succession weakened Spain's position in the Southeast. Not only did Spain lose Apalachee, but English influence over tribes far to the west of Carolina threatened to reduce Pensacola, in the words of one historian, "to an enclave in a British domain." Moreover, from their new base in Apalachee Englishmen could continue southward down the Gulf coast to Tampa Bay and the Keys. From there, as Florida Gov. Francisco de Córcoles y Martínez had warned the king, they could easily harass Spanish shipping.[54]

As England expanded at Spain's expense during the war, so did its French ally increase its presence on the Gulf. From Mobile, French traders made their way to interior tribes such as Choctaws, Chickasaws, and Alabamas via the Alabama-Tombigbee river system, and they gained influence among Indians as far east as

Pensacola and as far west as Caddo country along the Red River.[55] But lamentably for the French in Louisiana, the same war that offered the colony a reprieve from Spanish attack by uniting Spaniards and Frenchmen, also consumed French resources. The government-sponsored colony languished. Unable to attract colonists, it amounted to little more than a center for the Indian trade, whose residents depended upon Indians for food.[56] In 1712, before the war came to a close, Louis XIV attempted to infuse new energy into Louisiana by giving exclusive control of its economic affairs for fifteen years to a private trading company headed by the financier Antoine Crozat. As an independent money-making venture, rather than as a Crown colony and base for imperial expansion, French Louisiana continued to flounder, but it did provoke Spanish officials into reoccupying Texas.

Louisiana's new governor, Antoine de la Mothe, Sieur de Cadillac, who had founded Detroit in 1701, pinned his hopes for the colony's prosperity on trade with Spanish neighbors. His hopes seemed dashed when the War of the Spanish Succession ended in 1713 and Spain closed its ports to its former ally. That summer, however, a remarkable letter from a Franciscan missionary in New Spain arrived at Mobile, a letter that kept alive Cadillac's plans for trade with New Spain and altered the political geography of North America.

The Spaniard's letter asked for French help in reestablishing missions among the Tejas Indians. Its author, Francisco Hidalgo, had served in Texas with Damián Mazanet two decades before. He regretted leaving the deteriorating missions and had promised the Caddos that he would return one day with more missionaries. In 1700, he had helped to found the mission of San Juan Bautista on the Rio Grande (at present Guerrero—thirty miles down river from today's Eagle Pass). There, poised on the northeastern edge of New Spain, he had retained a lively interest in returning to make a fresh start among the Tejas, but Spanish officials had offered no encouragement. Hence, as Hidalgo later told the viceroy, "seeing that all the means I had taken had failed, a happy thought occurred to me."[57] Hidalgo did not elaborate fully on his "happy thought," but he had apparently invited French officials to send missionaries into Texas, calculating that their presence would provoke a Spanish counterresponse, as it had done in La Salle's day. If this was Hidalgo's plan, it worked brilliantly. Hidalgo later remembered writing two letters to the governor of Louisiana. It was one of those audacious letters that reached Cadillac in Mobile in the summer of 1713.[58]

Cadillac responded by sending one of his most experienced and shrewdest traders, Louis Juchereau de Saint-Denis, to find Hidalgo. A relative by marriage of Pierre LeMoyne, Sieur d'Iberville, the tall, flamboyant, Quebec-born Saint-Denis had come to Louisiana in 1700.[59] Officially, Cadillac authorized Saint-Denis to search for Hidalgo's mission "in reply to Hidalgo's letter of January 17, 1711," and to buy horses and cattle for Louisiana.[60] Privately, Cadillac hoped to exploit the opportunity to open contraband trade with Mexico. In the autumn of 1713, Saint-Denis ascended the Mississippi and Red rivers to the heart of the Caddo confederacy of Natchitoches, in what is today northwestern Louisiana. He had first visited the Natchitoches in 1700, while trying to find his way to the Spanish settlements, and he knew that his canoes would carry him no farther. Beyond the Natchitoches villages an enormous logjam, which Anglo-Americans would come to know as the Great Raft, blocked navigation on the Red River.[61] Saint-Denis, then, struck out overland for the west, to the Hasinai villages where he had also traded in the past. From there he continued across the uncharted forests and plains of Texas with three French companions and several Hasinai guides.[62]

Two members of Saint-Denis's party, the brothers Pierre and Robert Talon, had crossed Texas previously. As young boys, the two had survived the La Salle tragedy and had been adopted by Indians; Pierre lived with the Hasinais and Robert (born on La Salle's voyage to America) with the Karankawas. In 1690, León and Mazanet had taken the brothers from Indian custody and, through curious twists, the boys had made it back to France. There, the French minister of marine, Louis de Ponchartrain, had tried but failed to exploit the brothers' special knowledge by sending them back to the Gulf with Iberville on his initial journey to Louisiana in 1698. Now the Talons were finally back in Texas where Saint-Denis must have hoped their tattooed faces and knowledge of native languages would assure his party a safe passage.[63]

When Saint-Denis's little band showed up on the edge of the Spanish frontier at San Juan Bautista in July 1714, the elderly presidial captain, Diego Ramón, recognized immediately the threat that it posed. "If His Majesty does not intervene," Ramón explained to Father Hidalgo, "the French will be masters of all this land."[64] Officials in Mexico City agreed. Fearing that Frenchmen would flood northern New Spain with contraband and perhaps even invade its mining districts, the viceroy, the duque de Linares, ordered the reoccupation of East Texas as a buffer.

The force the viceroy sent to Texas did not correspond to the magnitude of the threat that Spanish officials imagined the French posed. In April 1716, about seventy-five persons crossed the Rio Grande near San Juan Bautista, at a ford appropriately named Francia, en route to found a colony. Capt. Domingo Ramón, one of the presidial commander's sons and the leader of the group, counted eighteen soldiers, ten Franciscans (including the instigator of the enterprise, Francisco Hidalgo), and assorted colonists and Indian guides. Among the colonists were a six-year old boy, a four-year-old girl, an infant, and seven women, one of whom had given birth on the way up from Saltillo and another of whom was married on the journey.[65] Astonishingly, Saint-Denis served as chief of supplies, drawing the same salary from the Spanish government as the expedition's leader. Although the resourceful Frenchman had arrived at San Juan Bautista unable to speak Spanish,[66] he had managed to ingratiate himself with his Spanish captors. While nominally under arrest in the comfort of Diego Ramón's house, he had courted the presidial captain's young granddaughter, Manuela Sánchez Navarro, and won her heart.[67] Sent on to Mexico City for interrogation, Saint-Denis had also wooed Spanish officials, persuading them of his ardor to become a Spanish subject and of his fidelity to the Spanish Crown. Instead of a prison term—the fate of many a French intruder before and after him—Saint-Denis returned to San Juan Bautista with the appointment of supply master on the proposed expedition. There he married Manuela. Although other women traveled with Domingo Ramón's expedition into Texas in 1716, Madame de Saint-Denis did not join her husband. She remained behind, soon to bear a child, the first years of her marriage marked by prolonged separations.[68]

Among the Hasinais, whom they continued to call "Tejas or Texias," Spaniards built four small wooden churches and the presidio of San Francisco de los Dolores in the summer of 1716. Saint-Denis, who apparently spoke the native language, had smoothed the way for the Hasinais' friendly reception of the friars, which included offering to share with them a peace pipe decorated with white feathers. But as Father Hidalgo noted, the Tejas resisted baptism "for they have formed the belief that the [holy] water kills them."[69]

After construction began in the Hasinai communities, Capt. Domingo Ramón continued eastward through the dense pine forests to Natchitoches, where he found that Frenchmen had built a stockade on an island in the middle of the Red River. Unbeknown to the Spaniards, the impetus for fortifying Natchitoches had been intelligence supplied by Saint-Denis, who appears to have played both sides to his advantage. Even while in Spanish custody, the wily trader had managed to keep Governor Cadillac informed of the Spaniards' plans. From San Juan Bautista, he had sent Cadillac a report via the Talon brothers, who had managed once again to slip across Texas, and from Mexico City, Saint-Denis had contrived to get word to Cadillac of Spain's intention to reoccupy Texas. Fearful that he would be squeezed between eastward-moving Spaniards and westward-moving Englishmen, and Louisiana reduced to Mobile, Cadillac had ordered the post constructed at Natchitoches in order to establish a French presence beyond the Mississippi.[70] It worked. Tacitly, Captain Ramón acknowledged Natchitoches as the limit of Louisiana, but he tried to assure that the French would go no farther. Just to the west of Natchitoches, Ramón founded two more missions in nearby Caddo communities: San Miguel de los Adaes and Dolores de los Ais.[71]

This time, Spain had come to Texas to stay. Alarmed by French expansion and the aggressiveness of French traders, Spain moved quickly to reinforce eastern Texas. "Your Excellency can see what a condition the French are placing us," Francisco Hidalgo wrote to the viceroy from the new mission of San Francisco de los Tejas. "They are slipping in behind our backs in silence, but God sees their intentions."[72] One of those Frenchmen who slipped by was Saint-Denis himself, who in the spring of 1717 recrossed Texas with a mule train of trade goods. Arrested for smuggling in collaboration with his new in-laws and confined in Mexico City until he escaped in the fall of 1718, Saint-Denis made his way back to Natchitoches, apparently stopping at the presidio at San Juan Bautista to visit his Spanish wife who joined him in Louisiana a few years later. He remained a key figure in Spanish-French relations on the Texas-Louisiana border until his death in 1744, despite his vain hope of retiring to Mexico with his wife and children (Manuela remained at Natchitoches until her own death in 1758).[73] Pursuing his private interests, Saint-Denis, like Father Hidalgo, had brought the Spanish and French empires together in North America—a remarkable exception to the general rule that the frontier's political boundaries expanded and contracted with decisions made by diplomats in Europe.

In late 1716, months after Ramón's party had established itself in East Texas, a new viceroy, the marqués de Valero, appointed a governor for Texas, Martín de Alarcón, and charged him to take further defensive measures. Alarcón was to keep a sharp eye on the bay where La Salle had established his fort—a place Frenchmen still seemed to covet. He was to open overland communication with Florida, thus connecting the Spanish colonies that French Louisiana had severed on the Gulf. Finally, he was to establish a new settlement on the San Antonio River, to serve as a way station between the Rio Grande and the East Texas missions.[74] The result was the beginnings of San Antonio, established in a country of broad vistas and gently rolling hills, covered with live oaks, chaparral, and mesquite—a landscape that contrasted sharply with the pine forests of East Texas.

Fray Antonio de San Buenaventura de Olivares, who accompanied Alarcón, had already chosen a lush site for the new community of San Antonio. A decade before, on a preliminary expedition into Texas, he had been impressed by the irrigation ditches and terraced fields that Coahuiltecan Indians had built near the headwaters of the San Antonio River. The single creek of San Pedro, which still flows into the San Antonio River, "could supply not only a village but a city," his diarist noted.[75] In the spring of 1718, Governor Alarcón marched into Texas and laid the foundations for a presidio, San Antonio de Béjar, and a mission named for the viceroy, San Antonio de Valero—its chapel later known as the Alamo. Nearby, he also established the chartered municipality of San Antonio (then called Béjar). Following the viceroy's orders, Alarcón designated San Antonio a *villa*, a status higher than a pueblo or village, but below a *ciudad* or city.[76] Notwithstanding its fine location and status—the only villa in Texas—and Father Olivares's shameless boast to the viceroy that Indians there wore "gold on their cloaks" and possessed "a mountain of silver," San Antonio did not immediately become the provincial capital.[77] Governors of Texas made their headquarters closer to the French nemesis.

Leaving colonists behind at San Antonio to begin planting and ranching, Alarcón continued into East Texas where he found the new missions on the verge of collapse. Soldiers had deserted and supplies had run so low that the padres were reduced to eating crows, which they shot out of trees. The Hasinais, well provisioned with French firearms and ammunition, trade goods, and horses, had proved uncooperative.[78] Alarcón reinforced the missions of eastern Texas with fresh supplies and tried to placate the Hasinais with gifts. He considered destroying the French post at Natchitoches, but

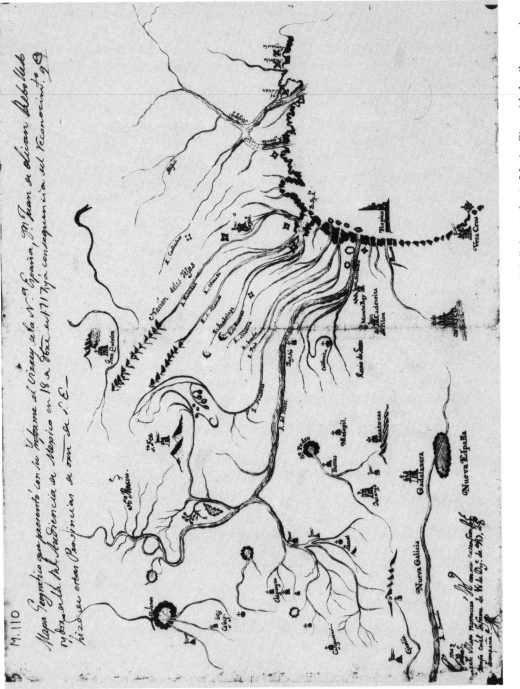

30. *Northern New Spain and the Gulf of Mexico drawn in 1717 by Juan de Oliván Rebolledo, a judge in Mexico City, with details concerning Texas based on information provided by Saint-Denis. Convinced of the vulnerability of Santa Fe and the mining towns of Nueva Vizcaya, Oliván Rebolledo projected a series of forts to protect approaches from the Gulf. Courtesy, J. P. Bryan Map Collection, Eugene C. Barker Texas History Center, University of Texas.*

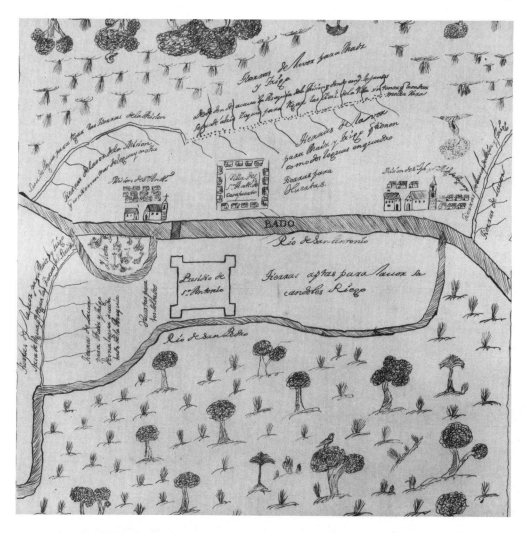

31. *The villa, presidio, and missions at San Antonio, surrounded by fields of wheat and corn, circa 1730. The villa actually developed at the site of the presidio, rather than beside the mission of San Antonio de Valero, as the marqués de Aguayo, who made this sketch, imagined it would. Courtesy, Institute of Texan Cultures, San Antonio.*

the missionaries apparently talked him out of the idea, arguing that it might cause an international incident.[79]

IV

In 1719, the year after Alarcón reinforced East Texas, a new war in Europe spilled over to America and put all of Spain's North American possessions in peril. In this so-called War of the Quadruple Alliance, Spain fought alone, for France aligned itself with England, Holland, and Austria to check Spanish ambitions in Italy. Both France and England regarded the conflict as an opportunity to divest Spain of its North American holdings, from its new outposts in Texas and Pensacola to its long-established colonies in New Mexico and Florida. Spanish officials harbored opposite intentions, hoping to make preemptive strikes that would eliminate their rivals from Carolina and Louisiana.

On the Atlantic coast, Spaniards anticipated renewed attacks from the Carolinians, who had laid waste much of Florida in the War of the Spanish Succession. St. Augustine's defenses had been strengthened in the interim, however, and Apalachee, lost in 1704, had been reclaimed. In 1718, in an effort to win the allegiance of the Lower Creeks, Spaniards had reestablished the coastal fort of San Marcos de Apalachee on Apalachee Bay (first built in the late 1670s with Apalachee labor but destroyed by pirates in 1682). Regarded as a link between Pensacola and St. Augustine, the Apalachee post endured as long as Spain held Florida.[80]

While Spain had strengthened its position in Florida, Carolina had lost ground. In 1719 Carolinians were still recovering from a devastating setback—a rebellion that they called the Yamasee War. In 1715, the Carolinians' abused and indebted Yamasee clients had turned against them. Joined by members of powerful inland tribes, particularly Lower Creeks, Yamasees and their allies had nearly destroyed the colony. After slaughtering hundreds of Carolinians, the Yamasees had withdrawn to Florida and joined the Spaniards, some settling near Pensacola and others at St. Augustine. That same year, Spanish agents had lured many Lower Creeks (still known to them as Apalachicolas), out of the English trading orbit and had brought them over to the Spanish side. For the moment, most of the tribes from Pensacola to Carolina leaned toward Spain; a delegation of seven Creek leaders even traveled from Pensacola to Mexico City in 1717 to offer allegiance to the viceroy.[81]

Devastated and deprived of key Indian allies, Carolinians were in no position to take the offensive against Spanish Florida during the War of the Quadruple Alliance. Instead, Carolinians anticipated an invasion from Florida and an assault by a Spanish armada being assembled in Havana specifically to attack Charleston.[82] Those attacks never came, for France unintentionally diverted Spanish attention to the Gulf. In May of 1719, a French fleet embarked from Louisiana and took Pensacola by surprise; the shocked Spanish *comandante* had not yet learned of the declaration of war. Easier to take than to hold, the rotting wooden fort at Pensacola changed hands two more times that year: the Spanish fleet originally destined for Charleston retook Pensacola, but France took it back again.[83]

Meanwhile, French officials in Louisiana conspired to expand westward at Spain's expense by invading New Mexico, which they incorrectly believed was rich in silver, and Texas as far as the Río Grande, where they wrongly imagined the existence of mines near San Juan Bautista.[84] The modest opening salvo of this ambitious campaign, however, seemed more of a whisper than a bang. In June 1719, a force of seven

Frenchmen from Natchitoches overwhelmed the mission of San Miguel de los Adaes, defended by a single soldier who had no prior knowledge of the war. The French invaders brought reports that their countrymen had seized Pensacola and that one hundred more French soldiers were on their way to Natchitoches to destroy the nearby Spanish missions. Undersupplied, nearly unarmed, and unable to depend on the loyalty of the pro-French Caddos, Spanish colonists, missionaries, and the twenty-five soldiers assigned to protect them abandoned the half dozen missions and two presidios they had built in East Texas. With their livestock, altar stones, and church vestments, they fled to San Antonio.[85]

In response to this French offensive, the king accepted the offer of a wealthy resident of Coahuila, the marqués de San Miguel de Aguayo, to reconquer Texas.[86] A Spanish-born nobleman who had become a marqués through a fortunate marriage to one of the richest widows in New Spain, Aguayo offered to journey into Texas as a "knight-errant," risking his life and his wife's fortune in what he saw as a "glorious" war.[87] Fearful that the French in Louisiana had grown prosperous, powerful, and a clear threat to northern New Spain, he probably reflected the concern of his contemporaries. Granted the title of captain general and governor of Coahuila and Texas, the marqués de Aguayo raised the most imposing force Spain would ever send into Texas—some five hundred men and enormous herds of horses, cattle, sheep, and goats.[88]

Initially, Felipe V ordered Aguayo not only to recapture East Texas, but to invade Louisiana in order to "force the French to abandon the territory they unjustly hold."[89] Meanwhile, a Spanish fleet was assembled in the Caribbean for a simultaneous invasion by sea. On the eve of his departure from Mexico, however, Aguayo received a disappointing change in instructions. Fighting had stopped in Europe and Felipe V, eager to rebuild his broken alliance with France, had called off the invasion of Louisiana. Aguayo was to limit himself to retaking eastern Texas, without using force.[90] In the heat of a Texas summer, the marqués de Aguayo rode across plains and prairies to confront the French in the woodlands on the edge of Louisiana. On the Neches River, at the end of July 1721, he met Saint-Denis, who had swum his horse across the river to the Spanish camp. Saint-Denis, who had distinguished himself in France's second offensive against Pensacola in 1719, had received a promotion to command the French post at Natchitoches early in 1721. He had planned a raid on San Antonio—a plan that had met with approval at high levels of government—but faced with Aguayo's superior force he decided instead to retreat. He agreed to abandon East Texas.[91]

Over the protest of Saint-Denis, the marqués de Aguayo built the fort of Nuestra Señora del Pilar de Los Adaes in the pine forest just twelve miles from Natchitoches (near present-day Robeline, Louisiana), leaving a 100-man garrison and six cannons behind. The wooden presidio of Los Adaes became the capital of Texas and held that position until the French flag came down over Louisiana. Aguayo also oversaw reconstruction of the nearby presidio of San Francisco that Domingo Ramón had established in 1716 among the Tejas, and the presidio that Alarcón had begun at San Antonio. In addition, he initiated construction of a new fortification at the scene of La Salle's failure on Matagorda Bay—which Spaniards had called the Bay of Espíritu Santo since Alonso de León had found it in 1690. Twice during the war, French forces had tried and failed to occupy Matagorda Bay.[92] To forestall further attempts by Spain's rivals to seize that symbolic spot, Aguayo ordered the presidio of Nuestra Señora de la Bahía del Espíritu Santo constructed on the very site of La Salle's Fort St. Louis. There, one of Aguayo's party reported, "we found nails, pieces of gun locks and fragments of other items used by the French."[93] When Aguayo rode out of Texas in 1722, the province had four presidios instead of one, over 250 soldiers instead of 50, ten missions including the six East Texas missions that had been abandoned in 1719, and the nucleus of a small civilian settlement beginning at San Antonio.[94] French provocation, then, had resulted in strengthening rather than weakening Spanish Texas.

The War of the Quadruple Alliance had repercussions in far off New Mexico, too, where officials anticipated a French offensive and made efforts to counteract it. Spanish authorities had long feared that Frenchmen would try to seize New Mexico. As early as the mid-1680s, one of the arguments advanced for reconquering New Mexico following the Pueblo Revolt was to keep it from falling into French hands.[95] This concern seemed especially well-founded when friendly Apaches brought reports into Santa Fe in 1695 of white men on the eastern plains.[96] In the years that followed, such reports multiplied. They reflected the visits of French traders from both the Illinois country and Louisiana to tribes on the Missouri, Kansas, Arkansas, and Red rivers. Although no Frenchmen reached Santa Fe, their trade goods and weapons did, causing New Mexicans and their Indian allies to feel the impact of French activities on the eastern horizon. In the hands of Pawnees, Missouris, and others, French firearms began to take a toll on friendly Apaches—Cuartelejos, Jicarillas, and Sierra Blancas. Then, too, the southward movement of Comanches—a group previously unknown in New Mexico—put additional pressure on the province. The right combination of Indians and Frenchmen could easily destroy New Mexico.

With the outbreak of war with France in 1719, New Mexico seemed more threatened than ever. That year, New Mexico Gov. Antonio Valverde y Cosío led a large expedition of Spanish troops, volunteers, and Indian allies to the northeast to punish Utes and Comanches. On the Arkansas River (in present-day southern Colorado), Cuartelejo Apaches told him the usual stories of Frenchmen on the plains, but one Apache, with a bullet wound in the belly, gave the governor especially alarming news. Farther north, among the Pawnees, the Indians reported Frenchmen had built two towns, each "as large as that of Taos"; they had armed the Pawnees and insulted the Spaniards, calling them "women."[97] The Frenchmen, Governor Valverde reported to the viceroy, seemed intent on pushing into New Mexico "little by little."[98]

The governor's disquieting report, coupled with the loss of Pensacola and East Texas to French forces that same year, prompted the viceroy, the marqués de Valero, to instruct New Mexico officials to take energetic measures against the French. Earlier the viceroy had urged New Mexicans to enter into an alliance with Apaches who, he argued, "could inflict considerable damage on the French and block their evil designs."[99] Now, in January 1720, he ordered Governor Valverde to establish a presidio at the Apache settlement of El Cuartelejo, apparently in today's western Kansas, and to launch another expedition to search out the French settlements among the Pawnees.[100]

Governor Valverde protested the order to advance to El Cuartelejo, arguing that a post 130 leagues beyond Santa Fe could not be adequately supplied or defended. It would, the governor bluntly told the viceroy, be "useless."[101] More tactfully, he suggested that the viceroy's advisors may have been mistaken. Perhaps they actually intended a garrison to be built among the friendly Jicarilla Apaches, whose adobes and irrigated farms lay just 40 leagues to the northeast of Santa Fe. The viceroy agreed

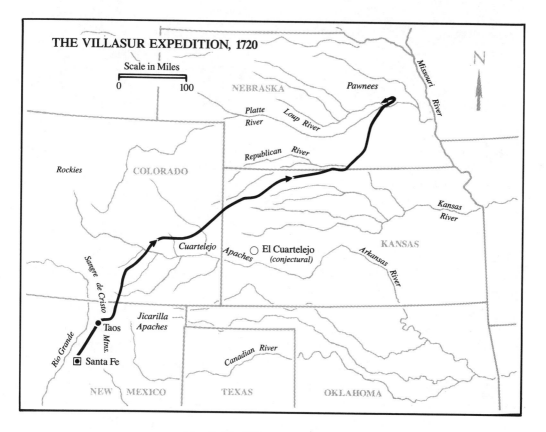

Map 7. The Villasur expedition, 1720.

32. In this detail of an extraordinary painting done on hide by an unknown artist, the Villasur party makes its last stand at the confluence of the Platte and Loup rivers. The delineation of features on the faces of the soldiers suggest that the artist knew them personally. Villasur lies dead beyond this scene; L'Archevêque is probably the hatless man facing forward in the main group. Photograph of "Segesser II," courtesy of the Palace of the Governors, Santa Fe.

with the governor,[102] but the New Mexico garrison, numbering fewer than one hundred men, suffered a disaster that in any case prevented it from carrying out the order.

In the summer of 1720, Pedro de Villasur led a small group of experienced New Mexico soldiers in search of the Frenchmen believed to be living among the Pawnees.[103] Along to serve as interpreter should the expedition encounter Frenchmen was the expatriate Jean L'Archevêque, one of La Salle's murderers. Eager to escape life among the Indians, L'Archevêque had thrown himself on the mercy of the Spanish expedition that found La Salle's fort in 1689. After interrogation in Mexico City and imprisonment in Spain, L'Archevêque had returned to New Spain as a Spanish subject and soldier in 1692, then joined Diego de Vargas in the reconquest of New Mexico. L'Archevêque had remained in Santa Fe, where he had married and worked as a merchant as well as a soldier. He had participated as an interpreter on several earlier expeditions to the plains.[104] This would be his last.

Traveling with his silver dishes, cups, and spoons, a silver candlestick, an inkwell, writing paper, quills, and a saltcellar, Villasur led the group, which numbered forty-five Spaniards and sixty Pueblo Indian auxiliaries, to the Pawnee country in today's Nebraska. At the confluence of the Platte and Loup rivers, as the Spanish party broke camp in tall grass early one morning, Pawnees and Otos surprised them. Eleven Pueblos and thirty-two Spaniards died, including Villasur and L'Archevêque.[105] Some of the survivors who straggled back to Santa Fe reported that Frenchmen fought with the Pawnees, but other survivors disputed the charge. New Mexicans did not return to investigate further or to seek revenge; the Santa Fe garrison had lost a third of its fighting force on the Platte. In the years that followed, reports of French activity on the plains east of New Mexico continued to reach Santa Fe, but with peace in Europe, such reports no longer produced alarm in Mexico City or Madrid and talk ended of establishing a permanent Spanish presence on the plains in today's Colorado.[106]

V

As the war of the Quadruple Alliance drew to a close, French negotiators received instructions to reach an accord that would push Louisiana's western boundary to the Rio Grande and its eastern border to Tampa Bay.[107] They failed. Despite setbacks on all frontiers, Spain emerged from the War of the Quadruple Alliance in 1721 with its North American possessions intact. Although New Mexico had failed to expand to the northeast and French traders drew ever closer, the Crown lost no ground in New Mexico itself. In Texas, the marqués de Aguayo had not only retaken the territory seized by the French at the outset of the war, but he had strengthened the defenses of the province. Pensacola, which had remained in French hands at the end of the war, reverted to Spain again as part of the treaty arrangements. St. Augustine and Apalacheee had not been threatened directly.

If Spain had suffered no permanent losses in the war, however, neither had it made the most of its own opportunities to drive the English out of the Carolinas or France out of Louisiana. Those failures proved costly in the long run, for Spain's imperial rivals used their North American bases ever more effectively to weaken Spain's commercial system, lure Indians out of the Spanish orbit, and challenge Spain for more territory.

"If we do not make one kingdom of all of this, nothing is secure," Florida governor Joseph de Zúñiga y Cerda had warned the king in 1704.[108] He and other officials who urged strong measures to preserve Spanish hegemony in North America had glimpsed the future. With France and England well established, nothing would again be secure.

7

Commercial Rivalry, Stagnation, and the Fortunes of War

*That these Indians get along so well with the English, Sir, is
because the latter do not oblige them to live under the bell in law
and righteousness, but rather, only as they wish. . . . The English
bring them guns, powder, balls, glass beads, knives, hatchets, iron
tools, woolen blankets and other goods.*
fray Alonso de Leturiondo to the king, St. Augustine,
Florida, ca. 1700

*The heathen of the north are innumerable and rich. They enjoy the
protection and commerce of the French; they dress well, breed horses,
handle firearms with the greatest skill.*
Col. Diego Ortiz Parrilla to the viceroy, San Luis
de Amarillas, Texas, 1758

A scant dozen miles or so from Saint-Denis's post at
Natchitoches, Spaniards built a small fort at Los Adaes in
1721, to halt French encroachment, weaken French influence among the neighboring tribes, and prevent French
traders from using Louisiana as a base for illicit commerce
with northern New Spain. Los Adaes, which also served as
the capital of the province of Texas, fell far from advancing
those goals. To the contrary, Frenchmen, who might have
easily destroyed the wooden fort, preferred to see it stand.[1]
Frenchmen, whose business Spain had hoped to undermine, dominated commerce on the forested Texas-Louisiana

frontier and Spaniards offered no competition. Surrounded by Caddo Indians armed with French weapons and loyal to French traders, unable to draw a labor pool from failed missions, and 800 miles from dependable sources of reasonably priced Spanish merchandise in Coahuila, Spanish officers, soldiers, and their families at Los Adaes had no choice but to turn to their French neighbors for supplies—traveling as far as New Orleans on occasion. Lest the community starve, Texas officials relaxed the normal prohibitions against dealing with foreigners and permitted the residents of Los Adaes to purchase food from the French. Trade in corn, beans, and other vegetables, however, provided cover for Frenchmen to smuggle foreign manufactures into Los Adaes, including guns and ammunition that the *adaeseños* sorely needed, in exchange for Spanish horses.[2]

The contradiction between the defensive posture of the small East Texas presidio and its dependence on its competitor appeared in especially stark relief during a squabble in 1735–36. During those years the commanding officer at Los Adaes, Joseph Gonzales, heatedly protested Saint-Denis's decision to move Natchitoches to

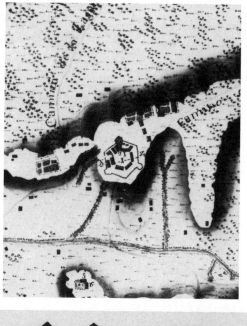

33. *The capital of Texas until 1770, Los Adaes consisted of a hexagonal wooden presidio (with the governor's house inside the walls), a scattering of houses, and a nearby mission chapel and friary (5 & 6). Details from a drawing by José de Urrutia in 1767. Courtesy, British Library and Museum of New Mexico, neg. no. 15051.*

the west bank of the Red River, into what Gonzales defined as Spanish territory. Following orders from his superiors, Gonzales backed up his words with deeds and prohibited all trade with Natchitoches. Los Adaes, however, could not survive the embargo. By cover of night, Gonzales allowed French grain into Los Adaes in order to feed his troops and their families.[3]

The reliance of Los Adaes on foreigners, which continued throughout its existence, was not unusual. Other Spanish frontier settlements fell into similar dependent relationships. During many years, residents of Pensacola turned to French Mobile for essential supplies.[4] Needy officials in St. Augustine sent vessels to both Mobile and New Orleans and also traded with Englishmen with whom relations were often tense. Indeed, at one juncture Spanish officers in St. Augustine obtained weapons from Carolina merchants in order to defend themselves in a war with those very same Carolinians.[5] Spanish dependency even extended to colluding with pirates and begging from Indians—humiliations that Spain's European rivals seldom knew. In 1718, a group of Lower Creeks traveled to the newly rebuilt Fort San Marcos de Apalachee where a Spanish agent had led them to believe they would receive gifts. Instead of impressing the Indians with Spanish largesse, and thus discouraging them from falling under the influence of English traders, the starving Spanish soldiers at the garrison implored their Creek visitors for food.[6]

Spain simply could not deliver the goods, either to its own subjects or to Indians, and its North American holdings stagnated. Unlike more populous areas of the Spanish empire, which enjoyed fabulous mineral wealth and responded to shortages by gearing up local production, frontier communities were too small, impoverished, and beleaguered to rally.[7] Caught in a vicious circle, the frontier communities remained small because they had little to attract immigrants and much to repel them. The shortage of merchandise for the Indian trade also hindered Spain's ability to expand its frontiers. Across the borderlands, from Florida to New Mexico, wherever English or French competition increased in the first two-thirds of the eighteenth century, Spain lost control of the Indian trade—the key to empire in North America. The expanding Spanish frontier sputtered and stalled, and in some areas rolled back. Ultimately, however, the gains and losses scored in commercial rivalries were cancelled out by the fortunes of war and the negotiations of distant diplomats who in 1762–63 redrew the map of European holdings in North America.

I

The economic malaise that afflicted Spain's North American colonies reflected the limitations of the Spanish economy itself. In the seventeenth century, severe structural problems had exacerbated Spain's trade imbalance, causing the kingdom's wealth and productivity to decline. Fed by bullion from America, spiraling inflation had raised the cost of Spanish manufactures and made them uncompetitive. Relatively inexpensive foreign goods flooded Spanish markets, leaving Spain dependent on foreign imports and unable to supply its own needs much less those of its colonial outposts. As Spain's manufacturing slipped, so did its ability to absorb raw materials exported from its colonies. Then, too, Spain's eroding economic status was reinforced by its loss of naval supremacy after the resounding defeat of the Spanish armada in 1588.[8]

For the colonies, the shortage of trade goods was aggravated by Spain's restrictive commercial policies, which aimed to benefit residents of Iberia at the expense of the colonials. A late medieval mercantile system, which endured with only minor adjustments until the late eighteenth century, limited the supply and raised the cost of imported goods throughout the empire. To protect its own manufacturers, Spain discouraged manufacturing in its colonies. To protect its mercantile guild and to facilitate the collection of tax revenues, Spanish policy generally limited trade to Spanish goods, handled by Spanish merchants, and carried on Spanish vessels. Moreover, to maintain tight control over commerce within its trading system, Spain permitted commercial vessels to call at only a few key ports in the New World.[9]

None of the natural harbors along the Texas coast were among them. Fearful of encouraging smuggling, Spain kept the Texas coast closed to legal shipping until the end of the colonial era, despite entreaties from officials who pointed out the benefits to commerce. As one critic noted in 1779, if Texas had failed to progress and its inhabitants had grown indolent, the explanation could be found in the regulations that closed ports and hindered the exportation of mules, hides, lard, tallow, wool, flour, grain, meats, salt, and other products. "What an abuse! Do you not have the sea so nearby?"[10]

Similar criticism came from New Mexico, where the sea was not nearby. As early as 1630, fray Alonso de Benavides had pointed to considerable savings in transportation costs that would result from opening a direct route from Santa Fe to a port on the Gulf, a few days' sail from Havana. A half century later, the Crown ordered the viceroy to investigate Benavides's idea, "since my royal treasury bears much expense for soldiers and carts."[11] Distance, danger, and bureaucratic inertia stalled the opening of a commercial route from New Mexico to the Gulf, and the same fate befell a scheme to make the Rio Grande navigable all the way to New Mexico.[12]

By law, goods bound from Spain for Texas, New Mexico, or anywhere else in New Spain, could enter the viceroyalty only at Veracruz. From there, merchandise destined for northern New Spain was hauled over a torturous mountain highway to Mexico City, then transported over rude roads to places such as San Antonio, Los Adaes, Santa Fe, Taos, or the edges of Pimería Alta where Jesuits had built missions in what is today Arizona. The cost of transportation, plus profits for numerous middlemen and additional internal customs duties (*alcabalas*) along the way, drove the price of some items to many times their value in Veracruz or Mexico City by the time they reached the frontier. One outspoken critic of the system described it as "economic slavery."[13]

Although Spanish vessels did land at St. Augustine and Pensacola (there was no way to deliver supplies to those places by land), their residents fared little better. Monopolies and regulations kept goods scarce in those ports, too, and unscrupulous merchants charged what the market would bear. The parish priest at St. Augustine complained directly to the king in 1700 that a bar of soap or a box of sugar might sell in St. Augustine for five times its value in Havana or New Spain.[14]

For suppliers and consumers alike, such artificially high prices made smuggling so attractive that perhaps two-thirds of all commerce throughout the Spanish empire consisted of illegal trade, much of it with foreigners.[15] In Spanish North America, contraband had been a conspicuous feature of commercial life from the beginning. In Florida, which foreign or domestic smugglers could readily approach by sea, illegal trade had begun in the sixteenth century. As early as the 1680s, illicit trade between Englishmen from Charleston and Spaniards in St. Augustine had become so important that one governor of Carolina declined to attack St. Augustine for fear war would disrupt smuggling operations. Throughout much of the eighteenth century, English merchants from as far as New York and Providence met little resistance from officials when they sold their wares in St. Augustine in exchange for gold, silver, deerskins, and oranges (oranges were a popular export from Florida through the 1730s, when Englishmen began to cultivate and market them too).[16] Across the borderlands, clandestine trade increased in the eighteenth century as English and French merchants grew more numerous and more proximate. Below-the-table deals became a mainstay of trade in those frontier communities with greatest access to foreign merchandise, as at Los Adaes where foreign-made manufactures far outnumbered those from Spain in the mid-eighteenth century.[17] Some foreign smugglers found their way over the plains to remote New Mexico, but distance protected Santa Fe from serious foreign competition and left its commerce almost entirely within the Spanish mercantile system.

In addition to its economic weakness and restrictive policies, Spain's colonial priorities assured the stagnation of its North American outposts. By the eighteenth century, Spain regarded its northernmost colonies in the hemisphere as essentially defensive. Lacking precious minerals and a large population of docile Indians to work plantations or mines, the colonies from New Mexico to Florida served primarily to protect adjacent areas—the sea lanes of the Gulf and the Atlantic and the mines of northern New Spain—rather than to produce minerals or agricultural wealth for export. By definition and in practice, the northern colonies were marginal and dispensable. In the negotiations ending the War of the Quadruple Alliance, for example, Spain had offered to give Florida to England in exchange for Gibraltar (which Spain had lost to England in 1713), but England had declined to make the swap.[18] Upon retaking Pensacola at the end of the same war, Spain had toyed with the idea of draining the harbor to render it useless to other nations, rather than incur the expense of rebuilding the ruined fort.[19] Spain continued to entertain that idea for another generation. Unable to finance the construction of a massive fort that would withstand a French or English assault, Spain kept only a token force at Pensacola largely "to maintain the right of possession."[20] Pensacola, which became a hub of fur trading activity when English merchants established a post there later in the century, remained nothing more than an isolated military base during its first six decades under Spain. Due in part to unfavorable soil and climate, commercial agriculture and ranching failed to develop; tree trunks destined to become ships' masts were Pensacola's only exports. With a military detachment of no more than 200 and a population of fewer than 800 in 1763, it appeared as a large annual deficit in the royal ledger.[21]

II

While Spain came to regard its North American colonies as defensive money-losing outposts of the large and tottering imperial trading system to the south, England and France saw North America itself as their main chance for profit in the Americas. In contrast to Spain, which formed its empire in the sixteenth century when European kingdoms put primacy on territorial acquisition through political and religious domination, England and France entered North America in an era of commercial expansion, when control of trade had become more important than control of territory. For Englishmen in particular, America was "a commercial enterprise." England's most successful colonies were joint stock ventures, developed in the seventeenth century when mercantile interests dominated a weak monarchical government that, compared to Spain's, left its subjects unhindered by regulations or taxes.[22] In the absence of gold and silver in French and English America, furs and hides appeared as the continent's most immediately remunerative commodity. Frenchmen and Englishmen competed with Spaniards and with one another for the loyalty of Indian trappers and hunters who would furnish furs and hides.

Popular images notwithstanding, Spaniards from Florida to New Mexico traded in animal skins—deer, buffalo, elk, antelope, or beaver, depending on the regional habitat.[23] At St. Augustine, a local trade in deerskins had begun as early as 1580, and in seventeenth-century Apalachee, deerskins served as currency. In New Mexico, Hispanics also traded in furs and hides from the beginning, and by the late eighteenth century, venturesome traders had made their way into the southern Rockies to obtain beaver pelts from Utes and had journeyed out to the eastern plains to trade with Comanches and Pawnees for buffalo hides. Trade in hides and furs was important to local Hispanic economies but appears to have been modest in comparison to French and English exports of animals skins. England and France had larger domestic markets that drove demand, and they enjoyed a number of other competitive advantages as well.[24]

Both France and England adhered to the prevailing mercantilism of the day and, in theory, operated closed trading systems along the same lines as Spain's. But France and

England enjoyed a greater capacity to produce and distribute goods, absorb raw materials, and generate capital.[25] In competition for Indian customers, then, France and England had the edge. In the colonies themselves, Frenchmen in Louisiana and Englishmen in the Carolinas did not antagonize their potential Indian trading partners by demanding that Indians alter their religion or their culture to the extent that Spaniards did.[26] Nor did Frenchmen and Englishmen imitate Spain's self-defeating policy of denying Indians muskets, powder, and shot—weapons that helped tip the balance of power across the Spanish frontier. Although bows had decided advantages over cumbersome and inaccurate muskets of the era, Indians coveted European firearms and ammunition, and Europeans and Indians alike tended to regard Indians with firearms as more dangerous than those with bows and arrows.[27]

The difference between Spain's policy of not giving or trading firearms to Indians, and the French-English use of weapons as trade goods, should not, however, be drawn too starkly. Spaniards commonly violated the Crown's prohibitions. Some unscrupulous private parties traded firearms to hostile Indians, and government officials in Florida, New Mexico, and Texas made firearms and ammunition available to mission Indians and other native allies when it suited Spanish purposes—sometimes openly and sometimes surreptitiously.[28] Perhaps a chronic shortage of guns and ammunition more than scruples against violating government prohibitions left Spaniards at a disadvantage in the Indian trade.[29] One ingenious Texas governor, whose need for guns was matched by his lack of scruples, solved the problem by obtaining firearms from French merchants at Natchitoches then exchanging them with Indians along the lower Trinity River for deer and buffalo skins, corn, and horses.[30] An enterprising Cuban carried out a similar operation in Apalachee, trading French muskets and liquor for Indian furs.[31]

Of the three European competitors for the trade of Indians, Englishmen offered the best deals. English traders paid the highest prices for Indian furs, and English goods—items such as knives, axes, scissors, combs, blankets, shirts, hats, and cloth, as well as firearms, gunpowder, and flints—were generally more abundant, better made, and less expensive than those from France or Spain. English trade goods were so plentiful, however, that traders tried to force them into inelastic Indian markets with the lure of liquor and debt. Those unscrupulous trading practices, combined with a frequent obtuseness to Indian custom, had dire consequences on occasion, as when Carolina traders provoked the Yamasees to revolt in 1715.[32]

In contrast to the English, the most skillful of French traders endeared themselves to Indians by treating them as equals, learning their language, marrying them, and making few claims on Indian lands.[33] Spaniards on the frontier appreciated the superior tactics of their French rivals. As one Franciscan observed, while the Spaniards "are engaged in vexing the Indians . . . your Frenchman will take off his shirt to give to them and to hold them to their allegiance."[34] But French behavior toward Indians, as one historian has reminded us, "was politic and should not be confused with affection."[35] French Indian policy could be cynical in the extreme, as when French traders promoted warfare between Indian peoples, hoping to weaken powerful tribes and create an unsafe climate for British traders who sought to penetrate Louisiana. Putting "these barbarians into play against each other is the sole and only way to establish any security in the colony," Jean-Baptiste LeMoyne de Bienville wrote in 1723.[36]

With its declining metropolitan economy, retrograde mercantile policies, and insistence on proselytizing its customers, Spain lost ground to its competitors. Although France had seized the heartland of the continent and its Indian trade, in the long run England proved to be Spain's most formidable rival—and France's as well. Demography and commerce worked in England's favor, as Spain discovered first in the Southeast.

III

The English and northern European population along the Atlantic seaboard grew stunningly, from some 72,000 in 1660 to 1,275,000 in 1760. Most immigrants moved into New England, the Chesapeake, and the middle Atlantic colonies, but a significant number of those white colonists, together with imported black slaves, settled along the Spanish rim.[37] There, they soon enjoyed vast numerical superiority and challenged Spain for control of Georgia, Florida, and the Indian trade along the Gulf from Apalachee to Pensacola. By 1700, just thirty years after its founding, the white population of South Carolina had reached some 3,800 (plus 2,800 black slaves), more than double the Spanish population of long-established Florida, which stood then at about 1,500. Over the next decades, the gap widened dramatically. By 1745, the number of Europeans in South Carolina was nearly ten times that of Florida (20,300 to 2,100).[38]

As the burgeoning English population pushed south and west, the borderlands between Florida and Carolina became a turbulent arena of contention between warring Europeans.[39] Spaniards and Englishmen each tried to win Indians over to their side with guns, ammunition, and alcohol as well as trade goods, and Indians played off one side against the other in order to extract the most favorable terms.

In the so-called American Treaty signed at Madrid in 1670, England abandoned all claims to the flat, forested country along a 150-mile stretch from just below Charleston south to St. Augustine. Nonetheless, Englishmen made repeated efforts to occupy this land, beginning with their destruction of the prosperous Spanish mission province of Guale in the 1680s and 1690s. Spaniards did not return to Guale after the Franciscan missions were devastated, and the remaining native inhabitants, Yamasees and Lower Creeks, abandoned the region when they went over to the Spanish side after the Yamasee War of 1715.[40] Carolinians, then, moved to fill the void in that depopulated land. In 1721 they built a small blockhouse, Fort King George, at the mouth of the Altamaha River near present Darien, Georgia. It stood there for the next six years, nearly provoking a war with Spain before Carolinians abandoned it.

In the 1720s, Spain tried to stave off the Carolinians' southward expansion. Florida officials tried negotiation, but met evasion and delay in Charleston. Meanwhile, they also turned for help to their former enemies, the Yamasees who had settled near St. Augustine. In a peninsula nearly devoid of missions and mission Indians, Florida officials had no choice. Since 1715 they had plied the Yamasees with gifts and trade goods—including guns and ammunition that Gov. Francisco Córcoles y Martínez had obtained from Charleston traders.[41] Some Yamasees were Christians who had fled years before from the Florida missions, but Spain now tried to retain their loyalty with the English technique of offering material incentives rather than spiritual rewards. In return for outfitting and rewarding them, officials in St. Augustine expected the Yamasees to harass farmers and traders along Carolina's southern border, but that strategy backfired. In 1728 Carolinians and their Indian allies retaliated by destroying the largest Yamasee village, Nombre de Dios Chiquito, on the very edge of St. Augustine, killing or capturing many Yamassees.[42]

Spain's failure to protect Indian clients "within a rifle-shot" of the great castillo of San Marcos, diminished Spanish prestige among tribes farther west, including the powerful Creeks who had become the key to controlling the Southeast.[43] Converted into professional hunters and slavers by the English market for deerskins and Indian slaves, Creeks raided deep into the Florida peninsula for game, extinguishing small tribes and driving refugees into St. Augustine from as far away as Tampa Bay.[44]

By the 1730s officials in St. Augustine could count on few effective Indian allies. Some of the Yamasees remained loyal to Spain until the end, living by hunting and farming near their homes in a few fortified villages "under the canon" of the castillo as one resident put it. Their dwindling numbers were augmented slightly by a polyglot, demoralized, and increasingly inebriated lot of Indian refugees.[45] By 1759, only seventy-nine Indians remained in two villages near St. Augustine; a third village of fewer than twenty-five Indians hung on at San Marcos de Apalachee.[46]

Meanwhile, Spain's hold on Florida was further weakened by the establishment in 1733 of Georgia, an English proprietary colony whose title granted it the territory between the Savannah and the Altamaha rivers, from the Atlantic to the Pacific. Led by James Oglethorpe, Georgia had expanded quickly from its main base at Savannah. Within a few years Georgians had moved southward toward Florida. First, the town of Frederica arose on St. Simons Island at the mouth of the Altamaha. Then, still farther south, fifty miles north of St. Augustine, Fort George went up at the mouth of the St. Johns River, a cypress-lined waterway of strategic importance to Florida since it curved sharply to the south, penetrated the hinterlands behind St. Augustine, and cut across the road to Apalachee.

Spain protested the English occupation of Guale and tried to negotiate a settlement, but received little satisfaction. Meanwhile, Spanish officials shored up the land and water approaches to St. Augustine and prepared to retake Guale by force. In 1734, Gov. Francisco de Moral built the twin wooden forts of Pupo and Picolata on opposite

sides of a ford on the slow-moving St. Johns River due west of St. Augustine, and he
stationed troops at outlying positions: Fort San Diego, some twenty miles north of St.
Augustine; Matanzas, twenty miles to the south; and Fort San Marcos de Apalachee,
far to the west where the Spanish flag continued to fly. These measures stretched the
200-man Florida garrison beyond its limits for a few years until reinforcements arrived from Cuba to triple the garrison's size and ease the strain.[47]

While Spain was able to strengthen its fortifications, it could not marshal the
economic resources to build relations with southeastern tribes. Instead, well-supplied
English traders easily got the upper hand. By the end of the 1730s, trade goods and
Oglethorpe's personal diplomacy had persuaded many Lower Creeks, Cherokees, and
Chickasaws to join him. They proved to be a considerable asset, particularly during
the bitter fighting that began with the so-called war of Jenkins' Ear in 1739 and
merged into the protracted War of the Austrian Succession (known as King George's
War in the English colonies).[48]

The war came home to Florida in the spring of 1740 when Oglethorpe invaded with
a force of over 2,000, including Indian allies, and easily took Spain's posts at San

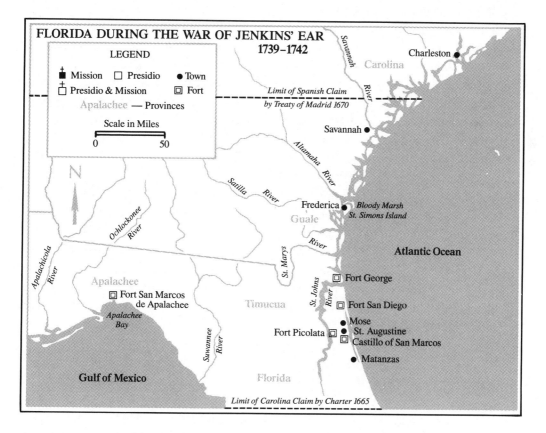

Map 8. Florida during the War of Jenkins' Ear, 1739–42.

Diego, Picolata, Pupo, and Mose—the latter a new, stone-walled village just two miles north of St. Augustine. Mose had been built by about 100 former black slaves and their families, who had fled Carolina to freedom with the encouragement of Florida officials in need of extra manpower.[49] Oglethorpe lay siege to Fort San Marcos, where most of the residents of St. Augustine and outlying villages had taken refuge. The castillo withstood bombardment for thirty-eight days, during which time Oglethorpe suffered a demoralizing setback. Spaniards, including black militia from Mose, stole out of the besieged fort at night, retook Mose, and inflicted heavy casualties. When reinforcements from Cuba arrived, Oglethorpe withdrew—just as his predecessor, James Moore, had done in the siege of 1702.[50]

In 1742, Spain retaliated. Gov. Manuel de Montiano, who had successfully defended St. Augustine against Oglethorpe, led the counteroffensive. With a flotilla outfitted in Cuba and carrying nearly 2,000 men, Montiano struck first at St. Simons Island, silencing the guns of the English fort and landing his troops on the south end of the island. Rattled, however, by an English victory at what came to be called Bloody Marsh, Montiano lost his nerve and retreated from the island before gaining his objective, the town of Frederica.[51] The war dragged on, and small-scale but inconclusive raids continued along the Florida-Georgia frontier until 1748. When the Treaty of Aix-la-Chapelle ended hostilities in Europe, Georgia remained in British hands.

Stagnant Florida barely survived these decades of contention with the steadily growing English colonies. Florida's missions never recovered from the English-Indian attacks at the turn of the century. To the contrary, the Franciscans steadily abandoned the province, unable to compete for Indians against the earthly rewards the English offered. By 1759, only ten friars remained.[52] Nor did the colony attract Hispanic settlers. Spain, which in the sixteenth century required adelantados to colonize at their own expense, now had to reverse its policy and dip into the treasury to promote settlement. The Crown offered free transportation, seed, tools, money, and tax relief but could not induce poor Galician peasants to volunteer to move to Florida in the 1730s. The Crown had greater success at moving Canary Islanders to St. Augustine in the late 1750s. They built flourishing farms on the northern edge of the city, where officials hoped they would fill the empty landscape, produce food for the garrison, and discourage English expansion.[53] By 1760, the Hispanic population of Florida had risen to just over 3,000. That year, the white population of the thirty-year-old Georgia colony stood at 6,000 (plus 3,600 black slaves); white South Carolinians, who had amounted to some 20,000 in 1745 now totaled 38,600 (plus nearly 60,000 black slaves).[54]

Until 1763, when Spain lost Florida to Britain for two decades, the province consisted of little more than its military garrisons and the population that served them. That year, officers, soldiers, and their wives, children, servants, and slaves (2,202 persons) constituted just over 70 percent of the population of eastern Florida (a total of 3,124 persons who lived from San Marcos de Apalachee to St. Augustine). Another

5 percent of the population (163 persons) depended directly on the military for the salaries that supported them or their families. The remaining 25 percent of the population consisted of merchants, tradesmen, farmers, and professionals and their families (759 persons), who depended directly on the military population to buy their products or services.[55]

The high percentage of the population dependent upon the public sector and the near absence of an industrial sector in small garrison towns like St. Augustine and Pensacola, contrasted sharply with the more commercially oriented English urban centers that had developed along the Atlantic coast.[56] St. Augustine, like any military base, depended on government support for its very survival. Its annual subvention, or situado, came to 116,127 pesos by 1749, and included military supplies, manufactured goods, currency, and even food. Harassed by hostile Indians and without the labor of mission Indians, the tiny community could not produce enough to feed itself, much less revive ranching and fur trading to produce a surplus of hides, tallow, dried meat, and furs for export as it had done in the previous century.[57] Officers continued to govern St. Augustine, and the western post at Fort San Marcos de Apalachee. Although St. Augustine had many of the features of a town it lacked a town council, or cabildo, common to the civilian government of Spanish communities.[58]

If St. Augustine could not feed or govern itself, it could mount an effective defense. When attack threatened, its garrison could be augmented quickly from Havana, and its troops and fortifications blocked English expansion below the St. Johns River. Englishmen did not test Florida's defenses again after 1740, nor did they need to. It became clear to Carolinians and Georgians that Florida's stagnant economy and modest population posed no offensive or commercial threat. Beginning in the 1740s, the Florida-Georgia border entered the longest period of calm that it had enjoyed since the founding of Charleston in 1670. Florida's governors lacked the resources to launch a new attack on Georgia, and Englishmen turned their attention to France, which became England's chief rival for world empire. The region below the Altamaha River became a neutral ground as England sought to avoid further imbroglios with Spain in order not to give its Bourbon monarch reason to team up with France, which represented a more immediate threat to English aspirations in southeastern America.[59]

IV

Through the mid-eighteenth century, at the same time that it sought to halt a seemingly inexorable English advance toward St. Augustine and Pensacola, Spain confronted aggressive French traders along the Gulf coast and on the high plains as far west as New Mexico. Compared to the bloody Anglo-Spanish rivalry in northern Florida and Georgia, the Franco-Spanish borderlands were tranquil after the War of the Quadruple Alliance ended in 1721. The beleaguered Bourbon monarchs of Spain and France, who needed one another's good will, entered into a series of so-called Family Compacts in 1733, 1743, and 1761 and tried to avoid the risk of new confrontations in North America. When a governor of Louisiana proposed to invade Texas and Mexico in 1753, higher authorities in France simply ignored him.

Spain never abandoned its assertion that France had no legal right to Louisiana, but rather than press that case, Spain settled for a policy of quiet containment. In 1735, for example, Spain protested when Saint-Denis moved Natchitoches from its site on an island to the western side of the Red River. Saint-Denis refused to budge, but Spain never pushed. In the 1750s, French traders moved into the valley of the lower Trinity River, territory that Spanish officials claimed was Texas. Spain countered peaceably, building the presidio of San Agustín de Ahumada and the mission of Nuestra Señora de la Luz de Orcoquisac near the mouth of the Trinity at Galveston Bay.[60] With Louisiana a fait accompli, the focus of Spanish-French contention in North America shifted to the control and economic exploitation of Indians.

In contrast to most of the English colonies, French Louisiana had grown haltingly in the first half of the eighteenth century. Badly governed, dependent on imports to feed itself, and costly to defend, Louisiana had become a financial liability for France and for the private stock companies that held monopolies there from 1712 to 1731. The hot, humid, mosquito-ridden coast had attracted few voluntary immigrants. By 1731, when the colony reverted to the Crown, its European population totaled about 2,000, including soldiers, convicts, vagrants, and other involuntary immigrants, together with an additional involuntary population of 3,800 black slaves. French Louisiana continued to grow slowly. By 1760, its European population reached about 4,000, and the number of black slaves came to 5,000.[61] The colony represented a net liability for France, never achieving France's persistent goal of turning it into a base for large-scale trade with the Spanish colonies.[62] Nevertheless, a small number of traders in this marginal colony did extend French influence far into the interior of North America.

Well beyond their initial footholds at Biloxi and Mobile, Frenchmen in search of furs and hides established a series of trading posts in native villages along the great river system that drains the heart of the continent. Nouvelle Orléans, established in 1718 on high ground on the east bank of the Mississippi 100 miles above the Gulf, became the colony's headquarters in 1722 and one of the hubs of an extensive trading network.[63] Saint-Denis's post at Natchitoches on the Red River marked the westernmost edge of that network, while its northern edge extended up the Mississippi, past a post established in 1714 on the bluffs at Natchez, to the Arkansas Post, built in 1721 on the lower Arkansas River to tap trade with the Quapaws. Far to the east, with Mobile as its hub, another trading network extended northward, up the Alabama-Tombigbee-Mobile river system. Upstream, 170 miles to the northeast of Mobile, Frenchmen built Fort Toulouse in 1717 near the junction of the Coosa and Tallapoosa rivers, hoping to neutralize the Carolinians' influence among the Alabamas and other bands of Creeks; for over four decades the traders at Fort Toulouse succeeded.[64]

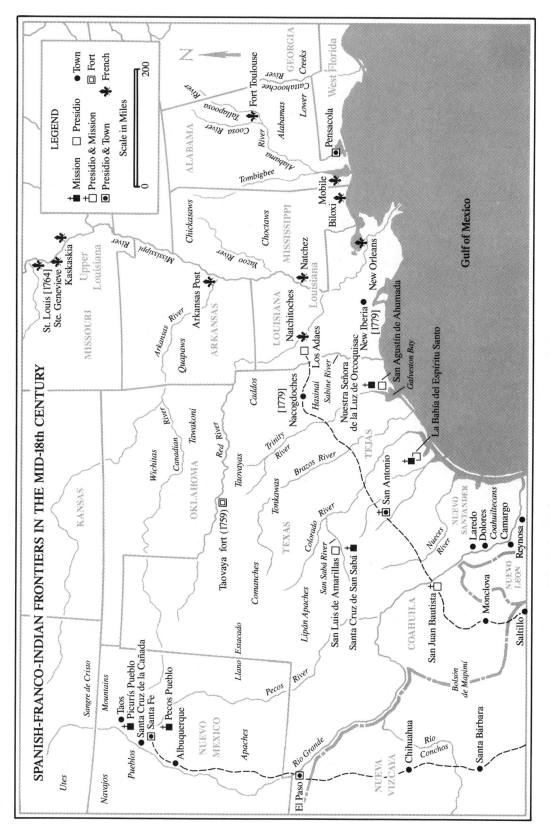

Map 9. Spanish-Franco-Indian frontiers in the mid-eighteenth century.

Louisiana also came to include the sparsely settled Illinois Country, or Upper Louisiana, a vaguely defined area lying south and west of Lake Michigan, with a scattering of settlements from Detroit down to Kaskaskia and Ste. Genevieve (St. Louis was not established until 1764). By midcentury, an additional 1,500 Frenchmen lived in this region, whose economy remained more closely linked to that of French Canada than to that of the lower Mississippi Valley.[65]

Out of the vast trading network of lower Louisiana, furs and hides obtained from Indian hunters made their way to New Orleans and Mobile and then to Europe to feed a growing leather industry. Deerskins formed the mainstay of this trade and also constituted French Louisiana's most consistently important export item.[66] The skillful French traders who harvested these furs and hides capitalized on Spain's weaknesses to win the allegiance of Indians along the Gulf and across the southern plains from Texas to the borders of New Mexico. Indians with French arms and markets made life uncomfortable for Hispanics; they also discouraged further Hispanic expansion onto the Great Plains.

V

The missions that Spain had employed to advance its North American frontiers early in the seventeenth-century faltered in the face of French competition in Texas, just as they had in Florida when English traders arrived on the scene. Franciscans in Texas suffered from many of the same impediments that missionaries had encountered in other times and places—epidemics, unruly soldiers, quarrels between representatives of the church and the state, and Indians' devotion to their own religions—but French competition added a new element that undermined Spanish missionary efforts in Texas from the outset. By giving natives a choice, French traders ended native dependency on Spaniards; by furnishing natives with arms, ammunition, and promises of protection, foreign traders gave natives additional means to maintain their independence.

In Texas, Franciscans had first learned this bitter truth when they returned to the Caddo country in 1716. The Hasinais, coached by Saint-Denis, had obligingly built churches and agreed to enter missions, but their subsequent actions betrayed their loyalties. They had refused to congregate into tight communities around the chapels as the Franciscans asked, and they had declined to receive baptism except on the point of death. The padres stood by helplessly, unable to force their will on the Indians. "We do not have a single gun," the two Franciscan leaders lamented, "while we see the French giving hundreds of arms to the Indians."[67] In desperation, the Franciscans concluded that they could achieve their ends only through force. They asked the king to send fifty soldiers for the "sole task" of burning Indians' houses of worship, forcing Indians "to assemble in their mission and build houses," and guarding the missions to prevent Indians from fleeing.[68]

The troops never came and the situation never improved. When a royal inspector visited eastern Texas in 1727, he reported quite simply that "there were no Indians in the missions."[69] Three of the six East Texas missions were soon abandoned and reestablished near San Antonio in 1731. The remainder hung on into the 1770s, even though Indians continued to decline baptism except "in the hour of death" when, as one priest speculated, "it is suspected that many ask for it as a natural remedy for obtaining bodily health."[70]

With meager material incentives, the friars understood that they could not induce armed Indians to settle voluntarily at missions. Caddos had a nearby French market for bear and deer skins, chamois, tallow and horses, and a trading partner with well-stocked shelves.[71] Spaniards, on the other hand, could barely fill their own larder. With all ports on the Gulf closed to legal shipping, supplies destined for Texas had to come a lengthy overland route by way of New Spain under harsh and dangerous conditions that raised transportation costs substantially, took a heavy toll on pack animals, and made the lives of men miserable. The marqués de Aguayo, for example, had been plagued by mosquitoes, chiggers, nettles, swollen streams, and mud on his way to East Texas in the summer of 1721, and by ice as he made his way back home. He had returned to the Rio Grande having lost all but 50 of the 4,000 horses he had brought to Texas.[72]

In contrast to French traders in Louisiana, who enjoyed the logistical advantages of navigable rivers that carried them into the heart of the continent,[73] Spaniards traveling into Texas from New Spain found that rivers caused irksome delays. In Texas, the main waterways flowed south by southeast, crossing the paths of travelers and often causing them to stop to build makeshift bridges or rafts. In full flood some Texas rivers could not be crossed by any means, and delays stretched into days and weeks. Martín de Alarcón, who had nearly drowned crossing the Guadalupe, had camped on the shores of the Trinity River for twenty-two days in 1718 until the river fell.[74] The ability to swim, which Alarcón had not acquired, was apparently an asset for travelers in Texas; one priest who traveled with Alarcón was chosen to return to Mexico for assistance "because he is a swimmer."[75]

The two Franciscan colleges that sponsored missions in Texas had planned to bridge the vast distances that separated East Texas from other Spanish provinces. On paper, they had divided the region between them. Friars from the College of Nuestra Señora de Guadalupe de Zacatecas would build a chain of missions southwesterly from East Texas to Tampico, and priests from the College of Santa Cruz de Querétaro would convert Indians to the northwest of East Texas, all the way to New Mexico.[76] The Franciscans, however, lacked sufficient gifts, trade goods, and manpower to compete for Indian loyalties. By 1750, many plains peoples, including Pawnees, Wichitas, and Comanches, had obtained French firearms directly or through Indian intermediaries. These Indians also had Spanish horses, and a strong aversion to Spaniards, whose reputation had preceded them.[77]

As French arms and Spanish horses spread across the Great Plains, native groups with access to them grew more powerful than their neighbors. A period of extraordinary disequilibrium followed. In Texas various groups of eastern Apaches, seasonal farmers who once dominated parts of the southern plains, were among the many groups whose lives and homes were disrupted. Too far west for easy access to French arms, they found themselves caught in a three-way squeeze. Highly mobile Comanches, migrating southward out of the Rockies onto the buffalo-rich grasslands, pushed Apaches from the north; Wichitas with French arms pushed them from the east, and Spaniards from the south. Of the Apaches' three adversaries, Spaniards with livestock had the most to offer, so Apaches fell on San Antonio after discovering it in 1720, and ran off livestock, especially horses. In 1732, in the midst of especially heavy Apache raids on San Antonio, the outnumbered and demoralized garrison begged the governor of Texas to negotiate a peace, "Otherwise, this Presidio, with its towns and Missions will be exposed to total destruction."[78]

Spain made several attempts to exert influence over the tribes to the north and west of the trail that ran from San Juan Bautista on the Rio Grande to San Antonio and to Los Adaes. In the hope of checking French influence among the Apache-like Tonkawas, who lived to the north of San Antonio, Spanish officials authorized the building of a mission and presidio in the mid-1740s. The effort, replete with bitter quarelling between friars and soldiers, failed after a decade, leaving little trace. On several occasions, the Tonkawas revealed their true loyalties, as in 1750 when they fled the missions in search of Frenchmen with trade goods who had been rumored to be nearby.[79] When the Tonkawa missions collapsed in the mid-1750s, the military garrison was moved to the northwest of San Antonio to protect missions that Franciscans intended to build among Lipán Apaches on the San Sabá River. This experiment at converting Apaches would end in a shocking tragedy and jolt Spaniards into a painful recognition of the weakness of their position on the interior plains.

Over the years, Lipán Apaches had expressed interest in missions on a number of occasions, but Gov. Jacinto de Barrios y Jáuregui and other officials in Texas had dismissed the Apaches' requests as insincere ploys to enlist Spanish aid against Comanches. In 1757, however, viceregal authorities responded favorably to Apache pleas by sending missionaries, soldiers, and their families to the San Sabá River (near present-day Menard). The gamble seemed worth it, for San Sabá held the potential of becoming the first of a series of mission-presidio complexes that would neutralize Apaches, expand the Spanish frontier farther north, and open the way for the discovery of mineral wealth or an overland trading route to Santa Fe.[80] Moreover, the Crown was not gambling entirely with its own money. A wealthy mine owner, Pedro Romero de Terreros, had volunteered to support the missionary side of the enterprise for three years, provided his cousin, fray Alonso Giraldo de Terreros, was put in charge.[81] In the spring of 1757, then, Franciscans built Santa Cruz de San Sabá, the first of three missions planned for the San Sabá River. Three miles away, soldiers built a log stockade, San Luis de Amarillas, with room enough for 300 to 400 persons, including the 237 women and children who would soon reside there.[82] At the padres' insistence, the fort went up across the river and three miles from the mission so that soldiers would not corrupt Indians.

Of that, there was no danger. However pleased they might have been with a Spanish military presence in the area, Apaches shunned the mission and put the Franciscans off with promises. Santa Cruz de San Sabá did not last a year. Comanches, incited by the Spaniards' alliance with their Apache enemies, and joined by Indians from several other tribes including Tonkawas and Hasinais, pillaged and burned the mission on March 16, 1758. The attackers killed 8 people including Father Terreros, who had stubbornly insisted on staying at the mission rather than taking refuge in the fort. The Comanches and their allies, estimated at 2,000, vastly outnumbered the soldiers, but did not attempt to take the presidio, calculating perhaps that a direct assault would cost them too many lives.[83]

For the viceroy and his advisors, the destruction at San Sabá cried out for revenge, lest the plains tribes lose respect for Spaniards and take Spanish inaction as license to attack other frontier posts. A year after the tragedy, the commander of the presidio at San Sabá, Col. Diego Ortiz Parrilla, led a sizable punitive expedition north to the Red River, deep in enemy territory. A Spanish-born officer who had fought in Morocco against the Moors and had served in the Indies since 1740 (most recently as governor of Sonora from 1751 to 1756), Ortiz had opposed the risky San Sabá venture from the beginning. Now, it became his duty to avenge Spanish honor, sullied as the consequence of someone else's bad decision. On the Red River, Ortiz found the Comanches and other tribes forewarned, well-equipped with French muskets, and waiting for him in a fortified village of the Taovayas—one of several Wichita peoples whom the Spaniards termed the Nations of the North. A French flag few over the Taovaya town, which was surrounded by a stockade and a moat (when Anglo-Americans discovered the site years later, they mistakenly called it Spanish Fort—a name it bears yet today). Following an initial skirmish in which he saw 52 of his men either killed, wounded, or deserting, Ortiz wisely organized an orderly retreat. Although he had over 500 men under his command, most were inexperienced civilians or Apache allies whose dependability he doubted.[84]

For Ortiz and his compatriots, these setbacks revealed that power on the Great Plains resided in the hands of Indians who owed no allegiance to Spain, but who had French guns, Spanish horses, and had understood European strategy well enough to construct a European-style fortification and to unite against the common enemy. There is no conclusive evidence to support the contention of some Spanish officials that "foreign political agents" encouraged the attack on San Sabá, or that Frenchmen coordinated the defense of the Taovaya village on the Red River.[85] Eyewitnesses left no doubt, however, that Comanches and their allies who destroyed the mission of San Sabá had been well equipped with "French arms, bullet pouches, and very large

34. When the wealthy Pedro de Terreros learned of the death of his cousin, he commissioned a commemorative painting. Executed in Mexico City circa 1763 by an artist or artists still unidentified, the large canvas (83" x 115") depicts eighteen events, as explained by an alphabetized key in the lower half of the scroll. This work of hagiography suggests not only that the two priests were martyred by barbarians, but by French-men who had armed them. This is the earliest known professionally rendered scene of a contemporary event in Texas. Courtesy, George P. Vlassis, President, New Phoenix Sunrise Corporation.

powderhorns," as a servant of Father Terreros testified immediately afterwards. Half of the 2,000 Indians who attacked the mission, fray Miguel de Molina estimated, carried firearms and one of the Comanche leaders wore a red jacket decorated like a French uniform.[86]

Two centuries before, Spaniards had had their way with Indians. Now they found themselves fighting a better armed, more mobile, and more savvy adversary. In Texas, Spanish soldiers believed the tables had turned rapidly, and that French arms had made the difference. Sgt. Joseph Antonio Flores, who left the fullest firsthand account of the events at San Sabá, testified that in his thirty years of service on the frontier "he had never seen or heard of hostile Indians attacking our forces in such numbers and so fully armed. Formerly the barbarians had fought with arrows, pikes, hatchets . . . and soldiers of the presidio held the advantage."[87] Whatever the relative merits of European versus native weapons, after the events at San Sabá, Spanish soldiers on the Texas frontier lamented that they faced "overwhelming numbers of the enemy armed with the same weapons as their own."[88] The shift in the balance of power led the commander of the presidio at La Bahía del Espíritu Santo to conclude that his position had become untenable. "The enemy [is] so superior . . . in firearms as well as in numbers, that our destruction seems probable."[89] At San Sabá, a number of men in the garrison petitioned their commander to abandon the site, lest Indians return and destroy it.[90]

Spanish forces remained at San Sabá to show Spanish resolve lest, as Col. Ortiz Parrilla argued, "with abandonment and retreat . . . spirit would be given to the barbarous enemies to return to their hostilities."[91] Soldiers replaced the wooden presidio with one of quarried limestone and dug a moat around it; Franciscans built two unauthorized missions among Lipán Apaches on the Nueces River, 100 miles west of the presidio; expeditions went out in search of a route to New Mexico; talk continued of working mines discovered at a place called Los Almagres. But ultimately, all of these projects failed. Comanches and their allies kept Spaniards holed up in the fort and picked off those soldiers who dared to venture out in small numbers. Finally, Spanish forces abandoned the presidio in 1769.

The Comanche attack on the mission of Santa Cruz de San Sabá in 1758, and Ortiz Parrilla's failure to extract retribution on the Red River, had brought a stunning halt to Spanish efforts to expand north and west of San Antonio. Those lands would remain part of a great *despoblado*—an area considered uninhabited by Spaniards but peopled by Apaches and increasingly by Comanches—a people unknown to Hispanics in Texas for the first four decades of the century.[92] In attempting to court Apaches in 1757, Spaniards in Texas had made a powerful new enemy in the Comanches.

VI

Missions did not fail everywhere in Texas, but the restrictive mission life, where one might receive four or five lashes for missing morning assemblies and worse punishment for more serious offenses, attracted mainly Indians who had nowhere else to turn. Particularly susceptible to the blandishments of Franciscans were small bands of hunters and gatherers, many of them Coahuiltecan-speaking peoples of the lower Rio Grande who represented an astonishing number of groups that have since become extinct. Squeezed between Hispanics moving northward and Apaches moving southward, some members of these small bands found food and refuge in the mission of San Antonio de Valero and in the four additional missions that had sprouted along the San Antonio River downstream from San Antonio between 1720 and 1731. "They are more concerned about having food in abundance than with any fear of life eternal," one Franciscan lamented.[93]

The five San Antonio missions were the most successful in Texas, but the number of converts remained small compared to early days in Florida or New Mexico. The native population of each of the five San Antonio missions seldom exceeded 300, and fluctuated with the seasons and from year-to-year. Sometimes epidemics or massive flights lowered the mission population drastically, as in 1737 and 1739. Indians fled the missions with frequency—"it is rare," one priest wrote in 1740, "if they do not flee . . . two or three times, sometimes going as far as 100 leagues away."[94] But pressure from Apaches discouraged many Indians from leaving the missions, and as Apaches grew more numerous in South Texas by midcentury the mission population of all five San Antonio missions stabilized at about a thousand. A few other missions along the coastal plain attracted modest numbers, but none achieved the potential that the dense native population of Texas seemed to offer.[95]

With day-to-day life made insecure by armed nomads, few docile natives to exploit, high transportation costs for exports and imports, and little evidence of precious metals, Texas also failed to attract colonists. "Our best defense consists in seeing to it that a place is inhabited. . . . Settlers will defend their own territory," two ecclesiastical leaders explained to the viceroy in 1722.[96] But Texas officials faced a familiar conundrum: there would be safety in numbers, but they could not raise the numbers without guarantees of safety.

As in the case of Florida, Spanish officials tried to break out of this bind by simultaneously increasing defenses and persuading the Crown to subsidize colonists from Spain or New Spain, including Hispanicized Indians from Tlaxcala who had been useful elsewhere on the frontier, including Santa Fe and Saltillo. The marqués de Aguayo, echoing an earlier recommendation from the king's own council, had urged the Crown to move 200 Tlaxcalans to Texas, plus 200 families from Galicia, the Canary Islands, or Cuba. "Without these families," the marqués wrote, "the survival of that province will be very difficult if not impossible."[97] The Crown responded quickly. In 1723, the king offered to resettle 200 families of Canary Islanders, providing them free transportation, livestock, tools, arms, land, their maintenance for a year, and the title of hidalgo. There was no shortage of peasant volunteers from the impoverished islands, but the project became ensnared in Spanish bureaucracy and the quota, which was raised to 400 families in 1724, was never filled. Eight years after the king issued his order, the first and last contingent of government-sponsored immigrants from the Canary Islands reached Texas. Fifty-five people from Tenerife, most of them children and teenagers, arrived in San Antonio in March 1731 after a year-long journey by way of Havana, Veracruz, and Saltillo.[98] Together with those colonists who had come to Texas with the early expeditions of Domingo Ramón, Martín de Alarcón, and the marqués de Aguayo, the islanders or *isleños* brought the Hispanic population of the province to perhaps 500, and that of San Antonio itself to about 300.[99]

At San Antonio the new families found temporary lodging in the homes of the older residents and immediately set to planting crops. Like other settlers of the eighteenth century, these Spanish peasants apparently arrived in North America without the illusions of quick wealth that had beguiled their sixteenth-century predecessors. Thus, only after the planting season did the isleños begin to organize a town and assign themselves lots. They revived San Antonio, founded in 1718 as the villa of Béjar, and renamed it the villa of San Fernando. They surveyed its municipal lands and formed a municipal government—the first and only civilian government in Spanish Texas (the capital of Texas remained at the presidial community of Los Adaes as long as France held Louisiana). Then, showing little gratitude toward their hosts, the isleños took control of the town government and lorded it over San Antonio's original soldier-settlers, to whose irrigated farmlands the isleños laid claim.[100]

Economic realities in the new villa of San Antonio, however, must have disappointed the new land-owning *hidalgos*. Without Indian laborers, the isleños did their own farming and ranching—dangerous enterprises, especially since they had no prior experience with ranching and did not know how to use a gun. In 1749, however, Apaches and Hispanics came to terms at San Antonio, literally burying a hatchet as well as a lance, six arrows, and a live horse in the plaza.[101] The detente signified by the destruction of these weapons of war permitted Hispanics to expand their ranches and irrigated farms along the San Antonio River in the 1750s. Ranching became the principal economic activity, but *tejanos* had little incentive to produce beyond their needs. Until the 1770s, when the expansion of silver mining raised demand for beef in northern Mexico and the American Revolution created a need in Louisiana, tejanos lacked viable external markets. Ranching, then, remained primitive, amounting to little more than an annual roundup of wild cattle on public lands. The isleños, then, joined their predecessors in eking out a hardscrabble existence that bore no resemblance to the lives of owners of great haciendas in some parts of northern Mexico.[102]

Locally, tejanos in San Antonio could not compete with the cheap communal labor and large-scale irrigated agriculture at the subsidized Franciscan missions. Mission Indians managed large herds on the open range and raised corn that the friars sold at bargain prices to the presidio. The Canary Islanders twice sent delegates to Mexico

City to petition the viceroy for a guaranteed market at the garrison and permission to hire Indian laborers from the missions, but Franciscans successfully lobbied against them.[103] Friars did hire townspeople to do specialized tasks at the missions, such as blacksmithing or carpentry, and mission Indians proved economically useful to San Antonio in some ways. On balance, however, the economic exchange was probably not mutually beneficial. Local merchants, for example, received little business from the nearby missions since the friars purchased supplies from central sources in larger cities to the south.[104]

The friars, the Canary Islanders, and the descendants of the community's first Hispanic settlers carried on a running feud over the valley's limited resources, until intermarriage and common interests eventually united both factions of townsfolk against the Franciscans. Into the late 1770s when new markets appeared in Louisiana, San Antonio remained a village of farmers, ranchers, and tradespeople who depended on the local garrison for trade and on the presidial store for merchandise. The military was the motor that ran the debt-ridden barter economy, but government regulations kept it sputtering. They required soldiers to buy from the commissary rather than from local merchants, and prohibited settlers from selling produce in the interior of Mexico, in Louisiana, or at trade fairs in neighboring provinces.[105]

Through natural increase and a trickle of immigration, Hispanic Texas grew slowly, its population rising from 500 persons in 1731 to 1,190 by 1760. Of those 1,190 persons, about 580 lived in San Antonio, 350 at Los Adaes, and some 260 at La Bahía.[106] Those figures do not include mission Indians or Hispanics who lived in the El Paso area, then part of New Mexico, or in the lower Rio Grande Valley, part of the new, neighboring province of Nuevo Santander—the precursor of the modern Mexican state of Tamaulipas.

The *colonia*, or colony, of Nuevo Santander had its beginnings when Spanish officials groped for a way to stop England from seizing a stretch of unpopulated Gulf coast during the War of Jenkins' Ear. Nuevo Santander, which in theory extended from the Tampico and Pánuco River to the edge of Texas at the Medina River (and later at the Nueces River), was settled with remarkable speed. For the first and only time officials in New Spain relied on colonists rather than missionaries and soldiers to settle a new territory. Led by José de Escandón, the novel colonization project began in 1749, and by 1755 Escandón had moved over 6,000 colonists into the colonia and established twenty-three towns and fifteen missions. Two of those towns, Laredo and Dolores, stood on the north side of the Rio Grande in present Texas, as did the ranches of many colonists who lived on the south side of the great river in communities such as Camargo and Reynosa.[107] Dolores soon folded, but Laredo grew modestly as the center of a region rich in grazing land for cattle, sheep, and goats. In 1767, with a population of less than 200, the community was elevated to the status of a villa and a municipal government was formed; twenty years later, in 1789, the town's population reached 708, just over half the size of San Antonio that same year.[108]

Texas itself languished as one of the least populated provinces on the northern frontier of New Spain. By 1790, when the Hispanic population of Texas stood at 2,510, Nuevo Santander had over ten times as many Hispanics and New Mexico, with 20,289, had eight times that number. Only the two Californias had fewer Hispanics than Texas. In 1790 San Antonio, La Bahía, and Nacogdoches (which had replaced Los Adaes as the principal settlement in East Texas), had non-Indian populations of roughly 1,500, 600, and 400, making them more akin in size to the small presidial towns of St. Augustine or Pensacola rather than the provincial capitals in central New Spain (Mexico City surpassed 110,000 in 1793; Puebla had nearly 53,000; Guanajuato had over 32,000).[109]

As in Florida, high percentages of Hispanics in Texas were soldiers or civilians who depended upon the military for their subsistence. The military, in turn, depended heavily on the Crown, which paid dearly for its failure to develop Texas economically, as the king's own auditor suggested.[110]

Texas, then, retained the character of a defensive outpost. Although friars and soldiers continued to draw up plans to build more presidios and missions to the north, Spanish Texas failed to grow beyond the three points that the marqués de Aguayo had reinforced in 1721—San Antonio, La Bahía, and Los Adaes.[111] The explanation for Spain's failure to develop Texas more fully lies not in the allegedly inhospitable nature of the Great Plains or the woodlands of East Texas, as some writers have suggested, but in distance, danger, and government policies that gave advantages to foreign rivals and in Spanish missions that retarded civilian economic growth.[112]

VII

Like Texas, New Mexico also failed to fulfill its original promise. By the mid-eighteenth century, the missions had lost their vigor and the number of Franciscans had declined. What Spaniards still referred to as "the spiritual and temporal conquest," never extended beyond El Paso and the narrow sphere of the Rio Grande Pueblos.[113] Although older, more complex and populous than Texas, New Mexico still had a scanty Hispanic population through the midcentury. In 1765, non-Indians numbered 9,580, of whom 3,140 lived in the El Paso district. That same year, Hispanicized Pueblo Indians and detribalized Indians were counted at 10,500 (of whom 1,600 lived in or near El Paso). Since it had become home to Spanish and Pueblo refugees following the Pueblo Revolt of 1680, the population of El Paso proper had grown to 2,635 by 1765 making it the largest urban center on the northern frontier. Santa Fe came a close second, with 2,324 (San Antonio, without its outlying missions, had about 1,000). New Mexico boasted four villas—Santa Fe (ca. 1610), El Paso (1680), Santa Cruz de la Cañada (1695), and Albuquerque (1706).[114]

In the 1700s, missionaries and settlers continued to exploit Pueblos, but common enemies—Navajos, Utes, Comanches, and Apaches—forced the Pueblos to make common cause with Spaniards. Most Hispanics and Pueblos were also united by two constants of daily life—fear and poverty. From near or far, observers characterized New Mexico as "little populated and poverty-stricken, although endowed with natural resources,"[115] features it had in common with Spain's other frontier provinces. In New Mexico, however, a smaller percentage of the overall population than in Florida or Texas were soldiers or military dependents.

New Mexicans carried on a vigorous trade with neighboring tribes, exchanging weapons, munitions, horses, and agricultural produce for furs, buffalo hides, meat, and slaves. Some of this bartering took place during colorful annual fairs at Taos or Pecos, where Utes and Comanches temporarily pitched their tents and settled in to trade. Comanches, one observer noted in 1760, brought "plunder they have obtained elsewhere," and even as some of them traded peaceably at Taos or Pecos, "others of their nation make warlike attacks on some distant pueblos."[116]

In addition to this local Indian trade, New Mexicans sent goods south to Chihuahua, but until the 1780s, distance, danger, and Spain's monopolistic policies deprived the *nuevomexicanos* of profitable external markets and hard currency. A few Chihuahua merchants, who controlled the New Mexico market, paid low prices for New Mexico's sheep, raw wool, buffalo hides, buckskins, pine nuts, pottery, and wool and cotton manufactures, and charged New Mexicans dearly for goods from Spain and central New Spain, advancing them on credit. The unfavorable balance of trade drained New Mexico of currency so that a barter economy prevailed—as was true in Florida and Texas as well. The Chihuahua trade, described by one outside observer in 1778 as "defective and corrupt," reduced New Mexico traders to permanent indebtedness, and left them "puppets of the Chihuahua merchants."[117] Unlike their counterparts in Florida and Texas, nuevomexicanos had little opportunity to buy or sell from French or English smugglers. Over 900 miles from Natchitoches, New Mexico remained relatively isolated from French traders in neighboring Louisiana.

Spanish officials had worried about French commercial penetration of New Mexico since the 1690s, but French merchants were slow to reach Santa Fe. In the mistaken belief that New Mexico was rich in minerals, private traders from Louisiana and the Illinois country made several attempts to find a way across the plains.[118] In 1719, Jean-Baptiste Bénard de la Harpe went as far as a Tawakoni village on the Canadian River in present-day Oklahoma, where he saw horses with Spanish bridles and saddles, but he proceeded no farther west. Comanches, eager to prevent their Apache enemies from benefiting from trade with Frenchmen, blocked the way. Five years later, the veteran explorer of the upper Missouri, Etienne Bourgmont, crossed the plains from a post he established on the Missouri, near present-day Miami, Missouri, but he got no farther than central Kansas before taking ill and turning back.[119]

Not until 1739 did French traders find the way to Santa Fe. That year, the brothers Pierre and Paul Mallet and six companions ascended the Missouri River by boat from the Illinois country to present South Dakota believing, as did their contemporaries, that the river led to New Mexico. When Arikara Indians told them they had gone too far north, they returned downstream to an Omaha village in northeastern Nebraska, where they purchased horses for an overland trip. Following Indian trails, they traveled through Nebraska, Kansas, and the Oklahoma panhandle, then crossed the Sangre de Cristo Mountains to Picurís Pueblo and Santa Fe. The Mallets apparently arrived without their merchandise, personal possessions, and most of their clothing—all lost in crossing a river (or so New Mexico officials said). Hungry for better terms of trade than the price-gouging Chihuahua merchants offered, and perhaps in doubt as to the current status of Spanish-French relations, New Mexican officials welcomed the bedraggled Frenchmen and lodged them in private homes while waiting for word from the viceroy concerning what to do with them. Lt. Gov. Juan Páez Hurtado took the two Mallet brothers into his house and fed them at his table for nine months until the answer came. The Mallets could leave. From Santa Fe, the brothers traveled to New Orleans by way of the Canadian and Arkansas rivers, carrying at least one shopping list from a trade-hungry New Mexican. The vicar of Santa Fe, Santiago Roybal, offered to buy goods from New Orleans with silver from Chihuahua. The Mallets also carried a letter from Juan Páez Hurtado to Louis de Saint-Denis at Natchitoches, suggesting how the Mallets might return legally.[120]

This evidence that New Mexicans would welcome trade, coupled with the Mallets' erroneous report of rich silver mines in New Mexico, drew a number of French merchants across the plains in the years that followed—including the brothers Mallet. Some of those Frenchmen apparently sold their wares to Hispanics and Indians on the periphery of New Mexico, but others met a less friendly reception than the Mallets had received in 1739. After learning that nearby Comanches had received muskets from French traders, New Mexico officials began to take a dim view of the Frenchmen.[121] Under the best of circumstances, New Mexicans had a precarious association with Comanches, who simultaneously traded and raided in the province. The relationship seemed certain to deteriorate, however, as Gov. Tomás Vélez Cachupín told his successor in 1754, if the "French of New Orleans" succeeded in ending the Comanches' "dependence upon us." War with Comanches and their allies would surely follow, the governor predicted, and end in New Mexico's "complete ruin."[122] This apocolyptic vision suggested that the liabilities of trade with Frenchmen outweighed its advantages. Those French merchants who followed the Mallet brothers to Santa Fe faced arrest and the confiscation of their merchandise—a fate that befell several of them, including Pierre Mallet, in 1751. Officials in New Spain detained these new arrivals indefinitely, hoping to discourage others from following them.[123]

The government in Madrid also did its part to chill French mercantile passions by urging the king of France to inform his subjects that venturing into New Mexico could bring the death penalty. The Spanish Crown spared the lives of two Frenchmen who had arrived in Santa Fe in 1752 only because of the "good harmony which today this crown has with that of France."[124] The stern words and deeds of Spanish officials seem to have discouraged French traders from venturing into New Mexico after 1753, although a few smugglers may have continued to come and go quietly, without official detection.[125] In remote New Mexico, then, Spain cut off a trickle of French commerce and reduced New Mexico to its single lifeline—the *camino real* or royal road that led to Chihuahua and points south. Not until the 1820s, with the opening of the Santa Fe Trail that connected New Mexico to the Mississippi Valley, did New Mexicans find an alternative to the Chihuahua trade.[126] By then, however, France was long gone.

VIII

With a few strokes of the pen in 1762 and 1763, European diplomats altered the political, economic, and social arrangements so painfully shaped by decades of contention and cooperation between European colonials and North American natives. Spanish officials who had labored long but unsuccessfully to check the growth of French influence from Louisiana learned that the French province had passed suddenly into Spanish hands. Conversely, Spaniards who had successfully defended Pensacola, San Marcos de Apalachee, and St. Augustine against Indians and foreigners, discovered that their king had surrendered Florida to Britain without a fight. The diplomatic arrangements of 1762–63 demonstrated that however vigorously or imaginatively frontier officials coped with foreign rivals, Indians, and the stifling effects of Spanish commercial policies, their success or failure could be determined by distant forces beyond their control. Individuals who lived on the frontier occasionally altered the course of empire, but more often than not Spain's imperial claims in North America waxed and waned with decisions made in Madrid and other European capitals.

On November 3, 1762, France ceded Louisiana west of the Mississippi to Spain, in perpetuity, in the secret Treaty of Fontainebleau. French motives for this offering remain murky, but one seems fairly clear: France was eager to get rid of Louisiana. The colony lost money consistently and had become more difficult to maintain after England seized Canada in what came to be known in Europe as the Seven Years' War (the French and Indian War in the English colonies). Formally declared in 1756, the Seven Years' War had involved only France and England at the outset. Spain had entered the war late, in January 1762, on the French side, then had promptly lost Manila and Havana to British fleets; it seemed likely to lose the Floridas, too, in the peace arrangements. In fulfillment of promises made before the war, and perhaps to compensate Spain for its losses, France offered at Fontainebleau to surrender western Louisiana to Spain.[127]

Reluctantly, and only after consulting with his ministers, Carlos III accepted Louisiana from his French cousin. The colony promised to remain a financial liability for Spain as it had been for France, but the same defensive strategy that had led Spain to advance into Texas to counteract the French thrust into the Mississippi Valley now prompted Carlos III to decide that he needed Louisiana no matter what the cost. One of his ministers, the conde de Aranda, pointed out that Spain could not afford to leave Louisiana in French hands or Spanish commerce would continue to suffer. Moreover, France might cede all of it to the English, "who would make the most of it." On the other hand, under Spanish control western Louisiana could become a bulwark against migrating Englishmen. The Mississippi River, Aranda argued, would form a "recognizable barrier, a good distance from the population centers of New Mexico."[128]

In the Treaty of Paris, which officially ended the war on February 10, 1763, England recognized Spain as the new owner of Upper and Lower Louisiana west of the Mississippi, together with the so-called Isle d'Orleans on the east side of the river—a substantial area from Bayou Manchac south, which gave Spain effective control over the river's mouth and the city of New Orleans. The Treaty of Paris left England as Spain's only European rival on the continent, because France surrendered to Great Britain the remainder of Louisiana to the east of the Mississippi and all of Canada. In that same treaty, England also acquired Florida from Spain. During the war, England had made no attempt to capture Florida, whose defenses at St. Augustine were apparently stronger than ever, but in 1763 England bartered it away from Spain in exchange for returning Havana, which it had taken from Spain the previous summer.[129] Faced with a choice between losing Cuba or Florida to the British, Spain surrendered Florida.

England took possession of Florida in 1763, splitting it into two administrative units, West Florida and East Florida, separated by the Apalachicola and Chattahoochee rivers. Protestant England permitted Spanish subjects to remain and practice their religion undisturbed, but few accepted the offer. Nearly all Florida families depended on the government payroll, directly or indirectly, and they followed orders from their king to evacuate the province. Eager to salvage its colonists in Florida, the Crown offered free transport to those willing to leave. Within a year, Spanish residents of Florida completed a painful exodus, selling their real estate at bargain prices to English speculators, and packing their movable belongings onto crowded vessels. At St. Augustine, over 3,000 Spanish subjects, including 83 Christian Yamassee Indians, 79 free blacks and mulattos, and 350 slaves, moved to Cuba. Only a few Spaniards remained behind, among them Luciano de Herrera who would later serve Spain as a spy in the English colony.[130]

Spain also evacuated Pensacola, the lone outpost in British West Florida. The orderly exodus was orchestrated by the luckless governor, Col. Diego Ortiz Parrilla, who had to mop up in Sonora following a large-scale Pima rebellion in 1751 and who had commanded the presidio of San Sabá during the Comanche raid of 1758 and the retreat on the Red River. Now he had to endure yet another humiliation. Under his supervision, some 700 refugees, including 108 Christian Indians, sailed from Pensacola to Veracruz to begin life anew in Mexico. Only one Spaniard stayed in Pensacola. Although Spain reacquired the Floridas twenty years later, few of the refugees from St. Augustine or Pensacola ever returned.[131]

In contrast to Spain's total evacuation of English Florida, few Frenchmen abandoned Spanish Louisiana. France did not encourage its former subjects in the Mississippi Valley to repatriate, but instead cooperated with Spain to strengthen Louisiana against further English expansion. The French colonials, however, refused to put out the welcome mat for their new sovereign. To the contrary, they tried to persuade France to reassert its control over the Mississippi Valley and they subverted Spain's efforts to effect a peaceful transition of power.

Louisianans lived in an uneasy political limbo from September 1764, when they learned of the Treaty of Paris, until a rainy Ides of March in 1766, when the first Spanish governor, Antonio de Ulloa, reached New Orleans. With Ulloa came an insubstantial force of about ninety men, and he waited in vain for a promised battalion. A highly respected French-speaking naval officer from Seville who had done pioneering scientific research in America as a young man and, most recently, served as a governor in Peru, Ulloa arrived with instructions to leave the French governmental structure intact. "No innovation will be made in the government," Carlos III had instructed Ulloa, "and no law or custom prevailing in the Indies will be applied."[132]

Ulloa followed his instructions. He established a curious system of joint rule with the last French governor, Charles Aubry, who, like most other French officeholders, retained his former position. Ulloa also attempted to incorporate the remaining French soldiers into the Spanish army and, to the astonishment of the French residents, he did not lower the fleur-de-lis or raise the red-and-yellow banner of Spain over the city. With this tactful occupation, Ulloa aimed to conciliate the French population upon which Spain would have to depend to make the colony thrive. Moreover, without adequate troops or funds at his disposal, Ulloa had no choice but to rely on friendly persuasion.

Whatever he gained by trying to keep the political transfer of Louisiana smooth, Ulloa lost with his abrasive economic reforms. Before a Spanish Louisiana could fulfill its intended purpose of shielding northern New Spain against English advances, its

35. Detail from a view of New Orleans, drawn by a British officer, Philip Pittman, in 1765. Courtesy, Louisiana State Museum.

36. Antonio de Ulloa. Courtesy, Museo Naval, Madrid.

economy needed strengthening and its meager population bolstered. Ulloa tried to achieve those ends by pulling the colony's commerce into the closed Spanish imperial trading system. He tried to close Louisiana's traditional markets within the French empire, end the contraband trade that French colonists had enjoyed with the English, and license Indian traders. Not surprisingly, Ulloa's efforts to regulate commerce antagonized Louisiana's powerful merchant elite. This group had savored freedom from trade restrictions under France, particularly after France had become distracted by war with England in the mid-1750s. Fearful that their economic interests and political influence would suffer under the new regime, the merchants' resistance to Ulloa stiffened. In October 1768 they led a popular revolt. They stirred up the "common folk of the city," Ulloa later reported, by telling them that instead of Bordeaux "they would have to subject themselves to drinking the wretched wine of Catalonia." This, Ulloa explained, was a potent issue since "those people are so given to drinking." Amid shouts of *vive le roi, vive le bon vin de Bordeaux,* and other expressions of French patriotism, Ulloa abdicated and retreated to Cuba. Fittingly, perhaps, he left on a French vessel since the only available Spanish ship was not seaworthy.[133]

Although rebel leaders subsequently justified their brief, bloodless, and boozy rebellion by appealing to their natural right to revolt against despots, most seemed eager to return to a neglectful French despotism rather than remain under a more vigilant Spanish variety.[134] They appealed to France to reassert its sovereignty over the colony but French officials, unwilling to antagonize their Spanish ally, declined to entertain the idea.[135]

Louisiana remained independent for nearly a year before Spanish forces returned. In August 1769 a new Spanish governor, Gen. Alejandro O'Reilly, arrived in New Orleans with a well-equipped armada of twenty-one ships and over 2,000 troops— more men than Spain would ever again send to the Mississippi Valley. An Irish soldier of fortune who had made a brilliant career in the Spanish military, O'Reilly easily reasserted Spanish authority. Taken completely by surprise, convinced of the futility of resistance, and not suspecting serious reprisals, French leaders in Louisiana welcomed the Spanish general. Backed up by the force for which Ulloa had pleaded but never received, O'Reilly raised Spain's banner over Louisiana's settlements for the first time, including those on the Spanish side of the Mississippi in Upper Louisiana—Ste. Genevieve and St. Louis. Ste. Genevieve had been founded about 1750, but St. Louis, established in 1764 by French fur traders at an advantageous location on a high bluff near the confluence of three great rivers—the Missouri, Illinois, and Mississippi— was destined to become the administrative and economic center of what Spaniards would call Illinois or Upper Louisiana.[136]

Swiftly and decisively, O'Reilly followed his instructions from the king to "make formal charge and punish according to the law the instigators and accomplices of the uprising." Within ten days he pressed charges against a dozen ringleaders and imprisoned them. All received due process, as O'Reilly's instructions required; all were found guilty and five were executed by a firing squad. French Louisianans and pro-French historians later vilified "Bloody O'Reilly," but there is no evidence that he acted vengefully as they charged. To the contrary, he declined to pursue still more conspirators, and he granted amnesty to most participants in the revolt.[137]

O'Reilly remained in Louisiana until late February 1770, but during his brief tenure he imposed a new order. He dismantled the French administrative structure and placed Louisiana under the captain general at Havana, as Florida had been before its loss to the British. He nullified French laws and replaced them with a legal code of his own. Castilian, he decreed, would replace French as the colony's legal language. Finally, he prohibited trade with all foreigners and foreign ports, expelled a number of foreign merchants, and reformed the colony's military structure.[138] Under his successors, Spain encouraged immigration as it had in Texas and Florida, but it did not attempt large-scale conversion of French-influenced Indians. Within a decade, Louisianans enjoyed economic prosperity under Spain, perhaps because Spanish officials adopted France's more liberal trading policies, opened Louisiana to direct trade with several Spanish ports, and welcomed non-Spanish immigrants. On the other hand, even without these policy changes, a growing contraband trade with neighboring Anglo-Americans had invigorated the province's economy. Although Louisiana's colonists prospered more under Spain than they had under France, the province remained a net liability for the Spanish Crown.[139]

Spain held title to Louisiana (including the Illinois country) for nearly four decades, but failed to Hispanicize it, much less profit from it. In contrast to Florida, where English colonists quickly took the places of departing Spaniards, Louisiana became Spanish more in name than in fact. French culture and language remained dominant because Frenchmen, who took the oath of allegiance to Spain, simply overwhelmed Spaniards numerically. Through incentives, Spanish officials managed to lure Canary Islanders to Louisiana in much larger numbers than they had to Florida or Texas. Beginning in the late 1770s, as war with England loomed, Spain sent some 2,000 Canary Islanders to Louisiana, as well as a trickle of emmigrants from other parts of Spain. A hundred or so colonists from Málaga, for example, founded New Iberia in 1779.[140] Despite these successes, Spanish immigrants never outnumbered the 5,700 Frenchmen who had lived in Louisiana in 1766 when Ulloa arrived to take possession of the province.[141] Moreover, fresh waves of French immigrants increased Louisiana's Gallic population during the Spanish regime. An indeterminate number of Frenchmen crossed the Mississippi into Louisiana to avoid British rule, while others fled to Louisiana from Haiti to escape a slave rebellion in the 1790s. Acadian refugees from Nova Scotia comprised the largest immigrant group, swelling the French population of Louisiana by perhaps 3,000.[142]

IX

The new imperial boundaries created in 1763 existed, of course, largely in the European imagination. European diplomats had ignored the realities of indigenous territorial claims, and they had ignored geography itself. However convenient the Mississippi River had seemed as a boundary line, it formed the core of a region with its own integrity.[143] Like other river basins, the Mississippi drew people together rather than dividing them. Spaniards and Englishmen shared navigation rights on the river and had common economic interests, and yet each power fortified its side of the river and thus created new points of tension. Meanwhile, within the territories that Spain and England called their own, native Americans continued to assert their own claims, often with gun and powder as well as bow and arrow. If Spain were to maintain its hold over the western half of the continent and develop it economically, it would have to find a way to control the so-called barbarous Indians—those natives who had successfully maintained their political and spiritual independence. Traditional institutions and strategies had failed not only on the plains of northern Texas and eastern New Mexico, but also across much of the southwestern rim of the continent.

8

Indian Raiders and the Reorganization of Frontier Defenses

There must be on land defense against so many barbarous Indians with whom no arrangements can be made because . . . they must try to defend their lands and liberty.
fray Alonso de Posada, 1686

I prohibit the commandant-inspector and the captains of presidios from granting them peace.
King Carlos III, 1772

A bad peace with all the tribes which ask for it would be more fruitful than the gains of a successful war.
Viceroy Bernardo de Gálvez, 1786

In March of 1766, the marqués de Rubí rode north from Mexico City to inspect the formal defenses of northern New Spain, a tour that consumed the next two years and took him over 7,600 miles. Since before Christmas, the marqués had waited impatiently for the viceroy to gather the maps, documents, technical assistance, and personnel necessary for a study of the far-flung frontier garrisons. At last he was on his way.

A newcomer to the American colonies, Rubí had arrived in New Spain in 1764 as part of a military mission sent by Carlos III to reorganize the defenses of the viceroyalty. Rubí was one of four field marshals assigned to this important team, headed by Lt. Gen. Juan de Villalba y Angulo and prompted by Spain's defeat in the Seven Years' War. By seizing the fortified city of Havana, England had revealed the weakness of Spain's defenses in its American colonies. In the next confrontation, England could just as easily land troops at Veracruz and invade the population center of New Spain—an area that Spain previously believed was secure. Spain's humiliation, however, had coincided with the beginning of the reign of the most dynamic, innovative, and American-oriented of its eighteenth-century Bourbon monarchs, Carlos III (1759–88). In North America, the king's wide-ranging and ultimately successful program called for regaining Florida, which the British had acquired as part of the peace settlement, and shoring up the defenses of New Spain, including its northern frontier.[1]

I

The marqués de Rubí would not have to study long to understand that northern New Spain represented one of the few places in the empire vulnerable to direct attack from adjacent non-Spanish lands. He knew that the northern fringes of the viceroyalty had seemed chronically insecure in contrast to central New Spain, and that the region faced a new set of problems: how to defend newly acquired Louisiana; what to do with Texas now that it no longer served as a buffer colony against French Louisiana; how to protect the northern reaches of the empire from Britain, which had acquired Canada from France in 1763; and how to fend off Russians and Englishmen who had begun to probe North America's Pacific shores. Old problems also persisted and had grown more acute. Across northern New Spain from the Gulf of California to Texas, in what officials in Mexico City had long called the interior provinces, Indian raiders took a terrible toll on Spanish settlements, and Spain's military forces seemed unable to deter them. Their lands threatened by the continuing expansion of the Spanish frontier, and their liberty at risk from slaving parties and missionaries, some Indians had powerful motives besides booty for attacking Hispanic settlements.[2] Since 1700, the Crown's expenditures for the defense of the interior provinces had nearly doubled, but Indian reprisals and depredations had also increased, particularly after midcentury when sporadic raids by Apaches seemed to accelerate into open warfare.[3]

Shortly after arriving in Mexico City in 1764, the head of Rubí's military mission, Lt. Gen. Juan de Villalba, had inquired into the condition of frontier presidios. They were notorious for their mismanagement, but Villalba concluded that the viceroy, the marqués de Cruillas, lacked interest in reforming them. Instead, Villalba charged, the viceroy had embezzled their funds.[4] Informed of Villalba's suspicions, and aware of the devastation that Indians had caused in the interior provinces, the Crown had ordered the marqués de Rubí to conduct a special reconnaissance. Along with Rubí went a military engineer to provide technical assistance. Nicolás de Lafora, a twenty-year army veteran and member of the Royal Corps of Engineers, would make maps and keep a diary. It was Lafora who pithily explained the purpose of the mission: to learn why Indians "are so audacious" and why soldiers seemed "of so little use."[5]

On April 11, 1766, a month after leaving Mexico City, Rubí and Lafora reached Durango, the capital of mineral-rich Nueva Vizcaya, where their inspection of presidios began and the journey became increasingly dangerous. Nueva Vizcaya had a Hispanic population that approached 50,000, making it the most populous territory in the north. Nonetheless, most of the province remained the domain of Indians hostile to Spaniards, especially around Chihuahua, 450 miles north of Durango, where the country was, in the words of Lafora, "infested by Indians."[6]

The marqués and his party blamed Indian depredations in Nueva Vizcaya exclusively on Apache bands that lived to the north—Lipáns and Natagés who raided from Texas and Coahuila, and Natagés, Faraones, and Gileños who came from southern New Mexico.[7] Pushed off the buffalo plains over the course of a century by Comanches with firearms and by Wichita peoples whom Spaniards knew collectively as the Nations of the North, Apaches had gradually moved into what is today southern Arizona and New Mexico and southwestern Texas. By the time that Rubí made his tour, Apaches had formed a wide band across the interior provinces, from Texas nearly to Sonora.[8] Across the Gran Apachería, as Spaniards termed the Apache-held lands, Rubí found numerous communities, mines, haciendas, ranches, and farms destroyed by Apaches or abandoned out of fear. Eager for horses, deprived of the buffalo hides and meat that had been their stock in trade, and often mistreated and enslaved by Spaniards, Apaches had turned to raiding. In northern Mexico they had found Spanish horses, mules, and cattle ready for the taking. In the course of their raiding, they had won admiration for their "amazing . . . conduct, vigilance, speed, order, and endurance," as Lafora noted, and they had also gained a reputation for indolence and "extreme cruelty."[9]

Spaniards, on the other hand, whom Apaches first encountered as slavers and who continued to enslave Indians despite royal injunctions, probably also enjoyed a reputation for extreme cruelty among Apaches.[10] In Arizona, for example, it was Spanish "custom" to cut off the heads of Apaches killed in battle. Lt. Col. Pedro de Allende boasted of leading a campaign out of Tucson in 1779 in which he killed a "war captain, whose head he cut off before the very eyes of the enemy. Then he charged the Apache line single-handed, with the head stuck on his lance."[11] As one prominent officer observed, "The Spaniards accuse the Indians of cruelty. I do not know what opinion they would have of us: perhaps it would be no better . . . if he [an Indian] avenges himself it is for just satisfaction of his grievances."[12]

After three months of research and interviews in Nueva Vizcaya, the marqués and his party left Chihuahua and continued northward through a devastated region. In mid-July they crossed into New Mexico at the ruins of the hacienda of Ojo Caliente, and a few days later they reached the Rio Grande at El Paso. The fifty or so troops on

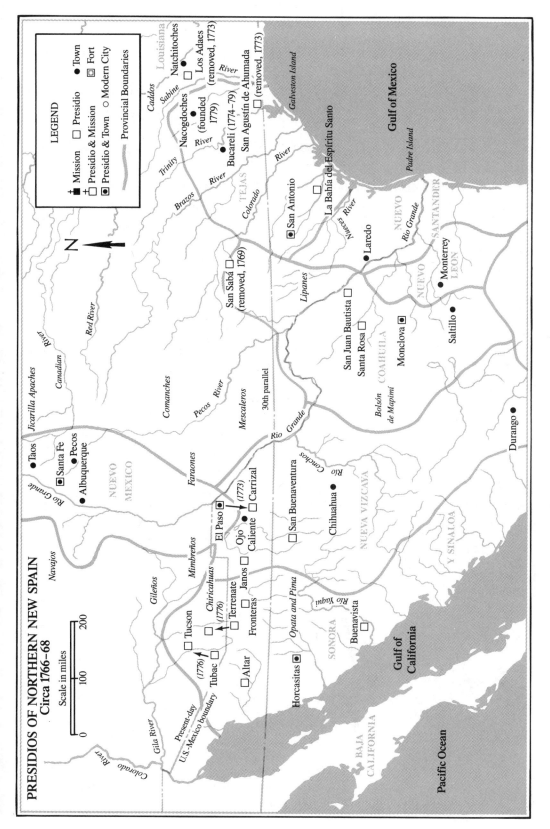

Map 10. *Presidios of northern New Spain, circa 1766–68.*

active duty had more than they could do to guard livestock, pursue Apache cattle thieves, and escort convoys along the camino real.[13] Nonetheless, Rubí believed that El Paso no longer needed a presidio because it had enough able-bodied men to form a militia to defend itself.[14] Many frontier communities relied on volunteer militia instead of paid soldiers, and some had both.

Leaving El Paso, Rubí's party crossed the Rio Grande on rafts on August 5 and warily continued to follow the camino real northward through Apache country. Nine days and some 250 miles later they passed through the first Hispanic settlements north of El Paso on the east side of the river, Las Nutrias and Tomé. On August 19, they

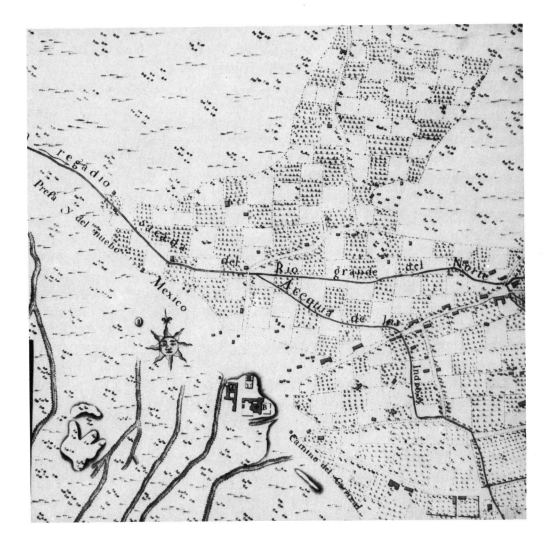

37. El Paso in 1766 with its adobe presidio (A), which consisted of nothing more than a captain's quarters and a guardhouse, the adobe church (B), and surrounding homes and fields. Drawn in 1766 by José de Urrutia. Courtesy, British Library and Museum of New Mexico, neg. no. 15065.

reached Santa Fe, the site of New Mexico's only garrison north of El Paso, established in 1693. New Mexico was an island surrounded by a sea of hostile tribes, as its officials never tired of reminding their superiors in Mexico City—although they failed to explain that Indian hostility was often provoked by their own slave trading or their encroachment on Indian lands. Indian hostilities had limited the province's growth: Apache bands to the south and southwest, Navajos to the west, Utes to the northwest, and Comanches to the northeast. Although New Mexicans lived in a state of "never-ceasing war . . . with the barbarians," as one governor put it,[15] not all of the "barbarians" made war on New Mexico at the same time, or they might well have destroyed the province.

Engineer Lafora dismissed the presidio of Santa Fe as "incapable of defense," but he found the New Mexicans, Pueblo Indians and Hispanics alike, "well prepared for war" against the "heathen nations" who surrounded them. "They learn to use weapons and ride horses when they are very young." Because the province suffered a chronic shortage of ammunition, however, the New Mexicans' weapons, Lafora lamented, consisted largely of lances, bows, and arrows.[16]

Although he had traveled some 1,800 miles in less than six months, Rubí had finished only the first leg of his journey when he completed his inspection of the presidio at Santa Fe. On September 15 he began to retrace his steps to the northern reaches of Nueva Vizcaya, then turned westward to examine garrisons at San Buenaventura and Janos. Continuing west, he crossed the Sierra Madre into Sonora, stopping at presidios at Fronteras, Terrenate, Tubac, and Altar.

Separated from Nueva Vizcaya in 1734 and, along with Sinaloa, made a separate administrative unit, Sonora itself had a Hispanic population of little more than 8,000 by the mid-1760s. Nearly all of Sonora's Hispanic residents lived below the present-day United States-Mexico border. In what is now Arizona, the Hispanic population, which probably did not exceed 600, lived in or near the presidio of Tubac, in the valley of the Santa Cruz River. In late December 1766, Rubí inspected Tubac and visited the nearby mission of Guevavi. As he had all along the way, he heard stories of depredations by Gileño Apaches and he found nearby *ranchos* deserted. North of Tubac, farther down the Santa Cruz Valley, the marqués noted that a Jesuit priest ministered to the Pima Indian communities at San Xavier del Bac and Tucson and that small detachments of troops from the Tubac garrison help defend those northernmost Spanish outposts on the Sonora frontier.[17]

After completing his inspection of the northern rim of Sonora, the marqués de Rubí turned south and east to review the presidios at Horcasitas (then the capital of Sonora) and Buenavista. Then he continued eastward to Nueva Vizcaya by a different route than he had come, recrossing the Sierra Madre and rejoining the camino real below Chihuahua. It was April 1767 and he had been gone from Mexico City for over a year, but another leg of the journey still awaited him.

Rubí headed toward Texas. Crossing Nueva Vizcaya, he made a long loop south

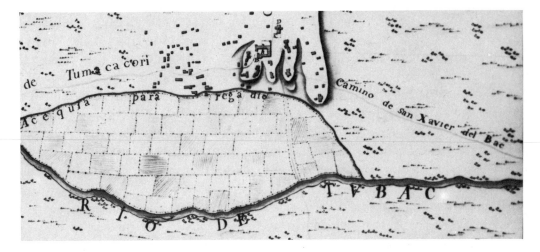

38. *Tubac in 1766, with its captain's house (A), guardhouse (B), military chapel, and cemetery (D and C). Detail from a drawing done in 1766 by José de Urrutia. Courtesy, British Library and Museum of New Mexico, neg. no. 15054.*

around the vast Bolsón de Mapimí—an arid region that Lafora described contradictorily as an "unpopulated land where enemy Indians and apostates from the missions take shelter and from which they set out to raid Nueva Vizcaya and Coahuila."[18] Beyond the Bolsón, Rubí passed through Saltillo, then turned north and entered the province of Coahuila where Spain's presence still rested lightly on the land. Lafora noted that the province contained "777 families of Spaniards, mestizos, and mulattoes," counting the troops at its three presidios—Monclova, Santa Rosa, and San Juan Bautista on the Rio Grande.[19] Although ostensibly at peace, Lipán and Natagé Apaches from the north of the Rio Grande made frequent raids into Coahuila and kept smaller rancheros impoverished by running off their stock. Rubí continued north to inspect presidios at Monclova and Santa Rosa, then crossed the Rio Grande with the help of Lipán Apaches and traveled another nine days to the presidio at San Sabá, which he reached in late July.

In the heart of dangerous Comanche country, the limestone presidio of San Luis de Amarillas had a large contingent of 100 men, but they had failed to protect the nearby mission from annihilation by Comanches in 1758. To Rubí and Lafora, then, a presidio at San Sabá seemed "of no advantage whatever"—a judgment that led to the garrison being removed from San Sabá in 1769.[20]

On August 8, five days' journey from San Sabá, Rubí came to San Antonio, whose garrison, however poorly equipped and undermanned, did seem worth maintaining. Although the presidio of San Antonio de Béjar consisted of little more than barracks and a few other structures built around a square in the center of town, the troops offered a measure of protection to the community and to five nearby missions, where some 800 Indians resided at the time of his visit. Frequent attacks by Comanches and the Nations of the North on livestock and herders left the townspeople in fear. Without protection, they would surely have abandoned San Antonio; indeed, many houses around the military plaza stood empty and provided cover for hostile Indians to approach the military buildings.[21]

East of San Antonio, it seemed to Rubí the king's money was badly spent on fortifications. Twelve days of hard travel took Rubí beyond the Neches River to the mission of Nacogdoches. Neither it nor the nearby mission at Los Ais had Indian neophytes. Lafora dismissed these missions as worse than "useless," because the maintenance of priests and soldiers to guard them wasted royal revenues.[22] At Los Adaes, on the very edge of Louisiana, which they reached on September 10, Rubí and Lafora found the presidio in complete disarray. The garrison of sixty-one shoeless soldiers, dressed in rags rather than uniforms, had only two serviceable muskets among them. Of 117 horses only 25 were fit to use. The presidial commander had siphoned off monies that should have supplied the troops and had sold the best horses to the French. Happily, this useless garrison had little to protect. Although Los Adaes still served as the governor's residence, it was no longer needed to shield Texas from Spain's Gallic rivals, who had surrendered Louisiana, nor did it protect Indians at the nearby missions, where Franciscans had failed to attract neophytes. A year after Rubí's visit, in August 1768, the acting governor of Texas decided to move his headquarters and the garrison to San Antonio, which had greater need for protection. Five years later, in 1773, Spain would abandon Los Adaes completely and designate San Antonio the new capital of Texas.[23]

Los Adaes marked the eastern terminus of Rubí's tour. There was no need for him to continue into Louisiana, where Gov. Antonio de Ulloa was conducting his own inspection and restructuring regional defenses. Louisiana would further develop its own elaborate system of fortifications, but its purpose would be to protect the province from England and then the United States, and responsibility for its design would fall to the captain general at Havana. Louisiana was never considered one of the internal provinces of New Spain.[24]

From Los Adaes, then, the marqués began his long trek back to Mexico City, stopping to inspect more presidios along the way. From Los Adaes he journeyed southward to the Gulf coast presidio of San Agustín de Ahumada on the lower Trinity River, arriving there on October 9. Built in 1756, near the mouth of the Trinity some 37 miles east of modern Houston, the post was to hold the coast against Frenchmen and to protect nearby missions. The missions, however, stood empty, as they had near Los Adaes, and Lafora pronounced the fort "useless."[25] Turning westward, the marqués followed the coastal plain to the presidio of Nuestra Señora de La Bahía del Espíritu Santo. Originally located at the site of La Salle's post on Matagorda Bay, it had stood since 1749 on the San Antonio River, some 100 miles downstream from San Antonio and 50 miles from the river's mouth, on a malaria-infested site near present

Goliad.[26] Despite its unhealthy location, two nearby missions had converts and the presidial community occupied a strategic place in a plan that Rubí had begun to formulate. Most of the Gulf coast, however, he believed was not worth occupying. Spanish policymakers, Rubí argued, had deceived themselves in the belief that they needed to occupy the Gulf from the Mississippi to Nuevo Santander, for the coast's shallow waters and unnavigable rivers provided a natural defense.[27]

From the presidio of La Bahía, Rubí continued westward. He crossed the northern reaches of Nuevo Santander, an area devoid of Hispanic settlement, to the town of Laredo on the Rio Grande, then journeyed upstream to the presidio of San Juan Bautista in Coahuila, arriving on November 22. After inspecting that post, he returned to Mexico City by an elliptical route that took him through Monterrey, Saltillo, Zacatecas, and across Mexico to the province of Nayarit, where he inspected one last presidio near the Gulf of California. On February 23, 1768, Rubí and his party entered Mexico City. Across the interior provinces of New Spain, they had inspected twenty-three of the king's twenty-four frontier posts and seen firsthand "the tremendous damage His Majesty's subjects suffer daily from the barbarians."[28]

II

The devastation that Rubí witnessed had occurred at a time when the military was in the ascendancy throughout the Spanish empire in general, and on the northern frontier of New Spain in particular.[29] By the 1760s, presidios or military bases, most of them fortified, had eclipsed missions to become the dominant institution on Spain's North American frontiers. Spaniards had long built fortifications in North America, beginning in Florida in the 1560s with the posts established by Menéndez de Avilés, and the chain of blockhouses built in the Carolinas and Tennessee by Juan Pardo. As Mexico's frontier moved north, presidios were constructed along the road from Mexico City to Zacatecas in the middle of the prolonged Chichimeca War (1550–90). But these tiny, rustic garrisons could not mount an effective offense against natives who enjoyed vast numerical superiority. Hence, Menéndez de Avilés and his wisest successors in Florida tried mightily not to provoke wars with Indians; in northern Mexico, officials turned to diplomacy to end the Chichimeca War. Nonetheless, despite their limited utility, fortifications served a useful defensive role for soldiers and civilians. The Crown continued to maintain them in small numbers. In sixteenth-century northern Mexico, they served as peace agencies and centers for distributing goods to Indians, a role that they would come to play again in the late eighteenth century.[30]

As Spain had advanced its North American frontiers in the seventeenth century, it had relied less on soldiers than on missionaries. Missions cost less than presidios and missionaries' methods seemed more in harmony with the Crown's policy of "pacificying" new lands instead of "conquering" them.[31] Moreover, the walls of mission churches and compounds met the needs of many communities for defense from external attack. Some missions were built more substantially than fortifications. One visitor to Mission San José at San Antonio, for example, noted with perhaps some exaggeration that "in beauty, plan, and strength . . . there is not a presidio along the entire frontier line that can compare with it."[32] In the seventeenth century, presidios had been erected more to ward off foreigners than to provide protection from Indians, as was the case with the castillo of San Marcos at St. Augustine and the small block-house built at Apalachee in 1657.[33] New Mexico, unthreatened by foreigners, had no presidio or professional soldiery until after the Pueblo Revolt. Following Spanish tradition, New Mexicans relied upon private or communal defenses. Some country homes in New Mexico resembled small forts, with walls, parapets, and towers. Towns, too, had fortified walls and towers; in smaller communities the windowless back sides of houses, built contiguously around a plaza, formed the town wall.[34] Mustering men to arms in seventeenth-century New Mexico had fallen to the encomenderos, who received no salary from the Crown (only in times of crisis had the Crown sent soldiers northward).

In the late seventeenth century, the destruction of the missions of Florida and New Mexico, the Indian rebellions that continued to ripple across northern Mexico, and the growing threat from foreigners had led Spain to increase and professionalize its military forces on the northern fringes of the empire and to construct fortifications on an ad hoc basis, in response to local crises. In 1681, survivors of the Pueblo Revolt had established a presidio at El Paso del Norte. When Diego de Vargas reasserted Spanish control over the Pueblo country in 1693, he had founded a presidio in Santa Fe, as authorized by the viceroy.[35] Since Spain had not restored encomiendas in New Mexico after the Pueblo Revolt, responsibility for defense had shifted to presidial troops paid by the king. On campaigns, the professional soldiery continued to be augmented by civilian volunteers, some organized into informal militia. In the eighteenth century, Pueblo Indians also joined the Spaniards in common cause against the tribes that Spaniards called barbaric—*indios bárbaros*.[36] Although civilians and Pueblo Indians bore much of the actual burden of defense, economic power and status in the province came to reside in the professional military with its access to the government payroll, as had been the case in Florida from the beginning.[37]

In Florida, the Crown had added a new military post at Pensacola in 1698 and had steadily increased support for the forts at St. Augustine, Pensacola, and their dependencies, professionalizing them and linking them to Havana under special regulations.[38] Since its missions had never recovered from the devastation that began in the late 1600s, and since it had also failed to attract colonists, Spanish Florida in the 1700s consisted of little more than military bases, soldiers, and a small number of civilians who, at least in St. Augustine, were also organized into militia.[39]

In Texas, Spain had depended almost entirely on missionaries in its initial attempt at settlement in the 1690s and lost the gamble. When Spaniards returned to Texas in

1716 to check the expansion of French Louisiana, presidios became conspicuous on a frontier where missionaries had little success. Similarly in Arizona, the presidio at Tubac was established in 1752, after the Pima revolt of the previous year revealed the need for a more forceful Spanish presence.

By the 1760s, when the marqués de Rubí made his tour of inspection, the military had become the dominant institution on the frontier, and war rather than "pacification" had become the prevailing mode of subduing intractable nomads. As Rubí learned to his sorrow, however, Spain's heightened military presence had failed to bring peace. First, decades of exposure to Europeans had transformed Apaches, Comanches, and other groups into more effective adversaries. Better armed and mounted than ever before, and increasingly cognizant of the fighting methods and capabilities of their Spanish adversaries, Plains Indians in particular proved increasingly formidable raiders.[40] Second, throughout the interior provinces of New Spain, the military operated with notorious inefficiency. Presidios had developed haphazardly, in response to local needs and without an overall plan. Each operated as the local fiefdom of its commanding officer, with little coordination of troop movements between presidios or standardization of weapons, ammunition, and uniforms. As Rubí discovered, many of the presidios were poorly situated. Officers commonly skimmed the payroll for personal profit, and soldiers suffered from poor training, shoddy equipment, acute poverty, and low morale.

Remedies for these ills had long since been prescribed as the result of a laborious tour of inspection conducted by Brig. Gen. Pedro de Rivera, who between 1724 and 1728 had gone over much the same ground as the marqués de Rubí.[41] The resulting *Regulations of 1729* had addressed the peculiar problems of the presidios of the interior provinces. Except for the rules regarding discipline, regulations that governed the regular army did not seem to apply to the Indian frontier where regular forces seldom served. In the "land of war," the presidios were usually manned by local recruits, who enlisted for one or more terms of ten years.[42] In coastal presidios such as those at St. Augustine and Pensacola, which were built as bastions against foreigners rather than Indians and which never became the nucleii of substantial civilian settlements, most of the troops came from outside the province—the majority from Spain itself.[43]

Pedro de Rivera's tour had given authorities in Mexico City and in Madrid fundamental knowledge of the frontier, and his report continued to be consulted for years afterwards.[44] Nonetheless, the *Regulations of 1729* had reflected Rivera's emphasis on economy over efficacy. They resulted in only minor changes and were honored mainly in the breach. In the early 1750s, Viceroy Revillagigedo concluded that the regulations had not only been ignored, but were out of date and largely unknown because few copies remained in circulation. Although he succeeded in dramatically restructuring the administration of the Florida presidios,[45] Revillagigedo's efforts to rewrite the regulations for the interior provinces failed. The official to whom he had entrusted the task died and Spain drifted into the Seven Years' War.[46] Thus, many of the same problems that Rivera had encountered remained to be addressed anew by Rubí. Moreover, they needed to be addressed urgently since Indian depredations had grown far worse. Rivera had regarded the indios bárbaros as little more than cattle thieves, a people susceptible to conversion with no special hatred for Spaniards; Rubí regarded them simply as enemies.[47]

III

In the 1760s, prospects seemed bright that the intractable problems of the frontier presidios might respond to the fresh initiatives supported by Carlos III and his ministers. Rubí's extraordinary tour resulted in a new set of regulations for the frontier presidios and a new strategy for defending the interior provinces. Promulgated provisionally in Mexico in 1771, and officially by Carlos III the following year,[48] the *Regulations of 1772* replaced those of 1729 and remained in force as long as Spain's empire endured in North America.[49] Reflecting the thinking of Rubí and his staff, as well as of many of his compatriots, the *Regulations of 1772* emphasized force over

39. Carlos III (1759–88). From Manuel Rivera Cambas, Los gobernantes de México *(Mexico, 1872–73). Courtesy, DeGolyer Library, Southern Methodist University.*

diplomacy. Indeed, by authorizing an offensive war against pagans, the Crown departed for the first time since 1573 from its ill-enforced but well intentioned policy of peaceful expansion.[50] In military terms, the *Regulations of 1772* offered essentially European solutions to American problems.

Like Pedro Rivera before him, Rubí had advocated more efficient use of military resources rather than costly military escalation. At the heart of Rubi's recommendations,[51] which the king adopted due in no small part to the savings they promised, was the idea of an impregnable "cordon of presidios" spaced uniformly across the frontier from the Gulf of California to the Gulf of Mexico.[52] As rational and geometrical as it was unrealistic, the plan called for the construction of fifteen fixed posts, located at 100-mile intervals, to run roughly along the 30th parallel from Altar in Sonora to La Bahía in Texas. Much of the way, the cordon approximated the future U.S-Mexican border, with nearly all of the anticipated presidial sites located just below the present border. The plan required moving many garrisons, such as Tubac, in order to space them apart at uniform distances, and abandoning others to the south and north of the cordon. It did allow a few exceptions. The presidio of La Bahía in Texas, would serve as the cordon's eastern anchor even though it was "more than one degree outside of the line."[53] Much farther north of the line, and not forming a part of it, presidios were also to remain at Santa Fe and San Antonio, each to form "a separate frontier."[54]

Although it disrupted the harmonious proportions of his design, Rubí recognized that fortifications at Santa Fe and San Antonio were necessary to protect the substantial populations of Hispanic settlers and Hispanized Indians in their vicinities. Moreover, as officials repeatedly pointed out, these provinces served as the first line of defense for the richer provinces to the south.[55] The highly exposed garrisons at both Santa Fe and San Antonio were to have seventy-six soldiers instead of the forty-three assigned to the presidios on the line and were to be linked to the cordon by outlying detachments—one stationed at Robledo, between Santa Fe and El Paso, and one at Cíbolo, between San Antonio and La Bahía. Presidios at Santa Fe and San Antonio would bring the total to seventeen; seven presidios were to be shut down entirely, representing a substantial savings to the Crown.

Rubí also recommended modifying the presidial fortifications. Their designs seemed anachronistic by European standards and their materials and strategic sites appeared deficient. The presidio at San Sabá exemplified many of the weaknesses that offended the sensibilities of these European-trained officers. The limestone fort stood on a site between two deep gulches, or *barrancas*, that provided cover for hostile Indians approaching it. Ditches and perimeter walls designed to protect the presidio seemed better suited as sanctuaries for forces that might attempt to assault it. The structure itself, a square enclosure, had towers on two corners from which troops could cover the approaches to the four walls. One of the towers, however, did not protrude sufficiently from the two adjacent walls to give defenders an angle to fire along them, and the towers' poorly constructed parapets, made of piles of unmortared stones, seemed likely to collapse under enemy fire.[56]

For the marqués de Rubí and his staff, serious flaws in construction and choice of site were endemic to frontier presidios, and the king agreed. He required that future presidial fortifications be built nearer water and pasturage and constructed according to standardized designs drawn up by the engineer Nicolás de Lafora.[57] The new specifications exceeded local resources, however, and were usually ignored or modified. The Santa Fe presidio, for example, was rebuilt in 1791 of adobe rather than stone as Lafora's plan required; after eighteen years, its walls began to collapse. Some of the newer presidios were constructed of better materials and with more sophisticated designs than their predecessors, but that seldom made them more effective.[58] Old as well as new presidios enjoyed reputations as secure places of refuge from hostile Indians, due less to the refinements of design than to Indian reluctance to incur heavy losses by laying siege to a fortification, however crudely constructed. Indians never overran a fortified presidio in a direct attack, but that was usually not their goal. Rather than occupy a position, they generally favored swift attacks to capture horses or gain revenge. Even at San Sabá, the numerous Comanches and their allies who seized the mission in 1758 stopped short of a direct assault on the nearby presidio.[59]

The *Regulations of 1772* also adhered to European ideals rather than local realities in their prescriptions for soldiers. They described in detail standardized modes of dress, weapons, and accoutrements and spelled out the number of horses that each soldier must have—"six serviceable horses, one colt, and one mule."[60] According to one estimate, the regulations required the properly equipped presidial soldier to carry 123 pounds of accoutrements, in addition to food and water. This heavy equipment included a knee-length sleeveless leather coat, designed to deflect Indian arrows. Made of seven layers of buckskin, the coat alone weighed 18 pounds and served, in the words of one historian, "as both a life-preserver and a strait-jacket."[61] This distinctive coat, however, gave the frontier troops their name, *soldados de cuera*, or "leather-jacketted soldiers." Ideally, then, the individual presidial soldier was a mounted arsenal leading his own cavalcade. Like the presidios themselves, soldiers functioned well as defense units, but their weighty equipment prevented them from effective pursuit, and the cloud of dust that their animals raised made it difficult for them to launch surprise attacks.

Since soldiers had to purchase their own uniforms, weapons, saddlery, and mounts, as well as feed and clothe themselves and their families, the *Regulations* also addressed the problems of assuring a supply of fairly priced, high-quality goods at remote frontier commissaries and of distributing equitably the military payroll to the troops. For two centuries, these closely related problems had defied solution in Florida, northern Mexico, and other corners of the empire. Officers had commonly extorted pay from their own soldiers or paid them in shoddy goods at inflated prices. In New

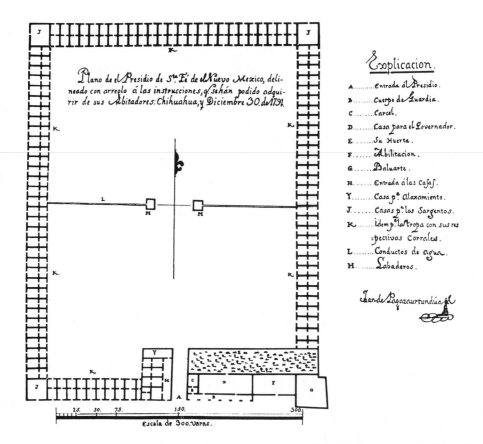

40. Plan of the Presidio of Santa Fe, 1791. From Marc Simmons, Spanish Government in New Mexico *(Albuquerque: University of New Mexico Press, 1969). Courtesy, Marc Simmons and the University
of New Mexico Press.*

Mexico, as one Franciscan described the situation in 1760, soldiers' pay amounted to
400 pesos a year, but they saw none of it in cash. They received 150 pesos in the form of
"clothing of the poorest quality, and the remainder is paid in supplies; whether they
want them or not they must take them."[62] Soldiers who challenged the system seldom
won a fair hearing, for frontier governors were themselves officers and often personally involved in extortion and price-gouging.[63] Quarrels over the spoils turned officer
against officer, and consumed time that might have been spent on conducting Indian
wars. Meanwhile, the system demoralized ordinary soldiers, whose prosperity had
come to depend on their own ability to raise their food and to find other sources of
income.

Little wonder, then, that the *Regulations of 1772* devoted considerable attention to
ways of safeguarding presidial payrolls and supplies from corrupt officers, including
the outright prohibition that governors and presidial commanders "are not to participate in any manner whatsoever in the buying of provisions and equipment for their

41. *A* soldado de cuera, *drawn circa 1803 by Ramón de Murillo to accompany a proposal to cut the heavy thigh-length leather coat to jacket size, as shown here. Courtesy, Archivo General de Indias, Seville (Uniformes 71).*

garrisons."[64] Notwithstanding the efforts of some frontier commanders to end shabby practices, the *Regulations* did little to weed corruption out of a society in which public office had long been regarded as a legitimate source of private profit. Soldiers continued to see their pay siphoned off through the cupidity and mismanagement of their officers and suppliers.[65]

Finally, the *Regulations* also sought to set higher standards of military conduct and to improve military instruction and drill. These new rules apparently had some effect in professionalizing the frontier forces, but local realities mitigated against their full implementation. Overworked soldiers, whose duties often took them away from presidios, had little time for training, and officers and soldiers born in the provinces had low regard for European military drill. Yet, notwithstanding that their training seemed shabby by European standards, there is reason to believe that the presidial forces were better suited than the regular army for arduous frontier service. Some observers described them as skilled horseman, courageous, and remarkably tough. An officer writing in 1776 admired the "hardiness, courage and steadfastness. . . . They will endure risk, fatigue or hunger."[66]

Most of the articles in the *Regulations of 1772*, then, offered traditional European military solutions to uniquely American problems. Those solutions might improve the frontier army's efficiency, but they fell short of a prescription for containing Indian raiders who enjoyed numerical superiority and had few fixed positions to attack. Rubí had tacitly acknowledged the unlikely prospects for a strictly military strategy. Although he had recommended a "continuous offensive war" aimed at exterminating Apaches and other intractable tribes, he had also advocated taking women and children prisoner so that hostile Indians could not reproduce themselves.[67] He also recommended forming alliances with Comanches and the Nations of the North, whom he saw as enemies of the Apaches. Rubí's understanding of the limitations of a military approach was also clear in his argument for building a defensive line of presidios. Spain, he said, should attempt to control only those regions that it actually occupied—"what should be called the dominion and true possession of the king."[68] A retreat to the 30th parallel, Rubí recognized, ran "contrary to the rule of pushing domination forward," but he suggested that Spain needed first to consolidate its position by filling in the open spaces that separated the interior provinces from New Spain's population centers before expanding farther north to Canada or to California.[69]

IV

Like the *Regulations of 1729*, the *Regulations of 1772* might have been quietly ignored as expressions of royal intent had they not received support at the highest levels of government and included a provision for a high-ranking officer to enforce them. Inspired by a plan drawn up by José de Gálvez, a special emissary sent to New Spain by Carlos III in 1765, the *Regulations of 1772* called for the immediate appointment of a *comandante inspector*, or inspector in chief, who would provide central command for the frontier army.[70] The inspector in chief had authority to force presidial captains to implement the new regulations, to plan comprehensive strategies, and to launch coordinated offenses that involved forces from presidios in several provinces. Large-scale coordination had not been a feature of frontier military policy, and Apaches and other tribes had taken advantage of Spanish disunity to attack one province then flee to another for sanctuary.

The inspector in chief had jurisdiction over the presidios throughout the interior provinces: Texas, Coahuila, New Mexico, Nueva Vizcaya, Sonora, Sinaloa, and Alta and Baja California.[71] In 1769, Spain had begun to occupy Alta California, establishing presidios at San Diego and Monterey to forestall foreign settlement on the Pacific coast. In practice, the new California presidios received little personal attention from the inspector in chief, whose preoccupation with depredations by Indians left him with little time to contemplate theoretical incursions by foreigners in remote California.

First to occupy the office of inspector in chief was an Irishman, Lt. Col. Hugo O'Conor. One of the many Wild Geese—Irish Catholics who fled to the continent to

seek service with the enemies of England—Dublin-born O'Conor had found a home
in the Spanish army. He had come to New Spain in 1765 to join the military mission of
Lt. Gen. Juan de Villalba and had held a number of posts on the northern frontier
including that of provisional governor of Texas from 1767 to 1770, during the time the
marqués de Rubí had inspected the province. Among some Indians, his red hair earned
him the nickname *capitán colorado* or "Captain Red."[72] O'Conor was promoted to
colonel and named inspector in chief of the interior provinces in September 1772,
after the king approved the new *Regulations*.[73] O'Conor owed this appointment to his
influential older cousin, Field Marshal Alejandro O'Reilly, who had imposed Spanish
rule on Louisiana in 1769.[74]

Making his headquarters in Nueva Vizcaya, the most central of the interior provinces, O'Conor worked vigorously on all fronts. At the same time that he led several
coordinated offensives against Apaches and other tribes, he traveled widely to oversee
the complex realignment of the frontier presidios, making many of the changes recommended by Rubí. Easier to imagine than to orchestrate, the relocation of presidios
entailed more than moving military personnel and equipment. It also required trans-
porting soldiers' families and other civilians, marshaling scarce labor for new construction, and maintaining a solid defensive posture during the transition.[75]

To the north of the present U.S.-Mexico border, O'Conor moved or shut down all
but three presidios—those at Santa Fe, San Antonio, and La Bahía. In New Mexico,
O'Conor moved the El Paso garrison south to Carrizal in northern Nueva Vizcaya. In
Sonora, Terrenate was moved in 1776, from an inhospitable rocky hill below the
present-day border, some fifty miles north to the San Pedro Valley, not far from
present Tombstone. In this exposed position, Apaches pounded it badly, inflicting
heavy casualties and preventing the soldiers from harvesting their crops or completing
the elaborate structure. Within five years, the site was abandoned and the garrison
retreated to still another site farther south.[76] In 1776, also following O'Conor's
orders, the Tubac garrison moved forty miles north to the Pima village of Tucson,
beyond the line that Rubí had recommended. Tucson had a good supply of wood,
water, and the labor of mission Indians who had already fortified the village, and it also
stood along a newly opened overland route to California. The fate of the new presidio
at Tucson hung in the balance for many years, but it survived several Apache assaults to
become the center of a small community of Hispanics, Pimas, and peaceful Apaches by
the century's end.[77]

This costly repositioning of men and fortifications did little to win a reprieve for
Hispanic communities to the north of the line. In the 1770s, Indians killed at least 243
Hispanics in New Mexico alone—the most in any decade in the century. There,
Pedro Fermín de Mendinueta led numerous campaigns of Hispanics and Pueblo
Indian allies against hostile Indians and won occasional victories during a decade as
governor, but at the end of his term the situation remained gloomy. Indian depreda-
tions, he reported in 1777, had reduced New Mexico "to the most deplorable state and

greatest poverty."[78] Short of men, horses, and arms to mount an effective offense, Mendinueta advocated a defensive posture, a local variant of Rubí's strategy. All of New Mexico, Mendinueta said, was a frontier zone, excessively exposed to Indian attacks because settlers insisted on living in scattered ranches and farms. He urged that they be compelled to live in tight communities, in imitation of the Pueblos, where they might at least defend themselves effectively. In addition, he needed two more presidios, one at Taos, New Mexico's most northerly settlement.[79]

O'Conor's most vexing problems to the north of the line, however, involved the Texas-Louisiana frontier. There, he had to shut down the presidios of San Agustín de Ahumada and Los Adaes, where he once served as captain and acting governor, and supervise a Spanish retreat from an area that no longer served a defensive purpose since Louisiana had passed into Spanish hands.[80] As the *Regulations of 1772* required, soldiers, missionaries, and some 500 settlers from the area around the decaying wooden presidio of Los Adaes, many of them recent arrivals from Spanish Louisiana, were forced to resettle in San Antonio, the new capital of Texas, in 1773. The unhappy refugees immediately petitioned to return to their former homes, but O'Conor refused to permit it. He feared that East Texas would become a center for contraband trade with Englishmen and the source of more firearms for Indians. Meanwhile, the group's leader, a prosperous rancher and smuggler named Antonio Gil Ybarbo, journeyed to Mexico City where he convinced the viceroy, Antonio María de Bucareli, that settlers in East Texas would help maintain friendly relations with Indians and keep on the lookout for Englishmen.

Bucareli overruled O'Conor. In 1774 the viceroy permitted the settlers to return to eastern Texas—but only as far as the Trinity River, some 175 miles from Natchitoches. Where the trail from San Antonio to Los Adaes crossed the Trinity, Ybarbo and his compatriots founded the town of Nuestra Señora de Pilar de Bucareli, named after their viceregal patron. Five years later, after Comanches menaced the community, the settlers moved on their own initiative, farther east to the site of the old mission of Nacogdoches. The new town of Nacogdoches, founded in early 1779, came to rival San Antonio in importance through the end of the colonial period for it became, as O'Conor had predicted, an important center for contraband. Spain did not establish another presidio in East Texas, but Ybarbo was put on the payroll as an Indian agent.[81]

O'Conor's concern that Hispanic settlements in East Texas would become centers for contraband firearms and powder had been well founded. Shortly after acquiring Louisiana from France, Spanish officials had recognized the futility of using missionaries or military means alone to control the colony's large Indian population or to defend its new border with England at the Mississippi.[82] Instead, Spanish officials sought to win the loyalty of Louisiana tribes through trade, and thus prevent their defection to the British. To do so, Spain found it expedient to continue the French policies to which Indians had been accustomed. Thus, upon taking charge of Loui-

siana in 1767, Gov. Antonio de Ulloa had authorized the sale of firearms and munitions to "those nations accustomed to obtaining them," although he had prohibited
the sale of alcohol.[83] "The method followed here to keep them peaceful and friendly is
to give them presents . . . and to assure them that trade will be kept up," Ulloa had
explained to a dubious Hugo O'Conor, who then held the position of governor of
Texas.[84]

To implement the French policy in Louisiana, Spain licensed many of the French
traders themselves, who had stayed on to become Spanish subjects. Chief among them
was Athanase de Mézières, related by his first marriage to the powerful family of St.
Denis. In 1769, O'Reilly had put De Mézières in charge of the sensitive Natchitoches
district where Saint-Denis once reigned. There, Indian hostility toward Spaniards
had run deep, but De Mézières and his agents had effectively countered it, not only in
western Louisiana, but across northern Texas. By dispensing or withholding trade, De
Mézières had won alliances for Spain with a number of the well-armed Wichita
peoples whom the Spaniards termed the Nations of the North, including Tawakonis
and Taovayas. Until the death of De Mézières in 1779, Natchitoches, not San Antonio, directed Indian policy in the northern reaches of Texas.[85] Meanwhile, to the
east, Spaniards had welcomed Indians from the English side of the Mississippi, hoping
to draw them into the Spanish orbit to erect a barrier of loyal Indians who would block
English expansion.

The French model that Spain adopted for Louisiana troubled Spanish officials in
the interior provinces of New Spain. Most worrisome to them, ever greater numbers
of arms and ammunition seemed to filter westward into the hands of Indians hostile to
Hispanic frontiersmen. By 1772, Viceroy Bucareli understood that Comanches and
Apaches as well as the Nations of the North had such an "abundance of guns, powder
and ball," that many had abandoned their traditional weapons. The firearms, Bucareli
had learned, came not only from English traders beyond the Mississippi, but from
Spanish Louisiana itself.[86] Despite such disquieting reports, neither Bucareli nor
O'Conor had sufficient authority to prevent Louisiana traders from operating among
Texas tribes, or to alter Spain's new policy in Louisiana.[87] Louisiana did fall within the
viceroyalty of New Spain, but it came under the immediate supervision of the captain
general of Havana and had its own military regulations, army, and militia. Spain's
troops on the Mississippi, stationed there more to defend Louisiana, Texas, and New
Mexico from British invasion than from Indians, lay outside of O'Conor's jurisdiction.[88] Thus two Indian policies, one bellicose and one based on trade and negotiation, coexisted uncomfortably.

Despite the ongoing tensions on the Texas-Louisiana frontier, O'Conor and Bucareli optimistically believed that by exerting force and following Rubí's plan of creating
a line of presidios "from sea to sea," they were making substantial progress in pacifying
the frontier.[89] Few officials close to the scene, however, would have agreed. The
realignment of presidios had diverted the military from campaigns against hostile

Apaches, whose depredations increased in some areas during O'Conor's tenure, and the impregnable cordon line of presidios had proved remarkably permeable. Rubí himself had described the presidio at San Sabá as a place that "affords as much protection to the interests of His Majesty in New Spain as a ship anchored in mid-Atlantic would afford in preventing foreign trade with America."[90] The same observation might have applied to most of the fortifications spaced at 100-mile intervals along the line. Apaches traveled between them with ease, continuing to plunder to the south of the cordon where they now found some communities undefended because their presidios had been abandoned or moved.[91]

V

O'Conor had further plans to bring greater military pressure to bear on Apaches, but his work was interrupted by an announcement from Madrid that dramatically changed the governing structure of the interior provinces of New Spain. In May of 1776, Carlos III removed the interior provinces from the viceroy's jurisdiction and brought them under the Crown's direct control. As inspector in chief of the interior provinces, O'Conor would continue to supervise military affairs, but he would now serve under an official with broad civil and military authority, a person who combined the offices of governor and commander in chief (*comandante general*) and who reported directly to the king. Disappointed at being passed over for the position, O'Conor apparently feigned illness and resigned as inspector in chief in January 1777.[92]

This new administrative structure, the Comandancia General of the Interior Provinces of New Spain, had been under study since José de Gálvez proposed it in 1768. Carlos III had approved it in principle in 1769 and alluded to it in the *Regulations of 1772*.[93] The plan was not implemented, however, until Gálvez assumed the position of secretary of the Indies, on January 30, 1776; three and a half months later, Carlos III created the Comandancia General.[94]

An autonomous government for the interior provinces promised to improve the efficiency of the region's administration and to promote its economic growth—major goals of Bourbon administration. Carlos III saw a clear link between the growth of the frontier population and the region's ability to defend itself. Distant and preoccupied with other matters, Mexico's viceroys had not and could not give adequate personal attention to the development of the far north. Upon taking office in 1772, for example, Viceroy Bucareli had complained of "the chaos of difficulties which enclose me in the confused management of these vast provinces . . . I walk in shadows."[95] Unfortunately, the viceroy and the new commander in chief continued to walk in shadows for their lines of authority overlapped. The Comandancia General was semi-autonomous at best. Although independent of the viceroy in theory, the Comandancia General remained within the Viceroyalty of New Spain, and its commander in chief was required to keep the viceroy informed of his activities and he depended on the viceroy for supplies. All supplies and communications bound for the Interior Provinces continued to enter Mexico through Veracruz.[96]

First to head the Comandancia General of the Interior Provinces was another foreigner with connections in high places, French-born Teodoro de Croix, nephew of the marqués de Croix, the former viceroy of New Spain.[97] His jurisdiction included the Californias, Sonora, Sinaloa, Nueva Vizcaya, New Mexico, Texas, and Coahuila— the same area over which O'Conor had had military supervision.[98] Teodoro de Croix had served in the Spanish army for nearly thirty years before receiving his appointment to the interior provinces in 1776, but his prior experience in New Spain had been brief, coinciding with the years that his uncle had served as viceroy, from 1766 to 1771.

Croix began his long tenure as governor and commander in chief, which lasted from 1776 to 1783, believing in a military solution to the Indian problem—as Rubí and O'Conor had before him. Appalled at the notion of defending an 1,800-mile frontier with fewer than 2,000 troops, Croix appealed repeatedly to the king and the viceroy for more soldiers; meanwhile, he laid plans for a massive offensive against Apaches. Croix's instructions required him to abide by the *Regulations of 1772*, and he continued O'Conor's program to curtail the abuses that Rubí had identified. Like Rubí and O'Conor, Croix believed in a rational arrangement of presidios, but he regarded the new line as badly conceived and porous and he relocated some of the

42. Teodoro de Croix. From Alfred Barnaby Thomas, ed. and trans., Teodoro de Croix and the Northern Frontier of New Spain, 1776–1783 *(Norman: University of Oklahoma Press, 1941). Courtesy, University of Oklahoma Press.*

presidios.[99] Croix also studied his predecessors' reports, toured much of his jurisdiction, and began to make more efficient use of the resources available to him. In so doing, he drew on the years of experience of the frontier officers who served under him. As a result, he began to modify the frontier army to meet frontier conditions, rather than trying to impose rigid European modes of warfare onto the frontier.[100]

One of Croix's most important innovations was the creation of special "light troops," or *tropa ligera*, in 1778. Croix's tropa ligera operated without the rigid eighteen-pound leather jacket, the three-pound lance, the four-pound shield, and some of the other gear that regulations required. Less encumbered than the leather-jacketted soldiers, the light troops moved more rapidly, required fewer horses, and could fight on foot. They also needed fewer supplies. Croix used the savings from this and other innovations to increase the number of troops under his command by nearly 50 percent, from some 1,900 to 2,840.[101] He employed these additional troops not only to defend the line, but also to form a second tier of defense below the line in order to intercept Indians who poured through it and to maintain pressure on hostile tribes who lived below the line—an unpleasant reality largely overlooked by the *Regulations of 1772.*

Another of Croix's innovations was to work actively to shift the balance of power by building alliances. He began, for example, to implement a strategy, suggested by the marqués de Rubí and others, to ally with Comanches and to turn their enmity toward Apaches to Spain's advantage.[102] Croix adopted that policy only after weighing the alternative—making an alliance with the Lipán Apaches, and enlisting their aid against the Comanches. At the same time he courted Comanches, Croix instructed officials in Texas and Louisiana to enlist the aid of the Nations of the North, who had recently been won over to the Spanish side, so they might join Comanches to make war on Apaches.[103]

By enlisting more Indian allies and raising the numbers and efficiency of the presidial troops, Croix hoped to launch a concerted, coast-to-coast offensive that would exterminate the Apaches—a policy that the marqués de Rubí had also advocated, the *Regulations of 1772* had endorsed, and O'Conor had begun. As in the case of O'Conor, Croix's plans to launch a large-scale campaign against Apaches were thwarted by events beyond his control. In orders of February 20, 1779, the secretary of the Indies, José de Gálvez, explained to Croix that imminent war with England prevented Spain from sending reinforcements to the interior provinces. Gálvez instructed Croix to abandon plans for an offensive and to concentrate on defense.[104]

Croix's final years as commander in chief of the Comandancia General of the Interior Provinces coincided with Spain's war with England. Inventive by necessity as well as disposition, he continued to implement reforms and economies that made the frontier military more efficient, including the creation of presidial companies manned by Indian auxiliaries. His immediate successors, Felipe de Neve (1783–84) and José Antonio Rengel (1785–86), benefited from those reforms as the crisis with England passed and they resumed offensive war against the Apaches.[105] Croix's successors, however, also enjoyed an increasingly flexible Indian policy that marked the end of military escalation and the beginning of a new era of relatively peaceful relations with the indios bárbaros in the interior provinces.

VI

The likelihood of war with England and its claim on scarce resources had apparently prompted José de Gálvez to reevaluate Spanish Indian policy in the interior provinces. Gálvez had concluded that military victory over the Apaches was impossible, at least for the moment. Instead of offensive war, he had urged Croix in 1779 to win the allegiance of Apaches and other hostile tribes through diplomacy, gifts, and trade, so that they would come to prefer the Spanish way of life over their own. To make trade more attractive and to increase Indian dependency on Spaniards, Gálvez reversed a long-standing policy and suggested that firearms be traded to Indians.[106]

Gálvez's instructions of 1779 represented a shift in official policy based on long experience. In practice, Spanish officers and officials had displayed greater pragmatism than is usually supposed, including in the distribution of arms to friendly Indians and in the use of diplomacy and trade. In northern New Spain two centuries before, officials had determined that war against the Chichimecas was unwinnable and had abandoned warfare in favor of diplomacy. In the interior provinces the most successful Indian policy had been crafted by officers such as New Mexico Gov. Tomás Vélez Cachupín, who emphasized trade, fair treatment, and alliances.[107] Most recently, as Gálvez knew, the French trading model had worked remarkably well in Louisiana and its success there had probably been behind his decision to urge a similar policy for the interior provinces in 1779.

As secretary of the Indies, José de Gálvez had received favorable reports on the French policy in Louisiana from his young nephew and protégé, Bernardo de Gálvez, whose appointment as acting governor José de Gálvez had arranged in late 1776.[108] Bernardo de Gálvez had firsthand experience in both Louisiana and the interior provinces. As a precocious and well-connected young officer assigned to Chihuahua, he had acquired a deep and respectful understanding of Apaches along with an arrow wound in his arm and a lance wound in his chest.[109] Several years later, as acting governor of Louisiana, Bernardo de Gálvez had the opportunity to observe, as he explained to his uncle, "the way in which the English and the French treat or have treated their Indians," making them utterly dependent on Europeans. Through trade and gifts, Indians had received "sundry conveniences of life of whose existence they previously knew nothing, and which now they look upon as indispensable." Those conveniences included guns and gunpowder which, Gálvez believed, had caused Indians to forget the use of the bow and arrow, and to depend on Europeans for the means to hunt and to defend themselves.[110]

43. Bernardo de Gálvez. From Manuel Rivera Cambas, Los gobernantes de México *(Mexico, 1872–73). Courtesy, the Vargas Project, University of New Mexico.*

In 1778, Bernardo de Gálvez had urged his uncle to adopt the Louisiana model for the interior provinces. Although he had no illusions that trade would alter Indian cultures rapidly, he thought it better than a costly and ineffective war. Through trade, he argued, "the King would keep them very contented for ten years with what he now spends in one year in making war upon them."[111] Conversely, he doubted that Spain's relatively few troops could win a war against Apaches in the interior provinces—"an expanse equal to that from Madrid to Constantinople."[112] Bernardo de Gálvez was not the first high-ranking official to recommend that Spain adopt French Indian policies, including trade in guns and munitions, but it was probably his recommendations that prompted José de Gálvez to bring the Indian policy of the interior provinces into greater harmony with that of Louisiana.[113]

Whatever their source, José de Gálvez's temporary orders of 1779 became the foundation of a new Indian policy for the interior provinces—one that his nephew would articulate with exquisite cynicism in a more permanent document seven years later—the famous *Instructions of 1786.* As a result of his heroic conduct during the American Revolution and his uncle's penchant for nepotism, Bernardo de Gálvez succeeded his father, Matías de Gálvez, as viceroy of New Spain in 1785. Enjoying his uncle's confidence, Bernardo de Gálvez was also given direct responsibility for the

Comandancia General of the Interior Provinces, which temporarily lost their semi-autonomous status. After reviewing Spain's Indian policy, the new viceroy issued a set of instructions to the commander in chief of the Interior Provinces, Jacobo Ugarte, that reiterated his sentiments, and those of his uncle, that Spain could not win a war against the Apaches.[114] The escalation of military expenditures, the increase of troops, the rearrangement of presidios, the passage of "wise rules" for governing the Interior Provinces and the management of military forces, had produced little result.[115]

Gálvez's *Instructions* cogently summarized recent Spanish policy, reconciled conflicting practices, and offered some innovations.[116] Henceforth, Spanish Indian policy would have three facets: first, the maintenance of military pressure on Indians, to the point of exterminating Apaches if necessary; second, continued reliance on building alliances—"the vanquishment of the heathen," he coldly noted, "consists in obliging them to destroy one another";[117] third, Indians who sought peace were to be made dependent on Spaniards through gifts and trade. Gifts, he continued to believe, were cheaper than war and more effective than the "useless reinforcements of troops."[118]

Bernardo de Gálvez surpassed his uncle in providing a reasoned rationale for increasing Indian dependency, a policy that he termed "peace by deceit."[119] He ordered, for example, that those Indians who had no acquaintance with alcohol be introduced to it and encouraged to acquire a taste for it, "creating for them a new necessity which will oblige them to recognize their dependence upon us more directly."[120] Like his uncle, he urged that Indians be furnished with firearms and ammunition, but he specified that guns be made of poorly tempered metal with long barrels that would make them awkward to use and easy to break. Natives, then, would depend upon Spaniards for repairs or replacement. As to ammunition, Gálvez believed that Indians should be given an abundance of it. The more they used powder and shot, he believed, the less they would use the arrows. Soon, they would "begin to lose their skill in handling the bow," which Gálvez correctly believed was a more effective weapon than the firearm.[121] In short, Gálvez planned to use tried-and-true English and French practices to destroy the basis of native culture as the first step toward turning nomadic

44. A Spanish escopeta—*a light, smoothbore, muzzle-loading musket widely used on the frontier of New Spain in the eighteenth century. Courtesy, Arizona Historical Society, Tucson.*

Indians into Spaniards, accomplishing with the iron fist and the velvet glove what missionaries had been unable do to do through less violent and cynical means.

Modified and refined, the *Instructions of 1786*, together with the *Regulations of 1772*, governed Spanish-Indian relations on the northern frontier for the remainder of the colonial period. Like other official policies, however, they were not fully implemented. Strapped for funds and arms for its own army, Spain never had sufficient resources to buy a peace. Nor is there evidence that Spain provided significant amounts of alcohol to Indians. To the contrary, Gálvez's recommendation regarding liquor was not adopted and officials continued the traditional Spanish policy of restricting the distribution of alcohol, even in Louisiana. The new policies apparently met greatest success in areas where Spain did not have to compete with English or American traders,[122] but across northern New Spain Gálvez's *Instructions* did establish clear rules under which some of Spain's ablest officers could play a new game. Henceforward, minor infractions of the peace by individual Indians were to be overlooked as Spanish Indian policy followed Gálvez's dictum: "A bad peace . . . would be more fruitful than the gains of a successful war."[123]

VII

Trade, treaties, and toleration, previously subordinate to force, became the cornerstones of a new French-inspired Indian policy. Rarely used on earlier frontiers by Spaniards, written treaties came into vogue, implying respectful dealings between sovereign peoples and replacing the earlier Spanish assumption that Indians were vassals of the king.[124] Along with silver-headed canes, or *bastones*, uniforms, and suits of clothing, Spanish officials began to bestow banners and medals on Indian leaders. These secular symbols of allegiance to the Spanish Crown were distributed wherever Indians had come to expect them from Frenchmen or Englishmen; Spain had to compete.[125]

The new policy began to show results in the interior provinces well before Bernardo de Gálvez reformulated it in 1786. One of the most notable successes occurred in New Mexico under the leadership of Juan Bautista de Anza, a third generation presidial officer whose father had been killed by Apaches on the Sonora frontier. As governor of New Mexico from 1778–87, Anza won an enduring peace with Comanches, who had been the scourge of the province since midcentury. In February of 1786, Anza and Ecueracapa, the designated leader of one of the main bands of the so-called western Comanches (including Yamparikas and Yupes), signed a treaty of peace and alliance that lasted for the next generation. Anza skillfully negotiated this agreement without rupturing longtime Spanish alliances with two groups whose enmity toward Comanches was well known: the flexible Jicarilla Apaches who farmed and hunted in the Sangre de Cristos of northern New Mexico, and Utes who lived in the Rockies to the northwest of New Mexico. Once he had come to terms with Comanches, Anza went on to lay the foundation for an alliance with Navajos, who were soon persuaded to turn on their former allies, the Gileño Apaches.

Anza owed these feats of diplomacy in part to the military pressure that he had exerted on Comanches. In 1779, accompanied by the usual contingent of Pueblo allies, he had led Spanish forces into southeastern Colorado where he smashed a Comanche camp and killed a prominent war chief, Cuerno Verde. The unusual victory had apparently earned him the grudging respect of Comanches as well as of other tribes. In the next few years, as Comanche bands sought to make peace with Anza, he patiently insisted that he would not negotiate unless all Comanche leaders participated. Anza's diplomatic success also benefited from the initiative of his counterpart in Texas, Gov. Domingo Cabello, who had signed a treaty with the eastern Comanches the previous autumn, after using his alliances with the Nations of the North to bring more pressure on them. To a considerable extent, then, the military reforms and greater coordination between frontier provinces had paid dividends for New Mexico.[126]

But Spaniards had entered into agreements with Comanche bands on previous occasions. Gov. Tomás Vélez Cachupín had negotiated peace agreements in 1752 and 1762, as had Gov. Pedro Fermín de Mendinueta in 1771.[127] Anza and his successors, however, were able to maintain the peace with Comanches in large part because peace rather than war had become the goal of Spanish policy, because Spaniards now had more to offer Comanches than the absence of war, and because Comanches themselves saw benefits in the new arrangements. New Mexico officials now offered arms, ammunition, and gifts, including clothing, hats, mirrors, orange paint, indigo, knives, cigars, and sugarloaves.[128] They also offered access to trade fairs, cooperation against mutual enemies, and more equitable and consistent treatment than Indians had been accustomed to receiving in the past. An important part of the deal that Anza offered Ecueracapa in 1786 was the promise to regulate the trade fair at Taos, where Comanches often felt cheated by double-dealing New Mexican traders.[129]

Anza's successor, Fernando de la Concha, a Spanish-born career officer who served as governor of New Mexico from 1787–93, continued to use the liberal dispensation of gifts and regulated trade to maintain alliances with the Comanches, Utes, and Jicarilla Apaches, and to strengthen relations with Navajos.[130] Through the end of his term, Concha believed that all four allied tribes remained firmly in the Spanish orbit. He singled out Comanches, once viewed by Spaniards as faithless, for special praise: "in this tribe one finds faith in the treaties that it acknowledges, true constancy, [and] good hospitality."[131]

Under Concha, Comanches and Navajos in particular joined with Spanish forces to increase military pressure on Gileños, Chiricahuas, Mimbreños, and other Apaches. Meanwhile, Apaches were squeezed from the south. From Sonora and Nueva Vizcaya, Spaniards and their Opata and Pima allies coordinated campaigns against Apaches with New Mexicans and their Indian allies. The war against these indios bárbaros, who

45. The Comanche warrior His-oo-san-chees, "The Little Spaniard," described by George Catlin as "half Spanish . . . being a half-breed." A lithograph based on a painting by Catlin, 1834. Catlin, North American Indians *(1844). Courtesy, the Vargas Project, University of New Mexico.*

refused to conform to the ways of so-called civilized people, was waged without pity. Beginning at least as early as 1787, Spaniards offered rewards for pairs of Apache ears.[132] By the 1790s it was common to ship Apache prisoners of war, including women and children, from New Spain to Havana, so they might never escape and return to their people as earlier deportees to Mexico City had done. Shackled, incarcerated en route, and exposed to new diseases, most failed to survive the ordeal of the journey to the Caribbean. Those who did generally spent the remainder of their lives in some form of forced labor.[133]

As the balance of power shifted in favor of the Spanish forces, many Apaches began to sue for peace and its attendant benefits—not only in southern New Mexico, but across the northern frontier. The turning point in the Apache-Spanish relations occurred during the administration of the experienced and exceptionally able Jacobo de Ugarte, who served as commander in chief of the Interior Provinces from 1786–90.

On the western front, in Sonora and western Nueva Vizcaya, Spaniards regarded many of the bands of Gileños, Chiricahuas, and Mimbreños as at peace by mid-1790.[134] On the eastern front, from southeastern New Mexico through Texas, a shakier and uneven peace reigned with Faraones, Mescaleros, and Lipanes.[135]

Peace with these different Apache bands was never as firm or as enduring as that with Comanches, but raids and occasional outbreaks of war notwithstanding, contemporaries recognized that they had entered a new era. A number of Apaches accepted the Spaniards' offer to make peace more attractive than war and settled in *establecimientos de paz*—peace establishments that resembled later-day Indian reservations. By 1793, some 2,000 Apaches de paz, or *mansos*, had settled onto eight establecimientos—one just outside the walls of the presidio at Tucson.[136] As they had since the sixteenth century, Spanish policymakers still envisioned turning Indians into town-dwelling Spanish Catholics who farmed, ranched, and practiced familiar trades. Even when issuing the harshest of military orders, the Crown never failed to remind officials that religious conversion was the principal reason for Spain's presence on the frontiers of empire. Where missionaries had failed among nomads, however, soldiers were to play the role of benevolent Indian agents. To Apaches who agreed to surrender and settle in establecimientos, soldiers were to distribute weekly rations of corn, meat, tobacco, and sweets and to offer instruction in the ways of Spaniards. Much as Franciscans had tried to enter into Indian cultures by learning their languages, Spanish officers now stressed speaking native languages and making greater use of interpreters to assure accurate communication.[137]

Viewed in the most optimistic light, the establecimientos de paz could themselves become agencies to pacify other nomads. As New Mexico Governor Concha explained in 1792, prosperous settlements of Apaches would weaken the resistance of bands who remained "dispersed in the empty Sierras with nothing but wild foods to eat, stealing to live." Those Apaches would find Spanish life irresistible and "solicit peace in order to enjoy the same benefits as their companions."[138]

A considerable gap existed, of course, between the ideal and the real. Critics argued that soldiers corrupted Apaches and failed to teach them to farm or ranch—although some Apaches already possessed those skills—and that Indians who enjoyed Spanish largesse continued to raid at will. Franciscans in particular argued that the system neglected the Indians' spiritual welfare.[139] Many Indians, on the other hand, found settled life confining or in conflict with their values. A group of Comanches, for example, installed themselves in new houses at San Carlos de los Yupes on the Arkansas River in southeastern Colorado in 1787 but moved away in less than a year when a woman died and custom required family and friends to abandon the site of a death.[140] Raiding, which brought prestige as well as economic benefits to Apaches, also proved difficult to forswear.[141] A settlement of Gileño Apaches on the Rio Grande, near Sabinal, lasted for just four years, from 1790–94.[142] But despite some failures and defections, a number of the Apache reservations enjoyed a long life, especially in Sonora, and endured even through times of scarcity when Spaniards failed to fulfill their promises of food and supplies.[143] Two generations later, American officials inaugurated a reservation system with similar characteristics, unaware of the earlier Spanish experiments.[144]

VIII

In the last decade of the eighteenth century, then, the northern frontier of New Spain entered a period of relative peace that owed more to diplomacy and a mutual desire for peace and trade than to military and administrative reform.[145] Military escalation, coordinated punitive expeditions, and administrative restructuring had not in themselves forced Indians to negotiate. The military buildup had reached its height under Teodoro de Croix by the early 1780s; thereafter, the number of soldiers and the number and position of presidios remained static.[146] The advantages of a centralized command for the interior provinces had diminished after 1786, when José de Gálvez placed the northern frontier back under the immediate supervision of the viceroy, his nephew. Thereafter, the office of commander in chief underwent numerous redefinitions of jurisdiction in relation to viceroys and to other frontier commanders. The frequency of these administrative changes mitigated against continuity of policy, intensified bureaucratic infighting (generally intense in any event), and lessened the efficiency of military operations.[147]

The mantle of peace had fallen over the frontier mainly because Spanish and Indian leaders had come to believe, as Bernardo de Gálvez hoped they would, that they had more to gain from peace than from war. Spanish officials had arrived at this understanding slowly, only after Indians had forced them to the bargaining table and extracted from them more gifts, fairer and more open trading arrangements, and dependable alliances. Only then did a significant number of Indian leaders agree that peace would bring greater benefits than raiding or warfare.[148]

Once they had reached agreement, leaders on both sides worked at maintaining friendly relations. Individually or in small groups, Spaniards and Indians alike continued to commit murder, mayhem, and theft, but most of their spokesmen tried to prevent such episodes from degenerating into war. In response to criticism in 1799, Commander in Chief Pedro de Nava justified forbearance toward individual Comanches because the alternative would be war, "an error of very serious consequences." Comanche warriors, he noted, far outnumbered Spanish forces.[149] For their part, Nava reported, Comanche leaders understood that Spanish punishment of individual Indians who committed crimes would not be a reason "to break the peace."[150] Indeed, in order to maintain peaceful relations with Spaniards, Comanche leaders themselves ostracized or punished individuals who crossed the bounds of acceptable behavior.[151]

Out of such understandings, one-time adversaries began to develop personal relationships and deeper mutual respect. Spanish officers began to abandon the notion popular in military circles that Apaches and other recalcitrant tribes understood only force and possessed a "natural wild disposition which differs little from the fierce beasts."[152] Some Spanish officers began to describe Apaches more sympathetically. One veteran, for example, speculated in 1796 that Apache raiding might have "originated in former times by the excesses and avarice of the colonists themselves."[153] "If the Indians had a defender who could represent their rights on the basis of natural law," another officer wrote in 1799, "an impartial judge could soon see that every charge we might make against them would be offset by as many crimes committed by our side."[154]

At heart, however, economic interests and mutual security united Spaniards and Indians, and the new peace served those interests well. In Arizona, New Mexico, and to a lesser extent in Texas, the 1790s ushered in two decades of prosperity for merchants and artisans, and expansion for Hispanic stockraisers and farmers (and miners in Arizona), who moved onto lands where they had once feared to tread. Travel became safer, making it possible to open direct routes between the frontier communities of Tucson, Santa Fe, and San Antonio. With a single companion, Pedro Vial pioneered a trail from San Antonio to Santa Fe in 1786–87 (a distance of over 700 miles), and in 1795, Capt. José de Zúñiga opened a long-sought pack train route from Tucson to Santa Fe, much of it through Apache country and mountainous terrain.[155] Discovered late in the colonial period, these routes did not become important highways of commerce, but their opening is further evidence of a new economic vitality.

In itself, the decrease in Spanish-Indian hostilities had not promoted economic growth or the expansion of trade routes—the impetus came from a number of circumstances including a growing demand for grain, livestock, and textiles in the revived silver mining districts of Chihuahua and Sonora. But the decline in Indian hostilities had been a necessary precondition for expansion, and the ongoing infusion of capital to provide gifts to Indian allies stimulated production in Sonora and New Mexico.[156]

In the interior provinces, the imperfect alliances formed with Comanches, Apaches, Navajos, and other tribes endured until the chaotic decade of the 1810s. Then, when rebellion in Mexico diverted resources away from the frontier and made it difficult for Spanish officials to continue to buy peace or offer a steady supply of trade goods, hardwon alliances began to disintegrate. On the northeastern frontier in particular, the intermural quarrels between Spanish royalists and Spanish insurgents, both of whom solicited the Indians' aid, made Spaniards undependable allies in the 1810s.[157] Indians, themselves, then, became less predictable and more susceptible to the blandishments and wares of itinerant Anglo-Americans.

9

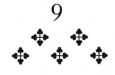

Forging a Transcontinental Empire: New California to the Floridas

Certain foreign Powers . . . now have an opportunity and the most eager desire to establish some Colony at the Port of Monterrey.
Viceroy Croix and Visitador Gálvez to the king, Mexico, Jan. 23, 1768

The king has determined that the principal object of his arms in America during the present war will be to drive [the English] from the Mexican Gulf and the neighborhood of Louisiana.
José de Gálvez to Bernardo de Gálvez, [Madrid], Aug. 29, 1779

In contrast to the consolidation and accommodation that became the foundation of a cautious new policy toward intractable Indians during the long reign of Carlos III, expansion and high-risk belligerence characterized Spain's efforts to counter the influence of its European rivals in North America. Initially, at least, this aggressive stance brought positive results. By the time Carlos III died in 1788, Spain had reacquired Florida, planted new settlements on the Pacific from San Diego to San Francisco, and strengthened its claims to the Northwest Pacific coast as far as Alaska.

Remarkably, the dynamic force behind Spain's imperial policy in North America was one individual, José de Gálvez, whose singular determination and ability led to the founding of New California in 1769. That achievement, in turn, furthered his own meteoric rise to prominence in the Spanish court. In 1776 Carlos III appointed him secretary of the Indies, the keystone position in the colonial bureaucracy, where he presided over the reinvigorated Council of the Indies. Enjoying the confidence of the Bourbon monarch with the most ambitious program for imperial reform, Gálvez exercised greater influence than any secretary of the Indies before or after him.[1] All of the Indies fell under his care, but until his death in 1787 Gálvez maintained an especially close watch on affairs across the northern fringes of the empire, the region that he knew firsthand.

I

José de Gálvez had spent six years in New Spain as inspector general, or *visitador general*, with an extraordinary assignment. His instructions, which gave him authority over the viceroy himself in some matters, charged him with carrying out a wide-ranging inspection, or visita, and with recommending sweeping administrative and economic reforms to the king. Gálvez had arrived in New Spain on August 25, 1765, as the harbinger of a new order, his delegation intended to complement the military mission of Lt. Gen. Juan de Villalba and the marqués de Rubí, which had come the year before. Carlos III planned to reform the old Hapsburg imperial system, making New Spain more efficient, productive, and profitable for the Crown. Driven by the passion for greater rationality and efficiency that characterized the monarchs of the Enlightenment, Carlos's predecessors, Felipe V (1700–1746) and Ferdinand VI (1746–1759), had streamlined the administration of Spain itself. Now, in the aftermath of the Seven Years' War, Carlos III and his ministers had begun to extend similar reforms to the American empire, including New Spain.[2]

José de Gálvez had not been the king's first choice for the sensitive position of inspector general, but Carlos III would have been hard-pressed to find his equal in audacity, dynamism, intelligence, ambition, and ruthlessness.[3] Born to a noble but impoverished family near Málaga on the south coast of Spain in 1720, Gálvez owed his early education to clergymen who had taken him out of the pastures where he tended sheep and educated him for the priesthood. Renouncing ecclesiastical life, Gálvez had turned to the study of law at the University of Salamanca and become a career bureaucrat in Madrid. Knowledge of French, acquired from his second wife, had apparently helped him gain a position with the powerful secretary of state, the marqués de Grimaldi, in the Francophile court of the Bourbons. Within a few years the relatively unknown Gálvez had won the confidence of Carlos III, who entrusted him with the delicate mission to New Spain.

In Mexico City, Gálvez took an early interest in New Spain's northern frontier. Gálvez carried secret instructions to investigate the viceroy's management of the frontier presidios, but in comparison to the marqués de Rubí, who saw the frontier's problems in largely regional military terms—an area threatened by hostile Indians—

46. José de Gálvez, from José Antonio Calderón Quijano, ed., Los virreyes de Nueva España en el reinado de Carlos III *(Sevilla, 1967), vol. 1. Courtesy, the Vargas Project, University of New Mexico.*

Gálvez had a broader international vision.[4] Russia, England, and Holland, in Gálvez's view, represented immediate threats to Spain's claims to the unoccupied Pacific coast of North America, all of which Spaniards termed "California." With the geography of the Rockies, the Great Basin, and the Sierras still a mystery to Europeans, it was easy for Gálvez to imagine that Englishmen, pushing westward from Canada and Louisiana, might soon find their way to California along great rivers, including the Colorado. "There is no doubt," Gálvez wrote in 1768, "we have the English very close to our towns of New Mexico and not very far from the west coast of this continent."[5] Gálvez also worried that if England's well-publicized search for a Northwest Passage succeeded, its mariners would slip easily into the Pacific. A book written by a Spanish Jesuit, the *Noticia de la California*, published in 1757, had warned of this very possibility, as well as of a threat from Russia.[6] For some years, Russian fur hunters had crossed Siberia into the Pacific Basin in search of sea otter pelts that fetched high prices in China. Details about this Russian expansion to the Pacific, spearheaded by Vitus Bering, had circulated widely in Europe. Indeed, in 1759 a Spanish Franciscan who had lived in Mexico and the Philippines, José Torrubia, published a book with the alarming title, *Muscovites in California*, in order to alert Spanish authorities to the danger.[7]

Out of this international perspective, Gálvez fashioned a broad strategy for frontier defense. He supported Rubí's plan for a cordon of defensive presidios, but he also embraced three other ideas, none entirely original but all aimed to defend the frontier through expansion rather than through consolidation. First, Gálvez proposed to strengthen Sonora and the peninsula that we know today as Baja California, building firm bases to push the frontier far to the northwest, beyond Rubí's presidial line. Second, Gálvez urged the creation of a highly independent military government for the three western interior provinces of Sonora, Nueva Vizcaya, and Baja California, with its capital near the junction of the Gila and Colorado rivers at present Yuma. This separate administrative structure, Gálvez argued, would promote the development of those territories, "abundant and rich by nature, that could within a few years form a new empire, equal to or better than Mexico."[8] (On a larger scale, his plan eventually bore fruit when he became secretary of the Indies and created the Comandancia General of the Interior Provinces of New Spain in 1776). Third, once the western interior provinces were secure and flourishing, Gálvez would use them as a springboard to advance far up the Pacific coast to Monterey Bay. Since the voyage of Sebastián Vizcaíno in 1602–3, Spaniards had regarded Monterey as the most desirable harbor north of San Diego Bay.

The idea of defending California by occupying its principal harbor had been advanced over sixty years before by Eusebio Francisco Kino, a tireless Jesuit who had extended the mission frontier of Sonora northward into the land of the upper Pimas and explored the lower Colorado and Gila rivers, but his motives were religious rather than political. Although submerged by more compelling problems, Kino's idea had resurfaced from time to time.[9] The marqués de Rubí, with considerable justification, had dismissed a colony at Monterey as premature and unrealistic—one of several "monstrous projects" whose costs would outweigh its benefits.[10] José de Gálvez, on the other hand, not only supported a Spanish outpost at Monterey, but worked with gusto to bring it about.

In 1767, while Rubí was inspecting the northern presidios, Gálvez began on his own initiative to lay the foundations for expansion to the northwest. He took measures to streamline the administration of Sonora and the California peninsula, to promote economic activity in both provinces, and to quell Seri and Upper Pima Indians in Sonora, whose chronic resistance threatened to upset his expansive plans. With characteristic extravagance, Gálvez planned this Sonora campaign as the first phase of a large military operation that would extend into Nueva Vizcaya and New Mexico, bringing peace to the western interior provinces.[11]

Gálvez also planned a precipitous leap to Monterey, and he sent an emissary back to Madrid in May 1767, apparently to arrange the necessary royal authorization. Nearly a year later, in early April 1768, without yet having received the blessings of the Crown, Gálvez left Mexico City with Monterey his ultimate destination.[12] Within a month, however, a messenger overtook him with orders from Spain that could not have surprised him. Warned by the Spanish ambassador to Moscow that large numbers of Russians had landed on the California coast, the marqués de Grimaldi instructed Gálvez to find ways of "thwarting them however possible."[13] These orders must have come as music to Gálvez's ears. Although a covering letter from the viceroy

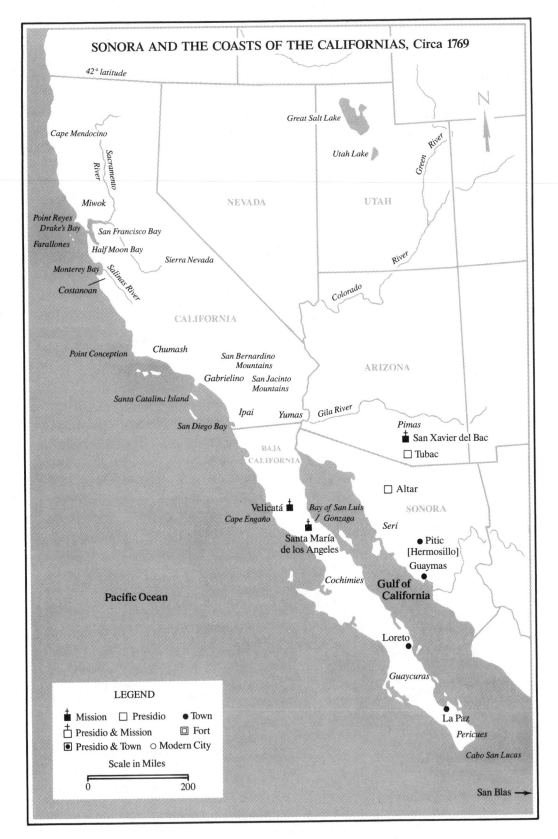

Map 11. *Sonora and the coasts of the Californias, circa 1769.*

prohibited Gálvez from personally continuing on to Monterey because he was needed in New Spain, Grimaldi's orders could be interpreted as authorization to occupy Monterey Bay.[14]

Legal obstacles to his ambitious plan behind him, Gálvez still faced enormous practical problems. Hostile Seris and Pimas impeded travel in Sonora, through which any expedition would logically pass, and no Spaniard had yet explored a route from Sonora to the Pacific coast. Hence, Gálvez and his advisors turned to the sea. Meeting at San Blas, a mosquito-infested shipyard and naval depot that Gálvez founded in May 1768, some sixty miles north of present-day Puerto Vallarta, they decided to send a naval expedition to plant a settlement and a presidio at Monterey.[15] With the California project his highest priority, the visitador moved his headquarters across the Gulf to the California peninsula in July 1768. There he hoped to marshall resources for an expedition that would complement the naval party by traversing the length of the 800-mile-long peninsula and continuing on to Monterey.[16] Gálvez quickly learned, however, that the barren peninsula lacked sufficient resources to support such an enterprise. California's missions, which might have been expected to supply Indian labor, produce, and livestock, were in shambles. Nor could Gálvez draw from Baja California's non-Indian population, for it numbered perhaps no more than 400 in this peculiar province of New Spain.[17]

For 164 years after the discovery of Baja California in 1533 by Cortés's pilot, Fortún Jiménez, Spaniards had failed to plant enduring colonies on the peninsula.[18] Into this void had come the Society of Jesus, whose missions already extended up the Pacific slope of New Spain. Beginning in Loreto in 1697, Jesuits had constructed a chain of seventeen missions and over forty visitas stretching from Cabo San Lucas, at the tip of Baja California, to Santa María de los Angeles, on the arid Gulf of California watershed inland from the Bay of San Luis Gonzaga—some 300 miles below the present U.S.-Mexico border. But no corresponding growth of towns or fortifications had taken place. In an unusual gesture, the Crown had granted the Jesuits nearly absolute control over Baja California, and the missionaries, hoping to keep Indians insulated from moral contamination, had restricted immigration to soldiers and their families who worked directly for the missions. Yet even with a virtual monopoly, the Jesuits could not create flourishing missions in an arid land. Most of the peninsular missions could not produce enough food to maintain Indians year round, and acute hunger became chronic among natives whose hunting and gathering strategies had been disrupted. In tight mission quarters, Indian peoples—Pericues, Guaycuras, and Cochimies—had succumbed to European diseases and their population had declined steadily from perhaps 40,000 in 1697 to some 7,000 in the missionized part of the peninsula by 1768.[19] Moreover, at the time of Gálvez's arrival, the peninsula's ordinarily impoverished missions were at an ebb, their storehouses depleted and their herds butchered.[20] Just months before, in one of the most wrenching events of the century in New Spain, government officials had ousted the Jesuits, the missions' overseers.

In 1767, Carlos III had ordered the Jesuits expelled from Spain and all of its colonies, a measure that the Portuguese and French crowns had already taken in 1759 and 1764. Carlos III had charged the Jesuits with sedition, but this appears to have been a pretext to eliminate the privileged and wealthy religious order that the king's ministers regarded as a powerful obstacle to urgent secular reforms.[21] In New Spain, Gálvez himself had played a key role in executing the king's orders to arrest the Jesuits, ship them out of the viceroyalty, and confiscate their properties—orders which officials guarded with great secrecy before carrying them out through much of New Spain on a single day, June 25, 1767. In Baja California, as in other remote places, the expulsion had taken longer; Jesuits had not left the peninsula until February 1768.

Gálvez had little use for missions, and initially he and his advisors did not regard them as central to the Monterey enterprise.[22] Like most Enlightened Spanish officials, he believed that church control of property had hindered the generation of wealth and that missions had slowed the transformation of Indians into producers and consumers. In Baja California, Gálvez exceeded the logic of his convictions by trying quixotically to convert the former mission Indians into Spanish townsfolk, residents of utopian communities. Indians, however, declined to follow his script.[23] In the end, with his troops tied up in the Sonora campaign, Gálvez had to turn to missionaries for help, for missionaries represented the only group experienced in managing Indians at low cost. Missionaries came to play a central role in the settlement of New California, even though the province was founded in an increasingly secular age just two years after the expulsion of the Jesuits. Many officials continued to share Gálvez's antipathy toward missions but hoped to reform them by permitting non-Indians to live at the missions and so hasten the acculturation process.[24]

II

In the scantily populated California peninsula, Gálvez had the good fortune to find two talented men to lead the expedition to Monterey—Capt. Gaspar de Portolá, upon whose dedication to duty Gálvez could rely, and fray Junípero Serra, whose religious zeal Gálvez could exploit. Gálvez placed Portolá in overall command of the expedition, while Serra took charge of the religious contingent.

The second son of a minor Catalonian nobleman, Gaspar de Portolá had thirty years of military experience behind him in Europe when he arrived in Mexico with the military reinforcements sent in 1764. In 1767, the tall, lifelong bachelor, a captain of dragoons, had been assigned to Baja California. He arrived with sealed orders to arrest and expel the Jesuits—a task he completed with courtesy—and to assume the first governorship of what he would soon call "this miserable peninsula." Portolá would have many reasons to dislike his assignment in California, but he stood ready, as he later put it "either to die or to fulfill my mission."[25]

In April 1768, a few months after Portolá had shipped the last of the Jesuits to the mainland, Junípero Serra had crossed over to the California peninsula at the head of a small group of Franciscans, sent to take charge of the former Jesuit missions. The fifty-five-year-old friar from Mallorca had given up a professorship of philosophy in 1749 to convert Indians and seek martyrdom in the Indies. Death had eluded him (in 1758 he came within a hair's breadth of being sent to the Apache mission of San Sabá in Texas), but the asthmatic, five-foot-two-inch-tall friar mortified his body, often punishing himself by walking and aggravating the painful varicose ulcers in his legs when he might instead have ridden, wearing "rough hair shirts, made either of bristles or with points of metal wire," flagellating himself to the point of bleeding, and burning the flesh on his chest with a lighted candle.[26] In an era when many Franciscan clergy had grown soft, Serra embodied the hard-edged zeal that had characterized the earliest Spanish missionization in America; time and chance would make him one of the best known and most controversial priests in American history.[27]

Plagued by bad luck and perhaps sabotage by mariners reluctant to sail, the Portolá expedition provided its members, all of them men, with numerous opportunities to mortify their flesh. During the first half of 1769, what Gálvez once termed the "Sacred Expedition," set out in stages to meet the Russian threat.[28] Two new brigantines commandeered from the Sonora campaign, along with men and materiel, set out from La Paz, where they had undergone final preparations under Gálvez's personal scrutiny. The *San Carlos* sailed in January 1769 under command of Vicente Vila, followed the next month by the *San Antonio* under Juan Pérez. Having departed well past what they understood to be the optimum season for sailing north, both vessels met heavy seas and the usual contrary winds and currents that slowed their progress, lengthened their time at sea, and made their crews vulnerable to scurvy. Of the ninety men on the two ships, only sixteen were healthy enough to attend to the sick by the time the vessels dropped anchor in San Diego Bay. The *San Antonio* arrived on April 11 and the *San Carlos*, which had left a month earlier but suffered greater misfortunes, on April 30.[29]

Meanwhile, two land parties moved up the peninsula toward San Diego Bay. On March 24, the Mexican-born Capt. Fernando de Rivera y Moncada, commander of the garrison at Loreto, led twenty-five leather-jacketted presidial soldiers and some forty mission Indians from a camp in good pasturage at Velicatá, 30 miles beyond Santa María, the northernmost of the Jesuit missions. For 52 days and 250 miles, hungry and thirsty much of the way, Rivera's men picked their way through country unknown to Europeans, and arrived at San Diego on May 14. At the same time, the second land expedition, about seventy men including Gaspar de Portolá and Junípero Serra, made their way up the peninsula from Loreto to the camp at Velicatá, arriving there on May 13, just as the first party approached San Diego. Two days later, Portolá and Serra set out for San Diego. Making rapid progress over the newly broken trail, they arrived in forty-six days, on July 1.[30]

When the land parties reached San Diego, they expected to see a fortification and mission already in place; instead they found a hospital and a cemetery. The men who had arrived by sea, Portolá explained to the viceroy, were "immobilized and in so unhappy and deplorable a state as moved my deepest pity." Thirty-one had died of scurvy by early July, and twenty more would succumb to the disease, or a related illness, in the months ahead.[31]

Gálvez's instructions had called for both sea and land expeditions to continue to Monterey after their rendezvous at San Diego, but the sailors could not complete the assignment. With a skeleton crew, the *San Antonio* returned to San Blas for supplies, while the *San Carlos* rode anchor for want of enough crewmen to set sail. Eager to beat the winter snows and the Russians, Portolá decided to continue to Monterey by land, without support from the vessels. It was, as he recognized, "a rather bold decision" for he had few rations.[32] He hoped, however, that a third ship dispatched by Gálvez to Monterey, the *San José*, would meet them with supplies; only later did he learn that the *San José* had vanished without a trace.

Portolá's band, some sixty able-bodied men and a train of pack mules, left San Diego on July 14 to break a new trail along a coast known to Spaniards only from the sea. They passed easily through the Los Angeles basin despite several frightful earthquakes—one "lasted about half as long as an Ave María," the prayerful Portolá noted in his diary.[33] Beyond San Luis Obispo, mountains met the sea and made the coast inaccessible. The party turned inland and continued north over rugged mountain trails, then followed the broad Salinas River valley back to the coast near the latitude of Monterey. There, they recognized from nautical descriptions dating back to the voyages of Vizcaíno, the northern and southern landmarks of Monterey Bay, Point Año Nuevo and Point Pinos. The broad sandy roadstead of the bay itself, however, did not measure up to their heightened expectations. They scoured the area, unable or unwilling to recognize the fine sheltered harbor that Vizcaíno had described and whose virtues may have seemed more evident from sea than from land.[34] On October 4, eighty days out of San Diego, the perplexed Portolá held the first of a series of *juntas*. Supplies were running low and many of the men were ill. Should they proceed, or carry out a strategic retreat? He asked for a formal statement of opinion and a vote from each of his fellow officers, Capt. Rivera y Moncada, Lt. Pedro Fages, and the military engineer Miguel Costansó, as well as from two priests who traveled with the expedition. Supposing they had not gone far enough, they decided unanimously to rest for a few days, then press on.[35]

Continuing up the coast, they came to Half Moon Bay where Portolá could see landmarks that he recognized from Vizcaíno's descriptions—the Farallones, Point Reyes, and Drake's Bay. Portolá knew then, without a doubt, that he had gone too far, but the mistake proved serendipitous for it led them to discover San Francisco Bay. In early November some of Portolá's men, who had climbed into the hills above Half Moon Bay to hunt, sighted from land the magnificent bay whose narrow entrance, later known to Americans as the Golden Gate, camouflaged it from the sea. The

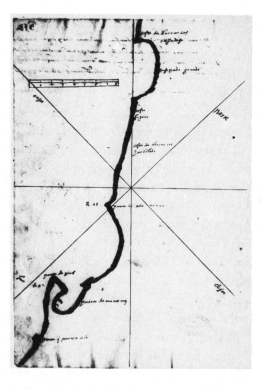

47. The port of Monterey as drawn by Enrico Martínez in 1603. If Portolá had had this chart with him instead of a verbal description, it seems far more likely that he would have recognized the bay. Courtesy, Archivo General de Indias, Seville, and W. Michael Mathes.

Golden Gate itself eluded Portolá's party, too; it was not discovered for another year, and not until 1775 did a Spanish ship sail through it. However dimly they understood its geography, members of Portolá's party recognized the significance of San Francisco Bay itself. Fray Juan Crespi described it without hyperbole as so large that "doubtless not only all the navies of our Catholic Monarch, but those of all Europe might lie within the harbor."[36] Thereafter, San Francisco Bay, the finest natural harbor on the Pacific Coast, figured into Spanish calculations for expansion.

Lost, nearly out of supplies, and his faith diminished in connecting with the supply ship *San José*, Portolá convoked another junta on November 11. The leaders decided to turn back to Point Pinos and search again for Monterey. The bay, however, continued to elude their recognition. Mystified, Portolá concluded that the harbor must have been "stopped up" by sand dunes.[37] Although they had failed to fulfill their individual orders from Gálvez to find Monterey, the officers decided on December 5 to return to San Diego.[38] Subsisting almost entirely on the meat of their pack mules, which they butchered daily toward the end, the group reached San Diego on January 24, 1770, "smelling of mules" as Portolá later recalled.[39] They had suffered great hardships, and some of the men had been so ill that they had received last rites, but all returned alive.

In San Diego, the immediate future of the enterprise hung in balance. Serra had established the mission of San Diego de Alcalá on June 16, two days after Portolá had left for Monterey. Ipai Indians, however, whose first encounter with Spaniards dated back to the arrival of Juan Rodríguez Cabrillo in 1542, had largely ignored the mission, preferring to pilfer the Spanish camp for gifts they apparently expected, and finally attacking it. Meanwhile, scurvy had continued to take a toll; only twenty men remained to greet Portolá's returning band. As supplies grew precariously low, the expedition's leaders quarreled acrimoniously, with Portolá reluctantly setting March 20 as the last possible date for a strategic retreat before lives would be lost, and Serra insisting on remaining, whatever the personal cost. Not until March 19, when the returning *San Antonio* was sighted, was it clear that they could stay.[40]

Reprovisioned, the indefatigable Portolá ordered the *San Antonio* to find the elusive Bay of Monterey, while he led sixteen soldiers to search for it again by land. This time, his expectations perhaps diminished, he recognized the bay without difficulty. On June 3, 1770, Portolá established a presidio at Monterey "to occupy the port and defend us from attacks by the Russians, who were about to invade us."[41] Within the palisaded compound that enclosed the garrison, the Spaniards also established the mission of San Carlos, naming it for the king. Although its harbor had not measured up to their expectations, Monterey remained, as José de Gálvez had planned, the capital of what Spaniards called Alta or New California.

Portolá stayed in Monterey until July 9, then left for Mexico on the *San Antonio* to give a firsthand report to the viceroy. Like a good soldier, Portolá had done his duty, but he apparently remained skeptical about the value of the entire enterprise. Several years later, he reportedly observed that the two settlements in New California would be too costly to maintain by land or by sea and inadequate to ward off the Russians.[42] On both counts, time proved him correct, but Portolá, who served for another sixteen years in the royal army, never returned to California to gauge the accuracy of his prophecy.

III

The success or failure of New California as a bastion against Russian expansion seemed to depend on the rapid delivery of reinforcements, food, and supplies. No one understood the precarious condition of San Diego and Monterey better than Capt. Pedro Fages, a fellow Catalán whom Gaspar de Portolá had left to preside over the new province. Fages, who had come to New Spain with the military mission of 1765, had sailed to California on the ill-fated *San Carlos*, at the head of twenty-five men—part of a special unit of Catalonian Volunteers. Thirteen of his men had died of illness within a matter of months, but Fages himself had survived to make both marches up the coast to Monterey with Portolá.[43] Fages knew the country and understood that his token force, separated by the 450 miles between San Diego and Monterey, could not defend their own positions from a concerted attack by Indians, much less by Russians.

Initially, California's coastal peoples (perhaps the most culturally and linguistically varied in North America) had received Spaniards with cautious but friendly curiosity. Growing familiarity, however, soon bred contempt. Ignorant of native customs, Spaniards offended Indians with their bad manners and their pilfering of Indian grains and animals; most offensive, Spanish soldiers violated native women. Unaccompanied by Hispanic women, the soldiers had been "condemned to perpetual celibacy," in the words of the engineer Miguel Costansó, but many soldiers refused to accept that sentence.[44] A few, with hearty encouragement from Junípero Serra, married Indian converts at the missions; other soldiers simply raped Indian women. "It is," Junípero Serra lamented, "as though a plague of immorality had broken out."[45] The soldiers' sexual violence toward Indian women, either more excessive than on earlier frontiers or better documented, hardened Franciscan resistance to integrating non-Indians into the new mission communities.

Notwithstanding the hostility that they provoked, the vastly outnumbered Spanish occupying force survived the initial years. Guns and horses had not yet spread across mountains and deserts to the Indians of the Pacific and, most important, the coastal bands and tribes lived in small villages with little tradition of organized warfare and no centralized political structures or confederacies that would have facilitated unified resistance against outsiders.[46] Spaniards, then, did not need elaborate military campaigns or diplomatic arrangements, as they had elsewhere, but managed to control some of the native Americans with rewards and punishments. Since they had few gifts at first, the Spaniards relied heavily on intimidation, crushing the first signs of Indian resistance with whippings, burnings, and executions—lest Indians achieve a victory and "come to know their power" as one officer later put it.[47] Such harsh treatment invited retribution. In 1775, the familiar pattern began. The Ipais burned the mission at San Diego and killed its priest—the first of several Indian rebellions along the coast.[48]

The Spaniards hung on, but just barely, enduring chronic hunger, deprivation, and anxiety. Their first attempts at agriculture failed. They had yet to understand California's climate and terrain, and they could not exploit the knowledge of the coastal Indians who were not farmers in the European sense, but who managed game and plant life with techniques that Spaniards did not fully comprehend. Livestock also remained in short supply, as did tools, artisans, and Indian labor. Franciscans had founded five missions by 1774, but with few gifts they made few converts. At San Diego, the friars had baptized only 83 Ipai by the autumn of 1773; at San Carlos near Monterey, the second oldest mission, they had baptized 162.[49] Friars and soldiers blamed each other for their troubles, thus intensifying the customary tensions between church and state. By 1773, Junípero Serra had managed to get the viceroy's ear and have Pedro Fages removed from office. His replacement, Fernando de Rivera y Moncada, an accomplished officer who had served the Jesuits in Baja California, proved even more unacceptable to the friars than had Fages. Nonetheless, the arrival of Rivera y Moncada's party in 1774 raised the non-Indian population of New California to about 180 and helped make it more secure. Rivera y Moncada had traveled by way of Baja California with some 51 soldier-settlers from Sinaloa, including some of the first Hispanic women and children to come to California—7 women had preceded them by sea that spring.[50]

It seemed clear to many that the remedy for Spain's problems in California lay in finding a dependable overland route from New Spain to import troops, married colonists and single women, livestock, and supplies.[51] Baja California had exhausted its resources in supplying the Portolá expedition, and the tragic voyages of the *San Antonio*, *San Carlos*, and *San José* had demonstrated the horrifying cost of sending ships against the prevailing winds and currents. Even the journey across the difficult waters of the Gulf of California was fraught with peril. Until an all-land route could be opened, New California would remain, in effect, an island.

José de Gálvez had understood the problem from the first and had turned his prodigious energy to solving it. After launching Portolá's expedition from the California peninsula, Gálvez had crossed the Gulf of California to Guaymas in the first days of May 1769 to assume personal command of the campaign against Seri and Pima rebels. A road to New California, he reasoned, required peace in Sonora. By mid-July, however, Gálvez's health had begun to deteriorate. The weight of his responsibilities, he believed, had taken a toll. Indeed, by autumn he had begun to show the first serious signs of mental collapse. At Pitic (present Hermosillo), while on campaign against the Seris, he had emerged from his tent at two o'clock in the morning to explain to a nearby officer that St. Francis of Assisi had sent a written communication explaining the incompetence of his military leaders. Gálvez thereupon revealed his own plan to "destroy the Indians in three days simply by bringing 600 monkeys from Guatemala, dressing them like soldiers, and sending them against Cerro Prieto," the rebel stronghold.[52] Gálvez apparently continued to lose touch with reality, taking on the identity of prominent personages from Montezuma to the king of Sweden, and of religious figures including St. Joseph and God himself. Gálvez's secretary believed that the visitador had slowly come to understand that he lacked the means to realize his ambitious plans and that his depression descended into temporary insanity.[53]

By May 1770, José de Gálvez had returned to Mexico City, recalled by the concerned viceroy. Gálvez slowly regained his health and again turned his attention to California. In June 1771 he and the viceroy, the marqués de Croix, sent to the Crown a plan for developing an overland route to California. By then, Spanish-Indian relations on the Sonora frontier seem to have entered a period of relative calm, making exploration possible.[54] When the visitador and the viceroy returned to Spain later that year, however, plans to open a Sonora-California route fell by the wayside.

The new viceroy, Antonio María de Bucareli, did not share Gálvez's or Croix's enthusiasm for the troubled and costly California enterprise. Bucareli let two years go by before pressure from the Spanish court and entreaties from frontier officials and Franciscans convinced him of the need to strengthen coastal defenses against a new Russian threat and to occupy the valuable Bay of San Francisco, whose shores Spaniards had continued to explore by land.[55] In September 1773, after protracted deliberations, including a conversation with Junípero Serra who had traveled to the viceregal capital to plead the case for California, the cautious Bucareli, a consummate bureaucrat, granted the year-old request of a frontier presidial officer, Capt. Juan Bautista de Anza, for permission to open a trail "to the new establishments of San Diego and Monte Rey."[56] Now fully alert to the dangers on the coast, Bucareli also authorized a naval expedition to sail beyond San Francisco to search for foreigners and to select sites for further Spanish defensive settlements. The viceroy saw these land and sea expeditions as of a piece.[57]

Strapped for officers, men, and ships, Bucareli entrusted the naval exploration to an experienced pilot, Juan Pérez, and a single vessel that would double as a supply ship, the frigate *Santiago* made in San Blas. A Mallorcan who had worked the Manila galleon route, Pérez had sailed the *San Antonio* to San Diego in 1769 and had made three subsequent trips to deliver supplies from San Blas to New California. In January 1774, Pérez set out from San Blas on a voyage whose destination the viceroy hoped to keep secret, but that quickly became known as "going to Russia." After dropping supplies off at San Diego and Monterey, Pérez set his course far from the continent, then beat his way north beyond 42° north latitude—the present boundary of Oregon and California and the previous high point of Spanish exploration. Unable to comply with the viceroy's optimistic instructions to proceed to 60° north, Pérez made his northernmost landfall near the present-day Canadian-Alaskan boundary, at about 55° north. From there, he cruised south for a closer look at the coastline of what is now British Columbia, Washington, and Oregon. He could not, however, comply with his orders to inspect the coast carefully in search of foreigners or to stop frequently to take formal possession of sections of the coastline and mark it with wooden crosses. Bad weather, crippling scurvy, and fear of the icy, uncharted coastal waters forced him to stay far from shore. He did, however, establish Spanish claims to the northwest coast and identify a number of key places, including Nootka Sound off Vancouver Island, which would soon become a point of international contention, and Mt. Olympus, which he christened "Cerro Nevado de Santa Rosalía." A half century later, American heirs to Spain's claims to the Pacific Northwest would use Pérez's voyage to assert 54°40' as the northern boundary of the Oregon Country.[58]

Meanwhile, the same month that Pérez had set out from San Blas "for Russia," Capt. Juan Bautista de Anza left to open a land route to California. Ambitious and unusually able, Captain Anza would later win acclaim for his Indian policy in New Mexico, but in 1774 this third-generation veteran of the Sonora frontier commanded the presidio of

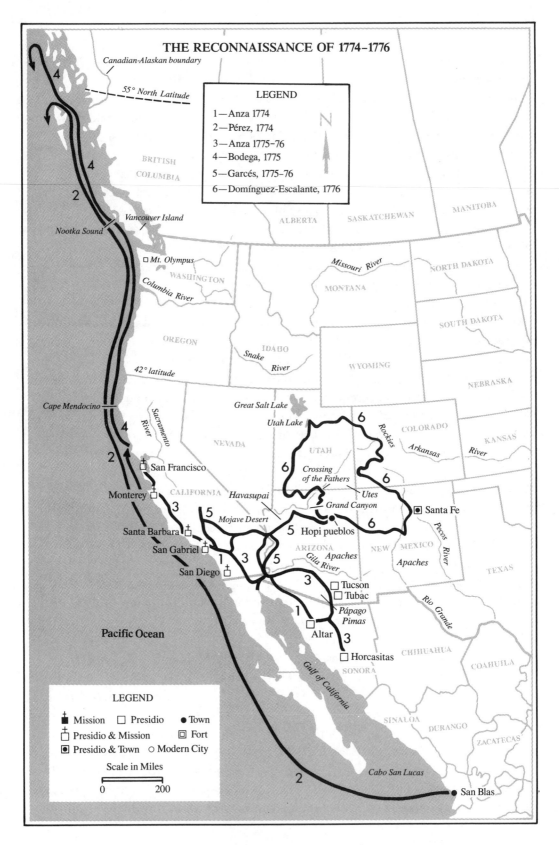

Map 12. The reconnaissance of 1774–76.

Tubac, then the northernmost in Sonora. Anza's small party included twenty-one soldiers and two priests, one of whom had already explored the first part of their intended route. Francisco Garcés, one of many Franciscans sent to Sonora to take charge of the former Jesuit missions of Pimería Alta, had made an extraordinary series of forays alone on horseback from the mission of San Xavier del Bac into the desert country of the Lower Colorado between 1768 and 1771. On the last of these journeys, Garcés had traveled within sight of the mountains that separate the Colorado Desert from the California coast and had learned from Indians that white men lived over the mountains. Garcés's discoveries, together with reports from Indians, had convinced Anza that the distance from Sonora to Monterey, as he told the viceroy, "can not be so great as formerly has been estimated, or the way so difficult."[59]

Anza had two guides on his search for a trail to the coast. First, the viceroy had honored Anza's request that Garcés should accompany him. Second, as he led his small band across the Sonora Desert by way of Altar in early 1774, Anza acquired an unexpected Indian guide, Sebastián Tarabal, who had recently come the way Anza wanted to go. A Cochimí Indian, Tarabal had fled from the new Franciscan mission of San Gabriel on the Pacific. Anza pressed Tarabal into service and continued to the

48. Juan Bautista de Anza. Copy of an oil portrait said to have been painted in Mexico City in 1774 and retained over several generations by Anza descendants. Courtesy, Collection of the Palace of the Governors, Museum of New Mexico, which now holds the original, and the Vargas Project, University of New Mexico.

Colorado where he met with a "friendly reception" from Yuma Indians, who helped his soldiers ford the river. Continuing westerly, Anza tried to penetrate what he soon regarded as the "impassable sand dunes" of the Colorado Desert, but neither Garcés nor Tarabal, whose wife had perished on his earlier crossing of the dunes, could see him through.[60] Lost and parched, Anza's group turned back to the river after ten days. On a second try, they managed to skirt the dunes and reach a point on the western edge of the desert (not far from today's Anza-Borrego State Park), where Tarabal saw familiar landmarks. The Cochimí led the Spaniards to water, then through the San Jacinto Mountains into the Los Angeles basin to San Gabriel. Anza had opened some 600 miles of new trail, but he rested only briefly at Mission San Gabriel, then rode north to Monterey and back to Tubac, completing a round trip of some 2,000 miles in five months. From Tubac, Anza continued an additional 1,500 miles to Mexico City, as his instructions required, to report personally to the viceroy.

Later, Anza's enemies argued that Sebastián Tarabal had discovered the route to California and challenged Anza's right to make that claim.[61] For the time being, however, Anza's feat won him honors and had important consequences for New California. Viceroy Bucareli recommended Captain Anza for a promotion to lieutenant colonel and ordered the enthusiastic officer to repeat the trip. This time, Bucareli instructed Anza to lead a group of soldiers, colonists, and their families over the new route and to select a site for a presidio on San Francisco Bay.[62]

Again, the viceroy coupled Anza's overland expedition with a maritime reconnaissance, this time sending out three vessels from San Blas, each commanded by young naval lieutenants recently transferred from Spain specifically to reconnoiter the northern reaches of the California coast. One vessel, the California supply ship *San Carlos*, commanded by Juan de Ayala, stopped at Monterey to deliver its cargo and a message from Bucareli that Anza was bringing colonists, then went on to explore San Francisco Bay—the first European ship to enter the Golden Gate and demonstrate its navigability.[63] Two other ships, the *Sonora* under Juan Francisco de la Bodega y Quadra and the *Santiago* commanded by Bruno de Hezeta, continued northward. Against great odds, the heroic Bodega y Quadra pushed the tiny *Sonora* up the Alaskan coast to 58°30′, near present-day Juneau, taking possession of the coast for Spain at four points, including on Prince of Wales Island at a place that still bears the name of the viceroy, Bucareli Sound. But the same difficulties that had plagued Juan Pérez (who now served as pilot on the *Santiago* and was one of the many sailors to die of scurvy on the expedition), prevented either Bodega or Hezeta from making careful charts that would establish an indelible Spanish claim to the coast. Hezeta, for example made the first-known European sighting of the mouth of the Columbia River, which appeared on subsequent maps as the "Entrada de Hezeta," but his failure to explore the river, coupled with the lack of publicity about the expedition, made the discovery easy for other nations to ignore. Seventeen years later, when the American Robert Gray explored the river and named it Columbia for his ship, the name stuck, even on Spanish maps, and helped strengthen American claims to the Pacific Northwest.[64]

While the three ships traveled north in the spring and summer of 1775, Anza finished recruiting colonists and proceeded to follow his instructions brilliantly. In the autumn, as the vessels with their sick crews returned to San Blas, Anza led 240 people, most of them women and children from Sinaloa, over desert and mountain, through drought, cold, snow, and rain. When they reached the coast at San Gabriel in January 1776, the party numbered 242. At least eight pregnant women had set out for San Francisco. One woman, the mother of seven, had died during childbirth, but three children born on the trail had survived. From San Gabriel, Anza journeyed north to San Francisco, where the viceroy had instructed him to select the site for a presidio. Mission accomplished, Anza returned to Tubac and to Mexico City. He received another promotion, to the governorship of New Mexico, an office that he held with distinction from 1778 to 1787.[65]

IV

At the same time that Viceroy Bucareli had authorized Anza to open a trail from Sonora to Monterey, he had encouraged exploration of a route between Santa Fe and Monterey—a project supported by knowledgeable persons from Junípero Serra in California to José de Gálvez in Madrid.[66] This work proceeded from two directions. The task of seeking a route eastward from California to Santa Fe fell to fray Francisco Garcés, a tenacious, patient, and experienced young priest who accomplished alone what Europeans ordinarily did in teams. Although born and reared in a village in Aragón, Garcés possessed unusual ability to travel through the lands of potentially hostile Indians. A fellow Franciscan, Pedro Font, noted that Garcés "appears to be but an Indian himself." He could sit with Indians for hours, and "with great gusto," eat Indian foods that Font found "nasty and dirty." "God has created him," Font concluded, "solely for the purpose of seeking out these unhappy, ignorant, and rustic people."[67]

Early in 1776, the Indian-like Garcés traveled up the Colorado River from the Yuma crossing to the Mojave villages at present Needles, trying apparently to put himself closer to the latitudes of Monterey and Santa Fe. From Needles, Garcés explored to the west and the east. First, he persuaded Mojaves to lead him over a well-worn trading trail through the Mojave Desert and over the San Bernardino Mountains to Mission San Gabriel. Garcés then returned to Needles, by way of the San Joaquín Valley, and continued eastward toward Santa Fe. Guided by Havasupai, Yavapai, and other Indians and fed and sheltered by them in exchange for gifts of white shells and tobacco, the tough Franciscan horseman crossed the Colorado Plateau of central Arizona, traveling south of the Grand Canyon. He nearly made it to New Mexico before his progress ended abruptly at the mesa-top pueblo of Oraibi, the largest of the Hopi villages. Hopis had never returned to the Spanish fold following the Pueblo Revolt of 1680, and unlike other Indians whom Garcés encountered, they refused to accept gifts or to give him food, water, or shelter. Garcés made camp on a dirty street corner, heated some corn gruel, or *atole*, over a fire he made from corn shucks, and bedded down. He spent two nights there. Then, on July 4, 1776, the same day that rebel representatives from the British colonies on the other side of the continent approved a declaration of independence, Garcés rode out of the pueblo fearing for his life. Lacking sufficient supplies and guides to continue to Santa Fe, he went back the way he had come.

Garcés had effectively opened a trail to New Mexico. Although he failed to make the last leg of the journey, one of his letters did. Before he left Oraibi, Garcés wrote a letter to the Franciscan priest at Zuni, "although I did not know his name."[68] An Acoma Indian whom Garcés apparently met at Oraibi carried the missive to Zuni, the most westerly of the New Mexico missions, and eventually it reached its minister, fray Silvestre Vélez de Escalante who, by remarkable coincidence, was in Santa Fe preparing to find a way to Monterey.[69]

The young Escalante was one of several New Mexico priests who had received instructions from Mexico City to seek a route to the California coast. In 1775, Escalante had traveled from Zuni to the Hopi pueblos to learn more about the country to the west. Like Garcés, he too had met a chilly reception, especially at Oraibi. Hopis had not threatened him with death, but at Walpi the men had assaulted his sensibilities with a dance in which, as Escalante noted in his diary, "the only part of their bodies that was covered was the face, and at the end of the member it is not modest to name they wore a small and delicate feather subtly attached." Appalled by this "horrifying spectacle," Escalante left the next day, convinced that only military force could bring the depraved and obstinate Hopi back into the Spanish fold.[70]

Garcés's letter caught up with Escalante in Santa Fe in late July 1776, as he and his superior, Francisco Atanasio Domínguez, prepared to embark on their own search for a route to Monterey. Discouraged by the aridity of the land and the belligerence of Indians due west of Santa Fe, they had planned to explore what they believed would be a more direct route to the northwest. The arrival of Garcés's letter, with the news that he had traveled directly across Arizona, did not change their plans. The two priests, who hoped to lay the groundwork for new missions among the Utes as well as find the way to the coast, decided that "the knowledge we could acquire of the lands through which we traveled would represent a great step forward and be of use in the future."[71]

Domínguez and Escalante never reached Monterey, but they did gather a fund of knowledge on an epic journey into the Great Basin. Setting out from Santa Fe on July 29 with eight companions, including Bernardo Miera y Pacheco, a soldier-cartographer, and Andrés Muñiz, an interpreter who had traded in the Ute country, they rode up much of the length of what is today western Colorado, then westward into Utah. By September 23 they had reached Utah Lake and the site of future Provo. Utes told them of the Great Salt Lake to the north, but they did not visit it. Instead, they traveled southwesterly toward California until October 8, when they decided to turn back. Near present Milford, Utah, they reckoned themselves in the

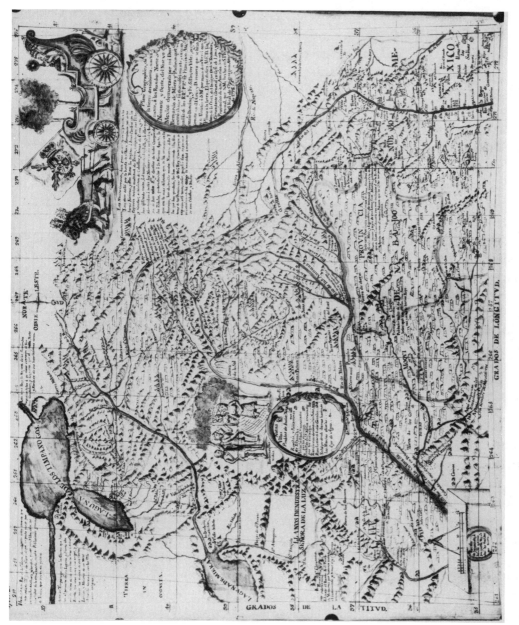

49. Out of the Domínguez–Escalante expedition came the first European map to depict the Great Basin based on firsthand experience. The cartographer, Bernardo Miera y Pacheco, misunderstood some geographical features that he had not seen directly, such as supposing that the Great Salt Lake and Utah Lake were a single body of water, Lake Timpanogos. Detail from one of six known manuscript copies. Courtesy, Museum of New Mexico, neg. no. 92063.

latitude of Monterey, but their reading of longitude, as Escalante noted, indicated that "we had many leagues left to us toward the west." Moreover, snow had begun to fall, leaving them "in great distress, without firewood and extremely cold." When the snow stopped, they could see that it had covered the mountains and would surely block the passes that led to the coast. Some of the men, however, insisted on continuing—Miera thought that they were but ten days from Monterey—and so on October 11 they settled the question by "casting lots" as an indication of "God's will." God sent them southward toward the Grand Canyon, across the Colorado River at a ford called thereafter the Crossing of the Fathers (a place now under the waters behind Glenn Canyon Dam), and through the lands of the Hopis. They returned to Santa Fe on January 2, having covered in five months on horseback some 1,800 miles, much of it through country previously unknown to Europeans.[72]

The explorations of Garcés and Domínguez-Escalante demonstrated the impracticality of reinforcing New California from New Mexico. Viceroy Bucareli had optimistically calculated that twenty days separated Santa Fe from Monterey; when traders began to ply a route from Santa Fe to Los Angeles in the 1820s, a normal trip took closer to two months.[73] New Mexicans in search of furs and slaves continued to trade in the Great Basin, but most of the country seen by the Franciscan explorers of 1776 was never revisited by official Spanish expeditions. Serious geographical misconceptions, such as the existence of a great river, the Buenaventura, that flowed westward from the Rockies directly to the Pacific, remained to confound a later generation of explorers.[74]

V

With the failure of the New Mexico connection, the future of California rested squarely on the route that Anza had opened from Sonora. Spanish officials took measures to secure that route by occupying the critical Yuma crossing of the Colorado River at its junction with the Gila River. José de Gálvez had argued in 1771 for an outpost at that spot, and the wisdom of his view seemed clearer as Spaniards came to know the country. Essential to holding the Yuma crossing were some 3,000 Quechan Indians, whom Spaniards knew as Yumas. Without the friendship of the Yumas, Garcés had warned, "it would not be easy to maintain the establishments at Monterey except at great expense to the Royal Treasury."[75] Anza had depended upon the Yumas, "the tallest and most robust that I have seen in all the provinces," to build rafts for him and his men and to move his stock across the river,[76] and he had cultivated one Yuma leader, Olleyquotequiebe (whose name meant "wheezy one"—perhaps he was an asthmatic), and named him Salvador Palma. On route home from his second overland journey to California in the fall of 1776, Anza had taken Palma to Mexico City where officials regaled him, dressed him in splendid clothes at the king's expense, and baptized him in the main cathedral. The viceroy regarded Palma and the Yumas as the key to Spanish expansion to the northwest, and Palma, a man of broad vision, saw considerable benefits for himself and his people if the gift-giving Spaniards could be induced to settle among the Yumas and protect them from their enemies. Palma, then, asked for missionaries and Spanish arms. Within a matter of months, José de Gálvez, now secretary of the Indies, ordered that Palma's request be granted.[77]

Responsibility for fulfilling Gálvez's orders to send missionaries and troops fell to Teodoro de Croix, who as the first general in chief of the newly created Comandancia General of the Interior Provinces had immediate responsibility for matters that previously would have fallen on the viceroy's shoulders. Distracted by rebellious Seris and the perennial depredations of Apaches, Croix stalled for two years until pressure from Franciscans forced his hand. Then, his response was feeble, partly because Spain's involvement in war with Great Britain severely limited his resources. Rather than establish presidios or missions on the Colorado, Croix authorized two fortified villages, each with twenty-five government-subsidized families of soldiers, colonists, and artisans, as well as two Franciscans each. Croix limited the friars' authority to the spiritual realm. They could try to persuade the Yumas to move into the two Spanish settlements and live like Christians, but the priests could make no claim on Indian labor or property. Like Gálvez, Anza, and others, Croix deplored the coercive nature of traditional missions, and he regarded mission Indians as worse off than slaves who, he said, "may hope to buy their freedom and become owners of material goods."[78]

By mid-January of 1780, the two small villages of soldiers, settlers, and missionaries had been established on the California side of the Colorado some 250 miles beyond the nearest garrison: Purísima Concepción, on a hill across the river from today's Yuma, and San Pedro y San Pablo de Bicuñer, about 10 miles upstream near present Laguna Dam.[79] These hybrid communities lasted only six months. On the morning of June 17, 1781, while Father Garcés said Mass, Yumas began to attack Spaniards. Within three days, the Yumas had destroyed the towns, beaten the four missionaries to death with war clubs, including Garcés, and killed many of the Spanish soldiers. The toll of dead or permanently missing Spaniards came to nearly a hundred. The Yumas spared women and children, but left many of them permanently scarred. Four years later, María Montiello, the wife of the ranking officer, still recalled vividly "the night my heart was broken, when my beloved husband was clubbed to death before my very eyes."[80]

Catalyst for the revolt had been the demands on Yuma hospitality and pasturage made by colonists and livestock bound that summer for the coast of New California. Most of this group, led by Capt. Fernando Rivera y Moncada, had moved on before the revolt started, but they represented only the most recent indignity for the disillusioned Yumas. Spanish arrogance, failed promises, corporal punishment, and demands for food and arable land had aroused anger throughout the Yuma community, alienating even the cooperative Salvador Palma. For their part, the Franciscans blamed Croix for sanctioning a low-budget enterprise and for limiting their control over the temporal lives of the Yumas in violation of custom and law; Croix blamed Anza and the Franciscans for misrepresenting Yuma docility.[81]

Later that year, Croix sent Pedro Fages of the Catalonian Volunteers, then stationed at Pitic in Sonora, at the head of a small force of soldiers and Pima and Pápago volunteers, to ransom the Spanish survivors and subdue the Yumas. Mixing diplomacy with treachery, Fages rescued some of the captives and also inflicted damage on the Yuma's villages but failed to humble the Yumas themselves.[82]

Spain never again made a serious effort to regain the Yuma crossing. First, war with Apaches and other tribes took priority over the Yumas—"it is necessary to forget those Indians for the moment" Viceroy Bernardo de Gálvez proclaimed in 1786.[83] Soon it became difficult to remember them. Spanish leadership at the highest levels shifted to a new generation with the deaths of Bernardo de Gálvez, José de Gálvez, and Carlos III in 1786, 1787, and 1788, respectively, and the military command of the volatile Comandancia General of the Interior Provinces lacked continuity. Even as relative peace came to the Apache frontier, projects to reopen the Sonora route failed to get off the drawing board because Spain had more pressing concerns closer to the edge of the Anglo-American frontier.[84] Much as the Comanche attack on San Sabá a generation before had dashed Franciscan plans to build a chain of missions from San Antonio to Santa Fe, the Yuma rebellion of 1781 had brought an abrupt halt to Garces's dream of extending missions up the Lower Colorado River and into central Arizona.

VI

Closing the Sonora route made New California dependent upon the sea once again and stunted its growth. In the few years it was open, however, the trail to Sonora had nurtured the fledgling colony to a point where it could sustain itself. The cattle and horses that Anza and Rivera had driven over the trail soon made California self-sufficient in domestic livestock, then multiplied beyond local needs; families who came with Anza and Rivera formed two farming communities that lessened California's dependence upon imported grains; and additional soldiers reinforced California's pitifully small garrisons.

The 242 soldiers and civilians who arrived with Anza in 1776 probably doubled the non-Indian population of California, and they founded two communities on San Francisco Bay—one military and one civil.[85] Led by Lt. José Joaquín Moraga, the newcomers built the presidio of San Francisco in 1776 on a high cliff overlooking the mouth of the bay—New California's third presidio after San Diego and Monterey. If San Francisco "could be well settled like Europe there would not be anything more beautiful in all the world," fray Pedro Font exclaimed. Under Spain, however, San Francisco never amounted to more than a small military post and a mission, San Francisco de Asís, also established in 1776.[86] The newcomers also established a town,

50. San Francisco presidio, drawn by the Russian artist Louis Choris, who visited California in 1816 with the Russian naval officer Otto Von Kotzebue, Voyages pittoresque autour du mond par Louis Choris *(Paris, 1822). Courtesy, California Historical Society, North Baker Library, San Francisco, FN–25092.*

the first in New California, near the southern tip of the bay in a broad sheltered valley chosen for its agricultural potential. Fourteen families who had come with Anza, nine of them headed by soldiers chosen because they had experience as farmers, founded San Jose in 1777.[87]

In 1781, more than 60 soldiers, colonists, and their families came overland to California and, like Anza's group, founded a civil and a military community. Organized in Sonora and Sinaloa by Fernando Rivera y Moncada, the new recruits traveled north in two groups. One crossed the Gulf of California and journeyed up the long trail through the California peninsula to Mission San Gabriel. Nearby, some of its members received plots of land at California's second civil settlement, Los Angeles, founded late that year.[88] Meanwhile, the larger of the two groups entered California by way of the Sonora desert and the Yuma Crossing—most of the party having left Yuma before the Indians began to kill Spaniards that summer. In 1782, soldiers and their families from this contingent built New California's fourth presidio at Santa Barbara, situated to hold a narrow point along the coastal trail to Monterey where numerous Chumash Indians could easily cut communication between north and south.[89]

Col. Felipe de Neve, one of the many Spanish-born officers who had arrived in New Spain in 1764, had overseen this unusual spurt of civil-military expansion in New California. When the Crown had ordered Neve to Monterey as governor in 1776, it recognized that New California had become more important than the old. The two

51. A leather-jacketted soldier at Monterey, sketched by one of the artists on the Malaspina expedition, 1791. Courtesy of the Museo de America, Madrid, and Iris Engstrand.

Californias comprised a single political unit, the Province of the Californias, but prior to 1776 the governor had resided at Loreto on the peninsula, while the lieutenant governor served in Monterey. After José de Gálvez became secretary of the Indies in 1776, the Crown reversed the two positions. Neve, governor at Loreto since 1775, made the 1,300-mile journey overland from Loreto to Monterey, the new seat of provincial government, arriving in February 1777; Rivera y Moncada traveled south to Loreto, which became the permanent residence of the lieutenant governor.[90]

Felipe de Neve regarded New California's importance to the Crown as chiefly strategic, notwithstanding royal rhetoric that gave preeminence to converting natives, and he sought to make California more self-reliant and thus more secure. He had planned the two civil settlements of San Jose and Los Angeles as farming communities that would provide grain and vegetables for the nearest presidios: San Francisco and Monterey in the north, and San Diego and Santa Barbara in the south.[91] Since California's presidios existed as much to defend the coast from foreigners as to protect the province from Indians, Neve drew up special regulations to address the province's peculiar needs.[92] In theory, the fortifications of the Californias formed part of the Interior Provinces of New Spain and fell under the *Regulations of 1772*, but in practice they functioned in isolation from the presidial cordon that ran across northern New Spain. In this respect, they resembled the garrisons of Louisiana and Florida, but in miniature. In 1794, for example, during a time of tension with England, the total military complement of all four presidios of New California was 218 men, including officers (the presidio at St. Augustine alone commonly had twice that number).[93] As physical structures, the California presidios also remained modest, never fulfilling the ambitious designs of military planners.[94]

Like other enlightened officers, Neve had scant regard for missions. From the first, the new missions in California were supposed to differ radically from the old in that they would be open to Hispanic residents who would help acculturate Indians. Elsewhere in New Spain, the notion of separate "republics" of Indians and Hispanics had long since broken down in practice and in theory. Franciscans in California, however, had come largely from Spain. They held the Mexican-born Hispanic settlers in low regard, and they deplored the soldiers' sexual exploitation of Indian women. The friars fought successfully to maintain segregated mission communities, to the disgust of Neve who echoed the sentiments of his immediate superior, Teodoro de Croix, by declaring the "fate" of the mission Indians "worse than that of slaves."[95] A pragmatist like Gálvez, Neve planned to use missionaries to expand the Spanish sphere in Cal-

52. Soldiers and Indians working outside of the walls of the presidio of Monterey. Sketch by José Cardero, 1791. Courtesy of the Bancroft Library and Iris Engstrand.

ifornia, but to minimize Franciscan influence in the economic and political life of the province. Over Franciscan objections, Neve succeeded in founding civilian towns at San Jose and Los Angeles. He failed, however, to nudge the friars into beginning the process of secularizing missions—that is, converting them into parishes with parish-supported secular priests and dividing the communal property among the Indians.[96]

Neve left the governorship of California in September 1782 to succeed Teodoro de Croix as commander in chief of the Interior Provinces. The Franciscans outlasted him in California and prevailed in their view that missions had to be maintained because Indian converts were not ready to compete in the Hispanic world. "The mission Indians should be free from guardianship in ten years," Gov. Diego de Borica complained in 1796, "but those of New California, at the rate they are progressing, will not become so in ten centuries."[97]

By the time of Junípero Serra's death in 1784, his successor and former student from Mallorca, Francisco Palóu, could report to José de Gálvez that "the spiritual conquest had something of the rapid progress that your Excellency wished."[98] By then, New California had nine missions, presided over by eighteen Franciscans, and together

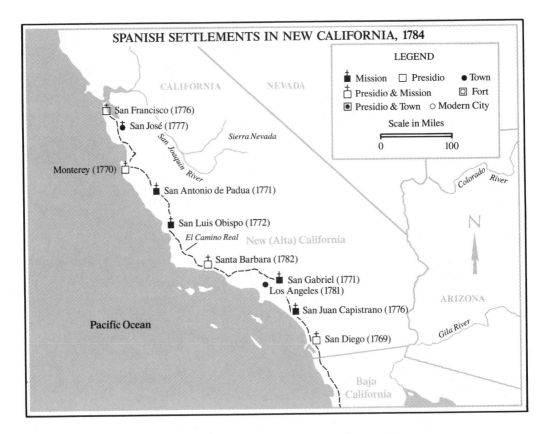

Map 13. Spanish settlements in New California, 1784.

they produced agricultural surpluses (the prosperity of individual missions varied, depending in part on the managerial capabilities of individual priests). Even Felipe de Neve had to acknowledge that the missions had "surpassed expectation . . . they have made fertile and fecund a portion of land which they found uncultivated wastes."[99] By the 1780s, supply vessels that once brought bulky grains to California could use cargo space for tools, clothing, and luxury goods from chocolate to snuff, and with their surpluses, missionaries produced revenue to pay for these imports. With more material goods at their disposal, the Franciscans found it easier to recruit Indians to the missions, and with increased Indian labor came increased productivity, enabling the friars to build more missions and increase the numbers of neophytes.[100]

In California, the friars had struck a bonanza of potential converts. With perhaps 300,000 Indians within the boundaries of the present state, California had the highest population density of any area of North America.[101] Moreover, reminiscent of the first decades of Spanish missionary activity in America, the friars in California did not have to compete for Indian loyalties with European rivals bearing trade goods. At the time of Serra's death in 1784, the Franciscans had some 4,650 Indians residing in their nine missions.[102] The number of Indians baptized by Franciscans exceeded this figure by far, of course, but some of those Indians had fled the missions notwithstanding the friars' attempts to restrain them or hunt them down. Other baptized Indians had died prematurely in the missions.

To the friars' consternation, Indian recruits probably survived mission life in California for only ten to twelve years. "They live well free but as soon as we reduce them to a Christian and community life . . . they fatten, sicken, and die," one Franciscan lamented.[103] As elsewhere, the tight mission quarters contributed to the spread of fatal European diseases. When one California governor tried to inspect the women's sleeping rooms, he found them so "small, poorly ventilated, and infested" that he had to leave. "It was not possible for me to endure them, even for a minute."[104] High infant and child mortality skewed the age patterns and, together with syphilis that often resulted in sterility, caused Indian birth rates to decline. In and out of missions between San Diego and San Francisco, the Indian population of the coastal region fell from some 60,000 in 1769 to perhaps 35,000 in 1800; the overall Indian population of what is today California may have fallen from 300,000 in 1769 to 200,000 by the end of the colonial era in 1821.[105]

Declining Indian populations, which doomed missions to extinction in Pimería Alta and Texas in the late eighteenth century, did not sound a death knell for the Franciscans' California enterprise. The populous interior of California continued to yield Indian recruits and the mission population rose steadily. By 1800 the number of missions in New California had reached eighteen, and the resident population had climbed to 13,500. In 1821, the last year of Spanish rule over California, the mission population crested—twenty missions had over 21,000 Indian residents. The mission economies had also continued to prosper. Since diseases carried off a larger proportion of the young and the old at the missions, an unusually high percentage of their resident populations tended to be in their most productive years, between the ages of nineteen and forty-nine. The mission economies, then, profited from the low ratio between workers and their dependent young or elderly.[106]

Paradox and irony surrounded the New California missions. They expanded even as Indians died. They functioned in a traditional manner, despite the efforts of enlightened officials to reform them. They became the dominant Spanish institution in an era when government officials sought to minimize their influence, and in a place that Spain regarded principally as a defensive outpost against foreign intruders.

In large part, missionaries in New California owed their curious preeminence to the failure of the military-civilian sectors to develop correspondingly—a failure that pleased many of the friars. After the Yuma revolt of 1781 and the establishment of California's fourth presidio, at Santa Barbara in 1782, no large influx of soldiers or colonists arrived, no additional presidios were built, and only one more town was established—a half-hearted effort in 1797 to establish a villa near mission Santa Cruz, named Branciforte for the viceroy.[107] The closing of the Sonora road in 1781 had made California dependent once again on the sea for all communication with New Spain, and the province offered no attractions that would prompt immigrants to make the arduous ocean voyage. To the contrary, missions and presidios both stood as obstacles to economic opportunity for would-be colonists in a dangerous and distant land. Missions occupied most of the arable coastal land, from San Diego to San Francisco, and the friars monopolized Indian labor and worked assiduously to stifle the growth of civil towns and of private ranches.[108] Meanwhile, as in Texas, the managed economy of the military government set prices that affected both supply and demand. As one of the friars explained, a settler could not sell grain or other surplus crops to anyone except the quartermaster at "absurdly low prices" fixed by law, "while being charged exorbitantly for whatever goods he can procure."[109]

Even without military price-fixing, however, *californios* had no viable external markets. More isolated than Spain's other North American provinces, Californians lived even beyond the reach of smugglers, foreign or domestic, until the early nineteenth century.[110] Until then, California's sole links with markets were a few government-owned vessels. In 1793 the military engineer Miguel Costansó lamented the monopolistic practices that limited ship building and noted that "maritime trade on the West Coast does not exist today."[111]

As on its other strategic frontiers in North America, Spanish officials knew that immigration was "the only effective means of assuring the possession and retention of that territory,"[112] and they tried to draw colonists to California—particularly single women and married couples. As elsewhere, officials offered material incentives to colonists, much as "the King gives a soldier arms for the defence of the nation."[113] Even with vigorous recruiting, however, they attracted only a few artisans and their families, who stayed for several years to instruct Indians in crafts, and a token number of colonists from New Spain desperate to better their condition. No single women responded to Gov. Diego de Borica's requests for "young healthy maids."[114] Unable to find volunteers, officials sent married convicts, prostitutes, orphan boys and girls, and other unfortunates to New California, where they might be rehabilitated and increase the Hispanic population at the same time. The province developed an unsavory reputation as a Spanish Botany Bay, which diminished still further its appeal to potential immigrants.[115]

Although immigration never exceeded a trickle, the Hispanic population of California grew at a healthy rate, from 990 in 1790, to 1,800 in 1800, and 3,200 in 1821.[116] In contrast to the mission Indians, Hispanics in California enjoyed remarkably low infant mortality.[117] When the Spanish era ended in 1821, most of the 3,200 californios were descended from those immigrants who had arrived before 1782.[118] All lived along the 500-mile stretch of coastal plain between San Diego and San Francisco, concentrated in or near one of the province's three municipalities—Los Angeles, San Jose, or Branciforte, or at one of New California's four military posts—San Diego, Santa Barbara, Monterey, or San Francisco.

However sparse their numbers and few their communities, Hispanics had seized control of the California coast from the native Americans and established a firm Spanish presence to preclude settlement by other European powers. The individual sacrifices of dutiful Spanish soldiers, dedicated Franciscans, and ambitious colonists had made the dream of José de Gálvez come true. Moreover, in the great reconnaissance of 1774–76, Anza, Garcés, and Domínguez-Escalante had opened new trails across the continent and the Pérez and Hezeta-Bodega expeditions had established Spanish claims beyond California to Alaska. Spain, however, with its limited resources strained by crises throughout its empire, had reached the limits of its ability to strengthen and expand its presence in or beyond California. In North America alone, the push to New California had coincided with the rising costs of defending northern New Spain from Indian raiders and with involvement in a new war against Great Britain that shifted the focus of Spanish attention in North America away from the Pacific to the Mississippi Valley and the Gulf coast.

VII

When thirteen of England's American colonies rebelled in 1775–76, they presented Spain with a chance for revenge after the humiliating defeat of the Seven Years' War, as well as opportunities for gain from England's distress. Spain's primary interest lay in Europe, particularly in regaining Gibraltar and Minorca, which it had lost to England in 1713. In North America, however, war with Britain also gave Spain a chance to drive England out of the lower Mississippi Valley and regain the Floridas.

For José de Gálvez, then serving as secretary of the Indies, the chance to make the Gulf of Mexico once again a Spanish lake took priority over fighting implacable tribes in the interior provinces, or bolstering California. In 1776, Gálvez instructed Teodoro de Croix to cancel plans for an ambitious offensive against Apaches and he ordered Viceroy Bucareli to halt further exploration on the Pacific coast. Later that year, Gálvez had to reverse the latter order when Spanish intelligence reported that one of Britain's most celebrated naval officers, Capt. James Cook, had sailed out of Plymouth in search of the Northwest Passage. Fearing that England would challenge Spanish claims to the Pacific coast beyond San Francisco, Gálvez asked Bucareli to send vessels up the Pacific to find and arrest Cook—a mission Spanish mariners never accomplished. The next year, when the threat from Cook had passed, Gálvez renewed his orders to stop further exploration on the Pacific.[119]

No sympathy for the cause of the rebel English colonies lay behind Spain's animus toward Britain. On the contrary, Spanish officials correctly saw that the revolutionaries' success would establish a dangerous precedent for its own American colonials.[120] Hence, although the Anglo-American rebels adopted the Spanish *peso* as their unit of currency in November 1776, and sought an alliance with Spain, Madrid resisted their overtures. When Spain finally entered the war against Britain in 1779, it was as an ally of France rather than of the thirteen colonies. The Bourbon monarchies of France and Spain were still bound together by the Third Family Compact of 1761.

Despite its antipathy for the Anglo-American rebels' cause, Spain informally supported them against the common British enemy for several years before it officially entered the war. While maintaining a semblance of neutrality, Spain smuggled guns and ammunition to the rebels and sent subsidies and loans through agents. Spain also supported a network of spies, directed from a distance by José de Gálvez. Juan de Miralles, for example, posing as a Cuban merchant, sent hundreds of reports on rebel activities out of Philadelphia, and Luciano de Herrera, one of the few Spaniards who had remained in St. Augustine after its evacuation in 1763, snooped around the British garrison and the harbor, picking up information about British troop movements that he hoped would lead to Florida's restoration to Spain.[121] Still further Spanish resources went to buy the allegiance of Indians from Illinois to Louisiana and Florida, to sponsor the emigration of Spaniards from the Canary Islands, Málaga, and other parts of Spain to shore up Spanish Louisiana, and to build up the army on the west bank of the Mississippi and in New Orleans in the event of an anticipated English attack.[122]

After Spain broke relations with England in June 1779, its military costs rose dramatically and drained cash from Spain's hard-pressed North American colonies. Californios girded for a British invasion that never came, and they contributed 4,216 pesos to a war tax (2,000 of which came from Governor Neve alone and much of the rest from soldiers' salaries).[123] *Sonorenses* contributed 22,420 pesos, of which 459 came from the fledgling presidio of Tucson; *nuevomexicanos* contributed 3,677 pesos.[124] Whatever Texas contributed was probably offset by the windfall that *tejanos* received by the demand for beef to feed the large Spanish army in neighboring Louisiana. Between 1779 and 1782, Texas *vaqueros*, or cowboys, drove some 9,000 head of cattle from private and mission ranches along the San Antonio River through dangerous Indian country in response to urgent requests from Louisiana officials.[125]

Louisiana and its valuable prize, New Orleans, faced an imminent British invasion when Spain entered the war in the summer of 1779, an eventuality that José de Gálvez had anticipated by reinforcing the province and by putting his talented twenty-nine-year-old nephew, Bernardo de Gálvez, in the governorship in late 1776. With the encouragement of an American agent in Louisiana, the money-raising merchant Oliver Pollack, Bernardo de Gálvez had assisted the American rebels from the first and had corresponded secretly with many of its leaders, including the governor of Virginia, Patrick Henry. By 1779, Gálvez knew from intercepted dispatches of the British plans to invade. Rather than stand tight and defend Louisiana, as his advisors suggested, Gálvez took the offensive. Royal orders soon vindicated his decision: "The king has determined," José de Gálvez wrote to his nephew, "that the principal object of his arms in America during the present war will be to drive [the English] from the Mexican Gulf and the neighborhood of Louisiana."[126]

Bernardo de Gálvez executed the king's orders with *brillo*. His objectives were across the river in neighboring West Florida, which had remained staunchly British. Heavily subsidized, sparsely populated, and occupied by sizable British garrisons, neither West nor East Florida had reasons to rebel and little prospect of success if they made the attempt. Like Quebec, Newfoundland, and Nova Scotia, and a dozen West Indian islands that included Jamaica and Barbados, the two Floridas had become havens for loyalists fleeing from the thirteen rebel colonies.[127]

Gálvez struck swiftly and surprised the numerically superior but scattered British

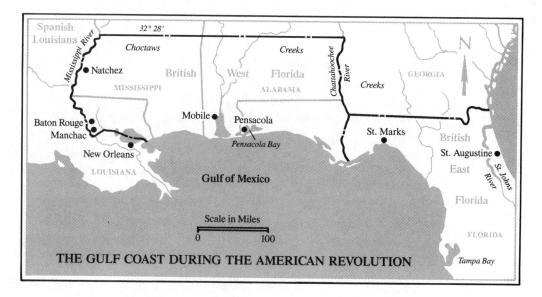

Map 14. The Gulf Coast during the American Revolution.

forces in West Florida, who were poised for an attack from American rebels rather than from Spaniards. In August and September 1779, Gálvez swept the lower Mississippi and its lakes clear of British ships and cleared the east side of the river of British forts at Manchac, Baton Rouge, and Natchez. With both sides of the Mississippi under Spanish control, Gálvez then turned his attention to Britain's two Gulf coast ports in West Florida, Mobile and Pensacola. In January 1780, with reinforcements from Havana, he led land and naval forces against Fort Charlotte at Mobile. He forced its surrender on March 12, before British forces approaching by land could relieve it.[128] Leaving José de Ezpeleta to defend Mobile from a British counterattack, Gálvez finally took aim at Pensacola, the administrative and commercial capital of British West Florida.[129]

In March 1781, a year after Mobile fell, Gálvez brought a force of over 7,000 men to bear on Pensacola—some arriving by sea from Cuba and others by land and sea from New Orleans and Mobile. Gálvez had launched this offensive the previous autumn, but a hurricane devastated his fleet as it crossed from Havana, and he had to begin preparations anew. This gave British forces and their Creek allies in Pensacola ample time to reinforce Ft. George against a long siege. Nonetheless, Gálvez took the fort. On May 8, sixty-one days after the siege had begun, a Spanish grenade ignited a gunpowder magazine in the Queen's Redoubt that guarded Ft. George on the north. Spanish forces, which included blacks and mulattos, poured into the redoubt and bombarded the fort until the British commander ended the carnage by raising a white flag. The last British stronghold on the Gulf had fallen, thanks to a lucky strike. Gálvez had but a two-day supply of cannonballs remaining—he had already stretched his supply by reusing spent English cannonballs.[130]

Gálvez's stunning victories on the Mississippi and the Gulf seemed an answer to the public prayers that Carlos III had ordered for the success of his troops. In California, Father Serra had prescribed a weekly liturgy with the invocation, "That Thou wouldst be pleased to humiliate the enemies of our Holy Church."[131] Much of the earthly credit for humiliating Spain's enemy belonged to Carlos III and his ministers, whose military reforms, especially in Cuba, had provided striking power that Spain had lacked a generation before.[132] Most of the glory, however, went to Bernardo de Gálvez. At a critical juncture as the Spanish fleet had approached Pensacola Bay, Gálvez's own naval commander had refused to risk running his vessels aground on the sandbar at the bay's narrow entrance and exposing them to enemy fire from shore. Gálvez had disagreed and had ended the stalemate by flamboyantly leading two ships and two gunboats into the harbor through enemy fire and shaming his own naval officers into following him. For this feat, Carlos III honored Gálvez with a title, the conde de Gálvez. "To perpetuate in your posterity the memory of the heroic action in which you, alone, forced your entry into [Pensacola] Bay," Carlos III wrote to Gálvez, "you may put as a Seal in your coat of Arms . . . the Motto: 'I ALONE.' "[133] Gálvez also received a series of promotions, to governor and captain general of Louisiana and

53. *An engraving of* The Capture of Pensacola *by Bernardo de Gálvez.* Recueil d'estampes repre-
sentant les différents événmens de la guerre qui a procuré l'indépendance aux Etats Unis
de l'Amérique *(Paris, 1784). Courtesy, Special Collections, John C. Pace Library, University
of West Florida.*

West Florida in 1781, to governor and captain general of Cuba in 1784, and finally to
viceroy of New Spain in 1785 where, among other achievements, he reformulated
frontier Indian policy in his famous *Instructions of 1786.*[134]

Bernardo de Gálvez's successes, combined with effective Spanish defenses of Manchac, Natchez, St. Louis, and the Illinois country against British-Indian invasions and
loyalist rebellions,[135] prevented Britain from seizing New Orleans and the Mississippi
Valley and contributed to the Anglo-American victory.[136] In the peace accords signed
at Paris in 1783, the thirteen rebellious colonies won official British recognition of
their independence and a western boundary that extended to the Mississippi—farther
west than Spain would have preferred. In those same accords, Britain officially recognized West Florida as a Spanish possession. Britain also surrendered East Florida to
Spain, even though St. Augustine still remained British at the end of the war. Augmented by refugees, East Florida's population had grown to some 7,000 mostly loyal
British subjects and 10,000 black slaves,[137] but without West Florida, England had
little use for East Florida. Moreover, it represented a sop to Spain, which had held out
in vain for Gibraltar, even though it had failed to capture it in the war.[138]

With East and West Florida restored to the empire and settlements firmly planted along the California coast from San Diego to San Francisco, the Spanish frontier in North America had become transcontinental.[139] Great Britain, Spain's chief rival, had been held at bay on the west coast and eliminated from the eastern seaboard to the Mississippi Valley. Britain still held its Canadian provinces and had claims to the Pacific Northwest, but along the continent's southern rim Spain had won the long fight for empire against England and France—just in time to face a new American contestant.

10

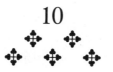

Improvisations and Retreats: The Empire Lost

A new and independent power has now arisen on our continent. Its people are active, industrious, and aggressive. . . . It would be culpable negligence on our part not to . . . thwart their schemes for conquest.
Juan Gassiot to Felipe de Neve Arizpe, Sonora,
October 9, 1783

I would also like to eradicate . . . the notion that it matters not if we surrender or lose our territories because they are unpopulated, produce nothing, or burden the royal treasury.
Report of José Cortés, Mexico City, 1799

Due to its proximity and interests . . . the United States must always be our natural and permanent enemy.
Félix Calleja to the President of Spain and the Indies,
Mexico City, Oct. 29, 1808

When Vicente Manuel de Zéspedes arrived at St. Augustine to assume the governorship of East Florida in the early summer of 1784, the future seemed bright. The sixty-four-year-old colonel from La Mancha, a veteran of over forty years of military service in the Indies, had lived to see Spain revenge itself after the humiliating losses of the Seven Years' War. Under the dynamic leadership of Carlos III and his able ministers, Spain had reasserted itself in North America. It had acquired Louisiana in 1762, expanded to New

271

California in 1769, seized the lower Mississippi and the Gulf coast in 1779–81, and gained title to both Floridas in 1783. Once again, Spain controlled the Bahama Channel, and both shores of the Mississippi. Farther west, Spain had reformed the administrative structure of the interior provinces of New Spain and had reformulated commercial and military policies that had begun to improve its relationships with independent Indian peoples.[1]

It must have been with some pride, then, that Governor Zéspedes watched British artillery salute the white flag with the Burgundy cross as it flew over the Castillo of San Marcos—a fort that had never fallen to an enemy.[2] On July 14, 1784, two days after the formal transfer of St. Augustine and its fort, British officials held a ball in Zéspedes's honor. While violins played minuets into the small hours of the morning at St. Augustine so, by coincidence, did they play that very night in Madrid's Plaza Mayor, where the return of the Floridas was one of several events acclaimed in a lavish ball and public ceremonies. As the festivities wound down in Madrid, the king had a choice of retiring to extravagantly appointed rooms in the massive Palacio de Oriente or to his nearby country palace at El Pardo. In St. Augustine, Governor Zéspedes, his wife and two daughters, went home to a dilapidated official residence on the town's nondescript plaza. The once-grand governor's house had deteriorated during years of British neglect and stood, as Zéspedes lamented, "nearly in ruins." Vandals had torn off wooden framework for firewood, the roof leaked in every room in the house, ceilings and walls were stained, and lizards, roaches, and crickets scurried through the corridors.[3]

Notwithstanding the great gains made under Carlos III, Spain's empire in North America was as precarious and porous as the governor's house, and far more difficult to repair. Spaniards remained a distinct minority within each of Spain's North American provinces. Indians, who communicated easily with one another over well-defined trading trails and watercourses from the Gulf to the Great Lakes and from the Atlantic to the Mississippi, outnumbered Spaniards everywhere except perhaps in New Mexico.[4] Spain's borderlands had also begun to be invaded quietly by westering Anglo Americans. Neither wilderness nor international boundaries seemed to impede them, and their own government could not control them.

Zespedes, who governed Florida from 1784–90, first encountered the American frontiersmen just fifty miles above St. Augustine, where the St. Marys River separates Georgia from East Florida. In the early 1780s, Americans had begun to trade and settle on the Spanish side of the river, joining a smattering of British loyalist families who had remained behind in Spanish territory. After touring the region in 1787, Zéspedes explained to his home government that he found the American backwoodsmen "nomadic like Arabs and . . . distinguished from savages only in their color, language, and the superiority of their depraved cunning and untrustworthiness." They were a distinctive people, he reported, called "crackers" in English—a term still used pejoratively in rural Georgia and Florida for impovershed whites. American

54. *The governor's house in St. Augustine, which faced the plaza and, beyond that, the bay. Watercolor sketch, Nov. 1764, orig. in British Library, Kings Maps, cxxii862a. Courtesy, St. Augustine Historical Society.*

frontiersmen, Zéspedes believed, chose the wilderness life of Indians in order "to escape all legal authority," and they had inherited the insatiable appetite for land of their British forbears. From his listening post at St. Augustine, Zéspedes picked up public and private reports of American schemes to expand farther into Spanish territory.[5]

Many knowledgeable Spanish officials shared Zéspedes's view of American frontiersmen and regarded the independent United States as a more immediate threat to Spanish hegemony than France or England had been.[6] The Americans' expansionist reputation extended even to the western edge of the continent. At Arizpe, Sonora, in October 1783, before he had learned that the last of the peace accords had been signed in Paris, Juan Gassiot, the senior member of the secretarial staff of the commander in chief of the Interior Provinces, warned of the "new and independent power [that] has arisen on our continent." Gassiot characterized the Anglo Americans as "active, industrious, and aggressive," willing to go to great lengths to trade with Indians and to build forts among them. Spain would have to take measures to block their advance before they "gained the frightening advantage of more acquired territory and many [Indian] allies." An admirer of republican institutions, Gassiot saw the United States as unified, inspired, and decisive, while, he said, Spain's "spirit of aggrandizement, insatiable in the age of our *conquistadores*, is now a thing of the past." The Americans, he argued, also enjoyed the advantage of proximity: "We must wait, not only for decisions but also for the means to carry them out, to come from more than 2,000 leagues [over 5,000 miles] away."[7]

Gassiot's specter of American economic and territorial expansion at Spain's expense was also evident to British and French observers in the 1780s. Publicly and privately, Anglo Americans boasted that Providence had marked them to occupy the entire continent; circumstances had given them the means as well as the will to fulfill what they saw as their manifest destiny.[8] Before the rebellion of 1776, the populations of the thirteen English continental colonies had grown stunningly, and that growth continued so that the United States outstripped not only Spain's most proximate colonies in North America, but New Spain itself. In 1790 the population of the United States and New Spain both stood at about 3.7 million (the U.S. figure did not include Indians, who comprised 60 percent of the population of New Spain, but it did include black slaves). By 1820, the population of the United States had increased to 9,600,000 (still not counting most Indians), while New Spain's had grown to 6,200,000.[9]

Most dangerous for Spain, large numbers of Americans poured over the Appalachians in pursuit of territory and trade in the Mississippi Valley. The population of Kentucky, for example, jumped spectacularly, from perhaps 12,000 in 1783 to over 73,000 in 1790, and to 221,000 by 1800 (it became a state in 1792). The Americans, it seemed to one Spanish official in Louisiana in 1794, were "advancing and multiplying . . . with a prodigious rapidity."[10] Louisiana, Spain's most populous North American province, probably had over 50,000 non-Indian inhabitants in 1800—a figure that included more Frenchmen, Englishmen, Americans, and Germans than Spaniards.[11]

The American economy also grew with extraordinary vigor during these years, surpassing even that of New Spain, the most prosperous colony in the Spanish empire. New Spain had made remarkable strides in mining and commerce in the eighteenth century and boasted more millionaires than any other part of the hemisphere, but despite the reforms of Carlos III, Spanish regulations, policies, institutions, and values continued to stifle entrepreneurial activity and commerce. In contrast, by the time of the rebellion against England, Anglo-American society had become highly commercial and secular, "with the major focus," as one historian has put it, "upon production, profit, trade, and consumption."[12] By 1800, the economy of the agrarian United States was twice as productive as that of New Spain.[13]

Anglo-American demographic and economic growth put Spain on the defensive in North America, prompting officials to improvise new policies and practices. Executing these policies, however, proved exceedingly difficult as the empire staggered through several decades of catastrophic decline under inept leadership. Madrid's colonial administration lost momentum after the death of José de Gálvez in 1787, the division of his ministry into two departments, and then its abolition in 1792. The monarchy itself was crippled with the death of Carlos III in 1788 and the succession to the throne of his phlegmatic son, Carlos IV (1788–1808). Within a year after Carlos IV came to power, Parisians stormed the Bastille and held his Bourbon cousin,

Louis XVI, and his family as prisoners in the Tuileries Palace. As key members of the Spanish court recognized, the French Revolution posed a serious challenge to royal authority in Spain as well. For a time, Carlos IV's ministers managed his government ably, but his incapacity to govern became painfully evident in 1792 when his faithless and domineering wife, María Luisa, maneuvered him into appointing her lover, twenty-five-year-old Manuel Godoy, as his chief advisor. Within months, the vain, politically inexperienced Godoy foolishly brought Spain into war against the regicidal French Republic. French troops swept across the Pyrenees into Spain's northern provinces and forced Godoy to sue for peace in 1795. Spain then abandoned a recent partnership with England and resumed its traditional alliance with France; England, betrayed, went to war with Spain in 1796 and imposed a blockade that effectively cut off trade between Spain and its empire. Any hope of lifting that blockade, which lasted with only brief periods of respite until 1808, evaporated when England twice smashed Spanish fleets—first in 1798 at Cape St. Vincent and again at Trafalgar in 1805.[14]

The collapse of colonial trade, the decline of public revenue, and the growing expenses of war ruined the Spanish economy. Political collapse followed when Napoleon Bonaparte imposed his brother, Joseph, on the Spanish throne in 1808, after forcing Carlos IV and his son Fernando VII to abdicate. Most Spaniards opposed the French pretender, and six years of bitterly violent civilian resistance followed. Overwhelmed by British forces and the harassment of the populace, whose tactics bequeathed the name *guerrilla* to a type of warfare, King José abandoned his throne in 1814. Meanwhile, Spain's American colonies drifted rudderless, buffeted by competing claims for authority. Spain's ebb in the Old World gave rise to a tide of New World revolutions that swept away nearly all of its American colonies, including those in North America.

I

The French Revolution, the Napoleonic Wars, and the collapse of Spain had been beyond imagining when Spain reacquired the Floridas in 1783, at the height of Spanish power under Carlos III. Then, Spain quickly reestablished itself in East and West Florida, maintaining them as distinct political units. Col. Vicente Manuel de Zéspedes presided over East Florida from St. Augustine (1784–90) and Col. Arturo O'Neill, an Irish-born veteran of the battle of Pensacola, governed West Florida from Pensacola (1781–93). Spain never drew a clear line to separate the two Floridas, but West Florida extended easterly to include Apalachee Bay, which Spain shifted from the jurisdiction of St. Augustine to more accessible Pensacola. The Mississippi and the Isle of New Orleans continued to divide West Florida from Louisiana, but in practice, West Florida was governed as an extension of Louisiana, and the governor at Pensacola came under the de facto supervision of the governor-general at New Orleans, Col. Esteban Miró (1782–91). With brief exception, all three governors fell under the immediate purview of the nearby captain general of Cuba rather than the distant viceroy of New Spain.[15]

In both Floridas, the initial transition from English to Spanish rule went smoothly. Spanish officials, all of them military officers, met little of the resistance their counterparts had faced in trying to assert control over French Louisiana after the Paris Treaty of 1763. In West Florida, a substantial number of British loyalists remained along the Mississippi, especially above and below the old French fort at Natchez, but many British subjects had left Mobile and Pensacola following England's capitulations to Spanish forces under Bernardo de Gálvez in 1780 and 1781.[16] In St. Augustine, which Spain had not taken during the war, the Irish-born Spanish officer, Capt. Carlos Howard, nimbly defused a Loyalist plot to set up an independent government, enabling Governor Zéspedes to reoccupy East Florida with only 500 soldiers. By the end of 1785, after a year and a half of acrimonious exchanges between Zéspedes and the last British governor, most of the 7,000 British loyalists and their black slaves had departed or disappeared into the back country.[17]

The Floridas quickly became re-Hispanicized. Mobile, Pensacola, and San Marcos de Apalachee resumed their earlier roles as garrison towns and centers for the Indian trade but remained understaffed, impoverished, unhealthy, and isolated even from one another. Soldiers, few of whom arrived with families, commonly fell into despair, and many deserted or abandoned themselves to "inordinate Use of Ardent Spirits and bad Wine . . . and promiscuous Intercourse with lewd Women," if one American who spent a week at Pensacola in 1791 can be believed.[18] The Hispanic civilian population remained relatively small, stagnant, and heavily male in the three communities. Two decades after Spain's return, San Marcos de Apalachee had a population of 189 persons, of whom 3 were women. At Pensacola, the administrative center of West Florida, the number of civilians (not counting soldiers or slaves) barely exceeded 400 from 1784 to 1803.[19]

St. Augustine's civilian population also remained small, but it depended less on the military than it had during its first two hundred years under Spain. In 1786, St. Augustine and its immediate environs had a population of nearly 2,000, of whom 450 were soldiers (most without families) assigned to the castillo and about 300 more were persons who lived on the town's outskirts. The town itself contained about 400 black residents, slave and free, and some 775 whites—of whom no more than 100 were non-Hispanics.[20] The Spanish community included government officials and their families, a few Cuban merchants, and over 100 *floridanos*—members of old Florida families who were beginning to return from two decades of exile in Cuba.[21]

Nearly 500 Catholics from the Mediterranean, most of them from the island of Minorca or intermarried with Minorcans, constituted the largest and most cohesive group of Hispanics in St. Augustine. This group represented the survivors or descendants of 1,400 people who had set out from Minorca for British East Florida in 1768 to work as indentured servants on an indigo plantation at New Smyrna, seventy miles south of St. Augustine. Most had died from the harsh conditions of plantation life, but

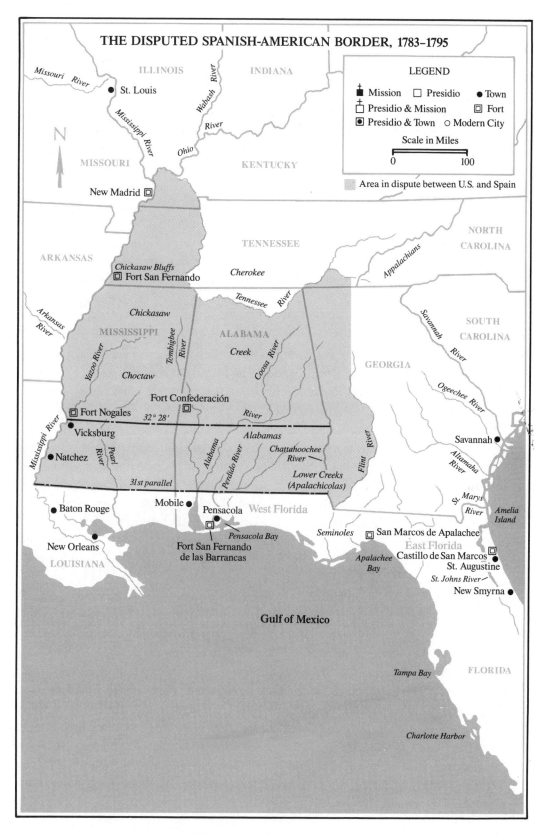

THE DISPUTED SPANISH-AMERICAN BORDER, 1783–1795

LEGEND

✝ Mission   ☐ Presidio   ● Town
⬒ Presidio & Mission   ◻ Fort
◙ Presidio & Town   ○ Modern City

Scale in Miles
0   100

▓ Area in dispute between U.S. and Spain

ILLINOIS
INDIANA
Missouri River
● St. Louis
Mississippi River
Wabash River
Ohio River
KENTUCKY
MISSOURI
N
New Madrid ◙

ARKANSAS
TENNESSEE
NORTH CAROLINA
Chickasaw Bluffs
◙ Fort San Fernando
Cherokee
Appalachians
Arkansas River
Chickasaw
Tennessee River
SOUTH CAROLINA
MISSISSIPPI
Yazoo River
Tombigbee River
ALABAMA
Creek
Coosa River
Savannah River
GEORGIA
Choctaw
Fort Confederación ◻
Ogeechee River
Fort Nogales ◙   32° 28'
River
● Vicksburg
Alabamas
● Natchez
Pearl River
Alabama River
Perdido River
Chattahoochee River
Flint River
Savannah ●
Altamaha River
Lower Creeks (Apalachicolas)
31st parallel
St. Marys River
Amelia Island
● Baton Rouge
Mobile ●
Pensacola ●
West Florida
Seminoles
San Marcos de Apalachee ◻
● New Orleans
Fort San Fernando de las Barrancas ◻
Pensacola Bay
East Florida
Castillo de San Marcos ◻
LOUISIANA
Apalachee Bay
St. Augustine
St. Johns River
New Smyrna ●

Gulf of Mexico

Tampa Bay
FLORIDA

Charlotte Harbor

Map 15. The disputed Spanish-American border, 1783–95.

the survivors had fled to British St. Augustine in 1777, where British officials had given them garden plots and allowed them to form a parish with their own priest. In 1781, after Zéspedes arrived, the Minorcans had taken an oath of loyalty to Spain, expressing pleasure at being "reunited with their rightful sovereign."[22] Minorca had belonged to Spain until 1713, when England acquired it; England had returned it along with the Floridas in 1783, and the Catalán-speaking Minorcans apparently continued to feel a close affinity to Spain.[23]

Beyond St. Augustine, San Marcos de Apalachee, Pensacola, and Mobile, Spanish officials governed provinces over which they had only nominal authority. Spanish claims notwithstanding, Spanish East Florida consisted of no more than a strip of land about twenty-five miles wide, between the St. Johns River and the Atlantic coast, and stretching ninety miles below the St. Marys River. The rest of East Florida was controlled by Creeks—commonly called Seminoles by the British in Florida, who had adopted and corrupted the Spanish word *cimmaron*, or "wild." By the late eighteenth century, whites knew nearly all Indians in Florida as "Seminoles," just as they earlier had attached the label "Creeks" to a variety of Indian peoples across the Southeast.[24]

Spanish West Florida, too, amounted to little more than small enclaves of Spanish settlement, with the interior of what is today the Florida panhandle, western Georgia, Alabama, and Mississippi dominated by Creeks, Choctaws, and Chickasaws, and many smaller groups such as those known to Europeans as Alabamas, Hitchitis, Shawnees, Tuskegees, and Yuchis. Numerous blacks who had fled from slavery on English plantations also lived in the interior of the Floridas. Some had formed their own communities; others had assimilated into Indian cultures or had become slaves of Creeks and other tribes.[25] Although periodic epidemics and warfare had continued to diminish their numbers, the southern tribes and their black kinsmen or slaves far outnumbered the Spanish residents of the Floridas. Creeks alone, the largest group, totaled between 20,000 and 40,000. Creeks and Seminoles together, Governor Zéspedes and his advisors conservatively estimated, could muster 1,000 fighting men—twice the number Spain had in St. Augustine or Pensacola.[26]

Against such odds, Spanish officials preferred to maintain harmonious relations with Indians. Moreover, Spain needed their friendship, for a series of Spanish governors hoped to use natives as human barriers against encroaching Anglo Americans, who claimed the northern reaches of West Florida as their own.

The treaties of Paris of 1783 had failed to specify a clear northern boundary for West Florida. England had recognized the southwestern boundary of the American Confederation as a line running along the 31st parallel, from the Mississippi River to the Chattahoochee—a long-forgotten border that had briefly separated Indian territory from West Florida after Britain acquired it in 1763. Spain, having received West Florida from Britain in a separate agreement, placed the line over a hundred miles farther north along 32°28', due east of the place where the Yazoo River entered the Mississippi at present Vicksburg. Spain clearly had the stronger argument, for 32°28' had been the British boundary of West Florida since 1764. Spain also claimed the east side of the Mississippi up to the Ohio and Tennessee rivers by virtue of its successful military operations against the British in that region during the American Revolution.[27]

At stake in this dispute were the fur-rich lands of the southern tribes, and frontage on the Mississippi River—lands and frontage so valuable that the state of Georgia nearly precipitated a war in 1785 by trying to expand its borders westward across the disputed borderlands to the Mississippi and take possession of the Spanish controlled district of Natchez. Although Georgia failed to establish the "County of Bourbon" on the Mississippi in 1785, the state continued to regard the disputed lands as its domain, and to sell pieces of what it called the Yazoo Strip to speculators.[28]

II

Initially, Spain tried to settle the boundary dispute with the United States, but the American government delayed, calculating correctly that time was on its side. In the meantime, Spanish officials improvised, taking radical measures to protect their border provinces from becoming overwhelmed by Anglo Americans. Spain had long since abandoned the idea of using missions to win over southern tribes, and the lengthy border made presidios impractical. Instead, Spanish policymakers tried to regulate commerce, promote immigration, and create a barrier of pro-Spanish Indians. These strategies were not new, but resourceful Spanish officials gave them a new twist, with the impetus for innovation usually coming from officials closest to the scene.[29]

First, Spain tried to stanch the flow of Americans into the Mississippi Valley by choking off their access to markets. In 1784 Spain closed the lower Mississippi to all but Spanish shipping—its right under the law of nations. The measure caused a furor among the self-styled "men of the western waters" in Kentucky and Tennessee, who could profitably market flour, bacon, and other bulky produce only by floating it on flatboats to the Gulf. Nonetheless, some of those Americans who risked the journey downriver discovered that modest payments opened markets in Spanish territory. Louisiana's commercial plantations, geared toward commodities for export, did not produce enough to feed the province, and so Gov. Esteban Miró welcomed American imports. Most Americans, however, regarded the use of the Mississippi, in the words of one Spanish officer, "as their legitimate patrimony," and they clamored for Spain to open it officially. To ease the pressure, Spain formalized Miró's policy in 1788 and allowed Americans to use the Mississippi, subject to payment of a 15 percent duty. American protests continued.[30]

Meanwhile, Spain had made even more remarkable commercial concessions to its subjects in the endangered borderlands. On January 22, 1782, the Crown permitted Spanish subjects in New Orleans and Pensacola to trade with certain French ports, hoping that goods from its French ally could supply the needs of its colonials and undercut British and American shippers and smugglers. This privilege, granted for ten years, was renewed and amplified in 1793. It was also extended to St. Augustine, where dissatisfaction with traditional trade restrictions ran deep and smuggling was rampant. Nowhere else in its empire did Spain relax its rigid mercantile system at this early date. Granted as temporary expedients, these concessions acknowledged the unhappy reality that Americans would continue to dominate the commerce of its border provinces if Spain or its allies could not supply their needs.[31]

The plan failed dismally. British manufactures and American foodstuffs continued to pour into the Gulf colonies in the 1780s—some smuggled by Americans, some delivered by French intermediaries, and some transported by American vessels that sailed to New Orleans boldly flying Spanish colors. After the French Revolution, as Spain's ability to supply goods deteriorated further, governors of Louisiana and the Floridas opened their provinces to American shipping on their own initiative. During the Spanish-English war of 1796–1802, Spain granted trading concessions to the neutral United States, the only nation that could supply goods and absorb the products of its colonies, allowing American merchants to make legitimate commercial inroads throughout Spain's border provinces as far west as California, and in South America and Spain itself.[32]

The large and proximate American markets gave a tremendous boost to the plantation economies of Louisiana and the Floridas, which sent cotton, indigo, tobacco, and sugar to American ports, along with naval stores, fruit, and furs. Commerce reached new heights, but much of the benefit went to the foreign-born export sector and the balance of trade worked in favor of the Americans. Hard currency, sent as annual subsidies from Spain, flowed to the United States. As Governor Zéspedes had described the situation at St. Augustine, "the money when it arrives does not remain among the inhabitants, for inevitably . . . the Americans receive it in payment for provisions."[33] Trade with the Americans, then, drained specie from Louisiana and the Floridas and left those provinces economically dependent upon the Americans long before the United States acquired them.[34]

Spanish officials also adopted an innovative immigration policy for its most endangered border provinces, with similar unfortunate results. From St. Augustine to St. Louis, local officials recognized that security depended on population: "The best fortification," Governor Zéspedes had argued, "would be a living wall of industrious citizens."[35] Efforts to encourage Canary Islanders and sympathetic Acadians to settle in Louisiana had achieved results, but Spain could not afford the subsidies that it needed to draw large numbers of Spaniards to its frontiers. When José de Gálvez authorized 50,000 pesos to promote immigration from Spain to East Florida in 1786, a desperate Governor Zéspedes spent it to feed his troops. Out of the experiment only five families of Canary Islanders came to St. Augustine.[36]

Unable to attract colonists from Spain or its American colonies, Spanish officials began in the mid-1780s to allow immigrants from the United States to settle in Louisiana and the Floridas and to obtain generous tracts of free land and access to the Mississippi. By 1788, local practice had become Crown policy as a result of lobbying by Gov. Esteban Miró, a career officer and veteran of the Mississippi and Gulf coast campaigns against the British, whose ten years in the governorship (1782–91) made him the most enduring Spanish governor of Louisiana.[37] Convinced that nothing could stop the flow of Americans and that it would be preferable to control it, Miró favored settling them in supervised communities where they could be assimilated—as at the fort at Natchez, or the fort established in Upper Louisiana (the Illinois country) at New Madrid in 1789 on the west side of the Mississippi near its confluence with the Ohio River.

The new Spanish policy required immigrants from the United States to take an oath of allegiance, but in a unique reversal of previous policy and practice, it did not insist that Protestants convert to Catholicism. Rather than discourage potential immigrants with such a requirement, the Crown relied upon Irish priests, some of them Spanish-trained, to convince American Protestants of the error of their ways and to instruct the immigrants' children, who "must positively be Catholics."[38] Subsidized by the Crown, many of those priests had already been sent to the Floridas, from St. Augustine to Natchez, to meet the demand for English-speaking priests.[39] Put off by the prohibition against public worship by non-Catholics and by laws against land speculation and political assembly, Americans never acquired Spanish citizenship in the numbers that Miró hoped, but legally or illegally, they came to Louisiana and helped swell its population from some 20,000 in 1782 to 45,000 a decade later. Natchez and environs, rich in tobacco plantations, became so populated with foreigners that the Crown ordered a governor assigned there in 1789. The appointee, Carlos III specified, must possess "a knowledge of foreign languages employed by the inhabitants"—a requirement fully met by the urbane, English-educated officer Manuel Gayoso de Lemos, who governed the Natchez district from 1789 until his promotion to governor-general of Louisiana in 1797.[40]

Spanish officials had by no means been unanimous in supporting this risky and paradoxical strategy of importing aliens and heretics to ward off aliens and heretics. The barón de Carondelet, who succeeded Miró as governor-general of Louisiana in late 1791, doubted the loyalty of American expatriates. He feared that they would enable the United States to seize Louisiana "without unsheathing the sword."[41] Such a notion had not escaped American leaders. In a private letter to President George Washington, Secretary of State Thomas Jefferson had praised the liberal Spanish immigration policy as "the means of delivering to us peaceably, what may otherwise cost us a war."[42] In retrospect his words seem prophetic. From Upper Louisiana to East Florida, immigrants from the United States began to Americanize Spain's border provinces long before the United States acquired those territories politically.[43]

Whatever the risks of trying to transform Anglo Americans into loyal vassals of the

Crown, the obvious indifference or disloyalty of many Anglo American frontiersmen to their own government had encouraged Spanish officials to believe it could be done. During the 1780s, some Americans plotted to create their own independent nations beyond the Appalachians and to place themselves under Spanish protection. A number of American secessionists, with the young, smooth, double-dealing former brigadier general in the Continental Army James Wilkinson most prominent among them, sought the cooperation of Spanish officials in Louisiana. In Governor Miró, who dreamed of the "delivering up of Kentucky into his Majesty's hands," they found a willing accomplice.[44] Meanwhile, Madrid lent moral support but avoided direct assistance that might bring it into conflict with the United States.

Just as extraordinary circumstances on the North American frontier led Spain to depart radically from its normal commercial and immigration policies, so did Spanish officials adapt time-honored Indian policy to new frontier exigencies. Happily for Spain, its interest in protecting its claims by blocking the southwesterly flow of Americans coincided with that of many tribal leaders, who regarded the burgeoning American population as a threat to their hunting lands. Out of that mutual interest came a series of Spanish-Indian alliances, which infuriated American frontiersmen, but slowed American expansion across much of the region.

The first of these Spanish-Indian pacts was initiated by a young Creek leader, Alexander McGillivray. Raised by his French-Creek mother of the prominent Wind clan and educated in Charleston and Savannah by his father, a well-to-do Scottish Indian trader, McGillivray bridged two worlds—as did many leaders of southern tribes in his day.[45] He was only one of many leaders in a decentralized society of villages and clans, but his unusual background made him a prominent spokesperson with outsiders, and his ability to garner resources from those same outsiders enhanced his influence among Creeks. Immediately after learning of the retrocession of Florida to Spain, McGillivray had written to the Spanish governor of West Florida, Arturo O'Neill, extending congratulations and asking for Spanish protection against Americans in Georgia who coveted Creek lands. McGillivray, who owned a plantation on the Coosa River, made it clear that he had something to offer in return for Spanish protection. "The Crown of Spain," he explained, "will Gain & Secure a powerful barrier in these parts against the ambitious and encroaching Americans."[46]

McGillivray had struck the right cord. Spanish officials moved quickly to accept his offer. At Pensacola, in June 1784, several Spanish officials signed a treaty of alliance with "the Creek Nations," with McGillivray representing the Creeks. Later that month in Mobile, Spanish officials signed similar treaties with leaders of the Alabamas and the Choctaws, and in July with Chickasaws.[47] In the fall, Governor Zéspedes smoked "the peace pipe" with Seminole and Creek leaders at St. Augustine, expressing hope "that you and all the Indian people will be as good friends of the Spanish as you have been of the English."[48]

Written treaties with the southern tribes represented a departure from prior Spanish policy and were followed by treaties signed with Comanches in Texas and New Mexico in 1785 and 1786. Born of necessity, these documents signified a shift away from Spain's sixteenth-century presumption that Indians owed allegiance to the Crown. As Governor Gayoso explained from Natchez in 1792, Indians were "free and independent nations . . . under His Majesty's protection."[49] Thus, in the same years that Spain relied on traditional missions and presidios to Hispanicize California's coastal peoples, it responded to different imperatives elsewhere in the borderlands with written treaties that promised protection and trade and with tolerance toward religious and cultural differences.

As in the past, trade goods and gifts held Spanish-Indian alliances together. "Indians," McGillivray had explained to Governor O'Neill, "will attach themselves to & Serve them best who Supply their Necessities"—an observation that he might have made about whites as well.[50] Trade with Europeans had become more essential to the southern tribes than ever before. Easy credit and access to European markets had transformed them into societies of debt-ridden commercial hunters in relentless pursuit of deerskins. With the passage of time, their role in international markets had shifted from that of trading partners to mere producers. Gunpowder and guns had become essential to the economies of the Creeks, Choctaws, and Chickasaws, as had European tools that facilitated sewing, cooking, and farming. Finally, many of the southern tribesmen had also developed an unquenchable thirst for liquor. Unscrupulous Anglo-American traders, themselves members of a heavy-drinking society, were pleased to try to meet Indian demands for alcohol and thus extract the best terms of exchange from stupefied clients.[51]

Although southern tribes had become more dependent than ever on European goods, Spain remained ill-equipped to supply them. Much as Spanish officials in Louisiana had turned to experienced Frenchmen to maintain continuity in the Indian trade, Spanish governors in the Floridas turned to Scotsmen.[52] Governor Zéspedes not only allowed a firm headed by two British loyalists, William Panton and John Leslie, to continue to monopolize trade with Creeks and Seminoles in St. Augustine as they had in the last days of British rule, but he took the extraordinary measure of permitting the two Scotsmen to import British trade goods—a decision sanctioned by his superiors even though it violated Spanish policy. Zéspedes regarded this arrangement with Panton, Leslie & Co. as a temporary expedient that would end shortly, when Spain trained its own Indian agents and produced its own goods for the trade.[53]

That day never came. Instead, Panton, Leslie & Co. expanded their operations westward, establishing posts at San Marcos de Apalachee, Pensacola, Mobile, and finally high on the Mississippi at Fort San Fernando (present-day Memphis) in 1795. Indian hunters throughout this vast trading network furnished Panton, Leslie & Co. with over half the deerskins sold on the London market by 1792. Through its generosity to Spanish officials, the company had received privileges that enabled it to crush competition, and through William Panton's friendship with Alexander McGillivray, a silent partner in the firm, they won over key Indian leaders, even among the distant Chickasaws.[54]

Spanish officials never fully trusted the company, however, suspecting quite rightly that the partners would put business above national loyalty. Indeed, the Spanish governors posted a scattering of their own Indian agents to watch both the Indians and the Scots.[55] But what was good for the Company proved good for the Crown. Although Panton and Leslie flooded the Floridas with British merchandise, they helped maintain the allegiance of the southern tribes. McGillivray, for example, who may have profited more from his Spanish alliance than any other Indian leader, requested and received secret shipments of arms and munitions from the Spanish governors in New Orleans, Pensacola, and St. Augustine, laundered through the stores of Panton, Leslie & Co. He used those arms so effectively in 1786 to defend Creek lands against the spurious claims of Georgians moving west of the Ogeechee River that Spain feared its role as an arms supplier would be regarded by the Americans as a hostile act.

Spanish officials soon recognized the limits of their success in negotiating with the southern tribes. Although more abundant than ever before, trade goods never seemed sufficient, and by 1794, annual gifts to Indians in Louisiana and West Florida cost 55,000 pesos, or 10 percent of the total budget for those provinces.[56] Then, too, competition from Anglo Americans increased after 1789 when the fragmented United States abandoned the Articles of Confederation and adopted a strong central government that could take a tougher position in negotiating with Indians. Like other tribal leaders, McGillivray tried to play both sides of the field and traveled to New York in 1790 to sign a favorable treaty with the Americans. Until his death at Panton's store in Pensacola in 1793, after long bouts of illness, the Indian leader drew stipends from both American and Spanish officials.[57]

Whatever its failings, the peculiar policy of using a company of Scottish merchants to trade British goods to American Indians helped Spain to achieve its goal of building a coalition against American expansion. The arrangement worked well through the early 1790s, reaching its high-water mark with the Treaty of Nogales. In October 1793, Governor Carondelet convoked representatives of several tribes, including Cherokees, Chickasaws, Choctaws, and Creeks, at Fort Nogales, built two years before at the mouth of the Yazoo River in Choctaw territory. There, native American representatives signed a document that on paper if not in fact, unified the major southeastern tribes into a confederation. This treaty of mutual assistance obliged the tribes "to contribute on their part to the preservation of [Spain's] Dominion throughout all the provinces of Louisiana and both Floridas."[58]

The Treaty of Nogales fashioned by Governor Carondelet represented a more bellicose policy than the essentially commercial alliances of Miró before him. Carondelet, an energetic but impulsive and erratic career officer who succeeded Miró as governor-general of Louisiana in late 1791 and held the post until 1797, had good reason to be more pugnacious. With the outbreak of the French Revolution had come rumors that Jacobins in Louisiana would revolt, and when Spain went to war against France in 1793, reports had reached the governor that Americans would take the opportunity to seize the Mississippi. Indeed, while Spain was distracted in Europe, private American citizens, supported by French agents in the United States, hoped to drive Spain out of Louisiana and both Floridas. In St. Augustine, Gov. Juan Nepomuceno de Quesada (1790–95) put down an open rebellion from foreign-born residents whom he described as dissatisfied "with all monarchical government."[59] In Louisiana, Governor Carondelet took vigorous measures to protect the Mississippi, assembling a fresh water fleet to patrol it and building more forts along its banks. Spanish military power alone could not defend the North American frontier, Carondelet believed, and so he planned, however naively, to unite the factious southern tribes and use them "to make the most destructive war" on the Americans.[60]

The Treaty of Nogales cleared the way for Carondelet to expand Spain's military presence deeper into the territory in dispute with the United States. In Choctaw country, on the Tombigbee River over 200 miles north of Mobile, the governor built Fort Confederación in 1794—named for the Indian confederation created by the Treaty of Nogales, and in 1795 he built Fort San Fernando de las Barrancas on the strategic heights of Chickasaw Bluffs (present-day Memphis) on the Mississippi, where Panton and Leslie also opened a store.[61]

III

No matter how shrewdly officials on the scene worked to improvise policies to contain the Anglo Americans, Spain's rapid eclipse in Europe in the 1790s left it unable to sustain its position in North America. To the contrary, Spain yielded a sizable part of its North American claims in three major diplomatic setbacks, as it sought to appease England in 1790, the United States in 1795, and France in 1800.

The first sign of retreat in North America occurred on the Pacific Northwest coast, where England forced Spain to surrender its exclusive claims through an episode at Nootka Sound, an obscure spot on Vancouver Island. The troubles at Nootka originated with the 1778 visit of the celebrated Capt. James Cook to the Pacific Northwest. In his published journal, Cook had told of the fortunes to be made by marketing the silky pelts of Northwest coast sea otter in Canton. His report had brought merchant vessels from several nations racing to the coastal waters off present Oregon, Washington, and British Columbia. Alarmed by this activity, the viceroy of New Spain, Manuel Antonio Flores, on his own initiative sent Capt. Esteban José Martínez in 1789 to warn foreigners away from this region that Spain claimed by right of prior discovery but did not yet occupy. Flores ordered Martínez to establish a base at Nootka Sound, on today's Vancouver Island—then believed to be on the North American mainland. Flores had evidence that Russians or Englishmen might occupy this spacious harbor, and he also foresaw that Americans might try to establish themselves on the Pacific "above our possessions of Texas, New Mexico, and the Californias" and thus "obtain the richest trade of Great China and India."[62]

When Esteban Martínez arrived at Nootka Sound in early May of 1789, he found American and British vessels already anchored there. More continued to arrive. One British trader, Capt. James Colnett, professed to carry orders from George III to take possession of the region on the strength of Captain Cook's discoveries. Captain Martínez objected strenuously, noting that Juan Pérez had discovered Nootka in 1774, four years before Cook; Martínez had served under Pérez on that voyage. Martínez and Colnett began to discuss their differences amicably, but in Martínez's cabin the morning after a late night of drinking "freely," as Colnett put it, the two headstrong men lost their tempers. Even without the aid of an interpreter, Martínez understood the meaning of what sounded to him like "Gardem España" [God Damn Spain]. Although he had received instructions to avoid words and actions that "might bring about a clash," Martínez arrested Colnett, seized two British ships and their crews, and sent them to Mexico.[63]

The incident at Nootka grew into an international crisis. Hoping to gain commercial concessions from Spain, English officials whipped up latent anti-Spanish sentiment at home and threatened war abroad. Spain in turn appealed to its French ally for help, but the French Revolution had begun and the French National Assembly had little enthusiasm for past alliances made by monarchs. Spain, then, declined to play its weak hand and capitulated to British demands at the Escorial in October 1790. In this so-called Nootka Convention, Spain agreed to share the Pacific Northwest with Britain, return British property seized at Nootka, and make reparations. Appeasement averted an almost certain and potentially disastrous war for Spain, but its relinquishment of exclusive sovereignty of a portion of America's Pacific coast also marked the beginning of its slow withdrawal from North America.[64]

The significance of this setback is clearer in retrospect than it was to contemporaries, for Spain did not immediately abandon its interest in the Pacific Northwest. From distant New Orleans in the early 1790s, Governor Carondelet envisioned an overland route up the Missouri River to "near Nootka Sound," where Spain would establish a settlement "to prevent the English or the Russians from establishing themselves or extending themselves on those coasts."[65] He offered a large cash prize to the first Spanish subject to reach the Pacific from the Missouri. Carondelet's project grew out of his interest in blocking the advance of Canadian-based British fur traders all along the Upper Missouri—in preventing them from extending their smuggling operations into New Mexico, Louisiana, or invading Spanish Upper Louisiana in time of war. Anticipating Thomas Jefferson's outfitting of the Lewis and Clark expedition, a group of merchants in the intensely French town of Spanish St. Louis (the nerve center of Upper Louisiana or the Illinois country) formed the Missouri Company and sent three exploring parties toward the Pacific between 1794 and 1796. The most successful apparently got no farther than the Mandan villages in present North Dakota. Known to the St. Louis-based traders since 1790 when Jacques d'Eglise visited them, the Mandans possessed bridles and saddles from New Mexico, but the Spanish also found British traders in the Mandan villages.[66]

Although Spanish-sponsored overland expeditions failed to reach Nootka from Upper Louisiana, Spaniards had continued to visit the Pacific Northwest by sea. In 1791 and 1792, teams of Spanish scholars and artists examined the region's native peoples, topography, flora, and fauna, as part of the brilliant five-year, around-the-world scientific expedition that Alejandro Malaspina had begun from Cádiz in July 1789. In quest of knowledge rather than treasure, these Renaissance explorers had motives quite different from those of their sixteenth-century counterparts. In at least one respect, however, there was continuity. Two of the exploring vessels, the last that Spain would send to the region, were also to make a careful reconnaissance of the Strait of Juan de Fuca "to decide once and for all" if a strait connected the Pacific and Atlantic. The idea of the mythic Strait of Anián had surfaced again.[67]

Spain also maintained political interests in the coast north of California. Although the Nootka Convention granted England rights to the Pacific Northwest, it had not precluded Spain from also establishing itself in the region, nor had it established a clear northern boundary for Spanish California. England claimed that the agreement permitted it to range freely down the coast to San Francisco Bay, the northernmost Spanish settlement. Spain hoped to place the boundary farther north, at the Straits of

55. Dances held by Chief Tlu-pa-na-nootl for Malaspina, on the beach at Nootka, 1791. Wash drawing, probably by Tomás de Suria. Courtesy, Museo Naval, Madrid, and Robin Inglis.

Juan de Fuca on the North American mainland, in order to hold the British at a distance from California and New Mexico. Toward that end, in 1792 Spain established a short-lived settlement at Neah Bay, commanding the entrance to the Straits of Juan de Fuca on what is today the Washington State side.[68]

Meanwhile English and Spanish negotiators arrived at the thriving village of Nootka in the summer of 1792 to work out the details of the convention. They failed. Although his position was weak, Spain's negotiator, Juan Francisco de Bodega y Quadra, a hospitable and cunning naval officer, veteran mariner, and head of the Naval Department of San Blas, charmed his worthy opponent, George Vancouver, into a stalemate.[69] Negotiations shifted back to European drawing rooms, where chilly English-Spanish relations had warmed. The French execution of Louis XVI in 1793 had driven England and Spain into an alliance, and the rare rapprochement allowed the two monarchies to resolve the long-standing Nootka controversy. England reserved its right to trade along the coast, Spain surrendered its exclusive claim to the region, and both sides agreed to leave unresolved the question of California's northern boundary. On March 23, 1795, ceremonies at Nootka brought the quarrel to a formal end, with both sides abandoning the site.[70]

Spain had lacked the resources and the muscle to appropriate more than scientific knowledge in this remote corner of the Pacific. It never extended its towns, ranches,

56. *Two tent-like structures mark the Spanish settlement under construction at Neah Bay (then Núñez Gaona), the earliest European settlement in what is now Washington state. The Spanish corvette* Princesa, *and the goletas* Sutil *and* Mexicana *are in the foreground with Indian vessels. Ink drawing by José Cardero. Courtesy, Museo de America, Madrid, and Robin Inglis.*

presidios, or missions north of San Francisco Bay.[71] Possession, as Spain had discovered elsewhere, did not reside in papal bulls, prior discovery, scrupulous attention to acts of possession, or the planting of wooden crosses. Sovereignty depended on occupancy, and occupancy depended on economic development. Capable officers close to the scene had proposed ways to use private companies to compete for a share of the profits that foreigners reaped from the sea otter trade but Spain failed to nurture private enterprise. Bureaucratic obstacles to entrepreneurial activity, an essentially reactive policy, and ongoing crises in the mother country prevented Spain from competing with its rivals in the Pacific Northwest—much as Spain failed in the Floridas and the Mississippi Valley, where it yielded still more ground.[72]

IV

On July 22, 1795, a few months after the cordial ceremonies at Nootka, Spain betrayed its British ally. At Basel, Spain made a separate peace with the French Republicans, whose army had successfully invaded Spain after Godoy provoked a war. For this prudent surrender, Manuel Godoy received the title Prince of the Peace from Carlos IV and the enmity of Britain. As Spain resumed its traditional relationship with France, threat of war with Britain grew, and Godoy concluded that he needed the friendship or at least the neutrality of the United States. Without it, Spain would be hard-pressed to defend Mexico or any of its Caribbean possessions from a likely British assault. To win American favor, then, the Prince of the Peace reopened negotiations with the United States over the West Florida boundary and yielded to American demands.[73]

On October 27, 1795, in the Treaty of San Lorenzo del Escorial (best known to Americans as Pinckney's Treaty), Spain accepted 31° as the northern border of West Florida, thus abandoning its claims to the Ohio Valley and the one-hundred-mile strip below the Yazoo River, including the rich Natchez District. Spain also granted Americans the right to navigate the Mississippi to the sea without paying duties and with the additional right of unloading and storing goods for reshipment on oceangoing vessels at New Orleans or some other convenient place of deposit in Spanish territory.

From Godoy's vantage point, the Treaty of San Lorenzo represented a realistic surrender to new demographic and economic realities along the Spanish-U.S. frontier, and a tacit admission that Spain's policies had failed.[74] For the ever-optimistic Governor Carondelet in Louisiana, the treaty represented defeat snatched from the jaws of victory. First, it left Spain with nothing to offer to American secessionists, whose imminent success, he believed, would have divided and weakened the young American nation. Second, it cost Spain its hard-won alliances with the Creeks, Choctaws, and Chickasaws, whose lands now fell squarely into United States territory.[75]

If Spain lost the large southeastern tribes as a potential barrier against American expansion, the southern tribes lost the political leverage that their alliances with Spain had given them in their dealings with the United States. Their overhunted forests depleted of deer, native hunters possessed little of value to barter for alcohol and trade goods except their lands. Over the next several decades, American officials bribed, threatened, tricked, and forced Indian leaders, no matter how assimilated, to sign away their lands and emigrate beyond the Mississippi.[76] Meanwhile, as the deerskin trade declined, so did the profits of Panton, Leslie & Co. Reorganized by John Forbes after Panton's death in 1801, the company continued to operate in Spanish territory into the 1810s, but it slowly abandoned the Indian trade in favor of land speculation and became increasingly friendly to American interests, correctly anticipating the next shift in the political winds.

The Treaty of San Lorenzo, which was not implemented fully until 1798, marked only the beginning of Spain's retreat in the Mississippi Valley. Godoy had decided to withdraw still farther. He had become convinced of the futility of defending Louisiana from the United States, which refused to guarantee its territorial integrity as part of the San Lorenzo agreement. Spanish war vessels patrolled the Mississippi and forts dotted its banks, but Godoy judged them insufficient to defend 1,000 miles of river in the event of war. "You can't put doors on open country," he lamented.[77] Without Louisiana, Spain could shorten its line of defense and economize. Although commerce had increased dramatically on the Mississippi since Spain acquired Louisiana from France, the province still cost Spain far more than it garnered in revenues.

In December 1795, Godoy offered to trade Louisiana to France, reasoning that a friendly and powerful France would serve as a buffer between the United States and the rich mines of northern Mexico. Key French leaders, as Godoy knew, had never abandoned the vision of a Western empire. Thus, when he dangled Louisiana in front of the French Directory in December 1795, he asked in exchange for the return of the eastern half of the sugar-rich island of Santo Domingo to Spain. France declined the offer of Louisiana at that price, but soon got it at a bargain rate. In 1799, Napoleon Bonaparte seized control of the French government and began to pressure Carlos IV to surrender Louisiana as well as the Floridas to France. The king would not budge on the Floridas, but Napoleon did extort Louisiana from Spain in exchange for a throne in central Italy for María Luisa's brother—a promise that he never kept. On October 1, 1800, France and Spain reached this conditional agreement in an accord signed secretly at San Ildefonso. Two years later, on October 15, 1802, after angering Napoleon with further refusals to alienate the Floridas and with fruitless demands that Napoleon fill his part of the bargain in Europe, the hapless Carlos IV ordered officials in Louisiana to turn the province over to French emissaries.

Spain and France had tried with only limited success to conduct these negotiations in secret, in the well-founded belief that if the United States learned of them it would invade Louisiana to prevent the transfer. As one New York journalist noted in 1796, the United States had little to fear from "plodding Spaniards," but it needed to "prevent any powerful nation from making establishments in our neighbourhood."[78]

Anxious to keep Americans at arm's length from New Spain, Spain had also stipulated in the agreement at San Ildefonso that France not relinquish Louisiana to a third party. Within a year, Napoleon had broken that agreement, too. With his plans to restore the French empire in America shaken by his inability to crush an intractable slave rebellion in French Haiti and in need of American neutrality during hostilities with England, Napoleon quickly changed strategies and sold Louisiana to the United States. The deal was struck in Paris on April 30, 1803.

At the time of the sale to the United States, France had held Louisiana so briefly that its officials had yet to assume control of the government at New Orleans. On November 30, in the Spanish-built cabildo or city hall, on what is today Jackson Square, Spanish officials surrendered the province to France. In the same room a few weeks later, on December 20, French officials transferred possession of Upper and Lower Louisiana to a delegation from the United States. Symbolic but emotional ceremonies at St. Louis on March 9 and 10, 1804, and at New Madrid on March 18, 1804, formalized the completion of the process in Upper Louisiana.[79]

Spaniards did not abandon Louisiana wholesale, as they had the Floridas in 1763, but many departed for Texas, West Florida, or other Spanish-held lands, some probably bearing the sentiments expressed by one Spanish officer toward "ambitious, restless, lawless, conniving, changeable, and turbulent" Americans: "I am so disgusted with hearing them that I can hardly wait to leave them behind me."[80]

V

Spain declared the United States' purchase of Louisiana invalid on the grounds that Napoleon lacked title—he had not fulfilled his part of the agreement made at San Ildefonso in 1800 and had no right to alienate Louisiana to a third party. For the next decade, Spanish officials tried to regain Louisiana, but more pressing problems quickly presented themselves. For its part, the United States not only dismissed Spanish allegations of the illegality of its new acquisition but asserted that its purchase of Louisiana included most of West Florida and all of Texas. Those extravagant American claims, coupled with the same demographic, economic, and political pressures from the United States that had forced Spain to retreat in the lower Mississippi Valley, continued to keep Spain on the defensive in the opening decade of the nineteenth century.[81]

Spain and France had never formalized the borders of their North American possessions with precision, and the documents transferring Louisiana from Spain to France in 1800 and from France to the United States in 1803 described the boundaries in ambiguous and contradictory language. Spain, then, had much to negotiate with the new owners of Louisiana, but the Americans' expansionist president, Thomas Jefferson, seemed to prefer coercion to negotiation.

East of the Mississippi, the United States insisted that Louisiana extended to the

Perdido River, which had separated Spanish Florida from French Louisiana prior to 1762. This claim had murky legal basis. It ignored the twenty-year existence of British West Florida and Napoleon's government disavowed it. Nonetheless, for strategic and commercial reasons, it would appear, the Jefferson administration tried to bully Spain into surrendering West Florida or selling it to the United States (for good measure, the United States tried to buy East Florida as well). In 1804, Jefferson sent troops to the edge of West Florida, whose American residents far outnumbered Hispanics or Frenchmen, and threatened war. Only when convinced that military action would, in the words of one of his cabinet officers, "appear unjustifiable in the opinion of mankind and even of America," did the American president back down just short of war.[82]

West of the Mississippi, Spain also faced an aggressive United States. Jefferson claimed that Louisiana stretched to the Rockies (encompassing the entire watershed of the Mississippi-Missouri and their tributaries), and to the Rio Grande (including eastern New Mexico, northern Nuevo Santander between the Rio Grande and the Nueces, and all of Texas). Manuel Godoy, on the other hand, took the position that Louisiana extended no farther to the southwest than Natchitoches on the Red River, the site of St. Denis's old trading post. To the northwest, he argued, Louisiana did not include the Illinois country or extend up the Missouri. In short, Spain regarded Louisiana as encompassing little more than present-day Louisiana, eastern Arkansas, and eastern Missouri.[83]

Because the United States claimed lands that its citizens had yet to explore and that it dimly understood, Jefferson sponsored exploration at government expense. Meriwether Lewis and William Clark journeyed up the Missouri River from St. Louis to the mouth of the Columbia River in 1804–6, and Thomas Freeman and Peter Custis led a group in 1806 up the Red River, whose source they mistakenly expected to find near Santa Fe. In 1806, in a closely related enterprise, Gen. James Wilkinson sent Zebulon Pike to seek the sources of the Arkansas and the Red rivers and to spy on the Spaniards in New Mexico.[84] Wilkinson, who had secretly remained in the Spanish service as "agent 13" since his involvement in secessionist schemes in the 1780s, had returned to American military service and become the ranking United States general in the West. He had escorted the American delegation that received Louisiana from France in New Orleans in 1803, and in 1805 Jefferson had dispatched him to St. Louis as governor of the Louisiana Territory—as the Americans called the upper part of the Louisiana Purchase. Wilkinson's exact purpose in sending Pike into Mexico, like many other shadowy dealings of this double agent, continues to elude full explanation.[85]

Spanish officials rightly surmised that the American government hoped to use explorers to win the friendship of Indians along navigable rivers of the Mississippi watershed and to extend the American domain at Spain's expense. Carlos Martínez de Irujo, Spain's minister to the United States, correctly understood that Jefferson wanted to push America's border "up to the coasts of the South Sea [the Pacific]."[86] Spanish officials also knew that the loss of Louisiana, however defined, had brought

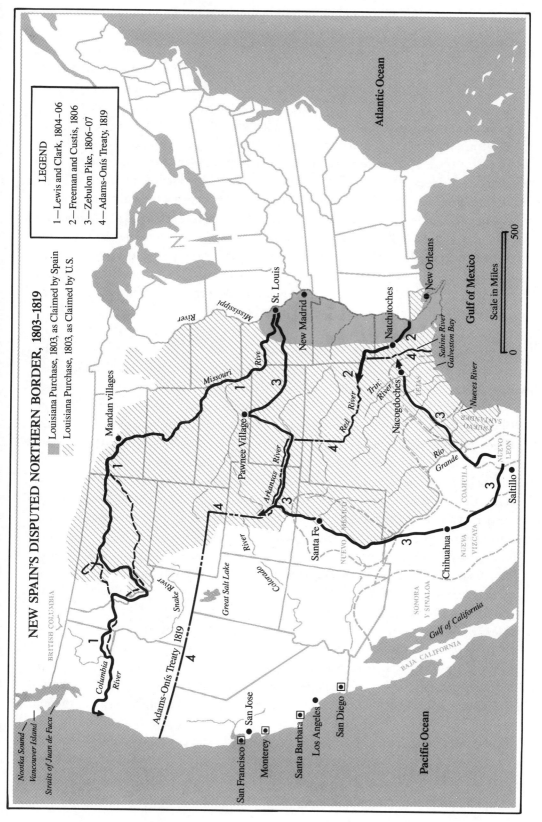

NEW SPAIN'S DISPUTED NORTHERN BORDER, 1803–1819

▨ Louisiana Purchase, 1803, as Claimed by Spain

▨ Louisiana Purchase, 1803, as Claimed by U.S.

LEGEND

1—Lewis and Clark, 1804–06
2—Freeman and Custis, 1806
3—Zebulon Pike, 1806–07
4—Adams-Onís Treaty, 1819

Map 16. New Spain's disputed northern border, 1803–19.

Americans closer to the rich mines of northern Mexico. In St. Louis in 1804, the last Spanish governor of Upper Louisiana, Carlos Dehault Delassus, reported that Americans "are already calculating the profit which they will obtain from the mines."[87]

Although American officials had taken pains to disguise their expeditions as scientific and to conceal their destinations, Spanish officials learned about these expeditions through agents, protested them, and tried to intercept them. In the case of Lewis and Clark, "Agent 13" had recommended secretly that Spain "force them to retire or take them prisoners."[88] Nemesio Salcedo, commander in chief of the Interior Provinces, sent orders to that effect to the governor of New Mexico, Fernando de Chacón, who dispatched at least four parties from Santa Fe between 1804 and 1806 to search for Lewis and Clark and to firm up Spanish alliances with peoples of the plains. Unlike his superiors in Madrid, who had little sense of North American geography, Salcedo understood the difficulty of apprehending Lewis and Clark. "Even though I realize it is not an easy undertaking," he had explained to Governor Chacón, "chance might proportion things in such a way that it might be successful."[89]

Chance favored none of the expeditions sent to find "Capt. Merry"—as Spaniards came to call Meriwether Lewis. Spanish troops had better luck intercepting the Freeman-Custis expedition. On July 29, 1806, some 635 miles up the Red River in what is today eastern Oklahoma, Francisco Viana and a detachment from Nacogdoches turned the Americans back.[90] Late that summer, an expedition from Santa Fe led by Lt. Facundo Melgares nearly crossed paths with Zebulon Pike at a Pawnee Village on the Republican River in what is today southern Nebraska. Melgares had made a broad sweep of the plains, hoping to learn the whereabouts of the expeditions of either Freeman and Custis or Lewis and Clark. His close encounter with Pike was accidental, but Pike turned it to his advantage by following Melgares's trail south to the Arkansas River. When Pike left Melgares's trace to search for the headwaters of the Arkansas in the southern Rockies, he became desperately lost. In late February 1807, Spanish troops rescued his shivering party, arrested them, and took them to Chihuahua where Nemesio Salcedo released them and allowed them to return home via Texas, to General Wilkinson. For permitting "those guilty to be freed," Salcedo received a reprimand from the Crown.[91]

Meanwhile Spaniards also gathered intelligence. Pretending to go on a hunting excursion, the marqués de Casa Calvo, the Spanish boundary commissioner and a recent governor of Louisiana, set out in 1805 from American New Orleans. With sixty-three persons, including two engineers, he intended to explore the bayous and rivers along the historic Louisiana-Texas border and to determine the site of the old presidio of Los Adaes. After Casa Calvo's departure, the American governor at New Orleans became suspicious of the Spaniard's purposes and tried but failed to intercept him on the Red River. When Casa Calvo concluded his mission and returned to New Orleans, the American governor summarily deported him.[92]

Spaniards, however, had already explored much of the area that Jefferson claimed as western Louisiana. On the northern plains beginning in the early 1790s, several Spanish trading expeditions had preceded Lewis and Clark far up the Missouri. On the southern plains between 1786 and 1793, Pedro Vial had blazed trails from San Antonio to Santa Fe, Santa Fe to Natchitoches via the Red River, and Santa Fe to St. Louis over what would come to be called the Santa Fe Trail in the 1820s.[93] The maps, diaries, and documents generated by these expeditions enabled Spanish officials to build their case from archival evidence, without further fieldwork. In response to royal orders, an elderly Mexican-born scholar, José Antonio Pichardo, prepared a thirty-one-volume, 5,127-page report on "The Limits of Louisiana and Texas." Copied and sent to Spain, Pichardo's treatise eventually aided Spanish negotiators in settling the boundary question with the United States.[94]

While both sides gathered intelligence, Jefferson sent troops toward the disputed Texas-Louisiana border, as he had to the edge of West Florida, and Nemesio Salcedo sent troops and militia to defend East Texas. Tensions mounted and bloodshed was narrowly averted in the autumn of 1806 when the respective commanders exceeded their orders and struck a deal. Gen. James Wilkinson and his counterpart, Lt. Col. Simón de Herrera, agreed to recognize a demilitarized zone between the Sabine River and the Arroyo Hondo near Natchitoches. (Wilkinson then sent a representative to Mexico City with a bill for over 150,000 pesos for his services, a sum the viceroy declined to pay). This Neutral Ground Agreement, as the Wilkinson-Herrera bargain came to be called, left the border question to await resolution by American and Spanish negotiators. Meanwhile, the neutral zone became a notorious home to fugitive slaves, outlaws, smugglers, and squatters from the United States and a staging ground for filibustering expeditions into Texas.[95]

Texas had clearly resumed its historic position as a buffer province, with Anglo Americans having replaced Frenchmen. Reawakened to the immediacy of the danger from Anglo Americans after the United States bought Louisiana, the Crown had planned in 1804 to send thousands of colonists from Spain and Santo Domingo to augment the province's 4,000 residents. The Crown also sought to provide more efficient leadership against the American threat to Texas by creating an eastern division of the Interior Provinces with the commander in chief directing operations from San Antonio. Spain's deteriorating situation in Europe, however, aborted both projects.[96] Responsibility for defending Texas, then, fell largely to officers in charge of the Comandancia General of the Provincias Internas, commanded from Chihuahua from 1803 to 1813 by the firm but gracious Nemesio Salcedo. Salcedo, whom Zebulon Pike described as of "stern countenance," had served in the king's army since his childhood in Spain, had tasted victory against the British in the Mobile and Pensacola campaigns, and then watched Spain's sad decline. His brother, Manuel Juan, had been the last Spanish governor of Louisiana before the Americans purchased it.[97]

Texas preoccupied Nemesio Salcedo and his subordinates, whose defensive measures resembled those adopted earlier in Louisiana. They welcomed Indians who wished to abandon American territory for Texas and hoped that small numbers of Alabamas, Cherokees, Chickasaws, Choctaws, Coushattas, Pascagoulas, and Shawnees would be the beginnings of an Indian buffer.[98] Officials in Texas also turned to a trading company run by foreigners in order to make gifts and trade goods more readily available to Indians. William Barr, an Irishman, and Peter Davenport, an American, performed the function that Panton and Leslie had earlier in the Floridas.[99] Then, too, Salcedo promoted immigration to East Texas from New Spain—most successfully at the new villa of Trinidad de Salcedo, founded in 1806 where the road from San Antonio to Nacogdoches crossed the Trinity River. For a time, he also opened Texas to former Spanish subjects from Louisiana—"unfortunate vassals who prefer his [Carlos IV's] rule to any other."[100] Under that dispensation, a few Americans who had become naturalized Spaniards, such as Daniel Boone, settled in Texas.[101]

Some Texas officials welcomed American immigrants from any quarter, pleased to increase the province's sparse population. Officially, however, Spain's traditional policy of excluding foreigners and foreign trade remained in force in Texas. Even in the 1780s and 1790s, when Spanish officials had invited Americans into Louisiana and the Floridas, private American citizens who ventured into the interior provinces had risked arrest, lengthy imprisonment, and death. Unlike some of his subordinates, Nemesio Salcedo saw no reason to allow Americans to trade or settle anywhere else in the interior provinces. The foreigners, Salcedo warned, "are not and will not be anything but crows to pick out our eyes."[102] Like his predecessors in Louisiana, however, Salcedo could not "put doors on open country." The well-publicized death of the veteran horse trader Philip Nolan, and the arrest of his men at the hands of Spanish troops in Texas in 1801, did not deter Americans, who continued to push into West Texas and Oklahoma to capture mustangs on the plains and to trade with Comanches, Taovayas, and Tawakonis. Other Americans trapped and traded near Santa Fe or smuggled along the California coast.[103]

VI

Whatever chance Salcedo and other officials had of protecting New Spain's northern perimeter from Anglo-American encroachment vanished after 1808, when Napoleon forced Carlos IV and his son Fernando VII to renounce their rights to the Crown. Across Spain, popular juntas organized against Napoleon's brother, Joseph, the "intruder king," governing themselves in the name of Fernando VII. The struggle against the French army of occupation left Spain without a clearly legitimate ruler and threw all of Spain's new world colonies into disarray. Fernando's return in 1814 restored only a semblance of order. During his absence, a liberal *Junta Central* had directed operations in his name, forming a constitutional government at Cádiz with representatives from the American provinces—including New Mexico and Texas, both of whom deplored their underdevelopment and their vulnerability to the "aggressions of the United States."[104] Fernando's refusal to recognize the constitution drawn up at Cádiz in 1812 or the representative provincial and municipal councils that it had legitimized, alienated many of his supporters and colonial administration broke down again. Finally, in 1820, the reactionary king survived a liberal military coup only by agreeing to govern under the new constitution.[105]

During the tumultuous decade of the 1810s, Spain's American colonies began to slip away. In those North American provinces that faced attacks from without as well as rebellion from within, Spain faced impossible odds—as it first discovered in West Florida.

Many of West Florida's numerous Anglo-American residents had taken an oath of allegiance to Spain, and they initially responded to the chaos in the peninsula by forming a junta to rule in the name of the deposed Fernando—as popular assemblies in Spain and elsewhere in Spanish America had begun to do. Quickly, however, some of those Anglo Americans showed their true colors. Encouraged by officials in Washington, they marched on Baton Rouge. In the middle of the night on September 23, 1810, amidst shouts that one Spaniard recognized as "Uurra! Waschintown!" the rebels easily overpowered the dilapidated Spanish fort at Baton Rouge and its twenty-eight defenders. The insurgents arrested the commandant, Carlos Dehault Delassus, and raised a flag with a lone star over the village. After declaring West Florida an independent republic, they petitioned the United States for annexation, and President James Madison responded quickly. He refused to recognize the rebel government but insisted that West Florida, as far as the Perdido River, had belonged to the United States since 1803. To restore order, President Madison sent troops to occupy Baton Rouge. Later, the Americans would incorporate the area from Baton Rouge to the Pearl River (the so-called Florida parishes) into Louisiana, which became a state in 1812.[106]

West Florida between the Pearl and Perdido rivers, also under siege by Americans and within the area claimed by Madison, remained in Spanish control for three more years. Vicente Folch, the Catalán-born governor at Pensacola, effectively directed the defense of Mobile in November 1810. Although he had few men or supplies and no prospect of obtaining them, he confused and divided his American adversaries and then defeated the whiskey-sotted remnants of one small invading army in a skirmish not far from town. The victory only delayed the inevitable, as Folch himself understood. Folch, who had begun service in the Mississippi Valley in 1787 under his uncle, Esteban Miró, believed that Spain could not hold West Florida and would do well to be rid of it. His assessment soon proved correct.[107]

In 1813, during the English-American War of 1812, United States forces under Gen. James Wilkinson captured Mobile without firing a shot—a preemptive strike aimed at stopping the British from taking the port. After the war, the Americans never returned Mobile. Instead, they incorporated the area between the Perdido and the

Pearl rivers into the Mississippi Territory (created in 1798). In 1817, Americans divided the area between the Perdido and the Pearl in half, putting Mobile and environs in the new territory of Alabama and leaving the remainder in the newly formed state of Mississippi). Pensacola also fell to the Americans during the war of 1812. In the fall of 1814, a detachment led by Andrew Jackson took Pensacola, which a small number of British troops had occupied despite Spain's neutrality. Jackson abandoned Pensacola after ousting the British but destroyed the town's fortifications, and Spain never rebuilt them. Demoralized over their dim prospects, some of Pensacola's residents probably emigrated, while the town continued to stagnate. Its poor soils and relative inaccessibility had made it unattractive to American settlers, compared to Natchez, Baton Rouge, or Mobile; its population in 1819, not counting the diminished garrison, stood at 992, of whom 343 were slaves.[108]

Echoes of the West Florida rebellion soon reverberated in East Florida and in Texas, where Spanish insurrectionists, American adventurers or *filibusteros*, and the United States government also combined in explosive mixtures. In 1812–13, some American residents of East Florida, backed by volunteers from Georgia and encouraged by the Madison administration, tried to establish an independent territory and have it annexed to the United States. These self-styled "patriots" took control of most of northeastern Florida—Amelia Island at the mouth of the St. Marys River and the rich cotton-producing lands between the St. Marys and St. Johns rivers—and lay siege to the diminished garrison at St. Augustine itself. Although a continuing influx of Anglo Americans and other foreigners had already transformed East Florida into an Anglo-American colony in all but name, the insurrection failed, leaving devastation in its wake.[109] Congress had refused to support Madison's aggression and Spanish officials in St. Augustine had marshalled the aid of free blacks and Seminoles who forced the so-called patriots to withdraw.[110]

Other filibustering attempts followed in East Florida, most notably another seizure of Amelia Island, whose population outstripped St. Augustine and which had become the commercial center of East Florida by the 1810s. Led by a Venezuelan general of Scottish origin, Sir Gregor MacGregor, a multinational revolutionary force established the Republic of the Floridas with its own constitution and printing press on Amelia Island in 1817. With a more accessible harbor than St. Augustine's, Amelia Island offered an ideal site to prey on Spanish shipping, and the "Republicans" soon acquired an experienced commander when Luis Aury, a privateer in the service of Mexican rebels, moved his base of operations there from Galveston Island. Three hundred Spanish troops and militia from St. Augustine failed to dislodge the rebels, but before the year was out the Americans did. The United States seized the island from the revolutionaries, whom it regarded as "piratical," but never relinquished it to Spain.[111]

Meanwhile, American adventurers and Spanish-American revolutionaries also invaded Texas, to the horror of the hapless junta that governed Spain from Cádiz. With tacit support and modest monetary aid from United States officials, Mexican insurgent Bernardo Gutiérrez de Lara led a small force of Americans into Texas in 1812. By the spring of 1813 his Republican Army of the North had captured San Antonio, the scene of an earlier local rebellion against royal officials.[112] The rebels assassinated Gov. Manuel Salcedo, the nephew of Nemesio Salcedo, and proclaimed Texas an independent nation, "free of the chains which bound us under the domination of European Spain."[113] In contrast to the Floridas, New Spain still maintained a large royalist army, which had recently crushed a popular rebellion sparked by Miguel Hidalgo in 1810. Forces led by José Joaquín Arredondo recaptured Texas in 1813 and, in a bloody purge, executed tejanos suspected of republican tendencies. The poorly provisioned troops also pillaged Texas, doing nearly as much harm to loyalists as they had to rebels. Texas never recovered. The Hispanic population, which had exceeded 4,000 in 1803, fell to fewer than 2,000 by 1820 and the town of Nacogdoches nearly expired.[114] The last Spanish governor of Texas, Antonio Martínez (1817–22), sent repeated appeals to his superior for relief from the "chaos and misery." But his appeals went unanswered. In its last years as a Spanish colony, Texas lay in ruins.[115]

While Spanish-American insurgents and American adventurers tore into East Florida and Texas with the approval of officials in the Madison administration, American diplomats took advantage of Spain's weakened condition to press America's claims to the Floridas and the western border of Louisiana. Negotiations, which had begun in earnest in 1816 after the restoration of Fernando, took on special urgency for Spain in the spring of 1818 when Gen. Andrew Jackson seized San Marcos de Apalachee and Pensacola. Jackson had accused Spanish officials of harboring Indians and bandits who raided in the United States, but by occupying Spanish territory, he had exceeded his instructions and his government soon required him to withdraw. Instead of apologizing for Jackson's violations of Spanish sovereignty, however, the American secretary of state, John Quincy Adams, blamed Spain for not keeping better order in the Floridas. The message to Spain was clear. Either control the Floridas, cede them to the United States in exchange for some advantage, or lose them. Spain had only one viable option.[116]

Spanish-American negotiations ended in Washington on February 22, 1819. John Quincy Adams and the Spanish envoy to Washington, Luis de Onís, agreed that Spain would cede East Florida to the United States and would tacitly recognize America's de facto control of West Florida; the United States would relinquish its claim to Texas and would assume claims of its citizens against Spain up to the amount of five million dollars. Adams and Onís also drew a clear line separating American and Spanish possessions. The boundary began at the Sabine River, which still separates Texas from Louisiana, and then followed a jagged northwesterly course along the Red and Arkansas rivers, before moving due west to the Pacific along the 42d parallel—today, the northern border of California, Nevada, and Utah. This agreement saved Texas for Spain and created a large buffer zone between Santa Fe and American territory, thus achieving two Spanish goals, but it cost Spain the Floridas and its claims to what would become known as the Oregon country.[117]

Gov. José Coppinger, who had served in St. Augustine since 1815, welcomed the transfer of East Florida to the United States after Adams and Onís reached an agreement. Frustrated by Spain's deteriorating position in East Florida, he looked forward to better days in Cuba or some other comfortable place in the empire. Instead, he now had to wait and worry about the prospect of an invasion from the United States. The United States Senate had ratified the Adams-Onís Treaty on February 24, 1819, two days after its signing; Spain delayed over a year and a half, until October 24, 1820—its officials caught up in intrigues over eleventh-hour land grants in Florida and its government in transition to a constitutional monarchy. Spain's delay infuriated Americans, and the agreement began to unravel. The Spanish chargé in Washington reported that the Americans regarded Spain with "mockery, scorn and contempt" and seemed likely to take Florida by force.[118] Finally, acrimonious exchanges ended, Spain ratified the treaty, and on July 10, 1821, Governor Coppinger ordered the Spanish flag lowered for the last time over the Castillo de San Marcos. That same day, Spanish officials, troops, and their families boarded vessels for Cuba.[119]

A week later, on July 17, a similar transfer took place at Pensacola. Officials there "burst into tears," according to one witness, "delivering up the keys of the archives, the vessels lying at anchor in full view, to waft them to their distant port."[120] Many civilian residents of Pensacola and St. Augustine remained behind—as did most pro-Spanish Indians, including some Seminoles who had declined the government's offer to move them to Texas.

Spain had good reason to want loyal Seminoles in Texas. Angered that the Adams-Onís Treaty had not delivered Texas to the United States, American westerners talked of taking it themselves. James Long, a drifter from Natchez, acted as well as talked. In 1819, he invaded Texas and declared it an independent republic, but Spanish troops under Col. Ignacio Pérez pushed him back into Louisiana before the year was out. In 1820, Long returned and established a new insurgent base on Galveston Bay, only to see his pretext for invasion vanish. Although free land rather than political principles motivated Long and his supporters, they had enveloped their cause in American revolutionary rhetoric, professing the wish to free Texas from "the yoke of Spanish authority . . . the most atrocious despotism that ever disgraced the annals of Europe."[121] On February 24, 1821, the Mexican-born officer Agustín de Iturbide launched a successful drive for Mexican independence. Throughout New Spain, royalist forces melted away, and the northern provinces from California to Texas became part of the newly independent nation without firing a shot. James Long had become a rebel without a cause.[122]

Located well beyond the immediate interest of the United States and its citizens, and isolated from Spanish-American insurgents as well, northern New Spain from New Mexico to California had experienced little of the violence that devastated Texas and the Floridas in the 1810s. A French privateer who purported to represent the insurgent cause had sacked Monterey in 1818, but from San Francisco to Santa Fe, the worst effects of the independence struggles had been economic. The crisis in Spain, and the violent 1810 rebellion in New Spain, had disrupted commerce, cut off supplies for soldiers and missionaries, diminished the flow of goods for the Indian trade, left unpaid the salaries of government officials, and made smuggling a necessity rather than an opportunity. Thus, Iturbide's declaration of independence had met no resistance from California to Texas. Instead, cautious frontier governors simply waited until the insurgents won, then they swore allegiance to the new government.

The reactions of Hispanics in the interior provinces to Mexican independence can never be fully known. Like their counterparts along the Gulf coast, however, many seem to have regarded the end of the Spanish era with ambivalence. They organized traditional celebrations as might have marked the coronation of a new sovereign, and cries of *viva la independencia*! echoed in the streets of San Antonio, Santa Fe, and Monterey, where *viva el rey*! had once sounded. Yet, even as optimists cheered their prospects for a better tomorrow without Spain, there were those who regarded the future with trepidation and the past with nostalgia. At Monterey, an assemblage watched in stony silence as the Spanish flag descended for the last time over the plaza, on April 11, 1822. The Spanish-born governor, Vicente de Sola, toothless, his hair and beard nearly white, stepped forward and swept the flag into his arms before it fell to the ground, then turned to a representative of the new government and explained: "They do not cheer because they are unused to independence."[123]

The ceremonies in Monterey in the spring of 1822 marked the end of an era. Centuries of struggle for the control of a continent had been undone in a decade that saw Spain lose all of its border provinces in North America, from Florida to California, as well as New Spain itself. In the old interior provinces of New Spain, however, the new era resembled the old in important ways. Independent Mexico now fell heir to the boundary agreed upon in the Adams-Onís negotiations, and to Mexico also fell the task of defending that boundary from an avaricious neighbor. Echoing warnings that Spanish officials had issued since the 1780s, Mexico's first minister to Washington reported in 1822 that, "the haughtiness of these Republicans, does not permit them to look upon us as equals . . . their conceit extends itself in my opinion to believe that their capital will be that of all the Americas."[124] Those themes continued to be heard in Mexican political circles, even after the United States annexed Texas in 1845 and took possession of the vast region from California to Texas in the victor's peace that followed the successful American invasion of Mexico in 1846–48.

11

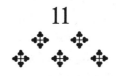

Frontiers and Frontier Peoples Transformed

Both from native seeds as well as from those brought over from Europe, the land produces an incredible quantity. . . . As for our cows, horses, [and] sheep . . . that have been brought over from Europe already, they breed very profusely.
fray Alonso de Benavides, 1634 writing about New Mexico

Their religious and civil usages manifest a predilection for the Spanish customs. There are several Christians among them . . . most of them speak and understand Spanish.
William Bartram among Creeks and Seminoles at Alachua Savanna, Florida, 1770s

Those people, reared in freedom and accustomed to independence, are no longer inclined to suffer with resignation.
Bernardo de Gálvez, ca. 1785–86, speaking of frontier soldiers

In 1826, a Pueblo Indian appealed to New Mexico officials to stop non-Indians from acquiring land belonging to his community. On behalf of the "principal citizens of the Pueblo of Pecos," *alcalde* Rafael Aguilar reminded Mexican officials that Pueblo Indians enjoyed the rights of "citizens of the new republic of Mexico," that Spain's law had guaranteed their ownership of four square leagues of land around their pueblo, and that non-Indians had violated the law by ursurping Pecos lands.[1]

302

Aguilar's petition, written in phonetic Spanish, was one of several formal complaints lodged in the 1820s by natives of Pecos to protect their farms and pastures. The petitions paid off. In 1829 the New Mexico legislature ordered non-Indians to vacate Pecos Pueblo lands.

Pueblo Indians, like the *pecoseños* for whom Rafael Aguilar spoke, had retained their own language, religion, and cultural identity throughout two and a quarter centuries of Spanish rule. Nonetheless, exposure to Hispanic neighbors and missionaries had added new dimensions to the Pueblos' culture, enabling them to meet Spaniards on common ground. By the end of the colonial era, Pueblo leaders such as Aguilar held Hispanic offices, understood how and when to appeal to Hispanic law, communicated with Hispanics in their language and on their terms, and identified themselves and their children with a Spanish surname and with Christian given names.[2]

Hispanic influences also extended to the heart of economic life at Pueblo communities such as Pecos. In addition to the corn, beans, squash, and cotton they had cultivated for centuries, Pueblos grew tomatoes, chiles, and new varieties of corn and squash brought by Spaniards from central Mexico, as well as exotic corriander, wine grapes, cantaloupe, watermelons, wheat, and other imports from the Old World. Pueblos also tended apricot, apple, cherry, peach, pear, and plum orchards, and raised sheep, goats, cattle, horses, mules, donkeys, oxen, and chickens—all previously unknown to them.[3] Eventually, as one historian has noted, the origin of some of the new foods "faded from memory . . . [and] came to be accepted as 'Indian food,' eaten in the kivas and named in rituals and prayers,"[4] but linguistically and ceremonially, Pueblos retained the identity of foods of foreign origin.[5]

In adopting these new crops and livestock, Pueblos had enriched their economy and diet.[6] Changes introduced by Spaniards, however, also had deleterious effects. Spanish-introduced diseases and raids by nomads riding Spanish-introduced horses had taken a toll at all the Pueblo communities. At Pecos itself, especially hard-hit by raiders from the Plains, the population had dwindled from a thousand or so in 1700 to fewer than 150 by century's end.[7] By 1829 it hardly mattered that Pecos won a legal victory against Hispanic encroachers, for the pecoseños were too few to prevent Hispanics from killing their stock, poisoning their water holes, and otherwise making their lives intolerable.[8] In the late 1830s, the residents of Pecos, numbering fewer than twenty, abandoned the town forever and moved far across the Rio Grande to Jémez Pueblo, which became their permanent home.

Although the story of Pecos Pueblo exemplifies the Hispanic impact on the Pueblo world, the details of the story are unique to Pecos. Even among Indians as seemingly similar as Pueblos, the effects of Hispanic influence varied greatly. Pueblos such as Abó and Quarai, for example, had become extinct earlier than Pecos; others, strengthened by their adaptions to the Hispanic world or isolated from it, have survived to the present day. Pueblos closest to Spaniards abandoned the tradition of matrilineal

57. Iron tools and weapons stood high on the list of European goods adopted by Indians. Indian Blacksmith Shop (Pueblo Zuñi). Lithograph based on a drawing by Richard H. Kern, 1851. Lorenzo Sitgreaves, Report of an Expedition down the Zuni and Colorado Rivers *(Washington, D.C., 1853).*

ownership of household and lands, while isolated pueblos came under less pressure to shift ownership to men in the Spanish fashion. Directly or indirectly, however, Hispanic influences transformed all of the Pueblo communities irrevocably—even the isolated Hopis, who never resubmitted to Spanish rule after the great revolt of 1680.[9]

I

Throughout North America, in ways large and small, Spanish influences changed the cultures of all native Americans who lived within trading distance of Spanish communities. In 1743, a Jesuit who visited a small group of Indians at the mouth of the Miami River in South Florida was surprised to find them speaking Spanish. Far from any Spanish mission or settlement, those Calusa and Key Indians had learned Spanish from sailors from Havana, with whom they traded.[10] In 1808, Capt. Francisco Amangual rode into an isolated Comanche village on the southern plains where he was greeted by "well dressed" chiefs wearing "long red coats with blue collars and cuffs, white buttons, [and] yellow (imitation gold) galloons."[11]

Change had been a constant feature of native life before the arrival of Europeans, but with their coming the pace of change accelerated throughout North America.[12] Rapid, profound change began immediately in the wake of initial Spanish-Indian contact, wherever alien infectious diseases killed high numbers of Indians and altered the societies of the survivors. The depth, pace, and quality of Spain's transforming influence on North American natives depended, however, on circumstances unique to time and place. Natives whom Spaniards had assembled in missions or reduced to slavery came under direct pressure to change; others felt Spanish influence indirectly, through markets, trade goods, or Spanish livestock. The extent to which change damaged or benefited a people also depended on the nature of their cultures, economies, and polities.[13] The horse, for example, brought about a transportation revolution for Apaches, Comanches, and other Plains peoples, enabling them to build more mobile and militarily powerful societies and to maintain a high degree of independence from Europeans; the horse also helped turn Cherokees, Chickasaws, Choctaws, Creeks, and other natives of the southern woodlands, into commercial hunters, contributing to their utter dependency on Europeans.

Geographical location itself shaped the direction that change would take. By the eighteenth century, farming peoples in southwestern America, who occupied margi-

58. Like many Indian peoples in the Southeast, this Caddo couple depicted near Nacogdoches about 1830 had adopted European clothing, although the man's ruffled shirt collar had long since gone out of vogue. Watercolor by Lino Sánchez y Tapia. Courtesy, Thomas Gilcrease Institute of American History and Art, Tulsa.

nal lands distant from strong markets, had a better chance to strengthen and enlarge their societies through selective adoption of Spanish introductions than did south-eastern natives. Pimas along the Gila River in what is today southern Arizona, for example, raised Spanish wheat, employed Spanish farm implements, increased food production, and sent surpluses to Hispanic markets. The Pimas' population grew by 50 percent over the course of the eighteenth and early nineteenth centuries, notwith-standing fatalities from new diseases; their villages increased from seven to eleven.[14] Apalachee farmers, on the other hand, had adapted remarkably well to Spanish mission life but were swept into the vortex of European wars and markets and annihilated along with other Florida tribes. Thus, while Pimas flourished in the desert of Arizona in the eighteenth century, Indians had largely disappeared from the rich meadows and game-filled forests of Florida.

Spain's goal, of course, had not been the annihilation of Indians, but rather their transformation into tax-paying Christians. The Crown had supported missions for that express purpose, but those institutions had the inherent limitation of separating Indians from the very society that Spanish policymakers wanted Indians to enter—reducing them "to the isolation of their wretched pueblos," as Juan Bautista de Anza said of the Pima missions.[15] Moreover, missionaries themselves had stood as obstacles to the full incorporation of Indians into Hispanic life. Convinced until the end of the colonial era that Indians at best were like smart children, and at worst "very limited in comprehension and lacking in reasoning ability," in the words of one Franciscan in Texas, the friars felt obliged "to determine everything that has to be done, even down to the very smallest details."[16] Paternalistic missionaries, who regarded Indians as "always children," and believed they could never achieve full religious understanding on a par with Europeans, much less become ordained, sought to protect Indians from the manifest dangers of life in the secular world.[17] Thus the friars aimed to build self-contained communities of Indians but did not prepare Indians to become self-reliant in Hispanic communities.

By the late eighteenth century, Spain had abandoned its unworkable plan to main-tain Indians and non-Indians in separate "republics." In the San Antonio missions, for example, the Indian population had declined, and intermarriage with Hispanics and the forces of acculturation had absorbed the remaining Indians to such an extent that the resident Franciscan at San Antonio de Valero wrote in 1792: "This mission cannot be called a mission of Indians but a gathering of white people." He urged that it be secularized—that is, converted to a parish with parish-supported secular priests and its lands divided among the remaining Indians. The next year, that was done. Later, a cavalry unit, the Flying Company of San José y Santiago del Alamo de Parras, moved into the mission and gave it the name for which it would become famous—the Alamo. The four remaining San Antonio missions were partially secularized in 1794—a process not fully completed for all the Texas missions until the 1820s.[18]

Just as Hispanics moved onto mission lands in some places, so did Indians move into

Spanish towns. In San Antonio, they constituted one-tenth of the population in 1790, according to that year's census. Some were former mission Indians and nearly all had been baptized. In Los Angeles pagan Indians or *gentiles*—whom Spaniards also termed *gente sin razón* or people without reason—lived and labored alongside the Hispanic people of reason—the *gente de razón*. On a sparsely populated frontier with a shortage of skilled laborers, those non-Christian Indians worked at a variety of Spanish trades, as masons, carpenters, plasterers, soapmakers, tanners, shoemakers, and blacksmiths. As the nature of their employment changed, so did the traditional divisions of labor between Indian men and women, thus altering their household structures and family lives.[19]

Indian women in particular became socially as well as economically integrated into Hispanic society in towns like Los Angeles. Perhaps as a result of what Gov. Pedro Fages deplored as the *"pernicious familiarity* that is had in the pueblo *with the gentile Indians,"* a number of Indian women married Spanish men. In 1784, when Los Angeles was just three years old, the first of these Indian brides, one María Dolores, received the sacraments of baptism and marriage in the same day. As a result of such marriages, as well as their more informal liaisons with Hispanic men, some mission and non-mission Indian women began to lose their ethnic identities in California and elsewhere along the northern frontier. Indian men, on the other hand, seldom married or lived with Hispanic women; in frontier communities where Hispanic males outnumbered them, Hispanic women had ample choices among their own kind.[20]

In many places, it seems likely that exposure to the market economy and the workaday world of Hispanic frontier society did more than missions to alter Indian society and culture.[21] Moored together in missions, Indians had little need to learn the ways of Spaniards or the Spanish language; adrift in the Hispanic world, many acquired Spanish—the key to Hispanicization—in order to survive and prosper. Indians who traded at Pensacola in 1822, one American noted, "are better acquainted with the Spanish language than either the French or English."[22] So equipped, Indians found many ways to get by in Spanish society—not all of them to the Spaniards' liking. Two Apalachees, for example, counterfeited a number of Spanish coins and passed them off successfully in St. Augustine before a shopkeeper discovered their ruse in 1695. In Spanish ranches, farms, and towns beyond the mission compounds, Indians learned to drink, swear, and gamble in the Spanish way, and to enjoy what Franciscans deplored as "this liberty by which they forfeit Christianity."[23]

In Arizona, New Mexico, and Texas, even some members of warring tribes such as Apaches, Comanches, and Kiowas, became partly assimilated into Spanish society. In one extraordinary case in California, an Apache, Manuel González, was appointed alcalde of San Jose! The process of assimilation of individual Indians (a process quite different from that of the accommodations made by Pueblos and other tribes), usually began with women and children whom Spaniards had captured or ransomed and taken into their households to become Christians and to provide cheap labor. In New

Mexico alone, such people constituted over 10 percent of the Hispanic population by 1750. Over time, many acquired land, skills as artisans, Hispanic spouses, and they or their children lived in the Spanish manner and began to blend into the lower strata of Hispanic society. Nonetheless, the tribal origins of these detribalized natives continued to mark them as outsiders, known in Arizona as *nixoras* and in New Mexico as *genízaros*. Authorities in New Mexico encouraged the genízaros to form new communities at Abiquiú, San Miguel del Vado, Belén, and other dangerous peripheral areas, where they were expected, ironically, to serve as a first line of defense against hostile tribes and as interpreters on military campaigns.[24]

In contrast to the English, Spanish policy and practice had made room for Indians within colonial society—even if on the bottom rung of the social ladder. Despite the social, racial, and legal barriers that blocked the full incorporation of Indians into Hispanic society, acculturation remained the goal of Spanish policy until the end of the colonial era. In 1811, the liberal Spanish Cortes of Cádiz took that policy to its logical conclusion by declaring the juridical equality of Indians and Spaniards throughout the empire. This new dispensation, which led one New Mexico governor to declare the Pueblo Indians "as Spaniards in all things," threw missionaries into confusion; how could they keep Spaniards in missions? The change came late and remained for independent Mexico to implement.[25]

There is little evidence, however, that most Indians wished to become "as Spaniards in all things." Not all natives preferred metal implements over sharp-edged flint tools, wished for crop-trampling Spanish livestock, or abandoned deeply held beliefs about the nature of god and man. Most Indians tried to adopt from Spanish culture only what they found useful, seeking to integrate the strange without disrupting the familiar.[26] But in the end, whether they chose innovation or resisted it, they had little control over the direction, scope, or consequences of change. Some, like the Pueblos, managed to accommodate themselves to the Spanish system and thereby assure their survival as a distinctive if much-changed people; most natives lived under less fortunate circumstances and saw their cultures degraded or annihilated. Meanwhile, individual Indians from a variety of backgrounds blended into the lower strata of Hispanic society, losing their ethnic identity with the passage of generations.

II

Whether Indians adopted features of Spanish culture, or assimilated into it, never again would their cultures be the same—nor would the natural world they inhabited. New characters on the North American stage, Spaniards had brought with them the means to change the stage itself. The Europeans had come with distinctive attitudes about using the land and animals, and they had brought a cornucopia of flora and fauna that set into motion profound ecological transformations. Never static or in perfect equilibrium, ecosystems are always in transformation. Indians, too, had altered the natural world, but Spaniards set into motion ecological changes as rapid and profound as the modern world has known.[27] The pace, depth, and qualities of Spanish-induced ecological changes varied depending on local circumstances, but the main outline of the story seems clear.

Early on, some Spanish-introduced plants established themselves on the North American continent faster than Spaniards themselves. In 1597, for example, Spanish explorers found Indians cultivating watermelons on the Ocmulgee River in Georgia, over 100 miles beyond any Spanish outpost; the next year, when Juan de Oñate arrived in New Mexico to begin permanent settlement, he encountered Pueblos growing watermelons.[28] Englishmen, who moved into Virginia, Carolina, and Georgia, discovered peach trees already growing wild or cultivated by Indians, who would come to regard peaches as native fruit. Introduced at the Spanish settlements along the Atlantic, peaches had apparently spread inland and northward over Indian trade routes.[29] Similarly, the American naturalist Dr. Peter Custis found exotic European plants growing wild as he journeyed far up the Red River in 1806, through what appeared to be virgin wilderness.[30] In California, notwithstanding its isolation from New Spain by sea and desert, at least three Old World plants had become established prior to the onset of Hispanic settlement in 1769.[31]

Domestic mammals imported from Iberia also roamed beyond the Spanish settlements, generally adapting with great ease to those temperate zones of North America that resembled their homeland. Introduced by Hernando de Soto, and then reintroduced by subsequent Spanish parties, omnivorous, long-legged range hogs of Extremadura multiplied like weeds in the well-watered Southeast. There they reverted to feral, ill-tempered animals that Anglo-American Southerners would call razorbacks. With little tolerance for hot, dry, open country, pigs did not become widely established from Texas to California, but there too they found ecological niches, even on the barren Channel Islands off the coast of Southern California where early mariners had deposited them to provide a source of meat for future visitors.[32]

More tolerant than pigs of heat and sun, cattle and horses spread readily across northern New Spain, especially in the ideal environments of the South Plains and coastal California. Before the establishment of permanent Spanish settlement in Texas, thousands of cattle and horses had already found it congenial. "The land is overrun with them," the French trader Louis Juchereau de Saint-Denis reported in 1715.[33] Guided by Indians, or leading their own unrecorded expeditions into the interior of the continent, Spanish mustangs or *mesteños* ranged into the Great Basin and onto the northern Plains well ahead of Spaniards.[34] Mountain and desert apparently halted the spread of horses and cattle into the Californias until the 1770s when Spaniards introduced them, and without human intervention they adapted less well in the Southeast. In Florida, mineral-deficient graze and diseases slowed the development of herds and stunted the growth of individual animals—even the tough barrel-shapped, humpless, New World breed that has come to be called *criollo*.[35] Ranches operated at or near the major Hispanic towns and missions in Florida, but at their peak in the late 1600s the herds were smaller than those in California or Texas at a later date. When they destroyed the Florida missions, Englishmen and Indians drove much of their livestock into South Carolina, where they blended with English stock. Feral horses and cattle remained in Florida, and Creeks and Seminoles had substantial herds by the late 1700s, but both animals remained scarce and expensive for Spaniards at St. Augustine.[36]

More susceptible than cattle and horses to heat, humidity, and predators, sheep did not adapt well to the Southeast. They multiplied, however, in the drier country around the San Antonio missions, in the high elevations of northern New Mexico, and along the temperate California coast.[37] In New Mexico, tough little *churros*, a breed despised in Spain for its low-yielding fleece, but more resistant to drought than cattle, became the province's most important and numerous domestic stock.[38] *Nuevomexicanos* reportedly preferred sheep over cattle and horses partly because their slowness and resistance to stampeding made them less attractive to Indian raiders.[39] A census of 1757 reported that Pueblos and Hispanos between them possessed seven times more sheep than cattle, and fifteen times more sheep than horses. The numbers were: 7,356 horses, 16,157 cattle, and 112,182 sheep.[40] Toward the end of the Spanish era, at a time of relative peace, the number of sheep in Hispanic New Mexico had exploded to well over 200,000 (not counting herds owned by Navajos and other Indians who lived beyond Spanish control), and Hispanic herders in search of fresh pasture had moved their flocks onto the eastern plains, perhaps as far as the present Texas Panhandle.[41] Unlike cattle, horses, and pigs, those domestic sheep did not range far beyond their Spanish caretakers. Sheep do not reproduce easily in a feral state or when their familiar surroundings and diet are disturbed.[42]

As they grew more numerous, European grazing animals began to rearrange the ecological mosaic of North America, especially in the arid and ecologically fragile Southwest, from California to Texas. Where sheep, cattle, and horses gathered in large numbers to graze or water, their sharp hooves trampled grasses to the roots and compacted soils, breaking down their structures. Along well-worn trails, water followed the paths of migrating animals. The higher the hills and inclines, the more that runoff from rain and snow eroded soils that had lost protective vegetation. Water runoff eventually carved deep gullies, or arroyos, which ran full in heavy rain but exposed parched, cracked earth in dry weather. "Gullying," as this phenomenon is known, carried water away rapidly, rather than allowing it to soak into the soil, and thus lowered water tables. Lush grasslands, dotted with trees and brimming with deer and other wildlife, began to diminish and, in some places, turned to desert.[43]

European livestock also began to alter the capacity of southwestern streams and rivers to support human life. The lower courses of the Gila, the Zuni, and the Puerco, for example, once supported luxuriant vegetation. Father Eusebio Francisco Kino, who introduced the first cattle and horses to the Pimas in the late 1600s, described the lower Gila as watering groves of cottonwoods and sustaining natives with "abundant fish and with their maize, beans, and calabashes."[44] Herds of alien animals, however, slowly consumed or broke down the vegetation that supported the Gila's banks. By the late nineteenth century, those banks had washed away, the stream bed had widened, and the river's lower course had grown sluggish—becoming in many places a great gash running through a barren landscape.[45]

The extent to which alien stock degraded the environment in the Spanish era is impossible to calculate. Sources offer few clues, and cooler climate and seasonal rainfall patterns in southwestern America may have mitigated the effects of overgrazing. Nonetheless, by 1820 the effects of overgrazing by feral animals and domestic herds must have been felt in the neighborhood of Hispanic and Indian communities alike. At Albuquerque, for example, spent grassland pushed some Hispanic ranchers westward into dangerous outlying areas with increased exposure to raids by nomads—westward to the Río Puerco in the 1750s and eastward into Tijeras Canyon in the foothills of the Sandía Mountains by the 1760s.[46] Near many missions, large herds exceeded the capacity of the land to sustain them. In 1818, for example, the mission at Tumacácori had more stock than could find water in the small, fragile Santa Cruz Valley—some 5,000 cattle, 2,500 sheep, 600 horses, 89 mules, and 15 donkeys.[47]

Wherever they went, Old World grazing animals transported Old World grasses—including Kentucky Blue grass and others that we have come to think of as 100 percent American. Old World grasses had adapted for centuries to close cropping and bare or compacted soil, and evolution had equipped them with seeds hardy enough to survive a journey through the digestive system of ambulatory quadrupeds, or with barbs or hooks that enabled them to hitch a ride. In California, for example, Mediterranean forage plants and weeds—bromes, common foxtail, curly dock, Italian ryegrass, red-stemmed filaree, sow thistle, wild oats, and others—spread slowly beyond the edges of Spanish settlement into northern California and the interior valleys of the San Joaquín and Sacramento. But the transformation of California's grasslands from native to alien species took decades and was perhaps only half complete by the beginning of the twentieth century.[48]

Old World grazing animals also contributed to the thinning of American forests and woodlands in some areas, for they needed pasture, and Old World draft animals—horses, mules, and donkeys—gave both natives and Hispanics the mobility to transport timbers and firewood over greater distances to their communities.[49] Whatever deforestation accompanied the introduction of European livestock, however, may have been offset by declining numbers of natives and the Spaniards' insistence that Indians stop setting large grass and brush fires. Spaniards understood the reasons why natives used fire. Indians in California, José Longinos Martínez noted, burned brush "for two purposes: one, for hunting rabbits and hares . . .; second, so that with the first light rain or dew the shoots will come up . . . upon which they will feed."[50] Nonetheless, Spanish officials in California, as elsewhere, prohibited what they regarded as needless destruction by fire of forest and scrub country.[51] Spaniards, however, had no interest in saving forests for their own sake and destroyed them near their settlements —as along the San Antonio River, where Spaniards and mission Indians hacked away the woods on both sides of the river for fourteen miles south of San Antonio to clear the land for pasture and farmland.[52] If the wood-intensive mining industry, common in some parts of New Spain, had become a significant enterprise along its North American frontiers, woodlands would have disappeared more rapidly.[53]

The florescence of European domestic mammals in North America probably had still other ripple effects on the natural world, but our knowledge of ecological change in this era remains rudimentary. Did the populations of large carnivors—the jaguar, wolf, and grizzly bear—decline more rapidly as Indian and Hispanic alike sought to protect livestock from predators?[54] Did the proliferating herds of cattle along the Gulf coast create an inhospitable environment for buffalo, or did Spaniards hunt them to excess for their tongues? Early explorers reported buffalo in profusion along the coastal plain below the Rio Grande, but the herds began to disappear from the Gulf in the eighteenth century.[55] Was deadly anthrax introduced to the buffalo population of the southern Plains through New Mexico in the 1670s?[56] To what extent did overgrazing by Spanish-introduced livestock create conditions that encouraged dense growth of mesquite and chaparral in the seventeenth and eighteenth centuries?[57] The work of historians, ethnobotanists, or zooarchaeologists has not yet revealed enough about the nature of flora and fauna at the outset of Spanish exploration and settlement to provide a baseline against which changes can be measured. Moreover, answers to such questions would necessarily be specific to locales rather than regions, thus yielding few generalizations.[58]

Sources written by Spanish contemporaries do not address, much less answer, such questions. Anthropocentric like other Europeans, Spaniards regarded the natural world as existing largely to serve them. Juan de Oñate, for example, remembered the Great Plains as "an earthly Paradise" because of its "abundance of cattle [buffalo], deer and other game for hunting and fishing."[59] Certain that the biological changes they had introduced were beneficial, and unburdened by questions about the negative consequences of ecological change, Spaniards took pride in Europeanizing the natural world with the "fruits of Spain."[60]

The natural world did serve Spaniards well in North America, thus validating their assumptions. Initially, Old World diseases had helped clear the continent for Spanish settlers and their domestic animals and crops, and those animals and crops made it substantially easier for Spaniards to establish themselves. Where European biota flourished, so did Spaniards, adapting readily to temperate zones as along the California coast, the high country of northern New Mexico where altitude mimics latitude and mocks the desert, and on the well-watered, fertile, and salubrious Texas coastal plain. In contrast, the desert Southwest and the semi-tropical Southeast proved unattractive to many European species and, therefore, less inviting to immigrants.[61]

In the main, of course, it was geopolitics and not the suitability of the land that brought Spaniards to North America. If the continent had held greater attractions in treasure or Indian labor, or if Spaniards had fewer alternatives in more desirable parts of the empire, they might have peopled North America in larger numbers and brought about swifter, more profound environmental transformations.

III

In March 1762, as she lay dying in her bed following a sudden illness, Juana Luján prepared her last will and testament. The pious and prosperous widow, who owned the sprawling Rancho de San Antonio near Santa Cruz de la Cañada in New Mexico, affirmed her faith in "everything that is upheld, believed and preached by our mother, the Holy Roman Catholic and Apostolic Church." She left instructions for her burial in the mission chapel of the Indian pueblo of San Ildefonso, and for prayers for the repose of her soul. Juana Luján itemized her property, which she bequeathed to her three children, all of them illegitimate. The size of her estate, valued at some 6,000 pesos, and the nature of her possessions, suggests that she was among the province's more affluent residents. She had owned a twenty-four-room home with its furniture, kitchenware, religious paintings and images, jewelry of gold, silver, and pearls, clothing made of fabrics imported from Europe, China, and Mexico, and land with its pastures, planted fields, garden, walled orchard, stable, corrals, livestock, and farm and ranching implements. Her will was duly witnessed, recorded, and its terms carried out two months after her death.[62]

Although they effected remarkable changes in the natural and native worlds, Spaniards had come to the frontiers of North America hoping to change little in their own lives except to enhance their wealth and status. Like other Europeans in America, they succeeded remarkably well—they transformed their environment far more than it transformed them, and they built new societies that owed more to inheritance from the Old World than to experience in the New World.[63] As the will of Juana Luján suggests, Spaniards of means on the North American frontier lived by Spanish law and custom, and surrounded themselves with traditional Spanish amenities. They organized the North American landscape into familiar shapes and measures, and they bestowed recognizable names on the land in order to incorporate it into their cosmos. They maintained time in familiar modes, marking their days by the Christian calendar and their hours by the bells of their churches. Within familiar time and space, they also reconstructed the hierarchical and patriarchal institutions of their homeland. One of those institutions was the household, where men held authority over wives and children, but where married women like Juana Luján owned separate private property and could pass it on to their heirs—a right English women did not enjoy.[64] Throughout their lives, they engaged in familiar routines of work and play and gave obeisance to the orthodoxies that characterized life in Christian communities in Iberia. When they grew ill, they turned to Iberian medical knowledge and medicines. When they died, they were buried by tradition, as was Juana Luján, in a simple shroud in emulation of Christ but in a place in or near the church that correspondeded to their status, for social distinctions followed Spaniards to the grave.[65]

On North American frontiers, however, Spaniards never reconstructed Spanish culture and institutions in unadulterated forms. First, Spanish civilization had crossed the Atlantic in "simplified" forms, which never reflected its full variety and complexity. Second, many Hispanic settlers had not come to the frontier directly from metropolitan Spain, but from peripheral areas such as Minorca, the Canaries, the Antilles, or New Spain, where Spanish culture had already been filtered through other distinctive environmental, economic, and social settings.[66] Then too, however much they wished to conserve the familiar, Spaniards' scanty numbers and resources left them with no choice but to make concessions to their strange new environment and, on occasion, to learn from natives, who understood local conditions better than they. Like Indians and other Europeans, Spaniards resisted change unless it offered clear benefits and did not challenge cherished beliefs or offend their sense of identity. Spaniards, then, avoided innovations that challenged their fundamental values, but when it became necessary they made modest adjustments in their material culture—in dress, diet, medicine, tableware, homes, and communities, which further transformed Hispanic culture on the frontier.[67]

From the outset Spaniards went to great lengths to maintain appearances, for dress signified status and distinguished Spaniards from Indians as well as from one another.[68] Setting off to conquer New Mexico with Juan de Oñate, for example, Capt. Luis de Velasco packed a wardrobe that included such items as linen handkerchiefs, numerous Cordovan leather boots and shoes, fancy hats, and six elegant suits—two of satin, one of silk, and one of "blue Italian velvet . . . trimmed with wide gold passementerie, consisting of doublet, breeches, and green silk stockings with blue garters with . . . gold lace."[69] Neither inconvenience nor expense diminished Spanish adherence to fashion on social occasions. "No Sonora Spaniard appeared in church without his mantle even if the heat were practically unbearable," one long-time resident of the province noted in the mid-eighteenth century.[70] "Many will go up to their ears in debt simply to satisfy their pride in putting on a grand appearance."[71] Frontier folk took pains to maintain valuable clothing and to pass it on to succeeding generations. Men saved suits and uniforms; women, such as Juana Luján, preserved plummed hats, silk stockings, and capes, shawls, hooped skirts, and dresses made of silks, velvets, British linens, and damask and decorated with silver braid, silver fringe, or gold thread.[72] Except for accessible coastal communities of Louisiana and the Floridas, then, fashions across the frontier would have seemed quaintly outdated to visitors. In California, Gov. Pablo Vicente de Sola was charmed in the 1810s to find women dressed in the style that he recalled from his youth in Castille.[73]

In day-to-day life, however, and especially in the more isolated areas, only the

*59. Wife of a soldier of Monterey, sketched by one of the artists on the Malaspina expedition, circa 1791.
Courtesy, the Museo de America, Madrid, and Iris Engstrand.*

upper and middle strata of society could afford to affect high style, in or out of date.
From California to Florida, when the shoes and boots of ordinary Hispanics wore
thin, they donned locally made Indian-inspired leather moccasins or moccasin-like
shoes. *Nuevomexicanos* copied a kind of footless stocking as well as a style of moccasin,
or *tegua*, from their Pueblo neighbors, and began to produce teguas for export to the
mining regions of northern Mexico. Among the *gente baja*, or poorer class, coarse
woolens, flannels, buckskins, and leather took the place of elegant fabrics for men, and
women dressed comfortably for work and travel, sometimes wearing short, decidedly
unstylish skirts.[74]

Necessity also drove Spaniards to adopt strange New World foods, because few
places in North America proved ideal for cultivating all of the staples of the Mediterranean diet and bulky foodstuffs could not be shipped economically to remote North
American outposts. After failing, for example, to raise wheat, olives, and grapes at St.
Augustine and Santa Elena, Spaniards turned to indigenous cultigens—maize,
beans, and squash—and supplemented them with adaptable foods from the Old

World—peaches, melons, and watermelons—and New World crops such as moschata squashes, chili peppers, and lima beans. Because sheep, Spaniards' preferred source of meat, did not thrive in their Atlantic colonies, Spaniards depended on fishing and on hunting deer, birds, and turtles while they husbanded their imported pigs, chickens, and cattle.[75]

By eating native foods as well as European imports, Hispanics probably enjoyed a richer, more varied diet than they would have had in Spain. Nonetheless, with wheat bread, olive oil, wine, and other familiar foods in short supply across much of the frontier, Spaniards at first believed themselves deprived—reduced to "herbs, fish and other scum and vermin" as one soldier in St. Augustine complained in 1573. In the hopes of winning official sympathy and shipments of familiar foods, residents of St. Augustine continued to represent their situation as desperate, even when they had ample nutrition.[76] As they grew more accustomed to native foods, however, the colonists' sense of privation may have diminished. In the Southeast, Hispanics quaffed the highly caffeinated native black tea, *cacina*, to the point of addiction.[77] In the Southwest, *chocolate*, *atole*, and *pinole* became favored drinks, and other Mesoamerican foods with Nahautl names and corn as the principal ingredient—*elotes*, *posole*, *tamales*, and *tortillas*—became mainstays of the Hispanic diet. Hispanics at all social levels altered the traditional Iberian diet in order to survive, but those at the lowest level made the greatest adjustments. "There is little difference between the food of the Indian and that of the common Spaniard," one German observer noted in Sonora.[78]

Along with their foods, Indians also introduced medicines to the Spaniards. Some, such as sassafras and tobacco, both of which grew in Florida, seemed so efficacious for a variety of ailments that Spaniards carried them to Europe. Others, such as a cactus fruit used as an antiscorbutic, peyote, or certain love potions, seem to have enjoyed only local use by Hispanics on the frontier. Spaniards who expanded their pharmacopoeia with native medicinal herbs did not, however, alter their theories about the causes and cures of disease or the practice of medicine. They transplanted their medical traditions intact from Iberia to the New World but extended them in anemic form to the frontier, where all but the largest towns and military posts lacked doctors and hospitals.[79]

Spaniards also adopted techniques and implements of food preparation from native Americans—most directly from Indian women who worked in Hispanic kitchens as servants, mistresses, or wives to a much greater extent than did Indian women in the English colonies. Indian influence on Spanish food preparation was greatest, of course, among Hispanics of the lowest socioeconomic strata, but even the home of the prosperous Juana Luján had six sets of grinding stones of the type that Indians used for preparing corn and a large flat griddle, or *comal*, for making Indian-style corn tortillas.[80] If many of the well-to-do ate with silver spoons or drank from ceramic cups and saucers imported from China, England, or Mexico, as did Juana Luján, less prosperous Hispanics ate from tableware made by local Indian potters—and in the

Southwest many ate with their hands or scooped their food with tortillas.[81] It was in "female activities with low social visibility," one anthropologist has suggested, that Spaniards allowed themselves to fall most readily under indigenous influences, including perhaps the use of Indian-made baskets, mats, and cloth for work regarded as women's. In the patriarchal Hispanic world, the high status associated with Spanish culture mitigated against an easy acceptance of native influences in such visible male activities as warfare or construction.[82]

In constructing new homes and public or ecclesiastical buildings in North America, Spaniards may have depended on Indian labor, but beyond some decorative touches, Indians had little influence on building techniques or the styles of Hispanic architecture.[83] To the contrary, Spanish churches, government buildings, and fortifications followed European conventions, and Spanish-built homes in North America resembled those of different regions of Spain. Poverty and shortages of skilled artisans and metal tools on the frontier, however, usually resulted in a simplification of styles for both public and private structures. With few exceptions, such as the ensemble of neoclassic residences built by the elite in New Orleans after the fires of 1788 and 1794 destroyed the old French structures, even the homes of the well-to-do seemed austere compared to those of the aristocracy in Spain or Mexico City. Most Hispanic frontiersmen lived in small, unadorned, functional houses, with a few multipurpose rooms in which they cooked, ate, entertained, and slept.[84]

Although they resisted native influences on their architecture, Spaniards did adapt European forms to local circumstances on the frontier. If Juana Luján, for example, lived in a home constructed of sun-fired earthen bricks or adobe, her counterpart in mid-eighteenth century St. Augustine would have lived in a house with walls made of shellstone, called coquina, or of a concrete-like mixture of sand, lime, and shell aggregate known as tabby. Most New Mexico homes had flat roofs constructed of timbers covered with earth; most homes in wetter St. Augustine had pitched roofs of straw or palm thatch.[85] The one-story, rectangular rooms of Juana Luján's spacious house probably stretched around a central courtyard or patio, as one might find in southern Spain. In St. Augustine, on the other hand, no homes had interior patios, but many had shady loggias, arcades, and balconies, as in parts of northern Spain; some St. Augustine houses rose to two stories—a style practically unknown in New Mexico, Texas, or California before 1821. Juana Luján's home had small windows and doors, appropriate to a place of cold winters and dry, mild summers where life spilled outdoors; homes in warm, humid St. Augustine had large, wood-grilled windows that projected out onto the street and caught cooling breezes.[86]

Simplification to the point of austerity also characterized the interiors of most public buildings and private homes. A few churches, such as San Xavier del Bac with its ornate, gilded baroque altar piece, had elaborate decor, and California mission chapels had bright motifs painted on interior walls late in the colonial era, but most church interiors seemed plain. "Its furniture, or adornment, is the absence of any," fray

60. St. George Street in St. Augustine, today. Photograph by Stanley Bond. Courtesy, Historic St. Augustine Preservation Board.

Francisco Atanasio Domínguez wrote of the parish church at Santa Fe in 1776. "The floor is bare earth packed down like mud. This is the usual floor throughout these regions."[87] Home interiors, also commonly floored with packed earth in the dry country, struck outsiders as "small and mean" and "scantily furnished" even at the end of the colonial era.[88] In or near prosperous and accessible New Orleans, a few high government officials, well-to-do merchants, and prosperous planters, Gov. Esteban Miró said, "lived in splendor," able to import crystal chandeliers and full-length mirrors trimmed with gold leaf.[89] Elsewhere on the frontier, even the affluent lived in relative simplicity. Juana Luján's twenty-four-room house had no movable wooden furniture other than her plank bed, a cabinet, a chest, two chairs, two benches, and writing desk.[90] She may have supplemented these meager furnishings with built-in adobe benches and cabinets, but her walls were otherwise unadorned except for a mirror and religious paintings on elkhides—the latter a commonplace adaption of indigenous materials now valued by collectors, but then scandalous to an ecclesiastical inspector from Durango who regarded religious paintings on hides as "improper" and "indecent."[91] Those less well off than Juana Luján had more spartan furnishings; they slept and sat on mats on the floor, as did the lower classes in Spain.[92]

Wooden furniture, expensive to import, was often made in towns, presidios, and missions by local craftsmen, who hewed to the standard designs, forms, and exacting proportions established by custom in the craft guilds of Spain or New Spain.[93] Nowhere in Spanish North America was furniture making, as well as other crafts, more advanced than in New Mexico, which had a large internal market, high transportation costs for imports, and a supply of skilled native labor. New Mexicans' ability to do fine carpentry was limited, however, by the shortage of iron tools and of iron itself for latches and hinges. Of the nine doors in Juana Luján's house, only four had metal latches and each was so valuable that she bequeathed one to the local priest to pay for Masses for her soul.[94] In furniture as in architecture, the styles of the Renaissance and the Baroque largely bypassed New Mexico, where furniture makers repeated late medieval motifs until the end of the eighteenth century, and where Indian craftsmen added occasional stylistic flourishes of their own.[95]

In the dry country, where Juana Luján ranched and farmed, streams or springs often proved insufficient for thirsty livestock and water-intensive crops. From San

61. A painting on hide of an image of St. Francis, of the type commonly found in colonial New Mexico. Courtesy, International Folk Art Foundation Collection in the Museum of International Folk Art, a unit of the Museum of New Mexico and the Vargas Project, University of New Mexico.

Antonio to the arid California coast, Spaniards built irrigation networks—dams, reservoirs, and ditches or *acequias*. To construct and manage these networks, which might be either private or public, Spaniards drew on Iberian precedents, borrowing little from those natives who had irrigated the land before them.[96]

Even as Spaniards altered the arid environment, that same environment modified the way Spaniards shaped the rural space. Lands designated for Indian towns and lands granted to individual Spaniards or to Spanish communities were necessarily much larger in the arid country than in well-watered regions, where it took less grazing land to sustain animals. Instead of regular square fields, long rectangular lots became commonplace in southwestern America, thus providing farmers and ranchers greater access to limited frontage on streams or acequias. As heirs divided estates, but maintained frontage on water courses, those long lots shrank, becoming narrower and less efficient. In the Southwest, land itself had little value without water. Rather than ask for a grant of land and water to go with it, as Spaniards would do ordinarily, Spaniards in the arid country might ask for the right to use water and the land to go with it.[97]

Spaniards also reorganized urban space in familiar ways. More than any other colonial power, Spain attempted to impose a uniform urban design on newly founded municipalities, which it regarded as central to colonization.[98] Royal regulations, promulgated in 1573, required officials throughout the empire to lay out new townsites in orderly grids, reflecting a rational Renaissance ideal that most of the labyrinthian medieval communities in Spain itself never achieved. Municipalities such as St. Augustine, Pensacola, San Antonio, El Paso, Santa Fe, Los Angeles, and San Jose were to reckon their boundaries at four leagues square. At the heart of each community would stand a principal plaza, laid out to the points of the compass, rectangular in shape to accommodate equestrian events, and faced by government and ecclesiastical buildings and shops. Beyond the plaza, surveyors generally divided the town into straight streets, designating uniform blocks and lots for houses and gardens. Still farther from the plaza, yet still within the municipal boundaries, stood private fields, municipal lands, and common pastures and woodlands.[99]

Wherever Spaniards formed municipalities in the western hemisphere, they repeated the general principles of this urban template with remarkable consistency. On the frontier, however, Spaniards often adapted municipal forms to local conditions, modifying the geometric urban ideal with organic elements. Over two hundred years after its founding, St. Augustine's narrow, irregular streets appalled Gov. Vicente Manuel de Zéspedes, who ordered an engineer to draw up plans to straighten them and to move the plaza closer to the center of town.[100] At Pensacola, military priorities caused town builders to modify the 1573 regulations.[101] At San Jose, common lands were never distributed as regulations required. At Santa Fe, Albuquerque, El Paso, and San Antonio, residents commonly built their dwellings where they chose rather than on orderly town blocks. (See figures 8-2, 11-7, and 11-9.) Indeed, to the dismay of Spanish officials, who regarded urban life as the ideal—"a microcosm of a larger

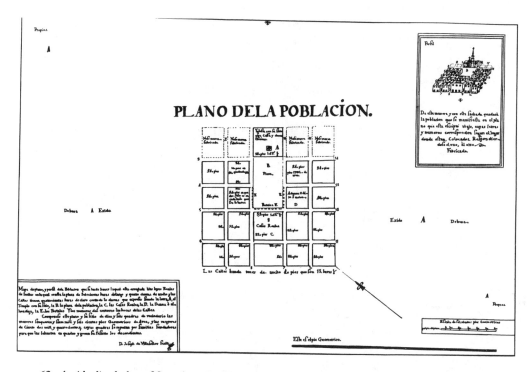

62. *An idealized plan of San Antonio, drawn circa 1730. Courtesy, Institute of Texan Cultures, San Antonio.*

imperial and ecclesiastical order"—Hispanic frontiersmen from Florida to California often preferred to live in the countryside, close to herds, watercourses, fields, and Indian laborers.[102] One traveler in 1754 noted that he had passed through Albuquerque, "or I might say the site of the villa of Albuquerque, for the settlers, who inhabit it on Sunday, do not live there. They must stay on their farms to keep watch over their cornfields."[103]

Spanish municipalities in North America lacked the most basic urban amenities as well as perfect order and symmetry. The cosmopolitan "new city" of New Orleans, rebuilt in the classic Spanish mode following the devastating fires of 1788 and 1794, stands as an exception. As the hub of a prosperous plantation economy and entrepôt for the Mississippi River trade, New Orleans grew from 3,000 in 1777 to over 8,000 in 1803 and could support sophisticated urban life. The city did not yet have a college or a library when the last Spanish officials left in 1803, but it boasted a cathedral and a splendid town hall. New Orleans' most affluent residents lived in mansions, rode in elegant coaches, and could enjoy newspapers, theater, raised sidewalks, street lights, an Ursuline Convent for the pious upbringing of their virginal daughters, and 'masked balls and a boisterous Carnival for those disinclined to suppress the sensual side of their natures.[104]

63. Plan of the town and presidio of San Antonio. Detail from a drawing by José de Urrutia, 1767. Courtesy, British Library and Museum of New Mexico, neg. no. 15052.

Other than New Orleans and perhaps St. Augustine, no Spanish community in North America enjoyed the rank of ciudad, or "city."[105] The most prominent of frontier municipalities remained villas, or towns—and those scarcely deserved the name. A visitor to San Antonio, for example, described the town in 1778 as a place that "resembles more a poor village than a villa." Its dirt streets, the scene of horse races and the haunt of wild dogs, were impassable after a heavy rain; the governor housed his family in a small jail for lack of an official residence; and the guard house at the garrison served not only as a dormitory for single soldiers, but as a prison and a workshop for gun repair, which everyone had to evacuate when its space was needed for some other purpose, as on the six occasions when the baronesa de Ripperdá, the governor's wife, gave birth there.[106]

With modest populations at the end of the colonial era, places such as Los Angeles (850), Santa Fe (6,000), San Antonio (1,500), and St. Augustine (1,500), could not boast of impressive cathedrals or public buildings, convents, seminaries, universities, libraries, theaters, newspapers, or presses—much less of the professors, nuns, lawyers, writers, and poets that such institutions supported elsewhere in Spanish America.[107] Except for very special occasions, these communities could not afford bullfights, then popular in Mexico and Spain. But townsfolk did amuse themselves with religious processions, fiestas, outdoor plays and pageantry, gambling at cards and dice, and *fandangos* in private homes, which the cabildo of San Antonio deplored because they "excite lust" and "give very serious offense to God."[108] Frontier municipalities, with the possible exception of New Orleans, also lacked almshouses and workhouses, for these towns remained too primitive to know the deep unemployment and crushing poverty that festered in the core of larger cities of Spanish or English America.[109]

If Spain's stunted communities in North America failed to develop into full-blown Spanish cities and towns, it was in part because they stood on a frontier where civilian initiative was discouraged and where private interests remained subordinate to those of the military. Whether maintained by the Crown to block hostile tribes from invading New Spain or to prevent Spain's European rivals from occupying key ports along the California, Gulf, and Atlantic coasts, Spain's North American communities continued to serve essentially defensive purposes until the end of the colonial era. Most frontier towns had perimeter walls, many were situated near a fortification or military barracks, and some—such as St. Augustine, Pensacola, Los Angeles, and San

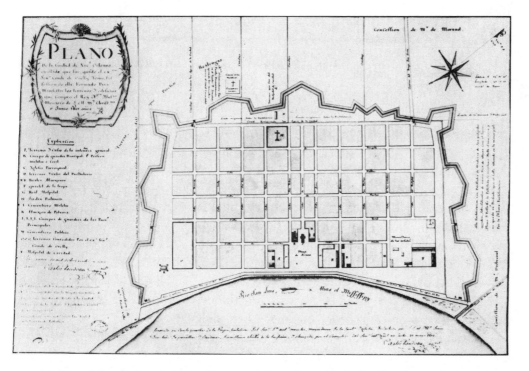

64. Plan of New Orleans in 1801. Courtesy, Archivo General de Indias, Seville, and the Spanish Colonial Resarch Center, University of New Mexico.

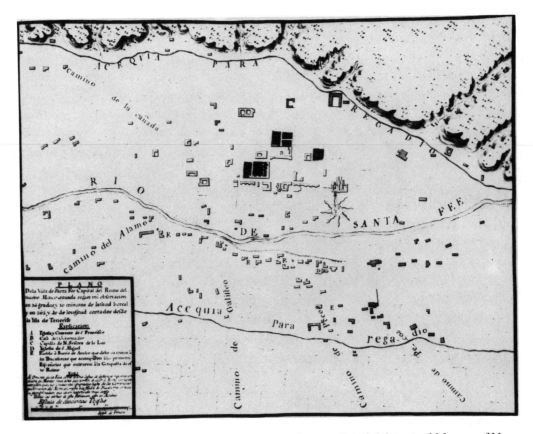

65. Plan of Santa Fe, 1766, drawn by José de Urrutia. Courtesy, British Library and Museum of New Mexico, neg. no. 15048.

Jose—existed almost entirely to serve nearby military bases. The latter had skewed economies and little need for trades or professions beyond those required to support the military.

All across the frontier, military officers—governors and their subalterns—dominated political life in civilian communities. Royal regulations required that the executive and judicial functions of municipalities be carried out by elected town councils, or cabildos, but such bodies had fallen into disuse. By the late eighteenth century, only San Antonio and New Orleans had functioning cabildos. Elected councils that once governed the old towns of Santa Fe and St. Augustine had become dormant, and new towns, such as San Jose and Los Angeles, functioned from the first without councils but with military officers supervising municipal affairs.[110]

Critics charged that military officers usurped the prerogatives of elected town councils because they regarded civilians as obstacles to their power. Officers, on the other hand, expressed scant confidence in civilians and argued that the unusual demands of frontier life required streamlined military command. When Gov. Diego de

Vargas of New Mexico founded the villa of Santa Cruz de la Cañada in 1695 and put in charge a single *alcalde mayor*, or chief magistrate, instead of establishing a cabildo, he explained that he gave the town "this style and form of government because of its being on the frontier."[111] Among other things, "being on the frontier" meant a shortage of able citizens to run municipal government. San Antonio had so few residents who could read and write that it elected illiterates to the cabildo in violation of the law and kept those persons in office longer than regulations permitted because there were no suitable candidates to replace them.[112] Military officers usually knew how to read and write, but were accused of petty despotism, corruption, and ignorance of the civil laws.[113]

Whether in the hands of civilians or military officers, municipal government left much to be desired in frontier communities and nowhere was its inadequacy clearer than in the administration of justice. In civil and criminal cases, frontier justice operated with an informality that surpassed legality. As one attorney in Durango noted, in New Mexico "very few contracts and judicial acts would remain standing . . . if we were to examine them for conformity to the law."[114] Law books could be found all across the frontier, but except for New Orleans few communities ever saw a trained lawyer or judge. Local courts or military justices could hear nothing more than minor civil and criminal cases and usually dealt with them fairly and adequately. Weighty cases or appeals required a journey of extraordinary length to a higher court in Guadalajara, Chihuahua, Monclova, San Luis Potosí, Mexico City, or Havana. Such cases became the subject of lengthy, costly, and frustrating litigation, "causing much injury to the parties and considerable delay," as one resident of St. Augustine complained.[115] Spaniards, then, had brought their system of justice to the frontier, but as with other features of Spanish life, Spanish law functioned on the frontier in a much simplified and imperfect form.

Many Spaniards on the frontier did not, of course, live in or near formal municipalities, but at military bases. In contrast to the westward-moving Anglo-American frontier, where the government usually established military posts to protect an advancing line of settlers, many of Spain's North American fortifications anchored territory so remote that it had little prospect of attracting significant numbers of Hispanic settlers. Presidial communities such as San Diego, Santa Barbara, Monterey, San Francisco, Tucson, San Fernando (Memphis), and Nogales (Vicksburg), took on the characteristics of small villages as soldiers, their families, and nonmilitary personnel settled around them, but they did not develop into municipalities until long after the Spanish era ended. Nor did they enjoy more than the essentials of Hispanic life.

Tucson is a case in point. Ranchers and farmers who lived on the outskirts of the fort paid no taxes or tithes, but neither did they derive benefits from a town government or a parish church (they used the military chapel). As a condition of owning land within a five-mile radius of the presidio, settlers were obliged to take up their own arms and mounts to campaign against Apaches. The community, the post commander, José de Zúñiga, reported in 1804, had no weaver, saddlemaker, or hatmaker, and "desperately needs a leather tanner and dresser, a tailor, and a shoemaker." The artisans who had recently completed the monumental baroque church of San Xavier del Bac just south of the presidio, "out here on the farthest frontier," as Zúñiga put it, had received double pay "because of the consequent hazard involved."[116]

IV

Whether they lived in towns, ranches, farms, or at military posts, Spaniards had succeeded remarkably in transplanting some of the amenities and artifacts of Iberia to the North American frontier. On alien ground and amidst alien peoples of the new continent, however, Hispanic culture and institutions had taken on simplified or hybrid forms. Spanish society underwent similar transformations, as Hispanic immigrants to North American frontiers tried with only partial success to replicate the hierarchical and patriarchal social structure they had known in Spain or in its more mature American colonies.

Since the early stages of settlement, American frontiers had offered opportunities to Hispanics for upward social mobility—first in the Caribbean, then in New Spain and Peru, and finally in peripheral areas such as North America. The followers of Menéndez de Aviles who settled at St. Augustine and Santa Elena in the 1560s, Oñate's colonists who pushed into the Pueblo country in 1598, the soldiers and settlers who made their way to Texas in the 1710s or to New California in the 1760s and 1770s, and the peasants from the Canary Islands who settled at San Antonio in the 1730s, had no difficulty establishing themselves near the top of the local social ladder. Except for a few transient government officials, no one occupied the rungs above them. Few Hispanic pioneers accumulated great wealth on the frontier, but many of the first settlers did acquire titles, land, and Indian servants—hallmarks of the elite in the Spanish-speaking world. Of course, latecomers to established frontier communities, often found opportunities closed to them and only got ahead with special skills or through fortuitous marriages.[117]

Racial purity, a requisite for elite status in Spain and its American colonies, proved less essential to upward mobility on the frontier than in core areas of the empire.[118] Throughout the Spanish empire, an individual's social status correlated strongly with his or her racial and ethnic origins. *Peninsulares*, those Spaniards born in Spain, held the key colonial offices and stood at the apex of colonial society. Criollos, children of Spaniards born in the Americas, ranked just below them. Both peninsulares and criollos were, of course, ethnic Spaniards or *españoles*, whose ancestry, it was presumed, betrayed no traces of Indian or black blood. Below the españoles, in descending order of status, were mestizos (persons who were part Indian and part español), mulattos, Hispanicized Indians, and freed or enslaved blacks.[119]

Españoles scorned mestizos, mulattos, Indians, and blacks, as much for their presumed social inferiority as for their race. Viceroy Luis de Velasco, for example, had urged Tristán de Luna to beware of the "half-breeds, mulattoes, and Indians" he was taking to Florida because "these will only serve to set the camp in confusion and eat up the supplies."[120] But colonizers embarking from New Spain could not be choosy. In addition to its predominantly Indian population and imported black slaves, Mexico had become home to a large number of mixed bloods, people of "broken color"—*color quebrado*—as they were called. Mixed bloods, together with blacks and Hispanicized Indians, composed the vast majority of the population of New Spain and, therefore, of immigrants to New Mexico, Texas, Arizona, and California. For example, only one-third of the men and one-forth of the women who founded San Jose and San Francisco in 1777 claimed to be ethnically Spanish, or españoles; of the initial forty-six residents of Los Angeles in 1781, only two identified themselves as españoles.[121] In contrast, in the Floridas and Louisiana, the majority of Hispanics had come directly from Andalusia, the Cantabrian provinces, or other parts of Spain, but there, too, mestizos, mulattos, and blacks, formed significant percentages of the Hispanic population.[122]

On the frontier, as throughout Spain's American empire, only españoles enjoyed all of the privileges that the Crown extended to its subjects. The law discriminated against "Negroes, mulattos, Indians, and mestizos and other dastardly persons," as Governor Zúñiga characterized St. Augustine's non-español residents in 1702.[123] At New Orleans, for example, municipal ordinances of 1766 forbade owners of cabarets to sell liquor to Indians, blacks, or mulattos; across the frontier the law prohibited public flogging of españoles as a punishment for crimes, but permitted it for mixed bloods, Indians, and blacks.[124] De facto segregation along socioracial categories also manifested itself in frontier communities. Indians, blacks, and mixed bloods lived on the edge of town or in certain neighborhoods, whereas españoles lived near the plaza. In some parishes, priests kept two sets of books—one for whites and one for non-whites. Some institutions, too, were segregated. St. Augustine had two separate militia companies in the mid-eighteenth century, one for mestizos and free mulattos and another for españoles.[125]

On the frontier, however, where record-keeping could be lax, mestizos, mulattos, and Hispanicized Indians found ample opportunity to transcend their official racial categories. Priests, officers, and civil officials responsible for recording a person's *casta* or caste, usually took a declaration of racial identity at face value or simply failed to take note of the caste of persons other than "españoles." In the later half of the eighteenth and early nineteenth centuries, priests and census takers paid greater attention to classifying people racially, yet still made those identifications casually and inconsistently. Antonio Salazar of Zacatecas, the master mason who directed work on the mission of San José at San Antonio, appears in four different documents between 1789 and 1794 with three different ethnic identities—Indian, mestizo, and Spaniard.[126] Inevitably, the frontier population became "whiter" as Indians and mulattos declared themselves mestizos, and mestizos described themselves as españoles. As one foreign resident of mid-eighteenth-century Sonora noted, "practically all those who wish to be considered Spaniards are people of mixed blood."[127]

Whitening occurred throughout Spain's empire, for a person's social status, or *calidad*, was never fixed solely by race, but rather defined by occupation and wealth as well as by parentage and skin color.[128] In frontier or rural societies, however, where institutions that maintained racial boundaries were relatively weak, it may be that social promotion occurred more rapidly than in urbanized, prosperous areas of New Spain. In California, for example, racial distinctions at the official level nearly disappeared in some communities by the end of the colonial era. At San Jose, Franciscans noted in 1814 that "the only two castes we know of here are the gente de razón and Indians. All the former are considered Spaniards." "Although it is well known that not all are genuine Spaniards," a priest at Santa Barbara wrote of the residents of the local presidio in 1813, "if they were told to the contrary they would consider it an affront."[129] In Texas, perhaps not to give affront, census takers simply listed all military personnel as "español," regardless of their racial origins. Indeed, español came to be such an elastic term in Texas that one finds in census reports: "Spaniard from Canada," "Spaniard from France," and "Spaniard from Corsica."[130]

The term *español*, however, never erased memories of a person's racial origins among his neighbors—not even for the well-to-do, such as the lieutenant governor of Texas, Antonio Gil Ybarbo, officially an español, but popularly known as a mulatto. In the heat of argument, "mulatto," "mestizo," or "Indian" might be hurled as insulting epithets and be considered grounds for slander.[131] Nor did the designation español ever become so elastic that it included all social inferiors, because, as everywhere, those in the upper strata of society needed people below them against whom they could define themselves. Black slaves and captive Indians pressed into servitude occupied the lowest social level. Near the bottom, but just above them, were poor mulattos, free blacks, and free Hispanicized Indians, whose opportunities to improve their calidad varied with local conditions. Black men in late-colonial Pensacola, for example, became free artisans and tradesmen, and a number of black women became mistresses of white men; in St. Augustine, on the other hand, Minorcan residents kept control of the trades for themselves and a higher percentage of blacks remained enslaved.[132]

Notwithstanding the continuing prejudices and discrimination against blacks, Indians, and those of "broken color," social mobility proved attainable for many Hispanic immigrants to the frontier. In sparsely populated lands of nearly chronic war, with primitive economies and little occupational differentiation, the military served as the chief vehicle for upward mobility.[133] Indeed, with the largest payroll on the North American frontier—and in some places the only payroll—the military enjoyed disproportionate influence. At St. Augustine, three-fourths of the population depended on the military payroll as late as 1813, and in California in the early 1810s, soldiers on active duty constituted half of the Hispanic adult male population (still more were retired soldiers).[134]

No matter how exploited by their officers, soldiers had access to salaries, benefits, booty, and pensions. Such sources of income, which few other frontiersmen enjoyed, helped offset their humble family origins and poverty and gave soldiers better prospects on the frontier than they might have enjoyed in Spain or in central Mexico, where competition was keener. Manuel Francisco Delgado, for example, rose through the ranks from private to captain over a thirty-three year career, becoming comandante of several presidios, including Santa Fe. At his death in 1815, his landed estate amounted to 24,891 pesos (including 100 pesos "loaned to His Majesty," the king of Spain!).[135] Excepting officers, few frontier soldiers could read or write, and many had come reluctantly to the coastal presidios. Taken from the prisons, galleys, and slums of the empire, some men worked as convict laborers at remote posts like Pensacola, from which there seemed no escape, and others were recruited directly into the army. Some deserted or continued to add to their reputations as malefactors, but those who combined ambition with skill, luck, or guile could make a respectable new life on the frontier. Hermengildo Sal, a convict conscripted into the army and sent to California, ended his military career as comandante at Santa Barbara and San Francisco. Like other officers, he would have been addressed by the honorific *don*, regardless of his ethnic or social origins or his previous criminal career.[136]

Of those soldiers who remained posted in a single community and retired on the frontier, significant numbers acquired land and moved into the local oligarchy by default.[137] Calidad clearly slowed some military careers, and one sergeant in Pensacola was denied promotion because the wives of other officers did not regard his wife as their social equal. In general, however, it appears that social level counted for less than ability in advancing or hindering soldiers' aspirations on the frontiers, where common danger and distance from authority encouraged solidarity and egalitarianism. "What does it matter to the Sovereign whether the one who serves him well be white or black if the color of his face is negated by the nobility of heart?" asked Bernardo de Gálvez. Indeed, among frontier soldiers, who had been "reared in freedom and accustomed to independence," Gálvez had detected what he regarded as "a defect of familiarity"—an excessive egalitarianism that bordered on insubordination and could not be found in the regular army. "The captains and officers," he lamented, "[have] found it necessary to call the soldiers comrades."[138]

Although a military career might advance a young man's social and economic position, it was not conducive to his establishing a family, the basic unit of Hispanic society. In posts with few Hispanic women, soldiers clearly had little prospect of finding ideal marriage partners. Such conditions existed not only in the initial phases of settlement, as along the California coast, but also at perennially undeveloped posts like San Marcos de Apalachee, which counted 168 adult males to 3 women as late as 1802. Deprived of Hispanic women, some soldiers found illicit outlets for their libidos—raping Indian women, consorting with prostitutes, and even more unspeakable crimes judging from the severity of the punishment. Governor Zéspedes shipped a half dozen soldiers out of St. Augustine in 1789 for having sexual relations with young boys; if found guilty, the soldiers could have been punished by death and their bodies burned.[139] In Santa Barbara, an eighteen-year-old soldier was caught in a compromising position with a mule; both were executed, their bodies purified by flame.[140]

Some soldiers came to the frontier with their wives, and others married there, but family life in general deviated from the norms of more settled areas. In posts with few Hispanic women, for example, even soldiers newly arrived from Spain were known to marry far beneath their station by taking Indian brides.[141] Even as the ratio of adult men and women approached parity, however, more men died prematurely in military communities than did woman, for soldiers often did dangerous work on the frontier. Residents of St. Augustine, for example, buried twice as many men as women in an average year. High adult male death rates offset the high birthrates that characterized most Hispanic communities in North America. The disproportionate deaths of grown males also left unusual numbers of orphans, single widows, remarried widows, and widows who served as heads of families.[142]

For civilians, too, conditions on the frontier altered what passed for normal family arrangements in more sophisticated parts of the empire. As their local societies became more complex and the range of potential marriage partners widened, as in New Mexico, frontier *arrivistes* tried to maintain or improve their position by contracting shrewd marriages for themselves or their children—a strategy for social advancement common to Spain and its empire. By marrying oneself or one's children to a social equal or a social better, españoles or putative españoles hoped to create family alliances that would preserve property, racial purity, honor, and position for the next generation. As a social and economic arrangement, marriage for the elites had little to do with romantic love or individual choice. Children, it was understood, could not marry without parents' permission (nor could soldiers and officers marry without the approval of their superiors). The use of marriage as a device for maintaining racial purity failed, however, across most of the frontier, where there simply were not enough españoles for the elite to perpetuate itself.[143]

Notwithstanding their isolation and the near absence of attorneys on the frontier, aristocrats and middling groups clearly understood the legal procedures, both civil and ecclesiastical, for betrothal, marriage, maintaining women's property as a separate entity within the marriage, and obtaining annulments or separations. Across the frontier, however, apparently to a greater extent than in Spain or in more settled areas of colonial Spanish America, all classes seem to have ignored inconvenient civil restrictions or religious and social conventions regarding marriage.[144] In Louisiana, for example, both governors Bernardo de Gálvez and Manuel de Gayoso violated the prohibition against marrying into local families during their term in office—Gayoso and his third wife, an American, Margaret Watts, married on the same day that their son was baptized.[145] Church officials, mindful of the shortage on the frontier of potential spouses of a certain calidad, often waived restrictions against marriage of close relatives, as in their favorable response to one New Mexican who begged a dispensation to marry his second cousin "for the lack of population in this miserable kingdom."[146] In places with no priests, as at Fort Miró in the 1790s (present-day Monroe, Louisana), frontiersmen entered into civil marriages in violation of ecclesiastical law.[147] Although church courts resisted granting separations to married couples for any reason except desertion (divorce as we know it did not exist), the mobility and anonymity of the frontier offered spouses an opportunity to begin married life anew, as bigamists.[148]

As elsewhere in Spain and its empire, Hispanics on the frontier did not limit their expressions of sexuality to the institution of marriage. Hispanic males, who commonly defined their masculinity by the sexual conquest of women, made a virtue of adultery, and men of means kept mistresses quite openly. For example, the captain of the presidio at La Bahía, Texas, lived with four women in succession—all married or related to soldiers in the presidio under his command and all mothers of his children. In a classic example of a double standard, men also sought to shield their wives, daughters, and sisters from the attentions of other males. A woman who lost her virtue was believed to have dishonored her family as well as herself, and so elites, who had the most honor to lose, went to great lengths to guard women. Governor Vicente Folch of Mobile, who caught his wife and a fellow officer in flagrante delicto, complained that protecting women from such perils was more difficult on the frontier than in Spain, where his family would have assisted him. He was probably right. Moreover, some of the most common occupations on the frontier, from soldier to herder, required that husbands absent themselves from home with frequency, thus increasing the vulnerability of their wives to the blandishments of predatory males. Finally, availability of Indian women servants who could be sexually exploited by their masters provided opportunities for adultery on the frontier that had no exact equivalent in Spain. There is no strong evidence, however, that the incidence of adultery or concubinage was higher on the frontier than among the upper classes of Spain, who regarded themselves as *gente decente*—as decent people.[149]

Among the lower strata of frontier society, the *gente baja*, an uncommonly high percentage of couples simply ignored the institution of marriage and lived together out of wedlock in informal unions or *barraganía*. Without property or honor to protect (and without illusions that their children would ever have the means to hold public office or ecclesiastical positions closed to illegitimate offspring), the poor saw little advantage in paying a fee to a priest to legitimize their relationship or their children.[150] Then, too, the *gente baja* had the example of priests who violated their vows of chastity in unseemly numbers and cohabited with women without benefit of the vows of marriage. In New Mexico, where Pueblo women customarily "offered their love and bodies in return for gifts and benefits," the padres apparently fell farther from grace than in any other frontier province. "The greater part of them live in concubinage," one official wrote in 1794. "All the pueblos are full of friars' children," a fellow Franciscan had lamented as early as 1671.[151]

A large number of illegitimate children derived from the consensual unions and casual couplings of laymen as well as priests. In Texas, 20 percent of children born in 1790 were illegitimate; in Pensacola in 1820, over one-fourth of the population was apparently illegitimate.[152] These percentages seem higher than those in Spain during the same era, but not necessarily higher than in other areas of Spanish America.[153] These children, illegitimate or legitimate, were reared in time-honored Hispanic ways, but with meager formal schooling and with a freedom that astounded outsiders. Even in New Orleans, the most cosmopolitan place on the frontier, Governor Carondelet observed that parents brought their children up "in a spirit of great liberty and total independence, so that, from the age of ten, they are allowed to run about alone, riding horses from house to house, and firing off their guns."[154]

In itself, the frontier milieu did not create these anomalous patterns in Hispanic society. It was Hispanics themselves who took advantage of the frontier to alter their lives or to resolve contending values that many of them had brought to the edges of the empire. Along with a fervent Christianity and belief in a family-centered, patriarchal, and hierarchical social structure, some Hispanics had sufficient skills, passions, or hypocrisies to subvert the constraints of Christianity and of the society of castes. The frontier, especially in its most insular places, simply provided greater opportunities for those individuals who wished to escape societal restraints. "By nature," as one historian has explained, "border zones, especially those that are far removed from the core, spawn independence, rebellion, cultural deviation, disorder, and even lawlessness."[155]

Isolation alone gave frontiersmen a certain degree of liberty. "Just as the light of the sun is less powerful at a distance and there is danger of darkness and shadows," the bishop of Puebla wrote to the king in regard to New Mexico, "so, at a distance, from your Majesty and your councils and the pontifical power, one finds provinces as remote as these exposed to great errors and misunderstandings."[156] In the vast spaces of the frontier, Hispanics who wished to keep their distance from vigilant officials could easily do so. At the most extreme, a small number of Hispanics went to live among pagan Indians. Perhaps, like two soldiers who deserted in Texas in 1716 to live with the Hasinais, "they wanted more to live with them than among Catholics."[157] Other Hispanics, such as those who traded with tribes on the Plains or with Utes in the Rockies, knew Indian languages, Indian ways, and moved with apparent ease between the two cultures. Their numbers, too, however, remained small.[158] Many more Hispanics simply made their homes in isolated places, not among Indians but far from the scrutiny of authorities. "They love distance which makes them independent," New

Mexico's Governor Concha conjectured, "in order to adopt the liberty and slovenliness which they see . . . in their neighbors the wild Indians."[159] In California, a Franciscan voiced a common complaint when he railed against the "spirit of independence" of those californios who had scattered beyond the towns into "remote regions without King to rule or Pope to excommunicate them."[160]

V

On the frontier, then, as in other parts of Spain's colonial empire, Hispanic society and culture never fully replicated Iberian models. Instead, material culture, institutions, social structure, and family life underwent modest transformations as tenacious Spaniards contended with native peoples and with one another to try to rebuild the old order in the New World. Hispanic colonists owed much more to the influence of Indians than did their English counterparts along the Atlantic coast, but Hispanic frontier culture and society did not represent a true synthesis of elements from native and Iberian worlds.[161] Sustained by the technological, economic, and political strength of a large state society, Spanish culture clearly prevailed over the cultures of native American tribal groups.

However much Spaniards might eat Indian foods, wear Indian footwear, take Indian wives or concubines, produce mestizo children, learn Indian languages, or live beyond the civility of Spanish urban life, the core of Hispanic frontier culture and society remained recognizably Hispanic and clearly intact. If Spanish political, economic, cultural, and social institutions seemed pallid all across the frontier, it was because Hispanic settlers suffered from isolation, poverty, sparse immigration, low imperial priorities, and Indian resistance, rather than because they had embraced the ways of native Americans. In contrast, those Indian societies impinged upon by influences from the more powerful and complex Spanish state were deeply transformed—frequently beyond recognition.[162]

Wherever Hispanic communities developed in North America, they left an enduring legacy. As Anglo Americans moved into the former Spanish possessions, they found institutional and cultural patterns so well established that it made more sense to adapt to them than to change them. From St. Augustine to San Francisco, not only did Spanish names endure (however badly pronounced), but so did the Hispanic communities and townspeople. With changes in transportation, "new towns" grew up at San Diego, Albuquerque, and San Antonio, but the "old towns" remained. In the countryside beyond the towns, Spanish private and communal land grants determined the shape of the land for years to come. Meanwhile, those Hispanics who remained in the former colonies passed their specialized knowledge on to Anglo-American newcomers—knowledge of local arts, architecture, foods, language, literature, laws, music, and the management of water and livestock in arid lands.

Until the large immigrations from Mexico and the Caribbean in the twentieth century, the Hispanic legacy in North America remained strong along the continent's southern rim less because of the power of Spain's presence than because Hispanics had made the initial European imprint on the region. "The first group able to effect a viable, self-perpetuating society are of crucial significance for the later social and cultural geography of the area, no matter how tiny the initial band of settlers may have been," one cultural geographer has explained.[163] But because Spanish North America never moved beyond the frontier stage in size or sophistication, and because it remained linked to a declining Spain, it stood vulnerable to its modernizing and predatory neighbor. Anglo Americans enjoyed not only demographic and economic advantages, but a mercantile ethos and a certitude in what they believed to be the superiority of their race, religion, and political institutions. Those conceits provided Americans with a rationalization for conquering and transforming the lands of their former Spanish neighbors, much as Spaniards' ethnocentric values had facilitated their domination of indigenous Americans several centuries before.

12

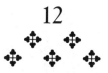

The Spanish Legacy and the Historical Imagination

The past is a foreign country whose features are shaped by today's predilections, its strangeness domesticated by our own preservation of its vestiges.
David Lowenthal, 1985

When Spain's hegemony over the southern rim of North America ended in 1821, its long tenure left an enduring legacy that extended beyond the tangible transformation of peoples and places. More abstractly, Spain's legacy also lingered in American historical memory, where it took on a life of its own. By its very nature, the past cannot be fully recaptured or replayed, but it can be partially remembered or reconstructed by individuals or groups who seek meanings in the past that will serve them in the present. The quest for a usable past has produced multiple interpretations of the Spanish experience on North American frontiers—constructions that have contended with one another over time to transform our understanding and to become in themselves powerful legacies of Spain's centuries in North America.

I

In the late eighteenth and early nineteenth centuries, Englishmen and Anglo Americans who wrote about the Spanish

335

past in North America uniformly condemned Spanish rule. History did not exist as a profession until the late nineteenth century, but a few Englishmen and Anglo Americans wrote histories of Spain's North American provinces, and others of their countrymen freely added historical dimensions to their writings about their travels or residence on the Spanish frontier. Centuries of Spanish misgovernment, these early English and Anglo-American writers believed, had enervated all of Spain's New World colonies, and Spain's misgovernment seemed the inevitable result of the defective character of Spaniards themselves.

From their English forebears and other non-Spanish Europeans, Anglo Americans had inherited the view that Spaniards were unusually cruel, avaricious, treacherous, fanatical, superstitious, cowardly, corrupt, decadent, indolent, and authoritarian—a unique complex of pejoratives that historians from Spain came to call the Black Legend, *la leyenda negra*. This Hispanophobia had deep roots in Europe. It had reached full flower in the sixteenth century among Protestants in northern Europe, where it had taken the form of propaganda against Spain's militant Catholicism and its highly successful imperialism, and it had continued to flourish in the earliest English-language histories of Spain's North American provinces.[1]

The Black Legend had crossed the Atlantic with northern Europeans bound for North America, and it predetermined their first impressions of their Spanish neighbors along the southern rim of the continent. When young Francis Baily from County Berkshire arrived at Chickasaw Bluffs in 1797 on a journey down the Mississippi, he expected the local comandante to treat him "insolently." To Baily's surprise, the official, Agustín Grande, invited his group to supper and "proved to be a very sociable sort of a man."[2] Baily was exceptional, however, for few Englishmen or Americans had their prejudices burdened by direct encounters with Spaniards. To the contrary, events beyond the Anglos' sphere reinforced their prior convictions. Quarrels over territory and the control of Indians from Florida to Louisiana kept historic Anglo-Hispanic enmities alive—first between Spain and England, and subsequently between Spain and the fledgling United States. Then, too, in the early nineteenth century the anti-Spanish rhetoric of Spanish-American revolutionaries revived and reinforced the Black Legend in the English-speaking world. American historian Jared Sparks had never visited Spain's colonies, but when he reflected in 1821 on their newly won independence, he pronounced them lacking "the materials and elements of a good national character."[3]

As Anglo Americans tried to understand the political, economic, religious, and social forces that had shaped the Spanish provinces from Florida to California, the Black Legend continued to color their judgment. The intensity with which Anglos of the late eighteenth or early nineteenth centuries disparaged the Spanish past in North America, however, varied according to circumstances that distinguished southeastern America from southwestern America.

One circumstance that influenced Anglo-American attitudes toward Hispanics was racial mixture. In southeastern America, where little Spanish-Indian blending had occurred, this was a moot issue. English-speaking visitors to New Orleans, Mobile, Pensacola, or St. Augustine seldom encountered mestizos.[4] They did meet mulattos and what they called mixed "races," but they used the word *race* loosely as a synonym for nationality. Such was the nature of Anglo-American prejudice, however, that even the mixture of persons of different nationalities appalled some Anglo Americans. The "mingling" of Spaniards, Frenchmen, and Englishmen at Pensacola, one observer noted, had produced creole males who were "listless and effeminate."[5]

From Texas to California, Anglo Americans were shocked to meet a predominantly mestizo population. Through much of the nineteenth century, Anglo Americans generally regarded racial mixture as a violation of the laws of nature, and many would have subscribed to the views of Thomas Jefferson Farnham, a New England attorney who toured California in the 1840s, and observed that a child of racially different parents was condemned biologically to "a constitution less robust than that of either race from which he sprang." Racial mixture in California, Farnham suggested, had produced "an imbecile, pusillanimous, race of men . . . unfit to control the destinies of that beautiful country."[6] Other Americans expressed similar sentiments, describing mestizos as "half-breeds" or "mongrels" and concluding that they were "degenerate." Rufus Sage, an American trapper, who visited New Mexico in the 1840s declared, "There are no people on the continent of America . . . more miserable in condition or despicable in morals than the mongrel race inhabiting New Mexico."[7] These Anglo-American commentators, who were almost always males traveling in male company, allowed their hormones to moderate their racist judgment and often exempted Hispanic females from their most pejorative remarks.[8]

In addition to race, another circumstance that shaped the depth of Anglo Americans' Hispanophobia was the degree to which they saw Hispanics as an obstacle to their ambitions. This issue, too, was of less importance in the Southeast than in the Southwest, for Spaniards and their descendants posed no serious challenge to Americans after the United States acquired Louisiana and the Floridas. To the contrary, Anglo Americans had outnumbered Spaniards in those provinces even while they still belonged to Spain, and a flood of American immigration continued to submerge those Hispanics who remained. In Florida, for example, Hispanics not only became a minority in Pensacola and St. Augustine, but by the 1830s those towns were eclipsed by the growth of Anglo dominated central Florida and the territory's new capital at Tallahassee. Hispanic influence seemed to survive only marginally in customs that Anglo outsiders soon adopted, such as dances, serenades, and festivals.[9] Thus when Anglo Americans in Florida talked about a "collision between the Races" or of a people who stood in the way of "the progress of the settlement of the country," it was Indians rather than Hispanics whom they had in mind.[10]

In the years immediately following the United States' acquisition of Louisiana and Florida, then, it served little purpose for Anglo Americans to denigrate the local

Hispanic population or its history. Indeed, compared to many of the fortune-seeking, rough-and-tumble American frontiersmen who drifted into Louisiana and Florida, the stable Hispanic community seemed virtuous. Reporting from Pensacola in 1822, Gov. William P. DuVal told President James Monroe that "the Spanish inhabitants of this country are the *best* even among the most quiet and orderly of our own citizens."[11] The few Americans who wrote about Florida in the half century after 1821 either praised the territory's Hispanic population or overlooked it entirely.[12] The so-called Minorcans at St. Augustine seemed especially admirable to Anglo-American writers, with the exception of Rev. Rufus Sewall, a Presbyterian minister. In his *Sketches of St. Augustine*, published in 1848, Sewall characterized the Minorcans as "of servile extraction" and lacking "enterprise," a judgment that he might have reconsidered after the Minorcans exercised sufficient enterprise to drive him out of town and to tear the offensive pages from the remaining copies of his book.[13]

The way in which Anglo Americans in the Southeast regarded their Hispanic contemporaries affected their view of history. In the absence of bitter contention with racially mixed Hispanics for political or economic power, Anglo-American writers merely repeated the conventional wisdom of the Black Legend, but without the vitriol that characterized similar writing about Spaniards in the Southwest. In Florida and Louisiana, writers condemned the "barbarities" of Hernando de Soto, the "demoniac malignity" of Pedro Menéndez de Avilés, and the "jealous and occlusive system" of the "perfidious Spaniards."[14] Amos Stoddard expressed a common sentiment when he wrote in his *Sketches, Historical and Descriptive, of Louisiana*, published in 1812: "Those who believe these people capable of self-government are much deceived."[15] Moreover, decades of Spanish rule, many observers argued, had retarded economic development. As Charles Vignoles crowed in his *Observations upon the Floridas* just two years after Spain ceded Florida to the United States: "Now that . . . the shackles which have hitherto impeded her improvement are taken off, we may rationally look forward to . . . prosperity, happiness and independence."[16] Indeed, several writers offered clear evidence of this assertion in Florida's recent past. When England held Florida from 1763 to 1783, Pensacola and St. Augustine had prospered, they argued. The return of Florida to Spain, as one contemporary put it, "operated as a blight over the whole land."[17] In the last years of Spanish rule, "gardens, fences, field and houses were suffered to grow up, with briars, or rot down, with time, or were burned up for fuel." By 1821, "the once flourishing [British] settlements of Florida, dwindled down to two dirty towns."[18]

However harsh, these assessments of the Hispanic past in the Southeast were often mitigated by suggestions that Spanish rule had virtues as well as defects. Several of the earliest Anglo-American writers praised Spain's relatively humane policy toward Indians, its speedy and inexpensive system of justice, and, paradoxically, the prosperity and good government that it brought to Louisiana.[19] The idea that Spain's relatively brief rule in Louisiana was "mild" and beneficent—a "golden age"—entered Anglo-American literature early and remained the dominant interpretation for the rest of the century.[20] Indeed, in interpreting Louisiana's past, Anglo-American writers were more likely to denigrate Frenchmen than Spaniards, so that France served as the scapegoat that Spain might have become.[21]

Southwestern America posed a different problem for Anglo Americans. The Spanish era had ended in 1821 with newly independent Mexico in control of the region, and Hispanics standing as an obstacle to American expansion—at least until the Texans' successful armed rebellion in 1836, and the United States invasion in 1846, which put New Mexico, Arizona, and California in American hands. Americans who wrote about the Southwest before midcentury interpreted the past in a way that justified their nation's expansionist aims. California, with its mild climate and Pacific ports, held special attractions for Americans, who denounced the californios and their history in the familiar rhetoric of the Black Legend.[22] William Shaler, captain of an American vessel that traded illegally along the California coast in 1803 while it still belonged to Spain, put the matter plainly. California and its "indolent" inhabitants had not progressed "under the degrading shackles of ignorance and superstition." California, he said, needed "nothing but a good government to rise rapidly to wealth and importance."[23] American readers understood which government he had in mind. In the Southwest, American expansionist designs combined with Hispanophobia and racism to produce a more vituperative portrait of Hispanics and their history than existed in the Southeast.[24]

Hispanophobia found its most strident and enduring rhetoric in Texas. Writing from the United States in the spring of 1836, where he had gone to seek aid for the cause of Texas independence, Stephen F. Austin drew the sides clearly. He characterized the conflict between Texas and Mexico as nothing less than "a war of barbarism and of despotic principles, waged by the mongrel Spanish-Indian and Negro race, against civilization and the Anglo-American race."[25] The bloodshed in Texas at the Alamo, Goliad, and San Jacinto, which had no parallel elsewhere in the borderlands, hardened attitudes on both sides and left a deep reservoir of Anglo-American hatred toward Mexicans and their Hispanic forefathers. As one Texas historian noted several years later, the "extermination [of Mexicans] may yet become necessary for the repose of this continent!"[26]

After their victory, Anglo-American rebels controlled not only Texas, but the writing of its history. They adopted the story line of their propagandists and added an additional twist—they portrayed themselves as heroic, a "superior race of men."[27] Heroes needed villains, and Texas's earliest historians found them full-blown, nurtured in the Hispanic past. The first detailed history of the Spanish era in Texas to appear in English (and the standard work until the twentieth century), concluded with a gloomy scene: "We have herein traced the history of Texas through the dim records

66. "Greasers," from Frank Triplett's Conquering the Wilderness *(New York, 1883). Courtesy, DeGolyer Library, Southern Methodist University.*

of a hundred and thirty-six years, rarely finding in that long period a congenial spot for human happiness. Ignorance and despotism have hung like a dark cloud over her noble forests and luxuriant prairies."[28]

Painting the Spanish era in dark hues enabled Texas historians to contrast it with the Texas rebellion. In essence, Texans revolted for political and economic reasons, but early Texas historians elevated the rebellion to a *"sublime collision of moral influences,"* "a *moral* struggle," and *"a war for principles."*[29] The inconvenient fact that some Mexicans had joined Anglo-American rebels in Texas was forgotten, and a repudiation of the Spanish past became an essential part of Texans' self-identity. Hispanophobia, with its particularly vitriolic anti-Mexican variant, also served as a convenient rationale to keep Mexicans "in their place." Hispanophobia lasted longer in Texas than in any of Spain's other former North American provinces. Well into the twentieth century it retarded the serious study of the state's lengthy Spanish heritage, leaving the field open to distortion and caricature.[30]

Elsewhere in the Southwest, a vigorous Hispanophobia also accompanied American expansionism, reaching a crescendo during the war with Mexico. But after the war, anti-Hispanic sentiment abated more rapidly in California, Arizona, and New Mexico than it did in Texas. Mexico had lacked the means to ship substantial numbers of troops into those distant provinces, as it had in Texas in 1835–36. Thus, despite some vigorous local resistance, California, Arizona, and New Mexico fell to United States forces rather easily, leaving little trace of bitterness among the victorious Anglo Americans.[31]

With or without rancor, however, Anglo Americans repudiated the Spanish past all across the borderlands, judging Spain's legacy an unmitigated failure and replacing its vestiges with their own institutions and culture. Even much of the widely respected Spanish civil law was rejected by the newcomers. As the California Senate concluded in 1850, the Spanish legal system "was based on the crude laws of a rough, fierce people, whose passion was war and whose lust [was] conquest."[32] Crossing America in 1877, an English journalist expressed surprise at the transformation of the old Spanish provinces. "The effacement of the Spanish element in New Orleans is enough," he wrote, "but its disappearance in California is even more complete. The *'nombres de España'* [España] only remain; the *'cosas'* thereof have entirely vanished."[33]

II

Spanish "things," however, had not vanished entirely. An appreciative view of Spanish culture ran like a feeble countercurrent through American thought and letters, represented most conspicuously in the works of Washington Irving and William H. Prescott. In the last two decades of the nineteenth century, war with Spain in 1898 notwithstanding, that current grew stronger until it became the mainstream. Indeed, in some areas of the old Spanish borderlands, things Spanish became not only appreciated, but fashionable, and a new historical sensibility came to rival the old Black Legend. Walt Whitman caught the spirit in a letter that he addressed to some of Santa Fe's leading citizens in 1883. "It is time to realize," Whitman wrote, "that there will not be found any more cruelty, tyranny, superstition, &c., in the *résumé* of past Spanish history than in the corresponding *résumé* of Anglo-Norman history." Whitman urged an appreciation of the "splendor and sterling value" of Hispanic culture in the Southwest, which he saw as enriching "the seething materialistic" ethos of the United States.[34]

California, populous and prosperous after the discovery of gold in 1848 changed it from a Hispanic Siberia to an American Mecca, became the center of a pro-Hispanic movement in America. In the Golden State, the reinterpretation of the Hispanic past became both cause and effect of a growing Hispanophilic sentiment. Whereas an earlier generation of Anglo Americans had portrayed californios as indolent, ignorant, and backward, Americans of the late nineteenth century reimagined the californios as unhurried, untroubled, and gracious. California's premier historian, Hubert Howe Bancroft, expressed this new sentiment succinctly in 1886: "Never before or since," he wrote of Hispanic California, "was there a spot in America where life was a long happy holiday, where there was less labor, less care or trouble."[35]

Bancroft's fictive, condescending, and still profoundly racist simplification of California's impoverished and often turbulent history had a counterpart in the sentimental historical fiction of Bret Harte, Helen Hunt Jackson, Gertrude Atherton, and others, who portrayed California for a wide readership. The californios, wrote Helen Hunt Jackson, had lived "a picturesque life, with more of sentiment and gaiety . . . than will ever be seen again on these sunny shores."[36] The theme was adopted by the old California families themselves. "There never was a more peaceful or happy people on the face of the earth than the Spanish, Mexican, and Indian population of Alta California before the American conquest," Guadalupe Vallejo wrote in 1890 for the popular *Century Magazine*.[37]

Whether Vallejo and other prominent descendants of old California families had helped to create this synthetic past, or simply reinforced it by repeating the new conventional wisdom, is not clear, but this remarkable turnabout in understanding California's Hispanic past coincided with changes in Anglo-American society as well as in the society of the californios. As the nation became more urbanized and industrialized in the late nineteenth century, many Americans recoiled from what they saw as excessive commercialism, materialism, vulgarity, and rootlessness and longed for pastoral values that they imagined had existed in a simpler agrarian America.[38]

In bustling California, which enjoyed unprecedented growth in the 1880s, newcomers found themselves rootless and often alienated. But writers, artists, architects, and scholars, who gave shape, meaning, and perspective to the historical experience, came to the rescue. By sanitizing California's Hispanic past, they made it an acceptable source of tradition and continuity for Anglo Americans, and a model of pastoral tranquility for those who wished to escape, at least in memory, to a less hurried era. "In these days of trade, bustle, and confusion . . . ," Guadalupe Vallejo lamented in 1890, "the quiet and happy domestic life of the past seems like a dream."[39] From conversations with his elders, Vallejo understood the old days as a "simple and healthful" time of plenty, when "their orchards yielded abundantly and their gardens were full of vegetables . . . beef and mutton were to be had for the killing, and wild game was very abundant."[40]

California's Mediterranean-like shores lent themselves to experimentation with transplanting Italian and Greek traditions (exemplified by the construction of the community of Venice on the Pacific in 1904–5, with its Renaissance palaces, canals, and gondolas), but only the Spanish past, even in a fictive reincarnation, had verisimilitude—"had behind it the force of history."[41] Conveniently, the force of history had also reduced the influence of California's Hispanic residents; by the 1880s californios comprised only a tiny percentage of the state's population. It became possible, then, for Anglo Americans to look back with nostalgia at the californios' past, because their descendants posed no challenge to Anglo dominance of politics, commerce, or social life.[42] Then, too, by focusing their admiration on historic Spain and premodern Spanish California, Anglo Americans could simultaneously and without contradiction have contempt for modern Spain, which they humiliated in the Spanish-American War.

Nostalgia for a vanished Hispanic past resembled a similar shift in Anglo-American attitudes toward Indians—in America in general and in California in particular. When writing about Hispanics, for example, the first generation of Anglo Americans in California seemed to take the Indians' side. In seeking to justify American expansion into Spanish and Mexican territory, those Americans condemned the californios as cruel exploiters of Indians. Anglo Americans who entered the state after the gold rush, on the other hand, rationalized their own behavior in pushing Indians off the land by portraying the natives as cruel and deserving of extermination.[43] By the late nineteenth century, however, Anglo Americans began to sentimentalize the race they had helped to annihilate. As one historian has noted, "the nostalgia and pity aroused by the dying race produced the best romantic sentiments."[44]

Nostalgia for the Spanish past also extended to the arts, artifacts, and architecture of the old californios, for the objects and monuments of the vanquished had become, in the words of one of our most astute cultural historians, " 'safe' to play with in recombinations emptied of previous vital meanings, as in tourist souvenirs, antiquarian reconstructions, or archaizing revivals."[45] Thus, just as they converted the californios' mundane daily lives into the picturesque "days of the *dons*," California romanticizers also reinvented their dwellings and places of worship. Immediately following the American conquest of California, what one writer has called "the Mansard malady and the Victorian virus" spread westward, replacing indigenous architectural styles. Then, in the 1880s, Anglo Americans began to appreciate and exaggerate what they had previously disdained. The californios of the Spanish era had lived in simple one-story adobes, many with flat, tar-covered roofs, and few with wooden floors, glass windows, fireplaces, or tree-shaded landscaping. Anglo Americans reimagined those modest structures as elegant two-story, red-tile-roofed structures, with carved woodwork and cantilevered balconies that looked into tree-filled patios where water played in fountains.[46]

The search for an authentic indigenous architecture led Anglo Americans to build such structures and also to apply features of the California missions to domestic and public buildings. This architectural style, which came to be called Mission Revival, had its origins in California in the 1880s, but its vocabulary of stucco walls, red tiles, arched logias, and bell towers, spoke to the nation as well as the state after the 1893 World Columbian Exposition in Chicago gave Mission Revival a wide audience. By the 1910s, mission-style railroad depots appeared in communities as far from California as Bismark, North Dakota, and Battle Creek, Michigan.[47]

California romanticizers also reimagined the missions and the missionaries, and the symbolic landscape of the "paths of the padres." Once despised by many Anglo Americans as bigoted zealots who imposed a corrupt Catholicism on recalcitrant natives, the Franciscans of Hispanic California came to be remembered as kindly Christians, ministering to devoted Indians. The mission structures themselves, most of them neglected since their secularization in the 1830s and falling into ruins, came to be

67. The chapel of San Carlos de Borromeo de Carmelo, circa 1880. Photograph by Carleton E. Watkins. Courtesy, California Historical Society, North Baker Library, San Francisco, FN–08423.

appreciated as picturesque. If priests had still said Mass in mission chapels, more austere Protestants might have found the iconography and ornamentation distasteful, but in ruins the missions seemed worthy of veneration. Led by the Association for the Preservation of the Missions, founded in Southern California in 1888, and galvanized by the flamboyant Charles Fletcher Lummis, Californians began to restore and embellish mission chapels, outbuildings, and grounds. Masquerading as historical preservationists, the rebuilders of California's missions often ignored the realities of archaeological and documentary records to produce the buildings and grounds that appealed to their imaginations and to the tastes of local businessmen.[48] The refurbishing of California's twenty-one missions included the "restoration" of the road that once linked them. Californians marked the historic *camino real* with over 450 iron mission bells, suspended eleven feet above the ground from graceful standards. The first of the mission bell markers was erected in 1906, by which time the missions had become, in the words of one specialist, "California's most conspicuous and influential cultural symbol."[49]

Ironically, if anticommercialism had provided part of the impetus for the nostalgic reinvention of the Hispanic past, it was commercialism that gave the new nostalgia and its adherents high public visibility. Properly laundered and packaged, California's picturesque Spanish heritage attracted tourists and gave its infant cities a patina of permanence and tradition. As Charles Lummis, Southern California's most exuberant Hispanophile, crassly put it: "The old missions are worth more money . . . than our oil, our oranges, or even our climate."[50] That message was not lost on the business community. The Southern Pacific Railroad promoted its north-south route by assuring travelers that the railroad followed the California mission trail where, among other wonders, newcomers might find the "ideal homesite for your castle in Spain."[51] On the Sunset Route from New Orleans to Los Angeles, the same railroad explained in a promotional pamphlet that "we take our way through the very heart of early missionary fields, where paganism has given place to Christianity."[52] By the 1940s, in Los Angeles alone, "the word 'mission' was to be found as part of the corporate name of over a hundred business enterprises," and there was "scarcely a community in Southern California . . . that does not have its annual 'Spanish fiesta'—where 'shoe salesmen and grocery clerks served you with a bit of scarlet braid on their trouser seams.' "[53] The most attractive of these events, John Steven McGroarty's famous

68. The chapel of San Carlos de Borromeo de Carmelo, photographed by Dr. Joseph A. Baird, Jr., in the 1950s. Courtesy, California Historical Society, North Baker Library, San Francisco, FN–16688.

"Mission Play," reportedly drew hundreds of thousands of spectators during its sixteen-year run, from 1912–28, at Mission San Gabriel.[54]

III

No other part of America witnessed the enthusiasm for things Spanish that manifested itself in yeasty Southern California, but many of the same ingredients could be found in other parts of southwestern and southeastern America: the decline of Hispanic economic and political power, newcomers' yearnings for pastoral traditions, anticommercialism, the ballyhoo of hucksters and publicists, and visible reminders of the Spanish past—particularly in the form of structures and people.

Nowhere outside of California did these elements combine more powerfully than in New Mexico. There, writers, artists, the Santa Fe Railroad, and Fred Harvey appropriated and marketed the refurbished symbols of a once-reviled people. In their hands, the tarnished Spanish past gained respectability. Santa Fe, once regarded as a miserable collection of mud hovels, came to be regarded as "the only picturesque spot in America yet undiscovered by the jaded globe trotter."[55] In addition to picturesque Santa Fe, New Mexico had picturesque Hispanics, picturesque Indians (many of them, partially Hispanicized), picturesque desert, and a tradition of arts and crafts that surpassed any other area of the old Spanish borderlands.

Hispanic art in New Mexico had found its most creative expression in the form of naive but powerfully evocative wooden carvings of saints, or *santos*, and paintings of saints on pine boards, known as *retablos*. The earliest foreign visitors to New Mexico dismissed these objects as either unworthy of mention or denigrated them as "unmeaning bits of ill-carved wood," "hideous dolls," or "miserable pictures of the saints."[56] In the twentieth century, the abstract, simple lines of these works came to be treasured, and the saintmakers, or *santeros*, regarded as heirs to one of the few indigenous artistic traditions in the United States.[57]

New Mexico's adobe churches and adobe homes underwent a similar metamorphosis in historical interpretation. At first, Anglo Americans had found adobe disgusting—a "degenerate Spanish (Mexican) style of architecture," one visitor to San Antonio opined.[58] In the last half of the nineteenth century, Americans and upper-class Hispanics imported fashionable domestic architecture from the East Coast and the Middle West—Greek Revival, Italianate, Queen Anne, and Colonial Revival—and they "Gothicized" adobe churches with ornate wooden trim. In the early twentieth century, however, Spanish-Pueblo styles were rediscovered and the so-called Santa Fe style slowly came into vogue. Churches began to be de-Gothicized and re-restored to approximate their original appearance.[59]

New Mexico's admiration for things Hispanic did not manifest itself entirely in refurbishing the old. New Mexicans also invented new historical traditions, including the now famous Santa Fe fiesta, an Anglo-American creation of the early twentieth

69. Beginning in the 1890s, a French priest, Antonine Docher, slowly transformed the church at Isleta pueblo, adding a covered balcony, replacing its flat roof with a pitched one of corrugated iron, and topping it all with wooden belfries, gables, and a dozen crosses. As photographed circa 1922. Courtesy, Elsa Brumm Collection, Museum of New Mexico, neg. no. 2669.

century that celebrated: "The Day of . . . Franciscan Missionaries and Martyrs," "The Day of the Conquerors," and the "Day of Spanish Romance."[60]

In some parts of southeastern America, the romanticization of the Hispanic past began earlier than in the Southwest.[61] With the end of the Civil War, the completion of railroad lines into the South, and the beginnings of Yankee tourism, the Hispanic past became a commodity to market if not a heritage to cherish. Histories and guide books sentimentalized local history and deemphasized or abandoned the Black Legend.[62] George Fairbanks's *History of Florida*, published in 1871, helped set the new tone. For example, instead of lingering on Hernando de Soto's harsh treatment of Indians as earlier writers had tended to do, Fairbanks explained it away as "a measure of policy" and presented De Soto as a "gallant adventurer."[63] Fairbanks asked his readers to admire "the perseverance and hardihood" of De Soto's band: "three hundred mounted men, on noble Andalusian steeds, richly caparisoned . . . all gentlemen and noble cavaliers, hidalgos of rank and scions of the noblest families of Spain."[64] Like his counterparts in California, Fairbanks sought to establish a link between the Spanish past and the American present. Instead of presenting Americans and Spaniards as antagonists, he portrayed Americans as heirs to a common tradition that began

70. *Diego de Vargas and the Franciscans, Santa Fe Fiesta, 1919. Photograph by T. Harmon Parkhurst.*
Courtesy, Museum of New Mexico, neg. no. 52375.

with De Soto: "The iron horse of an advancing civilization [of Anglo Americans] is startling those same pine forests with its shrill scream, indicating that fulfillment of that manifest destiny which was to strike forever from the land . . . the last remains of the aboriginal races."[65]

Fairbanks's views apparently influenced a guidebook published several years later, which described De Soto as "the most distinguished of the many brave leaders whose names are honored as discoverers of the Western World" and emphasized the expedition's adventures with an "Indian queen," and a "fair damsel" of Indian extraction.[66] Some promotional literature avoided the subject of the Spanish past completely and simply emphasized the antiquity and charm of the Spanish legacy.[67] One guide to St. Augustine compared its skies to Seville's, its sunlight to Granada's, and its moonlight to Valencia's, "where pinnacles and minarets . . . glitter in its beams on the Mediterranean shore."[68]

No southern community celebrated its Spanish past more enthusiastically than St. Augustine, which played upon its position as America's oldest continuously occupied European community. In 1885, for the benefit of wealthy winter tourists, the city's boosters invented a tradition of celebrating Ponce de León's "romantic" discovery of

Florida—with historic reenactments, parades, concerts, fireworks, and yacht races.[69] But primacy was not enough. Along with the rest of the Southeast, St. Augustine lacked two of the essential ingredients for a full-course Spanish revival such as communities in California and New Mexico enjoyed.

First, descendants of the region's earliest Hispanic settlers had long since vanished across much of the South, as had Hispanicized Indians. "Most tourists expect to find here a Spanish population," one guide to St. Augustine explained in 1892, but "the swarthy Spaniard stalks through the streets no longer."[70] In Louisiana, descendants of old Spanish families were still numerous and had retained much of their culture, but in the popular imagination they had become indistinct from Frenchmen, who had initially imprinted their culture on the region and who had dominated Louisiana culturally and demographically when the United States acquired it.[71]

Second, throughout the South, Spanish architecture—the most potent visual reminder of continuity with the Hispanic past—had also disappeared in large measure by the mid-nineteenth century. In contrast to the Southwest, the region had no ruins of Spanish missions to stir the souls of tourists. Some overzealous historians and amateurs tried to fill the void by portraying the remnants of prosaic nineteenth-century Georgia sugar mills as the romantic ruins of seventeenth-century Spanish

71. The Discovery of the Mississippi by De Soto A.D. 1541, *romanticized on a large canvas (144" x 216") by William H. Powell, 1853, hangs in the rotunda of the U.S. Capitol. Courtesy, Architect of the Capitol.*

THE FIRST EXCURSION TO FLORIDA LANDING OF PONCE DE LEON

72. *Ponce de León's discovery of Florida, as portrayed romantically in a brochure published for tourists by the Cincinnati Southern Railway,* Winter Cities in a Summer Land: A Tour through Florida and the Winter Resorts of the South *(1881). Courtesy, DeGolyer Library, Southern Methodist University.*

missions. That idea gained momentum during the first three decades of the twentieth century, until it ran squarely into a competing vision of Georgia's colonial origins. In the 1930s, the Georgia Society of the Colonial Dames of America sponsored an investigation that effectively exploded the myth of the Spanish mission ruins in Georgia. In the South, community standards limited the extent to which the past and its symbols could be reshaped.[72]

In the South, some domestic and public architecture did survive from the Spanish era, but it lacked the clear associations with Spain that characterized the Southwest's adobe ranchos, homes, and public buildings. New Orleans held the Southeast's most impressive ensemble of urban structures from the Spanish era, but like that city's culture and people, the Spanish buildings that dominated the French Quarter came to be remembered as French.[73] At Mobile, none of the buildings from the brief Spanish era (1780–1813) appear to have survived hurricanes, fires, and the local citizenry beyond the 1830s.[74] In Pensacola and St. Augustine, some early Spanish structures have remained, even though most were either destroyed or modified during the English occupation, from 1763 to 1783. Although Spaniards reoccupied both cities in 1784, Spanish architectural styles did not return with them. Americans who took possession of the two towns in 1821 found eclectic structures that could not be described as distinctively Spanish.[75] In St. Augustine, buildings from the Spanish era continued to disappear unmourned throughout the nineteenth century, replaced by styles current in the Northeast. Not until the 1930s did serious efforts get underway to preserve the city's Spanish architectural heritage.[76] Massive Spanish-built fortifications survived at Pensacola and St. Augustine, but they often conjured up unpleasant associations of "sepulchral donjons which tell of skeletons, manacles and inquisitorial torture of buried humanity."[77] Few visitors possessed the romantic imagination of Sidney Lanier, Georgia's celebrated poet, who noted in a promotional tract on Florida that the cannonballs at "the sweet old fort" of San Marcos "were only like pleasant reminders of the beauty of peace."[78]

Late in the century a "Spanish style" did become popular in Florida, but it owed less to continuity with the local past than to new influences from Spain, Mexico, and

73. The Hotel De León, today Flagler College. Courtesy, St. Augustine Historical Society.

California. Henry Flagler, a petroleum tycoon and Florida's most visionary developer, started the Spanish trend in Florida architecture in the late 1880s by building resort hotels at St. Augustine in an eclectic, theatrical style that his architects called Spanish Renaissance. Flagler's Hotel Ponce de León opened its doors in 1888, soon joined by the Alcazar and the Córdova, a Moorish-inspired concoction.[79] When Flagler moved farther south to Palm Beach in the 1890s, he abandoned not only St. Augustine but the "Spanish" style as well, which Floridians largely ignored until 1919 when the California architect Addison Mizner rediscovered that in Florida "the history, the romance and the setting were all Spanish." Mizner built the Everglades Club at Palm Beach—the first major structure in South Florida done in a style identified as Spanish—and his masterpiece, the community of Boca Raton.[80]

Mizner's conception of Florida's past, however, was as fictitious as Flagler's and represented little more than a local manifestation of a popular style that elaborated upon and supplanted Mission Revival. This so-called Spanish Colonial or Spanish Revival captured national attention with its dazzling display at the Panama-California Exposition in San Diego's Balboa Park in 1915. Spanish Revival, which ranged from Renaissance to Baroque and contained a generous admixture of influences from throughout the Mediterranean and Mexico, had few genuine antecedents in America north of Mexico. Unable to find, much less revive, significant numbers of elaborate

74. *Spanish Revival came to Kansas City in 1923, with the construction of Country Club Plaza. Courtesy, Missouri Valley Special Collections, Kansas City Public Library, Kansas City, Missouri.*

and decorative models in the nation's Hispanic past, American architects manufactured their own indigenous Hispanic architecture.[81]

However removed from historical realities its allusions to the past may have been, Spanish Revival's evocation of sense of place beguiled many Americans. In the 1920s and 1930s, Spanish-influenced churches, schools, banks, hotels, railroad stations, shopping centers, and assorted public buildings, many of them with Spanish names as well as Spanish styles, arose across the land—even in places with no significant link to the Spanish era such as Kansas City and Dallas.[82] By the 1920s, then, Americans had reimagined the Spanish past in the vocabulary of architecture as well as in prose, and the two forms of expression aided and abetted one another.[83] Spanish Revival has continued to reappear up to the present day, of course, with the current mode dismissed by some cynics as "Taco Deco" or "Mariachi Moderne."[84]

IV

The Hispanophobia of the first two-thirds of the nineteenth century has endured throughout this century, continuing to color our understanding of the past. Even at the height of American enthusiasm for things Spanish in the 1910s, bitterly negative interpretations of Spain's colonial empire in North America appeared in print. "There was something cruel, something radically wrong with the whole Spanish system of colonization," two well-intentioned Protestant missionaries, eager to "redeem" Mexican-Americans, wrote in 1916. "A race that was molded in the fanatical monastery schools is sufficient explanation of the medieval character of the population of the Southwest at the time of [its] incorporation into the union of the States."[85] Professional historians, however, usually expressed Hispanophobic sentiments with greater delicacy. Writing in the 1940s, for example, one historian praised Andrew Jackson's "stern" treatment of Spaniards in Florida, without which "Spanish customs, habits, and traditions would probably be much stronger in Florida today than they are."[86]

Among American writers of history, however, the pro-Spanish and often sentimentalized view of America's Hispanic past that emerged in the late nineteenth century has prevailed through most of this century. This viewpoint found its most authoritative expression in the prodigious research of Herbert Eugene Bolton and the large cadre of doctoral candidates that he trained while teaching at the University of California at Berkeley, between his arrival there in 1911 and his death in 1953. That Bolton worked in California and produced his crop of protégés there is not surprising. The seedbed of the Mission and Spanish revivals in America, California was also the most affluent state along the continent's southern rim. It could support libraries, researchers, writers, and readers as could no other state in the Southwest or the Southeast, and it had nourished the most vigorous historical writing on Hispanic North America even before Bolton's arrival.[87]

From his first days at Berkeley, Bolton's explicit goal was to enlarge the scope of

American history beyond its well-known English, Dutch, and French antecedents, to include the nation's Hispanic origins—a story that he, like a few others before him, regarded as important but little understood.[88] As he promoted that story, Bolton tried to compensate for what he regarded as the distortions of the Black Legend. He emphasized the heroic achievements of individual Spaniards and the positive contributions of Hispanic institutions and culture, often to a fault.[89] Through his solid scholarship ran an unabashed strain of sentimentality, as when he characterized the history of what he called "the Spanish Borderlands" as "picturesque" and "romantic,"[90] or when he uncritically endorsed the idea that the remnants of Georgia sugar mills were ruins of seventeenth-century missions.[91]

The Bolton school dominated American historical scholarship on the borderlands until the 1960s. His disciples and other like-minded historians reexamined Spain's frontier institutions and culture and found positive Spanish influences on many aspects of American life, including agriculture, mining, ranching, architecture, art, law, language, literature, and music.[92] Bolton himself had so celebrated Spain's contributions to America that he had written of "Spain's frontiering genius." Implicitly or explicitly, many of his disciples echoed him.[93] For example, Alfred Barnaby Thomas, a Bolton protégé who translated documents that revealed serious weaknesses in Spain's governance of its empire, lauded "the genius of Spanish civilization."[94] Herbert I. Priestley, another former student of Bolton's, reminded his readers in 1936 of the "debt" that Americans owed to Spain, "something like half of our present area having been brought into the fold of Christendom through the work of the Spanish pioneers."[95] As was characteristic of the Boltonians, Priestley neglected to point out that America's "debt" to Spain had come at a high price to native Americans.

Historians' pro-Spanish interpretation of America's Hispanic past has continued to serve commercial interests in communities across the Spanish rim of America up to the present day. It has also improved the image of the United States in the Hispanic world, as Bolton had argued it would—but apparently more in Spain than in Latin America.[96] As early as 1915, the distinguished Spanish historian Rafael Altamira identified and applauded those American historians who had broken away from the Black Legend—the traditional view of Spain as "a monstrous exception in the history of colonization."[97] Two years later, another Spanish scholar, Miguel Romera-Novarro, expressed similar sentiments, adding that "the North Americans should not be able to forget that two-thirds of their country has been Spanish territory."[98] He pointed with pride to Spaniards who first explored and settled the continent, to the existence of Spanish names on the land, and to the people in the United States "who still speak, feel, and think in Spanish."[99]

Spanish writers have continued to extol Spain's contributions to American history, some of them outdoing the Boltonians. In the *Spanish Presence in the United States*, first published in 1972, Carlos Fernández-Shaw painstakingly examined Spain's influence, state-by-state, on all aspects of American culture. He included lists of Spanish "firsts" in the United States, as well as monuments to individual Spaniards and identified numerous motels, hotels, and restaurants with Spanish names.[100] In their eagerness to bury the Black Legend, some Spaniards joined with Americans in creating a new one. For example, one Spanish scholar described Hernando de Soto's expedition as "not only the work of heroes and athletes; it was also the work of centaurs."[101]

V

Even as some Spanish scholars joined the Boltonians in looking with reverence if not with awe at Spain's towering achievements in North America, historians from several quarters began to chip away at Bolton's historical construction. Some struck at the very foundation of the Bolton school by challenging the claim that the Spanish past was relevant to the history of the United States. In an influential essay published in 1955, Earl Pomeroy argued that scholars had exaggerated the roles of Hispanics and other "local foreign groups" in respect to their relative importance. "Actually," Pomeroy wrote, "the native Spanish and Mexican elements in many parts of the West— particularly California where they are revered today—were small and uninfluential."[102] Echoing Pomeroy's argument, historian Moses Rischin dismissed historical interest in California's Spanish past as "eccentric and escapist." "Bolton," Rischin wrote, "contributed little that has enlarged the historical understanding of the United States."[103] American historians seldom took this position in print, but they implied through their work that the activities of Spaniards had little value for understanding the nation's history. Many studies, as John Caughey pointed out in 1965, treated the old Spanish provinces "as though they were an exotic prior figuration extraneous to all that developed later," and textbooks in American history have continued to give the Spanish era short shrift.[104]

More serious blows came from critics who granted the relevance of the Hispanic past, but who accused the Boltonians of misinterpreting it. From students of colonial Latin America came charges of Romantic excess. "There is [among the Boltonians] sometimes a tendency to minimize the unpleasant aspects of life and society," Eleanor Adams explained gingerly in 1954. Those who had studied the archival sources regarding colonial New Mexico, she said, "cannot feel that romantic idealization of a very human history is either necessary or advisable." To the contrary, New Mexico's colonial history "is one of failure in both the worldly and the evangelical senses."[105]

From another direction, some historians criticized the Bolton school for over-emphasizing Spaniards in the borderlands and losing sight of the fact that genetically and culturally the society of northern New Spain had been essentially mestizo or Mexican. Carey McWilliams, one of the earliest and most vocal of these critics, argued in 1948 that southwestern America had fallen under the spell of what he called "a fantasy heritage"—"an absurd dichotomy between things Spanish and things Mexican."[106] Those Anglo Americans who glorified the region's Spanish heritage while ignoring or discriminating against living Mexicans, McWilliams charged, were deluded by this fantasy. So, too, were those Mexican Americans who prefered to identify themselves as Spanish in order to disassociate themselves from refugees and job-seekers who had begun to pour across the border in large numbers during Mexico's turbulent revolution of the 1910s (the fantasy heritage had its counterpart in St. Augustine where descendants of Minorcans began in the 1950s to suggest their lineage to Spanish nobility).[107]

The world of scholars mirrored the schizoid view of Hispanics in southwestern America that McWilliams described. Bolton himself simultaneously celebrated "Spain's frontiering genius," while suggesting that Mexican "half-breeds—mestizoes or mulattoes" were naturally vicious and unruly.[108] In Bolton's day, social scientists who studied living Mexican Americans explained the group's relative poverty as a pathological condition caused by cultural deficiencies, including passivity, laziness, and an inability to look beyond the present.[109] At best, the fantasy heritage split the history of Hispanics in the Southwest into two disconnected parts, tacitly denying Mexican Americans their historic roots in the region. At worst, it implied that long-time residents with strong Indian features, or immigrants from Mexico, were inferior aliens in a new land. "Pure Spaniards," the eminent historian Walter Prescott Webb opined in 1931, had pushed the Spanish frontier northward, cutting "like a blade of Damascus steel," but as the frontier advanced and Spaniards mingled with "sedentary Indian stock, whose blood . . . was a ditch water," the steel lost its temper.[110]

Although a few specialists deplored the "fantasy heritage,"[111] their objections went largely unheeded until the late 1960s, when a small number of Chicano scholars set out to recapture the past for Mexican Americans. They had to start from scratch. Unlike peoples who invented enduring myths about themselves in their own lifetimes, such as the seventeenth-century Dutch or the eighteenth-century Anglo Americans, Hispanic elites on the impoverished frontiers of North America had produced a meager literature of self-glorification—one that most Chicano historians quickly rejected.[112] Sympathizing with the exploited rather than the exploiters, Chicano historians (like their Mexican counterparts) tended to identify themselves more closely with their Indian or mestizo ancestors than with Spaniards. Historian Manuel Servín charged that a "latent, anti-Mexican attitude" had permeated the work of Anglo-American historians—an anti-Mexican attitude that echoed the racism of españoles and would-be españoles in the Spanish colonial era.[113] Indeed, some of the most influential Chicano scholars adopted a long-range Indian perspective that reduced the entire three-century Spanish epoch to a relatively brief interlude. At the heart of that indigenous perspective was the powerful idea of a Chicano homeland called Aztlán.

Metaphorically if not in fact, some Chicano intellectuals embraced the idea that the American Southwest was Aztlán, the mythic ancestral home of the Aztecs. The Southwest, these scholars argued, had been the homeland of the Aztecs or Mexica peoples before they migrated southward to achieve greatness in central Mexico in the four-teenth century. Thus, the descendants of the Aztecs, Mexicans who had immigrated to the United States in the twentieth century, had simply returned home to the cradle of Mexican civilization when they crossed the border. This vision of the past contained more poetry than prose and offended a number of historians, Mexican Americans among them. It did, nonetheless, extend Chicano claims to the Southwest farther back in time than those of Spaniards or Anglo Americans, and it established Chicanos as natives rather than immigrants in the region.[114]

The myth of Aztlán became a powerful symbol for the Chicano movement, which sought to provide historical unity to the distinct experiences of *californios, arizonenses, nuevomexicanos,* and *tejanos* (curiously, the same myth had also been used for quite different political ends by an Anglo-American publicist in 1885, who apparently sought to suggest the savagery of Pueblo culture by portraying New Mexico as Aztlán).[115] Aztlán could not, of course, become a useful symbol of historical unity for all Hispanos in America in the twentieth century. The two other largest Hispanic

75. Protesting the Vietnam war, these students marched behind the banner of Aztlán in East Los Angeles on August 29, 1970, the day of the Chicano National Moratorium. Courtesy, Devra Anne Weber.

groups, *portoriqueños* and *cubanos*, had their own "homelands" offshore, and the diversity of America's Hispanic population made unity elusive if not impossible. Indeed, no single unified history of Hispanos in America emerged in the 1970s and 1980s, but rather there appeared histories of Hispanic groups, organized on the basis of national origin.[116] The value of Aztlán as a symbol had faded by the 1980s, but the solid historical scholarship that emerged from the Chicano movement has endured. Although some students of Mexican American history have dismissed the Spanish era as irrelevant,[117] others have plumbed the Spanish past to illuminate the present. In particular, a number of Chicano historians have explored themes that resonate with the problems of Mexicans in America, as well as with the concerns of contemporary social historians: migration, exploitation of labor and women, class struggle, racial mixture, racism, acculturation, accommodation, urban life, crime, punishment, family, faith, and the fortitude and adaptability of common folk who endure in times of rapid change and stress.[118] In so doing, they have transcended the view of New Spain's northern frontier as "romantic" or "picturesque" and have gone beyond seeing events solely through the eyes of explorers, missionaries, soldiers, or government officials.

In short, some Chicano historians, joined by a new generation of scholars in Spain and Mexico,[119] have come to see the historic southwestern borderlands as a complex mestizo frontier where the deep roots planted by early generations of Hispanic pioneers have facilitated the survival of subsequent generations under the most adverse conditions. Like the myth of Aztlán, this new historical construction provides continuity for Mexicans that the Romantic view denied them. Descendants of those Mexicans who remained in the region after the United States seized it in 1848, or who have entered it since, need no longer regard themselves as outsiders in a new land, but rather as residents of a "lost land." Moreover, possession of a homeland with a history that is their own has further empowered Mexicans in America to demand political and social justice and self-determination.[120] Nowhere has this been clearer than among the Hispano villagers of northern New Mexico. There, an expanded historical identity for a people whose ethnicity has been long marketed as a commodity for tourists has provided collective strength and converted lost rural land into a powerful symbol of ethnic resistence.[121] In southeastern America, conversely, no such symbol has emerged.

At the same time that Chicano historians attacked the Boltonians for elitism and romanticism, a growing group of scholars challenged the Bolton school for its failure to present Indian sides of the story. Bolton and his followers had by no means overlooked the impact of Spanish colonization on American Indians (and, indeed, were far more attentive to Indian history than their Turnerian counterparts), but they had slighted it. In some of their more exuberant efforts to whitewash the Black Legend, some traditional borderlands historians neglected to question stereotypical views that portrayed Indians as benighted, if not bedeviled and malevolent "untamed savages."[122] In their desire to find Spanish heroes, the Boltonians had often neglected to give Indians their due as rational historical actors who made choices that circumscribed the scope of Spaniards' actions. As they sought to demonstrate Spain's lasting contributions to America, borderlands scholars had frequently failed to make clear that Spaniards achieved many of their "successes" at agonizing cost to Indians.[123] Those ethnohistorians who sought to reconstuct the past of North American Indian groups have begun to deconstruct the traditional Eurocentric, triumphalist vision of the past and to offer in its place a multisided historical reality. Along the old Spanish rim, those scholars have been especially effective at taking us into the missions and reimagining them from Indian angles of vision.[124]

VI

In the 1980s, evidence of the Hispanophile view of the Spanish borderlands promoted by the Boltonians could still be found,[125] but it had fallen from fashion even among many scholars sympathetic to the field. Meanwhile, no new paradigm has taken its place. Instead, we have a variety of ways to understand the Spanish colonial era in American history. Hispanophobia and the Black Legend continued to have adherents, of course. "The Black Legend is in many respects an accurate interpretation of history," one distinguished historian bluntly explained in the nation's premier historical journal in 1988.[126] Some historians have continued to dismiss the Spanish past as irrelevant, while others insist that it needs to be more fully integrated into the nation's understanding of its history. Some Chicano scholars find the regional roots of their mestizo past on the Spanish frontier, and many ethnohistorians regard the European invaders with the reproachful gaze of the invaded. It is also possible to scrutinize the Hispanic past from the neglected perspectives of environment and gender.[127] If this is not confusing enough, these various historical reconstructions can also look very different depending upon the tools that historians choose, or the theoretical stance they adopt.[128] Finally, in well-nuanced work, a single historian might portray Spaniards from opposing viewpoints, as both conquerors and conquered, victors and victims.[129]

How, then, are we to comprehend the meaning of the Spanish frontier in North America? For those with an aversion to ambiguity or a strong need for absolute truth, the current answer is not comforting. There are many viewpoints, some of them contradictory and all of them valid, even if not of equal merit. This is not to deny the existence of an objective past or to doubt our ability to ferret out data and documents about the past. The past itself, however, has ceased to exist. What remains of importance is only our understanding of it, and that understanding, as historian Peter Novick has succinctly put it, "is in the mind of a human being or it is nowhere."[130] Lacking omniscience and possessing only a partial record of the past, we humans reconstruct time and place in highly imperfect ways, employing stories that often tell us more about the teller than the tale.[131] The Spanish legacy in North America, then, is not only what we have imagined it to be, but what we will continue to make of it. Like all historical terrain, the Spanish frontier seems destined to remain contested ground, transformed repeatedly in the historical imaginations of succeeding generations—much as the actual Spanish frontier and its peoples were transformed by several centuries of contention with the land and with one another, from the first landing of Ponce de León in 1513 to the end of the Spanish empire in North America in 1821.

Abbreviations

AB	Badger, R. Reid, and Lawrence A. Clayton, eds. *Alabama and the Borderlands from Prehistory to Statehood.* University: University of Alabama Press, 1985.
AHR	*American Historical Review*
AW	*Arizona and the West*
CC	Thomas, David Hurst, ed. *Columbian Consequences.* 3 vols. Washington, D.C.: Smithsonian Institution Press, 1989–91 (see bibliography for subtitles to individual volumes).
CDI(1):	*Colección de documentos inéditos relativos al descubrimiento, conquista y organización de las antiguas posesiones españolas de América y Oceanía . . .* (42 vols.; Madrid: 1864–1884).
CHSQ	*California Historical Society Quarterly* (this title has undergone slight variations over the years and has appeared since Spring 1978 as *California History*)
FE	Milanich, Jerald T., and Susan Milbrath, eds. *First Encounters: Spanish Explorations in the Caribbean and the United States, 1492–1570.* Gainesville: University of Florida Press, 1989.
FHQ	*Florida Historical Quarterly*
HAHR	*Hispanic American Historical Review*
HNAI	William C. Sturtevant, ed. *Handbook of North American Indians.* Vols. 8, 9, & 10. Washington, D.C.: Smithsonian Institution, 1978, 1979, & 1983 (see bibliography under Heizer and Ortiz for full cites to individual volumes).
JAH	*Journal of American History* (June 1914 to March 1964, appeared as *Mississippi Valley Historical Review*)
JAZH	*Journal of Arizona History*
JSDH	*Journal of San Diego History*
JW	*Journal of the West*
NMHR	*New Mexico Historical Review*
NS	Weber, David J., ed., *New Spain's Far Northern Frontier: Essays on Spain in the American West.* Albuquerque: University of New Mexico Press, 1979.
PHR	*Pacific Historical Review*

PM   Wood, Peter H., Gregory A. Waselkov, and M. Thomas Hatley, eds. *Powhatan's Mantle: Indians in the Colonial Southeast*. Lincoln: University of Nebraska Press, 1989.

RI   *Revista de Indias*

SCQ   *Southern California Quarterly* (1884–1917, title varies)

SWHQ   *Southwestern Historical Quarterly* (July 1897 to April 1912, appeared as the *Quarterly* of the Texas State Historical Association).

Tacachale   Milanich, Jerald T., and Samuel Proctor, eds. *Tacachale: Essays on the Indians of Florida and Southeastern Georgia during the Historic Period*. Gainesville: University Presses of Florida, 1978.

WHQ   *Western Historical Quarterly*

Notes

Most sources are cited in brief form in the notes, with full cites reserved for the bibliography. Exceptions include infrequently cited sources that do not bear directly on Spain in North America or that treat it tangentially, such as works that I consulted for background or for comparative or theoretical dimensions. Those exceptions are cited fully in the notes since they do not appear in the bibliography.

Introduction

The epigraph is from Whitman to Messrs. Griffin et al., Camden, New Jersey, July 20, 1883, in Walt Whitman, *The Complete Poetry and Prose of Walt Whitman*, 2 vols. (New York: Pellegrini & Cudahy, 1948), 2:402.

1. Bolton "Defensive Spanish Expansion," 61, calculated that "half of our national territory was once part of the Spanish empire." A still higher percentage might be asserted if one took all of the claims Spain made, from the sixteenth through the eighteenth centuries. Howard Mumford Jones, *O Strange New World: American Culture, the Formative Years* (New York: Viking, 1964), 80, suggested that "about two-thirds of the continental United States owes something to Spanish culture."

2. George R. Stewart, *Names on the Land: An Historical Account of Placenaming in the United States* (1st ed., 1945; San Francisco: Lexikos, 1982), 315. The name, "Cayo de Huesos," appears on a map of the Keys made by a Jesuit, Joseph Xavier de Alaña, based on his visit of 1743 (Sturtevant,

"Last of the South Florida Aborigines," 153).

3. The story is told by Campa, *Hispanic Culture*, 13, whose source is an eighteenth-century work.

4. For a recent comment on this failure, see Scardaville, "Approaches," 188–90. This theme is an old one. In the last century, for example, Hispanophile Charles Fletcher Lummis lamented the failure of textbooks to give Spaniards their due in American history (*Spanish Pioneers*, 11), and he sought to fill the gap. See, too, George Lipsitz, *Time Passages: Collective Memory and American Popular Culture* (Minneapolis: University of Minnesota Press, 1990), 32–33.

5. See, e.g., Clarence L. Ver Steeg, *The Formative Years, 1607–1763* (New York: Hill & Wang, 1964), and R. C. Simmons, *The American Colonies: From Settlement to Independence* (New York: W. W. Norton, 1976). One looks in vain for mention of California, New Mexico, or Florida in these volumes. Two recent books show greater

awareness of their geographical limits: Jack P. Greene and J. R. Pole, eds., *Colonial British America: Essays in the New History of the Early Modern Era* (Baltimore: Johns Hopkins University Press, 1984), and Meinig, *Shaping of America*, vol. 1. Pauline Maier, among others, has urged "abandoning the confines of British colonial America. Less needs to be learned about the British West Indies than about the Indians of the mainland, and about the Spanish borderlands, French Canada, and Louisiana, whose development played so critical a role in the dynamics of imperial conflict" (Pauline Maier, "Colonial History: Is It All Mined Out," *Reviews in American History* 13 [Mar. 1985]: 6).

6. Scardaville, "Approaches," 189.

7. The 1990 census counted 22.4 million Hispanics, of whom 13.3 million lived in the four southwestern states. Those states had higher concentrations of Hispanics than any other state: New Mexico, with 38.2 percent; California, 25.8 percent; Texas, 25.5 percent; and Arizona, 18.8 percent. (Colorado ranked fifth, with 12.9 percent.)

8. Thomas, *St. Catherines*, 3–10; Thomas, "Saints and Soldiers," 78–83, who provides a survey of known mission sites in the Southeast.

9. Richard C. Sandoval, ed., *One of Our Fifty Is Missing* (Santa Fe: New Mexico Magazine, 1986), 30.

10. Hodge makes this claim in Hodge, ed., *History of New Mexico by Gaspar Pérez de Villagrá*, 17. For the first printings of the work of Cabeza de Vaca, López de Gómara, and other early Spanish imprints, see Wagner, *Spanish Southwest*; for early imprints on the Southeast, see Brinton, *Notes on the Floridian Peninsula*, 1859.

11. Bolton did not coin the phrase, "the Spanish Borderlands," but he chose it from several titles suggested by his editor and gave it currency through his work. See Bannon, *Herbert Eugene Bolton*, 120–21, 129.

12. An unnamed referee's critique of the manuscript of Bolton and Marshall, *Colonization of North America*, quoted in Bannon, ed., *Bolton and the Spanish Borderlands*.

13. The quote is from Bolton, "Defensive Spanish Expansion," 33. This was a familiar theme of Bolton's, one that he expressed at least as early as 1920, in Bolton and Marshall, *Colonization of North America*, vi. See, too, Bolton to Allen Johnson, March 17, 1920, quoted in Bannon, *Herbert Eugene Bolton*, 135. Many historians have continued Bolton's lament. For a recent example, see Axtell, "Europeans," 621–32. Poyo and Hinojosa, "Spanish Texas," 393–416, argue that the nature of traditional Borderlands historiography, which emphasized frontier institutions such as presidios and missions to the near exclusion of the socioeconomic development of communities, isolated the field artificially from both United States and Latin American history. See, too, Scardaville, "Approaches," 188.

14. Bannon, *Herbert Eugene Bolton*, 283–90, contains a list of "Bolton's Academic Progeny," both M.A.'s and Ph.D.'s. I have taken my figures from this list.

15. Gibson, *Spain in America*, 189, reckoned that "it is probable that no other part of Colonial Latin America has stimulated so extensive a program of research." Since 1966, historiography has continued to be abundant. See Weber, "Bannon and the Historiography," 331–63.

16. Hudson, "Research," 12; Weber, "Bannon and the Historiography," 356–62.

17. On this point see Bernard Bailyn, "The Challenge of Modern Historiography," *AHR* 87 (Feb. 1982): 1–24; Thomas Bender, "Wholes and Parts: The Need for Synthesis in American History," *JAH* 73 (June 1986): 120–36; David Thelen, et al., "A Round Table: Synthesis in American History," *JAH* 74 (June 1987): 107–30; and many of the essays in Michael Kammen, ed., *The Past Before Us: Contemporary*

History Writing in the United States (Ithaca: Cornell University Press, 1980).

18. Some historians, for example, have used the term to mean the western borderlands, exclusively. Others use the term to include the nineteenth and twentieth centuries, extending it to well after the Spanish borderlands had ceased to be Spanish. For an extended discussion of this question, see Weber, "Bannon and the Historiography," 339–51.

19. See, e.g., geographer Sauer, *Sixteenth Century North America*; anthropologist Harold E. Driver, *Indians of North America* (1st ed., 1961; 2d rev. ed., Chicago: University of Chicago Press, 1969); and historian Quinn, *North America from Earliest Discovery*.

20. Michael Zuckerman, "Identity in British America: Unease in Eden," in Nicholas Canny and Anthony Pagden, eds., *Colonial Identity in the Atlantic World, 1500–1800* (Princeton: Princeton University Press, 1988), 115–57.

21. Weber, "Bannon and the Historiography," 341–44, 354–55; Poyo and Hinojosa, "Spanish Texas," 399; Caughey, "Herbert Eugene Bolton," 66. Latin American specialists have displayed a growing interest in regional history. See, e.g., Ida Altman and James Lockhart, eds., *Provinces of Early Mexico: Variants of Spanish American Regional Evolution* (Los Angeles: UCLA Latin American Center Publications, 1976).

22. Benjamin Keen, "Main Currents in United States Writings on Colonial Spanish America, 1884–1984," *HAHR* 65 (Nov. 1985): 661–70, comments on the Bolton school. Powell, *Tree of Hate*, remains the best introduction to the Black Legend in English. The debate continues. See Jacobs, "Communications," for the exchange between Jacobs and Axtell.

23. Norbert Elias, *Civilizing Process* (New York: Urizen Books, 1978), vol. 1, *The Development of Manners*, trans. Edmund Jeph-

cott, 1:192–93, who generalizes about Western Europe but draws most of his evidence from France. See, too, Bennassar, *Spanish Character*, 233–35.

24. The quote is from Elias, *Civilizing Process*, 194.

25. Fernando and Isabel to Columbus, Barcelona, May 29, 1493, in Gibson, ed., *Spanish Tradition*, 41.

26. The subject of the historian's risky role in rendering moral judgments about the past is the subject of a considerable literature, which includes such perdurable questions as historicism, determinism, and individual agency. For a guide to some of the sources and an interesting, recent debate concerning moral judgment and the writing of English-Indian relations, see Bernard Sheehan, "The Problem of Moral Judgments in History," *South Atlantic Quarterly* 84 (Winter 1985): 37–50, and James Axtell, "A Moral History of Indian-White Relations Revisited," in James Axtell, ed., *After Columbus: Essays in the Ethnohistory of Colonial North America* (New York: Oxford University Press, 1988), 9–33.

27. David Lowenthal, *The Past Is a Foreign Country* (Cambridge: Cambridge University Press, 1985), who drew his evocative title from the opening line of L. P. Hartley's poignant novel *The Go-Between* (London: Hamish Hamilton, 1953). See, too, James Deetz, *In Small Things Forgotten: The Archaeology of Early American Life* (Garden City, N.Y.: Anchor Press/Doubleday, 1977), 156–57.

28. Gutiérrez, *When Jesus Came*, 227.

29. Gibson, "Conquest," 12–13.

30. Specialists do not agree on dating the onset or ending of the Little Ice Age, but H. H. Lamb notes that "it is reasonable to regard the time from about 1550 to 1700 as the main phase for most parts of the world" (Lamb, *Climate: Present, Past and Future*, 2 vols. [London: Methuen & Co., 1972 & 1977], 2:463). Specialists who study North

America date the onset of the Little Ice Age at 1500 and even earlier, and place its end in the mid-nineteenth century. See Lawson, *Climate of the Great American Desert*, 80–87, who notes higher than average annual rainfall on the Plains, and Moratto, et al., "Archaeology," 147–61, who explain the importance of locale in determining microenvironments.

31. The story of the expansion of Europe, with an emphasis on the implantation of European institutions, characterized the Bolton school and the major overviews such as C. H. Haring's *The Spanish Empire in America* (New York: Oxford University Press, 1947). It remains influential and useful.

32. Perhaps the most forceful articulation of this viewpoint is Francis Jennings, *The Invasion of America: Indians, Colonialism, and the Cant of Conquest* (Chapel Hill: University of North Carolina Press, 1975).

33. See, e.g., Wolf, *Europe and the People without History*, and Spicer, *Cycles of Conquest*. On the question of literacy, see Todorov, *Conquest of America*; Jack Goody, *The Logic of Writing and the Organization of Society* (New York: Cambridge University Press, 1986); and my brief discussion of this in chapter 1.

34. For a guide to this literature, and an evaluation of it as it pertains to Latin America, see Steve J. Stern, "Feudalism, Capitalism, and the World System," *AHR* 93 (Oct. 1988): 829–72, and the exchange between Stern and Immanuel Wallerstein (ibid., 873–97). Sociologist Thomas Hall, *Social Change in the Southwest, 1350–1880*, examines these theories and argues for what he calls an "incorporation" model, which would place greater emphasis on the interaction between the colonized and the colonizers (242).

35. For the notion of the borderlands as an area beyond the "fringe" frontier, see Lockhart and Schwartz, *Early Latin America*, 287–89, and Cuello, "Beyond the 'Borderlands,'" 1–34.

36. William B. Taylor, "Between Global Process and Local Knowledge: An Inquiry into Early Latin American Social History, 1500–1900," in Olivier Zunz, ed., *The Worlds of Social History* (Chapel Hill: University of North Carolina Press, 1985), 115–89; Robert M. Netting, *Cultural Ecology*, 2d ed. (Prospect Heights, Ill.: Waveland Press, 1986) provides a fine introduction to ecological influences on cultural values.

37. See, e.g., Hulme, *Colonial Encounters*.

38. Like many historians, I have unabashed affection for *histoire événementielle* and an aversion to the reductionism of grand theory. I have sought to discover and explain patterns and relationships without deducing them from social theory. Insofar as I use theory as an explanatory device, it is in a spirit of eclecticism and in agreement with Clifford Geertz's remark that "calls for 'a general theory' of just about anything social sound increasingly hollow, and claims to have one megalomaniac" (Geertz, *Local Knowledge: Further Essays in Interpretive Anthropology* [New York: Basic Books, 1983], 4). Explanation in this book is embedded in narrative—a practice that seems to have regained respectability as the crudeness of the old narrative/analysis dichotomy has become clearer. See Allan Megill, "Recounting the Past: 'Description,' Explanation, and Narrative in Historiography," *AHR* 94 (June 1989): 627–53.

39. Bannon, *Spanish Borderlands Frontier*, 3.

40. Weber, "Turner," 80–81; Weber, *Mexican Frontier*, chap. 13. These works provide an introduction to the considerable literature on frontiers. See, too, Kenneth E. Lewis, *The American Frontier: An Archaeological Study of Settlement Pattern and Process* (Orlando: Academic Press, 1984), for the interesting use of a frontier model by an archaeologist.

41. Sauer, *Seventeenth Century North America*, 241–43; John, *Storms Brewed*, 181.

42. Limerick, *Legacy of Conquest*, has used this

paradigm effectively in explaining the American West, from the Spanish colonial era to the present, although she uses the word *conquest* rather than *contention*.

43. Frederick Jackson Turner's 1893 address, "The Significance of the Frontier in History," in Ray Allen Billington, ed., *Selected Essays of Frederick Jackson Turner* (Englewood Cliffs, N.J.: Prentice-Hall, 1961), 37–62, is, of course, the classic statement of this position.

44. For twentieth-century examples, see the essays in Oscar J. Martínez, ed., *Across Boundaries: Transborder Interaction in Comparative Perspective* (El Paso: Texas Western Press and the Center for Inter-American and Border Studies, 1986), particularly those by Ivo D. Duchacek and Ellwyn Stoddard.

45. Wolf, *Europe and the People without History*, ix.

46. Many Latin American specialists have made this point, see, e.g., Lockhart and Schwartz, *Early Latin America*, 288–29.

47. For an example of the idea of Indians as little more than a "challenge," see, e.g., Bannon, *Spanish Borderlands Frontier*, 5. My focus in this book is, of course, on Spaniards in certain places over time. I have made no attempt to write the history of individual Indian groups. I have, however, tried to take to heart the admonition of one ethnohistorian who commented that in writing about the missionaries and the missionized, "To know one without knowing all we can about the other may provide us with a lot of knowledge but not with much understanding" (Fontana, "Indians and Missionaries," 55). Understanding Indian motives, however, remains a considerable challenge, as Sheridan suggests: "How to Tell the Story," 168–89. Indeed, Calvin Martin asserts that the task of understanding native Americans in the past is impossible for non-Indian scholars since Indians do not fit "into the dominant culture's paradigm of reason and logic" (Martin, *The American Indian and the Prob-* *lem of History* [New York: Oxford University Press, 1987], 16).

Chapter 1: Worlds Apart

The epigraphs are, respectively, from Hallenbeck, *Journey of Fray Marcos*, 11; a Zuni tradition as told to Frank Cushing and quoted in Lowery, *Spanish Settlements*, 1:282; and from anthropologist Foster, *Culture and Conquest*, 1–2.

1. Quoted in Bolton, *Coronado*, 116–17. I have depended heavily on Bolton's biography, but it should be noted that another fine but underrated biography exists: Day, *Coronado's Quest*. Lecompte, "Coronado and Conquest," 279–304, is an engaging summary that takes a more hard-headed look at Coronado than Bolton did. For the deaths of several men, see the "Traslado de las Nuevas," in Hammond and Rey, eds. and trans., *Coronado Expedition*, 179.

2. Scholars have long believed this town to be Hawikuh, now in ruins. Documentary sources have been gathered together in Hodge, *History of Hawikuh*. Rodack has made a strong case that Coronado's guide, fray Marcos de Niza, visited another site, Kiakima, on an earlier visit and took Coronado there. See her "Cibola Revisited," 163–82. This identification, however, depends on the doubtful argument that fray Marcos actually saw one of the Zuni villages, and that Rodack has correctly identified that village (which depends upon the accuracy of fray Marcos's description); this would suggest but by no means prove that fray Marcos led Coronado to the same place he had visited earlier.

3. Coronado to the viceroy, Aug. 3, 1540, in Hammond and Rey, eds. and trans., *Coronado Expedition*, 171.

4. The single source that mentions this episode is Matías de la Mota Padilla, writing in the eighteenth century, apparently with access to original documents now lost. See Day [ed. and trans.], "Mota Padilla," 93. Castañeda, "Narrative," 218, mentions

Acomas drawing lines for the same purpose. Neither Castañeda nor Mota Padilla indicate how the Pueblos made this line, but Day, Bolton, and others have suggested that it was drawn with sacred cornmeal. This is confirmed by present-day Zuni use of lines of cornmeal to represent a physical structure (E. Richard Hart to Weber, Albuquerque, Aug. 4, 1988), and by past practice among the Hopis (Parsons, *Pueblo Indian Religion*, 1:363).

5. The requerimiento is discussed more fully later in this chapter. Riley, "Early Spanish-Indian Communication," 285–314, speculates that Coronado's interpreters were Pimas.

6. Coronado to the viceroy, Aug. 3, 1540, quoted in Hammond and Rey, eds. and trans., *Coronado Expedition*, 169. For the requerimiento, see ibid., 167–68, and for more details about Coronado's plight at Zuni, see the "Traslado de las Nuevas," ibid., 180–81.

7. In a suggestive but poorly documented article, Huff, "Coronado Episode," 119–28, first advanced the idea that Coronado interrupted the summer solstice ceremonies. Swagerty, "Beyond Bimini," was one of the first historians to integrate Huff's argument into a general narrative. Matilda Cox Stevenson, who saw the ceremonies in the late nineteenth century, described them in "Zuñi Indians," 148–62. These articles and the ethnohistorical aspect of this encounter were called to my attention by Swagerty, "Beyond Bimini." For native awareness of Spanish slave hunters, see Forbes, *Apache, Navaho, and Spaniard*, 7.

8. For the question of translation, see Riley, "Early Spanish-Indian Communication," 285–314.

9. For a fine summary of archaeological knowledge of the origins of Paleo-Indians in North America, see Chartkoff and Chartkoff, *Archaeology of California*, 24–37. For the physical uniformity of American Indians, see Crosby, *Columbian Exchange*,

19–21. In North America, archaeologists have found no human skeletal material predating 12,000 B.C., but new evidence, especially from the Monte Verde site in Chile, supports the view that the first wave of human migration occurred much earlier. For a summary of the literature, see the work of my colleague David J. Meltzer, to whom I am grateful for clarifying this complicated question: "Why Don't We Know When the First People Came to North America?" *American Antiquity* 54 (July 1989): 471–90. See, too, the readable and balanced overview, Brian M. Fagan, *The Great Journey: The Peopling of Ancient America* (New York: Thames & Hudson, 1987).

10. Castañeda, "Narrative," 254, 256. Subsequently, Spaniards would, of course, become acutely aware of linguistic and cultural differences between Pueblo communities.

11. For differences between Pueblos at the time of contact, see Dozier's discussion of "Base-Line Culture, about 1500," in his essay, "Rio Grande Pueblos," 103–22. Gutiérrez, *When Jesus Came*, xxx, argues for the commonality of Pueblo culture at the time of contact. For a summary of scholarly disputation over the nature of Pueblo society at the time of contact, see Wilcox, "Changing Perspectives," 378–410. For language, see Dozier, *Pueblo Indians*, 37, 181, and Cordell, *Prehistory of the Southwest*, 10–14. For the number of pueblos at the time of first contact with Spaniards, see Schroeder, "Rio Grande Ethnohistory," 47–48.

12. Shipley, "Native Languages of California," 80.

13. Wright, *Only Land*, 6.

14. For the Yumans, see the report of Alarcón's expedition, ca. 1540, in Hammond and Rey, eds. and trans., *Coronado Expedition*, 148. Snow, "Protohistoric Rio Grande Pueblo Economics," 362. The best single-volume overview of Indian cultures, ar-

ranged topically, remains Harold E. Driver, *Indians of North America* (1st ed., 1961; 2d rev. ed., Chicago: University of Chicago Press, 1969).

15. Wilcomb E. Washburn, *The Indian in America* (New York: Harper & Row, 1975), 11–13, 31–33, 55–56; Martin, "Metaphysics of Writing," 153–59. I offer these generalizations with full knowledge that they cover a great variety of exceptions on both Spanish and Indian sides. On the question of the variety of patterns of Indian land ownership and use, see Imre Sutton, *Indian Land Tenure: Bibliographical Essays and a Guide to the Literature* (New York: Clearwater Publishing, 1975), 25–34, and Shipek, *Pushed into the Rocks*, 11–18, 25.

16. For a review of the literature on this subject, see Upham and Reed, "Regional Systems," 57–76. Upham, however, brings a clear bias to this work. His deservedly controversial study, *Polities and Power*, argues that Zuni stood on the fringes of a complex, regional, economic and political system that flourished in the fourteenth century but collapsed a century before the Spaniards arrived. Finally see the insights of Lekson, *Great Pueblo Architecture*, 272–73.

17. Hudson, *Southeastern Indians*, 77–97, contains the best short introduction to this subject.

18. Frederick E. Hoxie, "The Indians versus the Textbooks: Is There Any Way Out?" *Perspectives* 23 (Apr. 1985): 21.

19. Jaime Vicens Vives, *Approaches to the History of Spain*, trans. Joan Connelly, 2d. ed. (Berkeley: University of California Press, 1972), remains one of the best short interpretive essays.

20. For the dominant role of Castile, see McAlister, *Spain and Portugal*, 74, 78. Castile's exclusive claim to the New World was not, contrary to popular belief, based on a special relationship between Isabel, Queen of Castile, and Columbus. I have simplified a complicated argument offered

by Stuart B. Schwartz, *The Iberian Mediterranean and Atlantic Traditions in the Formation of Columbus as a Colonizer* (Minneapolis: James Ford Bell Library, University of Minnesota, 1986), 9–10. For a discussion of the significance of Castilian possession of the New World, and a corrective of the view that the Indies remained the personal possession of the Crown of Castile, see Góngora, *Studies*, 33–67, 79–80. The Indies passed to the exclusive control of Castile after the death of Ferdinand in 1516 (ibid., 43). Luis Weckmann-Muñoz, "The Alexandrine Bulls of 1493: Pseudo-Asiatic Documents," in Fredi Chiappelli, ed., *First Images of America: The Impact of the New World on the Old*, 2 vols. (Berkeley: University of California Press, 1976), 1:201–9, argues that Alexander could not have divided the New World in 1493, for he did not know of its existence.

21. Anthropologist Foster, *Culture and Conquest*, 13, 21–33, emphasized diversity but concluded that "Spanish culture . . . in spite of marked regional variation, reflected a basic unity in belief, values, and customs" (28). Discussions of Spanish culture and character often resort to stereotypes that shed more light on the mentalité of their authors than on their subject. For an up-to-date guide to the literature, which emphasizes complexity over cliches, see Henry Kamen, *Golden Age Spain* (Houndmills, Eng.: Macmillan Education, 1988), 51–60, and Elliott, "Discovery of America," 46.

22. Bruce G. Trigger, "Early Native North American Responses to European Contact: Romantic versus Rationalistic Interpretations," *JAH* 77 (Mar. 1991): 1214.

23. For a good summary of conditions in Spain at the time of the discovery of America, see Lynch, *Spain under the Hapsburgs*, 1:1–37. For Spanish expansion, see McAlister, *Spain and Portugal*, 63–65, 75–107. Among the many good discussions of the

effect of the reconquista on the Spanish ethos and institutions, see Elliott, *Imperial Spain*, 56–76. For religious intensity, see Bennassar, *Spanish Character*, 81. McCarty, "Song of Roland," 380, n. 3, finds that " 'Santiago' was the war cry of the presidial troops of Hispanic Tucson against the Apaches throughout the Tucson presidio's history (1775–1856)." On Indians as Moors, see Gutiérrez, *When Jesus Came*, 194–95. Spaniards similarly confused Guanches with Moors in the Canaries in the late fifteenth century—Felipe Fernández-Armesto, *Before Columbus: Exploration and Colonization from the Mediterranean to the Atlantic, 1229–1492* (Philadelphia: University of Pennsylvania Press, 1987), 214.

24. See, e.g., the explanations of Las Casas and Oviedo for Ponce de León's failure in Florida, in Jackson, *Early Florida*, 16–17.

25. Genesis 1:28, quoted in Turner, *Beyond Geography*, 37. For the Spanish concept of barbarian at this time, see Anthony Pagden, *The Fall of Natural Man: The American Indian and the Origins of Comparative Ethnology* (Cambridge: Cambridge University Press, 1982), 15–23; for the complicated question of slavery, see ibid., chaps. 3, 4. See, too, Margaret T. Hodgen, *Early Anthropology in the Sixteenth and Seventeenth Centuries* (Philadelphia: University of Pennsylvania Press, 1964), 363. For the link between Christianity and dominion, see Dickason, "Old World Law," 52–78.

26. Jeremiah, 1:10, quoted in Góngora, *Studies*, 35, who finds this in the papal bull *Ineffablis et summi*, which entrusted the conquest of Africa to the king of Portugal. The quote from the May 4, 1493, papal donation comes from Gibson, ed., *Spanish Tradition*, 38, who reproduced the entire text in translation. For the theological and juridical underpinnings of belief in papal dominion over the world, see Pagden, *Fall of Natural Man*, 37–41.

27. The requerimiento is translated in many sources, one of the most accessible being Gibson, ed., *Spanish Tradition*, 58–60. For its antecedents, see among other sources Weckmann, *Herencia Medieval*, 2:406–7, and the interesting revisionist view by James Muldoon, "John Wyclif and the Rights of the Infidels: The *Requerimiento* Re-examined," *The Americas* 36 (Jan. 1980): 301–16.

28. These ideas are examined evocatively in Turner, *Beyond Geography* and in several of the essays in David Spring and Eileen Spring, eds., *Ecology and Religion in History* (New York: Harper & Row, 1974), including the seminal and controversial work by Lynn White, Jr., "The Historical Roots of Our Ecological Crisis," in Spring and Spring, eds., *Ecology and Religion in History*, 15–31.

29. Tedlock, "Zuni Religion," 499–508. This discussion assumes that Zuni religious beliefs have not changed significantly since the time of Coronado. In seeing the physical world as a spiritual place, Zunis apparently resembled other Pueblos. See Ortiz, *Tewa World*.

30. Coronado to the viceroy, Aug. 3, 1540, quoted in Hammond and Rey, eds. and trans., *Coronado Expedition*, 175.

31. Kessell, "Spaniards, Environment and the Pepsi Generation," 285–92.

32. Account of Hernando de Alvarado and fray Juan de Padilla, in Hammond and Rey, eds. and trans., *Coronado Expedition*, 183. On the Zuni preference for accommodation, see Goldman, "Zuni Indians of New Mexico," 313–53. One should not overstate the pacific nature of Zunis or other Pueblos. Simmons, "History of Pueblo-Spanish Relations," attacks the "stereotype of the Pueblo Indian as nonaggressive and essentially peaceful" (189). See, too, Forbes, *Apache, Navaho, and Spaniard*, 282, and Gutiérrez, *When Jesus Came*, 19, 25. For a good, balanced assessment, see Ferguson, "Emergence of Modern Zuni Culture," 342–44.

33. Wenhold, ed. and trans., *17th Century Let-*

ter, 11. For examples of Spanish obsession with gold, see Jackson, *Early Florida*, 77–88. For Cortés, see Weber, "Coronado," 232.

34. See, e.g., the elaborate rules for the taking of booty, and collateral documents, in Parry and Keith, eds., *New Iberian World*, 1:189–224. Góngora, "Conquistador," 1–32, outlines the continuities and discontinuities between Castilian experience at conquering Muslims, Africans, and Canary islanders and subsequent experiences in the New World, which altered Castilian patterns. See, too, Weckmann, *Herencia Medieval*, 2:403–6.

35. Quoted in Carlos M. Cipolla, *Guns, Sails and Empires: Technological Innovation and the Early Phase of European Expansion, 1400–1700* (New York: Pantheon Books, 1965), 132.

36. Irving A. Leonard, *Books of the Brave: Being an Account of Books and of Men in the Spanish Conquest and Settlement of the Sixteenth-Century New World* (Cambridge: Harvard University Press, 1949), esp. chaps. 2, 3.

37. Henri Baudet, *Paradise on Earth: Some Thoughts on European Images of Non-European Man*, trans. Elizabeth Wentholt (New Haven: Yale University Press, 1965).

38. Gonzalo Fernández Oviedo y Valdes, quoted in Jackson, *Early Florida*, 15.

39. For origins of the story, see Morison, *Northern Voyages*, 97–99; for Cabot, see Sauer, *Sixteenth Century North America*, 6.

40. Coronado to the viceroy, Aug. 3, 1540, quoted in Hammond and Rey, eds. and trans., *Coronado Expedition*, 170. See also Hodge, "Six Cities of Cíbola," 478–88. Hodge's view that only six pueblos existed in 1540 seems sustained by current scholarship. See, e.g., Ferguson and Hart, *Zuni Atlas*, 29, and Woodbury, "Zuni Prehistory," 469. Kintigh, *Settlement, Subsistence, and Society*, chaps. 5, 6, suggests that the question has not yet been settled.

41. Swagerty, "Beyond Bimini," 22–33.

42. Parry, *Age of Reconnaissance*, 53–99. For the wretched conditions of life aboard ship, see Taylor, "Spanish Seamen," 631–61,

and Carla Rahn Phillips, *Six Galleons for the King of Spain: Imperial Defense in the Early Seventeenth Century* (Baltimore: Johns Hopkins Press, 1978), 132–80.

43. Quinn, *North America from Earliest Discovery*, takes an especially strong position on the importance of European arms: "If European arms had not been so overwhelmingly superior to those of the indigenous peoples, the European impact on North America . . . would have been marginal only, as was the case in the sixteenth century in European relations with China" (73).

44. Quotes are respectively from Benavides, *Memorial . . . 1630*, 22, and Covington, ed., *Pirates, Indians and Spaniards*, 132.

45. Todorov, *Conquest of America*, 252, whose work informs this paragraph. I believe, however, that Todorov carries semiotics beyond empirical evidence when he states uncategorically that "the presence of writing favors improvisation over ritual" (248, 252). Aztec failure to comprehend the "other," to fully understand the threat represented by Cortés (see Todorov's chap. 2), may have had more to do with religion than with language. See, too, Jack Goody, *The Domestication of the Savage Mind* (Cambridge: Cambridge University Press, 1977). For a valuable caveat on the danger of dividing "cultures by the presence or absence of writing," see Hulme, *Colonial Encounters*, 268, n. 7.

46. Quoted in Hanke, *Aristotle and the American Indians*, 8. The reference is to Antonio de Nebrija's famous *Gramática*. When the Queen asked Nebrija, "What is it for?" the bishop replied on Nebrija's behalf.

47. Alarcón's Report, in Hammond and Rey, eds. and trans., *Coronado Expedition*, 133–34.

48. The "liars" quote is from Hernán Gallegos's Report of 1582, in Hammond and Rey, eds. and trans., *Rediscovery*, 79. Gallegos mentions on several occasions that his expedition told Indians that "we were children of the sun" (92); see, also, 72, 75, 77, 90, 94. Todorov has advanced the inter-

esting argument that Cortés's mastery of signs facilitated his conquest of the Aztecs, but North American natives seem to have had a less ritualized mode of discourse than the Aztecs and, therefore, may have had less difficulty in communicating directly with the Spaniards and in manipulating them rather than being manipulated by them.

49. Pedro de Castañeda, "Narrative," quoted in Hammond and Rey, eds. and trans., *Coronado Expedition*, 282.

50. Crosby, *Columbian Exchange*, 74–81, 95. The unevenness of the Columbian exchange emerges more clearly in Crosby's more recent book, *Ecological Imperialism*. See also Varner and Varner, *Dogs of the Conquest*, 33–34. Testimonies of Coronado and López de Cárdenas in Hammond and Rey, eds. and trans., *Coronado Expedition*, 327–28, 350–52.

51. Merbes, "Patterns of Health," 41–55.

52. Crosby, *Ecological Imperialism*, 197–98, 287, who points out that his list is "a matter of ambiguities and controversies" among scholars (342, n. 3). All of these diseases did not necessarily arrive in the western hemisphere in the sixteenth century. I have not included cholera and dengue fever, which certainly came later, or malaria, yellow fever, typhus, or syphilis, since scholars still disagree about their origins. See, e.g., Marshall T. Newman, "Aboriginal New World Epidemiology and Medical Care, and the Impact of Old World Disease Imports," *American Journal of Physical Anthropology* 45 (Nov. 1976, pt. 2): 667–72, who argues that typhus already existed in the New World; Dobyns, *Their Number Become Thinned*, 19, on the other hand, includes it in his list of European-introduced diseases. Dobyns chronicles waves of epidemics from many of these diseases (11–24). A number of studies have begun to illuminate this once neglected subject. For a cogent overview, see William H. McNeill, *Plagues and Peoples* (Garden City,

N.Y.: Anchor Press/Doubleday, 1976), esp. chap. 5.

53. Denevan, *Native Population*, 7. "Despite the disagreement about the size of the New World Indian population," Denevan notes, "there is little doubt about the massive and rapid drop in that population in the sixteenth century" (7).

54. Dobyns, *Their Number Become Thinned*, 12–13, argues the highest mortality rates. Other writers, such as Crosby, *Columbian Exchange*, 44, suggest that smallpox took 30 percent of the lives of previously unexposed populations. See, too, Crosby, "Virgin Soil Epidemics," 289–99, which offers additional societal and cultural explanations for high death rates associated with epidemics.

55. Quoted in Crosby, *Columbian Exchange*, 48 (see, too, 35–63). For similar expressions by Englishmen, see Crosby, *Ecological Imperialism*, 208, 215.

56. Denevan, *Native Population*, 3–4, 291.

57. The high figure comes from Dobyns, *Their Number Become Thinned*, 42, who defined North American natives as those "living north of civilized Mesoamerica." Dobyns weakened his argument by his remarkably careless use of sources and cannot be taken seriously. The conservative figures come from Thornton, *American Indian Holocaust*. A still lower figure, 4.4 million was suggested by Denevan, "Epilogue," 291. Both Thornton and Denevan define North America as the present United States, Canada, Greenland, and Alaska. For a more extensive discussion of the catastrophic impact of infectious disease, see chapter 2.

58. Elliott, *Imperial Spain*, 24, and Jerah Johnson and William A. Percy, *The Age of Recovery: The Fifteenth Century* (Ithaca, N.Y.: Cornell University Press, 1970), 13. Fernand Braudel, *The Structures of Everyday Life: Civilization and Capitalism, 15th–18th Century* (New York: Harper & Row, 1981), 47, suggests approximately

55 million for 1450 and 100 million for 1600.

59. Crosby, *Ecological Imperialism*, 137–38.

60. Arguments, of course, have been made on all sides. Quinn, *North America from Earliest Discovery*, 73, sees arms as the determining force. Crosby, *Ecological Imperialism*, argues that in the creation of "Neo-Europes," animals were "probably more important than superior military technology—certainly in the long run" (102–3). In *Columbian Exchange*, 35–36, Crosby suggests that disease was more effective than technology in facilitating the Spanish conquest of America.

Chapter 2: First Encounters

The epigraphs are from Quinn, ed., *New American World*, 1:231–32; "Relation of the Conquest of Florida Presented by Luys Hernández de Biedma in the Year 1544 to the King of Spain in Council," in Bourne, ed., *Narratives . . . of Hernando de Soto*, 2:21; and Cabeza de Vaca, *Adventures*, 60.

1. Quinn, *England*, 5–23. See, too, Sauer, *Northern Mists*.

2. The Europeans' initial failure to recognize what they had found led one historian to question whether Columbus's finding of America could be classified as a "discovery." See Edmundo O'Gorman, *The Invention of America: An Inquiry into the Historical Nature of the New World and the Meaning of Its History* (Bloomington: Indiana University Press, 1961), and Wilcomb E. Washburn, "The Meaning of 'Discovery' in the Fifteenth and Sixteenth Century," *AHR* 68 (Oct. 1962): 1–21, who takes O'Gorman and other scholars to task for failing to understand the meaning of the word *discovery* in the sixteenth century.

3. Estimates of the size of the population on Española at the time of Columbus's initial contact vary enormously, from a high of 8 million to a low of 60 thousand. The trend among scholars has been to accept higher figures. Linda A. Newson, "Indian Population Patterns in Colonial Spanish America," *Latin American Research Review* 20 (1985): 41–74, lists the major sources in the controversy (p. 69, n. 34) and analyzes regional variations in native population decline.

4. Weddle, *Spanish Sea*, 21–22.

5. Quinn, *North America from Earliest Discovery*, 139.

6. Oviedo y Valdés, *Historia general*, 1:486 (bk. 16, chap. 13). Samuel Eliot Morison misread Oviedo's account, first published in 1535, and noted that Oviedo believed Ponce's real motive was to find a remedy for *el enflaquecimiento del sexo*—weakening virility. In context, it is clear that Oviedo meant a loss of sense (*seso*), not a loss of sexual drive. I am grateful to Harry Kelsey for calling this to my attention. That error notwithstanding, Morison, *Southern Voyages*, 502–16, provides the best modern account in English, along with a discussion of sources.

Morison portrays Ponce as searching for a Fountain of Youth, as does Olschki, "Ponce de León's Fountain of Youth," 373, 377. Other scholars remain skeptical. See, e.g., Sauer, *Sixteenth Century North America*, 27. Some documents relating to the expedition are translated in Davis, "History of Juan Ponce de Leon's Voyages to Florida," 5–66, but this has been superseded by Lawson, *Discovery of Florida*, with an appendix that contains a fuller set of documents, many from archival sources, in both Spanish and English translations. Quinn, ed., *New American World*, 1:231–47, makes additional documents available. Murga, " 'Florida' So Named by Ponce de León," 33–60, attempts to sort out inconsistencies in the chronicles.

7. Servín, "Legal Basis for the Establishment of Spanish Colonial Sovereignty," 295–303, who identifies Holland as an exception. For Alaminos, see below, n. 11.

8. Dickason, "Old World Law," 52–3, 60–1, 67, 70–71, who analyzes French and Span-

ish thought of the sixteenth century and its antecedents on this question.

9. The most recent account of Ponce's voyage argues that his landfall on the coast of Florida was considerably below Charlotte Harbor and that he did not discover Yucatán on his return voyage, as some writers have suggested. See Weddle, *Spanish Sea*, 44–46, 51–53. For Ponce's relations with Indians, I relied upon Swagerty, "Beyond Bimini," 34–46. For the Calusas, see Widmer, *Evolution of the Calusa*.

10. Ponce de León to the Cardinal of Tortosa, Feb. 10, 1521, in Quinn, ed., *New American World*, 1:244. The sixteenth-century chronicler Herrera stated that Cortés's discovery rekindled Ponce's interest in Florida. See Herrera, quoted ibid., 1:246.

11. Weddle, *Spanish Sea*, 417, notes that Alaminos's "various achievements have often been recorded separately, without any attempt at consolidation" but Weddle overlooked an article by Parry, "Navigators of the Conquista," 61–70, which outlines Alaminos's career. Weddle offers valuable correctives, such as establishing Alaminos's age as 47 in 1522 (51), demonstrating that he was not a "boy" when he sailed with Columbus, as Parry suggested, and pointing out that Alaminos did not pilot the Garay expedition (417), as Morison claimed in his *Southern Voyages, 516–17*.

12. This account follows, in the main, Weddle, *Spanish Sea*, 95–108, which provides a good discussion of sources of this poorly understood expedition. No log of Pineda's expedition has come to light, but interpolating from other data Paul Hoffman disagrees with Weddle and suggests that the Mississippi may have been what Alvarez called the Río de Flores (Hoffman, "Nature and Sequence of the Spanish Borderlands," 49). See, too, Farmer, "Piñeda's Sketch," 110–14. Among the many writers who have repeated the story of Pineda careening his vessels on the Rio Grande is Hollon, *Southwest: Old and New*, 45. The

story of the fake clay tablet is told in Weddle, *Spanish Sea*, 107; for Garay's subsequent attempt to settle "Amichel," see ibid., 130–46.

13. Quinn, *North America*, 115–20 (evidence for this appears on Juan de la Cosa's map of 1500). Kelsey, "Planispheres of Sebastian Cabot," 49–51, offers strong evidence of the Cabots' 1494 voyage. A fine color reproduction of a copy of Cosa's manuscript map is in Shirley, *Mapping of the World*, xxiii (Shirley's caption, "from the original," is misleading).

14. Hoffman, "New Voyage," 415–26.

15. Hoffman, *New Andalucia*, 3–16. Hoffman's discovery of a new source, and his shrewd reading of older sources, enable him to identify Winyah Bay and other sites associated with this period more satisfactorily than any other historian has done to date.

16. Hoffman, *New Andalucia*, 16–21, 35–36.

17. Patent, June 12, 1523, to Ayllón, translated in Quattlebaum, *Land Called Chicora*, 136, and analyzed in Hoffman, *New Andalucia*, 34–40.

18. Hoffman, *New Andalucia*, 50–58; for translated documents, see Quinn, ed., *New American World*, 1:255–60.

19. For Montesinos, see, e.g., Hanke, *Spanish Struggle for Justice*, 17–18, 22, 23, and biographies of Montesinos and his two companions in O'Daniel, *Dominicans*, 1–16.

20. The site of San Miguel, and of Ayllón's first landing to the north, have been subjects of controversy. The exact sites remain unknown, but Hoffman, "Chicora Legend," 423, suggested that both sites were much farther south than Quattlebaum supposed. Hoffman, *New Andalucia*, 60–85 provides a fuller account, upon which I have depended.

21. The story of the "cloves" is told in Martyr, *De Orbe Novo*, 2:419–20.

22. Morison, *Northern Voyages*, 326–31, 336–37, provides a characteristically lively description, written as though there were no doubt that Gomes traveled from north to

south. For a more cautious interpretation and accompanying documents and bibliography, see Quinn, ed., *New American World*, 1:271–79. Both Morison and Quinn provide guidance to the standard sources on this expedition. Swagerty, "Beyond Bimini," 63–67, identifies the language group of the Indian captives (58 were taken) and comments on their fate.

23. Quinn, ed., *New American World*, 1:229. See, too, Lawrence C. Wroth, *The Voyages of Giovanni de Verrazzano, 1524–1528* (New Haven: Yale University Press, 1970).

24. The Ribero map is reproduced in color as plate 6 in Shirley, *Mapping of the World*, xxiv–xxv. Shirley's caption, which says that the map is "from the original in the Vatican Library," is misleading. The reproduction in Shirley is of a modern copy of the Ribero map. I am grateful to Harry Kelsey for calling this to my attention. The name Estevâ appears on the Ribero map, with the tilde over the *a* but without a final letter, thus indicating the omission of either the *o* in Portuguese or the *n* in Spanish.

25. See the report of recent archaeological findings in Tuck, Grenier, and Laxalt, "Discovery in Labrador," 40–71.

26. Martyr, *De Orbe Novo*, 2:419. Morison, *Northern Voyages*, 326–31, 336–37 (the quote from the Gomes map is on 329).

27. See, e.g., some of the evidence summarized by McGinty, "Ancient Oriental Mariners," 57–62.

28. The quotes are from Cortés's fourth letter to the king (Oct. 15, 1524), in Anthony Pagden, ed. and trans., *Hernán Cortés: Letters from Mexico* (1st ed., 1971; New Haven: Yale University Press, 1986), 328, 327. See, too, Holmes, *From New Spain*, 48–50, and Borah, "Hernán Cortés," 7–25, who demonstrates Cortés's dominant role in exploration of the Pacific coast of New Spain.

29. Holmes, *From New Spain*, 55–59. Holmes's overview is more accessible and current,

but less detailed than Wagner, *Spanish Voyages*.

30. The first quote is from Cutter, "Sources of the Name 'California,'" 233–44, who provides a fresh translation of the key passage from the *Sergas* and speculates on the origin of the word itself. The second quote is from a 1524 report of Cortés in Chapman, *History of California*, 64. For the latter application of the name to Alaska, see Cook, *Flood Tide of Empire*, 3. For Cortés's efforts to establish a settlement at La Paz see Mathes, ed. and trans., *Conquistador in California*.

31. The suggestion that Ulloa may have made it as far as San Diego continues to appear, as in Spate, *Spanish Lake*, 66, but does not deserve to be taken seriously. See Garrahy and Weber, "Francisco de Ulloa," 73–77. León-Portilla, *Hernán Cortés*, examines Cortés's voyages in broad context, with emphasis on cartography.

32. Cabrillo has long been incorrectly identified as a Portuguese mariner sailing for Spain—a notion so well established that it probably will continue to survive in the literature (see, for example, Spate, *Spanish Lake*, 66) despite good evidence to the contrary. See, e.g., Mathes, "Discoverer of Alta California," 1–8. The standard biography of Cabrillo has been Wagner, *Cabrillo*, but that has been supplanted by Kelsey, *Cabrillo*, who has corrected Wagner on many points, including Cabrillo's age, his probable place of birth, and the number of ships Cabrillo took. My brief account is based on Kelsey.

33. The log of the Cabrillo expedition has been lost, but some information can be gleaned from a summary of that log prepared by the famous sixteenth-century explorer Andrés de Urdaneta—not by Juan Páez as was previously believed (Kelsey, *Cabrillo*, 114–15). The Urdaneta summary has been printed in Spanish in a number of sources. The most accessible English translation is in Bolton, ed., *Spanish Explo-*

ration, 13–39, and quotations in this paragraph may be found on 23. The existence of a translation of a variant copy of the Urdaneta summary should be noted: Moriarty and Keistman, eds. and trans., *Summary Log of the Cabrillo Voyage*, but the editors do not make clear the need for their work or how it varies from previous translations.

34. Ipai, a name meaning "people," has come to be used by anthropologists to replace the Diegueño, a term of Spanish origin, to identify the peoples who occupied this coast and its hinterland in the 1600s. See Luomala, "Tipai-Ipai," 592–609.

35. Sources do not agree on whether Cabrillo broke an arm or a leg, but the latter seems more likely. See Wagner, *Cabrillo*, 27, Holmes, *From New Spain*, 110–13, and Kelsey, *Cabrillo*, 158. Historians have believed that Cabrillo died on San Miguel Island; Kelsey, *Cabrillo*, 157–59, makes a case for Santa Catalina. What appears to be his gravestone was found in 1901 on a nearby island. See Heizer, *California's Oldest Historical Relic*.

36. Spate, *Spanish Lake*, 59.

37. On the cartographical contribution of Cabrillo, see Kelsey, "Mapping the California Coast," 323. See, too, Shirley, *Mapping of the World*, xxvi, and Nunn, *Strait of Anian Concept*, 15. For the quality of Cabrillo's cartographical notes, see Kelsey, *Cabrillo*, 150.

38. Quinn, *North America from Earliest Discovery*, 206.

39. Cabeza de Vaca, *Adventures*, 125. Of several translations of Cabeza de Vaca's *Relación*, first published at Zamora in 1542, Covey's is the best and the most accessible. Covey notes differences between the 1542 and 1555 editions of the *Relación* and incorporates information from a valuable supplementary source, the "Joint Report" prepared apparently in 1537 by Cabeza de Vaca, Dorantes, and Castillo. The original Joint Report was lost, but most of it

was preserved by the sixteenth-century chronicler Gonzalo Fernández de Oviedo. At least three English translations of the Oviedo version have been published. The latest and most complete is a bilingual edition, Hedrick and Riley, trans. and eds., *Journey of the Vaca Party*. The best and most accessible Spanish edition is *La "Relación" o "Naufragios,"* Favata and Fernández, eds. My brief summary is based on these firsthand accounts, but informed by several secondary accounts including Swagerty, "Beyond Bimini," 133–222, who reveals much about Indian responses to Narváez and Cabeza de Vaca.

Cabeza de Vaca's journey has engaged the attention of popular writers as well as scholars. See, e.g., Terrell, *Journey into Darkness*. The best biography remains Bishop, *Odyssey of Cabeza de Vaca*, and I have relied upon it for background, such as the age of Cabeza de Vaca, who, Bishop says, was born between 1487 and 1494. Recent scholarship has called into question Bishop's reconstruction of Cabeza de Vaca's route in North America (see below, notes 49 and 50).

40. Narváez's *Capitulación*, Dec. 11, 1526, in *CDI*(1), 22:224.

41. The two quotes in this paragraph come from Cabeza de Vaca, *Adventures*, 33, 34. For reference to the ten women, see 139. For the ships, see Weddle, *Spanish Sea*, 189.

42. Parry, "Early European Penetration of Eastern North America," 93.

43. For Florida Indian archers in Spain, see Barrientos, *Pedro Menéndez de Avilés*, 24, who describes an episode of 1567. Parry, "Early European Penetration of Eastern North America," 93–94. Cabeza de Vaca, *Adventures*, 39, 42, 46. For descriptions of Indian archery and fighting skill by other sixteenth-century observers and chroniclers, see Jackson, *Early Florida*, 44–63. Purdy, "Weapons, Strategies, and Tactics," 265–66.

44. For the construction of the barges, see

Jackson, *Early Florida*, 46. Neither the construction site, nor any other associated with Narváez, has been definitely identified by archaeologists. Marrinan et al. "Expedition of Pánfilo de Narváez," 71–82; Weddle, *Spanish Sea*, 194 and 206, suggests Follet's Island rather than Galveston Island as the landing place.

45. Cabeza de Vaca, *Adventures*, 60. Wolff, "The Karankawa Indians," 2. W. Arens, *The Man-Eating Myth: Anthropology and Anthropophagy* (New York: Oxford University Press, 1979), 49–50, and Archer, "Cannibalism," 453–79. Anthropologists still disagree on the extent to which reports of cannibalism are exaggerated. Arens represents an extreme position; for a contrary view see Peggy Reeves Sanday, *Divine Hunger: Cannibalism and a Cultural System* (New York: Cambridge University Press, 1987). Hulme sees cannibalism as a category of discourse by which Europeans defined themselves against the "other": *Colonial Encounters*, 78–87.

46. Góngora, *Studies*, 63. See, too, Adorno, "Negotiation of Fear," 100–34, a penetrating analysis of his adaptive strategies with further insights into how by his contemporaries and later historians misread his account.

47. Cabeza de Vaca, *Adventures*, 128.

48. The prevailing view has them cross Texas in a circuitous route through the future sites of Austin and San Antonio, then make their way up the Pecos River into southeastern New Mexico before dropping southwesterly to cross the Rio Grande near the site of present El Paso. This was the route suggested by Hallenbeck, *Cabeza de Vaca*. Carl Sauer, *Sixteenth Century North America*, 108–25, agreed with the general route that Hallenbeck constructed, even while modifying it slightly. More recent work by anthropologists Alex D. Krieger and by the team of T. N. and T. J. Campbell strongly challenges the trans-Texas interpretation, bringing us closer to

the earlier views of Harbert [*sic*]Davenport and others, whom Hallenbeck challenged. The literature is judiciously surveyed by Chipman, "In Search of Cabeza de Vaca's Route," 127–48.

49. Hedrick and Riley, trans. and eds., *Journey of the Vaca Party*, 72, and 155. I have re-translated this passage, which Hedrick and Riley rendered too loosely.

50. Cabeza de Vaca, *Adventures*, 119. At the Spanish court, Cabeza de Vaca reportedly hinted at great riches in Florida. See Jackson, *Early Florida*, 97, citing the Fidalgo de Elvas. It is difficult to know, however, if Cabeza de Vaca implied this, or if observers inferred it.

51. Cabeza de Vaca, *Adventures*, 135.

52. Borah, "Hernán Cortés," 21–22.

53. Scholars disagree whether Esteban was an African or a dark-skinned Arab. The question may never be settled definitively, but evidence strongly suggests that Esteban was a black from the Arab world. Fray Marcos identified Esteban on at least five occasions as "Estevan, the black" (*Estéban, negro*), and, most telling, Cabeza de Vaca referred to Esteban as a "*black* Arab, native of Azamor." These statements, together with the references by other contemporaries to Esteban as a "black," have convinced most historians that Esteban was an African. See Weber, "Introduction," to Hallenbeck, *Journey of Fray Marcos*, xxvii–xxviii.

54. A letter by Rodrigo de Albornoz, Mexico City, Oct. 1539, quoted in Sauer, *Sixteenth Century North America*, 128, described rumors circulating in the capital. He did not quote fray Marcos directly.

55. "Narrative of Fray Marcos," in Hallenbeck, *Journey of Fray Marcos*, 34. For the skillful construction of fray Marcos's report, see Ahern, "Certification of Cíbola," 303–13.

56. Letter of fray Gerónimo Ximenez, Oct. 9, 1539, in Wagner, "Fr. Marcos," 223. See, too, the letter of Bishop Zumárraga, ibid.

Some contemporaries applied the name to the Zuni province, consisting of six towns, and some applied the name to the single Zuni town that Esteban and Coronado, and perhaps fray Marcos, visited. For a discussion of this question, see Riley, "Road to Hawikuh," 140–44. I have taken the origin of the word *Cíbola* from Sauer, *Sixteenth Century North America*, 131.

57. Wagner, "Fr. Marcos," 218–20. For the historiography of this question, see Weber, "Introduction," to Hallenbeck, *Journey of Fray Marcos*, xix–xxvii.

58. For a lengthy discussion of how these numbers are arrived at, see Hammond and Rey, eds. and trans., *Coronado Expedition*, 7–12. For the number of Franciscans (four ordained priests and two laybrothers) and their identities, long a subject of conjecture, see Chávez, *Coronado's Friars*. Chávez provides biographical sketches of five of these priests, not counting fray Marcos. For background on Coronado, see Bolton, *Coronado*, 19–20, and Day, *Coronado's Quest*, 22.

59. Inglis, "Men of Cíbola," 1–24, reports on a prosopographical study of Coronado's army, but his sample (25 percent) seems too small to support firm generalizations.

60. The route of Coronado, and that of Niza before him, remain the subject of dispute. A widely accepted reconstruction is by Sauer, "Road to Cíbola," 53–103. For a dissenting viewpoint, see Di Peso, *Casas Grandes*, 4:88–103, who places Coronado's route farther east than does Sauer. In a popular account, lavishly illustrated, Udall, *To the Inland Empire*, has reconstructed Coronado's route using some of the most recent conjectures.

61. Coronado to Viceroy Mendoza, Aug. 3, 1540, in Hammond and Rey, eds. and trans., *Coronado Expedition*, 170. For the size of Cíbola, I have used the estimate of population at Hawikuh in Hallenbeck, *Journey of Fray Marcos*, 40. It may be, as Rodack suggests, that Cíbola was the

nearby village of Kiakima (see my chapter 1, n. 2), but their sizes were probably similar. There is no firm evidence to indicate that Coronado was at the same village that Esteban visited and that fray Marcos claimed to have seen.

62. Castañeda, "Narrative," mentions the "seven" Hopi villages (pp. 213, 259), but the exact number of towns occupied by Hopis at this time is apparently no longer known. For a succinct summary of archaeological and historical knowledge of Hopis at this time, see Brew, "Hopi Prehistory," 514–23. Most Hopis apparently lived at the bases of their respective mesas, closer to their fields, until the 1690s when they moved to the mesa tops for protection against Spanish reprisals (Adams, "View from the Hopi Mesas," 325).

63. For the aesthetic values of sixteenth-century Europeans, see Keith Thomas, *Man and the Natural World: A History of Modern Sensibility* (New York: Pantheon, 1983), who draws examples from England, but who sees parallels among Spaniards (16). For the Tovar and López expeditions, see the Castañeda, "Narrative," 213–16, written some years later.

64. Bolton, *Coronado*, 153–68, provides a good account of the Alarcón expedition. The quote is from Castañeda, "Narrative," 211. See Alarcón's own account, in Hammond and Rey, eds. and trans., *Coronado Expedition*, 124–55. The next European to sail up the Colorado was the British Lt. R. W. H. Hardy, in the 1820s.

65. Bolton, *Coronado*, 201–12, provides a good account and a guide to sources for the tragedy at Arenal. For the number of pueblos destroyed, see Hammond and Rey, eds. and trans., *Coronado Expedition*, 22, n. 68. For the rape episode, see Castañeda, "Narrative," 225.

66. Castañeda, "Narrative," 221, reporting the Turk's description.

67. Scholars agree that Coronado reached the area of Lyons, but his precise route to and

from Quivira has been the subject of conjecture and controversy. Bolton's reconstruction of Coronado's route has been challenged by several writers. Wagstaff, "Coronado's Route to Quivira," 137–66, summarizes previous scholarship and proposes his own alternative, although he neglected to take into account Schroeder, "A Re-analysis of the Routes of Coronado and Oñate," 2–23. Two recent works discuss but do not attempt to reconstruct the route to Quivira: Strout, "The Coronado Expeditions," 2–31, and Udall, *To the Inland Empire*, xiv, 152–66. For Spanish expeditions from New Mexico onto the plains, from Coronado on, see Brandon, *Quivira*.

68. Coronado to the king, Oct. 20, 1541, in Hammond and Rey, eds. and trans., *Coronado Expedition*, 189, and Castañeda, "Narrative," 241. Kessell, *Kiva, Cross and Crown*, 22–24, places credence in this version of the story. It is also plausible that the Turk intended no duplicity, but that he and Coronado failed to understand one another. See Lecompte, "Coronado and Conquest," 295–300.

69. Castañeda, "Narrative," 236–37, 241.

70. Although the details of fray Juan de Padilla's death at Quivira are murky, first-hand accounts reveal that natives killed him. Luis de Ubeda, a laybrother, remained at Pecos; whether or not the natives killed him remains a matter of conjecture. See Angélico Chávez, *Coronado's Friars*, 64–74; Kessell, *Kiva, Cross and Crown*, 25–27.

71. Quoted in Bolton, *Coronado*, 379, whose biography tells the end of the story. The proceedings of the investigation are translated in Hammond and Rey, eds. and trans., *Coronado Expedition*.

72. Albornoz, *Hernando de Soto*, 10, 19, 217 (De Soto was born in 1500, and traveled to the New World as a page for Pedrarias in 1514). The inadequate and dated biography by Maynard, *De Soto and the Conquistadores* has been superseded by Albor-

noz, but the definitive biography in English has yet to be written.

73. Hoffman, *New Andalucia*, 88; Weddle, *Spanish Sea*, 422–24. My brief description of the De Soto expedition is based on a reading of the three surviving accounts by participants. These have been translated and gathered into two volumes: Bourne, ed., *Narratives . . . of Hernando de Soto*. Better known as literature but unreliable as a historical source is the classic account by Garcilaso de la Vega, purportedly based in large part on the reminiscences of an elderly participant and first published in 1605. The best edition in English is Vega, *Florida of the Inca*, ed. by the Varners. The definitive edition is Vega, *La Florida*, ed. by Hilton, which contains previously unknown corrections to the 1605 edition, as well as a balanced analysis of the historical value of Garcilaso's work. The same year that Hilton's edition appeared in Spain, Henige, "Context, Content, and Credibility," 1–23, reviewed the controversy, to the further detriment of the Inca's credibility.

74. For Cabeza de Vaca's arrival in Spain, and his subsequent career in Paraguay, see Bishop, *Odyssey of Cabeza de Vaca*, 167ff. De Soto's landing site is usually given as Tampa Bay, and most recent investigation points in that direction. See, e.g., Fairbanks, "Exploration to Settlement," 129–30; Milanich, "Notes on the Route of De Soto,"; and Mitchem, "Initial Spanish-Indian Contact," 52. Charlotte Harbor continues to have adherents: see Weddle, *Spanish Sea*, 230–31. The size of De Soto's landing party is difficult to determine, but I have accepted the conservative conclusion of Swanton, *Final Report*, 79–88, 98. On De Soto and the Genoese, see Pike, *Enterprise and Adventure*, 102, who provides no detail but who mentions Ponce de León as also receiving a loan from the Genoese.

75. De Soto to the Justice and Board of Magis-

trates in Santiago de Cuba, July 9, 1539, in Bourne, ed., *Narratives . . . of Hernando de Soto*, 2:162. Hudson, *Southeastern Indians*, 107, speculates that Ortiz "probably" spoke "a Timucuan language."

76. Hudson, *Southeastern Indians*, 77–96; Griffin, "Changing Concepts," 40–63; and Smith, "Mississippian Patterns," 64–79. I do not mean to suggest a uniformity of culture in this broad area. Archaeologists, for example, point to differences between coastal and inland cultures, and along the Gulf coast, to a mix of socioeconomic systems. See the various articles in Davis, ed., *Gulf Coast Prehistory*. Much of Florida is an exception to the pattern of agriculture in river bottoms. In an unpublished paper presented to the Society for American Archaeology, New Orleans, Apr. 1986, "Rivers as Centers, Rivers as Boundaries: Florida Variations on a Mississippian Theme," Gary Shapiro pointed out that most Florida rivers are poor environments for growing crops because they "issue from lowland swamps or from springs . . . [and] do not carry loads of silt or mineral nutrients."

77. Ranjel, "De Soto's Expedition," 2:117. Since this narrative was written by the chronicler Oviedo, it is difficult at times to separate Oviedo's moralizing from Ranjel's description.

78. Oviedo editorializing in Ranjel, "De Soto's Expedition," 2:60. (The translation says "slaying," but Oviedo's word was *montería*—hunting on horseback. For this point, I am grateful to Paul Hoffman.)

79. De Soto to the Justice and Board of Magistrates in Santiago de Cuba, July 9, 1539, in Bourne, ed., *Narratives . . . of Hernando de Soto*, 2:162. For Indian tactics, see Dye, "Warfare in the Sixteenth-Century Southeast," 211–22.

80. Only one site has been archaeologically identified with the De Soto expedition, but advances in archaeological and historical knowledge permit a more accurate yet still general and tentative tracing of the route than ever before. See Brain, "Archaeology of the Hernando de Soto Expedition," 96–107; Brain, "Introduction," xi–lxxii; Hudson, DePratter, and Smith, "Hernando de Soto's Expedition," 77–98; and Milanich, "European Entrada into La Florida," 3–29. I have followed the broad outline suggested by these writers, augmented by articles that describe segments of the route, as cited below.

81. For the electrifying 1987 discovery of De Soto's winter camp, see Ewen, "Soldier of Fortune," and two attractively illustrated articles: Ewen, "Anhaica," 110–18, and Mitchem, "Artifacts of Exploration," 99–109.

82. The quote is from Ranjel, "De Soto's Expedition," 2:99. The description of the canoe and the gifts is from the Gentleman of Elvas, the best edition of whose work is Robertson, ed. and trans., *True Relations*, 2:90–93. The location of Cofitachequi, once believed to be on the Savannah River, remains in dispute and suggestive documentary evidence has not been confirmed archaeologically. I have followed the impressive revisionist articles by Hudson, Smith, and DePratter, "From Apalachee to Chiaha," 65–77, somewhat revised in Hudson, Worth, and DePratter, "Refinements in Hernando de Soto's Route," 107–19, and in DePratter, "Cofitachequi," 134–56.

83. Ranjel, "De Soto's Expedition," 2:100; Hoffman, *New Andalucia*, 93–94.

84. At Chiaha, some writers believed De Soto had found the ancestors of Cherokees, but Hudson has found convincing evidence to the contrary: "Research," 15.

85. The quote is from the "Relation of . . . Luys Hernández de Biedma . . . ," in Bourne, ed., *Narratives . . . of Hernando de Soto*, 2:21. The parameters of Coosa are defined in Hally, Smith, and Langford, Jr., "Archaeological Reality of de Soto's Coosa," 121–38. They, like DePratter,

Hudson, and Smith, "From Chiaha to Mabila," put the principal town of Coosa in northwestern Georgia. Little and Curren, "Conquest Archaeology of Alabama," 186–87, put Coosa in northeastern Alabama. The site of Mabila, too, is disputed. DePratter, Hudson, and Smith, "From Chiaha to Mabila," 123, put it near present Selma. Little and Curren, "Conquest Archaeology of Alabama," 182–84, place it farther south near the confluence of the Tombigbee and Alabama rivers.

86. "Relation of . . . Luys Hernández de Biedma . . . ," in Bourne, ed., *Narratives . . . of Hernando de Soto*, 2:22.

87. Bolton, *Coronado*, 303–4, 356; Castañeda, "Narrative," 243. Schroeder, "Routes of Coronado and Oñate," 12–14, challenges Bolton's interpretation of Castañeda's account of this episode, but I do not find Schroeder's argument convincing. For the most recent interpretation of De Soto's route through Arkansas, see Morse and Morse, "Spanish Exploration of Arkansas," 197–210.

88. Sauer, *Sixteenth Century North America*, 170; Robertson, ed. and trans., *True Relations*, 218; Hudson, *Southeastern Indians*, 206–10.

89. "Relation of . . . Luys Hernández de Biedma . . . ," in Bourne, ed., *Narratives . . . of Hernando de Soto*, 2:37. The route of the party through Arkansas and Texas remains a matter of conjecture and disagreement among the few scholars who have studied the question. Sauer, *Sixteenth Century North America*, 177, relying on older sources, suggests that Moscoso might have reached the Brazos before turning back. More detailed efforts to reconstruct the route include: Strickland, "Moscoso's Journey"; Williams, "Moscoso's Trail"; and Woldert, "Expedition of Luis de Moscoso." Strickland believed they reached the Trinity River in southwestern Houston County; Williams argued that they traveled beyond Fort Worth, to pres-

ent Palo Pinto County; Woldert asserted that they went no farther than the forests of Nacogdoches County in East Texas. See, too, Williams, "New Evidence," 77–88. The most current hypothesis, written without acknowledging the earlier work of Sauer, Strickland, Woldert, or Williams, is Kenmotsu et al., "Moscoso and the Route in Texas," which suggests two alternatives, both of which end at the Colorado River near present-day Austin.

90. Swanton, *Final Report*, 83, 88. The exact numbers of those who came with De Soto, or left with Moscoso, are not known. Avellaneda, *Los sobrevivientes de la Florida*, identifies 257 survivors and speculates that the number 311 may be correct. That Indians slaves, or perhaps concubines, accompanied the survivors is usually overlooked, but later accounts mention two women from Coosa (Hudson, "Spanish-Coosa Alliance," 602, 626).

91. For Spanish secrecy, see, e.g., Parry, *The Age of Reconnaissance*, 105, and Holmes, *From New Spain*, 129–43. For the pilot's oath, see Carla Rahn Phillips, *Six Galleons for the King of Spain: Imperial Defense in the Early Seventeenth Century* (Baltimore: Johns Hopkins Press, 1978), 133.

92. See, e.g., Wheat, *Mapping the Transmississippi West*, 1:22, 47; Cumming, *Southeast in Early Maps*, 13; Martin and Martin, *Maps of Texas*, 13, 18, 25, 27, 77, 101; Jackson, Weddle, and DeVille, *Mapping Texas*, 14–15, and Cook, *Flood Tide of Empire*, 100. For an example of those who sailed from Seville benefitting from the exploration of their predecessors, see Kelsey, "Finding the Way Home," 147.

93. Barrientos, *Pedro Menéndez de Avilés*, 26, who completed this work in 1567; Hammond, "Search for the Fabulous," 17–33.

94. I am here borrowing a phrase from Todorov, *Conquest of America*, 49, who noted that Columbus "discovered America but not the Americans."

95. See, e.g., Jackson, *Early Florida*, 121–56,

for Spaniards casting blame. For a penetrating view of Cabeza de Vaca's adaptive strategies, see Adorno, "Negotiation of Fear," 100–134.

96. Elliott, *Old World and the New*, 14, a superb series of essays that should be supplemented by his essays: "Renaissance Europe," 11–23, and "Discovery of America," 42–64. See, too, Crosby, Jr., *Columbian Exchange*, 9–12, and Hulme, *Colonial Encounters*, 20–21. Although Spaniards of the first half of the sixteenth century can be characterized as representatives of the Early Renaissance, as Elliot does, much about their institutions and mentality suggest the Middle Ages. See Luis Weckmann, *Herencia Medieval*. A number of sources discuss the new round of Spanish inquiry that began in the mid-1530s, but see especially Anthony Pagden, *The Fall of Natural Man: The American Indian and the Origins of Comparative Ethnology* (Cambridge: Cambridge University Press, 1982), 57–200. For the English, see Bernard W. Sheehan, *Savagism and Civility: Indians and Englishmen in Colonial Virginia* (Cambridge: Cambridge University Press, 1980), 19–20. Matijasic, "Reflected Values," 31–50, argues that Europeans of this era saw Indians as multidimensional individuals and did not reduce them to the noble savage/savage dichotomy.

97. Antonello Gerbi, *Nature in the New World: From Christopher Columbus to Gonzalo Fernández de Oviedo*, trans. Jeremy Moyle (Pittsburgh: University of Pittsburgh Press, 1985), 7–8.

98. For "deculturation," see Smith, "Indian Responses," 135–49. On material culture, see Swagerty, "Beyond Bimini," 490, who also points out that a few Spaniards remained behind (508–9) and that genetic exchange had begun by 1543. Christopher L. Miller and George R. Hamell, "A New Perspective on Indian-White Contact: Cultural Symbols and Colonial Trade,"

JAH 73 (Sept. 1986): 311–28, offer an interesting assessment of Indian motives, including the observation that in the sixteenth century Indians "were not acquiring European goods primarily for what Europeans would have considered practical reasons," 341.

99. For sixteenth-century North America, sources are too limited to speak with assurance. Dobyns, *Their Number Become Thinned*, has been the most outspoken proponent of the scenario of early, large-scale population decline. In a convincing critique of Dobyns's book, Henige, "Primary Source," 305, excoriates Dobyns's cavalier use of sources, concluding that "there is virtually no documentary evidence to support the belief that epidemics repeatedly struck the Indians of Florida (or anywhere else in North America) before 1565." See, too, Henige's, "If Pigs Could Fly," 701–20. Dobyns replied to his critics in "More Methodological Perspectives," 285–99, and that in turn elicited rejoinders by Snow and Lanphear, and by Henige (ibid., 299–307).

Smith, *Archaeology of Aboriginal Culture Change*, confirmed Dobyns's view but did so on the basis of insubstantial evidence of population decline (84–85). In another study that appeared that same year, Ramenofsky found unambiguous archaeological evidence to support Dobyns's view that catastrophic population decline began in the lower Mississippi Valley in the sixteenth century with the De Soto entrada (*Vectors of Death*, 42–71). For the Southeast, see, too, Fairbanks, "Exploration to Settlement," 134–36; Crosby, *Ecological Imperialism*, 209–15; Dobyns, *Their Number Become Thinned*, 291–334.

100. Cabeza de Vaca, *Adventures*, 60. For Dobyns's analysis of this, see *Their Number Become Thinned*, 261. For a contrary view, see Henige, "Primary Source," 300.

101. Cowdrey, *This Land, This South*, 5.

102. Dobyns, *From Fire to Flood*, 48–56, specu-

lates that the decline of the densely populated Hohokam culture, the apparent ancestors of the Pimas, took place as a result of epidemics in early historic times, beginning in the 1520s and 1530s. Ezell, "History of the Pima," 150, agrees and provides further sources. Doyel, "Transition to History," 143, notes that "there is no archaeological evidence to support . . . the hypothesis that introduced European diseases caused a collapse of the Classic Hohokam." For the deep and ongoing division of scholarly opinion, see Minnis and Redman, eds., *Perspectives on Southwestern Prehistory*, 225–313, and Reff, *Disease, Depopulation, and Culture Change*, 13–14, 97–114, 243–45, who utilizes sources more judiciously than Dobyns and who views the decline of the Hohokam peoples as a gradual process, extending into the historic period. For the argument that smallpox reached the Southwest in the great pandemic of 1520–26 and subsequently with Coronado, see Upham, "Smallpox and Climate," 124–25, who relies on an epidemiological model. For a contrary view, see the commentary on Upham's article by Reff, "Introduction of Smallpox," 704–8, and Upham's reply, "Understanding the Disease History of the Southwest," 708–10.

103. See, e.g., Smith, *Archaeology of Aboriginal Culture Change*, chap. 4; Smith, "Aboriginal Population Movements," 21–34; Reff, *Disease, Depopulation, and Culture Change*, chap. 5; Ramenofsky, *Vectors of Death*, 173–74. Most scholars of California cautiously make no pronouncements about Indian demography until the beginning of Spanish colonization in 1769. See, e.g., Cook, "Historical Demography," and Castillo, "Impact of Euro-American Exploration and Settlement," 91–98 and 99–127. An exception is Hoover, "Archaeology of Spanish Colonial Sites," 94, who asserts population decline prior to the eighteenth century but offers no evidence. For later manifestations of population decline altering culture significantly, see for example, Ewers, "Influence of Epidemics," 111–12.

104. d'Escalante Fontaneda, *Memoir of D.o d'Escalente [sic] Fontaneda*, 21. This is the best edition of Fontaneda's account and includes a transcript of the original Spanish as well as corrections of the flawed translation by Smith.

Chapter 3: Foundations of Empire: Florida and New Mexico

The epigraphs are from Lyon, *Enterprise of Florida*, 215, 216, and Hammond and Rey, eds. and trans., *Don Juan de Oñate*, 1:335.

1. The best account of the landing is by Menéndez's chaplain, Francisco López de Mendoza Grajales, "Prosperous Voyage of . . . Pedro Menéndez de Avilés," 141–63. One other firsthand account by a participant, Menéndez's brother-in-law, Gonzalo Solís de Merás, is known: Connor, trans. and ed., *Pedro Menéndez de Avilés*. Connor includes translations of some of Menéndez's correspondence and explains the reason for bestowing the name of St. Augustine (83, n. 5). Menéndez himself mentions the ceremony of possession in a letter to Felipe II, Sept. 11, 1565, trans. in Quinn, ed., *New American World*, 2:393. My brief account of the beginnings of Florida is informed throughout by the standard work, Lyon, *Enterprise of Florida*. See, too, Arana, "Exploration of Florida," 1–16, and Connolly, "Four Contemporary Narratives," 305–34.

2. Le Moyne, "Narrative of Le Moyne," 114.

3. Some of the details in these paragraphs come from a letter Menéndez wrote to Felipe II, St. Augustine, Oct. 15, 1565, trans. in Quinn, ed., *New American World*, 2:395–404. The quote is on 397.

4. López de Mendoza Grajales, "Prosperous Voyage of Pedro Menéndez de Avilés," 158.

5. Menéndez to Felipe II, Oct. 15, 1565, in Quinn, ed., *New American World*, 2:398. Solís de Merás, Menéndez's brother-in-law, provides more details. Connor, trans. and ed., *Pedro Menéndez de Avilés*, 107–22.

6. In this sentence, I am not quoting Menéndez directly, but Lyon, *Enterprise of Florida*, 42, who describes his views. Lyon also discusses conflicting estimates of the number of French victims (ibid., 126–27). For Menéndez's public position, see his "reasons . . . for not being able to do anything other than what he did in Florida," ca. 1567, in Quinn, ed., *New American World*, 2:472.

7. Menéndez to Felipe II, St. Augustine, Oct. 15, 1565, Quinn, ed., *New American World*, 2:398.

8. Barrientos, *Pedro Menéndez de Avilés*, 3. For the 1560s as a time of unusual religious repression, see Kamen, "Toleration and Dissent," 18. For Felipe's reaction, see Hammond, ed. and trans., "French Document," 55–56.

9. Pierson, *Philip II*, 44. For Felipe's order to hang trespassers, see Lyon, "Captives of Florida," 2.

10. Felipe II to Menéndez, *Capitulación*, Mar. 20, 1565, in Connor, trans. and ed., *Pedro Menéndez de Avilés*, 259. For Menéndez's debts to earlier explorers, see Lyon, "Continuity in the Age of Conquest," 154–61.

11. Francisco López de Gómara, quoted in Elliot, "Spanish Conquest and Settlement," 149.

12. By 1574 Spaniards had established some 225 municipalities in America. See Nicolás Sánchez Albornoz, "The Colonial Population of Latin America," in Bethell, ed., *Cambridge History of Latin America*, 2:18.

13. For a discussion of this dichotomy and a guide to the literature, see Powell, *Tree of Hate*, esp. chaps. 2, 7. This point is forcibly refuted by Lyon, "Spain's Sixteenth-Century North American Settlement Attempts," 275–91.

14. Quoted in Kelsey, *Cabrillo*, 110.

15. See "A Comparison of Provisions of Various Sixteenth-Century Asientos," in Lyon, *Enterprise of Florida*, 220–23. Lyon does not include instructions to Ponce de León or Garay. For the former, see Davis, "History of Juan Ponce de León's Voyages to Florida," 9, 53; for Garay's instructions, which have apparently not been published in English, see *CDI*(1), 39:518.

16. Góngora, *Studies*, 17. Speaking of the reconquista, Góngora notes: "The Iberian 'conquests' . . . were, strictly speaking, 'searches,' attempts to win treasure and lands on the frontiers of Christendom. . . . As a result, in Spanish America, the urge to wander prevailed for some time over the tendency to permanent settlement."

17. For English behavior at Jamestown, and European attitudes toward manual labor, see the sources cited in chap. 5, n. 8.

18. The quote is from fray Toribio de Motolinia to Charles V, Tlaxcala, Jan. 2, 1555, in James Lockhart and Enrique Otte, eds., *Letters and People of the Spanish Indies, Sixteenth Century* (Cambridge: Cambridge University Press, 1976), 223. For Coronado's men, see below, n. 73. See, too, the notions about the natural wealth of North America that one scholar in Salamanca had gleaned from official reports by 1567: Barrientos, *Pedro Menéndez de Avilés*, 22–26.

19. The Crown's share of income in 1551–55 was 4,354,208 ducats; this fell to 1,882,195 ducats in 1556–60 (Pierson, *Philip II*, 33). This loss was not due to piracy alone. After 1565 the Crown's share began to rise again. See, too, Andrews, *Spanish Caribbean*, 81–85; Hoffman, *Spanish Crown*, 63–108.

20. Parry, *Spanish Seaborne Empire*, 44–45; Hoffman, *Spanish Crown*, 6. For the discovery of Bermuda, see Morison, *Southern Voyages*, 499–500.

21. Weddle, *Spanish Sea*, 246–48, summarizes the story. Details may be found in Arnold

and Weddle, *Nautical Archaeology of Padre Island*, and Arnold, ed., *Documentary Sources*.

22. Lyon, *Enterprise of Florida*, 29–30, 129, 142, 148–49.

23. Felipe II to officials in New Spain, Valladolid, Dec. 29, 1557, a previously unpublished document reproduced in Quinn, ed. *New American World*, 2:201–2, and Felipe II to Luis de Velasco, Dec. 29, 1557, ibid., 202–03. These orders do not mention a base on the Gulf, but subsequent events suggest it was part of the plan. Hoffman, *New Andalucia*, 69, identifies the Point of Santa Elena as Tybee Island, at that time.

24. Hoffman, "Legend, Religious Idealism, and Colonies," 59–71; Hoffman, *New Andalucia*, 25–39, 152–53, 326–27 *n.* 17.

25. For Felipe's bankruptcy, see Pierson, *Philip II*, 32.

26. Lyon, *Enterprise of Florida*, 49; Parry, *Age of Reconnaissance*, 97–98.

27. Velasco to Luna, Mexico, Oct. 25, 1559, in Priestley, ed. and trans., *Luna Papers*, 1:61. Priestley provides copies of the essential documents in both Spanish and English translation; his introduction has been the standard account. Priestley also told Luna's story in a romanticized biography, *Tristán de Luna*. Arnade, "Tristan de Luna," 210–22, summarized Priestley's work in lively fashion, adding no new detail. Hoffman, *New Andalucia*, 144–81, is rich in insights about the complex and evolving impulses behind the expedition and its geopolitical context. Hudson, Smith, DePratter, and Kelley, "Tristán de Luna Expedition," 119–34, use the most recent archaeological and historical findings to identify sites and native polities associated with the expedition with greater precision.

28. Weddle, *Spanish Sea*, 255, overstates his case when he says: "In both concept and execution Luna's expedition was more closely related to the De Soto expedition than has been generally realized." The point had already been made by Priestley, ed. and trans., *Luna Papers*, 1:xxi. Velasco's preparations included sending out two preliminary expeditions to survey the Gulf for the ideal site for a colony and assembling a fleet of thirteen ships, some newly constructed, carrying 240 horses and 1500 men, women, and children. Weddle, *Spanish Sea*, 259–60, notes a second preliminary voyage that earlier historians had overlooked.

29. Morales Folguera, *Arquitectura*, 21–27. For Velasco and the restless young men, see Hoffman, *New Andalucia*, 149, 155–56.

30. Felipe II to Luna, Toledo, Dec. 18, 1559, in Priestley, ed. and trans., *Luna Papers*, 2:17. Priestley used a copy of this document; Lyon, "Spain's Sixteenth-Century North American Settlement Attempts," 280, cites the original, as he does in the case of several documents that also appear in Priestley.

31. Hudson, "Spanish-Coosa Alliance," 599–626.

32. Felipe II to Viceroy Velasco, Sept. 23, 1561, in Bennett, comp., *Settlement of Florida*, 127–28.

33. Quinn, *North America from Earliest Discovery*, 240–61, provides a succinct overview of French activities and a guide to sources; Hoffman, *New Andalucia*, 206–15, points to French geopolitical motives. For the Spanish expedition to Charlesfort, see Wenhold, "Manrique de Rojas' Report," 45–62. The site of Charlesfort is not known with certainty. For England, see the good summary in Meinig, *Shaping of America*, 28–35.

34. For the failure of diplomacy, see Hoffman, *Spanish Crown*, 103–7, 110. The two quotes and their respective sources can be found in Hoffman's important article, "Diplomacy and the Papal Donation," 161. Neither are direct quotes.

35. Quinn, "Colonies in the Beginning," 22, referring to the response of Clement VII to an inquiry of 1533 from Francis I.

36. Hoffman, *New Andalucia*, 187–202; Lyon, *Enterprise of Florida*, 24–25, 34, 36, who also points out that Felipe relied on adelantados longer than historians have generally recognized.

37. Contrary to most modern accounts, Felipe II's initial motive for authorizing Menéndez to settle Florida had nothing to do with dislodging the French from Fort Caroline. The king had issued Menéndez a contract before he learned of the existence of the Protestant fort. Eugene Lyon made this discovery (*Enterprise of Florida*, 56). The adelantado contract did vary from the norm, most notably in that the Crown granted special trading privileges that would enable Menéndez to make money in the Caribbean to support his venture in Florida. In contrast to many adelantados, Menéndez had more experience than wealth. He and the Crown negotiated a solution to this problem (Lyon, *Enterprise of Florida*, 38–70). The number of persons who left Cádiz with Menéndez remains unclear, but it appears to have been close to 1,100, and perhaps as high as 1,500 (Ibid., 98–99). Another part of his fleet, which left from Spain's north coast, sailed separately and reached the Caribbean well after Menéndez.

38. Felipe II to Menéndez, *Capitulación*, Mar. 20, 1565, in Connor, trans. and ed., *Pedro Menéndez de Avilés*, 261.

39. Menéndez was born at Avilés in Asturias in 1519, and so was about forty-five when appointed adelantado. For his early career, see Lyon, *Enterprise of Florida*, 8–37. For his leadership, see ibid., 184. Schwaller, "Nobility, Family, and Service," 298–310, chronicles his family connections.

40. The quote is from Sauer, *Sixteenth Century North America*, 214. Lyon, "Continuity in the Age of Conquest," 156, provides concrete evidence that Menéndez "was an in-heritor of the knowledge of previous Spanish explorers." See also Lyon, "Pedro Menéndez's Strategic Plan," 1–14.

41. Menéndez to Felipe II, St. Augustine, Dec. 12, 1565, in Quinn, ed., *New American World*, 2:415. In April 1566 Menéndez had built Fort San Salvador on Parris Island. After a mutiny two months later, reinforcements arrived and built Fort San Felipe (Lyon, "Santa Elena," 2).

42. For Santa Elena, see Lyon, *Enterprise of Florida*, 156–57, 166. Lyon discusses the other forts of Tocobaga, San Antonio, Tequesta, Santa Lucía, San Agustín, San Mateo, and San Salvador throughout his book.

43. Menéndez de Avilés to Felipe II, St. Augustine, Oct. 15, 1565, and Havana, Dec. 12, 1565, in Quinn, ed., *New American World*, 2:398, 402, 415. Menéndez held similar views about North American geography even before he set sail to found St. Augustine. See Lyon, *Enterprise of Florida*, 42.

44. This remarkable story, based on recently neglected or unknown documents, emerged in a series of articles in the 1980s and is now told in full in Hudson, *Juan Pardo Expeditions*.

45. Menéndez to Felipe II, Havana, Jan. 30, 1566, in Quinn, ed., *New American World*, 2:422. Scholars seems to agree that the idea of the Strait of Anián first appeared in a pamphlet published in 1562 by the cartographer Giacomo Gastaldi and that it first appeared on a map in 1566 (by Bolognino Zaltieri). See Nunn, *Strait of Anian Concept*; Wagner, *Cartography of the Northwest Coast of America*, 1: 53–57; 2:426; and Mathes, "Mythological Geography of California," 320, who also quotes Urdaneta on this subject at some length (318–19). This piece of imaginary geography had several definitions—I am rather loosely equating it with the Strait of Bacalaos, to which Menéndez refers, and both of those waterways with the North-

west Passage. For finer distinctions, see Wagner, *Cartography of the Northwest Coast of America*, 2:426, and Mathes, "Apochryphal Tales," 53–54.

46. Vigneras, "Spanish Discovery of North Carolina," 401, who provides the best account of this expedition, along with translations of key documents. Hoffman, *New Andalucia*, 239, 246–50, suggests the chilling effect of the conversation with Urdaneta—a convincing explanation of Menéndez's diminished interest.

47. Luis de Quirós to Juan de Hinistrosa, Ajacán, Sept. 12, 1570, in Lewis and Loomie, *Spanish Jesuit Mission in Virginia*, 89. Lewis and Loomie provide a brief narrative of the expedition, together with transcriptions and translations of original documents, which remains the starting point for any study of this subject. I have relied upon it except where otherwise indicated. Marotti, "Juan Baptista de Segura," 267–79, provides a biography of Segura and argues that he was a flawed leader. The exact sites of the landing and the Jesuit mission remain unclear; Lewis's and Loomie's reconstruction is not definitive, but the best we have. Quinn, *North America from Earliest Discovery*, 282, finds it convincing.

48. Luis de Quirós to Juan de Hinistrosa, Ajacán, Sept. 12, 1570, in Lewis and Loomie, *Spanish Jesuit Mission in Virginia*, 90.

49. Ibid., 89.

50. Gradie, "Spanish Jesuits in Virginia," 131–56, offers the most satisfying account of Indian motivation.

51. Strong circumstantial evidence indicates that don Luis and Opechancanough were the same man. For the most complete exposition of that viewpoint, see Bridenbaugh, "Opechancanough," 5–49. For the quote, "He whose soul is white," see 16.

52. Pedro Menéndez Marqués to the Soldiers of the fort of St. Augustine, River of San Mateo, Sept. 7, 1570, in Connor, ed., *Colonial Records of Spanish Florida*, 1:3. For examples of desertions from Florida during

its first three years, see Lyon, *Enterprise of Florida*, 150–53, 166–67, 170, 180–81; Quinn, ed., *New American World*, 2:280–81; Lyon, "Florida Mutineers," 44–61.

53. The demise of Fort San Mateo and the other Florida posts are discussed in Lyon, *Enterprise of Florida*, 198–203. Regarding San Mateo, some firsthand accounts and guidance to sources can be found in Quinn, ed., *New American World*, 2:567–73. San Mateo was apparently never rebuilt. See Quinn, *North America from Earliest Discovery*, 281, and the report of Martin Diez, in Connor, ed., *Colonial Records of Spanish Florida*, 1:83. For the Jesuits, see the brief account in Gannon, *Cross in the Sand*, 32–34. Zubillaga has studied the Jesuit years in Florida in great detail in *La Florida* and made an extraordinary number of documents available in his *Monumenta Antiquae Floridae*.

54. Lyon, *Enterprise of Florida*, 182–94; Hoffman, *Spanish Crown*, 126–32.

55. Felipe II to Menéndez, *Capitulación*, Mar. 20, 1565, in Connor, trans. and ed., *Pedro Menéndez de Avilés*, 269.

56. Lyon, "Spain's Sixteenth-Century North American Settlement Attempts," 284–85.

57. Menéndez to Felipe II, Florida, Sept. 11, 1565, in Quinn, ed., *New American World*, 2:395.

58. The site was believed to be on Mound Key. Reilly, "Marriage of Expedience," 295–421, is a delightful and shrewd account of Menéndez's marriage with a fine summary of the literature on Calusa culture. Reilly argues that Carlos tricked Menéndez into the marriage in order to bolster his own political position. Reilly is not sufficiently critical, however, of the sources that attest to Menéndez's alleged reluctant participation in the arrangement. "Doña Antonia" was estimated to be thirty-five years old, which I judge to be the equivalent of "middle age" in the sixteenth century (Lewis, "Calusa," 19–49). For Menéndez's early

Indian policy, see Lyon, *Enterprise of Florida*, 118, 149, 155.

59. Lyon, *Enterprise of Florida*, 200, describes the Timucuan as "joyous" in their victory over the Spanish.

60. Testimony of Diego Ruiz, Jan. 17, 1573, in Connor, ed. and trans., *Colonial Records of Spanish Florida*, 1:61. See the testimony of Menéndez and others, ibid., 31–82.

61. Menéndez to the king, [Spain?], [1572], in Connor, ed. and trans., *Colonial Records of Spanish Florida*, 1:35.

62. Poole, "War by Fire and Blood," 115–37. The quote is on 136 *n.* 67.

63. Menéndez to the king, [Spain?], [1573], in Connor, ed. and trans., *Colonial Records of Spanish Florida*, 1:81.

64. Menéndez to his nephew, Pedro Menéndez Marqués, Sept. 7 and 8, 1574, Santander, quoted in full in Connor, trans. and ed., *Pedro Menéndez de Avilés*, 255.

65. Lyon, "Santa Elena," 6. Archaeological evidence, which reveals a richer material culture at Santa Elena, confirms the view that it was more prosperous than St. Augustine. See Deagan, "Archaeology of Sixteenth-Century St. Augustine," 30.

66. Most writers take the view that the Spanish defense of St. Augustine was little more than symbolic. Covington, "Drake Destroys St. Augustine," 81–93, offers a more sympathic interpretation. Quinn, ed., *New American World*, 5:39–52, reproduces key documents and provides guidance to bibliography.

67. Lyon, "Santa Elena," 15–16. For St. Augustine at this time, see Lyon, "St. Augustine 1580," 20–33, and Bushnell, "Noble and Loyal City," 27–40. For contemporary accounts, see Connor, ed., and trans., *Colonial Records of Spanish Florida*, and an eighteenth-century chronicle based on contemporary documents: Kerrigan, ed. and trans., *Barcía's Chronological History*, 146–84.

68. "Act of Taking Possession of New Mexico, April 30, 1598," in Hammond and Rey,

eds. and trans., *Don Juan de Oñate*, 1:335. Unless otherwise indicated, I have relied upon Hammond and Rey's summary of the Oñate enterprise. A firsthand description of the drama and ceremonies is in Hodge, ed., *History of New Mexico by Gaspar Pérez de Villagrá*, 129. Oñate's contract promised him the title of adelantado, but it was not granted until 1602, after he had fulfilled his part of the agreement. The letter of appointment is in Hammond and Rey, eds. and trans., *Don Juan de Oñate*, 2:766–77. The site of taking possession is commemorated at "La Toma," near present-day San Elizario, then on the south side of the Rio Grande but today, due to a shift in the river, on the American side (Timmons, *El Paso*, 14). No copy of the play, written by Capt. Marcos Farfan, is known to have survived.

69. "Act of Obedience and Vassalage by the Indians of Santo Domingo," in Hammond and Rey, eds. and trans., *Don Juan de Oñate*. The quotes in this paragraph are in vol. 1:339 and 340.

70. Gibson, "Conquest," 11–12, traces this idea to the fifteenth century. In theory, the requerimiento was not abolished as an instrument of policy until the adoption of the Orders for New Discoveries in 1573, see text at n. 75.

71. Ortiz, "San Juan," 278, 294; John, *Storms Brewed*, 43–46; Forbes, *Apache, Navajo, and Spaniard*, 95. For the findings of archaeologists at San Gabriel, see Ellis, "Long Lost 'City,'" 10–38 (Ellis has forgotten about prior European settlement in eastern North America). Jenkins, "Oñate's Administration," 63, argues that Oñate settled immediately at San Gabriel, not at San Juan, but Simmons, Oñate's most recent biographer, finds her evidence unconvincing. The date of the colonists' move from San Juan to San Gabriel is not clear, but Simmons, *Last Conquistador*, 148–49, finds it had occurred by 1600 if not before. For the shadowy information on the informal

beginnings and the formal founding of Santa Fe, see ibid., 182–81, 200. The town was not officially established until 1610.

72. Felipe's notation on a letter from Luis de Velasco to his Majesty, Oct. 14, 1595, Mexico, in Hammond and Rey, eds. and trans., *Don Juan de Oñate*, 1:58. Felipe II died on Sept. 13, 1598. There does not seem to be any contemporary evidence to support the widespread notion that Francis Drake's foray into the Pacific in 1579 prompted the settlement of New Mexico. See n. 80, this chapter.

73. Hammond and Rey, eds. and trans., *Obregón's History*, 228. Obregón did not use use the term *Anián*, but its Atlantic analogue, "strait of the codfish [or bacalaos]." See, too, Castañeda, "Narrative," 194.

74. This is not to say that Coronado's venture was completely forgotten. Details had blurred, as Castañeda makes clear ("Narrative," 192–93), but the recollection that he had found advanced civilizations remained alive in the minds of some officials. Vigil, "Bartolomé de las Casas," 45–57, describes Zorita's plan of 1558 to send missionaries into the lands Coronado had discovered.

75. "Ordenanzas de su Magestad hechas para los nuevos descubrimientos, conquistas y pacificaciones," July 13, 1573, in *CDI*(1), 16:143, 151, 154. Lyon, *Enterprise of Florida*, 24–25, has used a misdated version of these same regulations, in *CDI*(1), 8:484–538, and supposed that they were promulgated in 1563 instead of 1573 and thus applied to Menéndez. For background and context of these orders, which built on previous regulations, see Juan Manzano Manzano, *La incorporación de las indias a la Corona de Castilla* (Madrid: Ediciones Cultura Hispánica, 1948), 207–17. I discuss them further in chapter 4.

76. Hernán Gallegos's Report of 1582, in Hammond and Rey, eds. and trans., *Rediscovery of New Mexico*, 83 (see, too, 114). I

have relied upon Hammond and Rey's fine account of these events in their introduction to this valuable collection of documents. I have not, however, followed Hammond and Rey's argument that Chamuscado was the "de facto leader" of the expedition (7), a position that they base on Gallegos's testimony. Angélico Chávez, in an article that Hammond and Rey overlooked, raised serious questions about Gallegos's motives and argued convincingly that Chamuscado was not in charge: "Gallegos Relación Reconsidered," 1–21.

77. Hernán Gallegos's Report of 1582, in Hammond and Rey, eds. and trans., *Rediscovery of New Mexico*, 82–83.

78. The quote in this paragraph is from the letter of the archbishop of Mexico, Pedro Moya de Contreras, Oct. 26, 1583, in Hammond and Rey, eds. and trans., *Rediscovery of New Mexico*, 28; the king's order to issue a contract is dated Apr. 19, 1593, ibid.; for documents as well as analysis and guides to further sources on the Espejo expedition, see ibid., 15–28, 153–242. For Espejo and the Inquisition, see Conway, "Antonio de Espejo," 1–20, and Richard E. Greenleaf, *The Mexican Inquisition of the Sixteenth Century* (Albuquerque: University of New Mexico Press, 1969), 181–82.

79. Both Oñate and government officials refer to those regulations that bound his enterprise. See, e.g., Hammond and Rey, eds. and trans., *Don Juan de Oñate*, 1:2, 4, 8, 71–71, 77–80; 2:974, 976.

80. Some historians have asserted that Francis Drake's venture into the Pacific, discussed below, led to the settlement of New Mexico. See, e.g., Bolton, *Spanish Borderlands*, 169–70; Bolton, "Defensive Spanish Expansion," 44; Warren A. Beck, *New Mexico: A History of Four Centuries* (Norman: University of Oklahoma Press, 1962), 52; and Bannon, *Spanish Borderlands Frontier*, 33–34. None, however, have offered evidence to support that notion.

81. The best account of this group, which

came to its unhappy end in 1693, together with translations of key documents, appears in Hammond and Rey, eds. and trans., *Rediscovery of New Mexico*, 48–50, 298–326.

82. Castaño to the viceroy, on the Rio Grande, July 27, 1591, in Hammond and Rey, eds. and trans., *Rediscovery of New Mexico*, 308. For other pertinent documents, see ibid., 245–320; the editors provide a summary on 28–48. See, too, Schroeder and Matson, eds. and trans., *Colony on the Move*, which contain's Matson's translation of Castaño's "Memoria," along with a valuable explication by Schroeder who asserts that Castaño "complied in almost every detail with the Laws of Settlement of 1573" (4), an argument that I do not find persuasive. Castaño's "Memoria" mentions carts (*carretas*) on many occasions (31).

83. See the "Sentence Imposed on Castaño de Sosa, March 5, 1593," in Hammond and Rey, eds. and trans., *Rediscovery of New Mexico*, 317–19. The Council of the Indies, responding to an appeal, found Castaño innocent, but only after his death in the Philippines (ibid., 48). For Morlete's office, see Cutter, *Protector de Indios*, 28.

84. Luis de Velasco to Morlete, Mexico City, Oct. 1, 1590, in Hammond and Rey, eds. and trans., *Rediscovery of New Mexico*, 298–99. Hammond and Rey emphasize royal concern for the Indians' welfare as the motive for going to considerable lengths to apprehend Castaño (ibid., 48), but desire to protect the king's economic interests in New Mexico may have been equally important: "Thus we prevented the growth of obstacles to the exploration and pacification of New Mexico which might have resulted from his continued presence" (Viceroy Velasco's letter to Felipe II, Oct. 4, 1593, ibid., 319).

85. See, e.g., Hammond and Rey, eds. and trans., *Rediscovery of New Mexico*, 204, 271–75.

86. Gaspar de Zúñiga y Acevedo, conde de Monterrey, "Discussion and Proposal [1602]," in Hammond and Rey, eds. and trans., *Don Juan de Oñate*, 2:920.

87. Little is known of Oñate's early life. These biographical details come from Hammond, *Don Juan de Oñate and the Founding of New Mexico*, 13–18, which remained the standard biography until the appearance of Simmons's engaging *Last Conquistador*. Rumors that Oñate had squandered his fortune came to official attention from time to time, apparently spread by his enemies—see *Last Conquistador*, 33, 39. For Oñate's family background, see Chipman, "Oñate-Moctezuma-Zaldívar Families," 297–310.

88. Hammond, "Oñate's Effort," 321–30. For the amount Oñate claimed to spend in New Mexico, see his petition of 1617 in Hammond and Rey, eds. and trans., *Don Juan de Oñate*, 2:1125.

89. Felipe II to the viceroy of New Spain, Valencia, Jan. 26, 1586, in Hammond and Rey, eds. and trans., *Don Juan de Oñate*, 1:61. The king's treasury was, however, depleted by at least 115,906 pesos on Oñate's New Mexico venture and its aftermath, 1596–1609, not counting expenditures beginning with Governor Peralta. Nearly half that sum constituted direct support of the Franciscans (61,724 pesos). See Scholes, "Royal Treasury Records," 8–13, 16, 139–41, whose work on this question supersedes Bloom, "Spain's Investment in New Mexico," 11–12.

90. See the "Ordenanzas . . . para los nuevos descubrimientos, conquistas y pacificaciones," July 1573, in *CDI*(1), 16:150–51.

91. Estimates of the size of the initial colonizing party remain vague. Jones, *Los Paisanos*, 119, supposed 600 to 700. Capt. Luis de Velasco to the viceroy, Mar. 22, 1601, in Hammond and Rey, eds. and trans., *Don Juan de Oñate*, 2:608, mentions over 500 people in the initial years (before reinforcements arrived at the end of 1600). Although he sailed from Cádiz with more,

Menéndez landed at St. Augustine with some 800 men (Lyon, *Enterprise of Florida*, 114).

92. Juan de Oñate to the king, Apr. 7, 1599, in Hammond and Rey, eds. and trans., *Don Juan de Oñate*, 1:492.

93. For Espejo's view on supplying New Mexico by sea, see Mathes, *Vizcaíno*, 13.

94. Gonzalo Méndez de Canzo to Felipe III, St. Augustine, Feb. 3, 1600, in Quinn, ed., *New American World*, 5:97.

95. Velasco to the king, May 26, 1592, in Hammond and Rey, eds. and trans., *Rediscovery of New Mexico*, 314.

96. "Expedition to the North," Dec. 14, 1601, in Hammond and Rey, eds. and trans., *Don Juan de Oñate*, 2:746–60. The quote is on 758. See, too, Viceroy Velasco's instructions to Oñate, Oct. 21, 1595, ibid., 1:67. Oñate's exact route and destination have eluded a number of scholars. Susan C. Vehik has sifted through the arguments, correlated documentary and archaeological evidence, and posted several alternatives: "Oñate's Expedition to the Southern Plains," 13–33. For the carts, see also Brandon, *Quivira* 59–66.

97. For the quote in Spanish, and a photograph of the original inscription, see Slater, *El Morro*, 7.

98. Oñate must have known of official interest in the Pacific coast for he competed with Sebastián Vizcaíno for recruits (see Viceroy Monterrey to the king, Mexico, Dec. 20, 1595 and Feb. 28, 1596, in Hammond and Rey, eds. and trans., *Don Juan de Oñate*, 1:73 and 83. A soldier with Oñate in 1604–1605 is said by a contemporary to have previously accompanied Vizcaíno to California (Zárate Salmerón, *Relaciones*, 68). The connection between Spanish efforts to establish a settlement in California and Oñate's interest in the Pacific is usually not made by scholars.

99. Spanish activities in the Pacific during these years has been studied extensively. The most recent scholarly overview is Holmes, *From New Spain*, which contains references to earlier works. See, too, Kelsey, "Finding the Way Home," 145–64, and Kelsey, "Did Francis Drake Really Visit California?" 445–62, who notes the lack of conclusive evidence that Drake reached today's California. For Spanish fear that Drake had found the Strait of Anián, see Mathes, "Apochryphal Tales," 54.

100. The standard biography and assessment of the voyage is Mathes, *Vizcaíno*. Earlier writers have taken a dim view of Vizcaíno's accomplishments and motives, accusing him of egotistically disregarding Cabrillo's earlier work. Mathes effectively refutes these arguments (see, esp. 105 *n.* 58, and 166–70), but hostility to Vizcaíno remains imbedded in the literature. See, e.g., Spate, *Spanish Lake*, 112–15, who writes in ignorance of Mathes's book. A number of Vizcaíno letters are translated in Cutter, ed., *California Coast*.

101. Mathes, "Sebastián Vizcaíno," 5–6; Mathes, *Vizcaíno*, 170.

102. Oñate to the viceroy, San Bartolomé, Aug. 7, 1605, in Hammond and Rey, eds. and trans., *Don Juan de Oñate*, 2:1007.

103. Montesclaros to the king, Mexico, Oct. 28, 1605, ibid., 2:1010.

104. Oñate to the viceroy, San Bartolomé, Aug. 7, 1605, ibid., 2:1007.

105. Escobar's Report (mistitled a "diary,"), ibid., 2:1025 (see, too, 1029 for Escobar presenting this report to the viceroy).

106. Oct. 28, 1605, Mexico City, ibid., 2:1009.

107. Oñate to the viceroy, Mar. 2, 1599 (reporting on events of the previous year), ibid., 1:481.

108. See, e.g., Captain Velasco to the viceroy, Mar. 22, 1601, and the sworn testimony of several friars and officers, ibid., 2:609–10, 672–89. These sources do not specify the exact months in which these crimes against Indians occurred, but it seems safe to identify them with the first winter and the years that followed. See also n. 109.

109. Spaniards' ill treatment of Indians and their demands for food and blankets seem to have provoked the violence. See the documents relating to the trial of Indian prisoners, particularly the testimony of six Acomas, ibid., 1:464–67. Their testimony was, of course, self-serving but seems consistent with reports of similar abuses of Indians at other pueblos in the months and years that followed.

110. Quoted in Minge, *Acoma*, 4. For the challenge to Acoma, see Hodge, ed., *History of New Mexico by Gaspar Pérez de Villagrá*, 209.

111. Papers pertaining to the trial in Hammond and Rey, eds. and trans., *Don Juan de Oñate*, 1:428–79; the quote is on 477. For the number of deaths at Acoma, and Oñate's desire to make examples of the Acomas, see Forbes, *Apache, Navaho, and Spaniard*, 89–90. For the appearance of St. James, see Hodge, ed., *History of New Mexico by Gaspar Pérez de Villagrá*, 264–65, and Cutter, "With a Little Help from Their Saints," 127. For butchery as punishment in Spain see, e.g., Marvin Lunenfeld, *The Council of the Santa Hermandad: A Study of the Pacification Forces of Ferdinand and Isabella* (Coral Gables: University of Miami Press, 1970), 94–95. For the rebuilding of Acoma see Robinson, "Tree-Ring Studies," 99–106.

112. The quotes appear in Bernard W. Sheehan, *Savagism and Civility: Indians and Englishmen in Colonial Virginia* (Cambridge: Cambridge University Press, 1980), 168–69.

113. Oñate reached Quivira, but the native settlements that he described as Quivira were probably not the same as Coronado's. Schroeder, "Routes of Coronado and Oñate," 2–23, places Oñate's Quivira near present-day Ponca, Oklahoma.

114. Hammond and Rey, "Crown's Participation in the Founding of New Mexico," 293–309.

115. Montesclaros to the king, Mar. 31, 1605, in Hammond and Rey, eds. and trans., *Don Juan de Oñate*, 2:1002. See, too, Montesclaros to the king, Oct. 28, 1605, ibid., 1009-ll.

116. See Oñate's conviction, May 14, 1614, ibid., 2:1109–13.

117. Simmons, *Last Conquistador*, 188. Simmons finds no evidence to support the story that Apaches killed Oñate's son. See also Bloom, "Oñate's Exoneration," 175–92, which includes a letter from Oñate to the king, ca. Dec. 1623, and notes his considerable wealth. Oñate's last years in Spain have been further illuminated by the careful sleuthing of Beerman, "Death of An Old Conquistador," 305–19. For Menéndez, see Lyon, *Enterprise of Florida*, 192.

118. Gov. Pedro de Ibarra's instructions to Francisco Fernández de Ecija, St. Augustine, June 19, 1609, in Hann, "Translation of the Ecija Voyages," 22.

119. This became Spanish policy in 1612. See Wright, "Spanish Policy toward Virginia," 458. Wright, *Anglo-Spanish Rivalry*, 35–42, explains why Spain did not try to dislodge English colonists from Virginia. See, too, Quinn, ed., *New American World*, 5:56–68, 141–58, for more documents and Quinn's facile explanation that Spanish inaction toward Virginia resulted in part from "lethargy" (141).

120. Quinn, "Colonies in the Beginning," 10–34, concisely compares French, English, and Spanish interest in colonizing North America in the sixteenth century.

121. Bushnell, *King's Coffer*, 31–32.

122. Florida's shift from a proprietory to a Crown colony was gradual. See Lyon, "La visita de 1576," 197–210. For the anomalous situation of Florida under the Hapsburgs, when Florida was not part of any American administrative unit, see Bushnell, *King's Coffer*, 6–7.

123. Lyon, *Enterprise of Florida*, 183. See, too, Hoffman, "Study of Defense Costs," 401–22.

124. Sluiter, *Florida Situado*, argues that the situado arrived more regularly than previous writers have supposed. Bushnell, *King's Coffer*, 3–12, 63–74, provides a splendid explanation of the situado and its larger political, economic, and social context.

125. For the unhappy condition of the Florida settlers, see the depositions taken in 1573 by the Council of the Indies, in Connor, ed. and trans., *Colonial Records of Spanish Florida*, 1:81–101, and the pleas of various settlers to the king that they be granted permission to leave Florida, ibid., 1:131–85.

126. The investigation ordered in 1600 but conducted in 1602 is the subject of Arnade, *Florida on Trial*.

127. Fathers Pareja and Peñaranda to the king, St. Augustine, Nov. 29, 1607, quoted in Geiger, *Franciscan Conquest of Florida*, 212. See, too, 208–12. The question of the fate of baptized Indians also arose in the investigation of 1602 (Arnade, *Florida on Trial*, 71, 77).

128. See the king's notation at the end of Montesclaros to the king, Oct. 28, 1605, in Hammond and Rey, eds. and trans., *Don Juan de Oñate*, 2:1011. Several pieces of correspondence discuss the advisability of abandoning New Mexico, but the key documents are the recommendation of the Council of the Indies to the king, Madrid, July 2, 1608, and the king to Viceroy Luis de Velasco, Valladolid, Sept. 13, 1608, ibid., 2:1061–64, 1065–66.

129. Marqués de Montesclaros to the king, May 27, 1607, and Aug. 4, 1607, in Mathes, ed., *Californiana I*, 2:693–96, 703–5; Mathes, *Vizcaíno*, 108–20, 160–65; Spate, *Spanish Lake*, 115. See, too, Cutter, "Plans for the Occupation of Upper California," 78–90.

130. Matter, "Spanish Missions of Florida," 116, argues that from the death of Menéndez in 1574 until the British threatened Florida in the 1680s, "no significant development, except the growth of the Franciscan missions . . . occurred" (116) and that Florida was "a presidio surrounded by missions" (171–72). For a similar assessment of New Mexico, see Forbes, *Apache, Navaho, and Spaniard*, 175.

131. Chapter 99 of the Orders for New Discoveries of 1573 promised this title to those who established new settlements. Oñate's colonists became hidalgos in 1602 (Hammond and Rey, eds. and trans., *Don Juan de Oñate*, 2:974–75).

132. Murdo J. MacLeod, *Spanish Central America: A Socioeconomic History, 1520–1720* (Berkeley: University of California Press, 1973), 376, for example, notes an exodus from Guatemala when its mines played out.

133. Nicolás Sánchez Albornoz, "The Colonial Population of Latin America," in Bethell, ed., *Cambridge History of Latin America*, 2:16.

134. Quoted in Arnade, "Failure of Spanish Florida," 273. Census data is in Manucy, "Physical Setting of Sixteenth-Century St. Augustine," 46. For the number of men on the payroll, see Arnade, "Failure of Spanish Florida," 279.

135. Bushnell, *King's Coffer*, 3–4; Bushnell, "Noble and Loyal City," 44.

136. Corbett, "Population Structure in Hispanic St. Augustine," 267–68; Bushnell, "Noble and Loyal City," 51.

137. Jones, *Los Paisanos*, 111–12; Simmons, "Settlement Patterns," 101–3; and Simmons, *Last Conquistador*, 182–83, 200. For the beginnings of Santa Fe and El Paso see, too, Cruz, *Let There Be Towns*, 24–29, 36–41.

138. Oré, *Martyrs of Florida*, 43, ca. 1588. Contemporaries were well aware of the importance of intimidation. See, e.g., the

report of Pedro Menéndez Marqués to the Audiencia of Santo Domingo, St. Augustine, Apr. 2, 1579, in Connor, *Colonial Records of Spanish Florida*, 2:225, and Benavides, *Memorial . . . 1630*, 22.

Chapter 4: Conquistadores of the Spirit

The epigraphs are from Hammond and Rey, eds. and trans., *Obregón's History*, xxvii, and Hackett, ed., *Historical Documents*, 3:150–51.

1. The caravan departed on Sept. 4 and arrived in Santa Fe on the seventh Sunday after Easter (June 3), according to fray Estevan de Perea's, "True Report of the Great Conversion" (first published in 1632–33) in Bloom, ed. and trans., "Fray Estevan de Perea's *Relación*," 224–25. Thirty-one Franciscans left Mexico City (counting Perea), but one died on route and another four days after reaching Santa Fe (ibid.). On the long intervals between supply caravans, see Scholes, "Supply Service," 94–95.

2. Twenty friars were in New Mexico when the 1619 caravan arrived. By the end of the year, one had died and three had returned to Mexico, leaving a total of forty-six (Scholes and Bloom, "Friar Personnel," 70–71).

3. Franciscans who worked in Spanish North America were Observant Franciscans, of the Order of Friars Minor, as opposed to the Discalced, "barefoot" Franciscans, or to Capuchins or Conventuals, who also belong to the so-called First Order of St. Francis (Habig, "Franciscan Provinces," 89). In practice, Franciscans on the frontier often found it expedient to ride horses.

4. Bishop Juan de Zumárraga to his nephew, Aug. 23, 1539, speaking of Viceroy Mendoza's plans for the Coronado expedition, quoted in Rey, "Missionary Aspects," 23. Phelan, *Millennial Kingdom*, 29–38, is one of the finest accounts of early Franciscan activity written in English. The requirement that two priests accompany exploring

parties appeared in the Ordenanzas de Granada of Nov. 17, 1526, described in Gómez Canedo, *Evangelización*, 75–76. The New Laws of 1542 repeated that requirement. Dominicans had also accompanied early expeditions, such as those of Lucas Vázquez de Ayllón and Hernando de Soto (O'Daniel, *Dominicans*).

5. Gibson, ed., *Spanish Tradition*, 104–5. For an example of the ongoing expression of doubt about whether or not Indians had a soul, see Poole, "War by Fire and Blood," 126.

6. Gerónimo de Mendieta, quoted in Phelan, *Millennial Kingdom*, 69. See, too, Gibson, *Spain in America*, 68–74, and Parry, *Spanish Seaborne Empire*, 158–70, for good general discussions of Franciscan ideology and guides to the literature.

7. Phelan, *Millennial Kingdom*, 7–21.

8. Francisco Morales, "Los Franciscanos en la Nueva España. La época de oro, siglo xvi," in Morales, ed., *Franciscan Presence in the Americas* (Potomac, Md.: Academy of American Franciscan History, 1983), 77–80, explains the Crown's economic motives more clearly than have previous writers. In 1572 Felipe II appointed a secular cleric to the archbishopric of New Spain, a position that regular clergy had held to that time, and the new archbishop moved quickly to bring the nettlesome missionaries under control and secularize their missions. To hasten the process, the first Jesuits, a nonmendicant religious order, arrived in Mexico in 1572, charged with the responsibility of improving the quality of the secular clergy. See, too, Stafford Poole, *Pedro Moya de Contreras: Catholic Reform and Royal Power in New Spain, 1571–1591* (Berkeley: University of California Press, 1987), 66–87; 163–67, and John Frederick Schwaller, *The Church and Clergy in Sixteenth-Century Mexico* (Albuquerque: University of New Mexico, 1987), 81–109, on the important *Ordenanza del Patronazgo*.

9. Ricard, *Spiritual Conquest of Mexico*, 3, which remains the best single account in English of the mendicants' activities in central Mexico up to 1572. The process of secularization in the old Aztec realm was gradual and did not end until the nineteenth century. See Gibson, *Aztecs under Spanish Rule*, 110. For a more recent and succinct interpretive essay, see Liss, *Mexico under Spain*, 69–94.

10. "Ordenanzas de su Magestad hechas para los nuevos descubrimientos, conquistas y pacificaciones," July 13, 1573, in *CDI*(1), 16: 149–52; the quote is on 154. Much has been written about the evolution of this policy and the significance of these famous orders. For a discussion of their relationship to missionary endeavors, see Gómez Canedo, *Evangelización*, 74–82.

11. Gómez Canedo, *Evangelización*, 49–51, who explains this late sixteenth-century transition more clearly than other writers of whom I am aware, sees previous missionary efforts as located among Indians who had already been conquered. After 1573, he argues, missionaries would play the central role in conquest itself. A number of other writers see the mission as an institution that gained greater importance during the late 1500s. See, e.g., Bolton, "Mission as a Frontier Institution," 190–91, and Powell, *Soldiers, Indians, and Silver*, 188, 192–93, 208–9, 212. The view that the Orders of 1573 marked a radical change between an "encomienda-doctrina system" and a "new . . . mission system," as argued by Antonine S. Tibesar, "The Franciscan *doctrinero* versus the Francsican *misionero* in Seventeenth-Century Peru," *The Americas* 14 (Oct. 1957): 117, does not seem sustained by the evidence. The Orders of 1573 permitted granting of more *encomiendas* and the essential features of the mission, as described in Ricard's *Spiritual Conquest of Mexico*, were formed early in New Spain and transported to the frontier with little modification.

12. Liss, *Mexico under Spain*, 87, and Gibson, *Spain in America*, 80.

13. Dominicans unsuccessfully sought permission to extend their activities to New Mexico.

14. The number of "churches and monasteries [i.e., friaries]" is in Benavides, *Memorial . . . 1630*, 62, which contains a facsimile of the original edition of this memorial, published in Madrid in 1630 (164 of the Spanish facsimile corresponds to p. 62 of the translation). Earlier, Benavides also mentions the figure of fifty, but applies it just to churches (p. 33, corresponding to 121 of the Spanish facsimile). A more recent and smoother translation by Peter Forrestal, *Benavides' Memorial of 1630*, lacks the facsimile of the 1630 Spanish imprint. Riley, "Las Casas and the Benavides Memorial," 209–22, is essential to understanding the concluding sections of the *Memorial . . . 1630*. For women building walls, see Kubler, *Religious Architecture of New Mexico*, 7.

15. "The shape which all that which is settled has is that of a cross" (Fr. Juan de Pardo to the viceroy, Convento of San Francisco, Mexico, Sept. 26, 1638, in Hackett, ed., *Historical Documents*, 3:107). I have supposed the length of Pardo's imaginary cross to run east and west, but if one does not take the Hopi pueblos into account, fray Juan might have imagined the cross to have its base in the south.

16. The most detailed account of the first decades of missionary expansion among the Pueblos is Scholes and Bloom, "Friar Personnel," 319–36; 58–62.

17. Both quotes in this paragraph are from Bloom, ed. and trans., "Fray Estevan de Perea's *Relación*," 229–30, who provides a firsthand account of the expedition to Acoma, Zuni, and the Hopi country.

18. "Biography of Benavides," in Benavides, *Revised Memorial of 1634*, 1–17.

19. Benavides, *Memorial . . . 1630*, 34.

20. For the 500,000 figures, see Benavides,

Memorial . . . 1630, 62. One of Benavides's more statistically minded brethren tallied up the baptismal registers, probably in 1626, and found that the Franciscans had baptized 34,650 persons, presumably among the Pueblos alone (Zárate Salmerón, *Relaciones*, 53). On the method of baptism at this time, including the need for preliminary instruction, see Ricard, *Spiritual Conquest*, 83–95. For the English-Dutch threat, see Benavides, *Revised Memorial of 1634*, 167, 197–98.

21. Benavides, *Memorial . . . 1630*, 25. Fray Alonso describes the other miracles on 26–29.

22. Much has been written about the life of María de Jesús. The best critical biography is Kendrick, *Mary of Agreda*, which should also serve as a guide to other sources. Kendrick takes the position that the story of María reached New Mexico in 1629, with the supply caravan (31). That position has been more fully explicated by Donahue, "Mary of Agreda," 294–95, but evidence is circumstantial and depends chiefly on Benavides, *Revised Memorial of 1634*, rather than on other contemporary evidence.

23. Benavides, *Memorial . . . 1630*, 56–60, and Benavides, *Revised Memorial of 1634*, 92–96. In 1630, Benavides did not yet know the identity of the woman, dressed like a nun, who the Plains Indians said had preached to them.

24. María de Agreda to the friars of New Mexico, May 15, 1631, in Benavides, *Revised Memorial of 1634*, appendix 11, 140.

25. Benavides, *Revised Memorial of 1634*, 35 (also 99). Compare these passages to Benavides, *Memorial . . . 1630*, 62. With this firm evidence that God smiled on the Franciscans' work in New Mexico, Benavides traveled on to Rome. He revised and expanded his 1630 treatise on New Mexico, painting an even rosier picture. Instead of claiming 500,000 *potential* converts, for example, as he had done in 1630, Benavides now boasted that this number of "barbarous Indians have been converted to our holy Catholic faith." Benavides directed his revised treatise to Pope Urban VIII, whom he hoped to persuade to grant favors that would advance the missionary enterprise in New Mexico, elevate the province to the rank of a bishopric, and put Benavides in the new post (instead, Benavides received a bishopric for himself in Goa, Portuguese India).

26. María de Jesús to fray Pedro Manero, quoted in Kendrick, *Mary of Agreda*, 43–44, who also noted that her spiritual journeys were limited to the years 1620–23. See, too, Kendrick's analysis (35–40), who dismisses María's 1631 statement, which she was forced to sign "under obedience" (38), as "preposterous nonsense." María's repudiation of much of what Benavides reported that she said has gone unnoticed by most other writers.

27. Donahue, "Mary of Agreda," 309–13, and Kendrick, *Mary of Agreda*, 46–55.

28. See Wagner, *Spanish Southwest*, 2:342–56.

29. Donahue, "Mary of Agreda," 313–14.

30. Kendrick, *Mary of Agreda*, 19, mentions her early fasting and visions. See Rudolph M. Bell, *Holy Anorexia* (Chicago: University of Chicago Press, 1985), and Caroline Walker Bynum, *Holy Feast and Holy Fast: The Religious Significance of Food to Medieval Women* (Berkeley: University of California Press, 1987), which raises subtle questions about the relationship between anorexia and saintly behavior.

31. Bloom, ed. and trans., "Fray Estevan de Perea's *Relación*," 223, 230; Timmons, *El Paso*, 15–16; Spicer, *Cycles of Conquest*, 158, 162. Franciscan historians regard the period 1625–40 as the "golden age" of the New Mexico missions (Espinosa, "Our Debt," 84). See, too, Lynch, "Introduction" to *Benavides' Memorial of 1630*, xx, who uses the term *golden age* for New Mexico in Benavides's time. Scholes, *Troublous Times*, 195, noted that "From 1632 on, there was a definitive slowing down of the mission program."

32. For examples of padres' descriptions of

magical events, see Oré, *Martyrs of Florida*, 102–3, 113–14, 115, and Covington, ed., *Pirates, Indians and Spaniards*, 130–31. The episode of the bluish light is in Bushnell, "Archaeology of Mission Santa Catalina."

33. Geiger, *Franciscan Conquest of Florida*, 32–33.

34. Zubillaga, *La Florida*, 388–90, gives Indians substantial credit for the Jesuit withdrawal.

35. Matter, "Spanish Missions of Florida," 106, 117, 122, 345 *n.* 47, has made the most careful study of the statistics for these years yet finds them "confusing and incomplete." Most writers see 1675 as the high point of missionary activity in Florida (ibid., 340–41 *n.* 6); Gannon, *Cross in the Sand*, 57, 66–67.

36. Wenhold, ed. and trans., *Letter of Gabriel Díaz*, contains a facsimile of the bishop's letter of 1675 to Queen Mariana, which is the source of much of the following description. Florida and New Mexico lacked resident bishops; none visited New Mexico until 1760; two bishops inspected Florida in the 1600s, the first in 1606.

37. On Muskhogean and the bewildering changes of nomenclature and ethnicity among Southeastern Indians, see Wright, *Creeks and Seminoles*. For the identity of Timucuan languages, see Milanich, "Western Timucua," 61–62.

38. Milanich and Fairbanks, *Florida Archaeology*, 216–30, provides an authoritative overview.

39. Scholars once doubted that Indians in Guale dwelled in villages or engaged in significant agriculture, but current archaeological work has tended to place the Guale in the larger traditions that I describe, although the extent of their sedentism remains uncertain. See Jones, "Ethnohistory of the Guale Coast," 178–210. For recent archaeological advances in understanding what he terms "The Guale Problem," see Thomas, "Archaeology of Mission Santa Catalina de Guale," 57–64.

40. Matter, "Spanish Missions of Florida,"

108. Guale was the last province on the bishop's itinerary. To facilitate the reader's understanding of the chronological development of the missons, I have placed it first.

41. Survey of Guale by Pedro de Arcos, in Boyd, trans. and ed., "Enumeration of Florida Spanish Missions," 182–84, which provide more specific population figures than did the bishop. Not all natives counted by Arcos were mission Indians. In several villages he distinguishes between "men, women and children and pagans."

42. For the apparent tranquility of the Guale missions at this time, and their language differences, see Pearson, "Arguelles Inspection of Guale," 210–22. Lanning, *Spanish Missions of Georgia*, remains the standard account of the Georgia missions, but the subject merits a fresh study that will incorporate recent historical and archaeological research and move beyond Lanning's pro-Franciscan interpretation.

43. Prieto's own account of these years is in Oré, *Martyrs of Florida*, 112–19. For the larger context, see Geiger, *Franciscan Conquest of Florida*, 227–29. Little is known about Prieto, and biographical information regarding the padres who served in early Florida is scanty. Compare, e.g., the brief entries in Geiger, *Biographical Dictionary*, with the relatively full entries in Geiger's *Franciscan Missionaries*.

44. Survey of the missions of Apalachee and Timucua by Juan Fernández de Florencia, in Boyd, trans. and ed., "Enumeration of Florida Spanish Missions," 186–88.

45. Hann, *Apalachee*, 185 *n.* 6, 401–2.

46. The Díaz league was 2.6 miles (Matter, "Spanish Missions of Florida," 348 *n.* 65). By what may be a more direct route, the distance today from St. Augustine to Tallahassee is 205 miles.

47. Prieto in Oré, *Martyrs of Florida*, 118; Geiger, *Franciscan Conquest of Florida*, 229–30. The most authoritative account of the establishment of the Apalachee missions is Hann, *Apalachee*, 5–23.

48. Survey of the missions of Apalachee and Timucua by Juan Fernández de Florencia, in Boyd, trans. and ed., "Enumeration of Florida Spanish Missions," 184–86, suggests over eight thousand, but as Fernández noted, "I have not taken a census and they die daily, for which reason I have said a little more or less" (188). The figure may be much higher. Bushnell, " 'That Demonic Game,' " 4, suggests ten thousand.

49. San Luis de Talimali, 2.5 miles west of the State Capitol, is presently under excavation by the Florida Bureau of Archaeological Research and is open to the public. The diameter of the council house is 36 meters (Shapiro and Hann, "Documentary Image of the Council Houses," 519), while mission chapels did not exceed 26 by 13 meters (Jones and Shapiro, "Nine Mission Sites," 504, and Saunders," Ideal and Innovation," 527–42). For San Marcos, see Bushnell, "How to Fight a Pirate."

50. For the most up-to-date account of the founding and demise of these Apalachicola missions, see Hann, Apalachee, 47–50, 183–84.

51. Matter, "Spanish Missions of Florida," 110–11, 116; Matter, "Missions in the Defense of Spanish Florida," 32. Sturtevant, "Last of the South Florida Aborigines," 141–62, recounts a Jesuit attempt to build a mission at present Miami in 1743.

52. Since children did not usually receive this sacrament, the mission population of Florida may have exceeded this number. On the other hand, a rough estimate of the population of three main mission provinces (excluding Apalachicola), authorized by Gov. Pablo de Hita Salazar in 1675, suggested fewer Christian Indians—somewhat more than 10,000 (Boyd, trans. and ed., "Enumeration of Florida Spanish Missions," 182). Disparities between the statistics developed by Franciscans and civil officials were not unusual.

53. Both quotes are in Wenhold, ed. and trans., Letter of Gabriel Díaz, 12.

54. See, e.g., Spicer, Cycles of Conquest, 167, who compares the rapid imposition of the mission program on the Pueblos with the more gradual missionization in northwestern Mexico. The Crown apparently authorized as many as seventy friars for Florida, but the actual number usually stayed below fifty (Matter, "Spanish Missions of Florida," 417–18). In New Mexico, sixty-six was apparently the highest number authorized in the 1600s, a number seldom reached (Scholes, Troublous Times, 9).

55. For the Provinces of Florida, reports of Indians adopting the outward manifestations of Christianity come from several sources, including Bishop Díaz, who was no friend of the Franciscans (Wenhold, ed. and trans., Letter of Gabriel Díaz, 14). See, too, the account of Francisco Pareja, ca. 1616, in Oré, Martyrs of Florida, 126–29. Barth, Franciscan Education, 135–57, sees a shift away from compulsory reading and writing toward more vocational education in eighteenth-century Texas and California. For prayer and literacy in Spain, see Bennassar, Spanish Character, 73.

56. Benavides, Memorial . . . 1630, 19.

57. Barth, Franciscan Education, 339. For the sixteenth-century development of the idea of a hierarchical classification of mankind see John Rowe, "Ethnography and Ethnology in the Sixteenth Century," Kroeber Anthropology Society Papers 30 (1964): 1–19; Elliott, "Discovery of America," 53.

58. "Ordenanzas . . . para los nuevos descubrimientos, conquistas y pacificaciones," July 13, 1573, in CDI(1), 16:183. The "civilizing function of typical Spanish mission" is a central theme in the seminal essay by Bolton, "Mission as a Frontier Institution," 206. Ricard, Spiritual Conquest of Mexico, 290, writing of the first decades of missionization in Mexico, notes that Franciscans "would not countenance any attempt to Hispanize or Europeanize the natives," but he means this in a very restricted way. The Crown and the Fran-

ciscans had a different agenda by the late sixteenth century.

59. Schroeder, "Rio Grande Ethnohistory," 50; Kubler, *Religious Architecture of New Mexico,* 8; Milanich and Fairbanks, *Florida Archaeology,* 226; Hann, *Apalachee,* 239, 241–42. It is easy to overstate the extent of Franciscan instruction. Some writers, for example, have incorrectly credited friars with teaching Pueblos to make fireplaces, beehive ovens, and sun-dried adobe bricks; for a corrective, see Dozier, *Pueblo Indians,* 65.

60. Wenhold, ed. and trans., *Letter of Gabriel Díaz,* 12. See, too, Benavides, *Memorial . . . 1630,* 20, 21, 22, 23. An Englishman whose ship was wrecked on the Florida coast described Indians at the mission of Santa Catalina on Amelia Island in 1696 wearing "gowns and petticoats" of Spanish moss, "which at a distance or in the night look very neat" (Andrews and Andrews, *Jonathan Dickinson's Journal,* 67). For the shortage of cotton and cotton cloth, see Hann, ed. and trans., "Alonso de Leturiondo's Memorial," 178.

61. Matter, "Spanish Missions of Florida," 129, quoting a manuscript "Testimony and complaints by the provincial and definitors to the Governor of Florida," May-June, 1681. See, too, Oré, *Martyrs of Florida,* 130–31, and Benavides, *Memorial . . . 1630,* 66. Examples of Franciscan sacrifice abound; see the description of fray Blas de Montes in Oré, *Martyrs of Florida,* 66. For the decline in the vigor of the Church and the clergy, see Bennassar, *Spanish Character,* 80–85. That decline apparently contributed to the Franciscans' failure to fill the quota of seventy that the king provided for in Florida and was perhaps reflected, too, in a decline in the quality of Franciscans in Florida, as suggested by Matter, "Spanish Missions of Florida," 108–9, 86.

62. Juan de las Cabezas, Bishop of Cuba, to the king, St. Augustine, Florida, June 24, 1606, in Cabezas, "First Episcopal Visitation,"

457, who also alluded to scandalous conduct of some Franciscans.

63. Covington, ed., *Pirates, Indians and Spaniards,* 126.

64. "Ordenanzas . . . para los nuevos descubrimientos, conquistas y pacificaciones," July 1573, in *CDI*(1), 16:182–85, 186. For methods used by mendicants in New Spain in the first half century of missionization, see Ricard, *Spiritual Conquest,* 167–68, 176–93, and a Franciscan historian who draws many examples from New Spain, Gómez Canedo, *Evangelización,* 147–214: "Métodos y Medios de Evangelización." Borges, *Métodos misionales,* examined the methods of all religious orders in the sixteenth century. Notwithstanding the broad scope suggested by its title, Barth, another Franciscan historian, focuses largely on sixteenth-century New Spain in his *Franciscan Education.* The methods of converting Indians and maintaining them in missions that I describe here for Florida and New Mexico continued to be used in Alta California in the late eighteenth and early nineteenth centuries. See McGarry, "Educational Methods," 335–58. See, too, Polzer, *Rules and Precepts,* 39–58, who describes Jesuit methods, with some attention to Franciscans. The general strategy that he describes seems applicable to both orders. Spicer, *Cycles of Conquest,* 281–83, 288–98, 324–31, offers an interesting overview of missionary methods, contrasting the work of Jesuits in Pimería Alta and Franciscans in New Mexico, but it should be remembered that Jesuits began mission building in that area a century later than the Franciscans. Dominicans followed similar procedures. See, too, Felix M. Kesing, *The Ethnohistory of Northern Luzon* (Stanford: Stanford University Press, 1962), 224–26, 242–60.

65. The first quote is from Dominican Gregorio Beteta, 1549, who accompanied Luis Cáncer to Florida, quoted in Quinn, ed., *New American World,* 2:192; the second from *Testimonio* of fray Salvador de Guerra,

Jan. 23, 1668, in Scholes, ed. and trans., "Documents for the History of the New Mexican Missions," 199–200. Examples of gifts come from those distributed to the Hopis in 1629, Bloom, ed. and trans., "Fray Estevan de Perea's *Relación*," 232, and from Wenhold, ed. and trans., *Letter of Gabriel Díaz*, 13. Beginning in the late 1700s, Franciscans in California took pains not to baptize more Indians than they could feed. See Coombs and Plog, "Conversion of the Chumash Indians," 309–28.

66. Gutiérrez, *When Jesus Came*, 9; MacLachlin, *Spain's Empire*, 23.

67. To avoid confusion for the modern reader, I have generally used the familiar term *mission* as a synonym for *doctrina*. In seventeenth-century Florida and New Mexico, the terms had different meanings. A *misión* represented the initial stage of evangelizing; a *doctrina* represented an established Indian parish, including both *cabecera* and *visita* and presided over by a Franciscan *doctrinero*. Polzer, *Rules and Precepts*, 4–5, 47, identifies three stages of a mission's development: *entrada*, *conversión*, and *doctrina*, culminating with a secular phase—the *parroquia* or parish. The terminology employed by contemporaries, however, changed over time. In the eighteenth century, missionaries avoided the term *doctrina*, for once a mission became classified as a doctrina, or an Indian parish, it had taken the first step toward secularization (wherein Indians were no longer exempt from paying tithes and would be brought under episcopal control). See, e.g., Guest, *Fermín Francisco de Lasuén*, 141–42. By the eighteenth century, fray Diego Bringas noted, a misión and a conversión had become "essentially the same institution" (Matson and Fontana, eds. and trans., *Friar Bringas*, 47, 43). Bringas also objected vigorously to reclassifying the Pimería Alta missions as doctrinas.

68. Bushnell,   "Sacramental   Imperative,"

475–90; Elliott, "Discovery of America," 54–55.

69. Gannon, *Cross in the Sand*, 34–35; Zubillaga, *La Florida*, 378–80, and Oré, *Martyrs of Florida*, 119. Hann, "Demographic Patterns," 371, finds no evidence that friars used reducciones in Florida. Some entire towns, however, were moved to bring Indians nearer to the *camino real* (Spellman [pseud., Gannon], " 'Golden Age' of the Florida Missions," 365). In New Mexico, Governor Peralta arrived with instructions in 1609 to concentrate Pueblos into fewer and larger villages, but this seems to have occurred only at Jémez (Scholes, *Church and State*, 20–21). Kubler, *Religious Architecture of New Mexico*, 16–17, is insightful on this point. In New Mexico, Franciscans tried but generally failed to missionize nomads in the seventeenth century (Gómez Canedo, *Evangelización*, 107–12).

70. *Testimonio* of fray Salvador de Guerra, Jan. 23, 1668, in Scholes, ed. and trans., "Documents for the History of the New Mexican Missions," 198–99. See, too, the inventory of goods that the mission supply caravan brought to New Mexico in 1629, described in Bloom [ed. and trans.], "Fray Estevan Perea's *Relación*," 219–20.

71. Bushnell, "Ruling 'the Republic of Indians,' " 142. For the 1681 inventory and an analysis of it, see Hann, "Church Furnishings," 147–64, and Hann, *Apalachee*, 213–16, who takes exception to Bushnell's calculations. Although one might quibble over the arithmetic, her point, I believe is valid.

72. Gómez Canedo, *Evangelización*, 86–89; Bushnell, "Ruling 'the Republic of Indians,' " 139. For the use of women caciques, see Deagan, "Spanish-Indian Interaction," 299. Dozier, *Pueblo Indians*, 68, notes that the Pueblos established a "dual system of government," wherein "a set of secular officers served as a convenient facade behind which the more important and vital organization of native priests carried out the so-

cial and religious functions of the pueblo." Similarly in Florida, Hann, *Apalachee*, 101 n. 2, cites anthropologist Gary Shapiro's suggestion that the persons Spaniards believed were in charge were simply ambitious persons posing as leaders in order to advance their own interests. See, too, ibid., 110–12.

73. Oré, *Martyrs of Florida*, 106.

74. Richard C. Trexler, "From the Mouths of Babes: Christianization by Children in 16th Century New Spain," *Relgious Organization and Religious Experience*, J. Davis, ed. (New York: Academic Press, 1982), 115–35, and for New Mexico, see Gutiérrez, *When Jesus Came*, 74–84. For Florida, see Pedro Menéndez Márques to the Audiencia of Santo Domingo, St. Augustine, Apr. 2, 1579, in Connor, ed., *Colonial Records of Spanish Florida*, 2:227.

75. See, e.g., the law of Mar. 8, 1603, in the *Recopilación de leyes*, tomo I, lib. I, tit. XV, ley v, which makes it obligatory for doctrineros to learn Indian languages. See, too, Bolton, "Mission as a Frontier Institution," 203–4, and Schuetz, "Indians of the San Antonio Missions," 234.

76. Milanich and Sturtevant, eds., *Pareja's 1613 Confessionario*, 15. The editors make it clear that Pareja was not the only Franciscan in Florida to record texts in Timucuan, and the work of at least one other padre has survived (7–8). By 1572 Franciscans in New Spain had prepared at least eighty literary works in native languages—catechisms, grammars, dictionaries (usually copied by hand rather than printed) (Ricard, *Spiritual Conquest of Mexico*, 48). For Timucuan, see Milanich, "Western Timucua," 61–62.

77. Milanich and Sturtevant, eds., *Pareja's 1613 Confessionario*, 36, 38.

78. For Texas, see García, *Manual para administrar los santos sacramentos*, a Castilian-Coauiltecan manual. For California, see Kelsey, ed. and trans., *Doctrina and Confesionario of Juan Cortés*, who cites four other

bilingual manuscripts for California (3–4). No bilingual aid to instructing California natives appears to have been published at the time, but manuscript booklets such as that of Father Cortés (1798) probably existed at every mission, Kelsey believes. Among lists of extant books from New Mexico missions, no volume in a Pueblo language is cited. See, e.g., Adams and Scholes, "Books in New Mexico, 1598–1680," 226–70. Contemporaries in New Mexico, including one Franciscan, noted that written grammars did not exist for any of the languages of New Mexico. See the Testimony of fray Nicolás de Freitas, Feb. 21, 1661 [Mexico], and the Report of the Rev. Father Provincial of Santo Evangelio to the viceroy, Convent of San Francisco, March 1750, in Hackett, ed., *Historical Documents*, 3:136, 442, 445. The exception may be fray Gerónimo Zárate Salmerón. See Simmons, *Authors and Books*, 24.

79. This was apparently Pareja's *Catecismo, en Lengua Castellana, y Timuquana*. See the first hearing of Nicolás Aguilar, Mexico, Apr. 12, 1663, in Hackett, ed., *Historical Documents*, 3:139.

80. Borges, *Métodos misionales*, 544–50; Hann, *Apalachee*, 251; Gómez Canedo, *Evangelización*, 154–62. Although the supply of Franciscans with talent and energy to learn native languages never reached the demand, it is clearly an exaggeration to suppose (as did Bowden, *American Indians and Christian Missions*, 45, 51) that Spanish Franciscans had ceased to learn native languages by the time they reached the area of present-day North America. See, for example, Zárate Salmerón, *Relaciones*, 26; Hackett, ed., *Historical Documents*, 3:163; Kelly, *Franciscan Missions of New Mexico*, 63–64. But Franciscans in New Mexico acquired a reputation, perhaps unfairly, for reticence to learn Pueblo languages. See Adams, ed. and trans., *Bishop Tamarón's Visitation*, 18, 31, 78, who was unfriendly to Franciscans. For a fascinating look at the

failure of cross-cultural communication, see Vincente L. Rafael, *Contracting Colonialism: Translation and Christian Conversion in Tagalog Society under Early Spanish Rule* (Ithaca: Cornell University Press, 1988).

81. The quote is from Vélez de Escalante, "Letter to the Missionaries of New Mexico," 323. See also Adams, "Passive Resistance," 77–91. For the use of translators: Bloom ed. and trans., "Fray Estevan de Perea's *Relación*," 235; Hann, *Apalachee*, 107–8, 112.

82. Viceroy Martin López de Guana, Mar. 30, 1609, to Pedro de Peralta, in Bloom and Chaves, ed. and trans., "Ynstruccion a Peralta por Vi-Rey," 184 (the translation is defective at this place).

83. Hann, *Apalachee*, 250. Spicer, *Cycles of Conquest*, 425–27, takes a more negative view of the Pueblos' acquisition of Spanish than does Dozier, *Pueblo Indians*, 69. I have based my conclusion on Dozier and on the pueblo-by-pueblo survey reported in Adams and Chávez, eds. and trans., *Missions of New Mexico*, 51, 19, 71, 90, 98, 112 ff. For critical views of the Franciscans' efforts see, e.g., Adams, ed. and trans., *Bishop Tamarón's Visitation*, 79, and the Report of the Rev. Father Provincial of the Province of El Santo Evangelio to the viceroy, Convent of San Francisco, Mar. 1750, in Hackett, ed., *Historical Documents*, 3:439. See, too, Kelly, *Franciscan Missions of New Mexico*, 63–64. A few Pueblos, such as the mixed-blood governor of the Pueblo of Santa Ana, Bartolomé de Ojeda, wrote Spanish well. See Espinosa, ed. and trans., *Pueblo Indian Revolt*, 240–41.

84. Pius V to Menéndez, 1569, quoted in Gannon, *Cross in the Sand*, 34–35.

85. Quoted by fray Francisco de Zamora in Hammond and Rey, eds. and trans., *Don Juan de Oñate*, 2:675. See this and the testimony taken under oath at the meeting of Sept. 7, 1601, ibid., 672–89.

86. See, e.g., Geiger, ed. and trans., *Letter of Luís Jayme*, 42.

87. "Republic" had not yet taken on its present meaning of a state in which power is vested in the people but referred rather to a community of people with a common interest. For background on this, see Gómez Canedo, *Evangelización*, 140–43; Ricard, *Spiritual Conquest*, 153, 290; Bushnell, "Ruling 'the Republic of Indians,'" 138. The idea of separate republics broke down in the eighteenth century. See, especially, Guest, "Mission Colonization and Political Control," 97–116.

88. There are numerous examples of encroachment in New Mexico. See Jenkins, "Spanish Colonial Policy," 203. For the abundance of land in Florida, see Bushnell, "Ruling 'the Republic of Indians,'" 141.

89. MacLachlin, *Spain's Empire*, 30.

90. See the remarkably detailed list in the contract between the Crown and the Franciscans of 1631, translated in Scholes, "Supply Service," 100–105. For the wagons themselves, see Moorhead, *New Mexico's Royal Road*, 33. For the Florida missions, supplied more frequently than those of isolated New Mexico, see Bushnell, "Archaeology of Mission Santa Catalina de Guale."

91. Damián de Vega Castro y Pardo, St. Augustine, July 9, 1643, in Arnade, ed. and trans., "Florida in 1643," 175.

92. Bloom, "Spain's Investment in New Mexico," 13, whose estimate covers the period 1596–1697. With more documents available to him than were available to Bloom, Scholes calculated a deficit to the Crown of 1,759,268 pesos over a different time span (1586–1683) and estimated that 70 percent of that sum went to support the missionaries ("Royal Treasury Records," 159–60). These figures are meant to be suggestive, since Scholes and Bloom based their calculations on incomplete documentation. Sluiter, *Florida Situado*,

has made the fullest study of the Florida subsidy. He calculates 662,130 pesos for the decade 1611–1620, and 720,771 for the decade 1621–30 (6–9). According to Bloom's figures, the royal subsidy to New Mexico averaged 239,000 pesos per decade.

93. Benavides, *Memorial . . . 1630*, 68.

94. Bolton, "Mission as a Frontier Institution," 200.

95. This had been the case since the Chichimeca Wars in northern New Spain in the last half of the sixteenth century, if not before. Powell, *Soldiers, Indians, and Silver*, 211, notes that in the late 1500s, funds to support Jesuits and Franciscans on the Chichimeca frontier came from the royal treasury and were labeled "gastos de la paz de chichimecas."

96. Francisco Pareja, ca. 1616, quoted in Oré, *Martyrs of Florida*, 107; Matter, "Missions in the Defense of Spanish Florida," 27–29; Sluiter, *Florida Situado*, 6, 17–18.

97. Bolton, "Mission as a Frontier Institution," 194–99.

98. For Cáncer see O'Daniel, *Dominicans*. Vigil, "Bartolomé de las Casas," 45–57, describes a plan of 1558 for the nonmilitary pacification by Franciscans of the area from Florida to New Mexico. For the question of dependence upon soldiers, see especially Gómez Canedo, *Evangelización*, xvi–xvii, 82–86; Bolton, "Mission as a Frontier Institution," 201–2, and Guest, "An Examination of the Thesis of S. F. Cook," 57–59.

99. Bloom, ed. and trans., "Fray Estevan de Perea's Relación," 228. See, too, fray Isidro Félix de Espinosa, quoted in Gómez Canedo, *Evangelización*, 86.

100. For an extended and somewhat apologetic discussion of these questions in one borderland area, see Guest, "Examination of the Thesis of S. F. Cook," 1–77. Although the missions of Alta California were not established until the late eigh-

teenth century, Guest looks at sixteenth- and seventeenth-century antecedents, especially in Appendix II. See, too, Phelan, *Millennial Kingdom*, 9–10, and Sabine MacCormack, " 'The Heart Has Its Reasons': Predicaments of Missionary Christianity in Early Colonial Peru," *HAHR* 65 (Aug. 1985): 443–66, with its fine discussion of the theological questions surrounding the Christian tension between authority and reason.

101. Wenhold, ed. and trans., *Letter of Gabriel Díaz*, 14.

102. Unnamed Franciscan testimony of 1681, quoted in Matter, "Spanish Missions of Florida," 354 n. 9. See, too, ibid., 278–79.

103. Much has been written on this subject. See, e.g., Gómez Canedo, *Evangelización*, 177–78; Polzer, *Rules and Precepts*, 50. For New Mexico, see Scholes, *Troublous Times*, 11. For a sympathetic view of whipping as part of a system of rewards and punishments, see Keegan and Sanz, *Experiencia misionera*, 331–38.

104. This brutal act, committed at Oraibi in 1655, is described by Scholes as "the most flagrant case on record during the entire seventeenth century" (*Troublous Times*, 11–12). For Florida, see Hann, *Apalachee*, 256–59, and Bushnell, "Archaeology of Mission Santa Catalina de Guale." In sixteenth-century Mexico, Indians found guilty of idolatry might suffer torture, lifetime imprisonment, or execution, but such stern measures seem to have lessened by the eighteenth century (Gibson, *Aztecs under Spanish Rule*, 117–18).

105. Benavides, *Memorial . . . 1630*, 21 (see 102 for the Spanish version). Several Catholic historians have argued that whipping was mild and needed to be understood in the context of the times: Luzbetak, "If Junípero Serra Were Alive," 514; McGarry, "Educational Methods," 354–55; Guest, "Role of the Discipline," 1–68. Indians may not have

shared this view—see Archibald, "Indian Labor at the California Missions," 172–82. Questions of morality and severity produced a lively debate in California in the 1980s: Costo and Costo, eds., *Missions of California* (a largely polemical work); Meighan, "Indians and California Missions," 187–201; and Sandos, "Junípero Serra's Canonization," 1253–69.

106. The quote is from Covington, ed., *Pirates, Indians and Spaniards*, 142. Franciscans of that era commonly expressed this idea, and it is discussed in some of the secondary literature, such as Ricard, *Spiritual Conquest*, 284–90; Keegan and Tormo, *Experiencia misionera*, 325; and Polzer, *Rules and Precepts*, 44, who sees its strongest manifestation in missionary thought prior to the Enlightenment. Ricard, *Spiritual Conquest*, 286, notes that the friars "were particularly haunted . . . by the fear of a pagan-Christian syncretism."

107. Benavides, *Revised Memorial of 1634*, 63.

108. Fray Alonzo de Posadas to the Holy Office, May 23, 1661, in Hackett, ed., *Historical Documents*, 3:166, and Scholes, *Troublous Times*, 11. For New Spain, see Gómez Canedo, *Evangelización*, 162–69. For one example of the burning of idols in Florida, see fray Martin Prieto, in Oré, *Martyrs of Florida*, 115.

109. Statement of Nicolás de Freitas, Mexico, Jan. 24, 1661, in Hackett, ed., *Historical Documents*, 3:158. Freitas was condemning the kachina dances. Many other priests expressed this view of them.

110. Bushnell, "'That Demonic Game,'" 1–19.

111. Loucks, "Political and Economic Interactions," 55.

112. Bowden, *American Indians and Christian Missions*, 46–51, succinctly describes the similarities and differences between Catholicism and Pueblo religion.

113. William A. Christian, Jr., *Local Religion in Sixteenth-Century Spain* (Princeton: Princeton University Press, 1981), 3, 22, 42–47, 55–56, 147.

114. Inga Clendinnen, "Disciplining the Indians: Franciscan Ideology and Missionary Violence in Sixteenth-Century Yucatan," *Past and Present* 94 (Feb. 1982): 27–48; MacCormack, "Predicaments of Missionary Christianity in Early Colonial Peru," 451–52, 464. See, too, Henry Kamen, "Toleration and Dissent in Sixteenth-Century Spain: The Alternative Tradition," *Sixteenth-Century Journal* 19 (Spring 1988): 3–23, for a discussion of a long Spanish tradition, often a minority view, that coercion should not be used against unbelievers.

115. The quote is from the "Refutation of Charges," by Fermín Francisco de Lasuén, Monterey, June 19, 1801, in Archibald, "Indian Labor at the California Missions," 176 (the entire document is in Kenneally, ed. and trans., *Writings of Fermín Francisco de Lasuén*, 2:194–234). Although it is a late colonial example, Lasuén's eloquent defense of the use of force seems representative of padres' views in other times and places as well. See also, Guest, "Examination of the Thesis of S. F. Cook," 61–62; Elliott, "Discovery of America," 57.

116. Guest, "New Look at the California's Missions [*sic*]," 84, who examined what the friars read as well as what they wrote, is perhaps the finest examination of the mentalité of Spanish friars in North America.

117. See, too, John, *Storms Brewed*, 30, and the view of the Spanish jurist Juan de Solórzano Pereira, noted in Guest, "Examination of the Thesis of S. F. Cook," 57. John Leddy Phelan, *The Hispanization of the Philippines: Spanish Aims and Filipino Responses, 1565–1700* (Madison: University of Wisconsin Press, 1959), 54, also saw the threat of force as assisting missionaries in the Philippines. For an example of the view that Indians cooperated

voluntarily, see Kubler, *Religious Architecture*, 7.

118. Geiger, ed. and trans., *Letter of Luís Jayme*, 38.

119. The quote is Diego de Rebolledo in Hann, ed. and trans., "Rebolledo's 1657 Visitation," 85. Matter, "Missions in the Defense of Spanish Florida," 19–27, summarizes the conflict in early Florida. New Mexico had no garrison in the seventeenth century, but Franciscans often called upon the governor to dispatch military escorts of settler-soldiers to accompany the padres in the founding of new missions, while at the same time Franciscans took measures that seemed designed to drive all Spaniards out of New Mexico (Scholes, *Church and State*, 23–24, 71–72, 80, 89, 108). For examples of missionaries opposing the use of soldiers in Texas, see John, *Storms Brewed*, 188, and Gómez Canedo, *Evangelización*, 86. For a call for soldiers, see fray Andrés Varo, 1751, quoted in fray Pedro Serrano to the viceroy, 1761 [*sic*], in Hackett, ed., *Historical Documents*, 3:496.

120. Most authorities, and most Franciscans of the time, took the view that gifts and trade goods, such as iron tools, clothing, and ornaments, were powerful inducements. See, e.g., Hann, *Apalachee*, 123–33.

121. Mendoza to the king, Jacona, Apr. 17, 1540, in Hammond and Rey, eds. and trans., *Coronado Expedition*, 161. There are many examples of natives appealing to friars for help. See, e.g., fray Juan Sanz de Lezaún, Nov. 14, 1760, "Account of Lamentable Happenings in New Mexico," in Hackett, ed., *Historical Documents*, 3:477.

122. John, *Storms Brewed*, 56, suggests this possibility for the years 1607–8, when the Franciscans reported an unusual number of baptisms. See, too, ibid., 258–303.

123. A number of studies have reached this conclusion. See, e.g., Cushing, "Zuni and the Missionaries," 182, and Hu-DeHart, *Missionaries, Miners, and Indians*, 3. See also James Axtell, "Some Thoughts on the Ethnohistory of Missions," in Axtell, *After Columbus*, 51–52.

124. The quote is from anthropologist Shipek "California Indian Reactions," 485, who offers a delightful reconstruction of how Diegueño (Ipai) Indians probably responded to Franciscans. Native responses can only be reconstructed through an informed imagination, but on the points in these paragraphs, anthropologists seem to agree.

125. For the Pueblos, see Dozier, *Pueblo Indians*, 50; Loucks, "Political and Economic Interactions," 28–31.

126. Gutiérrez, *When Jesus Came*, 63, 77. See, too, Polzer, *Rules and Precepts*, 48. I do not mean to suggest that Indians prefered raising livestock to hunting, but only to suggest that the relative efficiency of keeping large animals contained may have impressed natives.

127. Dobyns, *From Fire to Flood*, 54, suggests this in the case of the Pimas. See, too, Smith, *Archaeology of Aboriginal Culture Change*, 126. Reff, *Disease, Depopulation, and Culture Change*, 260, argues that Jesuits' presumed curative powers were more attractive to Indians than any other inducement the Jesuits offered.

128. Gutiérrez, *When Jesus Came*, 71, 63. Like the Pueblos, Apalachees abstained from sexual activity to give them strength in warfare (Hann, *Apalachee*, 249).

129. For attempts to convert Apaches and other nomads in the 1600s, see, e.g., Forbes, *Apache, Navaho, and Spaniard*, 116–20, 128–29, 158, 159–60, and the episode recounted in John, *Storms Brewed*, 76. Four Franciscans to the Crown, Oct. 16, 1612, quoted in Bushnell, "Sacramental Imperative," 479–80.

130. Fray Silvestre Vélez de Escalante's diary, quoted in Adams, "Fray Silvestre," 136.

See also Adams, "Passive Resistance," 77–91.

131. This is, of course, a universal tendency, and there is widespread agreement among scholars that a syncretic religion developed among most natives in Spanish America. See, e.g., Barth, *Franciscan Education*, 339, Gibson, *Aztecs under Spanish Rule*, 100–101, 134. For Spanish North America, see Deagan, "Cultures in Transition," 112–14; Spicer, *Cycles of Conquest*, 506–8, 567–72; Schroeder, "Shifting for Survival," 239. This was also true in English America; see Axtell, "Some Thoughts on the Ethnohistory of Missions," in Axtell, *After Columbus*, 54.

132. Larson, "Historic Guale Indians," 135, and Thomas, "Saints and Soldiers," 119.

133. Gutiérrez, *When Jesus Came*, 163. For a modern reference to Jesus as a kachina, see Fergusson, *Dancing Gods*, 33. Among the Hopis, who resisted Christianity more staunchly than other Pueblos, Dockstader, *The Kachina and the White Man*, 11, found no case of a Kachina "taken over from white culture."

134. Hann, *Appalachee*, 239, 241, 243. Deagan, "Cultures in Transition," 113–14; Dozier, *Pueblo Indians*, 65–67. For one aspect of this question in a broader context, see John Super, *Food, Conquest, and Colonization in Sixteenth-Century Spanish America* (Albuquerque: University of New Mexico Press, 1988). Archaeologists in Florida have been especially vigorous in addressing these questions. For their tentative conclusions and an introduction to the large literature, see Reitz, "Zooarchaeological Evidence," 543–54, and Ruhl, "Spanish Mission Paleoethnobotany," 555–80.

135. See, e.g., Dozier, *Pueblo Indians*, 65, who probably understates the impact of material culture, but who notes that "the most tangible changes . . . affected the economy." For Florida, see the wide-ranging essay by Hilton, "El impacto español en

la florida," 249–70. Hann, *Apalachee*, 237–63, devotes a chapter to "Indian and Spanish Interaction and Acculturation," much of which represented missionary and Indian interaction.

136. Larsen et al., "Beyond Demographic Collapse," 409–28.

137. Deagan, "Spanish-Indian Interaction," 302. Sheridan, "Kino's Unforeseen Legacy," 157–60, cogently discusses the indirect impact on the Pimas of accepting European domestic animals and winter wheat. For the Pueblos, see Ford, "New Pueblo Economy," 73–91, and John, *Storms Brewed*, 67. See, too, Larson, "Historic Guale Indians" 133. Reff, *Disease, Depopulation, and Culture Change*, 254–59, dismisses the importance of European "innovations" including livestock, but even if one accepts his argument, it may be specific to the region that he studied. Archaeological evidence suggests that Spanish trade goods were not abundant, especially in comparison to those available through the French and English. See, e.g., Larson, "Historic Guale Indians" 135–38, and Merritt, "Beyond the Walls," 146–47, but the few trade goods that Spaniards did offer, together with those animals and plants that reproduced themselves, seem to me to be of great significance.

138. Examples are numerous. For Florida, see Covington, ed., *Pirates, Indians and Spaniards*, 130–31, and for New Mexico, see the well-known episode at the Hopi Pueblo of Awatovi in 1700 (Cordell, *Prehistory of the Southwest*, 354–55).

139. Fray Juan de Prada to the viceroy, Mexico, Sept. 26, 1638, in Hackett, ed., *Historical Documents*, 3:108. See, too, a similar comment by Francisco de Pareja, letter ca. 1616, in Oré, *Martyrs of Florida*, 106.

140. To Gov. Diego de Vargas, Bernalillo, Apr. 18, 1696, in Espinosa, ed. and trans., *Pueblo Indian Revolt*, 228. See, too, fray

Nicolás de Freitas to fray García de San Francisco, Cuarac, New Mexico, June 18, 1660, in Hackett, ed., *Historical Documents*, 3:150–51, quoted in the epigraph at the outset of this chapter.

141. For changes in burial customs, see, e.g., Deagan, "Cultures in Transition," 114, and Larson, "Historic Guale Indians," 134.

142. Spicer identified "compartmentalization" as specific to the Eastern Pueblos—a concept that has been well accepted but that did not occur among all native peoples for it depended upon the nature of indigenous society and the circumstances of contact with Spaniards ("Spanish-Indian Acculturation," 663–78). For a dissenting view, see Ellis's "Comment," *American Anthropologist* 56 (Aug. 1954): 678–80. Scholes, *Troublous Times*, 16, anticipated Spicer when he suggestively argued that in societies like those of the Pueblos, where "religion, village government, and social institutions were so closely interrelated . . . it was impossible to abolish any part without destroying the whole." For an extraordinary example of a Pueblo individual who publicly professed Catholicism, but who privately continued traditional practices, see Kessell, "Esteban Clemente," 16–17. Matter, "Mission Life," 418–20, provides a brief and balanced assessment of this question for Florida. For elements of syncretism in Spain, see William A. Christian, Jr., *Person and God in a Spanish Village* (New York: Seminar Press, 1972), and William A. Christian, Jr., *Local Religion in Sixteenth-Century Spain* (Princeton: Princeton University Press, 1981). See, too, James Axtell, "Were Indian Conversions *Bona Fide?*," in *After Columbus*, 100–121.

143. The rate and percentage of decline of the Pueblo population over the course of the seventeenth century cannot be stated with accuracy because estimates of the base population in 1600 vary wildly. See Schroeder, "Pueblos Abandoned in Historic Times," 254. The decline of numbers of Pueblos and their towns may have occurred quite early in the century, see Forbes, *Apache, Navaho, and Spaniard*, 139, 175, and fray Juan de Pardo to the viceroy, Mexico, Sept. 26, 1638, who estimated the Pueblos had declined from 60,000 to 40,000 due to smallpox "and the sickness that the Mexicans call *cocolitzli*" (Hackett, ed., *Historical Documents*, 3:108).

144. Bushnell, " 'That Demonic Game,' " 4, provides a good, brief discussion of the complicated question of the population of the Florida provinces in 1675 and guidance to sources. Her figures do not include Apalachicola. On the Timucua, see Deagan, "Cultures in Transition," 89–90, 95. See, too, Milanich, "Western Timucua," 59–88.

145. Hann, *Apalachee*, 163–66.

146. Authorities agree on this point. See, e.g., Dozier, *Pueblo Indians*, 63; Hann, *Apalachee*, 175–78, 180.

147. Part of a folktale from Santo Domingo that apparently originated at Zuni, told in Chávez, "Pohé-Yemo's Representative," 115, who identifies this figure as *Pohé-Yemo*. In Tewa, the correct name is *P'ose yemu*—"he who scatters mist before him" (Ortiz, "Popay's Leadership," 21).

148. There is substantial evidence of this among the Pueblos. See, e.g., Scholes, *Troublous Times*, 16, and Dozier, *Pueblo Indians*, 50.

149. Covington, ed., *Pirates, Indians and Spaniards*, 133. See, too, Hann, *Apalachee*, 12–13, 184. See Oré, *Martyrs of Florida*, 101, and Matter, "Spanish Missions of Florida," 74, for other examples from Apalachee, Apalachicola, Timucua, and Guale respectively.

150. Foote and Schackel, "Indian Women of New Mexico," 26–29; Gutiérrez, *When Jesus Came*, 14–19. For sexual miscon-

duct among priests and Hispanics in general, see my chapter 11.

151. For an example of a village fleeing, see the case of a Guale village cited in Gannon, "Conflicto entre iglesia y estado en Florida," 232. Benavides, *Revised Memorial of 1634*, 97, told of the urine and mice meat at Taos (he reported this as a murder attempt, but taoseños certainly would have used more lethal substances if they intended to kill the priest) and of the death of a priest at the Hopi Pueblo of Awatovi from what he believed to be poison (77). Both Florida and New Mexico had a substantial number of martyrs, some of whom died rather mysteriously.

152. Oré, *Martyrs of Florida*, 73.

153. These rebellions are discussed in greater detail in the next chapter.

154. For a fine case study from Alta California, see Sandos, *"Levantamiento!,"* 109–33.

155. The quotes are respectively from Gannon, *Cross in the Sand*, 37, Espinosa, "Our Debt," 84, and Bolton, "Mission as a Frontier Institution," 211 (Gannon altered his view and offered a less glowing portrait in an article, Spellman [pseud., Gannon], " 'Golden Age' of Florida Missions." For the identification of Gannon as Spellman, see Weber, "Blood of Martyrs; Blood of Indians," 440 *n.* 7. The historical literature abounds with praise for the padres, describing them, for example, as carriers of "the light of Christianity and the comforts of civilization to the untutored children of the forest . . . ." (Castañeda, "Sons of St. Francis," 289), and their work "one of the brightest chapters in human history" (Alfaro, "Spirit of the First Franciscan Missionaries," 49).

156. Zubillaga, *La Florida*, 430.

157. Archibald, "Indian Labor at the California Missions," 180.

158. For this argument, see, among others, Bolton, "Mission as a Frontier Institution," 211; Gómez Canedo, *Evangelización*, 143; and Kelsey, "European Impact," 511, who comes to this conclusion

after describing the story of the missions as "a tale of disaster."

159. Bolton, "Mission as a Frontier Institution," 211, For a similar comparison, see Cook, *Conflict*, 3–5.

160. Declaration of Luís de Quintana, Dec. 22, 1681, quoted in Forbes, *Apache, Navaho, and Spaniard*, 177; Dozier, *Pueblo Indians*, 50.

161. For a succinct and insightful view of sixteenth-century precedent, see León-Portilla, "Spiritual Conquest," 55–83. By resorting to force, the Christian preachers, as one Pueblo scholar has put it, "produced . . . a people hostile to Spanish Catholicism and civilization" (Dozier, *Pueblo Indians*, 55).

162. The quote is from Spellman [pseud., Gannon], " 'Golden Age' of Florida Missions," 355, who argues that there was no golden age. There is no shortage of critical views by scholars. See, e.g., Bowden, *American Indians and Christian Missions*, xvi; Heizer, "Impact of Colonization," 121–39; Matter, "Mission Life," 402, 418–20.

163. The first quote is from Matson and Fontana, eds. and trans., *Friar Bringas*, 31; the second is from Ortiz, "San Juan," 281, writing about seventeenth-century New Mexico; the third is from Fontana, "Indians and Missionaries," 58.

164. Polzer, *Rules and Precepts*, 53–54, 58, suggests missionaries did not fail in this task, but rather that the racially stratified non-Indian world beyond the mission was "probably incapable of preparing and accepting Indians into the more advanced forms of frontier society" (55). His position, however, seems to beg the question. For the other viewpoint, see Ricard, *Spiritual Conquest*, 153–54, 288–95.

165. Matter, "Missions in the Defense of Spanish Florida," 36, 32 *n.* 48, 37 *n.* 67, disagrees explicitly with Bolton on this point. See, too, Arnade, "Failure of Spanish Florida," 277.

166. In his classic essay, "Mission as a Frontier

Institution," Bolton acknowledged that "sometimes, and to some degree, they failed" (211), but in the main he concluded that the missions had succeeded in "extending, holding, and civilizing" the frontier (194). Bolton's conclusions need to be reexamined.

167. Gibson, *Aztecs under Spanish Rule*, 111–12; Nancy M. Farriss, *Maya Society under Colonial Rule: The Collective Enterprise of Survival* (Princeton: Princeton University Press, 1984), 68–79; Murdo J. MacLeod, *Spanish Central America: A Socioeconomic History, 1520–1720* (Berkeley: University of California Press, 1973), 120–142; Steve J. Stern, *Peru's Indian Peoples and the Challenge of Spanish Conquest: Huamanga to 1640* (Madison: University of Wisconsin Press, 1982), 51–79; Eugene H. Korth, S.J., *Spanish Policy in Colonial Chile: The Struggle for Social Justice, 1535–1700* (Stanford: Stanford University Press, 1968), 51–52, 60, 84.

Chapter 5: Exploitation, Contention, Rebellion

The epigraphs are from in Hackett, ed., *Historical Documents*, 3:162 (in which fray Nicolás de Freitas quotes or paraphrases the governor), and Boyd et al., *Here They Once Stood*, 27.

1. If the frontier is a place of freedom according to the conventional wisdom in the United States, recent scholarship, informed by world-systems theory, has gone in the opposite direction by portraying peripheries as places of coerced labor. For an elaboration on these ideas and guidance to the extensive scholarly literature behind then, see Lamar, "From Bondage to Contract," and Deeds, "Rural Work in Nueva Vizcaya," 425–49.

2. For friars' dependence on Indian labor in Florida and New Mexico in the 1600s see Matter, "Economic Basis," 31–38; Bushnell, *King's Coffer*, 24, 82, 99; Bushnell, "Archaeology of Mission Santa Catalina de Guale," chap. 9; Scholes, *Troublous Times*, 25–26, 58–61.

3. Hann, *Apalachee*, 142. Nicolás de Aguilar, who was hostile to the priests in New Mexico, also accused them of using Indians to weave and paint items that the padres sold. Aguilar to the Inquisition, Mexico, May 11, 1663, in Hackett, ed., *Historical Documents*, 3:144.

4. Report of the Rev. Father Provincial of the Province of El Santo Evangelio to the viceroy, Convent of San Francisco, Mexico, Mar. 1750, in Hackett, ed., *Historical Documents*, 3:447–48. For similar sentiments expressed by a friar in Florida, see Matter, "Mission Life," 417. Neophyte viewpoints on this and other matters are rare, and Indians would be unlikely to complain for fear of reprisals.

5. Hann, ed. and trans., "Rebolledo's 1657 Visitation," 87.

6. Scholes, *Troublous Times*, 26–27, 53. The friars themselves testified to this.

7. Luis de Velasco to the king, Dec. 17, 1608, in Hammond and Rey, eds. and trans., *Don Juan de Oñate*, 2:1068. There were, of course, exceptions. Many of Menéndez's colonists had come specifically to "plow and sow" and to ranch as well. Spanish attitudes toward manual labor have been much studied. See, e.g., Hanke, *Aristotle and the American Indians*, 13–14, and Bennassar, *Spanish Character*, 117–45.

8. Charles E. Bennett, *Laudonniére and Fort Caroline: History and Documents* (Gainesville: University of Florida Press, 1964), 22–23; Karen Ordahl Kupperman, *Roanoke: The Abandoned Colony* (Totowa, N.J.: Rowman & Allanheld, 1984), 38, 79–87; Kupperman, *Settling with the Indians: The Meeting of English and Indian Cultures in America, 1580–1640* (London: J. M. Dent & Sons, 1980), 17–18; Edmund S. Morgan, "The Labor Problem at Jamestown, 1607–1618," *AHR* 76 (June 1971): 595–611. See, too, James Axtell, *The Invasion Within: The Contest of Cultures in Colonial America* (New York: Oxford University Press, 1985), 51, and the shrewd remarks of Gary Nash, *Red, White, and*

Black: The Peoples of Early America (Englewood Cliffs, N.J.: Prentice-Hall, 1974), 47–49.

9. Nash, *Red, White, and Black*, 67, argues this point so forcibly that he may overstate the case.

10. Kessell, *Kiva, Cross and Crown*, 186. The form of encomiendas varied considerably on the frontiers of New Spain. See Gerhard, *North Frontier*, 9–10.

11. "Ordenanzas . . . para los nuevos descubrimientos, conquistas y pacificaciones," July 13, 1573, in *CDI*(1), 16:186, 159–60 (which mentions *repartimientos* and encomiendas).

12. The exact year in which the number of encomenderos was limited to thirty-five is not clear to me. Scholes, "Civil Government and Society," 79, says 1639, but provides no source. The hearing of Diego de Peñalosa, Mexico, June 25, 1665, in Hackett, ed. and trans., *Historical Documents*, 3:258, suggests that this occurred between 1640 and 1642. For the understanding prior to that time, see Benavides, *Revised Memorial of 1634*, 173.

13. Anderson, "Encomienda in New Mexico," 353–77, draws together much of the fugitive information on this subject, but this work is carelessly done and should be used with more than ordinary caution. The argument that the encomienda was not burdensome initially is made in Snow's interesting statistical analysis, "Note on Encomienda Economics," 347–57. John, *Storms Brewed*, 149, sees it as the source of "the greatest economic grievance of the Pueblos."

14. Foote and Schackel, "Indian Women of New Mexico," 20–23.

15. In the early stages of the conquest of America, labor or *servicio personal* was regarded as an acceptable form of tribute to encomenderos. In the mid-1500s, however, the Crown attempted to limit tribute to payment in kind and to emphasize other means of allocating labor (Gibson, *Spain in*

America, 60). Information on the practices of the encomenderos in New Mexico is quite incomplete but suggests common violation of the Crown's intent. An inventory of Gómez Robledo's encomiendas indicates that the pueblo of Tesuque did not pay tribute "because of service rendered on contract in lieu of tribute" (Kessell, *Kiva, Cross and Crown*, 186). See, too, the episode in Anderson, "Encomienda in New Mexico," 63. In Nuevo León, hunter-gatherers continued to pay tribute through forced labor to encomenderos into the 1700s, as Cuello "Persistence of Indian Slavery," 683–700, has demonstrated.

16. Foote and Schackel, "Indian Women of New Mexico," 24, 27–29; Gutiérrez, *When Jesus Came*, 155–56.

17. Scholes, *Troublous Times*, 42.

18. After the Pueblo Revolt, the Crown awarded one encomienda, but it failed to materialize. See Bloom, "Vargas Encomienda," 366–417.

19. Florida was not, then, established after the encomienda system was abolished, as Deagan has suggested ("Spanish St. Augustine," 22), but encomiendas were in disfavor by the 1560s. In 1563 the Crown denied Lucas Vázquez de Ayllón the right to encomiendas; two years later it gave Menéndez the right "to give repartimientos" to the settlers but did not mention encomiendas (Lyon, *Enterprise of Florida*, 24, 216). Although the terms *encomienda* and *repartimiento* were often used interchangeably in the early stages of the conquest, after the mid-1500s they seem to hold different meanings for the Crown (Gibson, *Spain in America*, 48–67). I do not find convincing Arnade's argument in "Failure of Spanish Florida," 276, that Florida was unsuitable for encomiendas due to the absence of a "culturally and politically advanced native structure." Deagan, "Spanish-Indian Interaction," 294, argues that the encomienda was "unnecessary" in Florida because "the colony had

no economic activities (such as mines or plantations) that required large-scale, intensive labor efforts, and it remained a subsidized military presidio . . ." (294). I believe she is partly correct. New Mexico, too, lacked mines and plantations, but the encomienda thrived because it was necessary to support soldier-citizens; in Florida soldiers were supported directly by the Crown. For Spain's weak position in Florida and hence its inability to impose the encomienda on Florida's natives see Lyon, *Enterprise of Florida*, 118, and Bushnell, *King's Coffer*, 37. Lyon ("Florida," 291) changed his view and suggested in 1990 that encomiendas existed in Florida "although no grants of encomienda have been found in the documents."

20. The collection of tribute was sporadic in Florida in the 1600s (Bushnell, *King's Coffer*, 97–99).

21. For Santa Fe, see Scholes, *Church and State*, 24; for St. Augustine, see Spellman [pseud., Gannon], " 'Golden Age' of the Florida Missions," 365–66.

22. Bushnell, *King's Coffer*, 98–99, and Bushnell, "Archaeology of Mission Santa Catalina de Guale."

23. For the repartimiento in seventeenth-century New Mexico, see Scholes, *Church and State*, 29–30, 73, 79, and Scholes, *Troublous Times*, 25, 29, 47–49. For good discussions of the repartimiento in Florida, see Bushnell, *King's Coffer*, 11–13, 16–25, 98–99, and Hann, *Apalachee*, 139–54. See also Bushnell, "Ruling 'the Republic of Indians,' " 143. TePaske, *Governorship of Spanish Florida*, 193–94, and Bushnell, *King's Coffer*, 97, 110–11, suggest that Indians were not as abused in Florida as elsewhere in the Spanish empire, a distinction in relativity that may have been lost on Florida Indians. Spellman [pseud., Gannon], " 'Golden Age' of the Florida Missions," notes that some Indians "died from the severity of their compulsory labor" (366). For royal prohibitions against using

Indians as burden bearers in Florida (1651 & 1656), see Matter, "Spanish Missions of Florida," 255–58, and for New Mexico see the viceregal orders to Gov. Juan de Eulate, Mexico, Feb. 5, 1621, in Bloom, ed. and trans., "Glimpse of New Mexico," 366, 376. In the latter document, the viceroy notes that women were not to be allotted in repartimiento (367).

24. In 1601 the Crown tried and failed to abolish the compulsory character of the repartimiento; the viceroy of Mexico ended all repartimientos except those in mines, effective Jan. 1, 1633 (Gibson, *Aztecs under Spanish Rule*, 233–35). For the hostility of the Franciscans and the church to this institution, see Stafford Poole, *Pedro Moya de Contreras: Catholic Reform and Royal Power in New Spain*, 1571–1591 (Berkeley: University of California Press, 1987), 179–82. For the survival of the repartimiento in late eighteenth-century New Mexico, see Morfí, *Account of Disorders*, 31–32. Simmons, "History of Pueblo-Spanish Relations," 183, argues that it was "of greater economic importance" than the encomienda in New Mexico. For its survival in another peripheral area, see Nancy M. Farriss, *Maya Society under Colonial Rule: The Collective Enterprise of Survival* (Princeton: Princeton University Press, 1984), 47–56.

25. Archibald, "Acculturation and Assimilation," 205–17, has a fine discussion of this subject. I have also drawn heavily from the work of Scholes, who focuses on the 1700s.

26. See, e.g., Scholes, *Church and State*, 73, 105.

27. The estimate for the 1600s is from Scholes, *Troublous Times*, 51. Statistics for the 1600s are not available, but census figures for 1749 show 1,350 Indian "slaves" belonged to a total Hispanic population of 4,170 in New Mexico—not counting the El Paso district (Kelly, *Franciscan Missions of New Mexico*, 19). Spaniards in Florida were also reported to have many Indian household servants, but the terms of their

servitude remain murky (Matter, "Spanish Missions of Florida," 271).

28. Gutiérrez, *When Jesus Came*, 180–90, contains a good discussion; the quotes are on p. 184. See, too, Scholes, *Troublous Times*, 51.

29. John, *Storms Brewed*, 63, asserts that most slaves were women and children. A considerable literature exists on the question of the legality of slavery. For the late sixteenth-century ecclesiastical debate, see Poole, " 'War by Fire and Blood,' " 115–37. The "Ordenanzas . . . para los nuevos descubrimientos, conquistas y pacificaciones," of 1573, 150, prohibited the taking of slaves, and these royal orders "governed conquests as long as Spain ruled her American colonies" (Hanke, *Spanish Struggle for Justice*, 131). Frontier officials understood the law very well. In Florida, for example, when Gov. Gonzalo Méndez de Canzo (1596–1603) requested permission to use captive Indians as servants, the king denied his request. See Matter, "Spanish Missions of Florida," 251.

30. Among the many examples of provoking natives into rebellion or launching slaving parties against them in seventeenth-century New Mexico, see Scholes, *Church and State*, 118–19, 132–34, 149, 150–51, 154–55, 160–61, and Forbes, *Apache, Navaho, and Spaniard*, 120–21. In Florida, the practice of enslaving hostile natives seems to have been less common than in New Mexico (or less record of it remains), but see the Yamasees' complaints against Spaniards, noted in Covington, "Stuart's Town," 9–10. Spanish officials on occasion permitted slavery; for example, when they allowed Apalachee mission Indians to enslave Apalachicola captives in order to discourage the Apalachees from slaughtering the Apalachicolas (Hann, *Apalachee*, 157–58).

31. For a good discussion of contemporary values and practices, see Ruth Pike, *Aristocrats and Traders: Sevillan Society in the Seventeenth Century* (Ithaca: Cornell University Press, 1972), 170–92, who finds that in Seville in 1565 there was one slave for every fourteen inhabitants (172). Although wealthier residents owned most of those slaves, slaveholding was not limited to the aristocracy.

32. For an example of Indian slaves in a Florida household, see Lyon, "St. Augustine in 1580," 24. See also Bushnell, *King's Coffer*, 21; Frederick P. Bowser, "Africans in Spanish American Colonial Society," in Bethell, ed., *Cambridge History of Latin America*, 2:357–59.

33. Decree of Sept. 26, 1714, Santa Fe, in Brugge, *Navajos in the Catholic Church Records*, xix. The slave trade in New Mexico in the seventeenth century has been little studied compared to the eighteenth. The one book-length study of the subject, Bailey, *Indian Slave Trade*, begins with the 1700s and is seriously flawed. Scholes's works remain the most authoritative for the early period, and the works upon which subsequent authors have relied. See *Church and State*, 73, 88, 118–19, 198; *Troublous Times*, 17, 30, 51–52, 218–19; and "Civil Government and Society," 84–85. Brugge, "Some Plains Indians," 181–88, and Brugge, *Navajos in the Catholic Church Records*, 17–32, provides statistical evidence of New Mexicans' enslavement of Indians from a variety of tribes.

34. Howard Mumford Jones, *O Strange New World: American Culture, the Formative Years* (New York: Viking, 1964), 79. Hanke, *Spanish Struggle for Justice*, is the best single outline of the debate and the body of law that emerged.

35. The quote is from Hann, ed. and trans., "Alonso de Leturiondo's Memorial," 177. The best study of this institution for any North American province is Cutter, *Protector de Indios*, 10, 21–40, 94, 108. Documentation regarding the role of the protector in New Mexico in the 1600s is so sparse that some historians believed the office did not exist—a notion that Cutter has

corrected (50). For Florida, see Matter, "Spanish Missions of Florida," 232–35, 277–78; Bushnell, *King's Coffer*, 111–12; Bushnell, "Patricio de Hinachuba," 3.

36. Matter, "Spanish Missions of Florida," 234–35; Cutter, *Protector de Indios*, 62.

37. For the venality of governors in general, see Woodrow Borah, ed., *El gobierno provincial en la Nueva España, 1570–1787* (Mexico: Universidad Nacional Autónoma de México, 1985), chap. 3. On frontier posts, which held special hardships, the media anata often went uncollected. In 1680 Florida governors were exempted from it, because Florida was declared a place of active war—of *guerra viva* (Bushnell, *King's Coffer*, 84).

38. Scholes, "Civil Government and Society," 82. For a suggestive analysis of this widespread practice, which overlooks its apparent illegality, see MacLachlin, *Spain's Empire*, 35–37. See, too, Kenneth J. Andrien, *Crisis and Decline: The Viceroyalty of Peru in the Seventeenth Century* (Albuquerque: University of New Mexico Press, 1985), who sees corrupt and inefficient administrators as the cause of Peru's fiscal crisis.

39. Historians agree that most governors in Florida and New Mexico in the 1600s used their office for personal profit. See, e.g., Scholes, *Church and State*, 70, and Bushnell, *King's Coffer*, 30–33. In New Mexico, *alcaldes mayores*, who often purchased their office from the governor, also distributed native labor under the repartimiento. Governors established workshops or *obrajes* using forced native labor in New Mexico (Scholes, *Church and State*, 117–18), a practice in which Florida governors apparently did not engage. Few published biographies treat governors of Florida or New Mexico prior to 1700. Among the exceptions is Held, "Hernando de Miranda," 111–30, who emerges as venal and self-serving.

40. Declaration of Capt. Andrés Hurtado, Santa Fe, Sept. 1661, in Hackett, ed., *His-torical Documents*, 3:188. For some of López's private ventures, see Scholes, *Troublous Times*, 47–49, who suggests that López was not exceptional, but that records for his administration are unusually good (34). See, too, Bloom, [ed. and trans.], "Trade-Invoice of 1638," 242–48.

41. López de Mendizábal quoted in Scholes, *Troublous Times*, 36–37, and Scholes's general statement, ibid., 256. For Rebolledo and Florida, see Bushnell, *King's Coffer*, 117.

42. Fray Juan Sanz de Lesaún, Nov. 4, 1760, "Account of Lamentable Happenings in New Mexico," in Hackett, ed., *Historical Documents*, 3:476. Simmons, *Spanish Government in New Mexico*, 62–63; TePaske, *Governorship of Spanish Florida*, 40–57.

43. Fray Estevan de Perea [to the Inquisition?], Mexico, Oct. 30, 1633, in Hackett, ed., *Historical Documents*, 3:131.

44. See, e.g., Lycett, "Spanish Contact and Pueblo Organization," 115–125.

45. The most detailed accounts of this contention are in Matter, "Spanish Missions of Florida," chaps. 7 and 8, whose subtitle, "Friars vs. Governors," suggests the importance of the theme, and in two splendid works by Scholes, *Church and State* and *Troublous Times*.

46. See, e.g., Matter, "Spanish Missions of Florida," 280.

47. Testimony of Thome Domínguez, Isleta, May 21, in Hackett, ed., *Historical Documents*, 3:178. For Eulate, see Scholes, *Church and State*, 72–73, 88; for López, see Scholes, *Troublous Times*, 61 ff. Hann, ed. and trans., "Rebolledo's 1657 Visitation," 84; Matter, "Mission Life in Florida," 414; Bushnell, "Archaeology of Mission Santa Catalina de Guale."

48. Francis of Asisi, quoted in Barth, *Franciscan Education*, 192–93.

49. Scholes, *Church and State*, 68, and Matter, "Spanish Missions of Florida," 262, who notes that the king usually sided with the friars (285). Gannon, "Defense of Native

American and Franciscan Rights," 449–52, recounts the episode from the friars' viewpoint.

50. Santa Fe, Feb. 21, 1639, in Hackett, ed., *Historical Documents*, 3:67. In explaining the Franciscans' intemperate use of power in New Mexico, I am following Scholes, *Church and State*, 15–17.

51. Scholes, *Church and State*, 26, 32, 47, 84–88.

52. The remarkable stories of these men are told most fully in Scholes, *Troublous Times*, chaps. 3–10. For the establishment of the Inquisition, see Scholes, "First Decade of the Inquisition," 195–241.

53. The story of his conflict with the clergy is told most fully in Gannon, "Conflicto entre iglesia y estado en Florida," 211–34. Bushnell, "Patricio de Hinachuba," 3, suggests, with good reason, that the governor had a "nervous breakdown." See, too, Arana, "The Day Governor Cabrera Left Florida," 154–63.

54. Scholes, *Troublous Times*, 249, 255–56; Matter, "Spanish Missions of Florida," 308.

55. Matter, *"Spanish Missions of Florida,"* 275–80, 282, notes that critics became especially vocal in Florida after 1675. See, too, Bushnell, "Patricio de Hinachuba," 3. For New Mexico, see López de Mendizábal, quoted or paraphrased in a statement of fray Nicolás de Freitas, Mexico, Jan. 24, 1661, Hackett, ed., *Historical Documents*, 3:162, and López de Mendizábal before the Inquisition, Mexico, May 10, 1663, and June 16, 1663, in Hackett, ed., *Historical Documents*, 3:196, 211–12.

56. The quote is from the *cabildo* of Santa Fe to the viceroy, Feb. 21, 1639, in Hackett, ed., *Historical Documents*, 3:67. See Scholes, *Church and State*, 128–33, for further detail, context, and analysis.

57. Bloom [ed. and trans.], "Royal Order of 1620," 297.

58. Vélez de Escalante, "Letter to the Missionaries of New Mexico," 322, 327. For the continuing controversy in Florida, see Matter, "Spanish Missions of Florida," 280, 389–90 *n.* 57.

59. Scholes, *Church and State*, esp. 28, 30, 32, 34, 42, 121, 138–39, 184. Gov. Luis de Rosas's assassination, initially believed to be the act of an aggrieved husband, was almost certainly a political act committed by his enemies, as Scholes and contemporary courts concluded (*Church and State*, 158–65). Physical attacks in Florida seem to have been rare, but personal verbal abuse was not (see, e.g., Matter, "Spanish Missions of Florida," 208), and Bushnell, "Archaeology of Mission Santa Catalina de Guale."

60. Bushnell, "Archaeology of Mission Santa Catalina de Guale," quoting a copy of a letter from Fuentes to a friar, 1682. For a similar episode in New Mexico, see Scholes, *Church and State*, 184. Friars prompted Guales to complain about civil officials (Matter, "Spanish Missions of Florida," 266–67, 270), and Rebolledo used Apalachees to provide one-sided testimony against the friars (Hann, ed. and trans., "Rebolledo's 1657 Visitation," 81–145).

61. Francisco de Salazar, Isleta, June 17, 1660, to fray Juan Ramírez, quoted in Scholes, *Troublous Times*, 89.

62. Gutiérrez, *When Jesus Came*, 22–25, 63.

63. Matter, "Mission Life in Seventeenth-Century Florida," 413, and Matter, "Spanish Missions of Florida," 315, 317. Gannon, "Conflicto entre iglesia y estado en Florida," 233. Arnade, "Failure of Spanish Florida," 278–79. Scholes, *Troublous Times*, 257–58. In a reckless and rambling attack on Scholes, which I do not find convincing, Garner, "Seventeenth Century New Mexico," argues that encomenderos and friars had common interests and were not in contention (48–49). He characterizes this period as a time of accommodation rather than conflict, arguing that up to 1670 "remarkably stable European-Indian relations prevailed" in New Mexico (51).

NOTES TO PAGES 133–34

64. Scholes, *Church and State*, 130–31, describes the conflict as having an "economic basis" in "rivalry over lands, labor, and the breeding of livestock." Matter, "Spanish Missions of Florida," notes that "dependence on Indian agriculture and labor . . . fostered and fed much of the church-state dissension" (315), although he argues that "jurisdictional conflict underlay all or most of the church-state dissension in Florida" (245).

65. These are summarized in a number of sources, including Matter, "Missions in the Defense of Spanish Florida," 20, 22, 26. The revolts in 1645 and the early 1680s in Guale have not been generally known but are mentioned in Bushnell, "Sacramental Imperative," 481.

66. Scholes, *Church and State*, 107–9, 137, 195; Forbes, *Apache, Navaho, and Spaniard*, 137, 142–43, 144.

67. Wilson, "Before the Pueblo Revolt," 118, argues that Spanish exploitation prompted revolts that Spaniards failed to report, but instead used Apaches as scapegoats to mask Pueblo unrest. Garner, "Seventeenth Century New Mexico," whose work Wilson ignores, takes the opposite view, arguing that until 1670 accommodation rather than conflict characterized Spanish-Pueblo relations (51). Many of the records from seventeenth-century New Mexico were lost in the Pueblo Revolt. Amy Bushnell believes that there were "many other Florida uprisings that are poorly documented" (Bushnell to Weber, June 1, 1989).

68. The Taos moved about 1640 into present-day Scott County, western Kansas. Most returned in 1662. See Forbes, *Apache, Navaho, and Spaniard*, 137, 156. After the failure of the Pueblo revolts, some Picuris again fled to El Cuartelejo, only to be enslaved by Apaches until 1706 when a Spanish party brought them back.

69. Forbes, *Apache, Navaho, and Spaniard*, 144, 163.

70. Wilson, "Before the Pueblo Revolt," 117–

18, suggests a more widespread drought than previously supposed. See also Simmons, "Pueblo Revolt," 12.

71. Fray Juan Bernal to the Inquisition, Santo Domingo, Apr. 1, 1669, quoted in Hackett, ed., *Historical Documents*, 3:272.

72. Spielmann, "Colonists, Hunters, and Farmers," 101–13.

73. Forbes, *Apache, Navaho, and Spaniard*, 158–61. Navajo and Apache motives cannot be stated with certainty. Reeve, "Seventeenth Century Navaho-Spanish Relations," 42–43, argued that Navajos did not raid the Pueblos for plunder, since they could have more easily obtained commodities through trade rather than through war, but he apparently did not know of Spanish efforts to restrict trade between unconverted Indians and Pueblos, nor did he take into account the drought and chronic shortages that might have left Navajos with fewer commodities of their own with which to trade.

74. Forbes, *Apache, Navaho, and Spaniard*, 160–76. In a revisionist work, Wilson, "Before the Pueblo Revolt," 114–17, argues that the Apaches' role in forcing the abandonment of these Pueblos has been exaggerated. Apaches, he suggests, attacked the missions rather than the Pueblos themselves. Details surrounding the abandonment of these so-called Saline Pueblos remain murky, and specialists disagree on such basic questions as how many were abandoned, when, and for how long, as well as on the more difficult question of Apache motivation. For an interesting analysis of causes, and the surprising conclusion that these pueblos carried the seed of their own destruction in a tendency toward internal divisiveness, see Vivian, *Excavations*, 151–54.

75. Bowden, *American Indians and Christian Missions*, 53–55, provides a lucid summary of the religious conflict. See, too, Forbes, *Apache, Navaho, and Spaniard*, 171–72.

76. Scholars generally agree that Pueblos

fought primarily for religious freedom, and in so doing they follow the interpretation laid out in the lengthy introduction to Hackett, ed., *Revolt of the Pueblo Indians*, upon whom I have also depended unless otherwise noted. Silverberg, *Pueblo Revolt*, is a popular account, undocumented but based on standard published sources. For examples of those who follow Hackett in presenting the issue of religion as the primary cause of the 1680 rebellion, see Forbes, *Apache, Navaho, and Spaniard*, 178, and Simmons, "Pueblo Revolt," 11–12. Exceptions include Garner, "Seventeenth Century New Mexico," who believes that historians have emphasized religious causation "far out of proportion to its actual relevance" (54), and Anderson, "Encomienda in New Mexico," who fails to identify religious persecution among his "main causes" of the rebellion (372). Lamar, "From Bondage to Contract," 298, overstates the case when he overlooks the religious dimension to identify the Pueblo Revolt as simply "a revolt of slave or bonded labor."

Most writers see Spanish demands for labor as adding significantly to Pueblo resentment and as an important cause of the revolt. See, for example, Scholes, *Church and State*, 194–96; Simmons, "Pueblo Revolt," 11; Sando, "Pueblo Revolt," 196. Dozier, *Pueblo Indians*, 71, suggests that the encomienda was "perhaps the most important cause of the revolt." Pueblo witnesses to the event identified both religious oppression and forced labor as causes. See, e.g., Sánchez, "Spanish-Indian Relations," 134, 137. For the role of Hopi tradition, see Wiget, "Truth and the Hopi," 184–85.

77. Sando, "Pueblo Revolt," 196, argues that Pueblos did not wish to kill the Spaniards but simply to force them to leave.

78. I follow Ortiz, "Popay's Leadership," 18–22, for identification of Popé (also spelled Popay) as a religious leader. A controver-sial article by fray Angélico Chávez, "Pohé-Yemo's Representative," 85–126, suggesting that the essential leadership of the Pueblos came from a mulatto, Domingo Naranjo, who impersonated the deity Pohé-Yemo, has been the subject of a closely argued rebutal by Beninato, "Popé, Pose-yemu, and Naranjo," 417–35. On the endogamy of Pueblo villages, see Dozier *Pueblo Indians*, 56. For the opposite view, see Wilcox, "Changing Perspectives," 382–85, who suggests that Pueblo communities may have been more closely linked than has been supposed. It seems to me, however, that those who claim that Pueblos lived in relatively autonomous communities have the stronger argument.

79. For a good account of Pueblo ambivalence and disunity, see John, *Storms Brewed*, 199–200, and for the example of Pecos, see Kessell, *Kiva, Cross and Crown*, 231–32. On Apache participation, see Forbes, *Apache, Navaho, and Spaniard*, 178–82. There is no evidence of substantial participation in the revolt by those Apaches (or, more properly, Athapascans) known as Navajos (McNitt, *Navajo Wars*, 18).

80. Otermín described his wounds in a letter to fray Francisco de Ayeta, Sept. 8, 1680, in Hackett, ed., *Revolt of the Pueblo Indians*, 1:105.

81. By Sept. 13, two parties of refugees, one from Santa Fe and one from Isleta, had joined together at Fray Cristóbal, some sixty miles south of Socorro. Anthropologist Dozier, from Santa Clara Pueblo, explained the Pueblos willingness to allow Spaniards to leave alive in terms of "compassion" (*Pueblo Indians*, 59), but it may also be that they did not wish to suffer further casualties.

82. Foote and Schackel, "Indian Women of New Mexico, 1535–1680," 30.

83. Declaration of Capt. Andrés Hurtado, Santa Fe, Sept. 1661, in Hackett, *Historical Documents*, 3:186–87.

84. Lic. Martín de Solís Miranda, Mexico, June 25, 1682, in Hackett, ed., *Revolt of the Pueblo Indians,* 2:382.

85. Some Pueblos rejected the effort to obliterate all things Spanish. See, e.g., the archaeological evidence discussed in Chávez, "But Were They All Natives?" 32, and the episode described in Sánchez, "Spanish-Indian Relations," 134–35. See, too, John, *Storms Brewed,* 106, and the extreme case of the Hopis, well explained in Adams, "View from the Hopi Mesas," 325–26.

86. Testimony of Pedro Naranjo, El Paso, Dec. 19, 1681, in Hackett, ed., *Revolt of the Pueblo Indians,* 2:247. For a fascinating interpretation of Naranjo's identity, see Chávez, "Pohé-Yemo's Representative," 99–102.

87. Otermín to fray Francisco de Ayeta, Sept. 8, 1680, in Hackett, ed., *Revolt of the Pueblo Indians,* 1:102.

88. Espinosa, *Crónica de los colegios de propaganda fide,* 123–24.

89. Paso del Río del Norte, Oct. 20, 1680, in Hackett, ed., *Revolt of the Pueblo Indians,* 1:206.

90. Otermín expressed incomprehension at the behavior of Christian Indians and attributed the rebellion to divine displeasure at Spaniards' sins. Letter to fray Francisco de Ayeta, Sept. 8, 1680, in Hackett, ed., *Revolt of the Pueblo Indians,* 1:94, 98, 103. For the devil, see Chávez, "Pohé-Yemo's Representative," 87–89, and Simmons, *Witchcraft in the Southwest,* 26–27.

91. Lic. Martín de Solís Miranda, Mexico, June 25, 1682, in Hackett, ed., *Revolt of the Pueblo Indians,* 2:402, quote called to my attention by Simmons, "Pueblo Revolt," 15.

92. Gibson, *Spain in America,* 186.

93. Forbes, *Apache, Navajo, and Spaniard,* 237–38.

94. Timmons, *El Paso,* 18; Burrus, "Tragic Interlude," 156, who reproduces a previously unknown census of 1684 that explains the economic conditions and possessions of each household in El Paso; Garner, "Dynamics of Change," 6–7.

95. Quoted in Forbes, *Apache, Navajo, and Spaniard,* 202 (see, too, 211).

96. See, e.g., Moorhead, *Presidio,* 19. Forbes, *Apache, Navajo, and Spaniard,* 200–224, called it the "Great Southwestern Revolt" and described it more comprehensively than have other writers. For the intensification of violent conflict in the regions immediately to the south of New Mexico at this time see Jones, *Nueva Vizcaya,* 97–115. Naylor and Polzer, eds., *Presidio and Militia,* 483–718, contains relevant documents in translation.

97. The identity of some of these smaller groups has been difficult to establish. Forbes argued that Janos and Sumas, for example were Apaches, a view that has been effectively rejected by Naylor, who demonstrates that they were Uto-Aztecan speakers ("Athapaskans They Weren't," 275–81).

98. Vargas to Mariana Villalba, Tlalpujaha, Mar. 22, 1686, in Kessell, ed., *Remote beyond Compare,* 130–31. This remarkable collection of newly discovered letters, together with Kessell's fresh biography, adds private dimensions to the Vargas known only by his public deeds.

99. For a short piece that suggests Spanish factionalism, see Sánchez, "Spanish-Indian Relations," 133–51. The reconquest of New Mexico has been chronicled in great detail. The account by Espinosa, *Crusaders of the Río Grande,* has never been surpassed and I have relied upon it. Vargas's campaign journal and related documents have been translated by Espinosa in *First Expedition of Vargas.* For use of Pueblo allies, see Jones, *Pueblo Warriors,* 40–43.

100. Slater, *El Morro,* 13. Whether Vargas personally made this inscription or not, he certainly had full knowledge of it. A photograph of the inscription appears in Leonard, ed. and trans., *Mercurio Volante,* facing 76.

101. Leonard, ed. and trans., *Mercurio Volante*, 88. Leonard includes a facsimile of the original 18-page pamphlet written in the summer of 1693, apparently with Vargas's campaign journal at hand, and published that same year.

102. For Spanish motivation in reoccupying New Mexico, see Espinosa, *Crusaders of the Río Grande*, 40, 46–48; Forbes, *Apache, Navajo, and Spaniard*, 236–37; Espinosa, "Legend of Sierra Azul," 113–58.

103. Chávez, *Our Lady of the Conquest*, esp. 21–28. For the symbolic meanings of this icon, the patroness of the annual Santa Fe Fiesta, see Grimes, *Symbol and Conquest*.

104. Fray Miguel Trizio to Vargas, Bernalillo, Apr. 17, 1696, in Espinosa, ed. and trans., *Pueblo Indian Revolt*, 226. Espinosa's work contains a fine overview of this period, in addition to a rich lode of primary sources, and I have followed his interpretation.

105. For military tactics and the use of Pueblo allies, see Jones, *Pueblo Warriors*, 57–60.

106. Adams, "View from the Hopi Mesas," 325–26, notes that refugees remained among the Hopis until years of drought in the 1730s created food shortages that sent them home.

107. Simmons, "History of Pueblo-Spanish Relations," 185–87, provides population figures and a good discussion of disruptions. See also Ferguson, "Emergence of Modern Zuni Culture," 340.

108. See, e.g., fray Andrés de Varo, 1751, quoted in fray Pedro Serrano to the viceroy, 1761 [*sic*] in Hackett, ed., *Historical Documents*, 3:492.

109. Dozier, *Pueblo Indians*, 71–78; Kessell, "Spaniards and Pueblos," 1:127–38; Flagler, "Governor José Chacón," 467–69. John, *Storms Brewed*, 138–39, 140–41, 149, 150, and 226–57, contains a good account of Spanish-Indian relations in "New Mexico, 1705–1733."

110. For the structural causes of the revolts of Florida mission Indians see, e.g., Matter, "Mission Life," 15, who sees forced labor as an important cause of native resentment, and Gannon, *Cross in the Sand*, 56–58. Religious persecution alone could cause rebellion, as suggested in Gradie, "Spanish Jesuits in Virginia," 147.

111. Wright, *Anglo-Spanish Rivalry*, 46–68—a fine overview of English expansion from Carolina and Spanish reactions to it. Crane, *Southern Frontier*, 1–81, remains of great value for those in search of a more detailed account.

112. For the situation in the last three Guale missions (and two missions of Timucuan-speaking Mocamo) in 1695, see Hann, "Twilight of the Mocamo and Guale Aborigines," 1–24.

113. Extracts from an inquiry of June 1705, in Boyd et al., *Here They Once Stood*, 81 (see, too, 53, 60, 75, 76, 79). This volume contains translations of a number of essential documents.

114. Col. James Moore to the Lords Proprietors, Apr. 16, 1704, in Boyd et al., *Here They Once Stood*, 94. I have depended on Matter's good overview of the demise of the Florida missions in "Spanish Missions of Florida," 199–201, 288–98, and on his article, "Missions in the Defense of Spanish Florida," 31–35, as well as Gannon, *Cross in the Sand*, 68–76; the documents in Boyd et al., *Here They Once Stood*; and Hann, *Apalachee*, 264–83 (whose work supersedes many other accounts and provides a fine guide to earlier literature).

115. For Spanish policy and practice in providing arms to Indians, see my chapters 6–8. For Yamasees' expressions of antipathy toward Spaniards at this time, see Covington, "Stuart's Town," 9–10.

116. Hann, ed. and trans., "Leturiondo's Memorial," 178.

117. Many writers have suggested that the Spaniards' abuse of neophytes contributed to their desertion to the English side. See, e.g., Matter, "Spanish Missions of Florida," 289, and Hann, *Apalachee*, 117, 227–33, and Boyd et al., *Here They*

Once Stood, 6–8, 19. This is evident even in works that are highly sympathetic to the missionaries, such as Lanning, *Spanish Missions of Georgia*, 201–9, and Gannon, *Cross in the Sand*, 73.

118. Quoted in Bushnell, "Patricio de Hinachuba," 6. For examples of Indian antagonism toward Christianity, see Bushnell, "Archaeology of Mission Santa Catalina de Guale."

119. Hann, *Apalachee*, 260–61, who makes this estimate after the most careful, recent study of the confusing and often contradictory evidence.

120. Bushnell, "Patricio de Hinachuba," 16. The quote is from Hinachuba to Antonio Ponce de León, Apr. 10, 1699, in Boyd et al., *Here They Once Stood*, 27.

121. A small number of Apalachees who survived near St. Augustine were apparently moved to Veracruz in 1763; those who had moved to Mobile in 1704 continued westward into Louisiana after Spain lost its possessions east of the Mississippi, and disappeared from the historical record after the 1830s (Covington, "Apalachee Indians Move West," 221–25).

122. Francisco de Florencia and Juan de Pueyo to the king, St. Augustine, Aug. 13, 1706, quoted in Boyd, ed. and trans., "Further Consideration of the Apalachee Missions," 477.

123. Arnade, "Failure of Spanish Florida," 280; Matter, "Spanish Missions of Florida," 286. Spanish explanations suggest that mission Indians in Apalachee joined the English because they feared for their lives if they stayed at the poorly defended missions (see, e.g., Francisco de Florencia and Juan de Pueyo to the viceroy, St. Augustine, July 16, 1704, in Boyd et al., *Here They Once Stood*, 61). No doubt, that was the case with many natives, but the defections had begun before the invasion of Apalachee and continued in following years; the reasons were probably more complex than Spaniards supposed or

wished to admit. Fitzhugh, "Commentary on Part IV," "Commentary on Part IV," in Fitzhugh, ed., *Cultures in Contact*, 275, argues that the mission process weakened the societies of Florida mission Indians, an especially fragile group in his view, to the point where they could not defend themselves.

124. Colonel Moore drew a distinction between Indians he enslaved and those who he "brought away." Col. James Moore to the Lords Proprietors, Apr. 16, 1704, in Boyd et al., *Here They Once Stood*, 94, but the disposition of the Florida Indians who voluntarily joined the Carolinians is not clear. At this time the Carolina trade in Indian slaves was unregulated; not until 1711 did Carolina officials rule that only Indians taken in war could be enslaved (Covington, "Some Observations," 14). On the Spanish side, Gov. Joseph de Zúñiga y Zerda, n.d. [ca. 1703] ordered that "all the pagans whom our Indians capture may be retained by them as slaves, and they may sell them" (Boyd et al., *Here They Once Stood*, 45).

125. Thomas Nairne, Report of 1708, quoted in Boyd, "Further Consideration of the Apalachee Missions," 464.

126. Bolton, "Spanish Resistance," 115–30, in Bannon, *Bolton and the Spanish Borderlands*, 148; TePaske, *Governorship of Spanish Florida*, 198–200.

127. Matter, "Spanish Missions of Florida," 299–306; Gannon, *Cross in the Sand*, 80–83. Geiger, *Biographical Dictionary*, 132–39, reproduces lists of missions and mission Indians from 1726 to 1738. In 1738, Manuel de Montiano counted 354 persons in eight mission communities. See, too, Deagan, "Spanish-Indian Interaction in Sixteenth-Century Florida," 291–92, for the rise and fall of native populations in the vicinity of St. Augustine in the eighteenth century.

128. Sturtevant, "Last of the South Florida Aborigines," 141–62.

129. TePaske, *Governorship of Spanish Florida*, 193–226, admirably analyzes the reasons for the failure of Spain's Indian policy in eighteenth-century Florida. See, too, my chapters 6, 7, 8, and 10.

Chapter 6: Imperial Rivalry and Strategic Expansion

The epigraphs are from Boyd, Smith, and Griffin, *Here They Once Stood*, 69, and Hatcher, ed. and trans., "Descriptions of the Tejas," 60–61.

1. For French interest in seizing all of New Spain in the late seventeenth century, see Folmer, *Franco-Spanish Rivalry*, 133–36. Clark, *Beginnings of Texas*, and Dunn, *Spanish and French Rivalry*, important pioneering works based on archival sources, have been largely superseded by later scholarship but still repay a careful reading.

2. I am following the fine reassessment of La Salle by Wood, "La Salle," 294–323, who concludes that La Salle did not deliberately distort geography to justify a scheme to invade New Spain, as some historians have argued, but rather that he made "a plausible geographical error" (312). Wood's argument has been reinforced by the recent discovery and publication of the journal of one Minet (his given name is not known). See Weddle et al., eds., *La Salle*, 7–8.

3. The quote is from La Salle to an unknown person, Oct. 1682, in Folmer, *Franco-Spanish Rivalry*, 144; La Salle proposed the number of Indians in 1684 (ibid., 150, 154). Wood, "La Salle," 314–15, explains that La Salle's scheme for gaining the support of 15,000 Indian allies was "optimistic" but not "fantastic," as some writers have suggested.

4. Quoted in Wood, "La Salle," 314. For the attitude of Louis XIV, see ibid., 311.

5. Shea [ed. and trans.], *Expedition of Don Dionisio de Peñalosa*, contains the fabricated account in Spanish and in English translation. Unbeknown to the editor of the 1964 reprint, Peñalosa's account had long since been discredited. See Hackett, "New Light on Don Diego de Peñalosa," 313–35, which reviews earlier scholarship. See, too, Weddle, *Wilderness Manhunt*, 16–22. Folmer, *Franco-Spanish Rivalry*, 139–54, seems to confuse chronology. Earlier interpretations of Peñalosa need to be tempered by conclusions subsequently reached by Wood, "La Salle." See, too, Thomas, ed. and trans., *Alonso de Posada Report*, 12–13.

6. Bolton, "Location of La Salle's Colony," 171–89, correctly identified the location of the fort on a hill on the right bank of Garcitas Creek about five miles from its mouth on Lavaca Bay, an extension of Matagorda Bay. Despite arguments for other sites, his work has been sustained. See Weddle, *Wilderness Manhunt*, 194, 223–24, and Weddle et al., eds., *La Salle*, 11.

7. Spaniards later gleaned this information from Indian informants. See Weddle, *Wilderness Manhunt*, 166–68.

8. Wood, "La Salle," 316–17. The news took even longer to reach England. See Coker, "English Reaction to La Salle," 129–35.

9. The remarkable story of how Spaniards learned of La Salle is told in Weddle, *Wilderness Manhunt*, 1–14.

10. The *informe* of Sebastián de Guzmán y Córdoba, [ca. 1686], quoted in Weddle, *Wilderness Manhunt*, 53.

11. Folmer, *Franco-Spanish Rivalry*, 126.

12. The marqués de Vélez and others, Junta de Guerra de las Yndias, Apr. 8, 1686, quoted in Weddle, *Wilderness Manhunt*, 89. Weddle provides a somewhat different translation of the same document on p. 13.

13. Weddle, *Wilderness Manhunt*, 24–25, 92. As late as the time of Tristán de Luna, it had that name (see my chapter 3). Alonso de León transferred the name Espíritu Santo to Matagorda Bay, when he found La Salle's fort there in 1690, and Espíritu Santo continued to be used for Matagorda Bay.

14. Except where indicated, I have based this account on Weddle's richly detailed *Wilderness Manhunt*. McWilliams, "Iberville at the Birdfood Delta," 127–40, convincingly argues that Spaniards did not see logs in the river's mouth, as earlier historians had assumed, but rather "mud lumps," a unique geological formation. In the interest of providing the general reader with a clearer image of a palisade, I have taken the liberty of using the term *bars of mud*. The log of the 1686 expedition is readily available in translation in Leonard, "Spanish Re-exploration of the Gulf Coast," 547–57, but Leonard's annotations are no longer accepted.

15. For biographical information, see Weddle, *Wilderness Manhunt*, 55.

16. On the naval expeditions of 1686–87, see the newly discovered diary of the chief pilot Enríquez Barroto, published in Weddle et al., eds., *La Salle*, 129–205. New information in this diary has prompted Weddle to modify some of his earlier conclusions.

17. For Géry's identity as a deserter from La Salle, see Weddle, *Wilderness Manhunt*, 188–89.

18. Alessio Robles, *Coahuila y Texas*, 301–58, and Jones, *Los Paisanos*, 23.

19. Karankawa motives are explained in Weddle, "Talon Interrogations," 224, 251.

20. León to the viceroy, Coahuila, May 16, 1689, in Gómez Canedo, ed., *Primeras exploraciones*, 137. Gómez Canedo includes many of the key documents for this period, including the itinerary of León's 1689 expedition (ibid., 118–30). Some of these documents have never been published in any language, but a few have appeared in English translation, as in Bolton, ed., *Spanish Exploration*, 345–423, and O'Donnell, trans., *La Salle's Occupation of Texas*, 5–14.

21. Quoted in Weddle, *Wilderness Manhunt*, 188.

22. For the testimony of L'Archevêque and his companion, May 1, 1689, see O'Donnell, trans., *La Salle's Occupation of Texas*, 15–20, and the summary in Weddle, *Wilderness Manhunt*, 195–97, 200–201. The only known eyewitness account of the destruction of the fort is that of the young Talon brothers, in Weddle et al., eds., *La Salle*, 237.

23. Bolton made this case clearly in an essay first published in 1930, noting that New Mexico was the only exception in North America. See "Defensive Spanish Expansion," 43.

24. Beginning with the work of Dunn, *Spanish and French Rivalry*, and continuing to the present, historians agree on this interpretation.

25. Mazanet to Sigüenza y Góngora, 1690, in Gómez Canedo, ed., *Primeras exploraciones*, 72; Castañeda, *Our Catholic Heritage in Texas*, 25, 31.

26. León to the viceroy, May 16, 1689, in Gómez Canedo, ed., *Primeras exploraciones*, 138.

27. For a brief, vivid description of Caddo culture, see John, *Storms Brewed*, 165–70. For more detailed accounts, see Bolton, *Hasinais* (the first publication of a manuscript completed in 1908 and not corrected or augmented by subsequent research), the fine study by Griffith, "Hasinai Indians," and Newcomb, *Indians of Texas*, 279–313. Hester, "Texas and Northeastern Mexico" 198–99, summarizes recent research.

28. Gilmore, "Indians of Mission Rosario," 231–44, offers a sensitive interpretation of the Karankawas. See, too, Newcomb, "Karankawa," 359–67.

29. For further sources and summaries of recent anthropological research on the Coahuiltecans, who have often been mistakenly viewed as impoverished, see Hester, "Texas and Northeastern Mexico," 193–96, and the more extensive piece by T. N. Campbell, "Coahuiltecans," 343–58. For Spanish-Coahuiltecan contact in the late seventeenth century, see the summary in John, *Storms Brewed*, 171–74.

30. Mazanet to Carlos de Sigüenza y Góngora, 1690, in Gómez Canedo, ed., *Primeras exploraciones*, 59 (this letter is translated in Bolton, ed., *Spanish Exploration*, 353–87).

31. The site was apparently near present-day Weches, due west of Nacogdoches, where it is commemorated with a replica of the chapel in Mission Tejas State Park.

32. Mazanet to Sigüenza y Góngora, 1690, in Gómez Canedo, ed., *Primeras exploraciones*, 70. Gómez Canedo (ibid., 26) argues that historians have exaggerated the difference in viewpoint between León and Mazanet.

33. Ibid., 26–28, and Alonso de León to the viceroy, Aug. 12 1689, ibid., 146–48. For the death of León, see Weddle, *Wilderness Manhunt*, 225.

34. Hatcher, ed. and trans., *Expedition of Don Domingo Terán de los Ríos*, 6, contains the instructions to the expedition, which put Mazanet in charge, the diaries of Terán and Mazanet, and other documents.

35. The quote is from Mazanet to Sigüenza y Góngora, 1690, in Gómez Canedo, ed., *Primeras exploraciones*, 70.

36. Trans. of fray Francisco Casañas to the viceroy, Aug. 15, 1691, in Hatcher, ed. and trans., "Descriptions of the Tejas," 295. Casañas estimated 3,000 deaths "among all the friendly tribes of the Tejias," in March 1691 alone (ibid., 303). The population of the Hasinai confederacy at this time is not known. John, *Storms Brewed*, 165, seems to suggest 8,000 for the "Caddo world," surely a substantial underestimate, and her figure for the number of persons who died in the epidemic (ibid., 189) is lower than than that of Casañas, who would have no reason to exaggerate.

37. Mazanet to the viceroy, Coahuila, Feb. 17, 1694, in Gómez Canedo, ed., *Primeras exploraciones*, 319. Gómez Canedo explains the demise of the Texas missions as a failure of Europeans (ibid., 30–31). For a fine secondary account written with sensitivity to the Indian point of view, see John, *Storms Brewed*, 187–93. For the death of Casañas, see Espinosa, ed. and trans., *Pueblo Indian Revolt*, 50, 250.

38. Juan Jordán de Reina, diarist on the Barroto-Romero expedition of 1686, quoted in Weddle, *Wilderness Manhunt*, 49. Good accounts of the three-way race for Pensacola appear in Ford, *Triangular Struggle*, chaps. 1, 2; Weddle, *Wilderness Manhunt*, chap. 20; and Folmer, *Franco-Spanish Rivalry*, 189–218. All are indebted to the pioneering work of Dunn, *Spanish and French Rivalry*. Luna had declared Pensacola "the best port in the Indies" (Arnade, "Tristán de Luna," 214).

39. Andrés de Pez, "Memorial," in Leonard, ed. and trans., *Spanish Approach to Pensacola*, 77–92, which Leonard believes was written by Sigüenza y Góngora. The quotes are, respectively, from 77 and 86. Holmes, "Andrés de Pez," 106–28, provides a more appreciative biography than does Leonard. For a less flattering view, see Weddle et al., eds., *La Salle*, 141 *n.* 28, 146.

40. "Opinion of the marqués de la Granja, Oct. 1690," in Leonard, ed. and trans., *Spanish Approach to Pensacola*, 103–11. The quote is on p. 109.

41. Report of Carlos de Sigüenza y Góngora, Mexico, June 1, 1693, in Leonard, ed. and trans., *Spanish Approach to Pensacola*, 193. Two expeditions reexplored Pensacola and the eastern Gulf in 1693, the most important being that of Pez and Sigüenza.

42. Ford, *Triangular Struggle*, 20–21.

43. Rule, "Jérôme Phélypeaux," 179–97, provides a good account of French motives. Ponchartrain quizzed the Talon brothers about the location of Spanish mines, as part of general preparations to send Iberville to Louisiana. He sent the transcript of the interrogation with Iberville, but not the brothers. Weddle et al., eds., *La Salle*, 219, 256.

44. See McWilliams, "Iberville at the Bird-food Delta," 127–40, and McWilliams, ed. and trans., *Iberville's Gulf Journals*, 32–33.

45. Rule, "Jérôme Phélypeaux," 186–87, 191.

The best account of Coxe's activities is William S. Coker's introduction to a book written by Coxe's son, Daniel Coxe, *Description of the English Province of Carolina*, xx–xxx.

46. Capt. Andrés de Arriola to the king, Pensacola, Dec. 1, 1698, quoted in Manucy, "Founding of Pensacola," 235. See, too, the Austrian engineer Jaime Franck to the Council of the Indies, Pensacola, Feb. 19, 1699, ibid., 237. Manucy's article offers no new interpretation but contains translations of these two gloomy letters. For English designs, see Ford, *Triangular Struggle*, 26–27, 46–47, 68–70.

47. For the dismal situation at early Pensacola, see Griffen, "Spanish Pensacola," 243–46, and Ford, *Triangular Struggle*, 31–32, 61, 76; for French aid, see ibid., 61, 72–75, 78–79. The quote is from François Le Maire, who served as a priest at Pensacola, 1712–25, in Jackson, Weddle, and De Ville, *Mapping Texas*, 25.

48. Spain's options, and this harsh judgment, are explained in Weddle, *Wilderness Manhunt*, 245–47.

49. Folmer, *Franco-Spanish Rivalry*, 219–25. In the paragraphs that follow, I have continued to rely on Folmer for the general outline of events in Louisiana. For the French reaction, see Rule, "Jérôme Phélypeaux," 192. For the reasons for the transfer to Mobile in 1702, see Higginbotham, *Old Mobile*, 1–53.

50. Arnade, "English Invasion of Spanish Florida," 29–37, is a concise overview.

51. Ford, *Triangular Struggle*, 80–86.

52. The viceroy to Alejandro Wauchope, Mexico, 1722, quoted in Griffen, "Spanish Pensacola," 256. See, too, ibid., 252–53, and Ford, *Triangular Struggle*, 78–82.

53. Crane, *Southern Frontier*, 71–98; Wright, Jr., *Anglo-Spanish Rivalry*, 62–68; TePaske, *Governorship of Spanish Florida*, 116–25.

54. Ford, *Triangular Struggle*, 85–86; the quote, dated 1710, is on p. 93.

55. For French influence near Pensacola at this time, see Ford, *Triangular Struggle*, 73.

56. Usner, "Frontier Exchange Economy," 169. The standard work on early Louisiana is Giraud, *History of French Louisiana*, vol. 1. Caruso, *Mississippi Valley Frontier*, is a lively account that emphasizes the early years of Louisiana but is somewhat dated.

57. Hidalgo to the viceroy, San Francisco de los Tejas, Nov. 4, 1716, in Hatcher, ed. and trans., "Descriptions of the Tejas," 53.

58. Ibid. Most sources say that Hidalgo wrote one letter and sent three copies of it. That was not Hidalgo's recollection; the text of Hidalgo's letters has apparently not been preserved (Weddle, *San Juan Bautista*, 15–17, 90–99). Folmer, *Franco-Spanish Rivalry*, 230–31, offers a different but unconvincing hypothesis to explain Hidalgo's actions.

59. The only book-length biography, Phares, *Cavalier in the Wilderness*, is marred by its romantic excesses and vague and uncritical use of sources. This part of Saint-Denis's career was told in detail by Clark, "Louis Juchereau de Saint Denis," 1–26, in an article that has stood the test of time and been only slightly corrected and embellished upon by subsequent writers.

60. The quote from the passport, dated Sept. 12, 1713, is from Folmer, *Franco-Spanish Rivalry*, 232.

61. Formed about 1200, when the Mississippi backed up to block and reverse the flow of the Red, the raft grew slowly, reaching nearly 100 miles in length by 1806 (Flores, "Ecology of the Red River," 19, and Meinig, *Shaping of America*, 195–97). For Saint-Denis on the Red in 1700, see Folmer, *Franco-Spanish Rivalry*, 218.

62. For geographical knowledge of Texas at this time, see Jackson, Weddle, and De Ville, *Mapping Texas*.

63. Weddle, "Talon Interrogations," 209–24, which also provides a valuable corrective to previous accounts of the composition of this party.

64. Ramón to Francisco Hidalgo, July 22, 1714, quoted in Weddle, "Talon Interrogations," 222.

65. Ramón, *Captain Don Domingo Ramón's Diary*, 4, 5, 8–9, 10. Weddle, *San Juan Bautista*, 106–21, provides a full, well-written, well-documented narrative of these years, augmenting the work of earlier historians. In addition to Ramón's diary, the other principal published primary source is Tous, ed. and trans., "Ramón's Expedition," 339–61.

66. Some writers have suggested that Saint-Denis spoke Spanish at this time (see, e.g., Weddle, *San Juan Bautista*, 103), but Ramón to Francisco Hidalgo, July 22, 1714, in Weddle, "Talon Interrogations," 222, states clearly that "the captain does not speak Spanish."

67. Little information about Manuela Sánchez exists and writers have confused her surname, her given name, and the identity of her parents. Saint-Denis himself said her name was "Manuela Sánchez," and frequent references to her in Natchitoches church records give her name as Emmanuela María Sánchez Navarro. She appears to have been the daughter of Capt. Ramón's daughter, hence the surname Sánchez Navarro. See Shelby [ed. and trans.], "St. Denis's Declaration," 169, and Chabot, *With the Makers of San Antonio*, 48, Jackson, Weddle, and DeVille, *Mapping Texas*, 71 *n.* 22, and Mills, *Nachitoches*.

68. Weddle, *San Juan Bautista*, 126, 140.

69. Hidalgo to the viceroy, San Francisco de los Tejas, Nov. 4, 1716, in Hatcher, ed. and trans., "Descriptions of the Tejas," 56. The "Tejas or Texias" quote is on p. 54; see, too, p. 61. Tous, trans. and ed., "Ramón's Expedition," 356, describes the peace pipe and Saint-Denis's preparations.

70. Saint-Denis's two missives to Cadillac, dated Feb. 21 and Sept. 7, 1715, are discussed in a variety of sources, including Folmer, *Franco-Spanish Rivalry*, 234–38. Weddle, "Talon Interrogations," 222, identifies the Talon brothers as the carriers of the first message.

71. Folmer, *Franco-Spanish Rivalry*, 239; Castañeda, *Our Catholic Heritage in Texas*, 2:66–67. The Ais and the Adaes did not belong to any of the three major Caddo confederacies. John, *Storms Brewed*, 165–66, identifies them as "independent Caddo groups."

72. San Francisco de los Tejas, Nov. 4, 1716, quoted in Hatcher, ed. and trans., "Descriptions of the Tejas," 60–61.

73. Shelby, "St. Denis's Second Expedition," 190–216. Manuela Sánchez did not join her husband at Natchitoches until sometime after 1721 (ibid., 214). Saint-Denis's wish to return to Mexico, expressed in Jan. 1744, is in Jackson, Weddle, and DeVille, *Mapping Texas*, 16. Manuela's burial is noted in Mills, *Nachitoches*, 101.

74. Alarcón's instructions are summarized in Céliz, *Diary of the Alarcón Expedition*, 17–19, 21–22. In making this account available, Hoffman provided a more sympathetic view of Alarcón, whose reputation had been besmirched by Father Olivares, "the habitual complainer" (ibid., 27). Hoffmann, ed. and trans., "Mezquía Diary," 312–23, adds no significant detail.

75. Espinosa, *Espinosa-Olivares-Aguirre Expedition*, 5.

76. For an extended discussion of the difference between a pueblo, villa, and ciudad, see Jones, *Los Paisanos*, 3, 10–11. Although Jones (ibid., 41) says that San Antonio was not initially designated a villa, Céliz, *Diary of the Alarcón Expedition*, 22, 23, 49, 55, 84, 86–87, makes it clear that Alarcón immediately founded a villa and that the expedition continued to refer to the new community as the villa of Béjar. In 1731, San Antonio was renamed the villa de San Fernando. See, too, Cruz, *Let There Be Towns*, 58, 64. To avoid confusing the modern reader, I consistently refer to the villa by its present name, San Antonio, rather than its earlier names of Béjar or San Fernando.

77. Olivares to the viceroy, ca. Oct. 1716, in Leutenegger, ed. and trans., "Two Franciscan Documents," 198.

78. Espinosa, *Crónica de los colegios de propaganda fide*, 725–26. Espinosa was an eye witness to these events.

79. Céliz, *Diary of the Alarcón Expedition*, 82–83 and Castañeda, *Our Catholic Heritage in Texas*, 2:106. On the other hand, Hidalgo to the viceroy, San Francisco de los Tejas, Nov. 4, 1716, in Hatcher, ed. and trans., "Descriptions of the Tejas," 59, recommended destroying the French post.

80. TePaske, *Governorship of Spanish Florida*, 122–25, 203–5; Ford, *Triangular Struggle*, 99. For the construction and demise of San Marcos, vividly explained, see Bushnell, "How to Fight a Pirate," 18–35; Boyd, "Fortifications at San Marcos," 3–34, is outdated but still the best overall history of the fort.

81. Crane, *Southern Frontier*, 255; Ford, *Triangular Struggle*, 94–97. The document that these writers cite regarding this latter episode provides no further information. See Gregorio de Salinas to Sgt. Juan de Ayala Escobar, Pensacola, Sept. 9, 1717, in Serrano y Sanz, *Documentos históricos*, 241–42.

82. Crane, *Southern Frontier*, 162–86; 217–18; Wright, *Anglo-Spanish Rivalry*, 71–73; TePaske, *Governorship of Spanish Florida*, 198.

83. Folmer, *Franco-Spanish Rivalry*, 253–57, outlines these events, Holmes, "Dauphine Island," 103–25, provides details.

84. Shelby, ed. and trans., "Projected French Attacks," 457–72.

85. Folmer, *Franco-Spanish Rivalry*, 265–67, 273–74; Castañeda, *Our Catholic Heritage in Texas*, 2:115–19. Contrary to the suggestion of some writers, the residents of east Texas had genuine reason for concern for their safety, as was explained in a joint letter of Isidro Félix de Espinosa and Antonio Margil de Jesús to the viceroy, mission of Purísima Concepción, Texas, July

2, 1719, and in Margil to Francisco de San Esteban, Mission San Antonio de Valero, Sept. 1, 1720, in Habig, ed., *Nothingness Itself*, 254–57, 273–74.

86. The expedition of the marqués de Aguayo is summarized in a number of sources, including Buckley's pioneering work, "Aguayo Expedition," 1–65, and Hackett, "Marquis of San Miguel de Aguayo," 193–214, who adds more detail from Aguayo's own correspondence. The best first-hand account is Santos, ed. and trans., *Aguayo Expedition into Texas*, upon which I have relied. A Spanish version of Peña's diary was published in 1722; a modern edition is in Porrúa Turanzas, ed., *Documentos para la historia eclesiástica y civil*, 1–86; also see Aguayo's own brief account, a letter to the king, Coahuila, June 13, 1722, ibid., 438–41.

87. Aguayo to the king, Coahuila, June 26, 1720, in Hackett, "Marquis of San Miguel de Aguayo," 200–201.

88. Weddle, *San Juan Bautista*, 161, notes that not until Santa Anna entered Texas in 1836 with Mexican troops did a larger force cross the Rio Grande.

89. Felipe V to the viceroy, Nov. 1, 1719, quoted in Folmer, *Franco-Spanish Rivalry*, 267. See, too, Castañeda, *Our Catholic Heritage in Texas*, 2:132–35.

90. Folmer, *Franco-Spanish Rivalry*, 259, wrote of negotiations in 1720, but the Treaty of the Hague, signed on Feb. 17, 1720, effectively ended the war. Negotiations did continue between France and Spain, however, with whom Felipe succeeded in signing a treaty of alliance on Mar. 27, 1721 (Felipe Gonzalo Anes, *El antiguo régimen: Los Borbones* [Madrid: Alianza, 1975], 349–50).

91. Santos, ed., and trans., *Aguayo Expedition into Texas*, 57. Folmer, *Franco-Spanish Rivalry*, 269–70, and Folmer, "Report on Louis de Saint Denis' Intended Raid," 83–88. Castañeda, *Our Catholic Heritage in Texas*, 2:140–41, suggests that Saint-Denis

decided not to offer resistance to a superior force. He may also have received orders not to take action that would upset peace negotiations.

92. In 1721, Antonio de la Peña referred to Matagorda as "La Bahía del Espíritu Santo which the French call San Bernardo" (Santos, ed. and trans., *Aguayo Expedition into Texas*, 66). Confusion continued over the name and location of this bay, which began in the era of La Salle. Although Spaniards located the ruins of La Salle's fort easily in 1721, Frenchmen had forgotten its location and had come to believe it had been on Galveston Bay, which they tried to occupy during the war! (Folmer, *Franco-Spanish Rivalry*, 274–75).

93. Santos, ed. and trans., *Aguayo Expedition into Texas*, 78.

94. Castañeda, *Our Catholic Heritage in Texas*, 2:142–48.

95. Espinosa, *First Expedition of Vargas*, 17.

96. The story of the French advance toward New Mexico, and many of the key documents from the Spanish side, are available in Thomas, ed. and trans., *After Coronado*, upon which all subsequent writers have depended heavily. John, *Storms Brewed*, 156, offers the perceptive suggestion that in 1695 New Mexicans may have been hearing belated reports of their own activities on the plains.

97. Valverde's campaign diary, 1719, in Thomas, ed. and trans., *After Coronado*, 132. The full term, "women *criconas*," was apparently still more derogatory, but neither Thomas nor I can translate it.

98. Valverde to the viceroy, Santa Fe, Nov. 30, 1719, in Thomas, ed. and trans., *After Coronado*, 141–45; the quote is on p. 144.

99. Order of the viceroy [to Valverde], Mexico, Aug. 1, 1719, in Thomas, ed. and trans., *After Coronado*, 138–39.

100. The viceroy's instructions of Jan. 10, 1720, can be inferred from Valverde's replies to the viceroy, Santa Fe, May 27, 1720, June 2, 1720, and June 15, 1720, in Thomas, ed. and trans., *After Coronado*, 154–62. Thomas placed Cuartelejo some fifty miles east of present-day Pueblo, Colorado, but archaeological evidence also points to Scott County, Kansas (Jones, *Pueblo Warriors*, 74 *n.* 16).

101. Valverde to the viceroy, Santa Fe, May 27, 1720, in Thomas, ed. and trans., *After Coronado*, 155.

102. The viceroy to Valverde, Mexico, Sept. 26, 1720, ibid., 234–39.

103. For the role of the Pueblos, see Jones, *Pueblo Warriors*, 96–105.

104. A sketch of L'Archevêque's remarkable life is in Weddle, *Wilderness Manhunt*, 173, 193–94, 196–98, and 249–52. See, too, Thomas, ed. and trans., *After Coronado*, 70, 88, 145.

105. There is some disparity in numbers of expeditionaries between different sources. I am following Hotz, *Indian Skin Paintings*, 183, 185, 203, who sorted through contradictory evidence and deepened our understanding of this tragedy with fresh pictorial evidence. I am also following Hotz's identification of the attackers as Pawnees and Otos (ibid., 158). John, *Storms Brewed*, 249, points to evidence that Kansas Indians committed the deed, but she apparently did not consult Hotz's work. See, too, Chávez, "Segesser Hide Paintings," 96–109.

106. See, e.g., the viceroy to the governor of New Mexico, expressing the king's concern, Mexico City, Oct 23, 1723, in Thomas, ed. and trans., *After Coronado*, 245–46.

107. Crane, *Southern Frontier*, 263.

108. Zúñiga y Cerda to the king, St. Augustine, Sept. 15, 1704, quoted in Boyd et al., *Here They Once Stood*, 69.

Chapter 7: Commercial Rivalry, Stagnation, and the Fortunes of War

The epigraphs are from Hann, ed. and trans., "Leturiondo's Memorial," 175, and Simpson and Nathan, eds. and trans., *San Sabá Papers*, 137.

1. Pedro de Rivera noted that French forces from Canada or Mobile could easily overwhelm the presidio, or simply take a detour around it (Naylor and Polzer, eds., *Pedro de Rivera*, 157–58).

2. Bolton, *Texas in the Middle Eighteenth Century*, 38–41. François Derbanne," Report of the Post of Natchitoches, June 12, 1724, in Bridges and DeVille, eds. and trans., "Natchitoches and the Trail to the Rio Grande," 256, who reported that in 1724 the residents of Los Adaes "were starving to death," and that the French sold them corn in addition to the "few guns and little powder" that they usually furnished them (Magnaghi, ed. and trans., "Texas as Seen by Governor Winthuysen," 177). For trade as far as New Orleans, and the exchange of Spanish horses, see Castañeda, *Our Catholic Heritage in Texas*, 4:238–39.

3. This episode is described in Griffith, "Hasinai Indians," 140–41.

4. Surrey, *Commerce of Louisiana*, 418–27. See, too, Griffen, "Spanish Pensacola," 262, and Coker, *Financial History of Pensacola's Spanish Presidios*, 20.

5. Gillaspie, "Sergeant Major Ayala y Escobar," 153, 164; Wright, *Anglo-Spanish Rivalry*, 78, 98, 100, 103, 105, 107; Surrey, *Commerce of Louisiana*, 27–30.

6. TePaske, *Governorship of Spanish Florida*, 204–5; Bushnell, "How to Fight a Pirate," 18–35.

7. Lang, *Conquest and Commerce*, 224.

8. Henry Kamen, *Spain in the Later Seventeenth Century, 1665–1700* (London: Longmans, 1980), 105, and Elliott, *Spain and Its World*, 215, who points to the historiographical debate surrounding the question of Spanish decline—a problem complicated by regional variations in the economy.

9. Many works describe the trading system; for cogent analyses of the theory and practice, see Stein and Stein, *Colonial Heritage of Latin America*, 44–53, and Murdo J. Macleod, "Spain and America: The Atlantic Trade," in Bethell, ed., *Cambridge History of Latin America*, 1:341–88.

10. Athanase de Mézières to Teodoro de Croix, Bexar, Oct. 7, 1779, in Bolton, ed., *Athanase de Mézières*, 2:293, 297, urging the opening of Matagorda Bay to legal commerce. For the continued restrictions and red tape in the late colonial era see Guice, "Trade Goods for Texas," 507–19; Faulk, *Last Years of Spanish Texas*, 98–99; Hatcher, *Opening of Texas*, 52; Hatcher, trans., "Texas in 1820," 64. Shipping to the Texas coast was permitted in times of crisis, as when the marqués de Aguayo marched into East Texas to retake it from the French.

11. For the later investigation, see Thomas, trans. and ed., *Alonso de Posada Report*, 8, 16, 52. The quote is on p. 16.

12. Revilla Gigedo, *Informe sobre las misiones*, 72.

13. Ramos de Arizpe from neighboring Coahuila (Benson, ed. and trans., *Report . . . Dr. Miguel Ramos de Arizpe*, 24, 40–44). See also Moorhead, *New Mexico's Royal Road*, 28–54.

14. Hann, ed. and trans., "Leturiondo's Memorial," 188.

15. MacLachlan, *Spain's Empire in the New World*, 160 n. 29.

16. Wright, *Anglo-Spanish Rivalry*, 58. For the extensive contraband from the beginning, see Lyon, "Santa Elena," 7. For the 1600s see Bushnell, *King's Coffer*, 89, 91. For the mid-1700s, see Harman, *Trade and Privateering*.

17. This statement cannot be substantiated from documentary evidence, of course, for successful smugglers leave few records, but we do have archaeological evidence. See, e.g., Corbin, "Spanish-Indian Interaction," 1:274, who points out that French and Chinese porcelain was more common than Mexican majolica at Los Adaes, and Fox, ed., *Traces of Texas History*, 84.

18. Wright, *Anglo-Spanish Rivalry*, 72.

19. Griffen, "Spanish Pensacola," 255.

20. This was Brig. Gen. Pedro de Rivera's recommendation to the viceroy in 1744 and, in my view, reflects Spanish practice toward Pensacola, if not Spanish policy. See Coker, ed., *Pedro de Rivera's Report*, 15. For the idea of abandoning the site, and Rivera's rejection of it, see ibid., 13–14.

21. Griffen, "Spanish Pensacola," 246–47, 261–62; Coker, *Financial History of Pensacola's Spanish Presidios*, 8.

22. The quote is from Lang, *Conquest and Commerce*, 227, who draws incisive comparisons. For elaboration, see Ralph Davis, *The Rise of the Atlantic Economies* (Ithaca, N.Y.: Cornell University Press, 1973), chap. 12, "England: The Untroubled Land." Eccles, *France in America*, 158, 166, notes that France moved into Louisiana for political reasons and that politics motivated France to remain, despite financial losses. But France persisted in attempting to turn Louisiana into a profit-making venture.

23. Most writers treat the fur trade as strictly English and French endeavors. See, e.g., Wolf, *Europe and the People without History*, chap. 6.

24. Lyon, "St. Augustine in 1580," 23; Hann, Apalachee, 148, 158, 240, 242–43; Weber, *Taos Trappers*, 12–31.

25. Stein and Stein, *Colonial Heritage of Latin America*, 4–26; Max Savelle, *Empires to Nations: Expansion in America, 1713–1824* (Minneapolis: University of Minnesota Press, 1974), 77–101.

26. I do not, of course, mean to suggest that Frenchmen and Englishmen had *no* interest in converting Indians. The Jesuits' vigorous efforts in French Canada and some of the English experiments are well known. James Axtell, *The Invasion Within: The Contest of Cultures in Colonial North America* (New York: Oxford University Press, 1985), examines French and English efforts to win Indian souls and, in the case of Englishmen, to "civilize" them. See, too, Bernard Sheehan, *Savagism and Civility: Indians and Englishmen in Colonial Virginia* (Cambridge: Cambridge University Press, 1980), 6, 116–43. The missionary impulse was weak, however, in Louisiana (Eccles, *France in America*, 158; John, *Storms Brewed*, 157–61, 196–98), and among Carolinians, who seemed to prefer enslaving Indians to converting them (Crane, *Southern Frontier*, 145–46, 166).

27. On both sides, perception proved more potent than reality; not until the late eighteenth century did key Spanish policymakers question the conventional wisdom and reevaluate the effectiveness of native arms. On this complicated question, see the good letter to the editor by Donald W. Matson and my reply in the *NMHR* 57 (Apr. 1982): 203–8; Schilz and Worcester, "Spread of Firearms," 1–10; and my chapter 8.

28. The prohibition against giving or trading arms to Indians was issued in 1521 by Carlos V. *Recopilación de leyes*, tomo II, lib. VI, tit. I, ley xxiv, and remained in force in theory until 1779 (see my chapter 8). For examples of private parties trading in firearms, see Jones, *Pueblo Warriors*, 55–56, 135–36, and for the arming of the Pueblos, see ibid., 61, 93, 116, 125. In Florida as early as 1676, Spaniards armed Apalachees for a raid on Chiscas (Hann, *Apalachee*, 186), and in 1680, when English-armed Indians raided Santa Catalina in Guale, they met resistance from forty mission Indians, sixteen of whom had firearms (Bushnell, "Archaeology of Mission Santa Catalina de Guale"). For an example of arming mission Indians in Texas, see Hatcher, ed., "Diary of a Visit of Inspections of the Texas Missions," 51.

In New Mexico, at least until the mid-1750s, officials apparently concealed the fact that Pueblos had arms (Jones, *Pueblo Warriors*, 123 n. 32). In Florida, on the other hand, Gov. Francisco Córcoles y

Martínez seems to have openly adopted such a policy in 1715, and his successors followed his lead to the best of their means (TePaske, *Governorship of Spanish Florida*, 198–200; Boyd, ed. and trans., "Diego Peña's Expedition," 7, 12, 23).

29. TePaske, *Governorship of Spanish Florida*, 205–6, argues the importance of the shortage of weapons for Florida policy, and his generalization seems to apply all across the frontier.

30. Bolton, *Texas in the Middle Eighteenth Century*, 336–37, describing the activities of Gov. Jacinto de Barrios y Jáuregui in the 1750s.

31. TePaske, *Governorship of Spanish Florida*, 217.

32. For interesting comparative commentary, see White, *Roots of Dependency*, 47–48, 57–59.

33. A number of writers have come to these conclusions. For a brief comparative overview, see TePaske, "French, Spanish, and English Indian Policy," 9–39, and Jaenen, "Characteristics of French-Amerindian Contact," 89–90.

34. Antonio de Bonilla, expressing in 1772 what I take to be the conventional wisdom of his day ("what room is there for doubt that the French are pleasing to the Indians?), and quoting the statement of a missionary from 1718, in West, ed. and trans., "Bonilla's Brief Compendium," 70.

35. White, *Roots of Dependency*, 49.

36. Ibid., 50.

37. Jack P. Greene, *Pursuits of Happiness: The Social Development of Early Modern British Colonies and the Formation of American Culture* (Chapel Hill: University of North Carolina Press, 1988), chaps. 3–6, and the table on pp. 178–79.

38. Wood, "Changing Population of the Colonial South," 38. See, too, Bernard Bailyn, *The Peopling of British North America: An Introduction* (New York: Alfred A. Knopf, 1986), 109–10.

39. The classic work on this contest is Herbert

E. Bolton's introduction to Bolton, ed., *Arredondo's Historical Proof.* The introduction alone was reprinted as a separate title: Bolton and Ross, *Debatable Land.*

40. Crane, *Southern Frontier*, 185, 254.

41. TePaske, *Governorship of Spanish Florida*, 199.

42. Ibid., 121–32, 208–9. Crane, *Southern Frontier*, 238–53, 263–72, emphasizes the Carolina side of the story. For a general description of the Yamasees, see Covington, "Yamasee Indians," 119–28, and for a remarkably detailed description, see Hann, "St. Augustine's Fallout," 180–96.

43. The quote is from fray Joseph de Bullones to the king, Oct. 5, 1728, in Hann, "St. Augustine's Fallout," 196.

44. For a recent summary of this early period of Creek history, with a fine analysis of the changes wrought by Europeans on Creek society, see Green, *Politics of Indian Removal*, 17–28, and for raiding in Florida, see Covington, "Migration of the Seminoles," 340–57.

45. The quote is from Pedro Sánchez Griñán, who lived in St. Augustine from 1731–42, in Scardaville and Belmonte, eds. and trans., "Florida in the Late First Spanish Period," 11. Hann, "St. Augustine's Fallout," 180–200, provides the most detailed picture of these peoples.

46. TePaske, *Governorship of Spanish Florida*, 224.

47. Chatelain, *Defenses of Spanish Florida*, 82–88.

48. Wright, *Anglo-Spanish Rivalry*, 74–86; TePaske, *Governorship of Spanish Florida*, 133–39, 209–15. Lanning, *Diplomatic History of Georgia*, is a more detailed chronicle of these years, written largely from the English side.

49. The encouragement was political rather than humanitarian. See Landers, "Spanish Sanctuary," 296–313, and Landers, "Gracia Real," 9–30.

50. TePaske, *Governorship of Spanish Florida*, 139–46.

51. Ibid., 146–52; Wright, *Anglo-Spanish Rivalry*, 87–100.

52. TePaske, *Governorship of Spanish Florida*, 190–91; Gannon, *Cross in the Sand*, 78–83.

53. Morales Padrón, "Colonos canarios en Indias," 424–29, reported that 700 Canary Islanders moved to Apalachee between 1757 and 1761, and TePaske, *Governorship of Spanish Florida*, 87–89, repeated that story. There is no evidence, however, that the Canary Islanders actually reached Apalachee during those years, although some apparently made it to St. Augustine (Gold, *Borderland Empires in Transition*, 67, 154, 156–57; personal correspondence, John H. Hann to David J. Weber, Tallahassee, Sept. 25, 1990 and Oct. 15, 1990; Jane Landers to Weber, Gainesville, Nov. 21, 1991).

54. Wood, "Changing Population of the Colonial South," 38, 59.

55. Marchena Fernández, "Guarniciones," 108–10.

56. Greene, *Pursuits of Happiness*, 185.

57. For Florida's ongoing need for support and its inability to feed itself, see TePaske, *Governorship of Spanish Florida*, 105, 87. For Florida's seventeenth-century ranching industry, see Arnade, "Cattle Raising," 116–24, and for richer detail and the evidence of exports see Bushnell, "Menéndez Márquez Cattle Barony," 407–31.

58. TePaske, *Governorship of Spanish Florida*, 26–27.

59. Wright, *Anglo-Spanish Rivalry*, 101–5; TePaske, *Governorship of Spanish Florida*, 154–55; Bolton and Ross, *Debatable Land*, 98–110.

60. Folmer, *Franco-Spanish Rivalry*, 293–97, 303–5. A more detailed account and guidance to further sources appear in Bolton, *Texas in the Middle Eighteenth Century*, and in Hackett [ed. and trans.], "Policy of the Spanish Crown," 107–45.

61. Usner, "Frontier Exchange Economy," 171. See, too, Wood, "Changing Population of the Colonial South," 39. The first

figures are from 1732. For the considerable literature on early forced and voluntary immigration see Brasseaux, "French Louisiana," 8–9.

62. On this later point, see Lemieux, "Mississippi Valley," 39–56. For an authoritative overview of these years, see Eccles, *France in America*, 158–72.

63. Clark, *New Orleans*, provides more than its title suggests.

64. Usner, "Frontier Exchange Economy," 168–71; Thomas, *Fort Toulouse*, xxviii–xxx, 1–38. TePaske, "French, Spanish, and English Indian Policy," 27, sees Mobile as the center of French Indian trade until 1763.

65. Eccles, *France in America*, 167; Surrey, *Commerce of Louisiana*, is dated but still of value.

66. Usner, "Deerskin Trade," 84.

67. Isidro Félix de Espinosa and Antonio Margil de Jesús to the viceroy, Mission Purísima Concepción, Texas, July 2, 1719, in Habig, ed., *Nothingness Itself*, 255.

68. Isidro Félix de Espinosa and Antonio Margil de Jesús to Mathías Sáenz de San Antonio, Guadalupe de Zacatecas, July 20, 1724, asking that this question be raised with the king, ibid., 304–6.

69. Naylor and Polzer, eds., *Pedro de Rivera*, 83–84. Hidalgo to the viceroy, San Francisco de los Tejas, Nov. 4, 1716, in Hatcher, ed. and trans., "Descriptions of the Tejas," 56, 57. See also John, *Storms Brewed*, 208–10, 222–23.

70. Hatcher, ed., "Diary of a Visit . . . to the Texas Missions," 65 (writing in 1768). See, too, ibid., 67–68.

71. See, too, the comments of Céliz, *Diary of the Alarcón Expedition*, 15, and Magnaghi, ed. and trans., "Texas as Seen by Governor Winthuysen," 175. Bolton, *Texas in the Middle Eighteenth Century*, 21, like many other writers, blamed the failures of Spanish missions in East Texas largely on the French trade. For the continued failure of the East Texas missions, see ibid., 100–101.

72. Santos, ed. and trans., *Aguayo Expedition into Texas*, 22, 36, 48, 52, 74; Isidro Félix de Espinosa and Antonio Margil de Jesús to the viceroy, Zacatecas, June 23, 1722, in Habig, ed., *Nothingness Itself*, 283–84.

73. Meinig, *Shaping of America*, 1:203.

74. Céliz, *Diary of the Alarcón Expedition*, 42, 54–55, 71–72, 84. See, too, Espinosa, *Crónica de los colegios de propaganda fide*, 725; Santos, ed. and trans., *Aguayo Expedition into Texas*, 48, 49, 52, 56. Conditions had not improved much a century later. See Sibley, *Travelers in Texas*, 27–28.

75. Hoffman, ed. and trans., "Mezquía Diary," 823.

76. Antonio Margil de Jesús to the viceroy, Mission Purísima Concepción, Texas, July 22, 1716, in Habig, ed., *Nothingness Itself*, 226.

77. John, *Storms Brewed*, 265–66, 287. For Indian aversion to Spaniards, see Benito Fernández de Santa Ana, Mission San Antonio, Feb. 20, 1740, to Pedro del Barco, in Leutenegger, ed. and trans., "Two Franciscan Documents," 205, and the similar observations of François Dion Deprez Derbanne, 1717, who had crossed Texas twice, in Bridges and DeVille, eds. and trans., "Natchitoches and the Trail to the Rio Grande," 251.

78. The garrison of San Antonio to Gov. Juan Antonio de Bustillo y Zeballos, presidio of San Antonio de Béjar, Dec. 4, 1732, quoted in Simpson and Nathan, eds. and trans., *San Sabá Papers*, xiii. The soldiers' dire view was seconded by a local priest, who noted the large number of arms and horses possessed by the Indians. For a detailed analysis of Apache activities in New Mexico and Texas during these years, see John, *Storms Brewed*, 256–303. Schilz, *Lipan Apaches*, adds nothing new to the story for these early years.

79. Bolton, *Texas in the Middle Eighteenth Century*, 43–55; 135–278. For more pithy accounts, see John, *Storms Brewed*, 276–92, and Weddle, *San Sabá Mission*, 30–35.

Starnes, *San Gabriel Missions*, adds little. For the search for the sites, see Gilmore, *San Xavier Missions*. Newcomb, *Indians of Texas*, 134, described the bands that came to be called Tonkawas as culturally similar to Apaches by the early nineteenth century, although they may have been a Coahuiltecan people.

80. For these motives, see Weddle, *San Sabá Mission*, 22, 103, 153. Although in present Texas, San Sabá was not then administratively in Texas, New Mexico, or Coahuila, but directly under the viceroy's jurisdiction. The discussion that follows is derived almost entirely from Weddle. I have provided citations only to statistics, quotes, or interpretations that might be controversial.

81. A number of writers have suggested that Pedro Terreros's interest in the missions at San Sabá had been heightened by reports of mines at Los Almagres, seventy-five miles to the west. The evidence does not support that connection. Patten, ed. and trans., "Miranda's Inspection," 231.

82. The figure is in Weddle, *San Sabá Mission*, 64.

83. Ratcliffe, " 'Escenas de Martirio,' " 506–34, examines the extraordinary painting of this episode, executed ca. 1763.

84. Ortiz's failure has often been described as a resounding defeat, but the most authoritative study judges it as "more in the nature of a standoff" (Weddle, *San Sabá Mission*, 129). For the number of men under Ortiz, see ibid., 118; for the number killed, wounded, or missing, see ibid., 125. Ortiz mentions his career in Morocco in a letter to the viceroy, San Luis de Amarillas, Apr. 8, 1758, in Simpson and Nathan, eds. and trans., *San Sabá Papers*, 138.

85. Weddle, *San Sabá Mission*, 112–14, 131, 139–40. Ortiz, not the most objective witness, reported that fourteen Frenchmen were seen in the fort on the Red River. The phrase "foreign political agents" shows up frequently in the testimony—see, e.g., Au-

ditor Domingo Valcárcel to the viceroy, Mexico, Apr. 6, 1758, in Simpson and Nathan, eds. and trans., *San Sabá Papers*, 32.

86. The quote is in the report of Joseph de Gutiérrez, presidio of San Luis, Mar. 21, 1758, Simpson and Nathan, eds. and trans., *San Sabá Papers*, 44. The estimates are in the report of fray Miguel de Molina, Mar. 22, 1758 (ibid., 85).

87. Presidio of San Luis, Mar. 21, 1758, in Simpson and Nathan, eds. and trans., *San Sabá Papers*, 53. For similar statements, see the testimony of Lt. Juan Galván and others, and Juan Leal, both on Mar. 22, 1758 (ibid., 66, 76), and Ensign Juan Cortinas, Mar. 28, 1758 (ibid., 117–18).

88. Testimony of Ensign Juan Cortinas, Mar. 28, 1758, ibid., 118.

89. Manuel de la Piscina to the viceroy, presidio of Nuestra Señora de Loreto, Mar. 24, 1758, in Simpson and Nathan, eds. and trans., *San Sabá Papers*, 35.

90. For the petition, ca. Mar. 27, 1758, see ibid., 107–9.

91. Ortiz to the viceroy, Nov. 8, 1760, quoted in Weddle, *San Sabá Mission*, 142.

92. Residents of San Antonio apparently first learned of Comanches in 1733 and made their first direct contact with them in 1743. Faulk, "Comanche Invasion of Texas," 12. For the despoblado, see Daniel, "Spanish Frontier in West Texas," 481–95.

93. Fernández de Santa Ana, Feb. 20, 1740, to Pedro del Barco, in Leutenegger, ed. and trans., "Two Franciscan Documents," 202.

94. Ibid.

95. Campbell and Campbell, *Indian Groups*, corrects earlier assumptions about the ethnicity of the mission Indians; in the incomplete mission records, the Campbells identify a great variety of groups, thirty-three at Concepción alone (67). For the best tabulation of population at these missions, see Schuetz, "Indians of the San Antonio Missions," 128. Schuetz takes too rosy a view of these missions, suggesting that they worked well because the padres did not repeat earlier mistakes and, therefore, did not have to resort to force. She does, however, report whips, stocks, shackles, and handcuffs at each mission, and that lashes were used (ibid., 242). For disease and flight, see Persons, "Secular Life," 58–59. The San Antonio missions have been the subject of considerable study, most of it written from Franciscan viewpoints and depicting happy Indians. See, e.g., Habig, "Mission San José," 503–16. The documents tell a different story, see, e.g., Benito Fernández de Santa Ana, *Letters and Memorials of . . . Fernández de Santa Ana*. The most detailed overview is Castañeda, *Our Catholic Heritage in Texas*, vol. 3. A balanced modern work has yet to appear, but the direction such a work will probably take is suggested by Hinojosa, "Friars and Indians," 7–25; Alfaro, "Spirit of the First Franciscan Missionaries," 49–66, is more traditionally triumphalist in tone.

96. Isidro Félix de Espinosa and Antonio Margil de Jesús to the viceroy, Zacatecas, June 23, 1722, in Habig, ed., *Nothingness Itself*, 290–91. For the explicit link between security and population see, e.g., Magnaghi, ed. and trans., "Texas as Seen by Governor Winthuysen," 179.

97. Aguayo to the king, Coahuila, June 13, 1722, in Porrúa Turanzas, ed., *Documentos para la historia . . . de Texas*, 444. Similar sentiments were repeated a few years later in the reports of Brig. Gen. Pedro de Rivera (Naylor and Polzer, eds., *Pedro de Rivera*, 161). With the exception of nine families brought to San Sabá in 1757, Tlaxcalans were apparently not used as immigrants in Texas (Simmons, "Tlascalans," 105–6).

98. For the most detailed and authoritative account, see Castañeda, *Our Catholic Heritage in Texas*, 2:268–301. Briefer and more

accessible is Cruz, *Let There Be Towns*, 59–63. The number of Islanders is often put at 56, because that number set out for Texas, but one young girl died on route at San Juan Bautista.

99. Jones, *Los Paisanos*, 47; Schuetz, "People of San Antonio," 73–83. De la Teja, "Land and Society in 18th Century San Antonio," puts the population of San Antonio between 242 and 310 on the eve of the arrival of the Canary Islanders.

100. Cruz, *Let There Be Towns*, 78; Spell, ed. and trans., "Grant and First Survey of the City of San Antonio," 82; De la Teja, "Forgotten Founders," 36–37. I am using the current name, San Antonio, to avoid confusion for the modern reader.

101. De la Teja, "Forgotten Founders," 38; Dunn, "Apache Relations in Texas," 262.

102. Myres, *Ranch in Spanish Texas*, 12–15; and Jackson, *Los Mesteños*, 32–85; De la Teja, "Land and Society in 18th Century San Antonio," 231–82.

103. For the Canary Islanders' view of their predicament, see Fernández de Santa Ana, "Memorial . . . Concerning the Canary Islanders," 275–76. The remainder of this memorial presents the Franciscan case. For the nature of mission agriculture, see Weniger, "Wilderness, Farm, and Ranch," 106–7.

104. Schuetz, "Indians of the San Antonio Missions," 297–301, argues that the missions benefited San Antonio economically. The question deserves further study, and a comparison with larger, more efficient missions, such as those of California, would be interesting. For a judicious consideration of this question in another setting, see Treutlein, "Economic Regime of the Jesuit Missions," 289–300. One of the most knowledgeable observers of northern New Spain suggested that the Franciscans themselves bore some responsibility for the failure of the frontier to develop economically: the marqués de Altamira, Opinion Concerning the Population of Nueva Vizcaya, Dec. 23, 1749, in Velázquez, [ed.], *El marqués de Altamira*, 76,

105. De la Teja, "Forgotten Founders," 27–38; "Land and Society in 18th Century San Antonio," 283–325, 330–39, 385–86; "Indians, Soldiers, and Canary Islanders," 81–96; and Poyo, "Canary Islands Immigrants of San Antonio," 41–58. Regulations continued to stifle growth until the end of the colonial era. See Mariano Sosa to Manuel Salcedo, May 26, 1810, in Castañeda, *Our Catholic Heritage in Texas*, 5:429, and Jackson, *Los Mesteños*, 507–10.

106. Gerhard, *North Frontier*, 341, whose figure for San Antonio may be low.

107. Jones, *Los Paisanos*, 65–78, summarizes the development of Nuevo Santander and provides guidance to sources. Jones inadvertently identifies the French instead of the English as the primary catalyst for the colony (ibid., 65). For a more detailed account, see Hill, *José de Escandón*, still the standard study. On the novelty of massive colonization, see Velázquez, *Tres estudios*, 88–91. For the northern boundary of Nuevo Santander, see Gerhard, *North Frontier*, 363.

108. Cruz, *Let There Be Towns*, 81–104; Hinojosa, *Borderlands Town in Transition*, 16. The Hispanic population of San Antonio, not counting mission Indians, was 1,295 in 1789 (Tjarks, "Comparative Demographic Analysis of Texas," 305, table 2).

109. For Texas population, see the table in Gerhard, *North Frontier*, 341; for New Mexico (including the El Paso District), see ibid., 322. For relative populations, see Jones, *Los Paisanos*, 240, whose figure of 30,953 for New Mexico includes Pueblo Indians (127). Gutiérrez, *When Jesus Came*, 167, contains valuable demographic analysis for New Mexico, but his figures do not include the populous El

Paso district. For the 1793 census of New Spain, see Humboldt, *Political Essay*, 33.

110. Maintaining a Spanish presence in Texas had cost the king 63,000 pesos a year, and the total bill had come to 3,000,000 pesos by 1747 (the marqués de Altamira, Auditor General de la Guerra, Opinion Concerning Not Changing the Missions of Texas, Jan. 28, 1747, in Velázquez, [ed.], *El marqués de Altamira*, 76). For the consequences of failing to establish towns, see Altamira's opinion of Jan. 31, 1750, to the viceroy, in Porrúa Turanzas, ed., *Documentos para la historia . . . de Texas*, 193. The extent of Texas's dependence on the military budget awaits a demographic study comparable to the one Juan Marchena has done for Florida.

111. For unfulfilled plans, see, e.g., West, ed. and trans., "Bonilla's Brief Compendium," 65, and John, "La situación y visión de los indios," 469.

112. Webb, *Great Plains*, argued that "defects in the Spanish colonial system" did not explain Spain's failure to expand onto the Great Plains (85). He offered two other reasons, the resistance of Plains Indians and "the country itself," which he said did not attract Spaniards (87). Webb and I agree only on the effectiveness of Plains Indians. In New Mexico, Spaniards moved onto the High Plains when danger from hostile Indians diminished late in the eighteenth century. Meinig, *Imperial Texas*, 26, 28, sees the woodlands of East Texas as uninviting to Hispanics.

113. The quote is from the marqués de Altamira, Opinion Concerning the Population of Nueva Vizcaya, Dec. 23, 1749, in Velázquez, [ed.], *El marqués de Altamira*, 116, who makes this general point, as does Kelly, *Franciscan Missions of New Mexico*, 26–35, 40–53, 92. By 1773, only sixteen Franciscans served twenty-one pueblos and three villas in the up-river settlements. Mendinueta to the viceroy, Santa Fe, Jan. 8, 1773, in Mendinueta, *Indian and Mission Affairs*, 18.

114. Cutter, ed. and trans., "An Anonymous Statistical Report," 347–52. These figures represent my analysis of this census, which was prepared apparently for the marqués de Rubí (see my chapter 8). The urban population included Hispanicized Indians. For a general overview of New Mexico's population, see Gerhard, *North Frontier*, 321–22, and the deeper analysis in Jones, *Los Paisanos*, 119–30, and Gutiérrez, *When Jesus Came*, 166–75, who does not include El Paso.

115. The marqués de Altamira to the viceroy, Mexico, Jan. 14, 1753, quoted in Thomas, ed. and trans., *Plains Indians and New Mexico*, 126. For the general agreement of visitors on this point, see Simmons, "'Misery' as a Factor in New Mexican Colonial Life," 227–30. For the continuing exploitation of Pueblos, see Vélez de Escalante, "Letter to the Missionaries of New Mexico," 321–22, 327–28; Adams, ed. and trans., *Bishop Tamarón's Visitation*, 26; Kelly, *Franciscan Missions of New Mexico*, 73–79.

116. Adams, ed. and trans., *Bishop Tamarón's Visitation*, 58.

117. The quotes are from Morfi, *Account of Disorders*, 15, 19, who condemned this trade with passion and perhaps exaggeration. See, too, Moorhead, *New Mexico's Royal Road*, 49–54.

118. Not all Frenchmen were so misinformed. François Dion Deprez Derbanne, "Report on the Post of Natchitoches," June 12, 1724, in Bridges and DeVille, eds. and trans., "Natchitoches and the Trail to the Rio Grande," had direct experience trading in northern New Spain and noted that "there is no silver in New Mexico, according to what the Spaniards say" (258).

119. These early efforts are described in a number of sources. See, especially, John,

Storms Brewed, 213–20, and 306–16, who has done the definitive work on early European-Wichita relations; Norall, *Bourgmont*, 28–80, 125–61; and Phillips, *Fur Trade*, 2:478–81.

120. The Mallet expedition has been described by numerous authors, but the best general source remains Folmer, "Mallet Expedition," 161–73, which contains a translation of an abstract of their lost journal, as well as letters from Santiago Roybal to Father Beaubois, Santa Fe, ca. 1740, and Paez Hurtado to Saint-Denis, Santa Fe, Apr. 30, 1740. For their route, Folmer is no longer adequate. See Blakeslee, "Mallet Expedition," 15–18, 14–16.

121. See the reports of 1748 in Folmer, "Contraband Trade between Louisiana and New Mexico," 265–66.

122. Vélez Cachupín to his successor, [Santa Fe], Aug. 12, 1754, in Thomas, ed. and trans., *Plains Indians and New Mexico*, 135.

123. Vélez Cachupín to the viceroy, Santa Fe, Mar. 8, 1750, quoted and paraphrased in Bolton, "French Intrusions into New Mexico, 1749–1752," 161–62.

124. Council of the Indies to the King, Madrid, Nov. 27, 1754, in Thomas, ed. and trans., *Plains Indians and New Mexico*, 87.

125. For the general outline of these French commercial ventures by their leading student, see Folmer, *Franco-Spanish Rivalry*, 297–303. For the immediate aftermath of the Mallet's expedition, see Blaine, "French Efforts to Reach Santa Fe," 133–57.

126. Brandon, *Quivira*, recounts pre-American activity along the trail.

127. For a recent summary of this complex affair and guidance to sources, see De-Conde, *This Affair of Louisiana*, 22–29, 293–94. Boulle, "Some Eighteenth-Century French Views," 26–27, explains that French motives are likely to remain

murky until more documentation becomes available, and that such explanations as the well-known "peace bribe" cannot be proven.

128. Quoted in Rodríguez Casado, *Primeros años de dominación española*, 43–44; see, too, ibid., 46–47. Although this work has been superseded in part by Moore, *Revolt in Louisiana*, it includes valuable appendices of documents and remains worth consulting.

129. Wright, *Anglo-Spanish Rivalry*, 107–10. For the strength of Florida at this time, see TePaske, *Governorship of Spanish Florida*, 156–58.

130. Cummins, "Luciano de Herrera," 43–57, which supersedes Lawson, "Luciano de Herrera," 170–76.

131. In addition to the evacuations of St. Augustine and Pensacola, some 70 residents of Fort San Marcos at Apachalee were withdrawn. Gold, *Borderlands Empires in Transition*, 23–106, 153–61, provides a detailed account. His work builds on several earlier studies, including Corbitt, "Spanish Relief Policy," 67–82.

132. Royal Order of May 1, 1765, quoted in Moore, *Revolt in Louisiana*, 43. I have relied heavily on Moore's interpretation of the troubled transition from French to Spanish rule. Carl Brasseaux, on the other hand, suggests that Moore's account has an inevitable pro-Spanish bias and that accounts written from the French side point to "confusion stemming from economic and governmental instability, especially Ulloa's administrative ineptitude, as the major cause of the rebellion" (Brasseaux, "French Louisiana," 15). For essential documents, see Kinnaird, ed., *Spain in the Mississippi Valley*.

133. The quotes, respectively are in Chandler, ed. and trans., "Ulloa's Account of the 1768 Revolt," 417, 418, 433, written immediately after his expulsion. See, too, Moore, *Revolt in Louisiana*, 161.

134. Moore, *Revolt in Louisiana*, 171, points to new evidence of proto-republican rhetoric from the rebels of 1768, but it is difficult to take this rhetoric seriously. Some of the rebels' rhetoric was also aimed at Ulloa himself, a martinet whose behavior some historians have viewed as an important cause of the revolt. Moore suggests that Ulloa's personality was not "the key element in the failure of his administration" (ibid., 11).

135. Boulle, "French Reactions to the Louisiana Revolution," 153.

136. Ekberg, *Colonial Ste. Genevieve*, and Foley, *Genesis of Missouri*, 26–27, 36–37.

137. The quote is from Carlos III to O'Reilly, Aranjuez, Apr. 16, 1769, in Texada, *O'Reilly and the New Orleans Rebels*, 46, who concludes that O'Reilly has been unfairly judged until recently (114–25). Torres Ramírez, *Alejandro O'Reilly*, 96–114, contains a clear but unanalytical summary of these events. Moore, *Revolt in Louisiana*, 185–215, provides a richer account.

138. Torres Ramírez, *Alejandro O'Reilly*, 115–83, and appendices that include O'Reilly's municipal ordinances for New Orleans and his regulations for judging civil and criminal cases in Louisiana (187–225). The doubts of some scholars that Spanish law completely superseded French law in Louisiana have now been laid to rest according to Arnold, *Unequal Laws*, 45.

139. Clark, *New Orleans*, 172.

140. Din, *Canary Islanders of Louisiana*, 25. For immigration from Málaga, see Din, "Lieutenant Colonel Francisco Bouligny," 187–202.

141. For the population in 1766, see Acosta Rodríguez, *La población de Luisiana española*, 33.

142. Brasseaux, *Founding of New Acadia*, 91, puts the number at between 2,600 to 3,000.

143. On this, see, e.g., Meinig, *Shaping of America*, 1:233.

Chapter 8: Indian Raiders and the Reorganization of Frontier Defenses

The epigraphs are from Thomas, ed. and trans., *Alonso de Posada Report*, 51; Brinckerhoff and Faulk, eds. and trans., *Lancers for the King*, 32 (speaking specifically of Apaches); Gálvez, *Instructions*, 38.

1. Christon I. Archer, *The Army in Bourbon Mexico, 1760–1810* (Albuquerque: University of New Mexico, 1977), 1–2, 8–10, a fine study that does not, however, include the troops on the northern frontier of New Spain. For a hemispheric view, which includes the northern borderlands of Spain's empire, see Julio Albi, *La defensa de las Indias (1764–1799)* (Madrid: Instituto de Cooperación Iberoamericana, 1987).

2. Historical sources for reconstructing Indian motives are scarce, but a number of writers have made reasonable conjectures. See, e.g., Velázquez, "Los indios gentiles," 116–23.

3. Navarro García, *José de Gálvez*, 60, 126, 213, which should be used in conjunction with Hernández Sánchez-Barba, *La última expansión*. Based heavily on archival sources, these books are indispensable for their rich detail.

4. Hernández Sánchez-Barba, *La última expansión*, 83, who reports that a subsequent investigation of the viceroy's conduct revealed that he had failed to release the annual payroll in 1765 (see, too, p. 194, which puts the year at 1762). Navarro García, *José de Gálvez*, 135–36, believes that Villalba's suspicions were not well founded.

5. Kinnaird, ed. and trans., *Frontiers of New Spain*, 44. Except where otherwise noted, I have relied on Lafora's account of Rubí's expedition, as edited and translated by Kinnaird. The Spanish text was first published in Alessio Robles, ed. *Nicolás de Lafora*. Lafora was one of seven military engineers who came to Mexico with Villalba in 1764. For a brief biography, see the pioneering study by Fireman, *Spanish Royal*

Corps of Engineers, 74–76. The Corps was founded in 1711, and only one member, Francisco Alvarez Barreiro, visited the borderlands prior to Lafora (ibid., 49–57). Rubí's career, before and after his important inspection, has yet to be studied. Kinnaird's account has mislead other writers into assuming that Rubí arrived in 1765 (see, e.g., Bannon, ed., *Bolton and the Spanish Borderlands*), or to assume that José de Gálvez gave Rubí his assignment (as does John, *Storms Brewed*, 377, and Park, "Spanish Indian Policy," 219–20). When the Crown issued Rubí's orders, on Aug. 7, 1765, Gálvez was on route to America (he arrived in New Spain on Aug. 25, 1765). Rubí's orders reached him by Dec. 1765.

6. Kinnaird, ed. and trans., *Frontiers of New Spain*, 69. Documents provide conflicting dates for Rubí's departure from Mexico City (Navarro García, *José de Gálvez*, 136). The Hispanic population in 1760 was, by one count, 47,150, plus 70,050 "pacified Indians." See Jones, *Los Paisanos*, 91, 240, and Jones, *Nueva Vizcaya*, chaps. 7, 8.

7. Kinnaird, ed. and trans., *Frontiers of New Spain*, 76–77.

8. Many writers have described this migration. For a convenient, authoritative introduction to the so-called western Apaches in a readable narrative, see Worcester, *Apaches*, 12–18; John, *Storms Brewed*, especially 258–303, provides a richly textured account of events on the southern plains.

9. The quotes are from Kinnaird, ed. and trans., *Frontiers of New Spain*, 216, 79, respectively.

10. The idea that Apaches were originally more interested in trade than in warfare, and that Spaniards provoked Apaches into hostility in the seventeenth century, has been advanced by a number of historians, including Scholes, *Troublous Times*, 17, and Forbes, *Apache, Navaho, and Spaniard*, 151, 160–61, 281–84. For some of the evidence that *nuevomexicanos* continued to enslave Apaches and other Indians into the eigh-

teenth and nineteenth centuries, see Brugge, *Navajos in the Catholic Church Records*, 17–32. The fact was noted and sometimes deplored by officials. See, e.g., Flagler, "Governor José Chacón," 469–70. Bailey, *Indian Slave Trade*, must be used with caution. See, too, my chapter 5.

11. Pedro de Allande y Saavedra to the king, ca. 1786, in McCarty, [ed. and trans.], *Desert Documentary*, 43–44, 45.

12. Gálvez, "Notes and Reflections on the War with the Apache Indians," 304. For Gálvez as author of this document, see John, "Bernardo de Gálvez on the Apache Frontier," 427–30.

13. Daniel, ed. and trans., "Diary of de la Fuente, January–July 1765," 260–281, and Daniel, ed. and trans., "Diary of de la Fuente, August–December 1765," 259–73.

14. Rubí, "Dictámenes," 40.

15. Miller, ed. and trans., "New Mexico in Mid-Eighteenth Century," 175.

16. The quotes in this paragraph are in Kinnaird, ed. and trans., *Frontiers of New Spain*, 91, 93.

17. Kinnaird, ed. and trans., *Frontiers of New Spain*, 128. For the population of Sonora, see Jones, *Los Paisanos*, 179–80, who notes a count of 8,284 in 1760 (Lafora himself gives no figure for Sonora). For the population of Tubac, which approached 500 at the time of Rubí's visit, see Kessell, *Friars, Soldiers, and Reformers*, 39.

18. Lafora's statement appears on a map that he prepared to accompany his report, which was redrawn for Kinnaird, ed. and trans., *Frontiers of New Spain*. The Bolsón is the area below the Rio Grande, bounded on the west by the Conchos River and the east by the Sierra Madre Oriental.

19. Kinnaird, ed. and trans., *Frontiers of New Spain*, 154.

20. Ibid., 151. Weddle, *San Sabá Mission*, 163–65, describes conditions at the fort at this time. Weddle argues that the fort did achieve its purpose by keeping San An-

tonio and the Rio Grande free of Indian attack (ibid., 162), a conclusion that might not hold up under careful scrutiny.

21. Kinnaird, ed. and trans., *Frontiers of New Spain*, 151, 160. Sibley, ed., "Across Texas in 1767," 615–16, describes the presidio and the town at the time of Rubí's visit. See, too, Buerkle, "Continuing Military Presence," 62–66, and Moorhead, *Presidio*, 156–57, 165.

22. Kinnaird, ed. and trans., *Frontiers of New Spain*, 166.

23. Vigness, "Don Hugo Oconor," 32. For the miserable conditions at the presidio, see Castañeda, *Our Catholic Heritage in Texas*, 4:238–39.

24. Morales Folguera, *Arquitectura*, 94. Louisiana did not fall under the captaincy general of Cuba officially until 1772, but the de facto relationship was clear in the 1760s (Cummins, "Spanish Administration in the Eastern Borderlands," 6).

25. Kinnaird, ed. and trans., *Frontiers of New Spain*, 171.

26. Ibid., 33. For the different locations of the fort, which was also on the Guadalupe River for a time, see O'Connor, *Presidio la Bahía*.

27. Rubí, "Dictámenes," 63–64.

28. Kinnaird, ed. and trans., *Frontiers of New Spain*, 44.

29. Marchena Fernández, *Oficiales y soldados*, 3–36.

30. Moorhead, *Presidio*, 3–26, provides a succinct overview. For the sixteenth-century, the works of Philip Wayne Powell are essential. See his "Genesis of the Frontier Presidio," 124–41, which summarizes some of his conclusions and provides references to his earlier work. See, too, Naylor and Polzer, eds., *Presidio and Militia*, vol. 1. The latter contains the most recent and complete published definition of a "presidio," a word that apparently did not come into usage in the Spanish language until 1570 in Morocco (ibid., 15–19) and that had different meanings in dif-

ferent times and places. Like other writers, Naylor and Polzer assert that " 'presidio' was not a mere synonym for *castillo* or *forteleza*," and they define presidios as "protective garrisons on frontiers" (18). That is generally true, but Spaniards sometimes used the word "presidio" to refer to the troops in places without protective structures. See Williams, "Architecture and Defense on the Military Frontier of Arizona," chap. 2, who correctly suggests that a presidio might best be defined as a military base. On the other hand, contemporaries *did* use presidio as a synonym for a *castillo* or *forteleza*—see the examples in Chatelain, *Defenses of Spanish Florida*, 151 *n*. 17, 152 *n*. 19.

31. As required by the Orders for New Discoveries issued by the Crown in 1573. See my chapter 4.

32. Morfi, *Excerpts from . . . History of . . . Texas*, 1:95. See, too, Eaton, "Gateway Missions of the Lower Rio Grande," 248.

33. The Apalachee fort was built in 1657 in response to the English seizure of Jamaica just two years before.

34. Simmons, "Settlement Patterns," 106–7. Williams, "Bastion, Baluarte y Torreón," argues that because much of the data on defense in contemporary written records concerns presidios, historians became fixated on the presidial system and overlooked other defensive structures.

35. In 1684, the presidio of El Paso del Norte was moved close to the Guadalupe mission (Timmons, *El Paso*, 18; Espinosa, *Pueblo Indian Revolt*, 37, 40). For the situation to the south and southwest of New Mexico, with documents illustrative of military activities including a rare journal from a campaign against Pimas and Apaches, see Naylor and Polzer, eds., *Presidio and Militia*, 1:483–718.

36. Jones, *Pueblo Warriors*. The evolution of militia on the frontier needs further study.

37. New Mexico's shift from an evangelical to a military colony is widely agreed upon by

historians. See, e.g., Scholes, "Civil Government and Society," 79–80; Garner, "Dynamics of Change," 8–11; and Gerhard, *North Frontier*, 10.

38. Marchena Fernández, "Guarniciones," 100–103. The Crown was slow to reform Florida's archaic military structure; not until 1749 did it bring Florida under the Regulations of Havana of 1719.

39. Scardaville, and Belmonte, eds. and trans., "Florida in the Late First Spanish Period," 9.

40. Williams and Hoover, *Arms of the Apachería*, argue that Apaches did not employ European tactics and that their adoption of European weapons was not decisive.

41. The regulations, along with other important documents, are translated and reproduced in the original Spanish text in Naylor and Polzer, eds., *Pedro de Rivera*.

42. Moorhead, *Presidio*, 179–80.

43. For St. Augustine and its dependent fortifications, see Marchena Fernández, "Guarniciones," 119–24.

44. Velázquez, "Los reglamentos," 3, 7, 28. Velázquez makes a better case for the long-range utility of Rivera's work than do Naylor and Polzer, eds., *Pedro de Rivera*, 19, who assert that it is a "misconception that Rivera's inspection was itself ineffective." Most historians, however, have not questioned the effectiveness of Rivera's inspection. Rather, they have noted that in the long run his work did not lead to fundamental reforms of the presidial system. See, e.g., Navarro García, *José de Gálvez*, 137.

45. The Reglamento of 1753, which made Florida a dependent outpost of Havana. Marchena Fernández, "Guarniciones," 101.

46. Velázquez, [ed.], "Los reglamentos," 29–36. The official who died was the *auditor de guerra*, the marqués de Altamira. For a more detailed consideration, see Velázquez, *El marqués de Altamira*.

47. Velázquez, "Los reglamentos," 37, 63–64.

48. *Reglamento é instrucción para los presidios que se han de formar en la linea de frontera de la Nueva España* (Madrid, 1772). For their publication in Mexico in 1771, see Moorhead, *Presidio*, 64. The most detailed expositions of the evolution of these documents are in Navarro García, *José de Gálvez*, 200–205, 215–20, and in Hernández Sánchez-Barba, *La última expansión*, 94–99. A translation of the *Regulations of 1772*, along with a facsimile of an 1834 Mexican imprint, is in Brinckerhoff and Faulk, eds. and trans., *Lancers for the King*.

49. Velázquez, "Los reglamentos," 70, 80, suggests that the 1772 regulations remained in force in independent Mexico until 1848, and some of their provisions did, but they were augmented in 1826 (Weber, *Mexican Frontier*, 108).

50. Velázquez, "Los reglamentos," 66, citing title 10.

51. Rubí made recommendations as he went along, but his principle recommendations were his "Dictámenes," written in Tacubaya, Apr. 10, 1768.

52. The details of this realignment were spelled out in the "Instrucción para la nueva colocación de presidios," that forms part of the *Regulations of 1772*, in Brinckerhoff and Faulk, eds. and trans., *Lancers for the King*, 49–67.

53. Brinckerhoff and Faulk, eds. and trans., *Lancers for the King*, 59.

54. Ibid., 61. The quote pertained to Santa Fe but can be applied to San Antonio as well.

55. See, e.g., Miller, ed. and trans., "New Mexico in Mid-Eighteenth Century," 180, and the report of Croix, 1781, in Thomas, ed. and trans., *Teodoro de Croix*, 106.

56. Moorhead, *Presidio*, 169–71, summarizing LaFora to Rubí, Aug. 12, 1767. Weddle, *San Sabá Mission*, 170, suggests that Rubí exaggerated the presidio's vulnerability.

57. The *Regulations of 1772* are vague on this point (Brinckerhoff and Faulk, eds. and trans., *Lancers for the King*, 63), but other

evidence suggests the existence of standardized designs that have not been found (Moorhead, *Presidio*, 165). For military architecture in the southeastern North America at this time, see Morales Folguera, *Arquitectura*, 77–162.

58. Moorhead, "Rebuilding the Presidio of Santa Fe," 123–42. Williams, "Fortress Tucson," 170–76, is also a fine case study. Williams, too, suggests that the newer presidios were probably not built exactly to the new specifications.

59. Moorhead, *Presidio*, 171, makes this point about San Sabá. Faulk, "Presidio," 67–76, argues that Indians never took a presidio "by direct attack," although he says they did occasionally penetrate presidial defenses "by stealth" (71). Notwithstanding their reluctance to engage in siege warfare, Indians did attempt to take presidios. Williams, "Fortress Tucson," 183, notes nine Apache assaults on the Tucson presidio between 1776 and 1856 (perhaps a record number for any presidio on the northern frontier), and Weddle, *San Sabá Mission*, 163–65, reports that Comanches attacked or lay siege to the presidio at San Sabá in 1764, 1767, and 1768. This question needs further study.

60. Brinckerhoff and Faulk, eds. and trans., *Lancers for the King*, 23.

61. Moorhead, *Presidio*, 186. See, too, ibid., 185–91.

62. Fray Juan Sanz de Leszaún, Nov. 4, 1760, "Account of Lamentable Happenings in New Mexico," in Hackett, *Historical Documents*, 3:474–75.

63. For Florida, see, e.g., Juan Núñez de los Ríos to Philip III, St. Augustine, Feb. 19, 1600, in Quinn, ed., *New American World*, 5:100–102. Bushnell, *King's Coffer*, 74, and Gillaspie, "Survival of a Frontier Presidio," 273–95. For the interior provinces, see Moorhead, *Presidio*, 201–8, and for a fine case study, see Warner, "Don Félix Martínez," 269–310.

64. Brinckerhoff and Faulk, eds. and trans.,

Lancers for the King, 13; Moorhead, *Presidio*, 209–11. Hernández Sánchez-Barba, *La última expansión*, 97, notes that the Laws of the Indies and earlier military regulations already contained such a prohibition.

65. Moorhead, *Presidio*, 211–19, summarizes efforts to enforce these sections of the *Regulations*. The abuses by officers of their soldiers mirrored abuses by civilian officials, particularly the *corregidores*, over the general populace. See, e.g., MacLachlan, *Spain's Empire in the New World*, 114–15.

66. Moore and Beene, eds. and trans., "Interior Provinces . . . Report of Hugo O'Conor," 278. See, too, Moorhead, *Presidio*, 178–200.

67. These are Lafora's words, but they reflect Rubí's thinking as well. Kinnaird, ed. and trans., *Frontiers of New Spain*, 217. See, too, Moorhead, *Presidio*, 60–61.

68. Rubí, "Dictámenes," 30.

69. Ibid., 43, 64, 76–77 (the quote is on p. 70).

70. Brinckerhoff and Faulk, eds. and trans., *Lancers for the King*, 37. This was not Rubí's idea; he would have put the vast region under three separate military commands (Rubí, "Dictámenes," 75). Gálvez first presented the plan to the Crown in 1768. For Gálvez's strategy explained in context, see my chapter 9. Carlos III approved the Gálvez plan in principle, but the *Regulations of 1772* put off its full implementation, noting that in the future such an office might be created for the interior provinces. On the other hand, the *Regulations of 1772* expanded the geographical scope of the inspector in chief beyond Gálvez's original idea by putting that official in charge of Texas, Coahuila, and New Mexico as well as Nueva Vizcaya, Sonora, and the Californias (Brinckerhoff and Faulk, eds. and trans., *Lancers for the King*, 37).

71. Sonora and Sinaloa were a single province from 1734 to 1830.

72. The most detailed biography in English, and a guide to sources, is in Moore and

Beene, trans. and ed., "Interior Provinces . . . Report of Hugh O'Conor," 267–69. See, too, Vigness, "Don Hugo Oconor," 31, which contains a brief biography.

73. The viceroy had put O'Conor in charge of implementing Rubí's proposals in 1771, but the king did not make the official appointment until Sept. 1772. In an article that treats O'Conor's first fourteen months in office, Christiansen, "Hugo O'Conor's Inspection," 159, notes that O'Conor did not receive his instructions and a copy of the *Regulations of 1772* until Mar. 1773.

74. O'Reilly had urged the viceroy to appoint O'Conor, describing him as like a son (O'Reilly to Viceroy Bucareli, Madrid, Sept. 25, 1772, quoted in Navarro García, *José de Gálvez*, 211). For O'Conor's birthplace and sobriquet, see ibid., 212, 198.

75. Christiansen, "Hugo O'Conor's Inspection," 161.

76. For an overview of the presidio's peripatetic history, see Kessell, "Puzzling Presidio," 21–46; for its five years in Arizona, see Williams, "Presidio of Santa Cruz de Terrenate," 129–48.

77. Dobyns, *Spanish Colonial Tucson*, 55–59; Williams, "San Agustín del Tucson," 113–21; and Williams, "Fortress Tucson," 168–87. O'Conor had selected the site and ordered the move in 1775. The order, dated Aug. 20, is in McCarty, [ed. and trans.], *Desert Documentary*, 26.

78. Mendinueta to Teodoro de Croix, Santa Fe, Nov. 3, 1777, in Thomas, "Governor Mendinueta's Proposals for the Defense of New Mexico," 35. See, too, Patrick, "Land Grants," 5–18, and Navarro García, *José de Gálvez*, 244–50, who chronicles Mendinueta's campaigns. For the number of Hispanos killed, see Brugge, *Navajos in the Catholic Church Records*, 30–31, table 3 (whose addition is in error). Brugge compiled his table from burial records, and speculates that some soldiers who died on campaigns may not be reflected in the records because their bodies were not brought back.

79. See, too, the more detailed report of adjutant-inspector Antonio de Bonilla, who endorsed Mendinueta's recommendations, but believed that a presidio at Taos was not necessary. Bonilla, however, had no firsthand experience in New Mexico (Thomas, [ed. and trans.], "Antonio de Bonilla," 183–209).

80. Hatcher, ed., "Diary of a Visit . . . by Fray Gaspar José de Solís," 65, described the presidio and missions as badly deteriorated.

81. The story has been told in a number of sources, among the most accessible is Bolton, *Texas in the Middle Eighteenth Century*, 377–446, which in its general outline of events has not been improved upon.

82. O'Reilly set the new tone when he shut down fortifications built by Governor Ulloa and withdrew many of the troops to New Orleans (Torres Ramírez, *Alejandro O'Reilly*, 129–41).

83. Quoted in Moore, *Revolt in Louisiana*, 94, who provides a fine summary of Spanish Indian policy in Louisiana during Ulloa's administration.

84. Ulloa to O'Conor, ca. Mar. 1768, quoted in Vigness, "Don Hugo Oconor," 31.

85. The key work on this subject remains Bolton, ed. and trans., *Athanase de Mézières*, who outlined De Mézières accomplishments (1:79–122), and who translated much of the rich documentation. The best narrative account is John, *Storms Brewed*, 383–430.

86. Antonio de Bucareli to Julián de Arriaga, Mexico, Oct. 27, 1772, in Velasco Ceballos, ed., *La administración de D. Frey Antonio María de Bucareli*, 1:70–71.

87. Bolton, ed. and trans., *Athanase de Mézières*, 1:108; Schilz and Worcester, "Spread of Firearms," 5.

88. Holmes, *Honor and Fidelity*, contains Holmes's chronicle of Louisiana military affairs, together with lists of those who

served in the infantry and militia in the Spanish period. Spain maintained a modest garrison in Louisiana, one that it could augment rapidly with reinforcements from Havana or Veracruz as the need arose. The size of the garrison increased from some 400 in 1770 (ibid., 20) to an authorized strength of 2,000 later in the century (ibid., 39). For the threat of British invasion as far as Texas and New Mexico, see Alejandro O'Reilly to Vicereoy Bucareli, Madrid, Sept. 25, 1772, quoted in Navarro García, *José de Gálvez*, 220.

89. The quote is from Moore and Beene, trans. and ed., "Interior Provinces . . . Report of Hugh O'Conor," 278, one of two of O'Conor's reports of his accomplishments that have been published (both employ similar language). The other is in González Flores and Almada, eds., *Informe de Hugo O'conor*. The latter is an incomplete version of a report of July 22, 1777 (the last two paragraphs and three tables of statistics are missing). The full document, a copy of which is in the De-Golyer Library at Southern Methodist University, is being edited and translated by Donald C. Cutter. A worthy subject for a biography, O'Conor's career as inspector needs further study and assessment. I am following the appraisal of O'Conor in Moorhead, *Presidio*, 74; for O'Conor's tenure from the viceregal perspective, see Bobb, *Bucareli*, 137–43, and many of the documents in Velasco Ceballos, ed., *La administración de D. Frey Antonio María de Bucareli*. For a more detailed account, see Navarro García, *José de Gálvez*, 221–43.

90. Quoted in Weddle, *San Sabá Mission*, 170.

91. Most scholars have judged the idea of the presidial line a failure. See, e.g., Park, "Spanish Indian Policy," 224–25.

92. Hernández Sánchez-Barba, *La última expansión*, 111, suggests that O'Conor's "illness" was not real.

93. For reference to the Crown's approval of the idea in 1769, see the "Informe del vir-

rey y el visitador general de Nueva España sobre la . . . comandancia general," Mexico, June 22, 1771, in Velázquez, [ed.], *La frontera norte*, 85. Brinckerhoff and Faulk, eds. and trans., *Lancers for the King*, 37. For the larger context of Gálvez's plan, see my chapter 9.

94. Historians have offered a number of unsatisfactory explanations for the timing of this decision (see, e.g., the discussion in Bobb, *Bucareli*, 144–45). Although it has yet to be clearly demonstrated, it appears that Gálvez promoted his pet project upon coming to power. See Hernández Sánchez-Barba, *La última expansion*, 111, 118; Navarro García, *José de Gálvez*, 275.

95. The interior provinces of Sinaloa, Sonora, and the Californias, Bucareli complained, "neither have their subsidies arranged, nor it is easily discovered how they are governed" (Bucareli to Alejandro O'Reilly, Mexico, Oct. 27, 1771, quoted in Bobb, *Bucareli*, 30).

96. Instructions of Carlos III to Teodoro de Croix, San Ildefonso, Aug. 22, 1776, in Velázquez, [ed.], *La frontera norte*, 131–39, spell out the responsibilities and the philosophy of the new position.

97. Thomas, ed. and trans., *Teodoro de Croix*, 17–18. The bulk of this book consists of Thomas's translation of a detailed report on each of the interior provinces, from Croix to José de Gálvez, Arizpe, Oct. 30, 1781. Like other writers, I have relied on Thomas's introduction, with its summary of Croix's tenure. I have not, however, always followed Thomas's interpretation. Steeped in Croix's correspondence, Thomas apparently adopted Croix's own point of view and made unnecessarily harsh judgments about Bucareli and O'Conor. For a more balanced view, see the fine summary in Moorhead, *Presidio*, 75–94, and Bobb, *Bucareli*, 147–55. A richly detailed account is in Navarro García, *José de Gálvez*, 275–425, who judges Croix's tenure as the high water mark of the provincias internas.

98. Initially, the appointment had followed Gálvez's 1768 plan precisely by including only Sonora, Sinaloa, Nueva Vizcaya, and the Californias. Subsequently, as the Comandancia underwent reorganization, its boundaries waxed and waned. For a time, for example, they included Nuevo León and Nuevo Santander.

99. The realignment is summarized in Moorhead, *Presidio*, 87–91.

100. Croix's idea of reducing the weight and number of soldiers' horses, discussed below, was not original with him. See, e.g., Kinnaird, ed. and trans., *Frontiers of New Spain*, 215, and Navarro García, *José de Gálvez*, 123, who points out that Bishop Pedro Tamarón also made such a recommendation in 1761.

101. Moorhead, *Presidio*, 82–83, 191–193, 91–92. Navarro García, *José de Gálvez*, 298, credits Bernardo de Gálvez with the idea. The tropa ligera augmented, but did not replace the leather-jacketted soldiers.

102. Moorhead, *Presidio*, 60–61; Thomas, ed. and trans., *Forgotten Frontiers*, 35–37, 45–46; Miller, ed. and trans., "New Mexico in Mid-Eighteenth Century," 173; John, *Storms Brewed*, 335.

103. Bolton, ed. and trans., *Athanase de Mézières*, 1:111, and the Councils of War at Monclova and San Antonio, Dec. 11, 1777, and Jan. 5, 1778, ibid., 2:150, 151, 156. Park, "Spanish Indian Policy," 225–26, who has wisely suggested that Croix's strategy represented a departure from that of his predecessors, although Park misunderstood the identity of the nations that comprised the "Nations of the North" (227).

104. For Gálvez's orders of Feb. 20, 1779, see n. 106 this chapter.

105. On June 27, 1782, as war with Britain drew to a close, the Crown ordered Croix to resume the offensive against the Apaches. Moorhead, *Presidio*, 85–100, summarizes Croix's last years, and the work of his two immediate successors.

106. The so-called Royal Orders of Feb. 20, 1779, have apparently not appeared in print and have been overlooked by many historians. See, e.g., Faulk, "Presidio," 67–76, who incorrectly describes the famous *Instructions of 1786* of Bernardo de Gálvez as the turning point in Spanish policy. The 1779 Orders are best summarized and analyzed in Moorhead, *Apache Frontier*, 120–23. Moorhead points out that the Feb. 20 orders anticipated the *Instructions of 1786* in many respects and that the latter "did not introduce drastic changes in Indian policy as some historians have intimated" (ibid., 123).

107. For Vélez Cachupín's successes and philosophy, see John, *Storms Brewed*, 320–35, and the relevant documents in Thomas, ed. and trans., *Plains Indians and New Mexico*, 61–166. For earlier Spanish distribution of guns and ammunition, see my chapter 7.

108. Appointed acting governor on Sept. 19, 1776, Bernardo de Gálvez assumed the position on Jan. 1, 1777, succeeding Gov. Luis de Unzaga. In Jan. 1779, Bernardo de Gálvez was promoted to governor (Caughey, *Bernardo de Gálvez*, 67, 152).

109. Navarro García, *José de Gálvez*, 191–96. Gálvez was born on July 25, 1746, in the Spanish province of Málaga like his uncle. He arrived in Chihuahua on Apr. 11, 1769 (ibid., 143, 188). For his views on Apaches, which derived from this experience, see Gálvez, "Notes and Reflections on the War with the Apache Indians," 302–5, and John, "Bernardo de Gálvez on the Apache Frontier," 427–30.

110. Bernardo to José de Gálvez, [New Orleans], Oct. 24, 1778, quoted in West, "Indian Policy of Bernardo de Gálvez," 100–101.

111. Ibid.

112. Bernardo to José de Gálvez, New Orleans, Oct. 24, 1778, in Hernández Sánchez-Barba, *La última expansión*, 122. This confidential letter appears to be the same quoted at length by West, "Indian

Policy of Bernardo de Gálvez," 100–101, but Hernández quoted a portion that West omitted.

113. West, "Indian Policy of Bernardo de Gálvez," 95–101, may have been the first to draw the connection between Gálvez's Louisiana experience and the development of policy in the interior provinces. For an example of another official with a similar vision, see Gov. Barón de Ripperdá to the viceroy, San Antonio, Apr. 28, 1772, in Bolton, ed. and trans., *Athanase de Mézières*, 1:269–70. Earlier suggestions were rejected as too risky.

114. Gálvez, *Instructions*. This edition includes the original Spanish-language version of the instructions. With the appointment of Gálvez, authority over the Interior Provinces reverted to the viceroy. The *Instructions* are summarized and placed in context in Moorhead, *Presidio*, 101–8. For Gálvez's heroic conduct, see my chapter 9.

115. Gálvez, *Instructions*, 27.

116. The extent to which Gálvez's *Instructions* represented a "new plan," as suggested by Faulk, "Presidio," 74, and Moorhead, *Presidio*, 100–101, needs clarification. In an earlier work, Moorhead more accurately characterized these instructions as a "synthesis" that "did not introduce drastic changes" but was "revolutionary in some few details" (*Apache Frontier*, 123).

117. Gálvez, *Instructions*, 37.

118. Ibid., 41.

119. Ibid.

120. Ibid., 47.

121. Ibid., 47–49.

122. Moorhead, The *Apache Frontier*, 128; Schilz and Worcester, "Spread of Firearms," 8; Holmes, "Spanish Regulation of Taverns," 160–64; Arnold, *Unequal Laws*, 66–71.

123. Gálvez, *Instructions*, 38.

124. Gibson, "Conquest," 1–15, suggests that although Spaniards entered into agreements with Indians, they generally did not negotiate formal, written treaties as did the English and French. Lyon, "Enterprise of Florida," 286–87, has found some sixteenth-century exceptions, but these seem rare. In the 1780s, however, written agreements became commonplace in Spanish North America due, almost certainly, to the influence of Spain's rivals not only on its policy, but on Indians themselves who demanded written instruments. See Kinnaird, "Spanish Treaties with Indian Tribes," 39–48 (a reply to Gibson); Sturtevant, "Spanish-Indian Relations," 73; Holmes, "Spanish Treaties with West Florida Indians," 140–54; and the treaties that Domingo Cabello and Juan Bautista de Anza signed with Comanches in 1785 and 1786, respectively, discussed below in this chapter. See, too, my chapter 10 at n. 49.

125. Ewers, "Symbols of Chiefly Authority," 272–86. If Spaniards distributed medals and banners earlier, the fact has eluded me. For Spanish understanding of English use of pacts with Indians and the need to emulate them, see Din, ed. and trans., *Louisiana in 1776*, 65–68.

126. Thomas, ed. and trans., *Forgotten Frontiers*, contains a summary of Anza's campaigns in New Mexico and translations of key documents, including Anza's own remarkable account of the forging of the Comanche peace and the Comanche treaty (329–31). Price, "Comanches [*sic*] Threat to Texas and New Mexico," 34–45, is a good summary of the published literature. John, *Storms Brewed*, 557–696, contains a richly detailed account of Anza's career and the events leading up to the making of both the Texas and New Mexico treaties. See, too, Faulk [ed. and trans.], "Spanish Comanche Relations," 44–53, for the terms of the treaty as described in Pedro de Nava to the viceroy, Chihuahua, July 23, 1799. Much of this same document is reproduced in Sim-

mons, ed. and trans., *Border Comanches*, 21–22, who speculates on internal reasons for Comanche interest in peace (p.14).

127. John, *Storms Brewed*, 324–25, 333–34, 471, and the relevant documents in Thomas, ed. and trans., *Plains Indians and New Mexico*. These do not appear to have been written agreements.

128. This list comes from Governor Concha, "Advice on Governing New Mexico," 238, 242.

129. See the Account of the Events Concerning Peace Conceded to the Comanche Nation, by Pedro Garrido y Duran, Chihuahua. Dec. 21, 1786, in Thomas, ed. and trans., *Forgotten Frontiers*, 305–6.

130. For the complicated Spanish relations with factions of these tribes at this time see Gunnerson, *Jicarilla Apaches*, 234–92; Reeve, "Navaho-Spanish Diplomacy," 200–235; McNitt, *Navajo Wars*, 30–36; and Foote, "Spanish-Indian Trade," 25–30.

131. Concha, "Advice on Governing New Mexico," 238. Benes, "Anza and Concha in New Mexico," 63–76, concentrates almost entirely on Concha's administration. August, "Balance-of-Power Diplomacy," 141–60, adds little more to the subject.

132. Park, "Spanish Indian Policy," 230.

133. For details of this story, see Archer, "Deportation of Barbarian Indians," 376–85, and Moorhead, "Spanish Deportation of Hostile Apaches," 205–20.

134. Moorhead, *Apache Frontier*, 170–99.

135. Ibid., 200–269.

136. Moorhead, *Presidio*, 260–61, whose chapter on establecimientos explains the evolution of the policy. The subject merits more study. See also, Dobyns, *Spanish Colonial Tucson*, 97–105.

137. Procedures for operating the Apache peace establishments were spelled out by Pedro de Nava in instructions of 1791. Nava emphasized gifts over trade and dictated policies left unaddressed by Bernardo de Gálvez in 1786. Moorhead, *Presidio*, 260–65, summarized Nava's instructions, and Jack S. Williams has transcribed and analyzed this unpublished document: "Pedro de Nava's Instructions" (unpublished ms, 1975), a copy of which he graciously put in my possession.

138. Concha to the viceroy, Santa Fe, July 22, 1792, quoted in Benes, "Anza and Concha in New Mexico," 73.

139. For examples of criticism, see Matson and Fontana, eds. and trans., *Friar Bringas Reports to the King*, 119–20, and Kessell, *Friars, Soldiers, and Reformers*, 200–201. For Apaches' prior practice of agriculture, see Wilson, "Southern Apaches as Farmers," 79–81.

140. Benes, "Anza and Concha in New Mexico," 65–66.

141. See, e.g., Goodwin, *Western Apache Raiding and Warfare*.

142. Benes, "Anza and Concha in New Mexico," 72–73; Moorhead, *Apache Frontier*, 284–85, mistakenly states that the settlement near Sabinal lasted just a few months.

143. On this latter point, see Cortés, *Views from the Apache Frontier*, 28–29, and Griffen, "Apache Indians," 184. Griffen, *Apaches at War and Peace*, 69–116, the most detailed study of such a reservation, provides guidance to additional sources. For Tucson, see Brinckerhoff, "Last Years of Spanish Arizona," 5–20.

144. Spicer, *Cycles of Conquest*, 45–46.

145. Spanish Indian policy and practice in the last decades of the Spanish era has yet to be studied in detail, but Elizabeth John has such a project well in hand. Her articles, "Nurturing the Peace," 345–69, and "La situación y visión de los indios," 465–83, offer preliminary views of her conclusions. See, too, the tentative overview of Spanish-Apache relations after 1790 in Moorhead, *Apache Frontier*, 283–90.

146. Moorhead, *Presidio*, 83.

147. Later changes in the Comandancia General are outlined in Moorhead, *Presidio*, 99–103, 111–12. The 1790s are explained in greater detail in Navarro García, *José de Gálvez*, 452–513, and for the period 1800–1820 in his *Las Provincias Internas*. For four of the key documents, from 1787, 1792, 1812, and 1819, see Velázquez, [ed.], *La frontera norte*, 198–209.

148. Indian motives must, of course, be regarded as specific to individual tribes and bands, and lack of records make historical reconstruction more conjectural than is usually the case. The possibility exists, for example, that some tribes, particularly Comanches and Lipán Apaches, were moved to make peace overtures because they had been weakened by a great smallpox epidemic of 1780–81. See Simmons, "New Mexico's Smallpox Epidemic," 324.

149. Pedro de Nava to the viceroy, Chihuahua, July 32, 1799, in Faulk [ed. and trans.], "Spanish Comanche Relations," 51.

150. Ibid., 53; John, "Nurturing the Peace," 346.

151. See, e.g., John, *Storms Brewed*, 671, 682–83.

152. Mendinueta to the viceroy, Santa Fe, Jan. 8, 1773, in Mendinueta, *Indian and Mission Affairs*, 19.

153. Matson and Schroeder, eds. and trans., "Cordero's Description of the Apache," 350.

154. Cortés, *Views from the Apache Frontier*, 30. See, too, John, "La situación y visión de los indios," 479–80. Similar sentiment had been expressed by Bernardo de Gálvez himself in his "Notes and Reflections on the War with the Apache Indians," ca. 1786; his views may have influenced officers down the line. Also see John, ed. and trans., "Cautionary Exercise in Apache Historiography," 302–5, and John, "Bernardo de Gálvez on the Apache Frontier," 427–30.

155. For their respective diaries, see Loomis and Nasatir, *Pedro Vial*, 262–87, and Hammond, [ed. and trans.], "Zúñiga Journal," 40–65 (Spanish versions are in Represa, ed., *La España ilustrada en el lejano oeste*, 29–41, 89–100). Simmons, "Spanish Attempts to Open a New Mexico-Sonora Road," 5–20, puts Zúñiga's journey in context.

156. Commercial growth in New Mexico has been explained most imaginatively in a dissertation by Frank, "From Settler to Citizen." For New Mexico, also see Kenner, *History of New Mexican–Plains Indian Relations*, 53–70, and Nostrand, "Century of Hispano Expansion," 365. For Arizona, see Dobyns, *Spanish Colonial Tucson*, 97–101; Brinckerhoff, "Last Years of Spanish Arizona," 14–17; and Officer, *Hispanic Arizona*, 70–88. Faulk, *Last Years of Spanish Texas*, 83–91, touches on this era in Texas, which did not undergo as vigorous an expansion as New Mexico or Arizona. Nacogdoches grew rapidly from 480 in 1790 to 660 in 1800 (McReynolds, "Family Life in a Borderland Community," 15), but that was due largely to proximity to the United States. San Antonio's economy seems to have become more vigorous, but its population remained static. De la Teja, "Land and Society in 18th Century San Antonio," 87–89, 323–30, explains this as a result of drought and epidemic (in contrast, Frank, "From Settler to Citizen," sees the epidemic in New Mexico as an asset, since it concentrated wealth). In comparison to New Mexico, Texas also lacked an Indian labor force equivalent to the Pueblos, and a population large enough to fend off Indians and produce at the same time.

157. John, "Nurturing the Peace," 361–65.

Chapter 9: Forging a Transcontinental Empire

The epigraphs are from "Plan para la creación de un Gobierno y Comandancia General . . .," in Treutlein, *San Francisco Bay*, 111, and Abbey, "Spanish Projects," 274.

1. For Gálvez's unique influence, see Guillermo Céspedes del Castillo, *América Hispánica (1492–1898)* (Barcelona: Editorial Labor, 1988), 317, and for the reinvigorated role of the Council over which he presided, see Mark Burkholder, "The Council of the Indies in the Late Eighteenth Century: A New Perspective," *HAHR* 56 (Aug. 1976): 404–23.

2. Gálvez's instructions appear in Priestley, *José de Gálvez*, 404–17. For a recent description and assessment of the Bourbon reforms, and guidance to earlier sources, see the fine interpretation by MacLachlan, *Spain's Empire in the New World*.

3. Priestley, *José de Gálvez*, contains biographical detail and remains the standard study in English of Gálvez's years in New Spain. A new study is long overdue. There are, of course, numerous studies of Gálvez, including biographical details surrounding him and his family. See, e.g., Isidro Vázquez de Acuña, *Historial de la Casa de Gálvez y sus Alianzas* (Madrid: privately printed, 1974). On the character of Gálvez, see the excessively praiseworthy analysis in Hernández Sánchez-Barba, *La última expansión*, 191–94, who wrote in apparent ignorance of Priestley's work. Navarro García, *José de Gálvez*, contains no analysis of Gálvez's character.

4. Hernández Sánchez-Barba, *La última expansión*, 83. The divergent views of Rubí and Gálvez are brought into clear relief in Navarro García, "North of New Spain," 201–15. Yet Navarro García draws the contrast too sharply; Rubí was aware of the Russian threat, but he regarded it as less serious than Gálvez did.

5. Gálvez's "Plan" of Jan. 23, 1768, cited below in n. 8. This passage is quoted in Cook, *Flood Tide of Empire*, 49, who provides a fine overview of Spanish perceptions of these foreign threats (44–48).

6. Facsimiles of the original edition and manuscript appear in Mathes, ed., *Obras californianas de Padre Miguel Venegas*.

7. Curiously, *I Mosoviti Nella California . . .* appeared in Italy. See Wagner, *Spanish Southwest*, 2:429–32.

8. These ideas were outlined in his "Plan para la creación de un Gobierno y Comandancia General . . . ," Jan. 23, 1768, which is summarized and quoted in several sources, including Hernández Sánchez-Barba, *La última expansión*, 114–16, from which I have taken the quote (115). The best English translation appears in Treutlein, *San Francisco Bay*, 109–17. See, too, the broader but related "Informe y plan de Intendencias . . . ," dated Jan. 15, summarized by Priestley, *José de Gálvez*, 289–92, and Navarro García, *José de Gálvez*, 91–94; 158–60. Both plans were signed by the viceroy, the marqués de Croix and Gálvez, Mexico, but Gálvez seems to have been their chief architect. Rubí, too, saw the need for a coordinated military command, but on a smaller scale (Rubí, "Dictámenes," 75).

9. Burrus, ed. and trans., *Kino's Plan*. This, and subsequent proposals were reviewed in the pioneering and still valuable work of Chapman, *Founding of Spanish California*, 14–44, and in Cutter, "Plans for the Occupation of Upper California," 79–90.

10. Rubí, "Dictámenes," 77–78.

11. On this latter point, see Hernández Sánchez-Barba, *La última expansión*, 197–98; Gálvez's other activities are outlined in the standard sources.

12. There is much confusion in the secondary literature regarding the extent to which Gálvez himself served as the catalyst for the settlement of New California, and the whole matter needs further study. For sources regarding the mission of Field Marshal Antonio Ricardos to Spain and for Gálvez's decision to go to Monterey, see Alan K. Brown's introduction to Boneu, *Gaspar de Portolá*, 29–30, who has discovered a document apparently missed by early students of Gálvez's California venture. Evidence continues to support Priestley's thesis that "the occupation of the upper California ports was the concep-

tion of Gálvez, and of him practically alone" (*José de Gálvez*, 253).

13. The royal orders, sent by Secretary Grimaldi to the viceroy, the marqués de Croix, El Pardo, Jan. 23, 1768, were forwarded by Croix to Gálvez, and reached him on May 6. See Navarro García, *José de Gálvez*, 162–63. The complete text is in Treutlein, *San Francisco Bay*, 2–3.

14. Gálvez to the marqués de Croix, San Blas, May 20, quoted in Priestley, *José de Gálvez*, 246.

15. This strategy was agreed upon at San Blas. For the proceedings, see Watson and Temple, eds. and trans., *Council Held at San Blas*, 19–23. See, too, Thurman, *Naval Department of San Blas*, 49–65.

16. Gálvez and his advisors intended to depend upon the ships but hoped they could also muster enough men and material to send by land. See Watson and Temple, eds. and trans., *Council Held at San Blas*, 19–23.

17. For the number of non-Indians, see Gerhard, *North Frontier*, 297.

18. For an authoritative overview of these years, see Mathes, "Baja California," 407–22.

19. Río Chávez, *Conquista y aculturación*, 224–26. For the entire peninsula, but not including the Colorado Desert or Delta, Jackson, "Epidemic Disease and Population Decline," 310, estimates a decline from about 60,000 in 1697 to 21,000 in 1762 and 12,300 in 1775. The only single-volume overview of this subject in English, Dunne, *Black Robes in Lower California*, paid scant attention to the missions' impact on the Indian population or to the pioneering works on this subject by Homer Aschmann, Sherburne F. Cook, and Peveril Meigs. In some respects, Dunne's work was out of date when it appeared.

20. The idea that military officials entrusted with the missions "looted" them has been effectively revised by Crosby, *Doomed to Fail*.

21. For an introduction to the literature on this subject, much of it polemical, see Magnus Mörner, ed., *The Expulsion of the Jesuits from Latin America* (New York: Alfred Knopf, 1965).

22. See Watson and Temple, eds. and trans., *Council Held at San Blas*.

23. Río Chávez, "Utopia in Baja California," 1–13. See Gálvez to Viceroy Bucareli, Mexico, Dec. 3, 1771, quoted in Hernández Sánchez-Barba, *La última expansión*, 217, for his own statement of his views on missions. For a fine case study of the internal political divisions surrounding this question, including Gálvez's pragmatic retreat, see Kessell, "Friars versus Bureaucrats," 151–59. The difficult transition from Jesuit to Franciscan control in Sonora, intimately tied to events in Baja California, is explored in McCarty, *Spanish Frontier in the Enlightened Age*.

24. Guest, "Mission Colonization and Political Control," 97–116, an important article that is far broader than its title suggests, and McCarty, *Spanish Frontier in the Enlightened Age*, 11–12.

25. The first quote is from Portolá to the viceroy, the marqués de Croix, Loreto, Feb. 3, 1768, quoted in Nuttall's authoritative account of Portolá's California years, "Gaspar de Portolá," 186. The second quote is from Portolá to the viceroy, San Diego, Apr. 17, 1770, in Boneu, *Gaspar de Portolá*, 398, a work distinguished for its genealogy, the contemporary documents that it contains, and the additional information provided by editor and translator Alan K. Brown.

26. The quote is from Palóu, *Palóu's Life of Serra*, 285–86, a biography by his contemporary and confidant, who talks of Serra's quest for martyrdom (285–86), and describes his self-mortification (279–80). Geiger, *Life and Times of Junípero Serra*, is the standard biography and a superbly detailed work.

27. For an introduction to the controversy, see

Sandos, "Junípero Serra's Canonization," 1253–69. Costo and Costo, eds., *Missions of California*, contains some valuable essays and text, but its excessively partisan tone does little to advance the debate.

28. Gálvez apparently used this term only once, in a letter to a priest, but writers have incorrectly seized upon it as though it were the official name of the expedition. See the shrewd comments by Treutlin, *San Francisco Bay*, 9. The question of sabotage is explored in Bernabeu Albert, "Viajes Marítimos."

29. The optimum sailing season, Gálvez and his advisors believed to be from June to mid-September. See Watson and Temple, eds. and trans., *Council Held at San Blas*, 21.

30. The best modern retracing of the mission trail through the peninsula is Crosby's delightful *King's Highway in Baja California*.

31. Portolá to Viceroy de Croix, San Diego, July 4, 1769, and Feb. 11, 1770, in Boneu, *Gaspar de Portolá*, 393, 320–21.

32. Ibid., 394.

33. Portolá's Journal, July 28, in Boneu, *Gaspar de Portolá*, 375. Several other expeditionaries kept accounts, the fullest being that of the engineer, Miguel Costansó, ibid., 159–298. The best-known journal of the expedition, translated in Bolton, *Fray Juan Crespi*, 59–273, has turned out to be so extensively edited by Palóu that it does not resemble Crespi's original. See Wood, "Juan Crespi," 230–31, for a lengthy bibliographical discussion.

34. Charts from the Vizcaíno expedition had not been published, but his verbal description of the California coast had been incorporated verbatim into a navigational guide, printed in Manila in 1734 and carried by Portolá: González Cabrera Bueno, *Navigación especulativa*, xiii–xiv, 335, and Mathes, *Vizcaíno*, 167. Portolá also carried Venegas's *Noticia de la California* (see above, text at n. 6), with an account by Torquemada of Vizcaíno's voyage (Nuttall, "Gaspar de Portolá," 188). Vizcaíno is often blamed for having exaggerated his description of Monterey, but that the Portolá party's failure to recognize it resulted from exaggerated expectations seems clear from Portolá's statement a year later, when he returned to find Monterey and noted that "Cabrera Bueno [was] not . . . mistaken in one tittle of the marks mentioned in his History" (Portolá to the viceroy, Monterey, June 15, 1770, in Boneu, *Gaspar de Portolá*, 399).

35. Boneu, [ed.], *Documentos secretos*, 29–33, who first published the previously lost accounts of these meetings.

36. Juan Crespi to Juan Andrés, [San Diego], Feb. 8, 1770, confusing the outer and inner bays, quoted in Stanger and Brown, eds., *Who Discovered the Golden Gate?*, 111. See, too, ibid., 19, 34, and Treutein, *San Francisco Bay*, 18–37.

37. Portolá to the viceroy, San Diego, Feb. 11, 1770, in Boneu, *Gaspar de Portolá*, 320.

38. For this third junta, see Boneu, [ed.], *Documentos secretos*, 55–63, and for Gálvez's orders, see ibid., 64–65.

39. "Conversación" of Portolá "con un amigo," Madrid, Sept. 4, 1773, in Boneu, [ed.], *Documentos secretos*, 162. This often-quoted document, first published in English in Chapman, *History of California*, 225–28, must be used with caution since it contains a number of errors and its author, Juan Manuel de Viniegra, had reason to discredit Gálvez. For the best analysis, see Brown's introduction to Boneu, *Gaspar de Portolá*, 33–34.

40. Among the many accounts of this highly romanticized episode, Geiger, *Life and Times of Junípero Serra*, 1:39–44, is notable for its balance. For Portolá, see Boneu, [ed.], *Documentos secretos*, 81–101.

41. "Conversación" of Portolá "con un amigo," Madrid, Sept. 4, 1773, in Boneu, [ed.], *Documentos secretos*, 163.

42. Ibid., 164.

43. Sánchez, *Spanish Bluecoats*, 58–70. Portolá to the viceroy, San Diego, Feb. 11, 1770,

reported the deaths of thirteen of the Catalonian Volunteers (Boneu, *Gaspar de Portolá*, 320–21).

44. Miguel Costansó to the viceroy, Sept. 5, 1772, in Bolton, *Anza's California Expeditions*, 5:11. On the initial reception that Indians in California might have given to Spaniards, see Shipek's imaginative, "California Indian Reactions," 480–93.

45. Serra to Bucareli, Mexico, Apr. 22, 1773, in Tibesar, ed., *Writings of Junípero Serra*, 1:341. See, too, May 21, 1773, ibid, 363, and Castañeda, "Comparative Frontiers," 287, 298 *n.* 19.

46. The literature on Indian cultures in what is now California is vast, and some of it highly ethnocentric. Brief, sensitive introductions to the subject and the literature are Rawls, *Indians of California*, 6–13, and Costo, "Indians before Invasion," 9–28. On the *relatively* pacific nature of the coastal peoples, see, too, Moriarty, "Accommodation and Conflict Resolution," 109–22; McCorkle, "Intergroup Conflict," 694–700; Edward Spicer, *The American Indians* (Cambridge: Belknap Press of Harvard University Press, 1982), 141.

47. Felipe de Neve to Bucareli, Monterey, Feb. 26, 1777, in Beilharz, *Felipe de Neve*, 83.

48. Castillo, "Native Response," 384–86; Heizer, "Impact of Colonization," 121–39.

49. For the number of Indians baptized at each of the missions see Palóu to Serra, San Carlos, Nov. 26, 1773, in Bolton, ed., *Historical Memoirs of . . . Francisco Palóu*, 4:319–27. Conditions in California at this time have been described by many writers, including the key contemporaries. See, e.g., Serra to Bucareli, Mexico, Mar. 13, 1773, and May 21, 1773, in Tibesar, ed., *Writings of Junípero Serra*, 1:295–327, 345–73, and Fages, *Description of California*.

50. Burrus, ed., *Diario del Fernando de Rivera y Moncada*, xlv. For an introduction to the controversy surrounding Rivera, see Servín, "California's Hispanic Heritage," 117–33. A recent examination of the number of Hispanics in California in 1775 puts the number at 182, counting 10 Indian women married to Spaniards (Mason, "Garrisons of San Diego Presidio," 403). A few months before Rivera's arrival, the *Santiago* brought 7 women and their families—"the first Spanish-speaking women to set foot in Alta California" (Castañeda, "Comparative Frontiers," 288).

51. These objectives were clearly understood by contemporaries, as in Miguel Costansó's report to the viceroy of Sept. 5, 1772, quoted in Bolton, *Anza's California Expeditions*, 5:8–11. Historians have agreed. See, e.g., Chapman, *Founding of Spanish California*, 92–94.

52. Juan Manuel de Viniegra, "Apuntamiento instructivo de la expedición que el ilmo. sor d. Joseph de Gálvez . . . . [Oct. 10, 1771], in [Portolá], *Crónicas del descubrimiento de California*, 274. This remarkable account, apparently published here for the first time, is by one of Gálvez's secretaries who had clear reason for malice against him. It is the only clear evidence of the nature of Gálvez's illness. The document is analyzed in Hernández Sánchez-Barba, *La última expansión*, 238–51, but he takes unwarranted credit (239, 240) for discovering it. Forty years earlier, Priestley, *José de Gálvez*, 279, summarized Viniegra's account.

53. Hernández Sánchez-Barba, *La última expansión*, 239–51, who suggests that Gálvez feigned illness in order to extricate himself from a game that he knew could not win. Navarro García, *José de Gálvez*, 178, offers no analysis.

54. The marqués de Croix and Gálvez to the king, Mexico, June 22, 1771, in Velázquez, [ed.], *La frontera norte*, 78; for the period of calm, see Hernández Sánchez-Barba, *La última expansión*, 251–56, and Navarro García, *José de Gálvez*, 181–85.

55. Although California fell under O'Conor's jurisdiction as inspector in chief, he concentrated on building defenses against Apaches and left the search for an overland route principally in the hands of the viceroy (Navarro García, *José de Gálvez*, 264–65). Bucareli has been praised as the force behind much of the activity in California, but his own biographer denies this and suggests that California historians have imputed to Bucareli their own enthusiasm for their subject. Bucareli, an efficient but unimaginative administrator, took little initiative and simply followed Gálvez's design (Bobb, *Bucareli*, 156–71). Treutlein, *San Francisco Bay*, 35–43, 47–53, chronicles further exploration of San Francisco Bay and provides an excellent analysis of the pressures on Bucareli.

56. See the deliberations and decision of the Council of War and Exchequer, Mexico, Sept. 9, 1773, with Bucareli's endorsement of Sept. 13, in Bolton, *Anza's California Expeditions*, 5:82–93 (the quote is on p. 91), and Bucareli to Arriaga, Sept. 26, 1773, ibid, 95–98. Chapman, *Founding of Spanish California*, 159, argues that Serra did not play a decisive role in the viceroy's decision.

57. Bucareli to Arriaga, Mexico, Sept. 26, 1773, in Bolton, *Anza's California Expeditions*, 5:96.

58. The two quotes in this paragraph, "Ir a la Russia," and "Cerro Nevado" are in Bernabeu Albert, "Juan Pérez," 286, 287, the best biographical sketch of Pérez. For a detailed account see Cook, *Flood Tide of Empire*, 54–69. For documents, maps, an assessment, and later American claims, see Beals, ed. and trans., *Juan Pérez*, esp. p. 41.

59. Anza to Bucareli, May 2, 1772, in Bolton, *Anza's California Expeditions*, 5:6. The first of these five volumes, a narrative, appeared separately as *Outpost of Empire*. The remaining four volumes contain translations of most of the official correspondence and diaries, giving weight to Bolton's assertion that "few episodes in early American history are so well documented" (ibid., x). Anza's trail breaking is summarized in Hague, *Road to California*, 58–67, and told more fully in Pourade, *Anza Conquers the Desert*.

60. Anza to the viceroy, Santa Olaya [on the Colorado River], Feb. 28, 1774, in Bolton, *Anza's California Expeditions*, 5:117.

61. Chapman, *Founding of Spanish California*, 415.

62. Bucareli to Arriaga, Mexico, Nov. 26, 1774, in Bolton, *Anza's California Expeditions*, 5:194–97.

63. One of the ship's boats was actually the first vessel to enter the bay. Treutlein, *San Francisco Bay*, 63–74; for firsthand accounts, see Galvin, ed. and trans., *First Entry into San Francisco Bay*.

64. Cook, *Flood Tide of Empire*, 69–79. For the diaries in the original, see Bernabeu Albert, ed., *Juan Francisco de la Bodega y Quadra*, and Beals, ed. and trans., *For Honor and Country*, with its detailed maps.

65. Treutlein, *San Francisco Bay*, 75–87, summarizes this journey and the quarrel between Anza and the ranking officer in California, Rivera y Moncada, that led Anza to leave California prior to the actual founding of San Francisco. In a report on the finding of Anza's grave in Arizpe, Bowman and Heizer, *Anza and the Northwest Frontier*, 52–73, also examine the myth that Anza founded San Francisco. On the women, see Castañeda, "Comparative Frontiers," 290–91.

66. Serra to Bucareli, Mexico, Mar. 13, 1773, in Tibesar, ed., *Writings of Junípero Serra*, 1:299. Gálvez to Arriaga, Madrid, Mar. 8, 1774, in Bolton, *Anza's California Expeditions*, 5:105–6.

67. The "simple and artless" quote is from a Father Cartagena to Bucareli, Jan. 29, 1773, and the remainder of the description from the 1775–76 diary of fray Pedro Font. Both are quoted in Kessell, "Making of a Martyr," 189, 190.

68. The quote is from the July 3d entry of a revised diary, in Garcés, *Record of Travels in Arizona and California*, 72. The Spanish version is available as Garcés, *Diario de exploraciones en Arizona y California*. Still valuable for its commentary and sources is Coues, trans. and ed., *On the Trail of a Spanish Pioneer*.

69. Garcés's letter, and related correspondence, are in Adams and Chávez, eds. and trans., *Missions of New Mexico, 1776*, 281–85. Although fray Silvestre's name is properly Vélez de Escalante, popular usage has rendered him simply Escalante.

70. Escalante's diary from 1775, in Adams, "Fray Silvestre," 132. Adams explains the circumstances of his journey.

71. Francisco Atanasio Domínguez to fray Isidro Murillo, Santa Fe, July 29, 1776, in Adams and Chávez, eds. and trans., *Missions of New Mexico, 1776*, 282; Escalante to Governor Mendinueta, Zuni, Oct. 28, 1775, in Thomas, ed. and trans., *Forgotten Frontiers*, 157. Adams, "Fray Francisco Atanasio Domínguez," 40–58, engagingly retells their story from familiar sources.

72. The quotes in this paragraph are from the *Domínguez-Escalante Journal*, 70–73. This new translation of the journal, with the most recent identification of sites, does not entirely supersede Bolton's *Pageant in the Wilderness*. Briggs, *Without Noise of Arms*, tells the story in an engaging narrative with splendid illustrations. For prior Spanish activity to the northwest of Santa Fe, see Weber, *Taos Trappers*, 23–24.

73. For Bucareli's estimate, see Adams, "Fray Silvestre," 103, who gives no source, but the viceroy had been advised that the distance was great. See Matheo Sastre to Bucareli, Horcasitas, Jan. 21, 1773, in Bolton, *Anza's California Expeditions*, 5:48–49. The engineer Miguel Costansó had prepared a report for the viceroy with quite accurate distances, but apparently too late to serve the Domínguez-Escalante expedition. A summary of Costansó's report is in Fireman, *Spanish Royal Corps of Engineers*, 110. The duration of the trip varied considerably, depending upon its purpose and the route chosen. See, e.g., Hafen and Hafen, *Old Spanish Trail*, 169, 185.

74. Cline, *Exploring the Great Basin*, 54–59; Goetzmann, *Exploration and Empire*, 51–52, 97, 129–30, 137.

75. Garcés, writing at Tubatama, Jan. 3, 1777, in Garcés, *Record of Travels in Arizona and California*, 92.

76. Anza to the viceroy, Colorado River, Feb. 9, 1774, in Bolton, *Anza's California Expeditions*, 5:118.

77. See Palma to Bucareli, Mexico, Nov. 11, 1776; Gálvez to Teodoro de Croix, El Pardo, Feb. 10, 1777, and Bucareli to Gálvez, Mexico, Feb. 24, 1777, in Bolton, *Anza's California Expeditions*, 5:365–76, 400, 409.

78. The quote is in a report on missions from Croix to José de Gálvez, Sept. 1778, in an unpublished manuscript by Gerald E. Poyo, "Conflict and Integration: Forces of Mission Secularization in Eighteenth Century Béxar." Croix's instructions regarding the Yuma settlements, dated Mar. 7, 1780, appear in full in Matson and Fontana, eds. and trans., *Friar Bringas Reports to the King*, 97–105. For Anza's views, see Kessell, ed. "Anza Damns the Missions," 53–63, and Anza to the viceroy, Nov. 20, 1776, in Bolton, *Anza's California Expeditions*, 5:386.

79. Yates, "Locating the Colorado River Mission," 123–30, which corrects the widespread misconception that the mission was downstream, near Pilot Knob.

80. McCarty, trans. and ed., "Colorado Massacre of 1781," 223.

81. Yuma viewpoints, as well as Spanish, are best analyzed in Forbes, *Warriors of the Colorado*, 192–200. For a Franciscan view, see, too, Matson and Fontana, eds. and trans., *Friar Bringas Reports to the King*, 84–87, 96–111. For Croix and Anza, see Chapman, *Founding of Spanish California*, 414.

82. Ives, ed., "Retracing the Route of the Fages

Expedition," 49–70, 157–70, and Ives, ed., "From Pitic to San Gabriel in 1782," 222–44.

83. Gálvez, *Instructions*, 58.

84. Chapman, *Founding of Spanish California*, 426.

85. The exact number of Spaniards in California in the 1770s remains a matter of conjecture and deserves further study. Burrus, "Rivera y Moncada," 693, notes that Rivera's diary contains "the names of countless pioneer families" not previously known to historians. The best study devoted exclusively to the population of California, Avilez, "Population Increases," relies heavily on the extraordinary pioneering work of Hubert Howe Bancroft and leaves much to be desired.

86. Treutlein, *San Francisco Bay*, 88–100, tells this story in detail, quoting liberally from contemporary sources. The quote from Font's diary is on p. 82. The full diary, rich in detail, is in Bolton, ed. and trans., *Font's Complete Diary*.

87. Winther, *Story of San José*, 3; Garr, "Frontier Agrarian Settlement," 93–94.

88. Kelsey, "Founding of Old Los Angeles," 326–39, explains that the settlers were put into possession of land as they arrived that summer, even before the founding date. The exact numbers of soldiers, families, and their colonists who arrived in California by the overland routes in 1781 is not known.

89. Beilharz, *Felipe de Neve*, 110–20.

90. Ibid., 16–19. The two Californias were not separated administratively until 1804.

91. Ibid., 42–43, 97–109.

92. Neve, *Reglamento para el gobierno de la Provincia de Californias*. These regulations of 1779 spelled out Neve's strategy and also explained the purpose of the new pueblos. See, too, Beilharz, *Felipe de Neve*, 85–96, and Junta de Generales to Julián de Arriaga, Madrid, Aug. 1, 1772, quoted in Hernández Sánchez-Barba, *La última expansión*, 99.

93. Servín, ed. and trans., "Costansó's 1794

Report," 222. Marchena Fernández, "Guarniciones," 101, puts the number in St. Augustine at 535 in 1763.

94. For the physical structures, see Whitehead, "Alta California's Four Fortresses," 67–94. For the California soldiery, whose lot resembled that of presidial forces across the frontier, see Campbell, "Spanish Presidio in Alta California," 63–77, and Campbell "First Californios," 583–95. Langellier and Peterson, "Lances and Leather Jackets," 3–11, writing in apparent ignorance of Campbell's work that appeared in the same journal, argue that historians have neglected the study of California presidios.

95. Letter of July 4, 1780, summarized by Galindo Navarro and quoted in Beilharz, *Felipe de Neve*, 52. Neve's interest in using missions to extend Spanish domain is clear in his *Reglamento para el gobierno de la Provincia de Californias*, 50–52. Guest, "Mission Colonization and Political Control," 97–116, explains the changing view of missions in Spain and New Spain and sees Franciscans from the College of San Fernando, who were responsible for the California enterprise, as especially conservative.

96. See, too, Garr, "Power and Priorities," 367; Campbell, "Spanish Presidio in Alta California," 75; Beilharz, *Felipe de Neve*, 64–65.

97. Quoted in Servín, "Secularization of the California Missions," 139.

98. Palóu to Gálvez, San Carlos, Sept. 6, 1784, in Bolton, ed., *Historical Memoirs of . . . Francisco Palóu*, 4:348.

99. Neve to Bishop Reyes, Dec. 29, 1783, in Geiger, *Life and Times of Junípero Serra*, 2:368–69. See, too, Serra's "Report on the Missions" [actually Carmel], July 1, 1784, in Tibesar, ed. and trans., *Writings of Junípero Serra*, 4:252–79; Costello and Hornbeck, "Alta California," 310; and Costello, "Variability among the Alta California Missions," 441.

100. Archibald, *Economic Aspects of the Califor-*

nia Missions, 48–55; Hornbeck, "Economic Growth and Change," 423–33. For a fine analysis of how one culture responded to perceived benefits of missionary life, see Johnson, "Chumash and the Missions," 366–68.

101. Costello and Hornbeck, "Alta California," 304.

102. Bowman, "Resident Neophytes," 145–46.

103. Mariano Payeras to the College of San Fernando, Purísima, Feb. 2, 1820, in Archibald, *Economic Aspects of the California Missions*, 157. The statistic, adjusted to account for high infant mortality and the high death rates of the elderly, is suggested by one large sample (Cook and Borah, "Mission Registers," 229).

104. Report of Gov. Diego de Borica, Monterey, June 30, 1797, in Florescano and Gil Sánchez, eds., *Descripciones económicas regionales de Nueva España*, 47.

105. I am using the estimates of Gerhard, *North Frontier*, 309. The classic studies of this question are in Cook, *Conflict*, to be supplemented by Cook, *Population of the California Indians*, 1–43. A daunting number of recent studies exist, some of which are suggested in Walker, Lambert, and DeNiro, "Effects of European Contact," 349–64. In addition, one should consult the many articles by Jackson, such as his "Patterns of Demographic Change," 251–72.

106. For population, see Bowman, "Resident Neophytes," 145–46. Franciscans built their twenty-first and last mission in California at Sonoma in 1823, at the beginning of the Mexican era. For the valuable insight about surplus labor, see Jackson, "Patterns of Demographic Change," 257–58. The most recent interpretation of California's missions, Monroy, *Thrown among Strangers*, 1–98, goes over much familiar ground, but with sensitivity to Indian responses and gender.

107. For Branciforte, see Guest, "Foundation of the Villa de Branciforte," 29–50, and Garr, "Villa de Branciforte," 95–109. Payne, "Villa de Branciforte," 403–10, contains no new information.

108. Servín, "Secularization of the California Missions," 133–37.

109. José Señán to the viceroy, May 14, 1796, in *Letters of José Señán*, 3–4. Mosk, "Price-Fixing in Spanish California," 118–22, and Guest, "Municipal Government in Spanish California," 309–10, 327–28.

110. Archibald, *Economic Aspects of the California Missions*, 115–41.

111. Servín, ed. and trans., "Costansó's 1794 Report," 228.

112. Pablo Sánchez, Salvador Fidalgo, and Miguel Costansó to the viceroy, Mexico, July 13, 1795, in Fireman, *Spanish Royal Corps of Engineers*, 208.

113. Servín, ed. and trans., "Costansó's 1794 Report," 226.

114. Borica made such requests in 1794 and 1798—quoted in Castañeda, "Comparative Frontiers," 288.

115. Guest, "Foundation of the Villa de Branciforte," 35–37; Garr, "Rare and Desolate Land," 133–44; Hutchinson, *Frontier Settlement*, 64–65. For the artisans, see Velázquez, *Notas sobre sirvientes de las Californias*, 13–63. For emphasis on women, see Hernández, "No Settlement without Women," 203–34.

116. Bancroft, *History of California*, 2:158.

117. Cook and Borah, "Mission Registers," 266, who find the infant mortality rate (100 to 150 deaths per 1,000 births) far below the ranges for mission-born Indians in California, or for French and English cases studied to date. Contemporaries commented on the high fertility of the californios. See, e.g., Servín, ed. and trans., "Costansó's 1794 Report," 227; Weber, *Mexican Frontier*, 218.

118. Chapman, *Founding of Spanish California*, 427.

119. Cook, *Flood Tide of Empire*, 84–99. The expedition that Gálvez ordered in 1776

did not get underway until 1779 and failed to find Cook.

120. For the impact of the Revolution, see Mario Rodríguez, *La revolución americana de 1776 y el mundo hispánico: ensayos y documentos* (Madrid: Editorial Tecnos, 1976).

121. Gold, "Governor Bernardo de Gálvez," 72–86; Cummins, "Spanish Espionage," 39–49; Cummins, "Luciano de Herrera," 43–57; Cummins, *Spanish Observers*, appeared while this book was in press.

122. Among accounts of Spain's diplomatic interests and early involvement with the rebels, the standard in English remains Bemis, *Diplomacy of the American Revolution*, 81–112. Wright, *Anglo-Spanish Rivalry*, 122–34, offers a succinct summary. The most satisfying recent study by a Spanish scholar is Ruigómez de Hernández, *El gobierno español*, but the classic work by Yela Utrilla, *España ante la independencia de los Estados Unidos*, still merits attention for its volume of published documents. For identification and appraisal of recent Spanish scholarship, see Cummins, "Spanish Historians," 194–205, and Hilton, "Las relaciones anglo-españolas," 851–63. James H. O'Donnell III, *Southern Indians in the American Revolution* (Knoxville: University of Tennessee Press, 1973), provides only glimpses of Spanish activities in this arena, a subject that deserves more study.

123. Langum, "Caring Colony," 218–19; Beilharz, *Felipe de Neve*, 82–83.

124. For Sonora and Tucson, see the tabulation in McCarty, [ed. and trans.], *Desert Documentary*, 51–56; for New Mexico, see Thomas, ed. and trans., *Forgotten Frontiers*, 42 n. 135.

125. Thonhoff, *Texas Connection*, 45–72, 75–76. Jackson, *Los Mesteños*, 120–23, 250–52, explains the legal impediments to this interprovincial trade.

126. José de Gálvez to Bernardo de Gálvez, Aug. 29, 1779, quoted in Abbey, "Spanish Projects," 274. Appointed acting governor on Sept. 19, 1776, Bernardo de Gálvez actually assumed the position on Jan. 1, 1777. For earlier advice given to Bernardo de Gálvez, see Diego Joseph Navarro to Gálvez, Havana, July 28, 1779, quoted in Caughey, *Bernardo de Gálvez*, 149. Caughey's work remains the standard account and has been augmented by recent studies rich in detail, especially Starr, *Tories, Dons, and Rebels*; Haynes, *Natchez District*; and Cummins's revisionist works, "Oliver Pollock's Plantations," 35–48, and "Oliver Pollock and George Rogers Clark's Service of Supply." Din, ed. and trans., *Louisiana in 1776*, 1, 28, chides historians for failing to note the influence of Francisco Bouligny on the reforms ordered by José de Gálvez.

127. Starr, *Tories, Dons, and Rebels*, 35–36, 47–48, 59, 230–31; Wright, *Florida in the American Revolution*, 16–23. For summaries of these works, see Starr, " 'Left as a Gewgaw,' " 14–27, and Wright, "British East Florida," 1–13.

128. Caughey, *Bernardo de Gálvez*, 149–87; Coker and Coker, *Siege of Mobile*.

129. Borja Medina Rojas, *José de Ezpeleta*, is an exhaustive study of Ezpeleta's work as governor and his preparations for the assault on Pensacola, which has been studied mainly from the perspective of Gálvez.

130. Caughey, *Bernardo de Gálvez*, 187–214. More recent sources, which embellish Caughey's work, appeared in conjunction with the 200th anniversary of the battle. For a clear exposition of the military aspects of the siege, see Coker and Coker, *Siege of Pensacola*. Parks, ed., *Siege! Spain and Britain*, contains several good essays, as does Coker and Rea, eds., *Anglo-Spanish Confrontation*. For further sources, see Servies, *Siege of Pensacola, 1781: A Bibliography*. Since 1981, the most important work to appear on the battle is Reparaz, *Yo Solo*, a sound, well-illustrated synthesis with up-to-date bib-

liography. Wilkie, "Gálvez's First Attempt to Attack Pensacola," 194–99, suggests that the hurricane that wrecked Gálvez's fleet in the fall of 1780 was worse than historians have supposed, but otherwise sheds little light. A previously unknown journal by a high-ranking eyewitness tells of Gálvez's shortage of ammunition: Saavedra, *Journal of Don Francisco de Saavedra*, xxxv, 168–69.

131. Quoted in Langum, "Caring Colony," 219. The king's order, which also reached Texas, is quoted in full in Thonhoff, *Texas Connection*, 58.

132. Kuethe, "Charles III," 64–77.

133. The elegant real cédula of May 20, 1783, recounting his exploits and granting his title, has been published in facsimile in a handsome edition by Woodward, ed. and trans., *Tribute to Don Bernardo de Gálvez*. The quote is on pp. 43 and 109. Beerman, " 'Yo Solo' not 'Solo,' " 174–84, explains that the second ship was captained by Riaño, Gálvez's brother-in-law, and that Gálvez's motto should have read "I alone, accompanied by my brother-in-law."

134. Discussed above in my chapter 8.

135. There is a large literature on this subject. For recent overviews and guidance to sources, see Kinnaird, "Western Fringe of Revolution," 253–70; Nasatir, *Borderland in Retreat*, 29–35; Din, "Arkansas Post," 3–30.

136. The relative value of Spain's contribution awaits detached study. Some Spanish scholars view Spain's role as pivotal. Ruigómez de Hernández, *El gobierno español*, 308, notes that Gálvez's campaigns "decided the future of North American independence." Most United States historians, on the other hand, do not regard Spain's role as militarily significant, as explained by Varona, "España e Hispanoamérica," 59–72. Indeed, the standard work by Willard M. Wallace, *Appeal to Arms: A Military History of the American Revolution* (New York: Harper &

Brothers, 1951), did not mention Gálvez or Pensacola; Don Higginbotham, *The War of American Independence* (Bloomington: Indiana University Press, 1971), 423, mentions Spanish military activity in a paragraph but ascribes no strategic significance to it. Thomason, *Spain: Forgotten Ally,* sought to redress what she saw as a void in the historiography by explaining Spain's financial and military contributions in detail, but she failed to assess their military significance.

137. East Florida's non-Indian population was about 4,000 in 1775 and rose to 17,000 in 1783, of whom about 10,000 were blacks (Wright, "British East Florida," 8–9).

138. Rea, "British West Florida," 76–77.

139. As throughout this book, I am using "continental" in the restrictive sense of the continent north of what is today Mexico.

Chapter 10: Improvisations and Retreats

The epigraphs are in: McCarty, ed. and trans., "The Sonora Prophecy of 1783," 318; Cortés, *Views from the Apache Frontier*, 46; and Enrique Lafuente Ferrari, *El Virrey Iturrigaray y los orígenes de la independencia de Méjico* (Madrid: Consejo Superior de Investigaciones Científicas, 1941), 431.

1. Several essays in *Charles III: Florida and the Gulf* (Coral Gables, Fla.: Count of Gálvez Historical Society, 1990), examine the achievements of Carlos III. See, especially Coker, "The Reign of Charles III," 19–33.

2. Zéspedes to Bernardo de Gálvez, St. Augustine, July 16, 1784, in Lockey, [ed. and trans.], *East Florida, 1783–1785,* 225, 230. The red-yellow-red flag, familiar in modern times, had its origins in a decree of 1785.

3. Tanner, *Zéspedes,* 33–36; Charles E. Kany, *Life and Manners in Madrid: 1750–1800* (Berkeley: University of California Press, 1932), 98–100. The quote is from Zéspedes to Juan Ignacio de Urriza, St.

Augustine, Sept. 16, 1784, in Lockey, [ed. and trans.], *East Florida, 1783–1785*, 278. Ware, "St. Augustine, 1784," 180–87, shows that Zéspedes made repairing his own house his first priority.

4. Tanner, "Land and Water Communication," 6–20, suggests the vast distances embraced by these communication systems. Cortés Alonso, "Geopolítica del sureste," 23–47, presents a fine panoramic view.

5. The quotes are from Zéspedes to Capt. Gen. Luis de las Casas St. Augustine, June 20, 1790, in Lewis [ed. and trans.], "Cracker—Spanish Florida Style," 191. See also, Tanner, *Zéspedes*, 129, 151–63.

6. See, e.g., the unsigned and undated treatise, "Reflexiones políticas sobre las costas de América . . ." [probably written by Felipe Bauzá y Cañas], in Mathes, ed., *Californiana IV*, 2:321–23, and Cortés, *Views from the Apache Frontier*, 42.

7. Juan Gassiot to Felipe de Neve, Arizpe, Sonora, Oct. 9, 1783, in McCarty, ed. and trans., "Sonora Prophecy," 318–19.

8. Albert K. Weinberg, *Manifest Destiny: A Study of Nationalist Expansionism in American History* (Baltimore: Johns Hopkins Press, 1935), esp. chaps. 1, 2; Reginald Horsman, *Race and Manifest Destiny: The Origins of American Racial Anglo-Saxonism* (Cambridge: Harvard University Press, 1981), 85–87; DeConde, *Affair of Louisiana*, 37–40. For a penetrating analysis of the innovative politics and ideology that made American expansion possible, see the forthcoming essay by Peter S. Onuf, "The Expanding Union," in David T. Konig, ed., *The Possession of Liberty: The Conditions of Freedom in the Early American Republic* (Stanford: Stanford University Press, 1993).

9. Weber, *Mexican Frontier*, 159; MacLachlan and Rodríguez O., *Forging of the Cosmic Race*, 197.

10. Baron de Carondelet, "Military Report," New Orleans, Nov. 24, 1794, in Robertson, ed., *Louisiana*, 1:297.

11. Reginald Horsman, *The Frontier in the Formative Years, 1783–1815* (New York: Holt, Rinehart and Winston, 1970), 5–6, 60. The population of Louisiana in the last decade of Spanish rule is impossible to estimate because so many Anglo Americans had swarmed into the territory (Acosta Rodríguez, *Población de Luisiana española*, 233). Some writers use the figure 50,000 for 1803—presumably for Lower Louisiana. See, e.g., Din, "Spain's Immigration Policy," 275 *n.* 57. The estimate of nationalities that outnumbered Spaniards is that of Gov. Manuel Gayoso (Din, "Spain's Immigration Policy," 272).

12. Jack P. Greene, *Pursuits of Happiness: The Social Development of Early Modern British Colonies and the Formation of American Culture* (Chapel Hill: University of North Carolina Press, 1988), 194.

13. Maclachlan and Rodríguez O., *Forging of the Cosmic Race*, 283–87; John H. Coatsworth, "Obstacles to Economic Growth in Nineteenth Century Mexico, *AHR* 83 (Feb. 1978): 81–83, 91–94.

14. These well-known events are treated in many sources. See, e.g., Manuel Tuñón de Lara, *Historia de España*, vol. 7: *Centralismo, ilustración y agonía del antiguo régimen (1715–1833)*, by Emiliano Fernández de Pinedo, Alberto Gil Novales, and Albert Dérozier (Madrid: Editorial Labor, 1980), 249–63, and Richard Herr, *Spain* (Englewood Cliffs, N.J.: Prentice-Hall, 1971), 65–71.

15. The brief exception occurred when Bernardo de Gálvez served as viceroy, 1785–86. See Corbitt, "Administrative System in the Floridas," 41–62, 57–67, for the finest discussion of the evolving and overlapping lines of authority, which confused even contemporaries. Corbitt explains that the Floridas and Louisiana constituted a captaincy general in this period, but since no captain-general governed them except that in Cuba (as several governors of Louisiana pointed out), and since East Florida oper-

ated with considerable autonomy, the "captaincy-general" seems to have existed more in theory than in practice (Beerman, "Arturo O'Neill," 29–41).

16. Starr, " 'Left as a Gewgaw,' " 26, estimates that one-half to two-thirds of the British population remained in West Florida.

17. Troxler, "Loyalist Refugees," 1–18, explains events largely from the loyalist side. For Howard's role, see Tanner, *Zéspedes*, 46–48, and Tanner, "Second Spanish Period," 15–42. The 7,000 figure is from Wright, "British East Florida," 8–9. Lockey, [ed. and trans.], *East Florida, 1783–1785*, contains a wealth of documents for these months of transition.

18. The quote is from Pope, *Tour*, 44. For the profound demoralization of the soldiers, see White, "View of Spanish West Florida," 139–42. San Marcos de Apalachee was apparently not reoccupied until 1787 (Boyd, "Fortifications at San Marcos," 16).

19. McAlister, "Pensacola during the Second Spanish Period," 290–91, 296, 300–303; Tornero Tinajero, "Estudio de la población de Pensacola," 541–44. Coker and Inglis, *Spanish Censuses of Pensacola*, provide the names of these individuals and give the population of San Marcos in 1802 (81).

20. Tanner, *Zéspedes*, 105–36, provides a good overview, but many particulars have been clarified by subsequent research. I am using the revised estimates by Johnson, "Spanish St. Augustine Community," 38–39, whose revisionist argument I am also following. Official enumerations of population must be regarded as approximations. For the black, military, and suburban populations, see Dunkle, "Population Change," 14–15.

21. Corbitt, "Spanish Relief Policy," 71–82, counts 132 *floridanos* in the 1786 census and traces subsequent efforts to repatriate them.

22. Quoted in Johnson, "Spanish St. Augustine Community," 52.

23. Griffin, "Minorcans," 61–83, provides a fine overview of this group. Although many of the immigrants included Italians and Greeks, intermarriage blurred ethnic lines, and they came to think of themselves as Minorcans, as did outsiders. Rasico, "Minorcan Population of St. Augustine," 160–84, analyses this incomplete census, which enumerated 475 Minorcans, but his work should be supplemented by Johnson, "Spanish St. Augustine Community."

24. Without surrendering its claims to sovereignty, Britain had recognized nearly all of East Florida as the domain of Creeks and Seminoles, and Governor Zéspedes retained that understanding (Wright, *Creeks and Seminoles*, 4–5, 86, 104, 107).

25. For blacks in the interior, see especially Wright, *Creeks and Seminoles*, 73–99.

26. Tanner, "Second Spanish Period," 20; for estimates of the number of Creeks, see Wright, *Creeks and Seminoles*, 126; for ongoing population decline during the eighteenth century, see Thornton, *Cherokees*, 5–40, who describes patterns that apply to more southerly tribes.

27. The motives and diplomacy on each side have been explored in detail in the classic works by Bemis, *Pinckey's Treaty*, 1–44, and Whitaker, *Spanish-American Frontier*, 8–13. Wright, *Florida in the American Revolution*, 113–23, provides an especially able summary.

28. Din, "War Clouds on the Mississippi," 51–76; Whitaker, *Spanish-American Frontier*, 123–39.

29. Whitaker, *Spanish-American Frontier*, remains the best account of American and Spanish strategy in English, although many of Whitaker's conclusions have been refined by subsequent scholarship. Sánchez-Fabrés Mirat, *Situación histórico de las Floridas*, is the best overview in Spanish. It is my own sense that policymakers closest to the scene were most innovative. A rich trove of documents for this era are translated in Kinnaird, ed., *Spain in the Mississippi Valley*, vols. 3, 4, which treat the years 1782–94.

30. The quote is from Francisco Bouligny to Miró, Natchez, Aug. 4, 1785, in Navarro Latorre and Solano Costa, *Conspiración española*, 183. For the policy, see Tyler, "Mississippi River Trade," 255–67; Whitaker, *Spanish-American Frontier*, 63–77, 101–2, 176–77. For Spain's juridical position, see Bemis, *Pinckey's Treaty*, 44.

31. In a pioneering work, Whitaker, ed. and trans. *Documents Relating to the Commercial Policy of Spain*, summarized Spanish policy (xix–lix), and provided transcriptions and translations of key documents. See also Miller, "Struggle for Free Trade in East Florida," 48–59; Tornero Tinajero, *Florida y los Estados Unidos*, 75–80.

32. Barbier, "Silver," 6–12; Javier Cuenca Esteban, "Trends and Cycles in U.S. Trade with Spain and the Spanish Empire, 1790–1819," *Journal of Economic History* 44 (June 1984): 521–43. For California, see Ogden, *California Sea Otter Trade*, 32–44.

33. Zéspedes to Juan Ignacio de Urriza, St. Augustine, Sept. 30, 1785, in Lockey, [ed. and trans.], *East Florida, 1783–1785*, 728. For the shortages of cash in St. Augustine, see Tanner, *Zéspedes*, 115. Lorente Miguel, "Commercial Relations," 177–91, moves beyond the anecdotal evidence of earlier studies. Acosta Rodríguez, "Crecimiento económico desigual," 735–57, sees dizzying growth limited largely to the foreign export sector.

34. Tornero Tinajero, *Florida y los Estados Unidos*, 65–126, makes this case convincingly for East Florida.

35. Zéspedes to Capt. Gen. Luis de las Casas, St. Augustine, June 20, 1790, quoted in Lewis [ed. and trans.], "Cracker—Spanish Florida Style," 202.

36. Tanner, *Zéspedes*, 112, 120, 138–39, 146–47, 210. For the settlement of Canary Islanders and Acadians in Louisiana, see my chapter 7.

37. Din, "Immigration Policy of Governor Esteban Miró," 155–75, supersedes earlier work on this subject, pointing out the previously unrecognized role of Miró. For land policy, see Arena, "Land Settlement Policies," 51–60. See the examples of Americans settling near Spanish Mobile in 1785, in Holmes, "Alabama's Forgotten Settlers," 87–97.

38. Gov. Manuel Gayoso, quoted by Arena, "Land Settlement Policies," 57.

39. Curley, *Church and State in the Spanish Floridas*, 164–211; Holmes, "Irish Priests in Spanish Natchez," 169–80; Din, "Irish Mission to West Florida," 315–334; and Coker, "Father James Coleman."

40. Decree of Jan. 7, 1789, quoted in Holmes, *Gayoso*, 29, 90–95. The population figure is in Din, "Immigration Policy of Governor Esteban Miró," 174 *n.* 54. Whitaker, *Spanish-American Frontier*, 157–62, explains the failure of the policy.

41. Carondelet to the conde de Aranda, June 10, 1792, quoted in Din, "Spain's Immigration Policy," 257.

42. Apr. 2, 1791, quoted in Deconde, *Affair of Louisiana*, 52. For Jefferson's interest in "conquering without war," see Robert C. Tucker and David C. Hendrickson, *Empire of Liberty: The Statecraft of Thomas Jefferson* (New York: Oxford University Press, 1990).

43. Tornero Tinajero, *Florida y los Estados Unidos*, 57.

44. The quote, dated Jan. 6, 1788, is from Bemis, *Pinckey's Treaty*, 124, who provides a good overview (109–48). Whitaker, *Spanish-American Frontier*, 90–122, 185–200, suggests that the intrigue was almost entirely American; Burson, *Stewardship of Don Esteban Miró*, 144–87, takes exception to Whitaker, noting that Miró's private correspondence indicated that he was involved with Wilkinson "with the knowledge if not always the advice of the Crown" (168). Navarro Latorre and Solano Costa, *Conspiración española*, who include many valuable documents in a lengthy appendix, wrote in ignorance of the work of Whitaker and Burson (156), but agree with Whitaker's position. See also Jacobs, *Tarnished Warrior*, 1–109.

45. Wright, *Only Land*, 234–37.

46. Little Tallassie, Jan. 1, 1784, in Caughey, *McGillivray of the Creeks*, 66. Caughey's work, consisting largely of correspondence to and from McGillivray, is preceded by a short biography. For interpretations of McGillivray in larger contexts (and guidance to the staggering scholarship on McGillivray), see Green, *Politics of Indian Removal*, 33–36; Wright, *Creeks and Seminoles*, 115–27; and the fine article by Watson, "Strivings for Sovereignty," 400–414.

47. Holmes, "Spanish Treaties with West Florida Indians," 140–43. Key provisions of the Treaty of Pensacola are in Caughey, *McGillivray of the Creeks*, 75–76. The Mobile Treaty is in Serrano y Sanz, *España y los Indios Cherokis y Chactas*, 82–85.

48. The quotes are from the "Talk" of Zéspedes to "the chiefs and warriors of the Lower Creeks and Seminoles," St. Augustine, Dec. 8, 1784, in Lockey [ed. and trans.], *East Florida, 1783–1785*, 429. See, too, 280–83. No written treaty resulted from these talks.

49. Gayoso de Lemos to Carondelet, Natchez, Mar. 24, 1792, quoted in Holmes, *Gayoso*, 157. See, too, my chapter 8; Gibson, "Conquest," 1–15; and Kinnaird, "Spanish Treaties with Indian Tribes," 39–49 (a response to Gibson). Berry, "Indian Policy of Spain in the Southeast," 462–77, offers an interpretation that remains unchallenged but has been amplified by subsequent research as exemplified by broad views such as Holmes, "Spanish Policy toward the Southern Indians," 65–82, and studies of individuals, such as White, "Indian Policy of Juan Vicente Folch," 261–75. Din and Nasatir, *Imperial Osages*, is less a study of the Osages than a chronicle of Spanish-Indian policy in Louisiana from 1763–1804.

50. Little Tallassie, Jan. 1, 1784, in Caughey, *McGillivray of the Creeks*, 65.

51. Wolf, *Europe and the People without History*, 194. The most penetrating explanation of the impact of this trade on specific Indian societies is in White, *Roots of Dependency*, 69–102; Wright, *Creeks and Seminoles*, 50–71, provides an especially rich description of the workings of the trade as well as its impact on the Creeks. For Americans' inordinately heavy drinking in this era (1790–1830), see Mark Edward Lender and James Kirby Martin, *Drinking in America: A History* (New York: Free Press, 1982), 46–48.

52. The former French officer and agent to the Choctaws, Jean de la Villebeuvre, is the best example. See Holmes, "Juan de Villebeuvre," 387–99; for others, see Holmes, "Spanish Policy toward Southern Indians," 68–69. For alcohol and the Indian trade in West Florida, see Holmes, "Spanish Regulation of Taverns," 160–64.

53. Tanner, *Zéspedes*, 80–104; Coker and Watson, *Indian Traders of the Southeastern Spanish Borderlands*, 63–65. Coker and Watson's work supersedes all else on this subject, and I have relied on it for the next paragraphs.

54. McGillivray also sent agents to other tribes, including the distant Chickasaws, to shore up their pro-Spanish factions and undermine their pro-American leaders. See, e.g., Gibson, *Chickasaws*, 80–88.

55. Wright, *Creeks and Seminoles*, 123.

56. White, "Indian Policy of Juan Vicente Folch," 270, 273; Holmes, "Spanish Policy toward Southern Indians," 69–70.

57. Caughey, *McGillivray of the Creeks*, 34–45; Green, *Politics of Indian Removal*, 35; Francis Paul Prucha, *The Great Father: The United States Government and the American Indians*, 2 vols. (Lincoln: University of Nebraska Press, 1984): 1:50–58.

58. The treaty is translated in Kinnaird, ed., *Spain in the Mississippi Valley* 4 (pt. 3):223–27. The quote is on p. 225 (art. 6). The documents in this volume treat what Kinnaird termed "Problems of Frontier Defense, 1792–1794." Governor Gayoso

toned down a more beligerant version of the treaty, see Holmes, *Gayoso*, 150–54.

59. July 5, 1795, quoted in Miller, "Rebellion in East Florida," 179. See, too, Miller, *Juan Nepomuceno de Quesada*, 113–66; Murdoch, *Georgia-Florida Frontier*; and related documents in Bennett, [ed. and trans.], *Florida's "French" Revolution*.

60. The quote is from Carondelet, "Military Report," New Orleans, Nov. 24, 1794, in Robertson, ed., *Louisiana*, 1:300. For Carondelet's policy in context, see Kinnaird, ed., *Spain in the Mississippi Valley*, 4:xxi–xxix, who suggests that Carondelet's beligerence grew out of necessity (xiv). Whitaker, *Spanish-American Frontier*, 163–70, regarded Carondelet's Indian policy as recklessly beligerent. Unlike his predecessor, Miró, or his successor, Gayoso, Carondelet has not been the subject of a published book-length biography. For a brief assessment and guidance to sources, see Brasseaux, "Baron de Carondelet," 64–70. Carondelet's military preparations are described in Nasatir, *Spanish War Vessels on the Mississippi*, a work that includes translations of contemporary documents.

61. Kinnaird, "Spanish Treaties with Indian Tribes," 47–48; Holmes, "Spain's Policy toward the Southern Indians," 71.

62. Flores to Secretary Antonio Valdés, Mexico, Dec. 23, 1788, quoted in Cook, *Flood Tide of Empire*, 130. The Nootka Crisis has been the object of considerable study. Archer, "Transient Presence," 3–32, noted the anti-Spanish bias in much of the literature and offered a fine corrective. That same year, Cook's more balanced work appeared; it remains the indispensable starting point. Pethick, *Nootka Sound Connection*, adds nothing new to the story.

63. For the heavy drinking, see Cook, *Flood Tide of Empire*, 169, 175; for "Gardem España," see ibid., 172; for Martínez's instructions, see ibid., 132.

64. Cook, *Flood Tide of Empire*, 200–249.

65. Carondelet to the duque de Alcudia, New Orleans, Jan. 8, 1796, in Nasatir, ed. and trans., *Before Lewis and Clark*, 2:388.

66. Ibid., 1:75–108 (p. 82 for the Mandans); Cook, *Flood Tide of Empire*, 434–41. See, too, Nasatir, *Borderland in Retreat*, chaps. 3, 4.

67. The quote is from Malaspina's instructions to the commanders of two vessels sent to the Pacific Northwest in 1792, quoted in Kendrick, ed. and trans., *Voyage of the SUTIL and MEXICANA*, 41. The splendid narrative of Cook, *Flood Tide of Empire*, examines the work of these scientists and offers guidance to sources. Cutter, "Spanish Scientific Exploration," 35–48, is the best short introduction to the subject. For detailed accounts of these expeditions in the larger context, see especially Arias Divito, *Las expediciones científicas españolas*; Engstrand, *Spanish Scientists in the New World*; and many of the essays in Peset, ed., *Culturas de la costa noroeste de América*, and Pino Diaz, ed., *Ciencia y contexto histórico nacional*. The firsthand account in English is Moziño, *Noticias de Nutka*. These Spanish scientists visited the California coast, too. See, especially, Cutter's two works, *Malaspina in California* and *California in 1792*.

68. Cook, *Flood Tide of Empire*, 349–52.

69. Archer, "Transient Presence," 31; Fireman, "Seduction of George Vancouver," 427–43.

70. Cook, *Flood Tide of Empire*, 409–23.

71. The one "Spanish" mission built north of San Francisco Bay was founded in 1823 at Sonoma, when independent Mexico governed California.

72. See Cook, *Flood Tide of Empire*, 197, 390, 524–26.

73. Bemis, *Pinckey's Treaty*, is the classic work, but I have followed Whitaker, *Spanish-American Frontier*, 180–84, 201–8, who corrected Bemis's analysis of Godoy's motives. See, especially, Whitaker, "New Light on the Treaty of San Lorenzo," 435–52. Armillas Vicente, *Mississipi*, ably sum-

marizes standard sources in English and in Spanish, emphasizing European diplomacy.

74. Whitaker, *Spanish-American Frontier*, 221; Kinnaird, "American Penetration into Spanish Louisiana," 220–21.

75. Whitaker, *Spanish-American Frontier*, 209–20.

76. White, *Roots of Dependency*, 95–96. Ronald N. Satz, *American Indian Policy in the Jacksonian Era* (Lincoln: University of Nebraska Press, 1975).

77. Quoted in Whitaker, *Mississippi Question*, 180. Whitaker's classic work also explains Godoy's policy in 1795–96 (ibid., 52–54). Nasatir, *Spanish War Vessels on the Mississippi*.

78. These complex and well-known negotiations are nicely summarized in DeConde, *Affair of Louisiana*, 75–105; the quote is on p. 81.

79. Foley, *Genesis of Missouri*, 139–40.

80. Capt. José Vidal to José Joaquín Ugarte, Concordia, Louisiana, Oct. 4, 1803, quoted in John, "Riddle of Mapmaker Juan Pedro Walker," 113. For examples of other requests to move from Louisiana to Texas, see Hatcher, *Opening of Texas*, 305–11; DeConde, *Affair of Louisiana*, 197. The population of Pensacola and Mobile swelled in 1804, apparently with officials and troops from Louisiana, but then dropped again (Coker and Inglis, *Spanish Censuses of Pensacola*, 6).

81. Brooks, "Spain's Farewell to Louisiana," 29–42.

82. Albert Gallatin to Jefferson, Sept. 12, 1805, quoted in DeConde, *Affair of Louisiana*, 225. For a good overview of the diplomatic issues, see ibid., 213–25, and Pratt, *Expansionists of 1812*, 60–69, for American motives. For American efforts to enlist Napoleon to pressure Spain see Egan, "United States, France, and West Florida," 227–52. For the American position, see Burns, "West Florida and the Louisiana Purchase," 391–416. Tucker and Hendrickson, *Statecraft of Thomas Jefferson*, 137–88, 235, 250, see a president obsessed with West Florida, but whose motives remain unclear.

83. Cook, *Flood Tide of Empire*, 456.

84. Flores, ed., *Jefferson and Southwestern Exploration*. Jackson, *Thomas Jefferson and the Stony Mountains*, xi, 98–267, is a fine summary and guide to the numerous sources. As Jackson notes, Pike "never thought of himself solely as an explorer. He was a spy—and proud to be one" (Jackson, ed. and trans., *Journals of Zebulon Montgomery Pike*, 1:viii).

85. Jackson, ed. and trans., *Journals of Zebulon Montgomery Pike*, 2:102–3. There is a large literature on Wilkinson. The best biography is Jacobs, *Tarnished Warrior*.

86. Martínez de Irujo to Pedro Cevallos, Washington, Dec. 2, 1802, in Nasatir, ed., *Before Lewis and Clark*, 2:714. Jefferson planned the Lewis and Clark expedition prior to purchasing Louisiana and that plan prompted the Spanish minister's observations.

87. Delassus to Casa Calvo, St. Louis, Aug. 10, 1804, in Nasatir, ed., *Before Lewis and Clark*, 2:743.

88. Wilkinson's secret report, "Reflections on Louisiana," as quoted in Cook, *Flood Tide of Empire*, 453, who also makes clear Wilkinson's influence on Spanish policy at this time.

89. Salcedo to Chacón, Chihuahua, May 3, 1804, ibid., 457.

90. Ibid., 446–90, provides a fresh and detailed overview of Spanish efforts to halt American explorers, revising the long-held notion that Melgares was searching for Pike. Cook explained the Melgares expedition "as a combined expedition to the Red River and the Pawnee country" (480), a point missed by Flores, ed., *Jefferson and Southwestern Exploration*, 125 *n.* 5, who oversimplified Cook's argument. See, too, Nasatir, *Borderland in Retreat*, chap. 7.

91. [Pedro Cevallos] to Nemesio Salcedo, San

Lorenzo, Nov. 21, 1807, in Jackson, ed. and trans., *Journals of Zebulon Montgomery Pike*, 2:279.

92. Holmes, "Marqués de Casa-Calvo," 324–39.

93. For these stories, together with translations of the pertinent diaries and documents, see Nasatir, ed. and trans., *Before Lewis and Clark*, and Loomis and Nasatir, *Pedro Vial*. Spanish texts are reproduced in Represa, ed., *España ilustrada en el lejano oeste*, 29–88, 101–16.

94. Carlos IV gave the order in May 1805; the incomplete treatise, nearly finished when Pichardo died in 1812, was never published in Spanish, but most of it has been translated in Hackett, ed. and trans., *Pichardo's Treatise*. The treatise arrived in Spain by 1817. See Brooks, *Diplomacy and the Borderlands*, 42, 75, 81. This was one of several such studies, see Coker, ed., *John Forbes' Description of the Spanish Floridas*, 1.

95. For the convoluted argument that the Rio Grande formed the western boundary of Louisiana, see Stenberg, "Western Boundary of Louisiana," 95–108, and Stenberg "Boundaries of the Louisiana Purchase," 32–64. Haggard, "Neutral Ground between Louisiana and Texas," 1001–1128, explains the agreement as well as its aftermath. For Wilkinson's "fee," see ibid., 1042–43. Castañeda, *Our Catholic Heritage in Texas*, 5:253–56, sees Spain's response as defensive. See, too, DeConde, *Affair of Louisiana*, 127–38, and for a more pro-American summary, see Faulk, *Last Years of Spanish Texas*, 121–26. Holmes, "Showdown on the Sabine," 46–76, provides perhaps the best account.

96. Hatcher, *Opening of Texas*, 83–84, 312–14, 333–34; Benson, "Bishop Marín de Porras," 30; Navarro García, *José de Gálvez*, 30–33. The population of Texas is in the report of Juan Bautista de Elguezabal, San Antonio de Bexar, Aug. 20, 1804, in Guice, [trans.], "Texas in 1804," 48. I use the term *reawakened* advisedly. Spain had

earlier plans to develop Texas against the American threat but did not implement them. They are outlined in Revilla Gigedo, *Informe sobre las misiones*, 72–74.

97. Navarro García, *José de Gálvez*, 3–4; Holmes, "Showdown on the Sabine," 47–48; Jackson, ed. and trans., *Journals of Zebulon Montgomery Pike*, 1:412–13.

98. Haggard, "Neutral Ground between Louisiana and Texas," 1082–89; Hatcher, *Opening of Texas*, 114–15, who also notes Nemesio Salcedo's refusal to admit a group of Apalachees! Everett, *Texas Cherokees*, 11–12. For the beginnings of the Choctaws' migration beyond the Mississippi, see White, *Roots of Dependency*, 93–99.

99. Haggard, "House of Barr and Davenport," 66–68; Guice, "Trade Goods for Texas," 507–19.

100. The quote is from Salcedo's order opening Texas to Louisiana, from a copy of Dec. 4, 1806, Béxar, in Hatcher, *Opening of Texas*, 311–12; see, too, ibid., 60–126.

101. For Boone, see ibid., 110–11, 322–23.

102. Nemesio Salcedo to Bernardo Bonavía, n.p., Aug. 21, 1809, ibid., 331. See also, Revilla Gigedo, *Informe sobre las misiones*, 73–74. Officials closest to the scene were more willing to compromise; see, e.g., ibid., 55–57, 297–300. Castañeda, *Our Catholic Heritage in Texas*, 5:285–36, augments Hatcher's standard account. For Texas governors Manuel Antonio Cordero (1805–8) and Manuel Salcedo (1808–13), see, too, Dunn, "Concern of the Spanish Government," 45–61, and Almaraz, *Tragic Cavalier*. In 1804, after the United States acquired Louisiana, Spain ordered a halt to American immigration to the Floridas. See Tornero Tinajero, *Florida y los Estados Unidos*, 57.

103. Wilson and Jackson, *Philip Nolan and Texas*, suggests that Nolan's motives were commercial and that charges that he was a spy are based on conjecture. Flores, ed., *Journal of an Indian Trader*, 3–30; Weber, *Taos Trappers*, 35–50; Nasatir, *Borderland*

in Retreat, chap. 5; Ogden, *California Sea Otter Trade*, 32–45. While all foreigners ran these risks, the treatment of individual Americans varied with individual circumstances. Liljegren, "Zalmon Coley," 263–86, is a case in point.

104. The quote is from Pedro Bautista Pino's *Exposición* of 1812 in Carroll and Haggard, eds. and trans., *Three New Mexico Chronicles . . .*, 37. No tejano went to the Cortes, but Texas was represented by Ramos de Arizpe from neighboring Coahuila (Benson, ed. and trans., *Report . . . Dr. Miguel Ramos de Arizpe*).

105. Timothy E. Anna, *Spain and the Loss of America* (Lincoln: University of Nebraska Press, 1983), examines the collapse of the metropolis and its increasingly dysfunctional colonial administration, which he sees as central to the loss of empire. For the impact of the Cádiz reforms on northern New Spain, see Weber, *Mexican Frontier*, 16–19.

106. For a recent summary of the situation in West Florida, see Clark and Guice, *Frontiers in Conflict*, 41–65. The more detailed treatment in Cox, *West Florida Controversy*, 388–403, remains indispensable; the quote is on p. 401. Arthur, *West Florida Rebellion*, is replete with detail and documents, including Madison's Oct. 27, 1810, proclamation. See, esp., pp. 113–14, and 134–35.

107. Cox, *West Florida Controversy*, 409–11, 437–86; White, *Vicente Folch*, 100–105.

108. McAlister, "Pensacola during the Second Spanish Period," 300–307, 310, 315–18, 324. For the sources and valuable correctives to the problematic statistics accepted by McAlister and other writers, see Coker and Inglis, *Spanish Censuses of Pensacola*, 91–93, 143.

109. Poitrineau, "Demography and the Political Destiny of Florida," 438–42; Marchena Fernández, "Guarniciones," 104, 112–14.

110. Pratt, *Expansionists of 1812*, 76–125, 189–246, placed these events in large perspective, but Patrick, *Florida Fiasco* provides a more richly detailed account with many correctives. For the Seminoles and Blacks, see ibid., 179–94, and Peters, *Florida Wars*, 27–45.

111. The quote is from a memo of James Monroe, Oct. 1817, in Griffin, *United States and the Disruption of the Spanish Empire*, 140. Bushnell, ed., *República de las Floridas* is a fine collection, with four essays that reevaluate this episode, explaining it in the context of the Spanish-American independence movement rather than as mere piracy, and providing guidance to numerous sources. For the importance of Amelia Island, see Tornero Tinajero, *Florida y los Estados Unidos*, 18–21, 80–83, 108–111.

112. The rebellion in San Antonio was in sympathy with that of Hidalgo in Mexico. See Chabot, *Texas in 1811*, and Haggard, "Counter-Revolution of Béxar," 222–35.

113. Constitution of Apr. 6, 1813, quoted in Warren, *Sword Was Their Passport*, 52. For official American involvement in Texas, see ibid., 31–32, and Gronet, "United States and the Invasion of Texas," 281–306. The standard narrative for events in Texas in this decade remains Garrett, *Green Flag over Texas*. For Salcedo's demise, see Almaraz, *Tragic Cavalier*, 171–72. For the measures ordered from Cádiz, see Ribes Iborra, [ed.], *Ambiciones estadounidenses*, 32–39.

114. Weber, *Mexican Frontier*, 9–10.

115. Antonio Martínez to the viceroy, Béxar, Jan. 20, 1821, and May 30, 1820, in Martínez, *Letters from Gov. Antonio Martínez*, 50, 48. See, too, Taylor, ed. and trans., *Letters of Antonio Martínez*, and Downs, "Governor Antonio Martinez," 27–43. Ribes Iborra, "Texas en las postrimerías," 194.

116. Jackson's foray and its results are exam-

ined in many sources, I am following Brooks, *Diplomacy and the Borderlands*, 139–50.

117. Ibid., 150–65. For the treaty's ambiguous resolution of the West Florida question, see ibid., 163–64.

118. Quotation from Mateo de la Serna, Oct. 15, 1819, ibid., 186.

119. Ibid., 170–89; Norris, "Squeeze," 109–10, 128–29.

120. Rachel Jackson to Mrs. Elizabeth Kingsley, Pensacola, July 23, 1821, in James Parton, *Life of Andrew Jackson*, 3 vols. (New York: Mason Bros., 1861), 2:604.

121. The preamble of the June 23, 1819, Texas Declaration of Independence, quoted in Warren, *Sword Was Their Passport*, 236, who summarizes Long's invasions of Texas, 233–54.

122. For Mexico's anomalous conservative rebellion, see Timothy E. Anna, *The Fall of the Royal Government in Mexico City* (Lincoln: University of Nebraska Press, 1978), and Anna, *The Mexican Empire of Iturbide* (Lincoln: University of Nebraska Press, 1990).

123. Quoted in Weber, *Mexican Frontier*, 8; these paragraphs are drawn from pp. 1–14. For earlier public celebrations, see the way in which the ascendency of Fernando VI was heralded in San Antonio and Santa Fe, in Cruz, *Let There Be Towns*, 141–43, and Adams, "Viva el Rey!," 284–90.

124. Manuel Zozaya, Dec. 26, 1822, quoted in Weber, *Mexican Frontier*, 12.

Chapter 11: Frontiers and Frontier Peoples Transformed

The epigraphs are in: Benavides, *Revised Memorial of 1634*, 38–39; Bartram, *Travels*, 118; and "Notes and Reflections on the War with the Apache Indians in the Provinces of New Spain," quoted in John, ed. and trans., "Cautionary Exercise," 311.

1. Alcalde Rafael Aguilar et al. to the diputación, Pecos, Mar. 12, 1826, discussed in Hall and Weber, "Mexican Liberals," 17. Aguilar may not have written this in his own hand.

2. In June 1828 a priest christened the son of Rafael Aguilar and his wife, Paula, as Juan Manuel (Hall, *Four Leagues of Pecos*, 54–55). For Pueblo Indian use of courts, see Cutter, *Protector de Indios*.

3. Ford, "New Pueblo Economy," 73–91, who summarizes archaeological as well as historical and ethnological evidence. See also, Dozier, *Pueblo Indians*, 65–66. Every pueblo did not adopt all of these plants and animals, of course.

4. John, *Storms Brewed*, 149. See, too, 105.

5. Ford, "New Pueblo Economy," 83–84, points out that "in the food classification system used by the Tewa[,] indigenous fruits are generally conceived as 'hot' but those from outside are 'cold'" (83).

6. See my chapter 4.

7. Kessell, *Kiva, Cross and Crown*, 455–58, examines the causes of the decline of Pecos. The date the pueblo was finally abandoned is not certain, but it is traditionally given as 1838. For population at Pecos, see the table on p. 342.

8. Pecos tradition suggests that Hispanics used these means (Hall, *Four Leagues of Pecos*, 60).

9. Dozier, *Pueblo Indians*, 65–71; Ferguson, "Emergence of Modern Zuni Culture," 346–47; Gutiérrez, *When Jesus Came*, 161; Adams, "Passive Resistance," 85–87.

10. Sturtevant, "Last of the South Florida Aborigines," 147.

11. Diary of Francisco Amangual, in Loomis and Nasatir, *Pedro Vial*, 482, called to my attention in Kenner, *History of New Mexican–Plains Indians Relations*, 57. See, too, Ahlborn, "European Dress in Texas," 6–9.

12. Schroeder, "Shifting for Survival," 239–55.

13. Spicer, *Cycles of Conquest*, 1–15, has one of the finest discussions of the various native responses to Hispanic influences and of the results of directed and undirected culture change. Hall, *Social Change in the Southwest*, has reexamined this question in light of more recent theories. For the Southeast, where scholarship on this question is thinner, see Sturtevant, "Spanish-Indian Relations," 41–94, and White, *Roots of Dependency*. For the interesting case of the Nootkas, see Cook, *Flood Tide of Empire*, 65–67.

14. Ezell, "Hispanic Acculturation," 134–35.

15. Kessell, ed. and trans., "Anza Damns the Missions," 58.

16. López, *Texas Missions in 1785*, 22. For a good sample of these attitudes, see the responses of California friars to a questionnaire, in Geiger, ed. and trans., *As the Padres Saw Them*.

17. The quote is from Matson and Fontana, eds. and trans., *Friar Bringas Reports to the King*, 57. Franciscans continued to express these ideas after the colonial period ended (Weber, *Mexican Frontier*, 46). For exclusion from the priesthood, see Stafford Poole, *Pedro Moya de Contreras: Catholic Reform and Royal Power in New Spain, 1571–1591* (Berkeley: University of California Press, 1987), 152–53.

18. The quote is López, "Report on the San Antonio Missions," 490. Hinojosa, "Religious-Indian Communities," 61–83. Almaraz, *San Antonio Missions*, 6, 55–56, ignores the disappearance of Indians by the 1790s as a cause of secularization (Weber, *Mexican Frontier*, 53–56).

19. Hinojosa and Fox, "Indians and Their Culture," 105–20; Phillips, "Indians in Los Angeles," 427–35; Mason, "Indian-Mexican Cultural Exchange," 124. Hurtado, *Indian Survival*, 8–9, 20–26.

20. The quote is in Mason, "Fages' Code of Conduct," 96. Emphasis is the governor's. Mason, "Indian-Mexican Cultural Exchange," 133–35, who also cites several marriages between Indian men from the mission and Hispanic women at Los Angeles in the 1820s. For other examples of Indian-Hispanic marriages, see below, n. 142.

21. For a full consideration of Spanish institutions and individuals as transmitters of Spanish culture, but one that does not compare missions with other institutions, see Spicer, *Cycles of Conquest*, 285–324. See, too, Radding de Murrieta, "Function of the Market," 155–69.

22. George A. McCall to "H," Cantonment Clincy, Jan. 6, 1823, in McCall, *Letters*, 56.

23. Luis Gil y Taboada and José María Zalvidea, San Gabriel, June 28, 1814, quoted in Mason, "Indian-Mexican Cultural Exchange," 132. For a similar observation, see Nentvig, *Rudo Ensayo*, 55–56. Hann, ed. and trans., "Apalachee Counterfeiters," 52–68.

24. The case of the Apache Manuel González is noted in Guest, "Municipal Government in Spanish California," 312. Gutiérrez, *When Jesus Came*, 171, 175, suggests that a third of the population of New Mexico were genízaros by the late eighteenth century, and he sees genízaros as social outcasts, but by his own data 36 percent were artisans by 1790 and 21 percent had acquired land (199–202). Archibald, "Acculturation and Assimilation," 205–17, argues for a much lower percentage due to assimilation. The best short introduction to this subject and its literature is Magnaghi, "Plains Indians in New Mexico," 86–95. See, too, Chávez, "Genízaros," 198–201; Dobyns et al., "What Were Nixoras?" 230–58; and Officer, *Hispanic Arizona*, 76. The extent to which this phenomenon existed in Texas is not clear, but for suggestive remarks see Hinojosa and Fox, "Indians and Their Culture," 109–110, and John, "Independent Indians," 131–35.

25. The quote is from Facundo Melgares, Santa Fe, Apr. 18, 1821, in Hall and

Weber, "Mexican Liberals," 7. See also, Weber, *Mexican Frontier*, 47. On the English, see Gary B. Nash, *Red, White, and Black: The Peoples of Early America* (Englewood Cliffs, N.J.: Prentice-Hall, 1974), 276–85, and Meinig, *Shaping of America*, 1:208.

26. For the rejection of livestock, see Bushnell, "Archaeology of Mission Santa Catalina de Guale." Hester, "Perspectives on the Material Culture," 219, 223, 225. See my chapter 4, for a consideration of this question in the mission context. For theoretical literature and a recent case study, see Judith Francis Zeitlin, "Ranchers and Indians on the southern Isthmus of Tehuantepec: Economic Change and Indigenous Survival in Colonial Mexico," *HAHR* 69 (Feb. 1989): 23–60, and León-Portilla, *Endangered Cultures*.

27. For the literature on this subject, which falls beyond the scope of my immediate concern, see Richard White, "Native Americans and the Environment," in W. R. Swagerty, ed., *Scholars and the Indian Experience* (Bloomington: Indiana University Press, 1984), 179–204.

28. Leonard W. Blake, "Early Acceptance of Watermelons by Indians of the United States," *Journal of Ethnobiology* 1 (Dec. 1981): 193–99.

29. Crosby, *Ecological Imperialism*, 156–57, who points out that the first French settlements may also have been a source of peaches; see also, Hann, *Apalachee*, 133.

30. Flores, "Ecology of the Red River in 1806," 36.

31. Crosby, *Ecological Imperialism*, 152–53, who identifies the three plants as curly dock, sow thistle, and red-stemmed filaree.

32. Sauer, *Sixteenth Century North America*, 161, 301; Crosby, *Columbian Exchange*, 77–79; Crosby, *Ecological Imperialism*, 173–76.

33. The quote is from a declaration of Louis Juchereau de Saint-Denis, June 22, 1715, in Jackson, *Los Mesteños*, 10. For a short introduction to the spread of Spanish horses from Florida to California by the authority on this subject, see Worcester, *Spanish Mustang*; for cattle, see Worcester, *Texas Longhorn*.

34. Crosby, *Ecological Imperialism*, 177, 182–83. Doolittle, "Las Marismas to Pánuco to Texas," revises the traditional notion of the source of Texas cattle, horses, and ranching techniques.

35. For a comparative view of the variety of adaptations of Spanish domestic mammals to different environments, see the zoo-archaeological evidence presented by Reitz, "Spanish Colonial Experience and Domestic Animals," 10–11. For English introductions, see Terry G. Jordan, *Trails to Texas: Southern Roots of Western Cattle Ranching* (Lincoln: University of Nebraska Press, 1981). John E. Rouse, *The Criollo: Spanish Cattle in the Americas* (Norman: University of Oklahoma Press, 1977), vii. See, too, the vivid description of diseased animals in Florida in Bartram, *Travels*, 132.

36. Arnade, "Cattle Raising in Spanish Florida," 116–24, who found 2,230 cattle reported for tax rolls in 1698–99—likely an undercount; Bushnell, "Menéndez Márquez Cattle Barony," 407–31; Scardaville and Belmonte, eds. and trans., "Florida in the Late First Spanish Period," 10; Tanner, *Zéspedes*, 52. The full explanation for the failure of cattle to thrive in Spanish Florida needs more study, for they flourished there at a later date. See Jordan, "North American Cattle Ranching Frontiers," chaps. 4, 6.

37. Charles Wayland Towne and Edward Norris Wentworth, *Shepherd's Empire* (Norman: University of Oklahoma Press, 1945), 44–52, 120, 122.

38. Baxter, *Las Carneradas*, 20.

39. Simmons, *Albuquerque*, 114.

40. Baxter, *Las Carneradas*, 42.

41. Ibid., 92–94. Denevan, "Livestock Numbers," 691–703, uses evidence that he acknowledges "is mainly in the form of unre-

liable estimates and is not conclusive" (699) to conjecture that there were two to three million sheep in New Mexico by the 1820s (698). Baxter, *Las Carneradas*, does not address Denevan's argument.

42. Towne and Wentworth, *Shepherd's Empire*, 19; Reitz, "Spanish Colonial Experience and Domestic Animals," 4–5.

43. Considerations of these complex questions in the Spanish era remain speculative for lack of empirical evidence. Most work touches lightly on the Spanish era and the processes are not fully understood for more recent times. See, e.g., Denevan, "Livestock Numbers," 691–95, 699–703; James Rodney Hastings and Raymund M. Turner, *The Changing Mile: An Ecological Study of Vegetation Change with Time in the Lower Mile of an Arid and Semiarid Region* (Tucson: University of Arizona Press, 1965), 30–32; Maitland Bradfield, *The Changing Patterns of Hopi Agriculture* (London: Royal Anthropological Institute, 1971), 24–29; William deBuys, *Enchantment and Exploitation: The Life and Hard Times of a New Mexico Mountain Range* [the Sangre de Cristos] (Albuquerque: University of New Mexico Press, 1985), 222–23; Weniger, *Explorers' Texas*, 1–29; Bernard L. Fontana, "Desertification of Papaguería: Cattle and the Papago," in Patricia Paylore and Richard A. Haney, Jr., eds., *Desertification: Process, Problems and Perspectives* (Tucson: University of Arizona Press, 1976), 59–69. For the considerable literature on arroyos, and the debate over their origins, see Ronald U. Cooke and R. W. Reeves, *Arroyos and Environmental Change in the American South-West* (Oxford: Clarendon, 1976), who compare southern Arizona with coastal California and propose a multicausal thesis. When the right climatic conditions and serious overgrazing coincide, desertification can occur within a generation. See Frank S. Crosswhite, "Dry Country Plants of the

South Texas Plains," *Desert Plants* 2 (Autumn 1980): 167.

44. Kino, March 1699, quoted in Amadeo M. Rea, *Once a River: Bird Life and Habitat Changes on the Middle Gila* (Tucson: University of Arizona Press, 1983), 17, who provides a number of firsthand descriptions of the Gila by Spanish observers.

45. For a case study of this phenomenon, see Dobyns, *From Fire to Flood*, 81–83. Dobyns summarized his argument in "Who Killed the Gila," 17–30. For the Río Puerco, next to the Pecos the longest tributary of the Rio Grande in New Mexico, see Jerold Gwayn Widdison, "Historical Geography of the Middle Rio Puerco Valley," *NMHR* 34 (Oct. 1959): 257–59, 272. For the Zuni River, see Bloom, ed. and trans., "Fray Estevan de Perea's *Relación*," 228.

46. Simmons, *Albuquerque*, 106–8.

47. Kessell, *Friars, Soldiers, and Reformers*, 237. Similar figures for Tumacácori exist for 1814 (ibid., 228) and 1820 (ibid., 244). Overcrowding also existed around the missions in Texas. See Weniger, *Explorers' Texas*, 13, 182–84.

48. Crosby, *Ecological Imperialism*, 153–54, and 287–89, who also explains the Great Plains as a "mysterious exception" (290). See, too, Cooke and Reeves, *Arroyos and Environmental Change*, 170–71; Conrad Bahre and David E. Bradbury, "Vegetation Change along the Arizona-Sonora Boundary," *Annals of the Association of American Geographers* 68 (June 1978): 150; and DeBuys, *Enchantment and Exploitation*, 224–26. For current research see West, "Early Historic Vegetation Change," 333–48.

49. Ford, "New Pueblo Economy," 74, 85–86; Dobyns, *From Fire to Flood*, 96.

50. Quoted in Stephen J. Pyne, *Fire in America: A Cultural History of Wildland and Rural Fire* (Princeton, N.J.: Princeton University Press, 1982), 416. See, too, Henry T. Lewis, *Patterns of Indian Burning in Califor-*

nia: Ecology and Ethnohistory, and its introductory essay by Lowell John Bean and Harry W. Lawton (Ramona, Calif.: Ballena Press, 1973), for the importance of grasses to protoagriculture in California.

51. I have relied on the argument in Pyne, *Fire in America*, esp. pp. 73–84, 415–17, 516–19. Pyne suggests that Indians whose agriculture did not depend on irrigation used fire most commonly (ibid., 73). See, too, Dobyns, *From Fire to Flood*, 43. For Indian use of fire in Florida and the Southeast, see, e.g., Hann, *Apalachee*, 127; Albert E. Cowdrey, *This Land, This South: An Environmental History* (Lexington: University of Kentucky Press, 1983), 14–15.

52. Weniger, *Explorers' Texas*, 180.

53. Dobyns, *From Fire to Flood*, 96. Terry G. Jordan and Matti Kaups, *The American Backwoods Frontier: An Ethnic and Ecological Interpretation* (Baltimore: Johns Hopkins University Press, 1989), argue that if Spaniards had the experience and technology of the Anglo-American backwoodsman, more southern forests may have yielded to their axes—an argument that they carry too far in asserting that Spaniards "knew nothing of forests and shunned them" (16).

54. David E. Brown, *The Grizzly in the Southwest: Documentary of an Extinction* (Norman: University of Oklahoma Press, 1985), 17.

55. Weniger, "Wilderness, Farm, and Ranch," 115; Weniger, "Natural History," in Weddle, ed., *La Salle*, 283; and Weddle, *San Juan Bautista*, 93.

56. Kenneth N. and Sally L. Owens, "Buffalo and Bacteria," *Montana Magazine* 37 (Spring 1987): 66.

57. "Mesquite invasions occur only after water tables are lowered . . . to a point which allows germination and growth of seedlings" (Dean A. Hendrickson and W. L. Minckley, "Ciénegas: Vanishing Climax Communities of the American Southwest," *Desert Plants* 6 [1984]: 167).

58. See, e.g., Jack M. Inglis, *A History of Vegetation on the Rio Grande Plain* (Austin: Texas Parks and Wildlife Dept., Wildlife Division, [1964]), an admirable study called to my attention by Don Chipman of North Texas University. For the problem of scale in writing environmental history, see Richard White's wide-ranging and clearheaded essay, "American Environmental History: The Development of a New Historical Field," *PHR* 54 (Aug. 1985): 319–23.

59. Oñate to the King, [Dec.] 1623, in Bloom, "Oñate's Exoneration," 187.

60. Turner, *Beyond Geography*, and Lynn White, Jr., "The Historical Roots of Our Ecological Crisis," in David and Eileen Spring, eds., *Ecology and Religion in History* (New York: Harper & Row, 1974), 15–31. The "fruits of Spain" quote is from Pedro Menéndez Marqués to the audiencia of Santo Domingo, St. Augustine, Apr. 2, 1579, in Connor, ed., *Colonial Records of Spanish Florida*, 2:227. See, too, Hodge, ed., *History of New Mexico by Gaspar Pérez de Villagrá*, 144; Benavides, *Revised Memorial of 1634*, 38–39; Pino, *Exposición*, in Carroll and Haggard, eds. and trans., *Three New Mexico Chronicles*, 219.

61. Crosby, *Ecological Imperialism*, 275, 304–7. See the perceptive comments in Hal Rothman, "Cultural and Environmental Change on the Pajarito Plateau," *NMHR* 64 (Apr. 1989): 188–90, and Reitz, "Spanish Colonial Experience and Domestic Animals."

62. Ahlborn, "Will of a Woman," 319–55 (the quote is on p. 338). Jenkins, "Some Eighteenth Century New Mexico Women," 337–40. Juana Luján's relative status cannot be clearly specified. She had amassed this property before the late-eighteenth century burst of prosperity came to New Mexico, and when little money circulated. In St. Augustine during these years, only 4 percent of the population earned more

than 400 pesos a year (Deagan, ed., *Spanish St. Augustine*, 43–44); toward the end of the century, one of the richest men in prosperous Lousiana died with an estate of 117,000 pesos (Burson, *Stewardship of Don Esteban Miró*, 240).

63. Although Frederick Jackson Turner stressed the impact of the frontier on American culture, American scholars see far greater continuity than change. See, e.g., Ray Allen Billington, *America's Frontier Heritage* (New York: Holt, Rinehart & Winston, 1966), 54; Jack P. Greene and J. R. Pole, "Reconstructing British-American Colonial History: An Introduction," in Greene and Pole, eds., *Colonial British America: Essays in the New History of the Early Modern Era* (Baltimore: Johns Hopkins University Press, 1984), 10, 14–16; and Andrew R. L. Cayton and Peter S. Onuf, *The Midwest and the Nation: Rethinking the History of an American Region* (Bloomington: Indiana University Press, 1990), 25–28, 42.

64. For a discussion of the application of the law in several cases in Juana Luján's New Mexico, see Rock, "*Pido y Suplico*,'" 148–51. For regional variations in practice, see McKnight, "Spanish Law," 367–406.

65. Koch, "Mortuary Behavior Patterning," 187–227, a rare study of Hispanic mortuary practices in Hispanic North America, finds strict adherence to tradition; Gutiérrez, *When Jesus Came*, 61; Bushnell, *King's Coffer*, 26. For an overview of Hispanic life and institutions among the nonmilitary population on the northern frontier of New Spain, see Jones, *Los Paisanos*.

66. The classic work on this subject remains Foster, *Culture and Conquest*. For a study of cultural diffusion, see Jordan, "North American Cattle Ranching Frontiers." Notwithstanding its regional variations, Spanish culture has an inherent unity, especially when considered in opposition to the cultures of Native Americans; it is in that sense that I use the term *Spanish cul-*

ture, with full awareness that one situtated in a purely Spanish context might talk instead of Basque, Catalán, or Castilian culture.

67. Although there is a large literature on native adaptation and acculturation to Hispanic culture, we have few studies of the impact of native Americans on Hispanics in North America. Scholes noted this deficiency in 1935 ("First Decade of the Inquisition," 225). A detailed consideration of Spanish culture would, of course, account for regional differences in Spanish culture.

68. Bushnell, *King's Coffer*, 26.

69. Inventory of July 10, 1597, in Hackett, ed., *Historical Documents*, 3:431.

70. Pfefferkorn, *Sonora*, 286. Spaniards themselves appear to have regarded the details of daily life as too commonplace to merit mention.

71. The quote is from Pfefferkorn, *Sonora*, 287. On the social importance of clothing, see Bushnell, *King's Coffer*, 26–27, and Gutiérrez, *When Jesus Came*, 205.

72. In addition to Ahlborn, "Will of a Woman," see the wills in Espinosa, *Shawls, Crinolines, Filigree*.

73. Bancroft, *California Pastoral*, 377. In New Orleans, more directly connected to Europe by sea, affluent residents affected the latest styles (Burson, *Stewardship of Don Esteban Miró*, 243–46).

74. For the simplification of clothing styles in New Mexico, see Boyd, *Popular Arts of New Mexico*, 220–33, for a characteristically insightful commentary, and Simmons, "Spaniards of San Gabriel," 44, who finds Spaniards dressing "in a style similar to that of the Pueblo Indians." For shoes, see Covington, ed., *Pirates, Indians and Spaniards*, 145, and Simmons, "Footwear of New Mexico's Hispanic Frontier," 223–231. Ahlborn, "European Dress in Texas," 8–18, is of use for clothing that in most respects had changed little since the late colonial period. Cisneros, *Riders across the*

Centuries, contains well-researched renderings of the clothing and accoutrements of Hispanic men.

75. Scarry and Reitz, "Herbs, Fish, Scum, and Vermin," 343–51, is the most up-to-date summary of archaeological knowledge of this elusive subject for the sixteenth century. For continuing adaptation in the eighteenth century, see Reitz and Cuumba, "Diet and Foodways," 151–85.

76. The quote is in Scarry and Reitz, "Herbs, Fish, Scum, and Vermin," 344. See, too, ibid., 351–55; Ford, "New Pueblo Economy," 86–87; and John Super, *Food, Conquest, and Colonization in Sixteenth-Century Spanish America* (Albuquerque: University of New Mexico Press, 1988), 80. For the complaints of starvation at St. Augustine as "part of the subsistence strategy," see Reitz and Cuumba, "Diet and Foodways," 152.

77. Hann, *Apalachee*, 130; Hudson, *Southeastern Indians*, 226–28.

78. Pfefferkorn, *Sonora*, 288; Reitz and Cuumba, "Diet and Foodways," 151–85, present archaeological evidence that suggests a strong correlation between diet and socioeconomic status.

79. Although of uneven quality, the literature on medical theory and practice on the Spanish frontier is large. See, e.g., Straight, "Medicine in St. Augustine," 731–41; Holmes, "Spanish Medical Care," 463–68; Ives, A "Lost Discovery," 101–14; Scholes, "First Decade of the Inquisition," 208, 218, 220; and Scardaville and Belmonte, eds. and trans., "Florida in the Late First Spanish Period," 16. For additional sources from the Southwest, see Weber, *Mexican Frontier*, 404. For the medical conservatism of Spaniards as well as Frenchmen and Englishmen, see Ronald L. Numbers, *Medicine in the New World: New Spain, New France, and New England* (Knoxville: University of Tennessee Press, 1987).

80. Ahlborn, "Will of a Woman," 346, 349, 350. For *metates* and *comales* in the homes

of early residents of San Antonio, see Cruz, *Let There Be Towns*, 157–58.

81. Ahlborn, "Will of a Woman," 346, 352, 353; Kenagy, "Stepped Cloud and Cross," 326–27; Mason, "Adobe Interiors," 259–60; Pfefferkorn, *Sonora*, 288; Hann, *Apalachee*, 245. For archaeological confirmation see Deagan, "Archaeology of Sixteenth-Century St. Augustine," 19; Deagan, ed., *Spanish St. Augustine*, 232–42; McEwan, "Sixteenth Century Spanish Foodways," 123–24, 127; South, "From Thermodynamics," 329–41.

82. Deagan, ed., *Spanish St. Augustine*, 123, 121. For baskets and cloth, which do not show up readily in the archaeological record, see Hinojosa and Fox, "Indians and Their Culture," 119–20. In southwestern America, Spaniards eventually did borrow some fighting techniques from their Indian adversaries.

83. For examples of Indian decorative influences see Kenagy, "Stepped Cloud and Cross," 327, 332; Neuerburg, *Decoration of the California Missions*, 7–8, 17, 54, 55, 58; Lee and Neuerburg, "Alta California Indians as Artists," 467–80; Schuetz, "Professional Artisans in the Hispanic Southwest," 24, 26–27. Kubler, *Religious Architecture of New Mexico*, 38–39, 48–49, 131–32, suggests some Indian influence beyond the merely decorative in the small fortress churches of seventeenth-century New Mexico (which lacked arches and domes).

84. For domestic architecture see Boyd, *Popular Arts of New Mexico*, 5–7, 25; Kirker, *California's Architectural Frontier*, 7–13; Morales Folguera, *Arquitectura*, 229–40, 255–58, 265–66, 275–78, 282–88; Tjarks, "Evolución urbana de Texas," 615–17; Robinson, "Colonial Ranch Architecture," 123–50. There is a large literature on mission architecture, but for its simplification on the frontier, see Kubler's classic, *Religious Architecture of New Mexico*, and Schuetz, "Professional Artisans in the His-

panic Southwest," 17–71, for her discovery of geometric proportions in the simplified baroque missions at San Antonio. Saunders, "Ideal and Innovation," 527–42, provides examples of adaptation but not of innovation.

85. I want to emphasize the word *most*. More adaptable and eclectic than many writers have supposed, some residents of St. Augustine had flat roofs of masonry or shingle-covered wooden roofs and Spaniards also built horizontal, notched log houses with pitched roofs in mountainous areas of New Mexico (Gritzner, "Hispanic Log Construction of New Mexico," 20–29).

86. For domestic New Mexican architecture, see Bunting, *Early Architecture in New Mexico*, 59–79, and the more insightful discussion in Boyd, *Popular Arts of New Mexico*, 2–30. For St. Augustine, see Manucy, "Changing Traditions in St. Augustine Architecture," 103–11. On this, as on other architectural questions, Grizzard, *Spanish Colonial Art and Architecture*, is disappointingly shallow.

87. Adams and Chávez, eds. and trans., *Missions of New Mexico*, 13–14; Fontana, "Biography of a Desert Church," 9, 20. Little descriptive or archaeological evidence of the decor of the Florida missions remains, but it seems clear that seventeenth-century chapels in Florida and New Mexico were relatively plain. Much of the painting of the California chapels was done late in the colonial era and in the 1820s (Neuerburg, *Decoration of the California Missions*, 10–11).

88. The quotes are from George H. von Langsdorf, a German who visited the home of Capt. Luis Argüello in 1806, quoted in Mason, "Adobe Interiors," 256. See, too, Weber, *Mexican Frontier*, 222.

89. Burson, *Stewardship of Don Esteban Miró*, 236–42 (the quote is on p. 242).

90. Ahlborn, "Will of a Woman," 341–55. This list is so detailed that is appears to include a complete inventory of her furniture. See, too, inventories of the possessions of two of the more prosperous residents of early San Antonio in 1736, in Cruz, *Let There Be Towns*, 156–58. Compare this to the artistocracy in Spain or Mexico: Marcelin Defourneaux, *Daily Life in Spain in the Golden Age*, trans. Newton Branch (Stanford: Stanford University Press, 1970), 149–50; Charles E. Kany, *Life and Manners in Madrid: 1750–1800* (Berkeley: University of California Press, 1932), 152–55; Doris M. Ladd, *The Mexican Nobility at Independence, 1780–1821* (Austin: Institute of Latin American Studies, University of Texas at Austin, 1976), 68–69.

91. Juan Bautista Ladrón del Niño de Guevara, 1817, quoted in Boyd, *Popular Arts of New Mexico*, 125; Ahlborn, "Will of a Woman," 347–48.

92. Mason, "Adobe Interiors," 244–47; Tjarks, "Evolución urbana de Texas," 615–17; Robinson, "Colonial Ranch Architecture," 132, 139; Boyd, *Popular Arts of New Mexico*, 21, 251; Kany, *Life and Manners in Madrid*, 153.

93. Taylor and Bokides, *New Mexican Furniture*, 6, 23–25, provides surprising evidence of adherence to standard forms from a study of wooden chests, "the most common surviving form of New Mexico furniture" (23). The "industrial" missions of California seemed especially productive at manufacturing furniture (Mason, "Adobe Interiors," 250, 255–56).

94. Ahlborn, "Will of a Woman," 330, 345. For the shortage of iron and the tools and hardware that were available, see Simmons and Turley, *Southwestern Colonial Ironwork*, 29, 116–34, 135–61.

95. Boyd, *Popular Arts of New Mexico*, 246–50; 258; Taylor and Bokides, *New Mexican Furniture*, 85–86, plates 94, 96. These examples of synthesis of Indian and Hispanic motifs seem exceptional. More Spanish-period furniture apparently remains to be

studied in New Mexico than elsewhere in the Spanish borderlands where few period pieces remain. See, e.g., Montero de Pedro, *Españoles en Nueva Orleans y Luisiana,* 147.

96. The Pueblos, who had their own traditional irrigation systems, apparently adopted Spanish custom and law for managing water (Meyer, *Water in the Hispanic Southwest,* 27–45; Simmons, "Spanish Irrigation in New Mexico," 135–50). Glick, *Old World Background,* notes the variety of regional practices in Spain.

97. Meyer, *Water in the Hispanic Southwest,* 76–82. For the middle Rio Grande Valley see Carlson, *Spanish-American Homeland,* 23–52. For the lower Rio Grande, see Robinson, "Colonial Ranch Architecture," 126–27.

98. Two of the most interesting commentaries on Spanish communities in comparison to the English and American phenomena are Reps, *Making of Urban America,* 26–55, and Stilgoe, *Common Landscape of America,* 33–43.

99. "Ordenanzas . . . hechas para los nuevos descubrimientos, conquistas y pacificaciones," July 13, 1573, in *CDI*(1), 16:142–87. Nuttall, ed. and trans. "Royal Ordinances," 743–53, 249–54, is highly misleading, for it includes only 17 of the 24 articles that concern new towns. A more recent translation is in Crouch, Garr, and Mundigo, *Spanish City Planning,* 1–65 (a work marred by errors), which includes more articles but which fails to compare discrepencies in three "original" manuscript versions and which renders its translation from an imprint. A definitive translation and commentary remains to be done. Meanwhile, for a fine exposition, see Francisco de Solano, "Significado y alcances de las Nuevas Ordenanzas de Descubrimiento y Población de 1573," in Gabriel Alomar, ed., *De Teotihuacán a Brasilia: Estudios de historia urbana iberoamericana y filipina* (Madrid: Instituto de

Estudios de Administración Local, 1987), 106–27. For the founding of three such municipalities in North America, see Cruz, *Let There Be Towns,* 70–73, 96–97, 109–12. Although St. Augustine was laid out before the 1573 codification, its norms were already the practice throughout Spanish America. The 1573 ordinances remained in force until the end of the colonial era, augmented in some cases by local officials, as in the case of New California. See Blackmar, *Spanish Institutions of the Southwest,* 153–63.

100. Montequin, "El proceso de urbanización," 634–36, 643–44. Thomas, "Spanish Missions of La Florida," 381, describes a number of ways in which St. Augustine departed from the 1573 regulations. See, too, Spell, ed. and trans., "Grant and First Survey of San Antonio," 73–89.

101. Reps, *Making of Urban America,* 42–43.

102. The quote is from Richard M. Morse, "The Urban Development of Colonial Spanish America," in Bethell, ed., *Cambridge History of Latin America,* 2:71. For dispersal from urban centers, see Bushnell, "Noble and Loyal City," 51; Simmons, "Settlement Patterns," 101–05, who suggests that this was true for Santa Cruz de la Cañada, Santa Fe, Albuquerque, and El Paso. See, too, Simmons, *Albuquerque,* 81–94, for Albuquerque's irregular beginnings. Tjarks, "Evolución urbana de Texas," 624–25, sees San Antonio as an exception, but a study of the 1767 plan of San Antonio (fig. 63), suggests otherwise. For San Jose, see Garr, "Frontier Agrarian Settlement," 97–98. See, too, Garr, "Villa de Branciforte," 101; and Garr, "Monterey: Planless Capital," 215–36. Monterey was not, however, a municipality. The dimensions and configuration of colonial towns at the time of their founding remains somewhat murky as is well illustrated in the case of Santa Fe. See Pratt, "Plaza in History,"

5–13; C. Snow, "Plazas of Santa Fe," 40–51; and C. Snow, "Santa Fe Plaza," 37–53.

103. Manuel Trigo quoted in Simmons, *Albuquerque*, 91.

104. Clark, *New Orleans*, 251–53; Morales Folguera, *Arquitectura*, 167–73, 200–229; Holmes, *Gayoso*, 200–213.

105. The status of St. Augustine is not entirely clear, but contemporary documents, including a royal decree, commonly refer to it as a "city" (Amy Bushnell to Weber, July 8, 1991).

106. The quote is from Morfi, *History of Texas*, 1:93, 92, and the descriptions from Tjarks, "Evolución urbana de Texas," 613–14, 635, based in part on Morfi's diary. Since Morfi despised the townspeople (2:417, 424–25), his harsh description of the villa might be dismissed, but others expressed similar sentiments. For similar observations from 1741 and 1779, see Fernández de Santa Ana, "Memorial . . . concerning the Canary Islanders," 278, and Bolton, ed. and trans., *Athanase de Mézières*, 2:293.

107. For urban amenities elsewhere, see Francisco de Solano, "La ciudad iberoamericana durante el siglo XVIII," 267, in Gabriel Alomar, ed. *De Teotihuacán a Brasilia: Estudios de historia urbana iberoamericana y filipina* (Madrid: Instituto de Estudios de Administración Local, 1987). Cathedrals existed, as in San Antonio and St. Augustine, but they were relatively modest. The population figures, which include rural residents who happen to live within broad municipal boundaries, are from Ríos-Bustamante and Castillo, *Illustrated History of Mexican Los Angeles*, 64; Gutiérrez, *When Jesus Came*, 170; Weber, *Mexican Frontier*, 1; Marchena Fernández, "Guarniciones," 112; Dunkle, "Population Change," 20 (who gives a figure of 1,383 for the town proper in 1815—the last census of the Spanish era).

108. Cabildo of San Antonio to Governor Cabello, 1783, quoted in Tjarks, "Comparative Demographic Analysis of Texas," 635–36. On bullfights, see ibid., 635; and Weber, *Mexican Frontier*, 237–38; Cruz, *Let Their Be Towns*, 139–43; and Adams, "Viva el Rey!," 284–92. New Orleans, in contrast, had more sophisticated entertainment in the Spanish era (Burson, *Stewardship of Don Esteban Miró*, 257–60).

109. Nash, *Red, White, and Black*, 230–32; Clark, *New Orleans*, 252.

110. Guest, "Municipal Government in Spanish California," 307–35. Bushnell, *King's Coffer*, 107, notes that St. Augustine, contrary to conventional wisdom, had a functioning cabildo in the seventeenth century; by the eighteenth century it had vanished (TePaske, *Governorship of Spanish Florida*, 26–27). For Santa Fe, see Simmons, *Spanish Government in New Mexico*, 166–67. Military usurpation of civilian political power is suggested in Cruz, *Let There Be Towns*, 144–48, but he does not develop this theme. Elective municipal government began to be restored on the frontier in the 1810s, due to initiatives from the liberal Cortes of Cádiz (Weber, *Mexican Frontier*, 16–17).

111. Quoted in Simmons, *Albuquerque*, 88, who notes that Albuquerque, too, had an *alcalde mayor* rather than a cabildo. See, too, Felipe de Neve's instructions to Pedro Fages, Saucillo, Sept. 7, 1782, in Beilharz, *Felipe de Neve*, 165–66. For a critique of military government, see Benson, trans. and ed., *Report . . . Dr. Miguel Ramos de Arizpe*, 30–31.

112. Hatcher, "Municipal Government of San Fernando de Bexar," 303–5; Simmons, *Spanish Government in New Mexico*, 171–73.

113. Benson, trans. and ed., *Report . . . Dr. Miguel Ramos de Arizpe*, 26–29. Such charges were commonplace throughout the empire—see Marchena Fernández, *Oficiales y soldados*, 13.

114. Rafael Bracho, Durango, ca. 1815, quoted in Cutter, *Protector de Indios*, 91.

115. Scardaville and Belmonte, eds. and trans., "Florida and the Late First Spanish Period," 7. For descriptions and assessments of the frontier judiciary, see especially TePaske, *Governorship of Spanish Florida*, 58–76; Simmons, *Spanish Government in New Mexico*, 176–80; Arnold, *Unequal Laws*, 54–59, 92–93; Basque, "Law and Order in Texas," 17–48; Langum, *Law and Community*, 30–33. For the presence of books and the near absence of lawyers, see McKnight, "Law Books on the Hispanic Frontier," 74–84, and McKnight, "Law without Lawyers," 51–65.

116. Report of José de Zúñiga, 1804, in McCarty, *Desert Documentary*, 86–92. The quote is on p. 91. For a similar comment in Texas, see Schuetz, "Professional Artisans in the Hispanic Southwest," 19. Moorhead, *Presidio*, 222–42, notes efforts to encourage civilian settlements at presidial sites in northern New Spain.

117. In some communities, an egalitarian poverty characterized the early years. Schuetz, "People of San Antonio," 78, has examined wills for the 1718–31 period and finds few economic differences between families. Governor Concha, "Advice on Governing New Mexico," 244, noted in 1794 that "these people with very little difference are each other's equals in fortune and birth." For the decline of opportunity in an established community, see Poyo, "Immigrants and Integration," 85–103.

118. Most scholars who have studied frontier society have advanced this argument.See Weber, "Turner," 75–78 (for a summary of the views of several specialists), Jones, *Los Paisanos*, 246, and the recent comments of Poyo and Hinojosa, "Spanish Texas," 411. It is difficult to test this generalization empirically, however, until we have a clearer picture of the flexibility of racial categories in other parts of Spanish America and more family studies that distinguish between actual racial identity and labels. For the current debate in New Spain and guidance to the enormous literature on the complicated questions of class, caste (terms which some writers find meaningless in colonial Latin America), and race, see Patricia Seed, "Social Dimensions of Race: Mexico City, 1753," *HAHR* 62 (Nov. 1982): 569–606; James Lockhart, "Social Organization and Social Change in Colonial Spanish America," in Bethell, ed., *Cambridge History of Latin America*, 2:265–313; Rodney D. Anderson, "Race and Social Stratification: A Comparison of Working-Class Spaniards, Indians, and Castas in Guadalajara, Mexico in 1821," *HAHR* 68 (May 1988): 209–443. Magnus Mörner's excellent summation, *Race Mixture in the History of Latin America* (Boston: Little, Brown, 1967), has become dated.

119. Using St. Augustine alone as an example, it is clear that peninsulares rather than criollos dominated the highest offices. See Marchena Fernández, "Guarniciones," 120, 122; Johnson, "Spanish St. Augustine Community," 41–42. For a revisionist view of the role of criollos, which needs to be tested in the borderlands, see Lockhart, "Social Organization and Social Change," 317–19. The term *mestizo* came to be synonymous with mixed bloods by the late eighteenth century, but I am using it in the narrower sense of Spanish-Indian mixtures (mestizo originally meant an individual of half-Indian and half-Spanish blood).

120. Velasco to Luna, May 12, 1559, quoted in Priestley, ed. and trans., *Tristán de Luna*, 1:xxxiii.

121. Forbes, "Hispano-Mexican Pioneers," 175–78; Temple, ed., "First Census of Los Angeles," 148–49. For the more complex question of the ethnic and racial composition of immigrants to New Mex-

ico, see Bustamante, "'Matter Was Never Resolved,'" 145–46.

122. In the most careful study of population origins in the southeastern borderlands, Corbett, "Migration to a Spanish Imperial Frontier," 414–30, found more immigrants from Spanish America, most of them mestizos, than had been supposed. Between 1658–91, 30 percent of the residents of St. Augustine had come from Spanish America (20 percent from New Spain alone); between 1692–1756, the percentage dropped to 10–13 (ibid., 418)—a figure that probably obtained in the second Spanish period, 1783–1821. See, too, Marchena Fernández, "Guarniciones," 119–28, and Landers, "African Presence," 315–27.

123. Quoted in Deagan, "*Mestizaje* in Colonial St. Augustine," 61.

124. Moore, *Revolt in Louisiana*, 56; Gutiérrez, *When Jesus Came*, 191; Basque, "Law and Order in Texas," 24, 27; Bustamante, "'Matter Was Never Resolved,'" 159.

125. Deagan ed., *Spanish St. Augustine*, 45, 104; Johnson, "Spanish St. Augustine Community," 28–29; Scardaville and Belmonte, eds. and trans., "Florida and the Late First Spanish Period," 9.

126. Officer, *Hispanic Arizona*, 77–78; Lockhart, "Social Organization and Social Change in Colonial Spanish America," 298; Tjarks, "Comparative Demographic Analysis of Texas," 293. Bustamante, "'Matter Was Never Resolved,'" 150–51, 158–59, and Gutiérrez, *When Jesus Came*, 190–206, offer different explanations for why race became a more important determinant of calidad after midcentury in New Mexico. For Salazar, see Schuetz, "Professional Artisans in the Hispanic Southwest," 31.

127. Pfefferkorn, *Sonora*, 284.

128. Anderson, "Race and Social Stratification," 2, 13; Gutiérrez, *When Jesus Came*, 205. Robert McCaa, "*Calidad, Clase*, and Marriage in Colonial Mexico: The Case

of Parral, 1788–90," *HAHR* 64 (Aug. 1964): 477–501, insists on separating "class" from "calidad."

129. Narciso Durán and Buenaventura Fortuny, San José, Nov. 7, 1814, and Ramón Olbés, Santa Barbara, Dec. 31, 1813, in Geiger, ed. and trans., *As the Padres Saw Them*, 13–14, 12, responding to a questionnaire from Cádiz, asking about the racial composition of local residents. See, too, Mason, "Indian-Mexican Cultural Exchange," 134.

130. Tjarks, "Comparative Demographic Analysis of Texas," 322–23, 326–27. See, too, De la Teja, "Indians, Soldiers, and Canary Islanders," 85; Gutiérrez, *When Jesus Came*, 196; Bustamante, "'Matter Was Never Resolved,'" 146–47.

131. Tjarks, "Comparative Demographic Analysis of Texas," 323 *n.* 45, 326; Scholes, *Church and States*, 126; Rock, "'Pido y Suplico,'" 147; Gutiérrez, *When Jesus Came*, 205–6.

132. Corbett, "Problem of the Household," 74.

133. Marchena Fernández, *Oficiales y soldados*, 35–36, notes that throughout Spanish America in the eighteenth century the army had served as a powerful vehicle for upward mobility.

134. Tornero Tinajero, *Florida y los Estados Unidos*, 61; Mason, "Adobe Interiors," 254. In Santa Fe or New Orleans, with larger, more diversified populations, the military enjoyed relatively less influence.

135. Delgado, "Spanish Ranker," 1–13 (the quote is on p. 13).

136. For the high illiteracy and humble backgrounds of soldiers, see, e.g., Marchena Fernández, "Guarniciones," 132–35, and Campell, "First Californios," 587–95. Dobyns, *Spanish Colonial Tucson*, 112, would disagree. For the common use of convicts, sources include Stern, "Social Marginality and Acculturation," 118–34; Coker, "Religious Censuses of Pensacola," 59–61; Corbett, "Migration to a

Spanish Imperial Frontier," 420, 427. For the story of Sal, see Campbell, "First Californios," 592. On the use of *don* for officers, see ibid., 590, and Deagan, ed., *Spanish St. Augustine*, 43.

137. As always in talking about a large expanse of space and time, the extent to which soldiers and officers could advance varied with circumstances. In St. Augustine, for example, the type and social status of soldiers varied considerably between the first and second Spanish periods, with fewer opportunites for troops after 1783 (Marchena Fernández, "Guarniciones," 131–33). In New Mexico, Garner, "Dynamics of Change," 8–11, advances (but does not substantiate) the interesting thesis that the elite, cut off from encomienda income after the seventeenth century, found a new source of government support as soldiers in the eighteenth. See, too, Moorhead, "Rebuilding the Presidio of Santa Fe," 133, who notes that the local soldiery were "rather patrician personnel" who required more than "the usual spartan accommodations." In New California, the rise of the soldiery to the local "nobility" occurred toward the end of the Spanish era and especially in the Mexican period when land and markets became available—later than is suggested by Campbell, "First Californios," 593. Generalizing from the case of San Antonio in 1779, Moorhead, *Presidio*, 241–42, suggests that civilians living near presidios may have been more affluent than soldiers, but as he notes, many civilians were retired soldiers.

138. Gálvez, "Notes and Reflections on the War with the Apache Indians," 311, 312. The case of the socially unacceptable wife is noted in White, *Vicente Folch*, 98. For the leveling influence of the frontier on the military, see also Campbell, "First Californios," 589–90, 594, and Concha, "Advice on Governing New Mexico," 244. For another complaint about near insubordination in the frontier military, see Tanner, *Zéspedes*, 187.

139. Tanner, *Zéspedes*, 167, 195; Holmes, "Do It," 20–21. Historians have not studied prostitution on the Spanish frontier, due perhaps to the scarcity of sources. One may only conjecture, for example, about why an inordinate number of women in Pensacola appear as seamstresses and laundresses in the 1820 census (McAlister, "Pensacola during the Second Spanish Period," 324). For the raping of Indian women, see my chapter 9.

140. Bancroft, *History of California*, 1:639–40, called to my attention by Kelsey, *Doctrina and Confesionario of Juan Cortés*, 15. The episode occurred in 1800. Neither sodomy or bestiality were unknown in Spain, of course. See Bennassar, *Spanish Character*, 207–12.

141. Deagan, "*Mestizaje* in Colonial St. Augustine," 58–59; Deagan, "Spanish-Indian Interaction," 305; Cruz, *Let There Be Towns*, 138–39. Castañeda, "Comparative Frontiers," 287, 298 *n.* 19, gives examples of six Catalonian volunteers who married Indian women in California. For the Catalonian origins of these men, compare Serra to Bucareli, Monterey, Aug. 24, 1774, and Feb. 5, 1775, in Tibesar, ed., *Writings of Junípero Serra*, 2:149, 237, and Sánchez, *Spanish Bluecoats*, 35.

142. The present state of research does not allow broad generalizations about the transplantation of Iberian family or household structure, which varied substantially with time and place. Some of the best work is by Corbett, "Population Structure in Hispanic St. Augustine, 1629–1763," *FHQ* 54 (Jan. 1976): 263–84, and Corbett, "Problem of the Household," 49–75. For the gender imbalance at San Marcos, see Coker and Inglis, *Spanish Censuses of Pensacola*, 81. Corbett's figure for high male death rates is based on samples from the first Spanish period.

See, too, Tornero Tinajero, "Estudio de la población de Pensacola," 545, 548; Poitrineau, "Demography and the Political Destiny of Florida," 435; Tjarks, "Comparative Demographic Analysis of Texas," 309, 310, 319. New Mexico stands as an exception (Tjarks, "Demographic, Ethnic and Occupational Structure," 62).

143. For Spain, see Bennassar, *Spanish Character*, 178–88; for a summary of the current state of knowledge about this complex subject, and for guidance to the literature in Spanish America, see Asunción Lavrín, "Introduction," to Lavrín, ed., *Sexuality and Marriage in Colonial Latin America* (Lincoln: University of Nebraska Press, 1990), 1–43. The most considered examination of the question of marriage for any region of the borderlands is Gutiérrez, *When Jesus Came*, esp. pp. 227–97, who finds a high degree of endogamy—a conclusion that Bustamante, "'Matter Was Never Resolved,'" seems to challenge. Elsewhere, one finds a high degree of exogamy. See, e.g., the suggestive comment of Poyo and Hinojosa, "Spanish Texas," 411; Poyo, "Canary Islands Immigrants of San Antonio," 46–47; De la Teja, "Indians, Soldiers, and Canary Islanders," 88; and Mason, "Indian-Mexican Cultural Exchange," 134.

144. Our present state of knowledge does not reveal the extent to which nuptual practices on the frontier differed from colonial norms—norms which varied, in any event, from urban to rural areas and among classes. Holmes, "Do it," 30, argues that "expediency dictated by frontier conditions obviated such things as marriage licenses [and] publication of the banns." Miranda, "Gente de Razón Marriage Patterns," 2, takes the opposite position, but she presents too idealized a view.

145. Holmes, "Do It," 30, and Holmes, *Gayoso*, 122–24. Bushnell, *King's Coffer*,

36, notes similar violations of regulations against marital alliances between the Crown's treasury officials and other government officials.

146. Antonio Chávez of Atrisco, 1718, quoted in Gutiérrez, *When Jesus Came*, 245. Miranda, "Gente de Razón Marriage Patterns," 14–15.

147. Baade, "Form of Marriage," 52–53, who also explains the applicability of the Tridentine form of marriage (the decree Tamestsi of 1563) to episcopal jurisdictions in Spanish North America.

148. Cummins, "Families in Crisis.; Scholes, "First Decade of the Inquisition," 207; Holmes, "Do It," 35–36; Rock, "'Pido y Suplico,'" 155–56.

149. The story of Luis Cazorla of La Bahía, is in Tjarks, "Comparative Demographic Analysis of Texas," 635. Folch's lament appears in Holmes, "Do It," 34. For adultery, see, too, ibid., 21–25; Scholes, *Troublous Times in New Mexico*, 3, 467, 217; Rock, "'Pido y Suplico,'" 152–56; Gutiérrez, *When Jesus Came*, 215–26, 235–38; Tjarks, "Comparative Demographic Analysis of Texas," 310; Bennassar, *Spanish Character*, 95–97, 195–201.

150. Borah and Cook, "Marriage and Legitimacy," 962–63; Tjarks, "Demographic, Ethnic and Occupational Structure," 67–70, and "Comparative Demographic Analysis of Texas," 310. By law, Hispanics could later marry and legitimize their children, an option closed to English colonials (McKnight, "Legitimation and Adoption," 135–50).

151. The first quote is Gutiérrez, *When Jesus Came*, who analyzes the padres' behavior in the context of Pueblo sexuality. The second quote is from Concha, "Advice on Governing New Mexico," (ibid., 249), and the third from fray Nicolás de Freitas, Feb. 21, 1671 (ibid., 123). Concha was no friend of the friars, but his view, and that of Gutiérrez, are corroborated by other sources. See, e.g., Vélez de Escalante,

"Letter to the Missionaries of New Mexico," 330, written in 1777.

152. Tjarks, "Comparative Demographic Analysis of Texas," 313. McAlister, "Pensacola," 325, indicates that "out of 379 persons whose parentage could be identified, 101 were illegitimate." See also, Gutiérrez, *When Jesus Came*, 199–202.

153. For comparison to Spain, see Bennassar, *Spanish Character*, 189–91, who reports comparable percentages for Valladolid (a special case), but lower percentages (below 10 percent) elsewhere. For Spanish America, see Lavrín, "Introduction," in Lavrín, ed., *Sexuality and Marriage in Colonial Latin America*, 12, 36–37 n. 29, and Thomas Calvo, "Warmth of the Hearth: Seventeenth-Century Guadalajara Families," ibid., 298.

154. Quoted in Curley, *Church and State in the Spanish Floridas*, 170. See, too, Miranda, "Hispano-Mexican Childrearing Practices," 311, 316.

155. Oscar J. Martínez, *Troublesome Border* (Tucson: University of Arizona Press, 1988), 2. The literature on this subject is vast. For a suggestion of its complexity, see Weber, *Mexican Frontier*, 280; Jerome O. Steffen, *Comparative Frontiers: A Proposal for Studying the American West* (Norman: University of Oklahoma Press, 1980), with his useful distinction between insular and cosmopolitan frontiers; and Alistair Hennessy, *The Frontier in Latin American History* (Albuquerque: University of New Mexico Press), 110–11.

156. Puebla, Nov. 25, 1640, in Hackett, ed. and trans., *Historical Documents*, 3:92.

157. Captain Domingo Ramón, report of 1716, quoted in Stern, "Social Marginality and Acculturation," 138, who provides examples and analysis of Hispanics who willingly took up life among pagan Indians (135–49).

158. See, e.g., Weber, *Taos Trappers*, 23–29, and Kessell, "Diego Romero," 12–16. Some Hispanics who lived in close prox-

imity to Indians in urban settings also developed close relationships, including the speaking of Indian languages (Mason, "Indian-Mexican Cultural Exchange," 131–33).

159. Concha, "Advice on Governing New Mexico, 1794," 250. See, too, Thomas, "Governor Mendinueta's Proposals for the Defense of New Mexico," 27–30, 38; Morfi, *Account of Disorders*, 12, 14; Simmons, "Settlement Patterns," 109–11.

160. Fray José Señán to the viceroy, May 14, 1796, in Señán, *Letters of José Señán*, 5.

161. Monroy, *Thrown among Strangers*, 96, asserts the emergence of a "syncretic culture" in California, but he later notes that "the fusion went only one way" (152), with Spaniards as the donor group.

162. "In contact situations marked by disparity in power and cultural complexity, the . . . major changes are found in the ways of the recipient group" (Foster, *Culture and Conquest*, 7).

163. Zelinsky, *Cultural Geography of the United States*, 13, explaining his "Doctrine of First Effective Settlement"—an idea endorsed by Meinig, *Shaping of America*, 221.

Chapter 12: The Spanish Legacy and the Historical Imagination

A large number sources in this chapter do not appear in the bibliography because they treat the Spanish era in North America tangentially, and I have cited them infrequently. The epigraph is from David Lowenthal, *The Past Is a Foreign Country* (Cambridge: Cambridge University Press, 1985), xvii.

1. For examples of such writing by Englishmen, see Roberts, *First Discovery and Natural History of Florida*, and Forbes, *California*. The English consul in Tepic, Forbes apparently never set foot in California, but his was the first book in English devoted entirely to California.

2. Baily, *Journal of a Tour*, 144. Grande com-

manded Campo de Esperanza on the Spanish side of the river (for other manifestations of distrust or dislike of Spaniards in Baily's writing, see ibid., 138, 150, 155, 167, 173–75, and 178).

3. Quoted in Hanke, "Introduction," to Hanke, ed., *Do the Americas Have a Common History?* 5. Powell, *Tree of Hate*, remains the best general introduction to this subject in English. For more detailed studies of aspects of this question, see Williams, *Spanish Background of American Literature*, 1:1–47; Raymund A. Paredes, "The Origins of Anti-Mexican Sentiment in the United States," *New Scholar*, 6 (1977): 139–65; Frances Fitzgerald, *America Revised: History Schoolbooks in the Twentieth Century* (New York: Vintage Books, 1980), 49; John J. Johnson, *A Hemisphere Apart: The Foundations of United States Policy toward Latin America* (Baltimore: Johns Hopkins University Press, 1990), 44–77.

4. Many residents of Louisiana in general and New Orleans in particular had Indian ancestry, although that was no longer recognizable to most outsiders by the early nineteenth century. See Usner, "American Indians in Colonial New Orleans," 108; Baily, *Journal of a Tour*, 168; Benjamin Henry Boneval Latrobe, *Impressions Respecting New Orleans: Diary & Sketches, 1818–20*, ed. Samuel Wilson, Jr. (New York: Columbia University Press, 1951). Following the Spanish evacuation of 1763, few mestizos seem to have returned to Pensacola or St. Augustine. Of the 700 persons reported in the Pensacola census of 1820, only 3 were identified has having Indian blood (Coker and Inglis, *Spanish Censuses of Pensacola*, 3); see, too, Sherry Johnson, "Spanish St. Augustine Community," 30. Ellen Call Long noted that "Spaniards and French had intermarried with the Indian; the result was an inferior type of man" (*Florida Breezes: or, Florida, New and Old*, intro. by Margaret S. Chap-

man [1st ed., 1883; facsimile, Gainesville: University of Florida Press, 1962], 66). But Long seems to have been reflecting abstractly on the past, for this lifelong resident of Tallahassee does not mention meeting such persons.

5. George A. McCall to "H," Cantonment Clinch, Nov. 8, 1822, in McCall, *Letters*, 14. For similar use of the term *race*, see Rachel Jackson to Elizabeth Kingsley, Pensacola, July 23, 1821, in James Parton, *Life of Andrew Jackson*, 3 vols. (New York: Mason Bros., 1861), 2:605, and Williams, *View of West Florida*, 77–78. For another example of effeminate used as a pejorative term, see ibid., 92, who incorrectly imagined that De Soto's men had survived in the wilderness and become "effeminate."

6. Quoted in Weber, "'Scarce More Than Apes,'" 295. See, too, ibid., 300. For the racist ideology of America in Farnham's day, see Reginald Horsman, *Race and Manifest Destiny: The Origins of American Racial Anglo Saxonism* (Cambridge: Harvard University Press, 1981).

7. Rufus B. Sage, quoted in Weber, ed., *Foreigners in Their Native Land*, 72, 73. Harsh commentary on the impact of *mestizaje* in New Mexico is abundant for this era. See, e.g., McCall, *Letters*, 499, writing from Santa Fe in 1850.

8. For the Southwest, see James H. Lacy, "New Mexico Women in Early American Writings," *NMHR* 34 (Jan. 1959): 41–51; Beverly Trulio, "Anglo-American Attitudes toward New Mexican Women," *JW* 12 (Apr. 1973), 229–39; Weber, "'Scarce More Than Apes,'" 296; and Rebecca McDowell Craver, *The Impact of Intimacy: Mexican-Anglo Intermarriage in New Mexico, 1821–1846* (El Paso: Texas Western Press, 1982). I am unaware of a secondary literature on this subject for the southeast, but see, too, Charles B. Vignoles, *Observations Upon the Floridas*, intro. by John Hebron Moore (1st ed., 1823; facsimile, Gainesville: University Presses of Florida,

1977), 115, writing about Hispanic women in St. Augustine in 1822.

9. Walter Sidney Martin, *Florida during the Territorial Days* (Athens: University of Georgia Press, 1944), 97, 104–5, 109. For the exodus of many Hispanics, see G. D. Worthington, secretary and acting governor of East Florida, to John Quincy Adams, St. Augustine, Dec. 11, 1821, and Jan. 8, 1822, in Clarence Edwin Carter, comp. and ed., *The Territorial Papers of the United States*, vol. 22, *The Territory of Florida, 1821–1824* (Washington, D.C.: United States Government Printing Office, 1956), 302, 329.

10. The quotes are from Fairbanks, *History of Florida*, 269, 374.

11. William P. DuVal to President James Monroe, Pensacola, Sept. 10, 1822, in Carter, comp. and ed., *Territorial Papers of the United States*, 22:532. See, too, DuVal to Monroe, Aug. 17, 1822, ibid., 508, and Andrew Jackson to John Q. Adams, Pensacola, Aug. 14, 1821, ibid., 153–54. Similarly, W. G. D. Worthington to John Q. Adams, St. Augustine, Jan. 8, 1822, characterized the local Hispanics as "a good, quiet, industrious people," ibid., 330.

12. See, e.g., Vignoles, *Observations upon the Floridas;* Anonymous [William Hayne Simmons], *Notices of East Florida*, intro. by George E. Buker (1st ed., 1822; facsimile, Gainesville: University of Florida Press, 1973), and Williams, *View of West Florida*, neither of which describe the territory's contemporary Hispanic residents.

13. R. K. Sewall, *Sketches of St. Augustine*, intro. by Thomas Graham (1st ed., 1848; facsimile, Gainesville: University Presses of Florida, 1976), 40, xvii–xxix. For more generous assessments, see Williams, *Territory of Florida*, 191; and Forbes, *Sketches, Historical*, 91, 104; and William Cullen Bryant, who described Minorcans in 1843 as "a mild, harmless race, of civil manners and abstemious habits" (quoted in Reynolds, *Standard Guide*, 18).

14. "Barbarities," is from Forbes, *Sketches, Historical*, 11; "demonaic malignity" is from Vignoles, *Observations upon the Floridas*, 18; "jealous . . . system" is from [Simmons], *Notices of East Florida*, 22; "perfidious Spaniards" is from Monette, *History . . . of the Valley of the Mississippi*, 1:97. See, too, Flint, *Condensed Geography and History*, 1:301–2, 313.

15. Stoddard, *Sketches, Historical and Descriptive, of Louisiana* (Philadelphia: Mathew Carey, 1812), 291.

16. Vignoles, *Observations upon the Floridas*, 34.

17. Williams, *View of West Florida*, 94.

18. Williams, *Territory of Florida*, 191 (who settled in Pensacola in 1820 and remained in Florida until his death, in 1856). See, too, Vignoles, *Observations upon the Floridas*, 18–19, and a Frenchman, C. C. Robin, who visited Pensacola in 1803 and made a similar observation: *Voyage to Louisiana, 1803–1805*, trans. Stuart O. Landry, Jr. (1st ed., Paris, 1907; New Orleans: Pelican Publishing Company, 1966), 1, 5.

19. For Indian policy, see Forbes, *Sketches, Historical*, 243–45, and Vignoles, *Observations upon the Floridas*, 130. For the system of justice, see Stoddard, *Sketches, Historical and Descriptive, of Louisiana*, 280–85. For Louisiana as prosperous and well-governed, see Monette, *History . . . of the Valley of the Mississippi*, 1:454–55, 65–69.

20. Gayarré, *History of Louisiana*, 627, notes: "I must call the attention of the reader to a singular anomaly . . . with all the foul abuses and tyrannical practices with which has been so long the general custom to reproach the government of Spain every where, her administration in Louisiana was as popular as any that ever existed in any part of the world . . . the golden age." For the "mildness" of Spanish rule, see too, Lowry and McCardle, *History of Mississippi*, 131; and Hamilton, *Colonial Mobile*, 262.

21. One historian writing in the 1850s, for example, commented on the characteristic

"indolence, drunkenness, and misery of the people, the knavery of the Government officers, and the neglect and recklessness every where apparent" (Greenhow, *History of Florida, Louisiana, Texas, and California*, 515–16; see, too, 551–52).

22. There is a large literature on Anglo-American stereotypes of the californios prior to the Mexican-American War. See, especially, Leonard Pitt, *The Decline of the Californios: A Social History of the Spanish-Speaking Californians, 1846–1890* (Berkeley: University of California Press, 1966), 14–18, and David J. Langum, "Californios and the Image of Indolence," *WHQ* 9 (Apr. 1978): 181–96. Langum argues that the negative image of californios was not the result of American racism, Protestantism, and expansionism. For a response to Langum, see Weber, "Here Rests Juan Espinosa," 61–68.

23. Quoted in Weber, ed., *Foreigners in Their Native Land*, 66–67.

24. For introductions to this subject, see Cecil Robinson, *With the Ears of Strangers: The Mexican in American Literature* (Tucson: University of Arizona Press, 1963), 1–131; Weber, " 'Scarce More Than Apes,' " 293–307; Horsman, *Race and Manifest Destiny*, 208–48.

25. Stephen F. Austin to L. F. Linn, New York, May 4, 1835, quoted in Weber, "Refighting the Alamo," 139, in Weber, *Myth and the History of the Hispanic Southwest*. See, too, Arnoldo de León, *They Called Them Greasers: Anglo Attitudes toward Mexicans in Texas, 1821–1890* (Austin: University of Texas Press, 1983), 1–13.

26. Henry Stuart Foote, *Texas and the Texans: or, Advance of Anglo-Americans to the South-West*, 2 vols. (Philadelphia: Thomas, Cowperthwait & Co., 1841), quoted in John H. Jenkins, *Basic Texas Books: An Annotated Bibliography . . .* (Austin: Jenkins Publishing Co., 1983), 164.

27. Foote, *Texas and the Texans*, 2:7.

28. Yoakum, *History of Texas*, 1:208. In generalizing about Spanish America, Yoakum drew heavily from William Robertson's *History of America* (1777). The earliest English-language histories of Texas skipped lightly over the events of the Spanish period as unworthy of investigation, but they villified Spaniards in general. See William Kennedy, *Texas: The Rise, Progress, and Prospects of the Republic of Texas*, 2 vols. (London: R. Hastings, 1841), and Foote, *Texas and the Texans*. See, too, Stephen Stagner, "Epics, Sciences, and the Lost Frontier: Texas Historical Writing, 1836–1936," *WHQ* 12 (Apr. 1981): 166–71.

29. Foote, *Texas and the Texans* 1:14 and 2:27. Italics in the original.

30. Stagner, "Epics, Sciences, and the Lost Frontier," 168; David Montejano, *Anglos and Mexicans in the Making of Texas, 1836–1986* (Austin: University of Texas Press, 1987), 223–25, 305; Weber, "Refighting the Alamo," 139, 149–51. For examples of oversimplification and its attendant distortions in twentieth-century Texas historiography, see George P. Garrison, *Texas: A Contest of Civilizations* (Boston: Houghton, Mifflin & Co., 1903), and the passages from Walter Prescott Webb's *Great Plains* (1931), and *Texas Rangers* (1935), in Weber, ed., *Foreigners in Their Native Land*, 75–78; and T. R. Fehrenbach, *Lone Star: A History of Texas and the Texans* (New York: Macmillan, 1968), 55.

31. Weber, ed., *Foreigners in Their Native Land*, 97–99, 117–31.

32. Quoted in Iris W. Engstrand's Introduction to Tyler, *Mythical Pueblo Rights Doctrine*, 4.

33. George A. Sala, *American Revisited . . .*, 2 vols. (London: Vizetelly & Co., 1882), 2:205, quoted in Earl Pomeroy, *In Search of the Golden West: The Tourist in Western America* (New York: Alfred A. Knopf, 1957), 35. Italics in original.

34. Whitman to Messrs. Griffin et al., Camden, New Jersey, July 20, 1883, in *The*

Complete Poetry and Prose of Walt Whitman,
2 vols. (New York: Pellegrini &
Cudahy, 1948), 2:402–3 (writing on
what he believed to be the occasion of
the 333d anniversary of the founding of
Santa Fe).

35. *California Pastoral,* 179, quoted in Langum,
"From Condemnation to Praise," 284.
Like many writers of his day, Bancroft
conflated the Spanish and Mexican eras of
California into a single "golden age."
Chapman, *Founding of Spanish California,*
418, 434–35, portrayed the closing decades
of the Spanish era in similar terms.

36. Quoted in Franklin Walker, *A Literary
History of Southern California* (Berkeley:
University of California Press, 1950), 126.
Walker is one of many scholars who has
examined the nostalgic writing of this era
in California, and the shift in perspective
that it represents. See, too, Langum,
"From Condemnation to Praise," 284–86;
Pitt, *Decline of the Californios,* 286–90;
Kevin Starr, *Americans and the California
Dream, 1850–1915* (New York: Oxford
University Press, 1973), 391–401. Starr
covers some of the same ground in *Inventing
the Dream: California through the Progressive
Era* (New York: Oxford University
Press, 1985). For Bancroft's racism and
contempt, see *California Pastoral,* 76–79,
180, 292.

37. Guadalupe Vallejo, "Ranch and Mission
Days in Alta California," *Century Magazine*
41 (Dec. 1890): 183, quoted in Weber,
ed., *Foreigners in Their Native Land,* 46.
Guadalupe Vallejo credited his uncle, Mariano
Guadalupe Vallejo, as the source of his
information.

38. Walker, *Literary History,* 121; Starr, *Americans
and the California Dream,* 395; Langum,
"From Condemnation to Praise,"
288–89; Nobel Prentis, quoted in Noggle,
"Anglo Observers of the Southwest Borderlands,"
129. See, too, Samuel P. Hays,
The Response to Industrialism, 1885–1914
(Chicago: University of Chicago Press,
1957); Leo Marx, *The Machine in the*

*Garden: Technology and the Pastoral Ideal in
America* (New York: Oxford University
Press, 1964); T. Jackson Lears, *No Place of
Grace: Antimodernism and the Transformation
of American Culture* (New York: Pantheon
Books, 1981).

39. "Ranch and Mission Days in Alta California,"
Century Magazine 41 (Dec. 1980),
quoted in Weber, ed., *Foreigners in Their
Native Land,* 47–48.

40. Ibid., 46.

41. Starr, *Americans and the California Dream,*
390. See, too, ibid., chap. 12: "An American
Mediterranean."

42. Weber, ed., *Foreigners in Their Native Land,*
148; Pitt, *Decline of the Californios,* 281,
284, 290.

43. James J. Rawls, *Indians of California: The
Changing Image* (Norman: University of
Oklahoma Press, 1984), explores this
theme in rich detail.

44. Robert F. Berkhofer, Jr., *The White Man's
Indian: Images of the American Indian from
Columbus to the Present* (New York: Alfred
A. Knopf, 1978), 88; Rawls, *Indians of
California,* 205.

45. Quoted in William Wroth, "Hispanic
Southwestern Craft Traditions in the 20th
Century," in Wroth, ed., *Hispanic Crafts of
the Southwest* (Colorado Springs: Taylor
Museum of the Colorado Springs Fine
Arts Center, 1977), 3.

46. The quote is from Trent Elwood Sanford,
*The Architecture of the Southwest: Indian,
Spanish, American* (New York: W. W.
Norton & Co., 1950), 247. The best discussion
of this phenomenon in California
is in Harold Kirker, *California's Architectural
Frontier: Style and Tradition in the
Nineteenth Century* (1st ed., 1960; rev. ed.,
Santa Barbara: Peregrine Smith, 1973), 1–
22.

47. Kirker, *California's Architectural Frontier,*
120–24; David Gebhard, "Architectural
Imagery, the Mission, and California,"
Harvard Architecture Review 1 (1980): 137–
45; Karen J. Weitze, *California's Mission Re-*

vival (Los Angeles: Hennessey & Ingalls, 1984), 134.

48. For Lummis's role as a publicist, see Edwin R. Bingham, *Charles Fletcher Lummis: Editor of the Southwest* (San Marino: Huntington Library, 1955), and the appreciative biography by two of his children, Turbesé Lummis Fiske and Keith Lummis, *Charles Fletcher Lummis: The Man and His West* (Norman: University of Oklahoma Press, 1975). For the fictive nature of much of the restoration work, see David Hurst Thomas, "Harvesting Ramona's Garden," 119–57.

49. John O. Pohlmann, "The Missions Romanticized," in John and LaRee Caughey, eds., *Los Angeles: Biography of a City* (Berkeley: University of California Press, 1976), 242. This article represents a distillation of Pohlmann's "California's Mission Myth" (Ph.D. diss., University of California, Los Angeles, 1974). A more accessible account of the marking of the Camino Real and the restoration of the missions is in the popularized account of George Wharton James, *In and Out of the Old Missions of California* (1st ed., 1905; rev. ed., Boston: Little Brown, & Co., 1927), 379–92. James was a participant in these events. John A. Berger, *The Franciscan Missions of California* (New York: G. P. Putnam's, 1941), has replaced James as the best popular account but provides a less satisfactory account of the restoration of the missions. The most recent popular introduction to this subject, with fine illustrations, is Dorothy Krell et al., *The California Missions: A Pictorial History* (1st ed., 1964; rev. ed., Menlo Park, Calif.: Lane Publishing Co., 1979). In addition to these more general works, many monographs and articles chronicle the story of the reconstruction of individual missions. See, e.g., C. Douglas Kroll, "The Decline and Restoration of Mission San Diego de Alcalá, 1821–1931," *SCQ* 68 (Winter 1986): 315–28.

50. A letter to the Santa Barbara *Morning Press*, quoted in Walker, *Literary History*, 132, who provides no date. See, too, Pitt, *Decline of the Californios*, 290.

51. *The Road of a Thousand Wonders* (San Francisco: Passenger Department, Southern Pacific Co., 1907), 26.

52. *Wayside Notes on the Sunset Route* (San Francisco: Passenger Department, Southern Pacific Co., 1908), 3.

53. Carey McWilliams, *Southern California Country* (New York: Duell, Sloan & Pearce, 1946), 79, 81.

54. Ibid., 78.

55. Agnes Laut, 1911, quoted in Pomeroy, *In Search of the Golden West*, 160. For an example of the commercial genre, see Fred Harvey, *The Great Southwest along the Santa Fe Trail*, 6th ed. (Kansas City: F. Harvey, 1921).

56. The quotes are respectively from W. W. H. Davis (1856) and Lt. W. H. Emory (1846), in Espinosa, *Saints in the Valleys*, 31, 30.

57. Espinosa, *Saints in the Valleys*, 35; Wroth, "New Mexican Santero," 273–84.

58. George McCall to "M," San Antonio, Jan. 10, 1850, in McCall, *Letters*, 488. Adobe in New Mexico received its share of disparaging remarks, too, as in Josiah Gregg, *Commerce of the Prairies*, ed. Max L. Moorhead (1st ed., 1844; Norman: University of Oklahoma Press, 1954), 144.

59. For a short introduction to this subject, see Bunting, *Early Architecture in New Mexico*, 101–2, and the examples in Kessell, *Missions of New Mexico*.

60. These were three of the five theme days for 1925. Marta Weigle and Peter White, *The Lore of New Mexico* (Albuquerque: University of New Mexico Press, 1988), 415–17, 431; Thomas E. Chávez, "Santa Fe's Own: A History of Fiesta," *El Palacio* 91 (Spring 1985): 6–17.

61. In contrast to the Southwest, there is little secondary literature on this subject. A few suggestive remarks are in George E.

Buker, "The Americanization of St. Augustine," in Jean Parker Waterbury, ed., *The Oldest City: St. Augustine, Saga of Survival* (St. Augustine: St. Augustine Historical Society, 1983), 174.

62. Although their prose became less choleric, some writers kept the Black Legend alive and well. Sidney Lanier, *Florida: Its Scenery, Climate, and History . . ., A Complete Handbook and Guide*, intro. by Jerrell H. Shofner (1st ed., 1875; facsimile, Gainesville: University of Florida Press, 1973), mixed romanticism (50, for example), with a bit of rhetoric concerning the Black Legend (64, 177, 193, 198). See, too, Richard L. Campbell, *Historical Sketches of Colonial Florida*, intro. by Pat Dodson (1st ed., 1892; facsimile, Gainesville: University Presses of Florida, 1975), 25, 33, 56, 152, and Spears, *History of the Mississippi Valley*, 157–61.

63. Fairbanks, *History of Florida*, 58, 73. Fairbanks considered his work "the first connected history of the State" (ibid., viii). While he romanticized the early explorers, he saw Spanish rule as regressive and Spaniards as "greatly deficient in industry and enterprise" (ibid., 241; 170, 245). Lowry and McCardle, *History of Mississippi . . .*, 8–15, contains another example of a glowing account of the De Soto expedition.

64. Fairbanks, *History of Florida*, 70.

65. Ibid., 71–72.

66. Anonymous, *Guide to Florida by "Rambler,"* intro. by Rembert W. Patrick (1st ed., 1875; facsimile, Gainesville: University of Florida Press, 1964), 35–36, 30, 37.

67. See, e.g., Anonymous, *Winter Cities in a Summer Land* (Cincinnati: Cincinnati, New Orleans, and Texas-Pacific Railroad, 1883), 26, and Harriet Beecher Stowe, *Palmetto-Leaves* (Boston: James R. Osgood and Co., 1873), 206, who lived near St. Augustine and described it as resembling "some little, old, dead-and-alive Spanish town, with . . . the indolent, dreamy stillness that characterizes life in Old Spain."

68. Reynolds, *Standard Guide to St. Augustine*, 26.

69. Thomas Graham, "The Flagler Era, 1865–1913," in Waterbury, ed., *Oldest City*, 192. Patricia C. Griffin, "The Impact of Tourism and Development on Public Ritual and Festival: St. Augustine, Florida, 1821–1987" (Ph.D. diss., University of Florida, Gainesville, 1988), 115–16, 120–29, decribes the event as celebrated sporadically until the 1920s, when it became an annual event (except for the depression years). Fairbanks, *History of Florida*, 2, described Ponce's discovery as "one of the romantic episodes of history." Anonymous, *Guide to Florida by "Rambler,"* 7, termed it "a most romantic incident of History."

70. Reynolds, *Standard Guide to St. Augustine*, 14.

71. Meinig, *Shaping of America*, 1:283, 221, who employs Zelinsky's useful "Doctrine of First Effective Settlement" (Zelinsky, *Cultural Geography of the United States*, 13–14). The descendants of Spanish Louisianans came to be categorized as Creoles, along with Frenchmen, and Creole culture was sentimentalized much as was the culture of the californios. See Tregle, "Early New Orleans Society," 26–27; Hamilton, *Colonial Mobile*, 812. For the survival of Hispanic culture in Louisiana, see Din, *Canary Islanders of Louisiana*.

72. For the rise of the mission myth in Georgia, see Marmaduke Floyd, "Certain Tabby Ruins on the Georgia Coast," in E. Merton Coulter, ed., *Georgia's Disputed Ruins* (Chapel Hill: University of North Carolina Press, 1937), 161–89. See, too, Thomas, "Saints and Soldiers," 78–81.

73. Williams, *Spanish Background of American Literature*, 1:311.

74. Elizabeth Barrett Gould, *From Fort to Port: An Architectural History of Mobile, Alabama, 1711–1918* (Tuscaloosa: University of Alabama Press, 1988), 21–103.

75. In St. Augustine, English influence con-

tinued until the end of the Spanish era, leaving a domestic architecture "that was neither Spanish nor English." Manucy, "Changing Traditions in St. Augustine Architecture," 132. In Pensacola, a "creole" style emerged, influenced apparently by the large French population. Coker and Inglis, *Spanish Censuses of Pensacola*, 8–9. See, too, Wilson, "Architecture in Eighteenth-Century West Florida," 102.

76. Fairbanks, *History and Antiquities of St. Augustine*, 101, 115. Reynolds, *Standard Guide to St. Augustine*, 9–12, 24. Robert N. Dow, "Yesterday and the Day Before, 1913 to the Present," in Waterbury, ed., *Oldest City*, 31–33.

77. Long, *Florida Breezes*, 36, reflecting on her youthful travels to Fort San Marcos near Tallahassee.

78. Lanier, *Florida*, 50.

79. Graham, "Flagler Era," 193–94. Pensacola did not undergo a Spanish revival.

80. Donald W. Curl, *Mizner's Florida: American Resort Architecture* (New York and Cambridge: Architectural History Foundation and MIT Press, 1984), 59–60.

81. Kirker, *California's Architectural Frontier*, 126–27; Sanford, *Architecture of the Southwest*, 248–53; John Buchard and Albert Bush-Brown, *The Architecture of America: A Social and Cultural History* (Boston: Little, Brown & Co., 1961), 366–67. The simplicity of design of most structures from the Spanish era gave architects little to draw on, although there were a few exceptional facades, as at San Xavier del Bac near Tucson, and many fine examples of imported architectural sculpture. See Grizzard, *Spanish Colonial Art and Architecture*.

82. For a general discussion of the Spanish architecture of this era, see Williams, *Spanish Background of American Literature*, 1:309–10. Newcomb, *Spanish-Colonial Architecture*, 36–39, and accompanying illustrations.

83. The influence of historians on these architectural revivals, and vice versa, merits fur-

ther exploration. Buchard and Bush-Brown, *Architecture of America*, 366, suggestively note in reference to the fabulous Spanish-Italian Renaissance-baroque estate of Vizcaya at Miami that "unfortunately taste of this sort was abetted by historians like Rexford Newcomb whose book *The Spanish House for America*, published at Philadelphia in 1927, offered illustrations of many houses of Spanish flavor to be seen in California, Florida, New Mexico and Arizona." Newcomb, however, was an architect who wrote history, rather than a historian who wrote about architecture.

84. Lawrence Cheek, "Taco Deco: Spanish Revival Revived," *Journal of the Southwest* 32 (Winter 1990): 491–98.

85. Robert McLean and Grace P. Williams, *Old Spain in New America* (New York: Association Press, 1916), 18, 16.

86. Martin, *Florida during the Territorial Days*, 31.

87. In 1929, the first year in which the U.S. census recorded per capita income on the state level, California's per capita income, at $995, was substantially higher than that of any other state in the sunbelt (Arizona took second place with $593 and Florida was third with $525). Because of its size as well as its wealth, California's total income represented 6.42 percent of total U.S. income; in contrast, Arizona and Florida represented .30 percent and .88 percent respectively. The economy of Texas, the only state along the old Spanish rim with a population larger than California's in 1929, represented 3.22 percent of the national income (*Historical Statistics of the United States: Colonial Times to the Present*, 2 vols. [Washington, D.C.: U.S. Department of Commerce, Bureau of the Census, 1975], 1:24–35 [Series A195–209, 243–45 [Series F297–348]).

88. See, in particular, Bolton's "Need for the Publication," 23–31, a collection of his most important essays on the borderlands. For Bolton's life, work, and complete lists

of his M.A. and Ph.D. students, see Bannon, *Herbert Eugene Bolton*. See, too, Weber, ed., *Idea of the Spanish Borderlands*. This idea of adding a Spanish dimension had been presented earlier, as in in 1883 by Walt Whitman (see the epigraph to the Introduction to this book), in 1893 by Lummis, *Spanish Pioneers*, 11, and in 1909 by William R. Shepard, "The Contribution of the Romance Nations to the History of the Americas," in Howard R. Cline, ed., *Latin American History: Essays on Its Study and Teaching, 1898–1965*, 2 vols. (Austin: University of Texas, 1967), 1:67.

89. Hanke, "Introduction," to Hanke, ed., *Do the Americas Have a Common History?* 22–23, 47.

90. Bolton, "Defensive Spanish Expansion," 32–33.

91. See Floyd, "Certain Tabby Ruins on the Georgia Coast," 174–76.

92. See, e.g., Shepherd, "Spanish Heritage in America," 75–85; Whitaker, "Spanish Contribution to American Agriculture," 1–14; Bernstein, "Spanish Influence in the United States," 43–65; Young, "Spanish Tradition in Gold and Silver Mining," 299–314; Worcester, "Significance of the Spanish Borderlands," 279–93.

93. Bolton, "Mission as a Frontier Institution," 211 (an essay first published in 1917).

94. Thomas, ed. and trans., *Teodoro de Croix*, 65–66.

95. Priestley, *Tristán de Luna*, 196.

96. Bolton and Marshall, *Colonization of North America*, v, argued that a less Anglocentric view of early America "is the inevitable result of the growing importance of our American neighbors" and Bolton later maintained that the idea of the Spanish borderlands was part of the larger idea of a hemispheric history. Hanke, "Introduction," to Hanke, ed., *Do the Americas Have a Common History?* 15–17. Bolton's most immediate concern was to improve the image of the United States in Latin America,

but Spanish intellectuals seem to have warmed to Bolton's pro-Hispanic writing more than Latin Americans, many of whom viewed Spain with ambivalence.

97. Altamira, "A manera de prólogo," in Carlos F. Lummis, *Los exploradores españoles del siglo xvi. Vindicación de la acción colonizadora española en América* (1st ed., Madrid, 1916; Mexico: Editorial Porrúa, 1981), ix.

98. Miguel Romera-Novarro, *El hispanismo en Norte-América* (Madrid: Renacimiento, 1917), 325. Romera-Novarro specifically credited H. H. Bancroft with this break, but he also praised a number of historians, including Bolton (see, too, ibid., 280). Romera-Novarro's work was called to my attention by Williams, *Spanish Background of American Literature*, 1:369.

99. Romera-Navarro, *El hispanismo*, 7.

100. Fernández-Shaw, *Presencia española*. See, too, Fernández-Florez, *Spanish Heritage*, and Cubeñas Peluzzo, *Presencia española e hispánica*. Some Spanish scholars have also sought to associate particular regions of Spain with Spanish achievements in North America. See, e.g., Piña, *Catalanes y Mallorquines*.

101. González Ruis, *De la Florida a San Francisco*, 257. See, too, ibid., 19, 20, 342. Although published in Argentina, this is the work of a Spaniard.

102. Earl Pomeroy, "Toward a Reorientation of Western History: Continuity and Environment," *JAH* 41 (Mar. 1955): 590.

103. Moses Rischin, "Beyond the Great Divide: Immigration and the Last Frontier," *JAH* 55 (June 1968): 51, 50. Rischin elaborated on this argument in "Continuities and Discontinuities in Spanish-Speaking California," in Charles Wollenberg, ed., *Ethnic Conflict in California History* (Los Angeles: Tinnon-Brown, 1970), 45–60, accurately quoting John Higham's dismissive evaluation of Bolton: "He gave a specious appearance of significance to a program of fragmentary

research." Higham, however, as I read him, directed that barb at Bolton's famous thesis that the Americas had a common history, not at Bolton's program of borderlands studies. See John Higham, *History: The Development of Historical Studies in the United States* (Englewood Cliffs, N.J.: Prentice Hall, 1965), 41.

104. Caughey, "Herbert Eugene Bolton," 66; Axtell, "Europeans," 621–32.

105. Adams, ed. and trans., *Bishop Tamarón's Visitation*, 22–23 (Adams had not been one of Bolton's students). For the ongoing criticism of the Bolton school by Latin Americanists, see, e.g., Cuello, "Beyond the 'Borderlands,'" 1–34; Scardaville, "Approaches," 188; Benjamin Keen, "Main Currents in United States Writings on Colonial Spanish America, 1884–1984," *HAHR* 65 (Nov. 1985): 662.

106. McWilliams, *North from Mexico: The Spanish-Speaking People of the United States* (1st ed., 1948; reprint ed., New York: Greenwood Press, 1968), 44.

107. Chávez, *Lost Land*, 84–99; Griffin, "Impact of Tourism and Development on Public Ritual and Festival," 131–37.

108. Bolton, "Mission as a Frontier Institution," 201, 211.

109. For a brief introduction to this question and some of its literature, see David G. Gutiérrez, "The Third Generation: Reflections on Recent Chicano Historiography," *Mexican Studies/Estudios Mexicanos* 5 (Summer 1989): 282–84.

110. Webb, *The Great Plains*, 1931, quoted in Weber, ed., *Foreigners in Their Native Land*, 76–77.

111. Chávez, *Lost Land*, 99–101, discusses the work of folklorist Arthur Campa in folklore and George Sánchez in sociology, in particular. Pitt, *Decline of the Californios*, published in 1968, was one of the first historians to take McWilliams seriously (see 288–96).

112. Simon Schama, *The Embarrassment of Riches: An Interpretation of Dutch Culture in the Golden Age* (1st ed., 1987; Berkeley: University of California Press, 1988); Edmund Morgan, *Inventing the People: The Rise of Popular Sovereignty in England and America* (New York: Norton, 1988). With the exception of a few works glorifying the achievements of individual frontiersmen, such as Villagrá's epic poem, Hodge, ed., *History of New Mexico by Gaspar Pérez de Villagrá*, or the effusive praise for Diego de Vargas in Leonard, ed. and trans., *Mercurio Volante*, most of the writing by frontiersmen or about the frontier concern themselves with the region's acute problems.

113. Servín, "California's Hispanic Heritage," 121. See, too, Servín, "Beginnings of California's Anti-Mexican Prejudice," 2–17, and García, "Chicano Perspective," 14–21, an explicit critique of the Bolton school, broader than its title suggests.

114. For a cogent explanation of the social and political context of this formulation, see Chávez, *Lost Land*, 129–31, 141–42, 147–48, and the illuminating essays in Anaya and Lomelí, eds., *Aztlán*. For a highly critical view, see Vigil, "New Borderlands History," 189–208.

115. Gutiérrez, "Aztlán, Montezuma, and New Mexico," 172–90, analyzing William G. Ritch's *Aztlán* (1885).

116. Alejandro Portes and Cynthia Truelove, "El sentido de la diversidad: Recientes investigaciones sobre las minorías hispanas en los Estados Unidos," in Rodolfo J. Cortina and Alberto Moncada, eds., *Hispanos en los Estados Unidos* (Madrid: Ediciones Cultura Hispánica, 1988), 33. Several other essays in this collection emphasize the diversity of Hispanos. Puerto Ricans and Cubans did not, of course, neglect their Spanish heritage in North America. José Agustín Balseiro, a Puerto Rican writer, has explained Spain's explorers as "men of epic heroism and fortitude" and the Spanish heritage in the United States as worthy of "our

grateful reverence," in his Introduction to Balseiro, ed., *The Spanish Presence in Florida* ([Miami]: A. Seemann Publishing Co., 1976), 17–18. For attempts at one-volume histories, see Harold J. Alford, *The Proud Peoples: The Heritage and Culture of Spanish-Speaking Peoples in the United States* (New York: David McKay, 1972), and L. H. Gann and Peter J. Duignan, *The Hispanics in the United States: A History* (Boulder: Westview Press, 1986).

117. Some did so explicity; see, e.g., Arthur Corwin, "Mexican-American History: An Assessment," *Pacific Historical Review* 42 (Aug. 1973): 271. Others did so implicitly. For example, Rodolfo Acuña, *Occupied America: The Chicano's Struggle toward Liberation* (San Francisco: Canfield Press, 1972), begins with the American conquest of the Southwest and neglects to explain how or why mexicanos were there in the first place. The earlier role of Hispanics as colonizers apparently did not fit neatly into his model of Chicanos as colonized. Matt S. Meier and Feliciano Rivera, *The Chicanos: A History of Mexican Americans* (New York: Hill & Wang, 1972), on the other hand, integrated the colonial period into the larger story and that model seems likely to prevail. Carlos E. Cortés adopted it in his essay on "Mexicans" in Stephan Thernstrom, ed., *Harvard Encyclopedia of American Ethnic Groups* (Cambridge: Harvard University Press, 1980), 697–719. For a fine analysis of the question of continuity, see Limerick, *Legacy of Conquest*, 253–58.

118. For a guide to some of the recent literature see Weber, "John Francis Bannon," 344–47, 356–58, and Poyo and Hinojosa, "Spanish Texas," 393–416. Recent examples include Monroy, *Thrown among Strangers*, and Poyo and Hinojosa, eds., *Tejano Origins*.

119. See, e.g., Marcelino C. Peñuelas, *Cultura hispánica en Estados Unidos. Los Chicanos*, 2d ed.(Madrid: Ediciones Cultura His-

pánica del Centro Iberoamericano de Cooperación, 1978), whose emphasis shifted considerably from the first edition published in 1964). As with Chicano scholars, Spaniards and Mexicans have evinced growing interest in Hispanics as an ethnic minority in America and have regarded the Spanish era as prologue. See, e.g., Alfredo Jiménez Núñez, *Los hispanos de Nuevo México. Contribución a una antropología de la cultura Hispana en USA* (Sevilla: Universidad de Sevilla, 1974), and Angela Moyano Pahissa, ed., *Protección consular a mexicanos en los Estados Unidos, 1849–1900* (Mexico: Secretaría de Relaciones Exteriores, 1989).

120. Chávez, *Lost Land*, sees this theme as well articulated in the late nineteenth and early twentieth century, but subordinated until it "remerged from the collective unconscious of the region's Mexicans" in the late 1960s (129). In exploring what he terms the "myth of the lost land," Chávez has also, of course, helped create it.

121. Sylvia Rodríguez, "Land, Water, and Ethnic Identity in Taos," in Charles L. Briggs and John R. Van Ness, eds., *Land, Water, and Culture: New Perspectives on Hispanic Land Grants* (Albuquerque: University of New Mexico Press, 1987), 322–23, 381–82, 387.

122. The quote is from Bolton, *Texas in the Middle Eighteenth Century*, 19. For the rise of ethnohistory in the 1950s, see Donald L. Parman and Catherine Price, " 'A Work in Progress': The Emergence of Indian History as a Professional Field," *WHQ* 20 (May 1989): 186–87. In an unpublished manuscript, Hurtado, "Herbert E. Bolton," analyzes Bolton's ethnocentrism within the context of his day. For a more appreciative view of the Boltonians' relationship to the emergence of ethnohistory, see John, "Crusading," 191–95.

123. Weber, "John Francis Bannon," 336–37.

124. For critiques of borderlands scholarship from ethnohistorical viewpoints, see Rollings, "In Search of Multisided Frontiers," 79–96; Sheridan, "How to Tell the Story," 168–89; the generous and wide-ranging view of Swagerty, "Spanish-Indian Relations," 36–78; Thomas, "Columbian Consequences," 3–7. For the missions from Indian viewpoints, see my chapter 4, and Weber, "Blood of Martyrs; Blood of Indians," 429–48, and Sandos, "Junípero Serra's Canonization," 253–69.

125. Perhaps the most prominent and eloquent recent example is Udall, *To the Inland Empire*, who in his passionate argument against the distortions of the Black Legend and in his attempt to cast Spaniards in a more favorable light than Englishmen exaggerates the Spaniards' humanitarianism and tolerance. But many other examples could be drawn from books and articles on discrete topics. See, e.g., Alfaro, "Spirit of the First Franciscan Missionaries," 49–66.

126. Jacobs in "Communications," *AHR* 43 (Feb. 1988): 283. In advancing this view, Jacobs joins distinguished company. See, e.g., Benjamin Keen, "The Black Legend Revisited: Assumptions and Realities," *HAHR* 49 (Nov. 1969). On the other side, see Lewis Hanke, "A Modest Proposal for a Moratorium on Grand Generalizations: Some Thoughts on the Black Legend," *HAHR* 51 (Feb. 1971): 112–27, and Powell, *Tree of Hate*, 117–44.

127. For environmental perspectives, see my chapter 11. For gender, see, e.g.: Hernández, "Nueva Mexicanas," 41–69; Rock, "'Pido y Suplico,'" 145–59; Gutiérrez, *When Jesus Came*; Castañeda, "Gender, Race, and Culture," 8–30.

128. See my Introduction.

129. See, e.g., Limerick, *Legacy of Conquest*, 222–58.

130. Peter Novick, *That Noble Dream: The "Objectivity Question" and the American Historical Profession* (Cambridge: Cambridge University Press, 1988), 582.

131. This epistemological phenomenon affects not only the social sciences and the humanities, but the so-called "hard" sciences as well, where knowledge is also socially constructed. See, e.g., Donna Haraway, *Primate Visions: Gender, Race, and Nature in the World of Modern Science* (New York: Routledge, 1989), and Thomas Laqueur, *Making Sex: Body and Gender from the Greeks to Freud* (Cambridge: Harvard University Press, 1990).

Select Bibliography

Although lengthy, this bibliography is not comprehensive. The literature is vast, and some older works are not included because they have been superseded. Unless I cite them frequently, titles that I consulted for background, or to provide comparative or theoretical dimensions, appear only in the notes. Since they treat Spain in North America tangentially, I have chosen not to add them to the bibliography.

By reading the documents from the era itself—the primary sources—I have tried to capture the spirit of time and place. A remarkable number of first-hand accounts have appeared in print. Here, too, the preponderance of titles are in English. Some Spanish manuscripts have never been published in Spanish, but even in cases where Spanish-language and English-language editions of primary sources exist, I have usually consulted the latter. The English-language editions are more accessible to North American readers and usually contain superior annotations, bibliographies, and indexes. Then, too, a facsimile or transcript of the original document often accompanies the translation in an English-language edition. Translation is, of course, an imperfect art and scholars whose interpretation of an event hangs on the precise meaning of a word or phrase must consult the original Spanish.

I have relied heavily on the interpretive works of fellow historians—the secondary sources. That most of the interpretive works in this bibliography are in English reflects the engagement of American scholars in their own national history. Spanish and Mexican historians have made important additions to this literature, but neither country supports professional historians in large numbers. In Spain, moroever, historians have responsibility for a longer national and imperial history than do their counterparts from the United States.

Primary Sources

Adams, Eleanor B., ed. and trans. *Bishop Tamarón's Visitation of New Mexico, 1760.* Albuquerque: Historical Society of New Mexico, 1954.

Adams, Eleanor B., and Angélico Chávez, eds. and trans. *Missions of New Mexico, 1776: A Description by Fray Atanasio Domínguez.* Albuquerque: University of New Mexico Press, 1956.

Alessio Robles, Vito. *Coahuila y Texas en la época colonial*. 1938. Mexico: Editorial Porrúa, 1978.

_____, ed. *Nicolás de Lafora, relación de viaje . . . .* Mexico: Editorial Robledo, 1939.

Andrews, Evangeline Walker, and Charles McLean Andrews [eds.] *Jonathan Dickinson's Journal*. 1945. New Haven: Yale University Press, 1961.

Arnold, J. Barto, III, ed. *Documentary Sources for the Wrecks of the New Spain Fleet of 1554*. Trans. by David McDonald. Austin: Texas Antiquities Committee, 1979.

Baily, Francis. *Journal of a Tour in Unsettled Parts of North America in 1796 & 1797*. Ed. by Jack D. L. Holmes. 1856. Carbondale, Ill.: Southern Illinois University, 1969.

Barrientos, Bartolomé. *Pedro Menéndez de Avilés, Founder of Florida, Written by Bartolomé Barrientos*. Trans. by Anthony Kerrigan. Gainesville: University of Florida Press, 1965.

Bartram, William. *The Travels of William Bartram*. Ed. by Francis Harper. 1791. New Haven: Yale University Press, 1958.

Beals, Herbert K., ed. and trans. *For Honor and Country: The Diary of Bruno de Hezeta*. Portland: West Imprints, Oregon Historical Society, 1985.

_____, ed. and trans. *Juan Pérez on the Northwest Coast: Six Documents of His Expedition in 1774*. Portland: Oregon Historical Society Press, 1989.

Benavides, Alonso de. *Fray Alonso de Benavides' Revised Memorial of 1634*. Ed. and trans. by Frederick W. Hodge, George P. Hammond, and Agapito Rey. Albuquerque: University of New Mexico Press, 1945.

_____. *The Memorial of Fray Alonso de Benavides, 1630*. Ed. by Frederick Webb Hodge and Charles Fletcher Lummis. Trans. by Mrs. Edward E. Ayer. Chicago: Privately printed, 1916.

Benavides' Memorial of 1630. Ed. by Cyprian J. Lynch. Trans. by Peter P. Forrestal. Washington, D.C.: Academy of American Franciscan History, 1954.

Bennett, Charles E. [ed. and trans.]. *Florida's "French" Revolution, 1793–1795*. Gainesville: University Presses of Florida, 1981.

_____, comp. *Settlement of Florida*. Gainesville: University of Florida Press, 1968.

Benson, Nettie Lee, ed. and trans. *Report that Dr. Miguel Ramos de Arizpe . . . Presents to the August Congress on the Natural, Political and Civil Condition of the Provinces of Coahuila, Nuevo León, Nuevo Santander, and Texas of the Four Eastern Interior Provinces of the Kingdom of Mexico*. Austin: University of Texas Press, 1950.

Bernabeu Albert, Salvador, ed. *Juan Francisco de la Bodega y Quadra: El descubrimiento del fin del mundo (1775–1792)*. Madrid: El Libro de Bolsillo Alianza Editorial, 1990.

Bloom, Lansing B., ed. and trans. "Fray Estevan de Perea's *Relación*." *NMHR* 8 (July 1933): 211–35.

_____, ed. and trans. "A Glimpse of New Mexico in 1620." *NMHR* 3 (Oct. 1928): 357–80.

_____, [ed. and trans.]. "The Royal Order of 1620 to Custodian Fray Esteban de Perea." *NMHR* 5 (July 1930): 288–98.

_____, [ed. and trans.]. "A Trade-Invoice of 1638 for Goods Shipped by Governor Rosas from Santa Fé." *NMHR* 10 (July 1935): 242–48.

Bloom, Lansing B., and Ireneo L. Chaves, ed. and trans. "Ynstruccion a Peralta por Vi-Rey." *NMHR* 4 (Apr. 1929): 178–87.

Bolton, Herbert Eugene [ed. and trans.]. *Anza's California Expeditions*. 5 vols. Berkeley: University of California Press, 1930.

———, ed. *Arredondo's Historical Proof of Spain's Title to Georgia: A Contribution to the History of One of the Spanish Borderlands*. Berkeley: University of California Press, 1925.

———, ed. and trans. *Athanase de Mézières and the Louisiana-Texas Frontier, 1768–1780*. 2 vols. Cleveland: Arthur H. Clark Co., 1914.

———, ed. and trans. *Font's Complete Diary, 1775–1776: A Chronicle of the Founding of San Francisco*. Berkeley: University of California Press, 1931.

———, ed. and trans. *Fray Juan Crespi, Missionary Explorer on the Pacific Coast, 1769–1774*. Berkeley: University of California Press, 1927.

———, ed. and trans. *Historical Memoirs of New California, by Fray Francisco Palóu, O.F.M.* 4 vols. Berkeley: University of California Press, 1926.

———, ed. *Spanish Exploration in the Southwest, 1542–1706*. New York: Scribner's, 1916.

Boneu Companys, Fernando, [ed.]. *Documentos secretos de la expedición de Portolá a California: juntas de guerra*. Lérida: Instituto de Estudios Llerdenses, 1973.

Bourne, Edward Gaylord, ed. *Narratives of the Career of Hernando de Soto . . . .* Trans. by Buckingham Smith. 2 vols. New York: A. S. Barnes & Co., 1904.

Boyd, Mark F., ed. and trans. "Diego Peña's Expedition to Apalache and Apalachicola in 1716: A Journal." *FHQ* 28 (July 1949): 1–27.

———, ed. and trans. "Enumeration of Florida Spanish Missions in 1675." *FHQ* 28 (Oct. 1948): 181–88.

———, ed. and trans. "Further Consideration of the Apalachee Missions." *The Americas* 9 (Apr. 1953): 459–79.

Bridges, Katherine, and Winston DeVille, eds. and trans. "Natchitoches and the Trail to the Rio Grande: Two Early Eighteenth-Century Accounts by the Sieur Derbanne." *Louisiana History* 8 (Summer 1967): 239–59.

Brinckerhoff, Sidney B., and Odie B. Faulk, eds. and trans. *Lancers for the King: A Study of the Frontier Military System of Northern New Spain, with a Translation of the Royal Regulations of 1772*. Phoenix: Arizona Historical Foundation, 1965.

Burrus, Ernest J. "A Tragic Interlude in the Reconquest of New Mexico." *Manuscripta* 29 (Nov. 1985): 154–65.

———, ed. *Diario del capitán comandante Fernando de Rivera y Moncada, con un apéndice documental [1774–1777]*. 2 vols. Madrid: José Porrúa Turanzas, 1967.

———, ed. and trans. *Kino's Plan for the Development of Pimería Alta, Arizona and Upper California: A Report to the Mexican Viceroy*. Tucson: Arizona Pioneers' Historical Society, 1961.

Bushnell, David, ed. *La República de las Floridas: Texts and Documents*. Mexico: Pan American Institute of Geography and History, 1986.

Cabeza de Vaca, Alvar Núñez. *Cabeza de Vaca's Adventures in the Unknown Interior of America*. Ed. and trans. by Cyclone Covey. New York: Crowell-Collier, 1961.

———. *La "Relación" o "Naufragios" de Alvar Núñez Cabeza de Vaca*. Ed. by Martin A. Favata and José B. Fernández. Potomac, Md.: Scripta Humanística, 1986.

Cabezas, Juan de las. "The First Episcopal Visitation in the United States (1606)." Trans. by V. F. O'Daniel. *Catholic Historical Review* 2 (Jan. 1917): 442–59.

Carroll, H. Bailey, and J. Villasana Haggard, eds. and trans. *Three New Mexico Chronicles* . . . . Albuquerque: Quivira Society, 1942.

Castañeda, Pedro de. "Narrative." In *Narratives of the Coronado Expedition, 1540–1542*, ed. and trans. by George P. Hammond and Agapito Rey. Albuquerque: University of New Mexico Press, 1940.

Céliz, Francisco. *Diary of the Alarcón Expedition into Texas 1718–1719*. Ed. and trans. by Fritz Leo Hoffmann. Los Angeles: Quivira Society, 1935.

Chandler, R. E., ed. and trans. "Ulloa's Account of the 1768 Revolt." *Louisiana History* 27 (Fall 1986): 407–37.

Coker, William S. "Four Contemporary Narratives of the Founding of St. Augustine." *Catholic Historical Review* 51 (Oct. 1965): 305–34.

_____, ed. *John Forbes' Description of the Spanish Floridas, 1804*. Pensacola: Perdido Bay Press, 1979.

_____, ed. *Pedro de Rivera's Report on the Presidio of Punta de Sigüenza, alias Panzacola, 1744*. Trans. by Vicki D. Butt et al. 1975. Pensacola: Pensacola Historical Society, 1980.

Coker, William S., and G. Douglas Inglis. *The Spanish Censuses of Pensacola, 1784–1820: A Genealogical Guide to Spanish Pensacola*. Pensacola: Perdido Bay Press, 1980.

Colección de documentos inéditos relativos al descubrimiento, conquista y organización de las antiguas posesiones españolas de América y Oceanía . . . . 42 vols. Madrid, 1864–84.

Concha, Fernando de la. "Advice on Governing New Mexico, 1794." Ed. and trans. by Donald E. Worcester. *NMHR* 24 (July 1949): 236–54.

Connor, Jeanette Thurber, ed. *Colonial Records of Spanish Florida*. Vol. 1: *1570–1577*; Vol. 2: *1577–1580*. Deland: Florida State Historical Society, 1925 & 1930.

_____, ed. and trans. *Pedro Menéndez de Avilés: Adelantado, Governor, and Captain-General of Florida. Memorial by Gonzalo Solís de Merás*. Deland: Florida State Historical Society, 1923.

Cortés, José. *Views from the Apache Frontier: Report on the Northern Provinces of New Spain by José Cortés, Lieutenant in the Royal Corps of Engineers, 1799*. Ed. by Elizabeth A. H. John. Trans. by John Wheat. Norman: University of Oklahoma Press, 1989.

Coues, Elliot, ed. and trans. *On the Trail of a Spanish Pioneer: The Diary and Itinerary of Francisco Garcés (Missionary Priest) in His Travels through Sonora, Arizona, and California, 1775–1776*. 2 vols. New York: Francis P. Harper, 1900.

Covington, James W., ed. *Pirates, Indians and Spaniards: Father Escobedo's "La Florida."* Trans. by A. F. Falcones. St. Petersburg: Great Outdoors Pub. Co., 1963.

Coxe, Daniel. *A Description of the English Province of Carolina, by the Spaniards call'd Florida and by the French La Louisiane*. 1722. Gainesville: University of Florida Press, 1976.

Cutter, Donald C., ed. and trans. "An Anonymous Statistical Report on New Mexico, 1765." *NMHR* (Oct. 1975): 347–52.

_____, ed. *The California Coast: A Bilingual Edition of Documents from the Sutro Collection*. Norman: University of Oklahoma Press, 1969.

Daniel, James M., ed. and trans. "Diary of Pedro José de la Fuente, Captain of the Presidio of El Paso del Norte, January–July, 1765." *SWHQ* 60 (Oct. 1956): 260–81.

_____, ed. and trans., "Diary of Pedro José de la Fuente, Captain of the Presidio of El Paso del Norte, August–December, 1765." *SWHQ* 83 (Jan. 1980): 259–73.

Day, A. Grove, [ed. and trans.]. "Mota Padilla on the Coronado Expedition." *HAHR* 20 (Feb. 1940): 83–110.

d'Escalante Fontaneda, Hernando. *Memoir of D.o d'Escalente [sic] Fontaneda Respecting Florida, Written in Spain about the Year 1575*. Ed. by David O. True et al. Trans. by Buckingham Smith. Coral Gables, Fla.: University of Miami Press, 1944.

Din, Gilbert C., ed. and trans. *Louisiana in 1776: A Memoir of Francisco Bouligny*. New Orleans: Louisiana Collections Series, 1977.

Espinosa, Isidro Félix de. *Crónica de los colegios de propaganda fide de la Nueva España*. Ed. by Lino Gómez Canedo. 1746. Washington, D.C.: Academy of American Franciscan History, 1964.

_____. *The Espinosa-Olivares-Aguirre Expedition of 1709*. Ed. by Paul J. Foik. Trans. by Gabriel Tous. Vol. 1, no. 3 of Preliminary Studies. Austin: Texas Catholic Historical Society, 1930.

Espinosa, J. Manuel, ed. and trans. *First Expedition of Vargas into New Mexico, 1692*. Albuquerque: University of New Mexico Press, 1940.

_____, ed. and trans. *The Pueblo Indian Revolt of 1696 and the Franciscan Missions in New Mexico: Letters of the Missionaries and Related Documents*. Norman: University of Oklahoma Press, 1988.

Fages, Pedro. *A Historical, Political, and Natural Description of California [1775]*. Ed. and trans. by Herbert Ingram Priestley. Berkeley: University of California Press, 1937.

Faulk, Odie, [ed. and trans.]. "Spanish Comanche Relations and the Treaty of 1785." *Texana* 2 (Spring 1964): 44–53.

Fernández de Oviedo y Valdés, Gonzalo. *Historia general y natural de las indias, islas y tierra firme del mar oceano*. 4 vols. Madrid: Imprenta de la Real Academia de la Historia, 1851–56.

Fernández de Santa Ana, Benito. *Letters and Memorials of the Father President Fray Benito Fernández de Santa Ana, 1736–1754*. Ed. by Marion A. Habig. Trans. by Benedict Leutenegger. San Antonio: Old Spanish Missions Historical Research Library, Lady of the Lake University, 1981.

_____. "Memorial of Father Benito Fernández concerning the Canary Islanders, 1741." Ed. by Marion Habig and Barnabas Diekemper. Trans. by Benedict Leutenegger. *SWHQ* 83 (Jan. 1979): 265–96.

Flores, Dan L., ed. *Jefferson and Southwestern Exploration: The Freeman and Custis Accounts of the Red River Expedition of 1806*. Norman: University of Oklahoma Press, 1984.

_____, ed. *Journal of an Indian Trader: Anthony Glass and the Texas Trading Frontier, 1790–1810*. College Station: Texas A&M University Press, 1985.

Florescano, Enrique, and Isabel Gil Sánchez, eds. *Descripciones económicas regionales de Nueva España: Provincias del Norte, 1790–1814*. Mexico: Instituto Nacional de Antropología e Historia, 1976.

Forbes, Alexander. *California: A History of Upper and Lower California from Their First Discovery to the Present Time*. London: Smith, Elder and Co., 1839.

Gálvez, Bernardo de. *Instructions for Governing the Interior Provinces of New Spain, 1786.* Ed. and trans. by Donald E. Worcester. Berkeley: Quivira Society, 1951.

_____. "Notes and Reflections on the War with the Apache Indians in the Provinces of New Spain, [ca. 1785–86]." In "A Cautionary Exercise in Apache Historiography." Ed. and trans. by Elizabeth A. H. John. *JAH* 25 (Autumn 1984): 301–15.

Galvin, John, ed. and trans. *The First Entry into San Francisco Bay, 1775: The Original Narrative, Hitherto Unpublished, by Fr. Vicente María* . . . . San Francisco: John Howell, 1971.

Garcés, Francisco. *Diario de exploraciones en Arizona y California en los años de 1775 y 1776.* Ed. by John Galvin. Mexico: Universidad Nacional Autónoma de México, 1968.

_____. *A Record of Travels in Arizona and California, 1775–1776.* Ed. and trans. by John Galvin. San Francisco: John Howell Books, 1965.

García, Bartholomé. *Manual para administrar los santos sacramentos.* Mexico, 1760.

Geiger, Maynard, ed. and trans. *As the Padres Saw Them: California Indian Life and Customs as Reported by the Franciscan Missionaries, 1813–1815.* Santa Barbara: Santa Barbara Mission Archive Library, 1976.

_____, ed. and trans. *Letter of Luís Jayme, O.F.M.: San Diego, October 17, 1772.* San Diego: Dawson's Book Shop for the San Diego Public Library, 1970.

Gibson, Charles, ed. *The Spanish Tradition in America.* New York: Harper Torchbooks, 1968.

Gómez Canedo, Lino, ed. *Primeras exploraciones y poblamiento de Texas (1686–1694).* 1968. Mexico: Editorial Porrúa, 1988.

González Cabrera Bueno, Joseph. *Navegación especulativa y práctica.* Facsimile, ed. by W. Michael Mathes. Madrid: José Porrúa Turanzas, 1970.

González Flores, Enrique, and Francisco R. Almada, eds. *Informe de Hugo O'Conor sobre el estado de las provincias internas del norte, 1771–1776.* Mexico: Editorial Cultura, 1952.

Guice, C. Norman, [trans.]. "Texas in 1804." *SWHQ* 59 (July 1955): 46–56.

Habig, Marion A., ed. *Nothingness Itself: Selected Writings of Ven. Fr. Antonio Margil, 1690–1724.* Trans. by Benedict Leutenegger. Chicago: Franciscan Herald Press, 1979.

Hackett, Charles Wilson, ed. *Historical Documents Relating to New Mexico, Nueva Vizcaya, and Approaches Thereto.* 3 vols. Washington, D.C.: Carnegie Institution, 1923–37.

_____, ed. and trans. *Pichardo's Treatise on the Limits of Louisiana and Texas.* 4 vols. Austin: University of Texas Press, 1931–46.

_____, [ed. and trans.] "Policy of the Spanish Crown Regarding French Encroachment from Louisiana, 1721–1762." In *New Spain and the Anglo-American West: Historical Contributions Presented to Herbert Eugene Bolton,* ed. by George P. Hammond et al. 2 vols. Los Angeles: Privately printed, 1932.

_____, ed. *Revolt of the Pueblo Indians and Otermín's Attempted Reconquest, 1680–1682.* Trans. by Charmion Clair Shelby. 2 vols. Albuquerque: University of New Mexico Press, 1941.

Hallenbeck, Cleve, ed. and trans. *The Journey of Fray Marcos de Niza.* 1949. Dallas: Southern Methodist University Press, 1987.

Hammond, E. A., ed. and trans. "A French Document Relating to the Destruction of the French Colony in Florida . . ." *FHQ* 39 (July 1960): 55–61.

Hammond, George P., [ed. and trans.]. "The Zúñiga Journal, Tucson to Santa Fé: The Opening of a Spanish Trade Route, 1788–1795." *NMHR* 6 (Jan. 1931): 40–65.

Hammond, George P., and Agapito Rey, eds. and trans. *Don Juan de Oñate: Colonizer of New Mexico, 1595–1628.* 2 vols. Albuquerque: University of New Mexico Press, 1953.

———, eds. and trans. *Narratives of the Coronado Expedition, 1540–1542.* Albuquerque: University of New Mexico Press, 1940.

———, eds. and trans. *Obregón's History of 16th Century Explorations in Western America.* Los Angeles: Wetzel Publishing Co., 1928.

———, eds. and trans. *The Rediscovery of New Mexico, 1580–1594: The Explorations of Chamuscado, Espejo, Castaño de Sosa, Morlete, and Leyva de Bonilla and Humaña.* Albuquerque: University of New Mexico Press, 1966.

Hann, John H., ed. and trans. "Apalachee Counterfeiters in St. Augustine." *FHQ* 67 (July 1988): 52–68.

———, ed. and trans. "Church Furnishings, Sacred Vessels and Vestments Held by the Missions of Florida: Translation of Two Inventories." *Florida Archaeology* 2 (1986): 147–64.

———, ed. and trans. "Translation of Alonso de Leturiondo's Memorial to the King of Spain." *Florida Archaeology* 2 (1986): 165–225.

———, ed. and trans. "Translation of the Ecija Voyages of 1605 and 1609 and the González Derrotero of 1609." *Florida Archaeology* 2 (1986): 1–80.

———, ed. and trans. "Translation of Governor Rebolledo's 1657 Visitation of Three Florida Provinces, and Related Documents." *Florida Archaeology* 2 (1986): 81–145.

Hatcher, Mattie Austin, ed. and trans. "Descriptions of the Tejas or Asinai Indians, 1691–1722." *SWHQ* 30–31 (Jan., Apr., July, and Oct. 1927): 206–18; 283–304; 50–62; 150–80.

———, ed. and trans. *The Expedition of Don Domingo Terán de los Ríos into Texas.* Vol. 2, no. 1 of Preliminary Studies. Austin: Texas Catholic Historical Society, 1932.

———, trans. "Texas in 1820." *SWHQ* 23 (July 1919): 47–68.

Hatcher, Mattie Austin, ed., and Margaret Kenney Kress, trans. "Diary of a Visit of Inspection of the Texas Missions Made by Fray Gaspar José de Solís in the Year 1767–1768." *SWHQ* 35 (July 1931): 28–76.

Hedrick, Basil C., and Carroll L. Riley, eds. and trans. *The Journey of the Vaca Party: The Account of the Narváez Expedition, 1528–1536, as Related by Gonzalo Fernández de Oviedo y Valdés.* Carbondale: University Museum, Southern Illinois University, 1974.

Hodge, Frederick Webb, ed. *History of New Mexico by Gaspar Pérez de Villagrá, Alcalá—1610.* Trans. by Gilberto Espinosa. Los Angeles: Quivira Society, 1933.

Hoffmann, Fritz, ed. and trans. "The Mezquía Diary of the Alarcón Expedition into Texas, 1718." *SWHQ* 41 (Apr. 1938): 312–23.

Hudson, Charles. *The Juan Pardo Expeditions: Exploration of the Carolinas and Tennessee, 1566–1568, With Documents . . . Transcribed, Translated, and Annotated by Paul E. Hoffman.* Washington, D.C.: Smithsonian Institution Press, 1990.

Humboldt, Alexander von. *Political Essay on the Kingdom of New Spain.* Ed. by Mary Maples Dunn. Trans. by John Black. New York: Alfred A. Knopf, 1972.

Jackson, Donald, ed. and trans. *The Journals of Zebulon Montgomery Pike, with Letters and Related Documents.* 2 vols. Norman: University of Oklahoma Press, 1966.

Jackson, W. R. *Early Florida through Spanish Eyes*. Coral Gables: University of Miami Press, 1954.

John, Elizabeth A. H., ed. and trans. "A Cautionary Exercise in Apache Historiography." *JAZH* 25 (Autumn 1984): 301–15.

Kelsey, Harry, ed. and trans. *The Doctrina and Confesionario of Juan Cortés*. Altadena, Calif.: Howling Coyote Press, 1979.

Kendrick, John, ed. and trans. *The Voyage of the SUTIL and MEXICANA, 1792: The Last Spanish Exploration of the Northwest Coast of America*. Spokane, Wash.: Arthur H. Clark Co., 1991.

Kenneally, Finbar, ed. and trans. *Writings of Fermín Francisco de Lasuén*. 2 vols. Washington, D.C.: Academy of American Franciscan History, 1965.

Kerrigan, Anthony, ed. and trans. *Barcía's Chronological History of the Continent of Florida . . . From the Year 1512 . . . until the Year 1722*. Gainesville: University of Florida Press, 1951.

Kessell, John L., ed. "Anza Damns the Missions: A Soldier's Criticism of Indian Policy, 1772." *JAZH* 13 (Spring 1972): 53–63.

_____, ed. *Remote beyond Compare: Letters of don Diego de Vargas to His Family from New Spain and New Mexico, 1675–1706*. Albuquerque: University of New Mexico Press, 1989.

Kinnaird, Lawrence, ed. and trans. *The Frontiers of New Spain: Nicolás de Lafora's Description, 1766–1768*. Berkeley: Quivira Society, 1958.

_____, ed., *Spain in the Mississippi Valley, 1765–1794*. In *Annual Report of the American Historical Association for the Year 1945*, 4 vols. Washington, D.C.: American Historical Association, 1946–49.

Le Moyne, Jacques. "The Narrative of Le Moyne." In *Settlement of Florida*, comp. by Charles E. Bennett. Gainesville: University of Florida Press, 1968.

Leonard, Irving Albert, ed. and trans. *The Mercurio Volante of Don Carlos de Sigüenza y Góngora: An Account of the First Expedition of Don Diego de Vargas into New Mexico in 1692*. Los Angeles: Quivira Society, 1932.

_____, ed. and trans. *Spanish Approach to Pensacola, 1689–1693*. Albuquerque: Quivira Society, 1939.

Leutenegger, Benedict, ed. and trans. "Two Franciscan Documents on Early San Antonio, Texas." *The Americas* 25 (Oct. 1968): 191–206.

Lockey, Joseph Byrne, [ed. and trans.]. *East Florida, 1783–1785: A File of Documents Assembled, and Many of Them Translated*. Ed. by John Walton Caughey. Berkeley: University of California Press, 1949.

López, José Francisco. "Report on the San Antonio Missions in 1792." Ed. by Marion A. Habig. Trans. by Benedict Leutenegger. *SWHQ* 77 (Apr. 1974): 486–98.

_____. *The Texas Missions in 1785*. Trans. by J. Autrey Dabbs. Vol. 3, no. 6 of Preliminary Studies. Austin: Texas Catholic Historical Society, 1940.

López de Mendoza Grajales, Francisco. "Memoir of the Happy Result and Prosperous Voyage of . . . Pedro Menéndez de Avilés." In *Laudonniére and Fort Caroline: History and Documents*, trans. by Charles E. Bennett. Gainesville: University of Florida Press, 1964.

McCall, George A. *Letters from the Frontiers, Written during a Period of Thirty Years' in the Army of the United States.* Intro. by John K. Mahon. 1868. Gainesville: University of Florida Press, 1974.

McCarty, Kieran, ed. and trans. "The Colorado Massacre of 1781: María Montielo's Report." *JAZH* 16 (Autumn 1975): 221–25.

———— [ed. and trans.]. *Desert Documentary: The Spanish Years, 1767–1821.* Tucson: Arizona Historical Society, 1976.

————, ed. and trans. "The Sonora Prophecy of 1783," *Journal of the Southwest* 32 (Autumn 1990): 316–20.

McWilliams, Richebourg Gaillard, ed. and trans. *Iberville's Gulf Journals.* University: University of Alabama Press, 1981.

Magnaghi, Russell M., ed. and trans. "Texas as Seen by Governor Winthuysen, 1741–1744." *SWHQ* 88 (Oct. 1984): 167–80.

Martin, James C., and Robert Sidney Martin. *Maps of Texas and the Southwest, 1513–1900.* Albuquerque: University of New Mexico Press for the Amon Carter Museum, 1984.

Martínez, Antonio. *Letters from Gov. Antonio Martínez to the Viceroy Juan Ruíz de Apodaca [1817–1821].* Ed. by Félix D. Alamaraz. Trans. by Virginia H. Taylor. San Antonio: Research Center for the Arts and Humanities, University of Texas, 1983.

Martyr, Peter. *De Orbe Novo: The Eight Decades of Peter Martyr D'Anghera.* Ed. and trans. by F. A. MacNutt. 2 vols. New York: G. P. Putnam's, 1912.

Mathes, W. Michael., ed. *Californiana I: Documentos para la historia de la demarcación comercial de California, 1583–1632.* 2 vols. Madrid: José Porrúa Turanzas, 1965.

————, ed. *Californiana IV: Aportación a la historiografía de California en el siglo XVIII.* 2 vols. Madrid: José Porrúa Turanzas, 1987.

————, ed. and trans. *The Conquistador in California: 1535. The Voyage of Fernando Cortés to Baja California in Chronicles and Documents.* Los Angeles: Dawson's Book Shop, 1973.

————, ed. *Obras californianas de Padre Miguel Venegas, S. J.* Prologue by Miguel León-Portilla. 5 vols. La Paz: Universidad Autónoma de Baja California Sur, 1979–1983.

Matson, Daniel S., and Bernard L. Fontana, eds. and trans. *Friar Bringas Reports to the King: Methods of Indoctrination on the Frontier of New Spain, 1796–97.* Tucson: University of Arizona Press, 1977.

Matson, Daniel S., and Albert H. Schroeder, eds. and trans. "Cordero's Description of the Apache—1796." *NMHR* 32 (Oct. 1957): 335–56.

Mendinueta, Pedro Fermín de. *Indian and Mission Affairs in New Mexico, 1773.* Ed. and trans. by Marc Simmons. Santa Fe: Stagecoach Press, 1965.

Milanich, Jerald T., and William C. Sturtevant, eds. *Francisco Pareja's 1613 Confessionario.* Trans. by Emilio F. Moran. Tallahassee: Division of History, Archives and Records Management, Florida Department of State, 1972.

Miller, Robert Ryal, ed. and trans. "New Mexico in Mid-Eighteenth Century: A Report Based on Governor Vélez de Cachupín's Inspection." *SWHQ* 79 (Oct. 1975): 166–81.

Mills, Elizabeth Shown. *Natchitoches: Abstracts of the Catholic Registers . . . 1729–1803.* New Orleans: Polyanthos, 1977.

Moore, Mary Lou, and Delmar L. Beene, eds. and trans. "The Interior Provinces of New Spain: The Report of Hugo O'Conor, Jan. 30, 1776." *AW* 13 (Autumn 1971): 265–82.

Morfí, Fray Agustín de. *Account of Disorders in New Mexico, 1778.* Ed. and trans. by Marc Simmons. Isleta: Historical Society of New Mexico, 1977.

––––––. *Excerpts from the Memorias for the History of the Province of Texas . . . by Padre Juan Agustín de Morfi.* Ed. and trans. by Frederick C. Chabot, with the assistance of Carlos Eduardo Castañeda. San Antonio: Naylor, 1932.

––––––. *History of Texas, 1673–1779.* Ed. and trans. by Carlos Eduardo Castañeda. 2 vols. Albuquerque: Quivira Society, 1935.

Moriarty, James R., and Mary Keistman, eds. and trans. *A New Translation of the Summary Log of the Cabrillo Voyage in 1542.* Occasional Paper no. 2. La Jolla, Calif.: San Diego Science Foundation, 1963.

Moziño, José Mariano. *Noticias de Nutka: An Account of Nootka Sound in 1792.* Ed. and trans. by Iris Wilson [Engstrand]. Seattle: University of Washington Press, 1970.

Nasatir, A. P., ed. *Before Lewis and Clark: Documents Illustrating the History of the Missouri, 1785–1804.* 2 vols. St. Louis: St. Louis Historical Documents Foundation, 1952.

Naylor, Thomas H., and Charles W. Polzer, eds. *1570–1700.* Vol. 1 of *The Presidio and Militia on the Northern Frontier of New Spain: A Documentary History.* Tucson: University of Arizona Press, 1986.

––––––, eds. *Pedro de Rivera and the Military Regulations for Northern New Spain, 1724–1729: A Documentary History of His Frontier Inspection and the* Reglamento de 1729. Tucson: University of Arizona Press, 1988.

Nentvig, Juan. *Rudo Ensayo: A Description of Sonora and Arizona in 1764.* Ed. and trans. by Alberto Francisco Pradeau and Robert R. Rasmussen. Tucson: University of Arizona Press, 1980.

Neve, Felipe de. *Reglamento para el gobierno de la Provincia de Californias/Regulations for Governing the Province of Californias.* Trans. by John Everett Johnson. 2 vols. San Francisco: Grabhorn Press, 1929.

Nuttall, Zelia, ed. and trans. "Royal Ordinances Concerning the Laying Out of New Towns." *HAHR* 4–5 (Nov. 1921; May 1922): 743–53; 249–54.

Oré, Luis Gerónimo de. *The Martyrs of Florida, 1513–1616.* Ed. and trans. by Maynard Geiger. New York: Joseph F. Wagner, 1936.

Palóu, Francisco. *Palóu's Life of Fray Junípero Serra.* Ed. and trans. by Maynard J. Geiger. Washington, D.C.: Academy of American Franciscan History, 1955.

Pareja, Francisco de. *Catecismo, en Lengua Castellana, y Timuquana.* Mexico, 1612.

Parry, John H., and Robert G. Keith, eds. *New Iberian World: A Documentary History of the Discovery and Settlement of Latin America to the Early 17th Century.* 5 vols. New York: Times Books, 1984.

Patten, Roderick B., ed. and trans. "Miranda's Inspection of Los Almagres: His Journal, Report and Petition." *SWHQ* 74 (Oct. 1970): 223–54.

Pfefferkorn, Ignaz. *Sonora: A Description of the Province.* Ed. and trans. by Theodore E. Treutlin. 1945. Tucson: University of Arizona Press, 1989.

Pope, John. *A Tour through the Southern and Eastern Territories of the United States of North*

America . . . Intro. by J. Barton Starr. 1792. Gainesville: University Presses of Florida, 1979.

Porrúa Turanzas, José, ed. *Documentos para la historia eclesiástica y civil de la Provincia de Texas o Nuevas Philipinas, 1720–79.* Madrid: José Porrúa Turanzas, 1961.

[Portolá, Gaspar de]. *Gaspar de Portolá: Crónicas del descubrimiento de California, 1769.* Ed. by Angela Cano Sánchez, Neus Escandell Tur, and Elena Mampel González. Barcelona: Universitad de Barcelona, 1984.

Priestley, Herbert I., ed. and trans. *Luna Papers: Documents Relating to the Expedition of Don Tristán de Luna y Arellano for the Conquest of La Florida, 1559–1561.* 2 vols. Deland: Florida State Historical Society, 1928.

Quinn, David Beers, ed. *New American World: A Documentary History of North America to 1612.* 5 vols. New York: Arno Press, 1979.

Ramón, Domingo. *Captain Don Domingo Ramón's Diary of His Expedition into Texas in 1716.* Trans. by Paul J. Foik. Vol. 2, no. 5 of Preliminary Studies. Austin: Texas Catholic Historical Society, 1933.

Ranjel, Rodrigo. "A Narrative of De Soto's Expedition." In *Narratives of the Career of Hernando de Soto . . .,* ed. by Edward Gaylord Bourne. Trans. by Buckingham Smith. 2 vols. New York: A. S. Barnes & Co., 1904.

Recopilación de leyes de los Reynos de las Indias. 4 vols. 1681. Madrid: Editorial Cultural Hispánica, 1973.

Represa, Amando, ed. *La España ilustrada en el lejano oeste: Viajes y exploraciones por las provincias y territorios hispánicos de norteamérica en el s. xviii.* Madrid: Junta de Castilla y León, 1990.

Revilla Gigedo, Conde de. *Informe sobre las misiones, 1793, e instrucción reservada al marqués de Branciforte, 1794.* Ed. by José Bravo Ugarte. Mexico: Editorial Jus, 1966.

Reynolds, Charles B. *The Standard Guide to St. Augustine.* St. Augustine, Fla.: E. H. Reynolds, [ca. 1892].

Ribes Iborra, Vicente, [ed.]. *Ambiciones estadounidenses sobre la provincia novohispana de Texas.* México: Universidad Nacional Autónoma de México, 1982.

Roberts, William. *An Account of the First Discovery, and Natural History of Florida.* Intro. by Robert L. Gold. 1763. Gainesville: University Presses of Florida, 1976.

Robertson, James Alexander, ed. *Louisiana under the Rule of Spain, France, and the United States, 1785–1807.* 2 vols. Cleveland: Arthur H. Clark Co., 1911.

———, ed. and trans. *True Relations of the Hardships Suffered by Governor Fernando de Soto and Certain Portuguese Gentlemen during the Discovery of the Province of Florida.* 2 vols. Deland: Florida State Historical Society, 1933.

Rubí, marqués de. "Dictámenes que de orden del exmo. sor. marqués de Croix, virrey de este reino, expone el mariscal de campo marqués de Rubí en orden a la mejor situación de los presidios . . ." In *La frontera norte y la experiencia colonial,* ed. by María del Carmen Velázquez. Mexico City: Secretaría de Relaciones Exteriores, 1982.

Saavedra, Francisco de. *The Journal of Don Francisco de Saavedra de Sangronis . . . .* Ed. by Francisco Morales Padrón. Trans. by Aileen Moore Topping. Gainesville: University of Florida Press, 1989.

Santos, Richard G., ed. and trans. *Aguayo Expedition into Texas, 1721: An Annotated Translation of the Five Versions of the Diary Kept by Br. Juan Antonio de la Peña*. Austin: Jenkins Publishing Co., 1981.

Scardaville, Michael C., and Jesús María Belmonte, eds. and trans. "Florida in the Late First Spanish Period: The 1756 Griñán Report." *El Escribano* 16 (1979): 1–24.

Scholes, France, ed. and trans. "Documents for the History of the New Mexican Missions in the Seventeenth Century," *NMHR* 4 (Jan. and Apr. 1929): 45–58; 195–201.

Schroeder, Albert H., and Dan S. Matson, eds. and trans. *A Colony on the Move: Gaspar Castaño de Sosa's Journal, 1590–1591*. Salt Lake City: School of American Research, 1965.

Señán, José. *The Letters of José Señán, O.F.M. Mission San Buenaventura, 1796–1823*. Ed. by Lesley Byrd Simpson. Trans. by Paul D. Nathan. San Francisco: John Howell Books, 1962.

Serrano y Sanz, Manuel. *Documentos históricos de la Florida y la Luisiana, siglos XVI al XVIII*. Madrid: Librería General de Victoriano Suárez, 1912.

Servín, Manuel P., ed. and trans. "Costansó's 1794 Report on Strengthening New California's Presidios." *CHSQ* 49 (Sept. 1970): 221–32.

Shea, John Gilmary, [ed. and trans.]. *The Expedition of Don Dionisio de Peñalosa . . . by Father Nicholas de Freytas*. 1882. Albuquerque: Horn & Wallace, 1964.

Shelby, Charmion Clair, ed. and trans. "Projected French Attacks upon the Northeastern Frontier of New Spain, 1719–1721." *HAHR* 13 (Nov. 1933): 457–72.

———, [ed. and trans.]. "St. Denis's Declaration Concerning Texas in 1717." *SWHQ* 26 (Jan. 1923): 190–216.

Shirley, Rodney W. *The Mapping of the World: Early Printed World Maps, 1472–1700*. London: Holland Press, 1984.

Sibley, Marilyn McAdams, ed. "Across Texas in 1767: The Travels of Captain Pagès." *SWHQ* 70 (Apr. 1967): 593–622.

Simmons, Marc, ed. and trans. *Border Comanches: Seven Spanish Colonial Documents, 1785–1819*. Santa Fe: Stagecoach Press, 1967.

Simpson, Lesley B., and Paul D. Nathan, eds. and trans. *The San Sabá Papers: A Documentary Account of the Founding and Destruction of San Sabá Mission*. San Francisco: John Howell Books, 1959.

Spell, Lota M., ed. and trans. "The Grant and First Survey of the City of San Antonio." *SWHQ* 66 (July 1962): 73–89.

Stanger, Frank M., and Alan K. Brown, eds. *Who Discovered the Golden Gate? The Explorers' Own Accounts*. San Mateo, Calif.: San Mateo County Historical Association, 1969.

Taylor, Virginia, ed. and trans. *The Letters of Antonio Martínez, the Last Spanish Governor of Texas, 1817–1822*. Austin: Texas State Library, 1957.

Temple, Thomas Workman, II, ed. "First Census of Los Angeles." *SCQ* 16 (1931): 148–49.

Thomas, Alfred Barnaby, ed. and trans. *After Coronado: Spanish Exploration Northeast of New Mexico, 1696–1727*. Norman: University of Oklahoma Press, 1935.

———, ed. and trans. *Alonso de Posada Report, 1686: A Description of the Area of the Present*

Southern United States in the Late Seventeenth Century. Pensacola: Perdido Bay Press, 1982.

————, ed. and trans. *Forgotten Frontiers: A Study of the Spanish Indian Policy of Don Juan Bautista de Anza, Governor of New Mexico, 1777–1787.* Norman: University of Oklahoma Press, 1932.

————, ed. and trans. *The Plains Indians and New Mexico, 1751–1778: A Collection of Documents Illustrative of the History of the Eastern Frontier of New Mexico.* Albuquerque: University of New Mexico Press, 1940.

————, ed. and trans. *Teodoro de Croix and the Northern Frontier of New Spain, 1776–1783: From the Original Document in the Archives of the Indies, Seville.* Norman: University of Oklahoma Press, 1941.

————. [ed. and trans.]. "Antonio de Bonilla and Spanish Plans for the Defense of New Mexico, 1772–1778." In *New Spain and the Anglo-American West,* ed. by George P. Hammond. 2 vols. Lancaster, Penn.: Privately printed, 1932.

Tibesar, Antonine, ed. *Writings of Junípero Serra.* 4 vols. Washington, D.C.: Academy of American Franciscan History, 1955–66.

Tous, Gabriel, ed. and trans. "Ramón's Expedition: Espinosa's Diary of 1716." *Mid-America* 12 (Apr. 1930): 339–61.

Vega, Garcilaso de la. *La Florida del Inca.* Ed. by Sylvia L. Hilton. 1605. Madrid: Historia 16, 1986.

————. *The Florida of the Inca.* Ed. and trans. by John Grier Varner and Jeannette Johnson Varner. 1605. Austin: University of Texas Press, 1951.

Velasco Ceballos, R., ed. *La administración de D. Frey Antonio María de Bucareli y Ursúa.* Vols. 29–30 of *Publicaciones del Archivo General de la Nación.* Mexico: Talleres Gráficos de la Nación, 1936.

Velázquez, María del Carmen [ed.]. *La frontera norte y la experiencia colonial.* Mexico: Secretaría de Relaciones Exteriores, 1982.

———— [ed.]. *El marqués de Altamira y las provincias internas de Nueva España.* Mexico City: El Colegio de México, 1976.

Vélez de Escalante, Fray Silvestre. "Letter to the Missionaries of New Mexico [Aug. 17, 1777]." Ed. and trans. by Eleanor B. Adams. *NMHR* 40 (Oct. 1965): 319–36.

Vignoles, Charles B. *Observations upon the Floridas.* Intro. by John Hebron Moore. 1st ed., 1823; facsimile, Gainesville: The University Presses of Florida, 1977.

Warner, Ted J., ed. *The Domínguez-Escalante Journal: Their Expedition through Colorado, Utah, Arizona, and New Mexico in 1776.* Trans. by Angélico Chávez. Provo: Brigham Young University Press, 1976.

Watson, Douglas S., and Thomas Workman Temple II, eds. and trans. *The Spanish Occupation of California: . . . Junta or Council Held at San Blas, May 16, 1768.* San Francisco: Grabhorn Press, 1934.

Weddle, Robert S., et al., eds. *La Salle, the Mississippi, and the Gulf: Three Primary Documents.* College Station: Texas A&M University Press, 1987.

Wenhold, Lucy L., ed. and trans. *A 17th Century Letter of Gabriel Díaz Vara Calderón, Bishop of Cuba, Describing the Indians and Indian Missions of Florida.* Smithsonian Miscellaneous Collections, vol. 95, no. 16. Washington, D.C: Smithsonian Institution, 1936.

West, Elizabeth H., ed. and trans. "Bonilla's Brief Compendium of the History of Texas." *SWHQ* 8 (July 1904): 3–78.

Wheat, Carl I. *Mapping the Transmississippi West*. 5 vols. San Francisco: Institute of Historical Cartography, 1957–63.

Whitaker, Arthur Preston, ed. and trans. *Documents Relating to the Commercial Policy of Spain in the Floridas, with Incidental Reference to Louisiana*. Deland: Florida State Historical Society, 1931.

White, David H. "A View of Spanish West Florida: Selected Letters of Governor Juan Vicente Folch." *FHQ* 56 (Oct. 1977): 138–47.

Williams, John Lee. *The Territory of Florida: or Sketches of the Topography, Civil and Natural History, of the Country* . . . . Intro. by Herbert J. Doherty, Jr. 1st ed., 1837; facsimile, Gainesville: University of Florida Press, 1962.

————. *View of West Florida: Embracing Its Geography, Topography, &c* . . . . Intro. by Herbert J. Doherty, Jr. 1827. Gainesville: University Presses of Florida, 1976.

Woodward, Ralph Lee, ed. and trans. *Tribute to Don Bernardo de Gálvez: Royal Patents and an Epic Ballad Honoring the Spanish Governor of Louisiana*. Baton Rouge: Historic New Orleans Collection, 1979.

Zárate Salmerón, Gerónimo. *Relaciones*. Trans. by Alicia Ronstad Milich. Albuquerque: Horn & Wallace, 1966.

Zubillaga, Félix. *Monumenta Antiquae Floridae (1566–1572)*. Monumenta Historica Societatis Iesu, vol. 66. Rome, 1946.

Secondary Sources

Abbey, Kathryn Trimmer. "Spanish Projects for the Recuperation of the Floridas during the American Revolution." *HAHR* 9 (Aug. 1929): 265–85.

Acosta Rodríguez, Antonio. "Crecimiento económico desigual en la Luisiana española." *Anuario de estudios americanos* 34 (1977): 735–57.

————. *La población de Luisiana española (1763–1803)*. Madrid: Ministerio de Asuntos Exteriores, 1979.

Adams, E. Charles. "Passive Resistance: Hopi Responses to Spanish Contact and Conquest." In *CC*, vol. 1.

————. "The View from the Hopi Mesas." In *The Protohistoric Period in the North American Southwest: A.D. 1450–1700*, ed. by David R. Wilcox and W. Bruce Masse. Tempe: Arizona State University Anthropological Research Papers, 1981.

Adams, Eleanor B. "Fray Francisco Atanasio Domínguez and Fray Silvestre Vélez de Escalante." *Utah Historical Quarterly* 44 (Winter 1976): 40–58.

————. "Fray Silvestre and the Obstinate Hopi." *NMHR* 38 (Apr. 1963): 97–138.

————. "Viva el Rey!" *NMHR* 35 (Oct. 1960): 284–92.

Adams, Eleanor B., and France V. Scholes. "Books in New Mexico, 1598–1680." *NMHR* 17 (July 1942): 226–70.

Adorno, Rolena. "Negotiation of Fear in Cabeza de Vaca's *Naufragios*." *Representations* 33 (Winter 1991): 100–34.

Ahern, Maureen. "The Certification of Cíbola: Discursive Strategies in *La relación del descubrimiento de las siete ciudades* by Fray Marcos de Niza (1539)." *Dispositio* 14 (1989): 303–13.

Ahlborn, Richard E. "European Dress in Texas, 1830: As Rendered by Lino Sánchez y Tapia." *American Scene* 13 (1972): 1–21.

———. "The Will of a Woman in 1762." *NMHR* 65 (July 1990): 319–55.

Albornoz, Miguel. *Hernando de Soto: Knight of the Americas*. New York: Franklin Watts, 1986.

Alfaro, Juan. "The Spirit of the First Franciscan Missionaries in Texas." *U.S. Catholic Historian* 9 (Spring 1990): 49–66.

Almaraz, Félix D., Jr. *The San Antonio Missions and Their System of Land Tenure*. Austin: University of Texas Press, 1989.

———. *Tragic Cavalier: Governor Manuel Salcedo of Texas, 1808–1813*. Austin: University of Texas Press, 1971.

Anaya, Rudolfo A., and Francisco A. Lomelí, eds. *Aztlán: Essays on the Chicano Homeland*. Albuquerque: Academia/El Norte Publications, 1989.

Anderson, H. Allen. "The Encomienda in New Mexico, 1598–1680." *NMHR* 60 (Oct. 1985): 353–77.

Andrews, Kenneth R. *The Spanish Caribbean: Trade and Plunder, 1530–1630*. New Haven: Yale University Press, 1978.

Arana, Luis Rafael. "The Day Governor Cabrera Left Florida." *FHQ* 40 (Oct. 1961): 154–63.

———. "The Exploration of Florida and Sources on the Founding of St. Augustine." *FHQ* 44 (July–Oct. 1965): 1–16.

Archer, Christon. "Cannibalism in the Early History of the Northwest Coast: Enduring Myths and Neglected Realities." *Canadian Historical Review* 61 (Dec. 1980): 453–79.

———. "The Deportation of Barbarian Indians from the Internal Province of New Spain, 1789–1810." *The Americas* 24 (Jan. 1973): 376–85.

———. "The Transient Presence: A Re-Appraisal of Spanish Attitudes toward the Northwest Coast in the Eighteenth Century." *BC Studies* 18 (Summer 1973): 3–32.

Archibald, Robert. "Acculturation and Assimilation in Colonial New Mexico." *NMHR* 53 (July 1978): 205–17.

———. *Economic Aspects of the California Missions*. Washington, D.C.: Academy of American Franciscan History, 1978.

———. "Indian Labor at the California Missions: Slavery or Salvation?" *JSDH* 24 (Spring 1978): 172–82.

Arena, C. Richard. "Land Settlement Policies and Practices in Spanish Louisiana." In *The Spanish in the Mississippi Valley, 1762–1804*, ed. by John Francis McDermott. Urbana: University of Illinois Press, 1974.

Arias Divito, Juan Carlos. *Las expediciones científicas españolas durante el siglo XVIII*. Madrid: Ediciones Cultura Hispánica, 1968.

Armillas Vicente, José A. *El Mississipi, frontera de España: España y los Estados Unidos ante el Tratado de San Lorenzo*. Zaragoza: Institución Fernando el Católico, 1977.

Arnade, Charles W. *Florida on Trial, 1593–1602*. Coral Gables: University of Miami Press, 1959.

––––––. "Cattle Raising in Spanish Florida, 1513–1763." *Agricultural History* 35 (July 1961): 116–24.

––––––. "The English Invasion of Spanish Florida, 1700–1706." *FHQ* 41 (July 1962): 29–37.

––––––. "The Failure of Spanish Florida." *The Americas* 16 (Jan. 1960): 271–81.

––––––. "Tristán de Luna and Ochuse (Pensacola Bay) 1559." *FHQ* 37 (Jan.–Apr. 1959): 210–22.

––––––, ed. and trans. "Florida in 1643 as Seen by Its Governor." *FHQ* 34 (Oct. 1955): 172–76.

Arnold, J. Barto, III, and Robert Weddle. *The Nautical Archaeology of Padre Island: The Spanish Wrecks of 1554*. New York: Academic Press, 1978.

Arnold, Morris S. *Unequal Laws unto a Savage Race: European Legal Traditions in Arkansas, 1686–1836*. Fayetteville: University of Arkansas Press, 1985.

Arthur, Stanley Clisby. *The Story of the West Florida Rebellion*. St. Francisville, La.: St. Francisville Democrat, 1935.

August, Jack. "Balance-of-Power Diplomacy in New Mexico: Governor Fernando de la Concha and the Indian Policy of Conciliation." *NMHR* 56 (Apr. 1981): 141–60.

Avellaneda, Ignacio. *Los sobrevivientes de la Florida: The Survivors of the De Soto Expedition*. Gainesville: P. K. Yonge Library, 1990.

Avilez, Alexander. "Population Increases into Alta California in the Spanish Period, 1769–1821." M.A. thesis, University of Southern California, 1955.

Axtell, James. "Europeans, Indians, and the Age of Discovery in American History Textbooks." *AHR* 92 (June 1987): 621–32.

––––––, ed. *After Columbus: Essays in the Ethnohistory of Colonial North America*. New York: Oxford University Press, 1988.

Baade, Hans W. "The Form of Marriage in Spanish North America." *Cornell Law Review* 61 (Nov. 1975): 1–89.

Badger, R. Reid, and Lawrence A. Clayton, eds. *Alabama and the Borderlands from Prehistory to Statehood*. University: University of Alabama Press, 1985.

Bailey, L. R. *Indian Slave Trade in the Southwest*. Los Angeles: Westernlore Press, 1966.

Bancroft, Hubert Howe. *California Pastoral, 1769–1848*. San Francisco: History Company, 1888.

––––––. *History of California*. 7 vols. San Francisco: History Company, 1884–90.

Bannon, John Francis, ed. *Bolton and the Spanish Borderlands*. Norman: University of Oklahoma Press, 1964.

––––––. *Herbert Eugene Bolton: The Historian and the Man*. Tucson: University of Arizona Press, 1978.

––––––. *The Spanish Borderlands Frontier, 1513–1821*. New York: Holt, Rinehart and Winston, 1970.

Barbier, Jacques A. "Silver, North American Penetration and the Spanish Imperial Economy, 1760–1810." In *The North American Role in the Spanish Imperial Economy, 1760–*

1819, ed. by Jacques Barbier and Allan J. Kuethe. Manchester: Manchester University Press, 1984.

Barth, Pious. *Franciscan Education and the Social Order in North America, 1502–1821*. Chicago: n.p., 1950.

Basque, Joseph. "Law and Order in Texas, 1776–1786." *El Campanario* 19 (Dec. 1988): 17–48.

Baxter, John O. *Las Carneradas: Sheep Trade in New Mexico, 1700–1860*. Albuquerque: University of New Mexico Press, 1987.

Beerman, Eric. "Arturo O'Neill: First Governor of West Florida during the Second Spanish Period." *FHQ* 60 (July 1981): 29–41.

———. "The Death of an Old Conquistador: New Light on Juan de Oñate." *NMHR* 54 (Oct. 1979): 305–19.

———. " 'Yo Solo' not 'Solo': Juan Antonio de Riaño." *FHQ* 58 (Oct. 1979): 174–84.

Beilharz, Edwin A. *Felipe de Neve, First Governor of California*. San Francisco: California Historical Society, 1971.

Bemis, Samuel Flagg. *The Diplomacy of the American Revolution*. 1935. Bloomington: University of Indiana Press, 1961.

———. *Pinckey's Treaty: A Study of America's Advantage from Europe's Distress, 1783–1800*. 1926. New Haven: Yale University Press, 1960.

Benes, Ronald J. "Anza and Concha in New Mexico, 1787–93: A Study in Colonial Techniques." *JW* 4 (June 1965): 63–76.

Beninato, Stefanie. "Popé, Pose-yemu, and Naranjo: A New Look at Leadership in the Pueblo Revolt of 1680." *NMHR* 65 (Oct. 1990): 417–35.

Bennassar, Bartolomé. *The Spanish Character: Attitudes and Mentalities from the Sixteenth to the Nineteenth Century*. Trans. by Benjamin Keen. 1975. Berkeley: University of California Press, 1979.

Benson, Nettie Lee. "Bishop Marín de Porras and Texas." *SWHQ* 51 (July 1947): 16–40.

Bernabeu Albert, Salvador. "Juan Pérez, Navegante y Descubridor de las Californias (1768–1775)." In *Culturas de la Costa Noroeste de América*, ed. by José Luis Peset. Madrid: Turner, 1989.

———. "Viajes marítimos y exploraciones científicas al Pacífico Septentrional, 1767–1788." Ph.D. diss., Universidad Complutense de Madrid, 1989.

Bernstein, Harry. "Spanish Influence in the United States, Economic Aspects." *HAHR* 18 (Feb. 1938): 43–65.

Berry, Jane M. "The Indian Policy of Spain in the Southeast, 1783–1795." *JAH* 3 (Mar. 1917): 462–77.

Bethell, Leslie, ed. *Colonial Latin America*. Vols. 1 and 2 of *The Cambridge History of Latin America*. Cambridge: Cambridge University Press, 1984.

Billington, Ray Allen, ed. *Selected Essays of Frederick Jackson Turner*. Englewood Cliffs, N.J.: Prentice-Hall, 1961.

Bishop, Morris. *The Odyssey of Cabeza de Vaca*. New York: Century Co., 1933.

Blackmar, Frank W. *Spanish Institutions of the Southwest*. Baltimore: Johns Hopkins Press, 1891.

Blaine, Martha Royce. "French Efforts to Reach Santa Fe: André Fabry de la Bruyère's Voyage up the Canadian River in 1741–1742." *Louisiana History* 20 (Spring 1979): 133–57.

Blakeslee, Donald J. "The Mallet Expedition of 1739." *Wagon Tracks: Santa Fe Trail Association Quarterly* 5 (Feb. and May 1991): 15–18; 14–16.

Bloom, Lansing B. "Oñate's Exoneration." *NMHR* 12 (Apr. 1937): 175–92.

_____. "Spain's Investment in New Mexico under the Hapsburgs." *The Americas* 1 (July 1944): 3–14.

_____. "The Vargas Encomienda." *NMHR* 14 (Oct. 1939): 366–417.

Bobb, Bernard E. *The Viceregency of Antonio María Bucareli in New Spain, 1771–1779.* Austin: University of Texas Press, 1962.

Bolton, Herbert Eugene. *Coronado on the Turquoise Trail: Knight of Pueblos and Plains.* Albuquerque: University of New Mexico Press, 1949.

_____. "Defensive Spanish Expansion and the Significance of the Borderlands." In *Bolton and the Spanish Borderlands*, ed. by John Francis Bannon. Norman: University of Oklahoma Press, 1964.

_____. "French Intrusions into New Mexico, 1749–1752." In *Bolton and the Spanish Borderlands*, ed. by John Francis Bannon. Norman: University of Oklahoma Press, 1964.

_____. *The Hasinais: Southern Caddoans as Seen by the Earliest Europeans*, ed. by Russell M. Magnaghi. Norman: University of Oklahoma Press, 1987.

_____. "The Location of La Salle's Colony on the Gulf of Mexico." *SWHQ* 27 (Jan. 1924): 171–89.

_____. "The Mission as a Frontier Institution in the Spanish American Colonies." In *Bolton and the Spanish Borderlands*, ed. by John Francis Bannon. Norman: University of Oklahoma Press, 1964.

_____. "Need for the Publication of a Comprehensive Body of Documents Relating to the History of Spanish Activities within the Present Limits of the United States." In *Bolton and the Spanish Borderlands*, ed. by John Francis Bannon. Norman: University of Oklahoma Press, 1964.

_____. *Outpost of Empire: The Story of the Founding of San Francisco.* New York: Alfred A. Knopf, 1931.

_____. *Pageant in the Wilderness: The Story of the Escalante Expedition to the Interior Basin, 1776.* Salt Lake City: Utah State Historical Society, 1950.

_____. *The Spanish Borderlands: A Chronicle of Old Florida and the Southwest.* New Haven: Yale University Press, 1921.

_____. "Spanish Resistance to the Carolina Traders in Western Georgia, 1680–1704." *Georgia Historical Quarterly* 9 (June 1925): 115–30.

_____. *Texas in the Middle Eighteenth Century: Studies in Spanish Colonial History and Administration.* 1915. Austin: University of Texas Press, 1970.

Bolton, Herbert Eugene, and Thomas Maitland Marshall. *The Colonization of North America, 1492–1783.* New York: Macmillan, 1920.

Bolton, Herbert E., and Mary Ross. *The Debatable Land: A Sketch of Anglo-Spanish Contest for the Georgia Country.* Berkeley: University of California Press, 1925.

Boneu Companys, Fernando. *Gaspar de Portolá: Explorer and Founder of California.* Ed. and trans. by Alan K. Brown. Lérida: Instituto de Estudios Llerdenses, 1983.

Borah, Woodrow. "Hernán Cortés y sus intereses marítimos en el Pacífico, el Perú y la Baja California." *Estudios de historia novohispana* 4 (1971): 7–25.

Borah, Woodrow, and Sherburne F. Cook. "Marriage and Legitimacy in Mexican Culture: Mexico and California." *California Law Review* 54 (May 1966): 946–1008.

Borges, Pedro. *Métodos misionales en la cristianización de América, siglo xvi.* Madrid: Consejo Superior de Investigaciones Científicas, 1960.

Borja Medina Rojas, Francisco de. *José de Ezpeleta, Gobernador de la Mobila, 1780–1781.* Sevilla: Escuela de Estudios Hispano-Americanos, 1980.

Boulle, Pierre H. "French Reactions to the Louisiana Revolution of 1768." In *The French in the Mississippi Valley*, ed. by John Francis McDermott. Urbana: University of Illinois Press, 1965.

———. "Some Eighteenth-Century French Views on Louisiana." In *Frenchmen and French Ways in the Mississippi Valley*, ed. by John Francis McDermott. Urbana: University of Illinois Press, 1965.

Bowden, Henry Warner. *American Indians and Christian Missions: Studies in Cultural Conflict.* Chicago: University of Chicago Press, 1981.

Bowman, J. N. "The Resident Neophytes (*Existentes*) of the California Missions, 1769–1834." *SCQ* 40 (June 1958): 138–48.

Bowman, J. N., and Robert F. Heizer. *Anza and the Northwest Frontier of New Spain.* Los Angeles: Southwest Museum, 1967.

Boyd, E. *Popular Arts of New Mexico.* Santa Fe: Museum of Mexico, 1974.

Boyd, Mark F. "The Fortifications at San Marcos de Apalache." *FHQ* 15 (July 1936): 3–34.

Boyd, Mark F., Hale G. Smith, and John W. Griffin. *Here They Once Stood: The Tragic End of the Apalachee Missions.* Gainesville: University of Florida Press, 1951.

Brain, Jeffrey. "The Archaeology of the Hernando de Soto Expedition." In *AB.*

———. "Introduction: Update of De Soto Studies since the United States De Soto Expedition Commission Report." In *Final Report of the United States De Soto Expedition Commission*, ed. by John R. Swanton. 1939. Washington: Smithsonian Institution Press, 1985.

Brandon, William. *Quivira: Europeans in the Region of the Santa Fe Trail, 1540–1820.* Athens: Ohio University Press, 1990.

Brasseaux, Carl A. *The Founding of New Acadia: The Beginning of Acadian Life in Louisiana, 1765–1803.* Baton Rouge: Louisiana State University Press, 1987.

———. "François-Louis Hector, Baron de Carondelet et Noyelles." In *The Louisiana Governors from Iberville to Edwards*, ed. by Joseph G. Dawson. Baton Rouge: Louisiana State University Press, 1990.

———. "French Louisiana." In *A Guide to the History of Louisiana*, ed. by Light Townsend Cummins and Glen Jeansonne. Westport, Conn.: Greenwood Press, 1982.

Brew, J. O. "Hopi Prehistory and History to 1850." In *HNAI*, vol. 9.

Bridenbaugh, Carl. "Opechancanough: A Native American Patriot." In *Early Americans*, ed. by Carl Bridenbaugh. New York: Oxford University Press, 1981.

Briggs, Walter. *Without Noise of Arms: The 1776 Domínguez-Escalante Search for a Route from Santa Fe to Monterey.* Flagstaff, Ariz.: Northland Press, 1976.

Brinckerhoff, Sidney B. "The Last Years of Spanish Arizona, 1786–1821," *AW* 9 (Spring 1967): 5–20.

Brinton, Daniel G. *Notes on the Floridian Peninsula, Its Literary History, Indian Tribes and Antiquities.* Philadelphia: Joseph Sabin, 1859.

Brooks, Philip Coolidge. *Diplomacy and the Borderlands: The Adams-Onís Treaty of 1819.* Berkeley: University of California Press, 1939.

_____. "Spain's Farewell to Louisiana, 1803–1821." *JAH* 27 (June 1940): 29–42.

Brugge, David M. *Navajos in the Catholic Church Records of New Mexico, 1694–1875.* Tsaile, Ariz.: Navajo Community College Press, 1985.

_____. "Some Plains Indians in the Church Records of New Mexico." *Plains Anthropologist* 10 (Oct. 1965): 181–88.

Buckley, Eleanor. "The Aguayo Expedition into Texas and Louisiana, 1719–1722." *SWHQ* 15 (July 1911): 1–65.

Buerkle, Ruth Cowie. "The Continuing Military Presence." In *San Antonio in the Eighteenth Century.* San Antonio: San Antonio Bicentennial Heritage Committee, 1976.

Bunting, Bainbridge. *Early Architecture in New Mexico.* Albuquerque: University of New Mexico Press, 1976.

Burns, Francis P. "West Florida and the Louisiana Purchase, An Examination into the Question of Whether It Was Included in the Territory Ceded by the Treaty of 1803." *Louisiana Historical Quarterly* 15 (July 1932): 391–416.

Burrus, Ernest J. "Rivera y Moncada, Explorer and Military Commander of Both Californias, in the Light of His Diary and Other Contemporary Documents." *HAHR* 50 (Nov. 1970): 682–92.

Burson, Caroline Maude. *The Stewardship of Don Esteban Miró, 1782–1792.* New Orleans: American Printing Co., 1940.

Bushnell, Amy Turner. "The Archaeology of Mission Santa Catalina de Guale: Missions and the Support System of a Maritime Periphery." *Anthropological Papers of the American Museum of Natural History,* forthcoming.

_____. "How to Fight a Pirate: Provincials, Royalists, and the Defense of Minor Ports during the Age of Buccaneers." *Gulf Coast Historical Review* 5 (Spring 1990): 18–35.

_____. *The King's Coffer: Proprietors of the Spanish Florida Treasury, 1565–1702.* Gainesville: University of Florida Press, 1981.

_____. "The Menéndez Márquez Cattle Barony at La Chua and the Determinants of Economic Expansion in Seventeenth-Century Florida." *FHQ* 56 (Apr. 1978): 407–31.

_____. "The Noble and Loyal City, 1565–1688." In *The Oldest City: St Augustine, Saga of Survival,* ed. by Jean Parker Waterbury. St. Augustine: St. Augustine Historical Society, 1983.

_____. "Patricio de Hinachuba: Defender of the Word of God, the Crown of the King, and the Little Children of Ivitachuco." *American Indian Culture and Research Journal* 3 (July 1979): 1–21.

_____. "Ruling 'the Republic of Indians' in Seventeenth-Century Florida." In *PM.*

————. "The Sacramental Imperative: Catholic Ritual and Indian Sedentism in the Provinces of Florida." In *CC*, vol. 2.

————. " 'That Demonic Game': The Campaign to Stop Indian Pelota Playing in Spanish Florida, 1675–1684." *The Americas* 35 (July 1978): 1–19.

Bustamante, Adrian. " 'The Matter Was Never Resolved': The *Casta* System in Colonial New Mexico, 1693–1823." *NMHR* 66 (Apr. 1991): 143–64.

Campa, Arthur L. *Hispanic Culture in the Southwest*. Norman: University of Oklahoma Press, 1979.

Campbell, Leon G. "The First Californios: Presidial Society in Spanish California." *JW* 11 (Oct. 1972): 583–95.

————. "The Spanish Presidio in Alta California during the Mission Period, 1769–1784." *JW* 16 (Oct. 1977): 63–77.

Campbell, T. N. "Coahuiltecans and Their Neighbors." In *HNAI*, vol. 9.

Campbell, T. N., and T. J. Campbell. *Indian Groups Associated with Spanish Missions of San Antonio Missions National Historical Park*. San Antonio: University of Texas at San Antonio, Center for Archaeological Research, 1985.

Canny, Nicolas, and Anthony Pagden, eds. *Colonial Identity in the Atlantic World, 1500–1800*. Princeton: Princeton University Press, 1988.

Carlson, Alvar W. *Spanish-American Homeland: Four Centuries in New Mexico's Río Arriba*. Baltimore: Johns Hopkins University Press, 1990.

Caruso, John Anthony. *The Mississippi Valley Frontier: The Age of French Exploration and Settlement*. Indianapolis: Bobbs-Merrill, 1966.

Castañeda, Antonia I. "Comparative Frontiers: The Migration of Women to Alta California and New Zealand." In *Western Women: Their Land, Their Lives*, ed. by Lillian Schlissel, Vicki L. Ruiz, and Janice Monk. Albuquerque: University of New Mexico Press, 1988.

————. "Gender, Race, and Culture: Spanish-Mexican Women in the Historiography of Frontier California." *Frontiers: A Journal of Women Studies* 11 (1990): 8–30.

Castañeda, Carlos E. *Our Catholic Heritage in Texas, 1519–1936*. 7 Vols. Austin: Von Boeckmann-Jones, 1936–58.

————. "The Sons of St. Francis in Texas." *The Americas* 1 (Jan. 1945): 289–302.

Castillo, Edward D. "The Impact of Euro-American Exploration and Settlement." In *HNAI*, vol. 8

————. "The Native Response to the Colonization of Alta California." In *CC*, vol. 1.

Caughey, John Walton. *Bernardo de Gálvez in Louisiana, 1776–1783*. Berkeley: University of California Press, 1934.

————. *McGillivray of the Creeks*. Norman: University of Oklahoma Press, 1938.

————. "Herbert Eugene Bolton." In *Turner, Bolton, and Webb: Three Historians of the American Frontier*. Seattle: University of Washington Press, 1956.

Chabot, Frederick C. *Texas in 1811: The Las Casas and Sambrano Revolutions*. San Antonio: Yanaguana Society, 1941.

————. *With the Makers of San Antonio: Genealogies . . . .* San Antonio: Privately printed, 1937.

Chapman, Charles Edward. *The Founding of Spanish California: The Northwestward Expansion of New Spain, 1687–1783*. New York: Macmillan Co., 1916.

_____. *A History of California: The Spanish Period*. New York: Macmillan Co., 1921.

Chartkoff, Joseph L., and Kerry Kona Chartkoff. *The Archaeology of California*. Stanford: Stanford University Press, 1984.

Chatelain, Verne E. *The Defenses of Spanish Florida, 1565 to 1763*. Washington, D.C.: Carnegie Institution, 1941.

Chávez, Angélico. *Coronado's Friars*. Washington, D.C.: Academy of American Franciscan History, 1968.

_____. "The Gallegos Relación Reconsidered." *NMHR* 23 (Jan. 1948): 1–21.

_____. "Genízaros." In *HNAI*, vol. 9.

_____. *Our Lady of the Conquest*. Santa Fe: Historical Society of New Mexico, 1948.

_____. "Pohé-Yemo's Representative." *NMHR* 42 (Apr. 1967): 85–126.

Chávez, John R. *The Lost Land: The Chicano Image of the Southwest*. Albuquerque: University of New Mexico Press, 1984.

Chávez, Thomas E. "But Were They All Natives?" *El Palacio* 86 (Winter 1980–81): 32.

_____. "The Segesser Hide Paintings: History, Discovery, Art." *Great Plains Quarterly* 10 (Spring 1990): 96–109.

Chiappelli, Fredi, ed. *First Images of America: The Impact of the New World on the Old*. 2 vols. Berkeley: University of California Press, 1976.

Chipman, Donald E. "In Search of Cabeza de Vaca's Route across Texas: An Historiographical Survey." *SWHQ* 91 (Oct. 1987): 127–48.

_____. "The Oñate-Moctezuma-Zaldívar Families of Northern New Spain." *NMHR* 52 (Oct. 1977): 297–310.

Christiansen, Paige W. "Hugo O'Conor's Inspection of Nueva Vizcaya and Coahuila, 1773." *Louisiana Studies* 2 (Fall 1963): 157–75.

Cisneros, José. *Riders across the Centuries: Horsemen of the Spanish Borderlands*. El Paso: Texas Western Press, 1984.

Clark, John G. *New Orleans, 1718–1812: An Economic History*. Baton Rouge: Louisiana State University Press, 1970.

Clark, Robert C. *The Beginnings of Texas, 1684–1718*. Austin: University of Texas Bulletin, 1907.

_____. "Louis Juchereau de Saint Denis and the Re-establishment of the Tejas Missions." *SWHQ* 6 (July 1902): 1–26.

Clark, Thomas D., and John D. W. Guice. *Frontiers in Conflict: The Old Southwest, 1795–1830*. Albuquerque: University of New Mexico Press, 1989.

Cline, Gloria Griffen. *Exploring the Great Basin*. Norman: University of Oklahoma Press, 1963.

Coker, William S. "English Reaction to La Salle." In *La Salle and His Legacy: Frenchmen and Indians in the Lower Mississippi Valley*, ed. by Patricia K. Galloway. Jackson: University of Mississippi Press, 1982.

_____. "Father James Coleman, Vicar and Ecclesiastical Judge, Parish of San Miguel de Panzacola, 1794–1822." Paper read at the symposium, "Spanish Missionary Heritage of the United States," San Antonio, Nov. 1990.

_____. *The Financial History of Pensacola's Spanish Presidios, 1698–1763*. Pensacola: Pensacola Historical Society, 1979.

———. "The Reign of Charles III and Its Effect Upon *La Florida*." In *Charles III: Florida and the Gulf*. Coral Gables: Count of Gálvez Historical Society, 1990.

———. "Religious Censuses of Pensacola, 1796–1801," *FHQ* 61 (July 1981): 54–63.

Coker, William S., and Hazel P. Coker. *The Siege of Mobile, 1780, in Maps.* . . . Pensacola: Perdido Bay Press, 1982.

Coker, William S., and Hazel P. Coker. *The Siege of Pensacola, 1781, in Maps* . . . . Pensacola: Perdido Bay Press, 1981.

Coker, William S., and Robert R. Rea, eds. *Anglo-Spanish Confrontation on the Gulf Coast during the American Revolution*. Pensacola: Gulf Coast History and Humanities Conference, 1982.

Coker, William S., and Thomas D. Watson. *Indian Traders of the Southeastern Spanish Borderlands: Panton, Leslie & Company and John Forbes & Company, 1783–1847*. Pensacola: University of West Florida Press, 1986.

Connolly, Matthew J. "Four Contemporary Narratives of the Founding of St. Augustine." *Catholic Historical Review* 51 (Oct. 1965): 305–34.

Conway, G. R. G. "Antonio de Espejo, as a Familiar of the Mexican Inquisition, 1572–1578." *NMHR* 6 (Jan. 1931): 1–20.

Cook, Sherburne F. *The Conflict between the California Indian and White Civilization, 1943–1946*. Berkeley: University of California Press, 1976.

———. "Historical Demography." In *HNAI*, vol. 8.

———. *The Population of the California Indians, 1769–1970*. Berkeley: University of California, 1976.

Cook, Sherburne F., and Woodrow Borah. "Mission Registers as Sources of Vital Statistics: Eight Missions of Northern California." In *Essays in Population History*, ed. by Sherburne F. Cook and Woodrow Borah. Vol. 3 of *Mexico and California*. Berkeley: University of California Press, 1979.

Cook, Warren L. *Flood Tide of Empire: Spain and the Pacific Northwest, 1543–1819*. New Haven: Yale University Press, 1973.

Coombs, Gary B., and Fred Plog. "The Conversion of the Chumash Indians: An Ecological Interpretation." *Human Ecology* 5 (Dec. 1977):3 09–28.

Corbett, Theodore G. "Migration to a Spanish Imperial Frontier in the Seventeenth and Eighteenth Centuries: St. Augustine." *HAHR* 54 (Aug. 1974): 414–30.

———. "Population Structure in Hispanic St. Augustine, 1629–1763." *FHQ* 54 (Jan. 1976): 263–84.

———. "The Problem of the Household in the Second Spanish Period." In *Eighteenth-Century Florida: The Impact of the American Revolution*, ed. by Samuel Proctor. Gainesville: University Presses of Florida, 1978.

Corbin, James E. "Spanish-Indian Interaction on the Eastern Frontier of Texas." In *CC*, vol. 1.

Corbitt, Duvon Clough. "The Administrative System in the Floridas, 1781–1821." *Tequesta* 1 (Aug. 1942 and July 1943): 41–62; 57–67.

———. "Spanish Relief Policy and the East Florida Refugees of 1763." *FHQ* 27 (July 1948): 67–82.

Cordell, Linda S. *Prehistory of the Southwest*. Orlando, Fla.: Academic Press, 1984.

Cortés Alonso, Vicenta. "Geopolítica del sureste de los Estados Unidos, 1750–1800." *RI* 12 (Jan.–Mar. 1952): 23–47.

Costello, Julia G. "Variability among the Alta California Missions: The Economics of Agricultural Production." In *CC*, vol. 1.

Costello, Julia G., and David Hornbeck. "Alta California: An Overview." In *CC*, vol. 1.

Costo, Rupert. "The Indians before Invasion." In *The Missions of California: A Legacy of Genocide*, ed. by Rupert Costo and Jeanette Henry Costo. San Francisco: Indian Historian Press, 1987.

Costo, Rupert, and Jeannette Henry Costo, eds. *The Missions of California: A Legacy of Genocide*. San Francisco: Indian Historian Press, 1987.

Covington, James W. "The Apalachee Indians Move West." *Florida Anthropologist* 17 (Dec. 1964): 221–25.

———. "Drake Destroys St. Augustine: 1586." *FHQ* 44 (July–Oct. 1965): 81–93.

———. "Migration of the Seminoles into Florida, 1700–1820." *FHQ* 46 (Apr. 1968): 340–57.

———. "Some Observations concerning the Florida-Carolina Indian Slave Trade." *Florida Anthropologist* 20 (Mar.–June 1967): 10–18.

———. "Stuart's Town, the Yamasee Indians and Spanish Florida." *Florida Anthropologist* 21 (Mar. 1968): 8–13.

———. "The Yamasee Indians in Florida, 1715–1763." *Florida Anthropologist* 23 (Sept. 1970): 119–28.

Cowdrey, Albert E. *This Land, This South: An Environmental History*. Lexington: University of Kentucky Press, 1983.

Cox, Isaac Joslin. *The West Florida Controversy, 1798–1813*. Baltimore: Johns Hopkins Press, 1918.

Crane, Verner W. *The Southern Frontier, 1670–1732*. 1928. New York: W. W. Norton, 1981.

Crosby, Alfred W., Jr. *The Columbian Exchange: Biological and Cultural Consequences of 1492*. Westport, Conn: Greenwood Press, 1972.

———. *Ecological Imperialism: The Biological Expansion of Europe, 900–1900*. Cambridge: Cambridge University Press, 1986.

———. "Virgin Soil Epidemics as a Factor in the Aboriginal Depopulation of America." *William and Mary Quarterly* 33 (Apr. 1976): 289–99.

Crosby, Harry W. *Doomed to Fail: Gaspar de Portolá's First California Appointees*. San Diego: San Diego State University, Institute for Regional Studies of the Californias, 1989.

———. *King's Highway in Baja California: An Adventure into the History and Lore of a Forgotten Region*. San Diego: Copley Books, 1974.

Crouch, Dora P., Daniel J. Garr, and Axel I. Mundigo. *Spanish City Planning in North America*. Cambridge: MIT Press, 1982.

Cruz, Gilbert R. *Let There Be Towns: Spanish Municipal Origins in the American Southwest, 1610–1810*. College Station: Texas A&M University Press, 1988.

Cubeñas Peluzzo, José Antonio. *Presencia española e hispánica en la Florida desde el descubrimiento hasta el bicentenario*. Madrid: Ediciones Cultura Hispánica, 1978.

Cuello, José. "Beyond the 'Borderlands' Is the North of Colonial Mexico: A Latin-Americanist Perspective to the Study of the Mexican North and the United States South-west." In *Proceedings of the Pacific Coast Council on Latin American Studies*, vol. 9, ed. by Kristyna P. Demaree. San Diego: San Diego State University Press, 1982.

———. "The Persistence of Indian Slavery and Encomienda in the Northeast of Colonial Mexico, 1577–1723." *Journal of Social History* 21 (Summer 1988): 683–700.

Cumming, William P. *The Southeast in Early Maps*. Princeton: Princeton University Press, 1958.

Cummins, Light Townsend. "Families in Crisis: Domestic Violence, Desertion, and Divorce in Spanish Texas and Louisiana." Paper read at the Texas State Historical Association, Dallas, Texas, Mar. 1991.

———. "Luciano de Herrera and Spanish Espionage in British St. Augustine." *El Escribano* 16 (Fall 1979): 43–57.

———. "Oliver Pollock and George Rogers Clark's Service of Supply: A Case Study in Financial Disaster." In *Selected Papers from the 1985 and 1986 George Rogers Clark Trans-Apalachian Frontier History Conferences*, ed. by Robert J. Holden. Vincennes, Ind., 1988).

———. "Oliver Pollock's Plantations: An Early Anglo Landowner on the Lower Mississippi, 1769–1824." *Louisiana History* 29 (Winter 1988): 35–48.

———. "Spanish Administration in the Eastern Borderlands, 1763–1800." *Proceedings of the Pacific Coast Council on Latin American Studies* 7 (1980–1981): 1–9.

———. "Spanish Espionage in the South during the American Revolution." *Southern Studies* 20 (Spring 1980): 39–49.

———. "Spanish Historians and the Gulf Coast Campaigns." In *Anglo-Spanish Confrontation on the Gulf Coast during the American Revolution*, ed. by William S. Coker and Robert R. Rea. Pensacola: Gulf Coast History and Humanities Conference, 1982.

———. *Spanish Observers and the American Revolution, 1775–1783*. Baton Rouge: Louisiana State University Press, 1991.

Curley, Michael J. *Church and State in the Spanish Floridas (1783–1822)*. Washington, D.C.: Catholic University of America, 1940.

Cushing, Frank Hamilton. "Zuni and the Missionaries: Keeping the Old Ways." In *Selected Writings of Frank Hamilton Cushing*, ed. by Jesse Green. Lincoln: University of Nebraska Press, 1979.

Cutter, Charles R. *The Protector de Indios in Colonial New Mexico, 1659–1821*. Albuquerque: University of New Mexico Press, 1986.

Cutter, Donald C. *California in 1792: A Spanish Naval Visit*. Norman: University of Oklahoma Press, 1990.

———. *Malaspina in California*. San Francisco: John Howell Books, 1960.

———. "Plans for the Occupation of Upper California: A New Look at the 'Dark Age' from 1602–1769." *JSDH* 24 (Winter 1978): 78–90.

———. "Sources of the Name 'California.'" *AW* 3 (Autumn 1961): 233–44.

———. "Spanish Scientific Exploration along the Pacific Coast." 1963. In *NS*.

———. "With a Little Help from Their Saints." *PHR* 53 (May 1984): 123–40.

Daniel, James M. "The Spanish Frontier in West Texas and Northern Mexico." *SWHQ* 71 (Apr. 1968): 481–95.

Davis, Dave D., ed. *Perspectives on Gulf Coast Prehistory*. Gainesville: Florida State Museum and University of Florida Press, 1984.

Davis, Frederick T. "History of Juan Ponce de Leon's Voyages to Florida: Source Records." *FHQ* 14 (July 1935): 5–66.

Day, A. Grove. *Coronado's Quest: The Discovery of the Southwestern States*. Berkeley: University of California Press, 1940.

De la Teja, Jesús Francisco. "Forgotten Founders: The Military Settlers of Eighteenth-Century San Antonio de Béxar." In *Tejano Origins in Eighteenth-Century San Antonio*, ed. by Gerald E. Poyo and Gilberto M. Hinojosa. Austin: University of Texas Press for the University of Texas Insitute of Texan Cultures at San Antonio, 1991.

_____. "Indians, Soldiers, and Canary Islanders: The Making of a Texas Frontier Community." *Locus* 3 (Fall 1990): 81–96.

_____. "Land and Society in 18th Century San Antonio de Bexar: A Community on New Spain's Northern Frontier." Ph.D. diss., University of Texas, 1988.

Deagan, Kathleen A. "Archaeology of Sixteenth-Century St. Augustine." *Florida Anthropology* 38 (Mar.–June 1985): 6–23.

_____. "Cultures in Transition: Fusion and Assimilation among the Eastern Timucua." In *Tacachale*.

_____. "*Mestizaje* in Colonial St. Augustine." *Ethnohistory* 20 (Winter 1973): 55–65.

_____. "Spanish-Indian Interaction in Sixteenth-Century Florida and Hispaniola." In *Cultures in Contact: The European Impact on Native Cultural Institutions, A.D. 1000–1800*, ed. by William W. Fitzhugh. Washington, D.C.: Smithsonian Institution Press, 1985.

_____. "Spanish St. Augustine: America's First 'Melting Pot.'" *Archaeology* 33 (Sept.–Oct. 1980): 22–30.

_____, ed. *Spanish St. Augustine: The Archaeology of a Colonial Creole Community*. New York: Academic Press, 1983.

DeConde, Alexander. *This Affair of Louisiana*. New York: Charles Scribner's Sons, 1976.

Deeds, Susan M. "Rural Work in Nueva Vizcaya: Forms of Labor Coercion on the Periphery." *HAHR* 69 (Aug. 1989): 425–49.

Delgado, Edmundo. "A Spanish Ranker in New Mexico: Captain Manuel Delgado of Santa Fe, 1738–1815." *NMHR* 66 (Jan. 1991): 1–13.

Denevan, William M. "Epilogue." In *The Native Population of the Americas in 1492*, ed. by William M. Denevan. Madison: University of Wisconsin Press, 1976.

_____. "Livestock Numbers in Nineteenth-Century New Mexico, and the Problem of Gullying in the Southwest." *Annals of the Association of American Geographers* 57 (4): 691–703.

_____, ed. *The Native Population of the Americas in 1492*. Madison: University of Wisconsin Press, 1976.

DePratter, Chester B. "Cofitachequi: Ethnohistorical and Archaeological Evidence." In *Studies in South Carolina Archaeology: Essays in Honor of Robert L. Stephenson*, ed. by Albert C. Goodyear III and Glen T. Hanson. Columbia, S.C.: Carolina Institute of Archaeology and Anthropology, 1989.

DePratter, Chester B., Charles M. Hudson, and Marvin T. Smith. "The Hernando de Soto Expedition: From Chiaha to Mabila." In *AB*.

Di Peso, Charles. *Casas Grandes: A Fallen Trading Center of the Gran Chichimeca*. 8 vols. Flagstaff, Ariz.: Northland Press, 1974.

Dickason, Olive Patricia. "Old World Law, New World Peoples, and Concepts of Sovereignty." In *Essays on the History of North American Discovery and Exploration*, ed. by Stanley H. Palmer and Dennis Reinhartz. College Station: Texas A&M University Press for the University of Texas at Arlington, 1988.

Din, Gilbert C. "Arkansas Post in the American Revolution." *Arkansas Historical Quarterly* 40 (Spring 1981): 3–30.

———. *The Canary Islanders of Louisiana*. Baton Rouge: Louisiana State University Press, 1988.

———. "The Immigration Policy of Governor Esteban Miró in Spanish Louisiana." *SWHQ* 73 (Oct. 1969): 155–75.

———. "The Irish Mission to West Florida." *Louisiana History* 12 (Fall 1971): 315–34.

———. "Lieutenant Colonel Francisco Bouligny and the Malagueño Settlement at New Iberia, 1779." *Louisiana History* 17 (Spring 1976): 187–202.

———. "Spain's Immigration Policy in Louisiana and the American Penetration, 1792–1803," *SWHQ* 76 (Jan. 1973): 255–76.

———. "War Clouds on the Mississippi: Spain's 1785 Crisis in West Florida." *FHQ* 60 (July 1981): 51–76.

Din, Gilbert C., and Abraham P. Nasatir. *The Imperial Osages: Spanish-Indian Diplomacy in the Mississippi Valley*. Norman: University of Oklahoma Press, 1983.

Dobyns, Henry F. *From Fire to Flood: Historic Human Destruction of Sonoran Desert Riverine Oases*. Socorro, N.M.: Ballena Press, 1981.

———. "More Methodological Perspectives on Historical Demography." *Ethnohistory* 36 (Summer 1989): 285–99.

———. *Spanish Colonial Tucson: A Demographic History*. Tucson: University of Arizona Press, 1976.

———. *Their Number Become Thinned: Native American Population Dynamics in Eastern North America*. Knoxville: University of Tennessee Press, 1983.

———. "Who Killed the Gila." *JAZH* 19 (Spring 1978): 17–30.

———, et al. "What Were Nixoras?" *Southwestern Journal of Anthropology* 16 (Summer 1960): 230–58.

Dockstader, Frederick J. *The Kachina and the White Man: The Influences of White Culture on the Hopi Kachina Cult*. 1954. Rev. ed., Albuquerque: University of New Mexico Press, 1985.

Donahue, William H. "Mary of Agreda and the Southwest [*sic*] United States." *The Americas* 9 (Jan. 1953): 291–314.

Doolittle, William E. "Las Marismas to Pánuco to Texas: The Transfer of Open Range Cattle Ranching from Iberia through Northeastern Mexico." *Yearbook, Conference of Latin Americanist Geographers* 13 (1987): 3–11.

Downs, Fane. "Governor Antonio Martínez and the Defense of Texas from Foreign Invasion, 1817–1822." *Texas Military History* 7 (Spring 1968): 27–43.

Doyel, David E. "The Transition to History in Northern Pimería Alta." In *CC*, vol. 1.

Dozier, Edward P. *The Pueblo Indians of North America*. New York: Holt, Rinehart and Winston, 1970.

_____. "Rio Grande Pueblos." In *Perspectives in American Indian Culture Change*, ed. by Edward H. Spicer. Chicago: University of Chicago Press, 1961.

Dunkle, John R. "Population Change as an Element in the Historical Geography of St. Augustine." *FHQ* 33 (July 1958): 3–32.

Dunn, Fabius. "The Concern of the Spanish Government of Texas over United States Expansionism, 1805–1808." *Louisiana Studies* 4 (Spring 1965): 45–61.

Dunn, William Edward. "Apache Relations in Texas, 1718–1750." *SWHQ* 14 (Jan. 1911): 198–274.

_____. *Spanish and French Rivalry in the Gulf Region of the United States, 1678–1702: The Beginnings of Texas and Pensacola*. Austin: University of Texas Press, 1917.

Dunne, Peter Masten. *Black Robes in Lower California*. Berkeley: University of California Press, 1952.

Dye, David H. "Warfare in the Sixteenth-Century Southeast: The De Soto Expedition in the Interior." In *CC*, vol. 2.

Eaton, Jack D. "The Gateway Missions of the Lower Rio Grande." In *CC*, vol. 1.

Eccles, W. J. *France in America*. New York: Harper & Row, 1972.

Egan, Clifford H. "The United States, France, and West Florida, 1803–1807," *FHQ* 48 (Jan. 1969): 227–52.

Ekberg, Carl J. *Colonial Ste. Genevieve: An Adventure on the Mississippi Frontier*. Gerald, Mo.: Patrice Press, 1985.

Elliott, J. H. "The Discovery of America and the Discovery of Man." In *Spain and Its World, 1500–1700: Selected Essays*, ed. by J. H. Elliott. New Haven: Yale University Press, 1989.

_____. *Imperial Spain, 1469–1716*. 1963. Harmondsworth, Eng.: Penguin Books, 1975.

_____. *The Old World and the New*. Cambridge: Cambridge University Press, 1970.

_____. "Renaissance Europe and America: A Blunted Impact?" In *First Images of America: The Impact of the New World on the Old*, ed. by Fredi Chiappelli. 2 vols. Berkeley: University of California Press, 1976.

_____. *Spain and Its World, 1500–1700: Selected Essays*. New Haven: Yale University Press, 1989.

_____. "The Spanish Conquest and Settlement of America." In *Colonial Latin America*, ed. by Leslie Bethell. Vol. 1 of *The Cambridge History of Latin America*. Cambridge: Cambridge University Press, 1984.

Ellis, Florence Hawley. "The Long Lost 'City' of San Gabriel del Yungue, Second Oldest European Settlement in the United States." In *When Cultures Meet: Remembering San Gabriel del Yunge Oweenge*. Santa Fe: Sunstone Press, 1987.

Engstrand, Iris H. W. *Spanish Scientists in the New World: The Eighteenth Century Expeditions*. Seattle: University of Washington Press, 1981.

Espinosa, Carmen. *Shawls, Crinolines, Filigree: The Dress and Adornment of the Women of New Mexico, 1739–1900*. El Paso: Texas Western Press, 1970.

Espinosa, J. Manuel. *Crusaders of the Río Grande: The Story of Don Diego de Vargas and the Reconquest and Refounding of New Mexico*. Chicago: Institute of Jesuit History, 1942.

_____. "The Legend of Sierra Azul." *NMHR* 9 (Apr. 1934): 113–58.

_____. "Our Debt to the Franciscan Missionaries of New Mexico." *The Americas* 1 (July 1944): 79–87.

Espinosa, José E. *Saints in the Valleys: Christian Sacred Images in the History, Life, and Folk Art of Spanish New Mexico*. 1960. Albuquerque: University of New Mexico Press, 1967.

Everett, Dianna. *The Texas Cherokees: A People between Two Fires, 1819–1840*. Norman: University of Oklahoma Press, 1990.

Ewen, Charles R. "Anhaica: Discovery of Hernando de Soto's 1539–1540 Winter Camp." In *FE*.

———. "Soldier of Fortune: Hernando de Soto in the Territory of the Apalachee, 1539–1540." In *CC*, vol. 2.

Ewers, John C. "The Influence of Epidemics on the Populations and Cultures of Texas." *Plains Anthropologist* 18 (May 1973): 104–15.

———. "Symbols of Chiefly Authority in Spanish Louisiana." In *The Spanish in the Mississippi Valley, 1762–1804*, ed. by John Francis McDermott. Urbana: University of Illinois Press, 1974.

Ezell, Paul H. "The Hispanic Acculturation of the Gila River Pimas." *American Anthropologist* 63 (Oct. 1961): 1–171.

———. "History of the Pima." In *HNAI*, vol. 9.

Fairbanks, Charles H. "From Exploration to Settlement: Spanish Strategies for Colonization." In *AB*.

Fairbanks, George R. *History and Antiquities of St. Augustine, Florida, Founded September 8, 1565*. 3d ed. Jacksonville: Horace Drew, 1881.

———. *History of Florida: From Its Discovery by Ponce de Leon, in 1512, to the Close of the Florida War, in 1842*. Philadelphia: J. B. Lippincott & Co., 1871.

Farmer, John. "Piñeda's Sketch." *SWHQ* 63 (July 1959): 110–14.

Faulk, Odie B. "The Comanche Invasion of Texas, 1743–1836." *Great Plains Journal* 9 (Sept. 1969): 10–50.

———. *Last Years of Spanish Texas, 1778–1821*. The Hague: Mouton & Co., 1964.

———. "The Presidio: Fortress or Farce?" 1969. In *NS*.

Ferguson, T. J. "The Emergence of Modern Zuni Culture and Society: A Summary of Zuni Tribal History, A.D. 1450 to 1700." In *The Protohistoric Period in the North American Southwest: A.D. 1450–1700*, ed. by David R. Wilcox and W. Bruce Masse. Tempe: Arizona State University Anthropological Research Papers, 1981.

Ferguson, T. J., and E. Richard Hart. *A Zuni Atlas*. Norman: University of Oklahoma Press, 1985.

Fergusson, Erna. *Dancing Gods: Indian Ceremonials of New Mexico and Arizona*. Albuquerque: University of New Mexico Press, 1931.

Fernández-Florez, Dario. *The Spanish Heritage in the United States*. Madrid: Publicaciones Españolas, 1971.

Fernández-Shaw, Carlos M. *Presencia española en los Estados Unidos*. 1972. Madrid: Ediciones Cultura Hispánica, 1987.

Fireman, Janet R. "The Seduction of George Vancouver: A Nootka Affair." *PHR* 56 (Aug. 1987): 427–43.

———. *The Spanish Royal Corps of Engineers in the Western Borderlands: Instrument of Bourbon Reforms, 1764 to 1815*. Glendale, Calif.: Arthur H. Clark Co., 1977.

Fitzhugh, William W., ed. *Cultures in Contact: The European Impact on Native Cultural Institutions, A.D. 1000–1800*. Washington, D.C.: Smithsonian Institution Press, 1985.

Flagler, Edward K. "Governor José Chacón, Marqués de la Peñuela: An Andalusian Nobleman on the New Mexico Frontier." *NMHR* 65 (Oct. 1990): 455–75.

Flint, Timothy. *Condensed Geography and History of the Western States or the Mississippi Valley*. 2 vols. Cincinnati: E. H. Flint, 1828.

Flores, Dan L. "The Ecology of the Red River in 1806: Peter Custis and Early Southwestern Natural History." *SWHQ* 88 (July 1984): 1–42.

Foley, William E. *The Genesis of Missouri: From Wilderness Outpost to Statehood*. Columbia: University of Missouri Press, 1989.

Folmer, Henri. "Contraband Trade between Louisiana and New Mexico in the Eighteenth Century." *NMHR* 16 (July 1941): 265–66.

———. "The Mallet Expedition of 1739 through Nebraska, Kansas and Colorado to Santa Fe." *Colorado Magazine* 16 (Sept. 1939): 161–73.

———. "Report on Louis de Saint Denis' Intended Raid on San Antonio in 1721." *SWHQ* 52 (July 1948): 83–88.

Folmer, Henry [Henri]. *Franco-Spanish Rivalry in North America, 1524–1763*. Glendale, Calif.: Arthur H. Clark Co., 1953.

Fontana, Bernard L. "Biography of a Desert Church: The Story of Mission San Xavier del Bac." *Smoke Signal* 3 (Spring 1961): 2–24.

———. "Indians and Missionaries of the Southwest during the Spanish Years: Cross Cultural Perceptions and Misperceptions." In *Proceedings of the 1984 and 1985 San Antonio Missions Research Conferences*. San Antonio: LEBCO Graphics, 1986.

Foote, Cheryl. "Spanish-Indian Trade along New Mexico's Frontier in the Eighteenth Century." *JW* 24 (Apr. 1985): 25–30.

Foote, Cheryl J., and Sandra K. Schackel. "Indian Women of New Mexico, 1535–1680." In *New Mexico Women: Intercultural Perspectives*, ed. by Joan M. Jensen and Darlis A. Miller. Albuquerque: University of New Mexico Press, 1986.

Forbes, Jack D. *Apache, Navaho, and Spaniard*. Norman: University of Oklahoma Press, 1960.

———. "Hispano-Mexican Pioneers of the San Francisco Bay Region: An Analysis of Racial Origins." *Aztlán* 14 (Spring 1983): 175–89.

———. *Warriors of the Colorado: The Yumas of the Quechan Nation and Their Neighbors*. Norman: University of Oklahoma Press, 1965.

Forbes, James Grant. *Sketches, Historical and Topographical, of the Floridas; More Particularly of East Florida*. Intro. by James W. Covington. 1821. Gainesville: University of Florida Press, 1964.

Ford, Lawrence Carroll. *The Triangular Struggle for Spanish Pensacola, 1689–1739*. Washington, D.C.: Catholic University of America Press, 1939.

Ford, Richard I. "The New Pueblo Economy." In *When Cultures Meet: Remembering San Gabriel del Yunge Oweenge*. Santa Fe: Sunstone Press, 1987.

Foster, George. *Culture and Conquest: America's Spanish Heritage*. Chicago: Wenner-Gren Foundation, 1960.

Fox, Daniel E., ed. *Traces of Texas History: Archaeological Evidence of the Past 450 Years*. San Antonio: Corona Publishing Co., 1983.

Frank, Ross. "From Settler to Citizen: Economic Development and Cultural Change in Late Colonial New Mexico, 1750–1820." Ph.D. diss., University of California, Berkeley, forthcoming.

Gannon, Michael V. "Conflicto entre iglesia y estado en Florida: Administración del Gobernador don Juan Márquez Cabrera, 1680–1687." In *La influencia de España en el Caribe, la Florida, y la Luisiana, 1500–1800,* ed. by Antonio Acosta and Juan Marchena. Madrid: Instituto de Cooperación Iberoamericana, 1983.

———. *The Cross in the Sand: The Early Catholic Church in Florida, 1513–1870.* Gainesville: University of Florida Press, 1965.

———. "Defense of Native American and Franciscan Rights." In *CC,* vol. 2.

García, Mario T. "A Chicano Perspective on San Diego History." *JSDH* 18 (Fall 1971): 14–21.

Garner, Van Hastings. "The Dynamics of Change, New Mexico 1680 to 1690." *JW* 18 (Jan. 1979): 4–13.

———. "Seventeenth Century New Mexico." *Journal of Mexican American History* 4 (1974): 41–70.

Garr, Daniel J. "A Frontier Agrarian Settlement: San José de Guadalupe, 1777–1850." *San José Studies* 2 (Nov. 1976): 93–105.

———. "Monterey: Planless Capital." In *Spanish City Planning in North America,* ed. by Dora P. Crouch, Daniel J. Garr, and Axel I. Mundigo. Cambridge: MIT Press, 1982.

———. "Power and Priorities: Church-State Boundary Disputes in Spanish California." *CHSQ* 57 (Winter 1978–1979): 364–75.

———. "A Rare and Desolate Land: Population and Race in Hispanic California." *WHQ* 6 (Apr. 1975): 133–44.

———. "Villa de Branciforte: Innovation and Adaptation on the Frontier." *The Americas* 35 (July 1978): 95–109.

Garrahy, Stephen T., and David J. Weber. "Francisco de Ulloa, Joseph James Markey, and the Discovery of Upper California." *CHSQ* 50 (Mar. 1971): 73–77.

Garrett, Julia Kathryn. *Green Flag over Texas: The Last Years of Spain in Texas.* 1939. Austin: Pemberton Press, 1969.

Gayarré, Charles. *History of Louisiana: The Spanish Dominion.* New York, Redfield, 1854.

Geiger, Maynard. *Biographical Dictionary of the Franciscans in Spanish Florida and Cuba, 1528–1841.* Vol. 21 of Franciscan Studies. Paterson, N.J.: St. Anthony Guild Press, 1940.

———. *The Franciscan Conquest of Florida, 1573–1618.* Washington, D.C.: Catholic University of America, 1937.

———. *Franciscan Missionaries in Hispanic California, 1769–1848.* San Marino, Calif.: Huntington Library, 1969.

———. *The Life and Times of Fray Junípero Serra, O.F.M.* 2 vols. Washington, D.C.: Academy of American Franciscan History, 1959.

Gerhard, Peter. *The North Frontier of New Spain.* Princeton, N.J.: Princeton University Press, 1982.

Gibson, Arrell M. *The Chickasaws.* Norman: University of Oklahoma Press, 1971.

Gibson, Charles. *The Aztecs under Spanish Rule: The Indians of the Valley of Mexico, 1519–1810.* Stanford: Stanford University Press, 1964.

_____. "Conquest, Capitulation, and Indian Treaties." *AHR* 83 (Feb. 1978): 1–15.

_____. *Spain in America*. New York: Harper & Row, 1956.

Gillaspie, William R. "Sergeant Major Ayala y Escobar and the Threatened St. Augustine Mutiny [1712]." *FHQ* 47 (Oct 1968): 151–64.

_____. "Survival of a Frontier Presidio: St. Augustine and the Subsidy and Private Contract Systems, 1680–1702." *FHQ* 57 (Jan. 1984): 273–95.

Gilmore, Kathleen Kirk. *The San Xavier Missions: A Study in Historical Site Identification*. Archaeological Program Report, no. 16. Austin: State Building Commission, 1969.

_____. "The Indians of Mission Rosario: From the Books and from the Ground." In *CC*, vol. 1.

Giraud, Marcel. *The Reign of Louis XIV, 1698–1715*. Vol. 1 of *History of French Louisiana*. Trans. by Joseph C. Lambert. 1st ed. in French, 1953. Baton Rouge: Louisiana State University Press, 1974.

Glick, Thomas F. *The Old World Background of the Irrigation System of San Antonio, Texas*. El Paso: Texas Western Press, 1972.

Goetzmann, William H. *Exploration and Empire: The Explorer and the Scientist in the Winning of the American West*. New York: Alfred A. Knopf, 1967.

Gold, Robert L. *Borderlands Empires in Transition: The Triple-Nation Transfer of Florida*. Carbondale: University of Southern Illinois Press, 1969.

_____. "Governor Bernardo de Gálvez and Spanish Espionage in Pensacola, 1777." In *The Spanish in the Mississippi Valley, 1762–1804*, ed. by John Francis McDermott. Urbana: University of Illinois Press, 1974.

Goldman, Irving. "The Zuni Indians of New Mexico." In *Cooperation and Competition among Primitive Peoples*, ed. by Margaret Mead. New York: McGraw-Hill, 1937.

Gómez Canedo, Lino. *Evangelización y conquista: Experiencia franciscana en hispanoamérica*. Mexico: Editorial Porrúa, 1977.

Góngora, Mario. "The Conquistador and the Rewards of Conquest." In *Studies in the Colonial History of Spanish America*, ed. by Mario Góngora, trans. by Richard Southern. Cambridge: Cambridge University Press, 1975.

_____. *Studies in the Colonial History of Spanish America*. Trans. by Richard Southern. Cambridge: Cambridge University Press, 1975.

González Ruis, F. [Felipe]. *De la Florida a San Francisco. Los exploradores españoles en los Estados Unidos*. Buenos Aires: Ibero-Americana, 1949.

Goodwin, Grenville. *Western Apache Raiding and Warfare*. Ed. by Keith H. Basso. Tucson: University of Arizona Press, 1971.

Gradie, Charlotte M. "Spanish Jesuits in Virginia: The Mission That Failed." *The Virginia Magazine of History and Biography* 96 (Apr. 1988): 131–56.

Green, Michael D. *The Politics of Indian Removal: Creek Government and Society in Crisis*. Lincoln: University of Nebraska Press, 1982.

Greenhow, Robert. *The History of Florida, Louisiana, Texas, and California . . . .* New York: Privately printed, 1856.

Griffen, William B. "Apache Indians and the Northern Mexican Peace Establishments." In *Southwestern Culture History: Collected Papers in Honor of Albert H. Schroeder*, ed. by Charles H. Lange. Santa Fe: Ancient City Press, 1985.

———. *Apaches at War and Peace: The Janos Presidio, 1750–1858*. Albuquerque: University of New Mexico Press, 1988.

———. "Spanish Pensacola, 1700–63." *FHQ* 37 (Jan.–Apr. 1959): 242–63.

Griffin, Charles Carol. *The United States and the Disruption of the Spanish Empire, 1810–1822*. New York: Columbia University Press, 1937.

Griffin, James B. "Changing Concepts of the Prehistoric Mississippian Cultures of the Eastern United States." In *AB*.

Griffin, Patricia C. "The Minorcans." In *Clash between Cultures: Spanish East Florida, 1784–1821*, ed. by Jacqueline Fretwell and Susan R. Parker. St. Augustine: St. Augustine Historical Society, 1988.

Griffith, William Joyce. "The Hasinai Indians of East Texas as Seen by Europeans, 1687–1772." In *Philological and Documentary Studies*, vol. 2. 1954. New Orleans: Tulane University Middle American Research Institute, 1977.

Grimes, Ronald L. *Symbol and Conquest: Public Ritual and Drama in Santa Fe, New Mexico*. Ithaca, N.Y.: Cornell University Press, 1976.

Gritzner, Charles F. "Hispanic Log Construction of New Mexico." *El Palacio* 85 (Winter 1979): 20–29.

Grizzard, Mary. *Spanish Colonial Art and Architecture of Mexico and the U.S. Southwest*. Lanham, Md.: University Press of America, 1986.

Gronet, Richard W. "United States and the Invasion of Texas, 1810–1814." *The Americas* 25 (Jan. 1969): 281–306.

Guest, Francis F.. "Cultural Perspectives on California Mission Life." *SCQ* 65 (Spring 1985): 1–65.

———. "An Examination of the Thesis of S. F. Cook on the Forced Conversion of Indians in the California Missions." *SCQ* (Spring 1979): 1–77.

———. *Fermín Francisco de Lasuén (1736–1803): A Biography*. Washington, D.C.: Academy of American Franciscan History, 1973.

———. "The Foundation of the Villa de Branciforte." *CHSQ* 41 (Mar. 1962): 29–50.

———. "An Inquiry into the Role of the Discipline in California Mission Life." *SCQ* 71 (Spring 1989): 1–68.

———. "Mission Colonization and Political Control in Spanish California." *JSDH* 24 (Winter 1978): 97–116.

———. "Municipal Government in Spanish California," *CHSQ* 46 (Dec. 1967): 307–35.

———. "New Look at the California's Missions [sic]." In *Some Reminiscences about Fray Junípero Serra*. Ed. by Francis J. Weber. Santa Barbara: Knights of Columbus, 1985.

Guice, C. Norman. "Trade Goods for Texas: An Incident in the History of the Jeffersonian Embargo." *SWHQ* 60 (Apr. 1957): 507–19.

Gunnerson, Dolores A. *The Jicarilla Apaches: A Study in Survival*. DeKalb: Northern Illinois University Press, 1974.

Gutiérrez, Ramón A. "Aztlán, Montezuma, and New Mexico: The Political Uses of American Indian Mythology." In *Aztlán: Essays on the Chicano Homeland*, ed. by Rudolfo A. Anaya and Francisco A. Lomelí. Albuquerque: Academia/El Norte Publications, 1989.

_____. *When Jesus Came, the Corn Mothers Went Away: Marriage, Sexuality, and Power in New Mexico, 1500–1846*. Stanford: Stanford University Press, 1991.

Habig, Marion A. "The Franciscan Provinces of Spanish North America." *The Americas* 1 (July and Oct. 1944; Jan. 1945): 88–96; 215–30; 330–44.

_____. "Mission San José y San Miguel de Aguayo, 1720–1824." *SWHQ* 71 (Apr. 1968): 503–16.

Hackett, Charles Wilson. "The Marquis of San Miguel de Aguayo and His Recovery of Texas from the French, 1719–1723." *SWHQ* 49 (Oct. 1945): 193–214.

_____. "New Light on Don Diego de Peñalosa: Proof That He Never Made an Expedition from Santa Fe to Quivira and the Mississippi River in 1662." *JAH* 6 (Dec. 1919): 313–35.

Hafen, LeRoy R., and Ann W. Hafen. *Old Spanish Trail: Santa Fé to Los Angeles*. Glendale, Calif.: Arthur H. Clark Co., 1954.

Haggard, J. Villasana. "The Counter-Revolution of Béxar, 1811." *SWHQ* 43 (Oct. 1938): 222–35.

_____. "The House of Barr and Davenport." *SWHQ* 49 (July 1945): 66–88.

_____. "The Neutral Ground between Louisiana and Texas, 1806–1821." *Louisiana Historical Quarterly* 28 (Oct. 1945): 1001–1128.

Hague, Harlan. *The Road to California: The Search for A Southern Overland Route, 1540–1848*. Glendale, Calif.: Arthur H. Clark Co., 1978.

Hall, G. Emlen. *Four Leagues of Pecos: A Legal History of the Pecos Grant, 1800–1933*. Albuquerque: University of New Mexico, 1984.

Hall, G. Emlen, and David J. Weber. "Mexican Liberals and the Pueblo Indians, 1821–1829." *NMHR* 59 (Jan. 1984): 5–32.

Hall, Thomas D. *Social Change in the Southwest, 1350–1880*. Lawrence: University Press of Kansas, 1989.

Hallenbeck, Cleve. *Alvar Núñez Cabeza de Vaca: The Journey and Route of the First European to Cross the Continent of North America, 1534–36*. Glendale, Calif.: Arthur H. Clark, 1940.

Hally, David J., Marvin T. Smith, and James B. Langford, Jr. "The Archaeological Reality of de Soto's Coosa." In *CC*, vol. 2.

Hamilton, Peter J. *Colonial Mobile: An Historical Study*. Boston: Houghton Mifflin, 1897.

Hammond, George P. *Don Juan de Oñate and the Founding of New Mexico*. Santa Fe: El Palacio Press, 1927.

_____. "Oñate's Effort to Gain Political Autonomy for New Mexico." *HAHR* 32 (Aug. 1952): 321–30.

_____. "The Search for the Fabulous in the Settlement of the Southwest." 1956. In *NS*.

Hammond, George P., and Agapito Rey. "The Crown's Participation in the Founding of New Mexico." *NMHR* 32 (Oct. 1957): 293–309.

Hanke, Lewis. *Aristotle and the American Indians*. London: Hollis & Carter, 1959.

_____. *The Spanish Struggle for Justice in the Conquest of America*. Philadelphia: University of Pennsylvania Press, 1949.

_____, ed. *Do the Americas Have a Common History? A Critique of the Bolton Theory*. New York: Alfred A. Knopf, 1964.

Hann, John H. *Apalachee: The Land between the Rivers*. Gainesville: University of Florida Press and Florida State Museum, 1988.

———. "Demographic Patterns and Changes in Mid-Seventeenth Century Timucua and Apalachee." *FHQ* 64 (Apr. 1986): 371–92.

———. "St. Augustine's Fallout from the Yamasee War." *FHQ* 68 (Oct. 1989): 180–96.

———. "Twilight of the Mocamo and Guale Aborigines as Portrayed in the 1695 Spanish Visitation." *FHQ* 66 (July 1987): 1–24.

Harman, Joyce Elizabeth. *Trade and Privateering in Spanish Florida, 1732–1763*. St. Augustine: St. Augustine Historical Society, 1969.

Hatcher, Mattie Austin. "The Municipal Government of San Fernando de Bexar, 1730–1800." *SWHQ* 8 (Apr. 1905): 227–352.

———. *The Opening of Texas to Foreign Settlement, 1801–1821*. Austin: University of Texas, 1927.

Haynes, Robert V. *The Natchez District and the American Revolution*. Jackson: University Press of Mississippi, 1976.

Heizer, Robert F. "Impact of Colonization on the Native California Societies." *JSDH* 24 (Winter 1978): 121–39.

———. *California's Oldest Historical Relic?* Berkeley: University of California, Robert W. Lowie Museum of Anthropology, 1974.

———, ed. *California*. Vol. 8. of *Handbook of North American Indians*. Ed. by William C. Sturtevant. Washington, D.C.: Smithsonian Institution Press, 1978.

Held, Ray E. "Hernando de Miranda, Governor of Florida, 1574–1577." *FHQ* 28 (Oct. 1949): 111–30.

Henige, David. "The Context, Content, and Credibility of La Florida del Inca." *The Americas* 43 (July 1986): 1–23.

———. "If Pigs Could Fly: Timucuan Population and Native American Historical Demography." *Journal of Interdisciplinary History* 4 (Spring 1986): 701–20.

———. "Primary Source by Primary Source? On the Role of Epidemics in New World Depopulation." *Ethnohistory* 33 (Summer 1986): 293–312.

Hernández, Salomé. "No Settlement without Women: Three Spanish California Settlement Schemes, 1790–1800." *SCQ* 72 (Fall 1990): 203–34.

———. "*Nueva Mexicanas* as Refugees and Reconquest Setters, 1680–1696." In *New Mexico Women: Intercultural Perspectives*, ed. by Joan M. Jensen and Darlis A. Miller. Albuquerque: University of New Mexico Press, 1986.

Hernández Sánchez-Barba, Mario. *La última expansión española en América*. Madrid: Instituto de Estudios Políticos, 1957.

Hester, Thomas R. "Perspectives on the Material Culture of the Mission Indians of Texas—Northeastern Mexico Borderlands." In *CC*, vol. 1.

———. "Texas and Northeastern Mexico: An Overview." In *CC*, vol. 1.

Higginbotham, Jay. *Old Mobile: Fort Louis de la Louisiane*. Mobile: Museum of the City of Mobile, 1977.

Hill, Lawrence F. *José de Escandón and the Founding of Nuevo Santander: A Study in Spanish Administration*. Columbus: Ohio State University Press, 1926.

Hilton, Sylvia-Lyn. "El impacto español en la Florida, siglos XVI y XVII." In *La influencia de España en el Caribe, la Florida, y la Luisiana, 1500–1800,* ed. by Antonio Acosta and Juan Marchena. Madrid: Instituto de Cooperación Iberoamericana, 1983.

———. "Las relaciones anglo-españolas en Norteamérica durante el reinado de Carlos III, revisión historiográfica." In *Coloquio Internacional Carlos III y su siglo: Actas.* Madrid: Universidad Complutense, 1990.

Hinojosa, Gilberto Miguel. *A Borderlands Town in Transition: Laredo, 1755–1870.* College Station: Texas A&M University Press, 1983.

———. "Friars and Indians: Towards a Perspective of Cultural Interaction in the San Antonio Mission[s]." *U.S. Catholic Historian* 9 (Spring 1990): 7–25.

———. "The Religious-Indian Communities: The Goals of the Friars." In *Tejano Origins in Eighteenth-Century San Antonio,* ed. by Gerald E. Poyo and Gilbert M. Hinojosa. Austin: University of Texas Press, 1991.

Hinojosa, Gilberto M., and Anne A. Fox. "Indians and Their Culture in San Fernando de Béxar." In *Tejano Origins in Eighteenth-Century San Antonio,* ed. by Gerald E. Poyo and Gilbert M. Hinojosa. Austin: University of Texas Press, 1991.

Hodge, Frederick Webb. "The Six Cities of Cíbola." *NMHR* 1 (Oct. 1926): 478–88.

———. *History of Hawikuh, New Mexico, One of the So-Called Cities of Cíbola.* Los Angeles: Southwest Museum, 1937.

Hoffman, Paul E. "The Chicora Legend and Franco-Spanish Rivalry in *La Florida,*" *FHQ* 62 (Apr. 1984): 419–38.

———. "Diplomacy and the Papal Donation, 1493–1585." *The Americas* 30 (Oct. 1973): 151–83.

———. "Legend, Religious Idealism, and Colonies: The Point of Santa Elena in History, 1552–1566." *South Carolina Historical Magazine* 84 (Apr. 1983): 59–71.

———. "Nature and Sequence of the Spanish Borderlands." In *Native, European, and African Cultures in Mississippi, 1500–1800,* ed. by Patricia K. Galloway. Jackson: Mississippi Department of Archives and History, 1991.

———. *A New Andalucia and a Way to the Orient: The American Southeast during the Sixteenth Century.* Baton Rouge: Louisiana State University Press, 1990.

———. "A New Voyage of North American Discovery: Pedro de Salazar's Visit to the 'Island of Giants.'" *FHQ* 58 (Apr. 1980): 415–26.

———. *The Spanish Crown and the Defense of the Caribbean, 1535–1585: Precedent, Patrimonialism, and Royal Parsimony.* Baton Rouge: Louisiana State University Press, 1980.

———. "A Study of Defense Costs, 1565–1585: A Quantification of Florida History." *FHQ* 51 (Apr. 1973): 401–22.

Hollon, W. Eugene. *The Southwest: Old and New.* New York: Alfred A. Knopf, 1967.

Holmes, Jack D. L. "Alabama's Forgotten Settlers: Notes on the Spanish Mobile District, 1780–1813." *Alabama Historical Quarterly* 33 (Summer 1971): 87–97.

———. "Andrés de Pez and Spanish Reaction to French Expansion into the Gulf of Mexico." In *La Salle and His Legacy: Frenchmen and Indians in the Lower Mississippi Valley,* ed. by Patricia K. Galloway. Jackson: University of Press of Mississippi, 1982.

———. "Dauphine Island in the Franco-Spanish War, 1719–22." In *Frenchmen and French Ways in the Mississippi Valley,* ed. by John Francis McDermott. Urbana: University of Illinois Press, 1965.

———. "Do It! Don't do it! Spanish Law on Sex and Marriage." In *Louisiana's Legal Heritage*, ed. by Edward F. Haas. Pensacola: Perdido Bay Press, 1983.

———. *Gayoso: The Life of a Spanish Governor in the Mississippi Valley, 1789–1799*. Baton Rouge: Louisiana State University Press for the Louisiana Historical Association, 1965.

———. *Honor and Fidelity: The Louisiana Infantry Regiment and the Louisiana Militia Companies, 1766–1821*. Birmingham: Louisiana Collection Series, 1965.

———. "Irish Priests in Spanish Natchez." *Journal of Mississippi History* 24 (Aug. 1967): 169–80.

———. "Juan de Villebeuvre and Spanish Indian Policy in West Florida, 1784–1797." *FHQ* 58 (Apr. 1980): 387–99.

———. "The Marqués de Casa-Calvo, Nicolás de Finiels, and the 1805 Spanish Expedition through East Texas and Louisiana." *SWHQ* 69 (Jan. 1966): 324–39.

———. "Showdown on the Sabine: General James Wilkinson vs. Lieutenant-Colonel Simón de Herrera." *Louisiana Studies* 3 (Spring 1964): 46–76.

———. "Spanish Medical Care in the Mobile District: Advanced or Retarded?" *Journal of the Florida Medical Association* 71 (July 1984): 463–68.

———. "Spanish Policy toward the Southern Indians in the 1790s." In *Four Centuries of Southern Indians*, ed. by Charles M. Hudson. Athens: University of Georgia Press, 1975.

———. "Spanish Regulation of Taverns and the Liquor Trade in the Mississippi Valley." In *The Spanish in the Mississippi Valley, 1762–1804*, ed. by John Francis McDermott. Urbana: University of Illinois Press, 1974.

———. "Spanish Treaties with West Florida Indians, 1784–1802." *FHQ* 48 (Oct. 1969): 140–54.

Holmes, Maurice G. *From New Spain by Sea to the Californias: 1519–1668*. Glendale, Calif.: Arthur H. Clark Co., 1963.

Hoover, Robert L. "The Archaeology of Spanish Colonial Sites in California." In *Comparative Studies in the Archaeology of Colonialism*, ed. by Stephen L. Dyson. Oxford: British Archaeological Review, 1985.

Hornbeck, David. "Economic Growth and Change at the Missions of Alta California, 1769–1846." In *CC*, vol. 1.

Hotz, Gottfried. *Indian Skin Paintings from the American Southwest: Two Representations of Border Conflicts between Mexico and the Missouri in the Early Eighteenth Century*. Trans. by Johannes Malthaner. Norman: University of Oklahoma Press, 1970.

Hu-DeHart, Evelyn. *Missionaries, Miners, and Indians: Spanish Contact with the Yaqui Nation of Northwestern New Spain, 1533–1820*. Tucson: University of Arizona Press, 1981.

Hudson, Charles. "Research on the Eastern Borderlands." Paper presented at the Columbus Quincentennial Conference on Archives and Records . . . 1492–1850, Washington, D.C., Sept. 23, 1987.

———. *The Southeastern Indians*. Knoxville: University of Tennessee Press, 1976.

———. "A Spanish-Coosa Alliance in Sixteenth-Century North Georgia." *Georgia Historical Quarterly* 73 (Summer 1989): 599–626.

Hudson, Charles, Chester B. DePratter, and Marvin T. Smith. "Hernando de Soto's Expedition through the Southern United States." In *FE*.

Hudson, Charles, Marvin T. Smith, and Chester B. DePratter, "The Hernando de Soto Expedition: From Apalachee to Chiaha." *Southeastern Archaeology* 31 (Summer 1984): 65–77.

Hudson, Charles, Marvin T. Smith, Chester B. DePratter, and Emilia Kelley. "The Tristán de Luna Expedition, 1559–61." In *FE*.

Hudson, Charles M., John E. Worth, and Chester B. DePratter. "Refinements in Hernando de Soto's Route through Georgia and South Carolina." In *CC*, vol. 2.

Huff, J. Wesley. "A Coronado Episode." *NMHR* 26 (Apr. 1951): 119–28.

Hulme, Peter. *Colonial Encounters: Europe and the Native Caribbean, 1491–1797*. London: Methuen, 1986.

Hurtado, Albert L. "Herbert E. Bolton, Ethnocentrism, and American History." Unpublished manuscript, July 1990.

———. *Indian Survival on the California Frontier*. New Haven: Yale University Press, 1988.

Hutchinson, C. Alan. *Frontier Settlement in Mexican California: The Híjar-Padrés Colony, and Its Origins, 1769–1835*. New Haven: Yale University Press, 1969.

Inglis, G. Douglas. "The Men of Cíbola: New Investigations on the Francisco Vázquez de Coronado Expedition." *Panhandle Plains Historical Review* 55 (1982): 1–24.

Ives, Ronald. "The Lost Discovery of Corporal Antonio Luis: A Desert Cure for Scurvy." *JAZH* 11 (Summer 1970): 101–14.

———, ed. "From Pitic to San Gabriel in 1782: The Journey of Don Pedro Fages." *JAZH* 9 (Winter 1968): 222–44.

———, ed. "Retracing the Route of the Fages Expedition of 1781." *AW* 8 (Spring and Summer 1966): 49–70; 157–70.

Jackson, Donald. *Thomas Jefferson and the Stony Mountains: Exploring the West from Monticello*. Urbana: University of Illinois Press, 1981.

Jackson, Jack. *Los Mesteños: Spanish Ranching in Texas, 1721–1821*. College Station: Texas A&M University Press, 1986.

Jackson, Jack, Robert S. Weddle, and Winston DeVille. *Mapping Texas and the Gulf Coast: The Contributions of Saint-Denis, Oliván, and Le Maire*. College Station: Texas A&M University Press, 1990.

Jackson, Robert H. "Epidemic Disease and Population Decline in the Baja California Missions, 1697–1834." *SCQ* 63 (Winter 1981): 308–46.

———. "Patterns of Demographic Change in the Missions of Central Alta California." *Journal of California and Great Basin Anthropology* 9, no. 2 (1987): 251–72.

Jacobs, James Ripley. *Tarnished Warrior: Major General James Wilkinson*. New York: Macmillan Co., 1938.

Jacobs, Wilbur R. "Communications." *AHR* 43 (Feb. 1988): 283–86.

Jaenen, Cornelius J. "Characteristics of French-Amerindian Contact in New France." In *Essays on the History of North American Discovery and Exploration*, ed. by Stanley J. Palmer and Dennis Reinhartz. College Station: Texas A&M University Press, 1988.

Jenkins, Myra Ellen. "Oñate's Administration and the Pueblo Indians." In *When Cultures Meet: Remembering San Gabriel del Yunge Oweenge*. Santa Fe: Sunstone Press, 1987.

———. "Some Eighteenth Century New Mexico Women of Property." *Hispanic Arts and Ethnohistory in the Southwest*, ed. by Marta Weigle. Santa Fe: Ancient City Press, 1983.

————. "Spanish Colonial Policy and the Pueblo Indians." In *Southwestern Culture History: Collected Papers in Honor of Albert H. Schroeder*, ed. by Charles H. Lange. Santa Fe: Ancient City Press, 1985.

John, Elizabeth A. H. "Bernardo de Gálvez on the Apache Frontier: A Cautionary Note for Gringo Historians." *JAZH* 29 (Winter 1988): 427–30.

————. "Crusading in the Hispanic Borderlands: An Essay Review." *Journal of the Southwest* 30 (Summer 1988): 190–99.

————. "Independent Indians and the San Antonio Community." In *Tejano Origins in Eighteenth-Century San Antonio*. Ed. by Gerald E. Poyo and Gilbert M. Hinojosa. Austin: University of Texas Press, 1991.

————. "Nurturing the Peace: Spanish and Comanche Cooperation in the Early Nineteenth Century." *NMHR* 59 (Oct. 1984): 345–69.

————. "The Riddle of Mapmaker Juan Pedro Walker." In *Essays on the History of North American Discovery and Exploration*, ed. by Stanley J. Palmer and Dennis Reinhartz. College Station: Texas A&M University Press, 1988.

————. "La situación y visión de los indios de la frontera norte de Nueva España (siglos XVI–XVIII)." *América Indígena* 65 (July–Sept. 1985): 465–83.

————. *Storms Brewed in Other Men's Worlds: The Confrontation of Indians, Spanish, and French in the Southwest, 1540–1795*. College Station: Texas A&M University Press, 1975.

Johnson, John R. "The Chumash and the Missions." In *CC*, vol. 1.

Johnson, Sherry. "The Spanish St. Augustine Community, 1784–1795: A Reevaluation." *FHQ* 68 (July 1989): 27–54.

Jones, B. Calvin, and Gary N. Shapiro. "Nine Mission Sites in Apalachee." In *CC*, vol. 2.

Jones, Grant D. "The Ethnohistory of the Guale Coast through 1684." In *The Anthropology of St. Catherines Island: 1. Natural and Cultural History*, ed. by David Hurst Thomas et al. *Anthropological Papers of the American Museum of Natural History* 55 (1978): 178–210.

Jones, Oakah L., Jr. *Nueva Vizcaya: Heartland of the Spanish Frontier*. Albuquerque: University of New Mexico Press, 1988.

————. *Los Paisanos: Spanish Settlers on the Northern Frontier of New Spain*. Norman: University of Oklahoma Press, 1979.

————. *Pueblo Warriors and Spanish Conquest*. Norman: University of Oklahoma Press, 1966.

Jordan, Terry G. *North American Cattle Ranching Frontiers: Origins, Diffusion, Differentiation, Adaptation*. Albuquerque: University of New Mexico Press, forthcoming.

Keegan, P. G. J., and L. Tormo Sanz. *Experiencia misionera en la Florida*. Madrid: Instituto Santo Toribio de Mogrovejo, 1957.

Kelly, Henry W. *Franciscan Missions of New Mexico, 1740–1760*. Albuquerque: University of New Mexico Press, 1941.

Kelsey, Harry. "Did Francis Drake Really Visit California?" *WHQ* 21 (Nov. 1990): 445–62.

————. "European Impact on the California Indian." *The Americas* 41 (Apr. 1985): 494–511.

_____. "Finding the Way Home: Spanish Exploration of the Round-Trip Route across the Pacific Ocean." *WHQ* 17 (Apr. 1986): 145–64.

_____. *Juan Rodríguez Cabrillo*. San Marino, Calif.: Huntington Library, 1986.

_____. "Mapping the California Coast: The Voyages of Discovery, 1533–1543." *AW* 26 (Winter 1984): 307–24.

_____. "A New Look at the Founding of Old Los Angeles." *CHSQ* 55 (Winter 1976): 326–39.

_____. "The Planispheres of Sebastian Cabot and Sancho Gutiérrez." *Terrae Incognitae* 19 (1987): 41–58.

Kenagy, Suzanne G. "Stepped Cloud and Cross: The Intersection of Pueblo and European Visual Symbolic Systems." *NMHR* 64 (July 1989): 325–40.

Kendrick, T. D. *Mary of Agreda: The Life and Legend of a Spanish Nun*. London: Routledge & Kegan Paul, 1967.

Kenmotsu, Nancy Adele, James E. Bruseth, and James E. Corbin. "Moscoso and the Route in Texas." In *The Expedition of Hernando de Soto in the West, 1541–1543: Proceedings of the De Soto Expedition Symposium*. Fayetteville: University of Arkansas Press, forthcoming.

Kenner, Charles L. *A History of New Mexican–Plains Indian Relations*. Norman: University of Oklahoma Press, 1969.

Kessell, John L. "Diego Romero, the Plains Apaches, and the Inquisition." *American West* 15 (May–June 1978): 12–16.

_____. "Esteban Clemente: Precursor of the Pueblo Revolt." *El Palacio* 86 (Winter 1980–81): 16–17.

_____. *Friars, Soldiers, and Reformers: Hispanic Arizona and the Sonora Mission Frontier, 1767–1856*. Tucson: University of Arizona Press, 1976.

_____. "Friars versus Bureaucrats: The Mission as a Threatened Institution on the Arizona-Sonora Frontier, 1767–1842." *WHQ* 5 (Apr. 1974): 151–59.

_____. *Kiva, Cross and Crown: The Pecos Indians and New Mexico, 1540–1840*. Washington, D.C.: National Park Service, 1979.

_____. "The Making of a Martyr: The Young Francisco Garcés." *NMHR* 45 (July 1970): 181–96.

_____. *Mission of Sorrows: Jesuit Guevavi and the Pimas, 1691–1767*. Tucson: University of Arizona Press, 1970.

_____. *The Missions of New Mexico since 1776*. Albuquerque: University of New Mexico Press, 1980.

_____. "The Puzzling Presidio San Phelipe de Guevavi, Alias Terrenate." *NMHR* 41 (Jan. 1966): 21–46.

_____. "Spaniards and Pueblos: From Crusading Intolerance to Pragmatic Accommodation." In *CC*, vol. 1.

_____. "Spaniards, Environment and the Pepsi Generation." 1973. In *NS*.

Kinnaird, Lawrence. "American Penetration into Spanish Louisiana." In *New Spain and the Anglo-American West*, ed. by George P. Hammond. 2 vols. 1932. New York: Kraus, 1969.

_____. "Spanish Treaties with Indian Tribes." *WHQ* 10 (Jan. 1979): 39–48.

_____. "The Western Fringe of Revolution." *WHQ* 7 (July 1976): 253–70

Kintigh, Keith W. *Settlement, Subsistence, and Society in Late Zuni Prehistory.* Anthropological Papers of the University of Arizona, no. 44. Tucson: University of Arizona Press, 1985.

Kirker, Harold. *California's Architectural Frontier: Style and Tradition in the Nineteenth Century.* 1960. Santa Barbara: Peregrine Smith, 1973.

Koch, Joan K. "Mortuary Behavior Patterning and Physical Anthropology in Colonial St. Augustine." In *Spanish St. Augustine: The Archaeology of a Colonial Creole Community,* ed. by Kathleen A. Deagan. New York: Academic Press, 1983.

Kubler, George. *The Religious Architecture of New Mexico in the Colonial Period and since the American Occupation.* 1940. Albuquerque: University of New Mexico Press, 1972.

Kuethe, Allan J. "Charles III, the Cuban Military, and the Destiny of Florida." In *Charles III: Florida and the Gulf.* Coral Gables: Count of Gálvez Historical Society, 1990.

Lamar, Howard. "From Bondage to Contract: Ethnic Labor in the American West, 1600–1890." In Steven Hahn and Jonathan Prude, eds., *The Countryside in the Age of Capitalist Transformation: Essays in the Social History of Rural America.* Chapel Hill: University of North Carolina Press, 1985.

Landers, Jane. "African Presence in Early Spanish Colonization of the Caribbean and the Southeastern Borderlands." In *CC,* vol. 2.

———. "Gracia Real de Santa Teresa de Mose: A Free Black Town in Spanish Colonial Florida." *AHR* 95 (Feb. 1990): 9–30.

———. "Spanish Sanctuary: Fugitives in Florida, 1687–1790." *FHQ* 62 (Jan. 1984): 296–313.

Lang, James. *Conquest and Commerce: Spain and England in the Americas.* New York: Academic Press, 1975.

Lange, Charles H., ed. *Southwestern Culture History: Papers in Honor of Albert H. Schroeder.* Santa Fe: Papers of the Archaeological Society of New Mexico, 1985.

Langellier, John Phillip, and Katherine Meyers Peterson. "Lances and Leather Jackets: Presidial Forces in Spanish Alta California, 1769–1821." *JW* 20 (Oct. 1981): 3–11.

Langum, David J. "Californios and the Image of Indolence." *WHQ* 9 (Apr. 1978): 181–96.

———. "The Caring Colony: Alta California's Participation in Spain's Foreign Affairs." *SCQ* 62 (Fall 1980): 217–28.

———. "From Condemnation to Praise: Shifting Perspectives on Hispanic California." *CHSQ* 61 (Winter 1983): 282–90.

———. *Law and Community on the Mexican California Frontier: Anglo American Expatriates and the Clash of Legal Traditions, 1821–1846.* Norman: University of Oklahoma Press, 1987.

Lanning, John Tate. *The Diplomatic History of Georgia: A Study of the Epoch of Jenkins' Ear.* Chapel Hill: University of North Carolina Press, 1936.

———. *The Spanish Missions of Georgia.* Chapel Hill: University of North Carolina Press, 1935.

Larsen, Clark Spencer, et al. "Beyond Demographic Collapse: Biological Adaptation and Change in Native Populations of La Florida." In *CC,* vol. 2.

Larson, Lewis H., Jr. "Historic Guale Indians of the Georgia Coast and the Impact of the Spanish Mission Effort." In *Tacachale.*

Lawson, Edward W. *The Discovery of Florida and Its Discoverer Juan Ponce de Leon*. St. Augustine: Edward W. Lawson, 1946.

Lawson, Katherine S. "Luciano de Herrera: Spanish Spy in British St. Augustine." *FHQ* 23 (Jan. 1945): 170–76.

Lawson, Merlin Paul. *The Climate of the Great American Desert: Reconstruction of the Climate of Western Interior United States, 1800–1850*. University of Nebraska Studies, New Series, no. 46. Lincoln: University of Nebraska Press, 1974.

Lecompte, Janet. "Coronado and Conquest." *NMHR* 64 (July 1989): 279–304.

Lee, Georgia, and Norman Neuerburg. "The Alta California Indians as Artists before and after Contact." In *CC*, vol. 1.

Lekson, Stephen H. *Great Pueblo Architecture of Chaco Canyon, New Mexico*. Albuquerque: National Parks Service, 1984.

Lemieux, Donald J. "The Mississippi Valley, New France, and French Colonial Policy." *Southern Studies* 17 (Spring 1978): 39–56.

León-Portilla, Miguel. *Endangered Cultures*. Trans. by Julie Goodwin Lawes. Dallas: Southern Methodist University Press, 1990.

———. *Hernán Cortés y la Mar del Sur*. Madrid: Instituto de Cooperación Iberoamericana, 1985.

———. "The Spiritual Conquest: Perspectives of the Friars and the Indians." In *Endangered Cultures*, by Miguel León-Portilla, trans. by Julie Goodwin-Lawes. Dallas: Southern Methodist University Press, 1990.

Leonard, Irving A. "The Spanish Re-exploration of the Gulf Coast in 1686." *JAH* 22 (Mar. 1936): 547–57.

Leone, Mark P., and Parker B. Potter, Jr., eds. *The Recovery of Meaning: Historical Archaeology in the Eastern United States*. Washington, D.C.: Smithsonian Institution Press, 1988.

Lewis, Clifford M. "The Calusa." In *Tacachale*.

Lewis, Clifford M., and Albert J. Loomie. *The Spanish Jesuit Mission in Virginia, 1570–1572*. Chapel Hill: University of North Carolina Press for the Virginia Historical Society, 1953.

Lewis, James A., [ed. and trans.]. "Cracker—Spanish Florida Style." *FHQ* 63 (Oct. 1984): 184–204.

Liljegren, Ernest R. "Zalmon Coley: The Second Anglo-American in Santa Fe." *NMHR* 62 (July 1987): 263–86.

Limerick, Patricia Nelson. *The Legacy of Conquest: The Unbroken Past of the American West*. New York: W. W. Norton, 1987.

Liss, Peggy K. *Mexico under Spain, 1521–1556: Society and the Origins of Nationality*. Chicago: University of Chicago Press, 1975.

Little, Keith J., and Caleb Curren. "Conquest Archaeology of Alabama." In *CC*, vol. 2.

Lockhart, James, and Stuart B. Schwartz. *Early Latin America: A History of Colonial Spanish America and Brazil*. Cambridge: Cambridge University Press, 1983.

Loomis, Noel M., and Abraham P. Nasatir. *Pedro Vial and the Roads to Santa Fe*. Norman: University of Oklahoma Press, 1967.

Lorente Miguel, Jesús. "Commercial Relations between New Orleans and the United States, 1783–1803." In *The North American Role in the Spanish Imperial Economy, 1760–*

1819, ed. by Jacques Barbier and Allan J. Kuethe. Manchester: Manchester University Press, 1984.

Loucks, L. Jill. "Political and Economic Interactions between Spaniards and Indians: Archaeological and Ethnohistorical Perspectives of the Mission System in Florida." Ph.D. diss., University of Florida, 1979.

Lowery, Woodbury. *The Spanish Settlements within the Present Limits of the United States.* 2 vols. New York, 1901 & 1905.

Lowry, Robert, and William H. McCardle. *A History of Mississippi* . . . Jackson, Miss.: R. H. Henry Co., 1891.

Lummis, Charles Fletcher. *The Spanish Pioneers.* Chicago: A. C. McClurg and Co., 1899.

Luomala, Katherine. "Tipai-Ipai." In *HNAI*, vol. 8.

Luzbetak, Louis J. "If Junípero Serra Were Alive: Missiological-Anthropological Theory Today." *The Americas* 41 (Apr. 1985): 512–19.

Lycett, Mark T. "Spanish Contact and Pueblo Organization: Long-term Implications of European Colonial Expansion in the Rio Grande Valley, New Mexico." In *CC*, vol. 1.

Lynch, John. *Spain under the Hapsburgs.* 2 vols. 1964. New York: New York University Press, 1984.

Lyon, Eugene. "The Captives of Florida." *FHQ* 50 (July 1971): 1–25.

———. "Continuity in the Age of Conquest: The Establishment of Spanish Sovereignty in the Sixteenth Century." In *AB*.

———. "The Enterprise of Florida." In *CC*, vol. 2.

———. *The Enterprise of Florida: Pedro Menéndez de Avilés and the Spanish Conquest of 1565–1568.* 1976. Gainesville: University of Florida Press, 1983.

———. "The Florida Mutineers, 1566–67." *Tequesta* 19 (1984): 44–61.

———. "Pedro Menéndez's Strategic Plan for the Florida Peninsula." *FHQ* 67 (July 1988): 1–14.

———. "St. Augustine in 1580: The Living Community." *El Escribano* 14 (1977): 20–33.

———. "Santa Elena: A Brief History of the Colony, 1566–1587." *Research Manuscript Series*, no. 193. Columbia: Institute of Archaeology and Anthropology, University of South Carolina, 1984.

———. "Spain's Sixteenth-Century North American Settlement Attempts: A Neglected Aspect." *FHQ* 59 (Jan. 1981): 275–91.

———. "La visita de 1576 y la transformación del gobierno en la Florida española." In *La influencia de España en el Caribe, la Florida, y la Luisiana, 1500–1800*, ed. by Antonio Acosta and Juan Marchena. Madrid: Instituto de Cooperación Iberoamericana, 1983.

McAlister, Lyle N. "Pensacola during the Second Spanish Period." *FHQ* 38 (Jan.–Apr. 1959): 290–91, 296, 300–303.

———. *Spain and Portugal in the New World, 1492–1700.* Minneapolis: University of Minnesota Press, 1984.

McCarty, Kieran. "A Song of Roland in Northwest Mexico." *AW* 28 (Winter 1986): 378–90.

———. *A Spanish Frontier in the Enlightened Age: Franciscan Beginnings in Sonora and Arizona, 1767–1770.* Washington, D.C.: Academy of American Franciscan History, 1981.

McCorkle, Thomas. "Intergroup Conflict." In *HNAI*, vol. 8.

McEwan, Bonnie. "Sixteenth Century Spanish Foodways in the Old World and in the Americas." In *Chaco to Chaco: Papers in Honor of Robert H. Lister and Florence C. Lister*, ed. by Meliha S. Duran and David T. Kirkpatrick. Albuquerque: Archaeological Society of New Mexico, 1989.

McGarry, Daniel D. "Educational Methods of the Franciscans in Spanish California." *The Americas* 6 (Jan. 1950): 335–58.

McGinty, Brian. "Did Ancient Oriental Mariners Sail to Our West Coast?" *American West* 20 (Nov.–Dec. l983): 57–62.

McKnight, Joseph W. "Law Books on the Hispanic Frontier." *JW* 27 (July 1988): 74–84.

———. "Law without Lawyers on the Hispano-Mexican Frontier." *West Texas Historical Association Year Book* 66 (1990): 51–65.

———. "Legitimation and Adoption on the Anglo-Hispanic Frontier of the United States." *Legal History Review* 53 (1985): 135–50.

———. "Spanish Law for the Protection of Surviving Spouses in North America." *Anuario de historia del derecho español* 57 (1989): 367–406.

MacLachlan, Colin M. *Spain's Empire in the New World: The Role of Ideas in Institutional and Social Change*. Berkeley: University of California Press, 1988.

MacLachlan, Colin M., and Jaime Rodríguez O. *The Forging of the Cosmic Race: A Reinterpretation of Colonial Mexico*. 1980. Berkeley: University of California, 1990.

McNitt, Frank. *Navajo Wars: Military Campaigns, Slave Raids, and Reprisals*. Albuquerque: University of New Mexico Press, 1972.

McReynolds, James Michael. "Family Life in a Borderland Community: Nacogdoches, Texas, 1779–1861." Ph.D. diss., Texas Tech University, 1978.

McWilliams, Richebourg Gaillard. "Iberville at the Birdfood Delta: Final Discovery of the Mississippi River." In *Frenchmen and French Ways in the Mississippi Valley*, ed. by John Francis McDermott. Urbana: University of Illinois Press, 1965.

Magnaghi, Russell M. "Plains Indians in New Mexico: The Genízaro Experience." *Great Plains Quarterly* 10 (Spring 1990): 86–95.

Manucy, Albert. "Changing Traditions in St. Augustine Architecture." In *Eighteenth-Century Florida: The Impact of the American Revolution*, ed. by Samuel Proctor. Gainesville: University Presses of Florida, 1978.

———. "The Founding of Pensacola—Reasons and Reality." *FHQ* 37 (Jan.–Apr. 1959): 223–41.

———. "The Physical Setting of Sixteenth-Century St. Augustine." *Florida Anthropology* 38 (Mar.–June 1985): 34–53.

Marchena Fernández, Juan. "Guarniciones y población militar en Florida oriental (1700–1820)." *RI* 41 (Jan.–June 1981): 108–10.

———. *Oficiales y soldados en el ejército de América*. Sevilla: Escuela de Estudios Hispanoamericanos, 1983.

Marotti, Frank, Jr. "Juan Baptista de Segura and the Failure of the Florida Jesuit Mission, 1566–1572." *FHQ* 63 (Jan. 1985): 267–79.

Marrinan, Rochelle A., John F. Scarry, and Rhonda L. Majors. "Prelude to De Soto: The Expedition of Pánfilo de Narváez." In *CC*, vol. 2.

Martin, Calvin. "The Metaphysics of Writing Indian-White History." *Ethnohistory* 26 (Spring 1979): 153–59.

Mason, William Marvin. "Adobe Interiors in Spanish California." *SCQ* 70 (Fall 1988): 235–64.

———. "Fages' Code of Conduct toward Indians, 1787." *Journal of California Anthropology* 2 (1975): 90–100.

———. "The Garrisons of San Diego Presidio, 1770–1794." *JSDH* 24 (Fall 1978): 398–424.

———. "Indian-Mexican Cultural Exchange in the Los Angeles Area, 1781–1834." *Aztlán* 15 (Spring 1984): 123–44.

Mathes, W. Michael. "Apochryphal Tales of the Island of California and Straits of Anián." *California History* 62 (Spring 1983): 52–59.

———. "Baja California: A Special Area of Contact and Colonization, 1535–1697." In *CC*, vol. 1.

———. "The Discoverer of Alta California: Joâo Rodríguez Cabrilho or Juan Rodríguez Cabrillo?" *JSDH* 19 (Summer 1973): 1–8.

———. "The Mythological Geography of California: Origins, Development, Confirmation and Disappearance." *The Americas* 45 (Jan. 1989): 315–41.

———. "Sebastián Vizcaíno and San Diego Bay." *JSDH* 18 (Spring 1972): 1–7.

———. *Vizcaíno and Spanish Expansion in the Pacific Ocean, 1580–1630*. San Francisco: California Historical Society, 1968.

Matijasic, Thomas D. "Reflected Values: Sixteenth-Century Europeans View the Indians of North America." *American Indian Culture and Research Journal* 11, no. 2 (1987): 31–50.

Matter, Robert Allen. "Economic Basis of the Seventeenth-Century Florida Missions." *FHQ* 52 (July 1973): 31–38.

———. "Mission Life in Seventeenth-Century Florida." *Catholic Historical Review* 67 (July 1981): 401–20.

———. "Missions in the Defense of Spanish Florida, 1566–1710." *FHQ* 54 (July 1975): 18–38.

———. "The Spanish Missions of Florida: The Friars versus the Governors in the 'Golden Age,' 1606–1690." Ph.D. diss., University of Washington, 1972.

Maynard, Theodore. *De Soto and the Conquistadores*. London: Longmans, Green and Co., 1930.

Meighan, Clement W. "Indians and California Missions." *SCQ* 69 (Fall 1987): 187–201.

Meinig, D. W. *Imperial Texas: An Interpretive Essay in Cultural Geography*. Austin: University of Texas Press, 1969.

———. *The Shaping of America: A Geographical Perspective on 500 Years of History*. Vol. 1 of *Atlantic America, 1492–1800*. New Haven: Yale University Press, 1986.

Merbes, Charles. "Patterns of Health and Sickness in the Precontact Southwest." In *CC*, vol. 1.

Merritt, J. Donald. "Beyond the Walls: The Indian Element in Colonial St. Augustine." In *Spanish St. Augustine: The Archaeology of a Colonial Creole Community*, ed. by Kathleen A. Deagan. New York: Academic Press, 1983.

Meyer, Michael C. *Water in the Hispanic Southwest: A Social and Legal History, 1550–1850*. Tucson: University of Arizona Press, 1984.

Milanich, Jerald T. "The European Entrada into La Florida: An Overview." In *CC*, vol. 2.

_____. "Notes on the Route of De Soto in Florida . . ." Unpublished report. Florida State Museum, Gainesville, 1986.

_____. "The Western Timucua: Patterns of Acculturation and Change." In *Tacachale*.

Milanich, Jerald T., and Charles H. Fairbanks. *Florida Archaeology*. New York: Academic Press, 1980.

Milanich, Jerald T., and Susan Milbrath, eds. *First Encounters: Spanish Explorations in the Caribbean and the United States, 1492–1570*. Gainesville: University of Florida Press, 1989.

Milanich, Jerald T., and Samuel Proctor, eds. *Tacachale: Essays on the Indians of Florida and Southeastern Georgia during the Historic Period*. Gainesville: University Presses of Florida, 1978.

Miller, Christopher L., and George R. Hamell. "A New Perspective on Indian-White Contact: Cultural Symbols and Colonial Trade." *JAH* 73 (Sept. 1986): 311–28.

Miller, Janice Borton. *Juan Nepomuceno de Quesada, Governor of Spanish East Florida, 1790–1795*. Washington: University Press of America, 1981.

_____. "Rebellion in East Florida in 1795." *FHQ* 57 (Oct. 1978): 173–86.

_____. "The Struggle for Free Trade in East Florida and the Cédula of 1793." *FHQ* 55 (July 1976): 48–59.

Minge, Ward Alan. *Acoma: Pueblo in the Sky*. Albuquerque: University of New Mexico Press, 1976.

Minnis, Paul E., and Charles L. Redman, eds. *Perspectives on Southwestern Prehistory*. Boulder: Westview Press, 1990.

Miranda, Gloria. "Gente de Razón Marriage Patterns in Spanish and Mexican California: A Case Study of Santa Barbara and Los Angeles." *SCQ* 63 (Spring 1981): 1–21.

_____. "Hispano-Mexican Childrearing Practices in Pre-American Santa Barbara." *SCQ* 65 (Winter 1983): 307–20.

Mitchem, Jeffry M. "Artifacts of Exploration: Archaeological Evidence from Florida." In *FE*.

_____. "Initial Spanish-Indian Contact in West Peninsular Florida: The Archaeological Evidence." In *CC*, vol. 2.

Monette, John W. *History of the Discovery and Settlement of the Valley of the Mississippi . . . .* 2 vols. New York: Harper & Bros., 1846.

Monroy, Douglas. *Thrown among Strangers: The Making of Mexican Culture in Frontier California*. Berkeley: University of California Press, 1990.

Montequin, Francois-Auguste de. "El proceso de urbanización en San Agustín de la Florida, 1565–1821: Arquitectura civil y militar." *Anuario de estudios americanos* 37 (1980): 583–647.

Montero de Pedro, *Españoles en Nueva Orleans y Luisiana*. Madrid: Ediciones Cultura Hispánica, 1979.

Moore, John Preston. *Revolt in Louisiana: The Spanish Occupation, 1766–1770*. Baton Rouge: Louisiana State University Press, 1976.

Moorhead, Max L. *The Apache Frontier: Jacobo de Ugarte and Spanish-Indian Relations in Northern New Spain, 1769–1791*. Norman: University of Oklahoma Press, 1968.

_____. *New Mexico's Royal Road: Trade and Travel on the Chihuahua Trail*. Norman: University of Oklahoma Press, 1954.

_____. *The Presidio: Bastion of the Spanish Borderlands*. Norman: University of Oklahoma Press, 1975.

_____. "Rebuilding the Presidio of Santa Fe, 1789–1791." *NMHR* 69 (Apr. 1974): 123–42.

_____. "The Spanish Deportation of Hostile Apaches: The Policy and the Practice." *AW* 17 (Autumn 1975): 205–20.

Morales Folguera, José Miguel. *Arquitectura y urbanismo hispanoamericano en Luisiana y Florida Occidental*. Málaga: Universidad de Málaga, 1987.

Morales Padrón, Francisco. "Colonos canarios en Indias." *Anuario de estudios americanos* 7 (1951): 339–441.

Moratto, Michael J., Thomas F. King, and Wallace B. Woolfenden. "Archaeology and California's Climate." *Journal of California Anthropology* 5 (Winter 1978): 147–61.

Moriarty, James Robert, III. "Accommodation and Conflict Resolution among Southern California Indian Groups." *SCQ* 56 (Summer 1974): 109–22.

Morison, Samuel Eliot. *The European Discovery of America: The Northern Voyages*. New York: Oxford University Press, 1971.

_____. *The European Discovery of America: The Southern Voyages*. New York: Oxford University Press, 1974.

Morse, Dan F., and Phyllis A. Morse. "The Spanish Exploration of Arkansas." In *CC*, vol. 2.

Mosk, Sanford A. "Price-Fixing in Spanish California." *CHSQ* 17 (June 1938): 118–22.

Murdoch, Richard K. *The Georgia-Florida Frontier, 1793–1796: Spanish Reaction to French Intrigue and American Designs*. Berkeley: University of California Press, 1951.

Murga, Vicente. "'Florida' So Named by Juan Ponce de Léon, the First to Name the Lands and Rivers of the Northern Continent of the New World." In *The Spanish Presence in Florida*, ed. by José Agustín Balseiro. [Miami]: A. Seemann Publishing Co., 1976.

Myres, Sandra L. *The Ranch in Spanish Texas, 1691–1800*. El Paso: Texas Western Press, 1969.

Nasatir, Abraham P. *Borderland in Retreat: From Spanish Louisiana to the Far Southwest*. Albuquerque: University of New Mexico Press, 1976.

_____. *Spanish War Vessels on the Mississippi, 1792–1796*. New Haven: Yale University Press, 1968.

Navarro García, Luis. *José de Gálvez y la Comandancia General de las Provincias Internas del norte de Nueva España*. Sevilla: Escuela de Estudios Hispano-Americanos, 1964.

_____. "The North of New Spain as a Political Problem in the Eighteenth Century." 1960. In *NS*.

_____. *Las Provincias Internas en el siglo XIX*. Sevilla: Escuela de Estudios Hispano-Americanos, 1965.

Navarro Latorre, José, and Francisco Solano Costa. *Conspiración española, 1787–1789?*. Zaragoza: Institución Fernando del Católico, 1949.

Naylor, Thomas H. "Athapaskans They Weren't: The Suma Rebels Executed at Casas Grandes in 1685." In *The Protohistoric Period in the North American Southwest: A.D. 1450–1700*, ed. by David R. Wilcox and W. Bruce Masse. Tempe: Arizona State University Anthropological Research Papers, 1981.

Neuerburg, Norman. *The Decoration of the California Missions*. Santa Barbara, Calif.: Beller-
ophon Books, 1987.

Newcomb, Rexford. *Spanish-Colonial Architecture in the United States*. New York: J. J.
Augustine, 1937.

Newcomb, W. W., Jr. *The Indians of Texas from Prehistoric to Modern Times*. Austin: University of Texas Press, 1961.

———. "Karankawa." In *HNAI*, vol. 9.

Noggle, Burl. "Anglo Observers of the Southwest Borderlands, 1825–1890: The Rise of a
Concept." *AW* 1 (Summer 1959): 105–41.

Norall, Frank. *Bourgmont: Explorer of the Missouri, 1698–1725*. Lincoln: University of
Nebraska Press, 1988.

Norris, David L. "The Squeeze: Spain Cedes Florida to the United States." In *Clash
between Cultures: Spanish East Florida, 1784–1821*, ed. by Jacqueline Fretwell and Susan
R. Parker. St. Augustine: St. Augustine Historical Society, 1988.

Nostrand, Richard L. "The Century of Hispano Expansion." *NMHR* 62 (Oct. 1987):
361–86.

Nunn, George E. *Origin of the Strait of Anian Concept*. Philadelphia: Privately printed,
1929.

Nuttall, Donald A. "Gaspar de Portolá: Disenchanted Conquistador of Spanish Upper
California." *SCQ* 53 (Sept. 1971): 185–98.

O'Connor, Kathryn Stoner. *Presidio la Bahía del Espíritu Santo de Zúñiga, 1721–1846*.
Austin: Von-Boeckmann-Jones, 1966.

O'Daniel, V. F. *Dominicans in Early Florida*. New York: United States Catholic Historical
Society, 1930.

O'Donnell, Walter, trans. *La Salle's Occupation of Texas*. Vol. 3, no. 2 of Preliminary
Studies. Austin: Texas Catholic Historical Society, 1936.

Officer, James E. *Hispanic Arizona, 1536–1856*. Tucson: University of Arizona Press, 1987.

Ogden, Adele. *The California Sea Otter Trade, 1784–1848*. Berkeley: University of California Press, 1941.

Olschki, Leonardo. "Ponce de León's Fountain of Youth: History of a Geographical
Myth." *HAHR* 21 (Aug. 1941): 361–85.

Ortiz, Alfonso. "Popay's Leadership: A Pueblo Perspective." *El Palacio* 86 (Winter 1980–
81): 18–22.

———. "San Juan." In *HNAI*, vol. 9.

———. *The Tewa World: Space, Time, Being and Becoming in a Pueblo Society*. Chicago:
University of Chicago Press, 1969.

———, ed. *New Perspectives on the Pueblos*. Albuquerque: University of New Mexico Press,
1972.

———, ed. *Southwest*. Vols. 9 & 10 of *Handbook of North American Indians*. Ed. by William
C. Sturtevant. Washington, D.C.: Smithsonian Institution Press, 1979 & 1983.

Palmer, Stanley H., and Dennis Reinhartz, eds. *Essays on the History of North American
Discovery and Exploration*. College Station: Texas A&M University Press for the University of Texas at Arlington, 1988.

Park, Joseph F. "Spanish Indian Policy in Northern Mexico, 1765–1810." 1962. In *NS*.

Parks, Virginia, ed. *Siege! Spain and Britain: Battle of Pensacola, March 9–May 8, 1781.* Pensacola: Pensacola Historical Society, 1981.

Parry, John H. *The Age of Reconnaissance: Discovery, Exploration and Settlement, 1450 to 1650.* New York: Praeger, 1969.

———. "Early European Penetration of Eastern North America." In *AB.*

———. "The Navigators of the Conquista." *Terrae Incognitae* 10 (1978): 61–70.

———. *The Spanish Seaborne Empire.* New York: Alfred A. Knopf, 1966.

Parsons, Elsie Clews. *Pueblo Indian Religion.* 2 vols. Chicago: University of Chicago Press, 1939.

Patrick, Elizabeth Nelson. "Land Grants during the Administration of Governor Mendinueta." *NMHR* 51 (Jan. 1976): 5–18.

Patrick, Rembert W. *Florida Fiasco: Rampant Rebels on the Georgia-Florida Frontier, 1810–1815.* Athens: University of Georgia Press, 1954.

Payne, Steven. "Villa de Branciforte." *Pacific Historian* 22 (Winter 1978): 403–10.

Pearson, Fred Lamar, Jr. "The Arguelles Inspection of Guale: December 21, 1677–January 10, 1678." *Georgia Historical Quarterly* 59 (Summer 1975): 210–22.

Persons, Billie. "Secular Life in the San Antonio Missions." *SWHQ* 62 (July 1958): 45–62.

Peset, José Luis, ed. *Culturas de la costa noroeste de América.* Madrid: Turner Libros, 1989.

Peters, Virginia Bergman. *The Florida Wars.* Hamden, Conn.: Archon Books, 1979.

Pethick, Derek. *The Nootka Sound Connection: Europe and the Northwest Coast, 1790–1795.* Vancouver: Douglas and McIntrye, 1980.

Phares, Ross. *Cavalier in the Wilderness: The Story of the Explorer and Trader Louis Juchereau de St. Denis.* Baton Rouge: Louisiana State University Press, 1952.

Phelan, John Leddy. *The Millennial Kingdom of the Franciscans.* 1956. Rev. ed. Berkeley: University of California Press, 1970.

Phillips, George Harwood. "Indians in Los Angeles, 1781–1875: Economic Integration, Social Disintegration." *PHR* 49 (Aug. 1980): 427–51.

Phillips, Paul Chrisler. *The Fur Trade.* 2 vols. Norman: University of Oklahoma Press, 1961.

Pierson, Peter. *Philip II of Spain.* London: Thames and Hudson, 1975.

Pike, Ruth. *Enterprise and Adventure: The Genoese in Seville and the Opening of the New World.* Ithaca, N.Y.: Cornell University Press, 1966.

Piña, Román. *Catalanes y Mallorquines en la fundación de California.* Barcelona: Editorial Laia, 1988.

Pino Diaz, Fermín del, ed. *Ciencia y contexto histórico nacional en las expediciones ilustradas a América.* Madrid: Consejo Superior de Investigaciones Científicas, 1988.

Poitrineau, Abel. "Demography and the Political Destiny of Florida during the Second Spanish Period." *FHQ* 66 (Apr. 1988): 420–43.

Polzer, Charles W. *Rules and Precepts of the Jesuit Missions of Northwestern New Spain.* Tucson: University of Arizona Press, 1976.

Poole, Stafford. "War by Fire and Blood: The Church and the Chichimecas, 1585." *The Americas* 22 (Oct. 1965): 115–37.

Pourade, Richard. *Anza Conquers the Desert.* San Diego.: Union-Tribune Publishing Co., 1971.

Powell, Philip Wayne. "Genesis of the Frontier Presidio in North America." *WHQ* 13 (Apr. 1982): 124–41.

———. *Soldiers, Indians, and Silver: North America's First Frontier War*. Berkeley: University of California Press, 1952.

———. *Tree of Hate: Propaganda and Prejudices Affecting United States Relations with the Hispanic World*. New York: Basic Books, 1971.

Poyo, Gerald E. "The Canary Islands Immigrants of San Antonio: From Ethnic Exclusivity to Community in Eighteenth-Century Béxar." In *Tejano Origins in Eighteenth-Century San Antonio*. Ed. by Gerald E. Poyo and Gilbert M. Hinojosa. Austin: University of Texas Press, 1991.

———. "Immigrants and Integration in Late Eighteenth-Century Béxar." In *Tejano Origins in Eighteenth-Century San Antonio*, ed. by Gerald E. Poyo and Gilbert M. Hinojosa. Austin: University of Texas Press, 1991.

Poyo, Gerald E., and Gilberto M. Hinojosa. "Spanish Texas and Borderlands Historiography in Transition: Implications for United States History." *JAH* 75 (Sept. 1988): 393–416

Poyo, Gerald E., and Gilberto M. Hinojosa, eds. *Tejano Origins in Eighteenth-Century San Antonio*. Austin: University of Texas Press, 1991.

Pratt, Boyd C. "The Plaza in History: Old World Ideals, New World Realities." *El Palacio* 94 (Winter 1988): 5–13.

Pratt, Julius W. *The Expansionists of 1812*. New York: Macmillan, 1925.

Price, Catherine. "The Comanches [*sic*] Threat to Texas and New Mexico in the Eighteenth Century and the Development of Spanish Indian Policy." *JW* 24 (Apr. 1985): 34–45.

Priestley, Herbert Ingram. *José de Gálvez, Visitor-General of New Spain (1765–1771)*. Berkeley: University of California Press, 1916.

———. *Tristán de Luna, Conquistador of the Old South: A Study of Spanish Imperial Strategy*. Glendale, Calif.: Arthur H. Clark Co., 1936.

Purdy, Barbara A. "Weapons, Strategies, and Tactics of the Europeans and the Indians in Sixteenth- and Seventeenth-Century Florida." *FHQ* 55 (Jan. 1977): 254–76.

Quattlebaum, Paul. *The Land Called Chicora: The Carolinas under Spanish Rule with French Intrusions, 1520–1670*. Gainesville: University of Florida Press, l956.

Quinn, David B. "Colonies in the Beginning: Examples from North America." In *Essays on the History of North American Discovery and Exploration*, ed. by Stanley H. Palmer and Dennis Reinhartz. College Station: Texas A&M Press for the University of Texas at Arlington, 1988.

———. *England and the Discovery of America, 1481–1620*. New York: Alfred A. Knopf, 1974.

———. *North America from Earliest Discovery to First Settlements: The Norse Voyages to 1612*. New York: Harper & Row, 1977.

Radding de Murrieta, Cynthia. "The Function of the Market in Changing Economic Structures in the Mission Communities of Pimería Alta, 1768–1821." *The Americas* 34 (Oct. 1977): 155–69.

Ramenofsky, Ann F. *Vectors of Death: The Archaeology of European Contact*. Albuquerque: University of New Mexico Press, 1987.

Rasico, Philip D. "Minorcan Population of St. Augustine in the Spanish Census of 1786." *FHQ* 66 (Oct. 1987): 160–84.

Ratcliffe, Sam D. " 'Escenas de Martirio': Notes on *The Destruction of Mission San Sabá.*" *SWHQ* 94 (Apr. 1991): 506–34.

Rawls, James J. *Indians of California: The Changing Image.* Norman: University of Oklahoma Press, 1984.

Rea, Robert R. "British West Florida: Stepchild of Diplomacy." In *Eighteenth-Century Florida and Its Borderlands,* ed. by Samuel Proctor. Gainesville: University Presses of Florida, 1975.

Reeve, Frank D. "Navaho-Spanish Diplomacy, 1770–1790." *NMHR* 35 (July 1960): 200–35.

————. "Seventeenth Century Navaho-Spanish Relations." *NMHR* 32 (Jan. 1957): 36–52.

Reff, Daniel T. *Disease, Depopulation, and Culture Change in Northwestern New Spain, 1518–1764.* Salt Lake City: University of Utah Press, 1991.

————. "The Introduction of Smallpox in the Greater Southwest." *American Anthropologist* 89 (Sept. 1987): 704–08.

Reilly, Stephen Edward. "A Marriage of Expedience: The Calusa Indians and Their Relations with Pedro Menéndez de Avilés in Southwest Florida, 1566–1569." *FHQ* 59 (Apr. 1981): 295–421.

Reitz, Elizabeth J. "The Spanish Colonial Experience and Domestic Animals." *Historical Archaeology* 26, no. 1 (1992): forthcoming.

————. "Zooarchaeological Evidence for Subsistence at La Florida Missions." In *CC,* vol. 2.

Reitz, Elizabeth J., and Stephen L. Cuumba. "Diet and Foodways of Eighteenth-Century Spanish St. Augustine." In *Spanish St. Augustine: The Archaeology of a Colonial Creole Community,* ed. by Kathleen Deagan. New York: Academic Press, 1983.

Reparaz, Carmen de. *Yo Solo: Bernardo de Gálvez y la toma de Panzacola en 1781.* Madrid: Serval/ICI, 1986.

Reps, John W. *The Making of Urban America: A History of City Planning in the United States.* Princeton: Princeton University Press, 1965.

Rey, Agapito. "Missionary Aspects of the Founding of New Mexico." *NMHR* 23 (Jan. 1948): 22–31.

Ribes Iborra, Vicente. "Texas en las postrimerías del tiempo hispánico, 1800–1820." *RI* 38 (Jan.–June 1978): 177–99.

Ricard, Robert. *The Spiritual Conquest of Mexico: An Essay on the Apostolate and the Evangelizing Methods of the Mendicant Orders in New Spain: 1523–1572.* Trans. by Lesley Bryd Simpson. Berkeley: University of California Press, 1966.

Riley, Carroll L. "Las Casas and the Benavides Memorial." *NMHR* 58 (July 1973): 209–22.

————. "Early Spanish-Indian Communication in the Greater Southwest." *NMHR* 46 (Oct. 1971): 285–314.

————. "The Road to Hawikuh: Trade and Trade Routes to Cibola-Zuni during Late Prehistoric and Early Historic Times." *Kiva* 41 (Winter 1975): 137–59.

Río Chávez, Ignacio del. *Conquista y aculturación en la California Jesuítica, 1697–1768.* Mexico: Universidad Nacional Autónoma de México, 1984.

————. "Utopia in Baja California: The Dreams of José de Gálvez." *JSDH* 18 (Fall 1972): 1–13.

Ríos-Bustamante, Antonio, and Pedro Castillo. *An Illustrated History of Mexican Los Angeles, 1781–1985*. Los Angeles: Chicano Studies Research Center, University of California, 1986.

Robinson, Willard B. "Colonial Ranch Architecture in the Spanish-Mexican Tradition." *SWHQ* 83 (Oct. 1979): 123–50.

Robinson, William J. "Tree-Ring Studies of the Pueblo of Acoma." *Historical Archaeology* 24, no. 3 (1990): 99–106.

Rock, Rosalind Z. " '*Pido y Suplico*': Women and the Law in Spanish New Mexico, 1697–1763." *NMHR* 65 (Apr. 1990): 145–59.

Rodack, Madelaine Turrell. "Cibola Revisited." In *Southwestern Culture History: Papers in Honor of Albert H. Schroeder*, ed. by Charles H. Lange. Santa Fe: Papers of the Archaeological Society of New Mexico, 1985.

Rodríguez Casado, Vicente. *Primeros años de dominación española en la Luisiana*. Madrid: Instituto Gonzalo Fernández de Oviedo, 1942.

Rollings, Willard. "In Search of Multisided Frontiers: Recent Writing on the History of the Southern Plains." In *New Directions in American Indian History*, ed. by Colin G. Calloway. Norman: University of Oklahoma Press, 1988.

Ruhl, Donna L. "Spanish Mission Paleoethnobotany and Culture Change." In *CC*, vol. 2.

Ruigómez de Hernández, María Pilar. *El gobierno español del despotismo ilustrado ante la independencia de los Estados Unidos de América: Una nueva estructura de la política internacional, 1773–1783*. Madrid: Ministerio de Asuntos Exteriores, 1978.

Rule, John C. "Jérôme Phélypeaux, Comte de Ponchartrain, and the Establishment of Louisiana, 1696–1715." In *Frenchmen and French Ways in the Mississippi Valley*, ed. by John Francis McDermott. Urbana: University of Illinois Press, 1965.

Sánchez, Jane C. "Spanish-Indian Relations during the Otermín Administration, 1677–1683." *NMHR* 58 (Apr. 1983): 134, 137.

Sánchez, Joseph P. *Spanish Bluecoats: The Catalonian Volunteers in Northwestern New Spain, 1767–1810*. Albuquerque: University of New Mexico Press, 1990.

Sánchez-Fabrés Mirat, Elena. *Situación histórico de las Floridas en la segunda mitad del siglo xviii (1783–1819). Los Problemas de una región de frontera*. Madrid: Ministerio de Asuntos Exteriores, 1977.

Sando, Joe. "The Pueblo Revolt." In *HNAI*, vol. 9.

Sandos, James A. "Junípero Serra's Canonization and the Historical Record." *AHR* 93 (Dec. 1988): 1253–69.

————. "*Levantamiento!* The Chumash Uprising Reconsidered." *SCQ* 67 (Summer 1985): 109–33.

Sauer, Carl O. *Northern Mists*. Berkeley: University of California Press, 1968.

————. "The Road to Cíbola." In *Land and Life*, ed. by John Leighly. Berkeley: University of California Press, 1963.

————. *Seventeenth Century North America*. Berkeley: Turtle Island Foundation, 1980.

————. *Sixteenth Century North America: The Land and the Peoples as Seen by the Europeans*. Berkeley: University of California Press, 1971.

Saunders, Rebecca. "Ideal and Innovation: Spanish Mission Architecture in the Southeast." In *CC*, vol. 2.

Scardaville, Michael C. "Approaches to the Study of the Southeastern Borderlands." In *AB*.

Scardaville, Michael C., and Jesús María Belmonte, eds. and trans. "Florida in the Late First Spanish Period: The 1756 Griñán Report." *El Escribano* 16 (1979): 1–24.

Scarry, Margaret C., and Elizabeth J. Reitz. "Herbs, Fish, Scum, and Vermin: Subsistence Strategies in Sixteenth-Century Spanish Florida." In *CC*, vol. 2.

Schilz, Thomas F. *The Lipan Apaches in Texas*. El Paso: Texas Western Press, 1987.

Schilz, Thomas Frank, and Donald E. Worcester. "Spread of Firearms among the Indian Tribes on the Northern Frontier of New Spain." *American Indian Quarterly* 11 (Winter 1987): 1–10.

Scholes, France V. *Church and State in New Mexico, 1610–1650*. Historical Society of New Mexico, Publications in History, vol. 7. Albuquerque: University of New Mexico Press, 1942.

———. "Civil Government and Society in New Mexico in the Seventeenth Century." *NMHR* 10 (Apr. 1935): 71–111.

———. "The First Decade of the Inquisition in New Mexico." *NMHR* 10 (July 1935): 195–241.

———. "Royal Treasury Records Relating to the Province of New Mexico, 1596–1683." *NMHR* 50 (Jan. and Apr. 1975): 5–23; 139–64.

———. "The Supply Service of the New Mexico Missions in the Seventeenth Century." *NMHR* 5 (Jan., Apr., and July 1930): 93–115; 186–210; 386–410.

———. *Troublous Times in New Mexico, 1659–1670*. Historical Society of New Mexico, Publications in History, vol. 11. Albuquerque: University of New Mexico Press, 1942.

Scholes, France V., and Lansing B. Bloom "Friar Personnel and Mission Chronology, 1598–1629." *NMHR* 19–20 (Oct. 1944; Jan. 1945): 319–36; 58–82.

Schroeder, Albert H. "Pueblos Abandoned in Historic Times." In *HNAI*, vol. 9.

———. "A Re-analysis of the Routes of Coronado and Oñate onto the Plains in 1541 and 1601." *Plains Anthropologist* 7 (Feb. 1962): 2–23.

———. "Rio Grande Ethnohistory." In *New Perspectives on the Pueblos*, ed. by Alfonso Ortiz. Albuquerque: University of New Mexico Press, 1972.

———. "Shifting for Survival in the Spanish Southwest." 1968. In *NS*.

Schuetz, Mardith Keithly. "The Indians of the San Antonio Missions, 1718–1821." Ph.D. diss., University of Texas at Austin, 1980.

———. "The People of San Antonio: Beginnings of the Spanish Settlement, 1718–1731." In *San Antonio in the Eighteenth Century*. San Antonio Bicentennial Heritage Committee, 1976.

———. "Professional Artisans in the Hispanic Southwest: The Churches of San Antonio, Texas." *The Americas* 40 (July 1983): 17–71.

Schwaller, John Frederick. "Nobility, Family, and Service: Menéndez and His Men." *FHQ* 66 (Jan. 1988): 298–310.

Serrano y Sanz, Manuel. *España y los Indios Cherokis y Chactas en la segunda mitad del siglo XVIII*. Seville: Tip. de la Guía Oficial, 1916.

Servies, James A. *The Siege of Pensacola, 1781: A Bibliography*. Pensacola: John Pace Library, 1981.

Servín, Manuel Patricio. "The Beginnings of California's Anti-Mexican Prejudice." In *An Awakened Minority: The Mexican-Americans*, ed. by Manuel Patricio Servín. Beverly Hills, Calif.: Glencoe Press, 1974.

————. "California's Hispanic Heritage: A View into the Spanish Myth." 1973. In *NS*.

————. "The Legal Basis for the Establishment of Spanish Colonial Sovereignty: The Act of Possession." *NMHR* 53 (Oct. 1978): 295–303.

————. "The Secularization of the California Missions: A Reappraisal." *SCQ* 47 (June 1965): 133–50.

Shapiro, Gary N., and John H. Hann. "The Documentary Image of the Council Houses of Spanish Florida Tested by Excavations at the Mission of San Luis de Talimali." In *CC*, vol. 2.

Shelby, Charmion Clair. "St. Denis's Second Expedition to the Rio Grande, 1716–1719." *SWHQ* 27 (Jan. 1924): 190–216.

Shepherd, William R. "The Spanish Heritage in America." *Modern Language Journal* 10 (Nov. 1925): 75–85.

Sheridan, Thomas E. "How to Tell the Story of a 'People without History': Narrative versus Ethnohistorical Approaches to the Study of the Yaqui Indians through Time." *Journal of the Southwest* 30 (Summer 1988): 168–89.

————. "Kino's Unforeseen Legacy: The Material Consequences of Missionization among the Piman Indians of Arizona and Sonora." *Smoke Signal* nos. 49–50 (Spring and Fall 1988): 151–67.

Shipek, Florence C. "California Indian Reactions to the Franciscans." *The Americas* 41 (Apr. 1985): 480–93.

————. *Pushed into the Rocks: Southern California Indian Land Tenure, 1769–1986*. Lincoln: University of Nebraska Press, 1987.

Shipley, William F. "Native Languages of California." In *HNAI*, vol. 8.

Sibley, Marilyn McAdams. *Travelers in Texas, 1761–1860*. Austin: University of Texas Press, 1967.

Silverberg, Robert. *The Pueblo Revolt*. New York: Weybright and Talley, 1970.

Simmons, Marc. *Albuquerque: A Narrative History*. Albuquerque: University of New Mexico Press, 1982.

————. "Authors and Books in Colonial New Mexico." In *Voices from the Southwest: A Gathering in Honor of Lawrence Clark Powell*, ed. by Donald C. Dickinson et al. Flagstaff: Northland Press, 1976.

————. "Footwear of New Mexico's Hispanic Frontier." In *Southwestern Culture History: Papers in Honor of Albert H. Schroeder*, ed. by Charles H. Lange. Santa Fe: Papers of the Archaeological Society of New Mexico, 1985.

————. "History of Pueblo-Spanish Relations to 1821." In *HNAI*, vol. 9.

————. *The Last Conquistador: Juan de Oñate and the Settling of the Far Southwest*. Norman: University of Oklahoma Press, 1991.

————. "'Misery' as a Factor in New Mexican Colonial Life." *Reflections: Papers on Southwestern Culture History in Honor of Charles H. Lange*, ed. by Anne V. Poore. Santa Fe: Ancient City Press, 1988.

————. "New Mexico's Smallpox Epidemic of 1780–81." *NMHR* 41 (Oct. 1966): 319–26.

————. "The Pueblo Revolt: Why Did It Happen?." *El Palacio* 86 (Winter 1980–81): 11–15.

————. "Settlement Patterns and Village Plans in New Mexico." 1969. In *NS*.

————. "Spaniards of San Gabriel." In *When Cultures Meet: Remembering San Gabriel del Yunge Oweenge*. Santa Fe: Sunstone Press, 1987.

————. "Spanish Attempts to Open a New Mexico-Sonora Road." *AW* 17 (Spring 1975): 5–20.

————. *Spanish Government in New Mexico*. Albuquerque, N.M.: University of New Mexico Press, 1968.

————. "Spanish Irrigation in New Mexico." *NMHR* 47 (Apr. 1972): 135–50.

————. "Tlascalans in the Spanish Borderlands." *NMHR* 39 (Apr. 1964): 101–110.

————. *Witchcraft in the Southwest: Spanish and Indian Supernaturalism on the Rio Grande*. Flagstaff: Northland Press, 1974.

Simmons, Marc, and Frank Turley. *Southwestern Colonial Ironwork: The Spanish Blacksmithing Tradition from Texas to California*. Santa Fe: Museum of New Mexico Press, 1980.

Slater, John M. *El Morro, Inscription Rock, New Mexico: The Rock Itself, the Inscriptions Thereon, and the Travelers Who Made Them*. Los Angeles: Plantin Press, 1961.

Sluiter, Engel. *The Florida Situado: Quantifying the First Eighty Years, 1571–1651*. Gainesville: University of Florida Libraries, 1985.

Smith, Bruce D. "Mississippian Patterns of Subsistence and Settlement." In *AB*.

Smith, Marvin T. "Aboriginal Population Movements in the Early Historic Period Interior Southeast." In *PM*.

————. *Archaeology of Aboriginal Culture Change in the Interior Southeast: Depopulation during the Early Historic Period*. Gainesville: University of Florida Press and Florida State Museum, 1987.

————. "Indians Responses to European Contact: The Coosa Example." In *FE*.

Snow, Cordelia Thomas. "The Plazas of Santa Fe, New Mexico, 1610–1776." *El Palacio* 94 (Winter 1988): 40–51.

————. "The Santa Fe Plaza: An Analysis of Various Theories of Its Size and Configuration . . ." In *Santa Fe Historic Plaza Study I: With Translations from Spanish Colonial Documents*, ed. by Linda Tigges. Santa Fe: Santa Fe City Planning Dept., 1990.

Snow, David H. "A Note on Encomienda Economics in Seventeenth-Century New Mexico." In *Hispanic Arts and Ethnohistory in the Southwest*, ed. by Marta Weigle. Santa Fe: Ancient City Press, 1983.

————. "Protohistoric Rio Grande Pueblo Economics: A Review of Trends." In *The Protohistoric Period in the North American Southwest: A.D. 1450–1700*, ed. by David R. Wilcox and W. Bruce Masse. Tempe: Arizona State University Anthropological Research Papers, 1981.

South, Stanley. "From Thermodynamics to a Status Artifact Model: Spanish Santa Elena." In *CC*, vol. 2.

Spate, O. H. K. *The Spanish Lake*. Minneapolis: University of Minnesota Press, 1979.

Spears, John R. *A History of the Mississippi Valley from Its Discovery to the End of Foreign Domination*. New York: A. S. Clark, 1903.

Spellman, Charles W. [pseud., Gannon]. "The 'Golden Age' of the Florida Missions, 1632–1674." *Catholic Historical Review* 51 (Oct. 1965): 354–72.

Spicer, Edward H. *Cycles of Conquest: The Impact of Spain, Mexico, and the United States on the Indians of the Southwest, 1533–1960.* Tucson: University of Arizona Press, 1962.

_____. "Spanish-Indian Acculturation in the Southwest." *American Anthropologist* 56 (Aug. 1954): 663–78.

_____, ed. *Perspectives in American Indian Culture Change.* Chicago: University of Chicago Press, 1961.

Spielmann, Katherine A. "Colonists, Hunters, and Farmers: Plains-Pueblo Interaction in the Seventeenth Century." In *CC,* vol. 1.

Starnes, Gary B. *The San Gabriel Missions, 1746.* Madrid: Ministry of Foreign Relations, 1969.

Starr, J. Barton. " 'Left as a Gewgaw,' The Impact of the American Revolution on West Florida." In *Eighteenth-Century Florida: The Impact of the American Revolution,* ed. by Samuel Proctor. Gainesville: University Presses of Florida, 1978.

_____. *Tories, Dons, and Rebels: The American Revolution in British West Florida.* Gainesville: University Presses of Florida, 1976.

Stein, Stanley J., and Barbara H. Stein. *The Colonial Heritage of Latin America: Essays on Economic Dependence in Perspective.* New York: Oxford University Press, 1970.

Stenberg, Richard. "The Boundaries of the Louisiana Purchase." *HAHR* 14 (Feb. 1934): 32–64.

_____. "The Western Boundary of Louisiana, 1762–1803." *SWHQ* 35 (Oct. 1931): 95–108.

Stern, Peter Alan. "Social Marginality and Acculturation on the Northern Frontier of New Spain." Ph.D. diss., University of California, Berkeley, 1984.

Stevenson, Matilda Cox. "The Zuñi Indians: Their Mythology, Esoteric Fraternities, and Ceremonies." In the *Twenty-third Annual Report of the Bureau of American Ethnology . . . 1901–1902.* Washington, D.C.: Government Printing Office, 1904.

Stilgoe, John R. *Common Landscape of America, 1580–1845.* New Haven: Yale University Press, 1982.

Straight, William M. "Medicine in St. Augustine during the Spanish Period." *Journal of the Florida Medical Association* 55 (Aug. 1968): 731–41.

Strickland, Rex W. "Moscoso's Journey through Texas," *SWHQ* 46 (Oct. 1942): 109–37.

Strout, Clevy Lloyd. "The Coronado Expeditions: Following the Geography Described in the Spanish Journals." *Great Plains Journal* 14 (Fall 1974): 2–31.

Sturtevant, William C. "The Last of the South Florida Aborigines." In *Tacachale.*

_____. "Spanish-Indian Relations in Southeastern North America." *Ethnohistory* 9 (Winter 1962): 41–94.

Surrey, N. M. Miller. *The Commerce of Louisiana during the French Régime, 1699–1763.* New York: Columbia University, 1916.

Swagerty, William R. "Spanish-Indian Relations, 1513–1821." In *Scholars and the Indian Experience,* ed. by W. R. Swagerty. Bloomington: Indiana University Press, 1984.

_____. "Beyond Bimini: Indian-White Relations in Sixteenth Century North America."

Unpublished manuscript, 1985, based on a Ph.D. diss., University of California at Santa Barbara, 1981.

Swanton, John R. *Final Report of the United States De Soto Expedition Commission.* 1939. Washington, D.C.: Smithsonian Institution Press, 1985.

Tanner, Helen Hornbeck. "The Land and Water Communication of the Southeastern Indians." In *PM*.

———. "The Second Spanish Period Begins." In *Clash between Cultures: Spanish East Florida, 1784–1821*, ed. by Jacqueline K. Fretwell and Susan R. Parker. St. Augustine: St. Augustine Historical Society, 1990.

———. *Zéspedes in East Florida, 1784–1790.* 1963. Jacksonville: University of North Florida Press, 1989.

Taylor, Lonn, and Dessa Bokides. *New Mexican Furniture 1600–1940: The Origins, Survival, and Revival of Furniture Making in the Hispanic Southwest.* Santa Fe, N.M.: Museum of New Mexico Press, 1987.

Taylor, Paul S. "Spanish Seamen in the New World during the Colonial Period." *HAHR* 5 (Nov. 1922): 631–61.

Tedlock, Dennis. "Zuni Religion and World View." In *HNAI*, vol. 9.

TePaske, John Jay. "French, Spanish, and English Indian Policy on the Gulf Coast, 1513–1763: A Comparison." In *Spain and Her Rivals on the Gulf Coast*, ed. by Ernest F. Dibble and Earle W. Newton. Pensacola: Pensacola Preservation Board, 1971.

———. *The Governorship of Spanish Florida, 1700–1763.* Durham, N.C.: Duke University Press, 1964.

Terrell, John Upton. *Journey into Darkness.* New York: William Morrow and Company, 1962.

Texada, David Ker. *O'Reilly and the New Orleans Rebels.* Lafayette: University of Southwestern Louisiana, 1970.

Thomas, Alfred B. "Governor Mendinueta's Proposals for the Defense of New Mexico, 1772–1778." *NMHR* 6 (Jan. 1931): 21–39.

Thomas, Daniel H. *Fort Toulouse: The French Outpost at the Alabamas on the Coosa.* Intro. by Gregory A. Waselkov. 1960. Tuscaloosa: University of Alabama Press, 1989.

Thomas, David Hurst. "The Archaeology of Mission Santa Catalina de Guale: 1. Search and Discovery." *Anthropological Papers of the American Museum of Natural History* 63, pt. 2 (1987): 47–161.

———. "Columbian Consequences: The Spanish Borderlands in Cubist Perspective." In *CC*, vol. 1.

———. "Harvesting Ramona's Garden: Life in California's Mythical Mission Past." In *CC*, vol. 3.

———. *St. Catherines: An Island in Time.* Atlanta: Georgia Endowment for the Humanities, 1988.

———. "Saints and Soldiers at Santa Catalina: Hispanic Designs for Colonial America." In *The Recovery of Meaning: Historical Archaeology in the Eastern United States*, ed. by Mark P. Leone and Parker B. Potter, Jr. Washington, D.C.: Smithsonian Institution Press, 1988.

———. "The Spanish Missions of La Florida: An Overview." In *CC*, vol. 2.

_____, ed. *Columbian Consequences*. Vol. 1: *Archaeological and Historical Perspectives on the Spanish Borderlands West*; Vol. 2: *Archaeological and Historical Perspectives on the Spanish Borderlands East*; Vol. 3: *The Spanish Borderlands in Pan American Perspective*. Washington, D.C.: Smithsonian Institution Press, 1989–91.

Thomason, Buchanan Parker. *Spain: Forgotten Ally of the American Revolution*. North Quincy, Mass: Christopher Publishing House, 1976.

Thonhoff, Robert H. *The Texas Connection with the American Revolution*. Burnet, Tex.: Eakin Press, 1981.

Thornton, Russell. *American Indian Holocaust and Survival: A Population History since 1492*. Norman: University of Oklahoma Press, 1987.

_____. *The Cherokees: A Population History*. Lincoln: University of Nebraska Press, 1990.

Thurman, Michael E. *The Naval Department of San Blas: New Spain's Bastion for Alta California and Nootka, 1767 to 1798*. Glendale, Calif.: Arthur H. Clark Co., 1967.

Timmons, W. H. *El Paso: A Borderlands History*. El Paso: Texas Western Press, 1990.

Tjarks, Alicia Vidaurreta. "Comparative Demographic Analysis of Texas, 1777–1793." *SWHQ* 77 (Jan. 1974): 291–338.

_____. "Demographic, Ethnic and Occupational Structure of New Mexico, 1790." *The Americas* 35 (July 1978): 45–88.

_____. "Evolución urbana de Texas durante el siglo XVIII." *RI* 33–34 (Jan. 1973–Dec. 1974): 605–36.

Todorov, Tzvetan. *The Conquest of America: The Question of the Other*. Trans. by Richard Howard. 1st ed. in French, 1982. New York: Harper & Row, 1982.

Tornero Tinajero, Pablo. "Estudio de la población de Pensacola: 1784–1820." *Anuario de estudios americanos* 34 (1977): 537–61.

_____. *Relaciones de dependencia entre Florida y los Estados Unidos (1783–1820)*. Madrid: Ministerio de Asuntos Exteriores, 1979.

Torres Ramírez, Bibiano. *Alejandro O'Reilly en las Indias*. Sevilla: Escuela de Estudios Hispano-Americanos, 1969.

Tregle, Joseph G., Jr. "Early New Orleans Society: A Reappraisal." *Journal of Southern History* 18 (Feb. 1952): 20–26.

Treutlein, Theodore E. "The Economic Regime of the Jesuit Missions in Eighteenth Century Sonora." *PHR* 8 (Sept. 1939): 289–300.

_____. *San Francisco Bay: Discovery and Colonization, 1769–1776*. San Francisco: California Historical Society, 1968.

Troxler, Carole Watterson. "Loyalist Refugees and the British Evacuation of East Florida, 1783–1785." *FHQ* 60 (July 1981): 1–18.

Tuck, James A., Robert Grenier, and Robert Laxalt. "Discovery in Labrador: A 16th-Century Basque Whaling Port and Its Sunken Fleet." *National Geographic* 186 (July 1985): 40–71.

Turner, Frederick. *Beyond Geography: The Western Spirit against Wilderness*. New York: Viking Press, 1980.

Tyler, Bruce. "The Mississippi River Trade, 1784–1788." *Louisiana History* 12 (Summer 1971): 255–67.

Tyler, Daniel. *The Mythical Pueblo Rights Doctrine: Water Administration in Hispanic New Mexico*. El Paso: Texas Western Press, 1990.

Udall, Stewart L. *To the Inland Empire: Coronado and Our Spanish Legacy*. Garden City, N.Y.: Doubleday & Co., 1987.

Upham, Steadman. *Polities and Power: An Economic and Political History of the Western Pueblo*. New York: Academic Press, 1982.

———. "Smallpox and Climate in the American Southwest." *American Anthropologist* 88 (Mar. 1986): 115–28.

———. "Understanding the Disease History of the Southwest: A Reply to Reff." *American Anthropologist* 89 (Sept. 1987): 708–10.

Upham, Steadman, and Lori Stephens Reed. "Regional Systems in the Central and Northern Southwest: Demography, Economy, and Sociopolitics Preceding Contact." In *CC*, vol. 1.

Usner, Daniel H., Jr. "American Indians in Colonial New Orleans." In *PM*.

———. "The Deerskin Trade in French Louisiana." In *Proceedings of the Tenth Meeting of the French Colonial Society*, ed. by Philip P. Boucher. Lanham, Md.: University Press of America, 1985.

———. "The Frontier Exchange Economy of the Lower Mississippi Valley in the Eighteenth Century." *William and Mary Quarterly* 44 (Apr. 1987): 165–92.

Varner, John Grier, and Jeannette Johnson Varner. *Dogs of the Conquest*. Norman: University of Oklahoma Press, 1983.

Varona, Frank de. "España e Hispanoamérica: Aliados olvidados de la revolución americana." In *Hispanos en los Estados Unidos*, ed. by Rodolfo J. Cortina and Alberto Moncada. Madrid: Ediciones de Cultura Hispánica, 1988.

Vehik, Susan C. "Oñate's Expedition to the Southern Plains: Routes, Destinations, and Implications for Late Prehistoric Cultural Adaptations." *Plains Anthropologist* 31 (Feb. 1986): 13–33.

Velázquez, María del Carmen. "Los indios gentiles apóstatas enemigos." In *Tres Estudios sobre las provincias internas de Nueva España*, ed. by María del Carmen Velázquez. Mexico City: El Colegio de México, 1979.

———. *Notas sobre sirvientes de las Californias y proyecto de obraje en Nuevo México*. Mexico City: El Colegio de México, 1985.

———. "Los reglamentos." In *Tres Estudios sobre las provincias internas de Nueva España*, ed. by María del Carmen Velázquez. Mexico City: El Colegio de México, 1979.

———. *Tres estudios sobre las provincias internas de Nueva España*. Mexico City: El Colegio de México, 1979.

Vigil, Ralph E. "Bartolomé de las Casas, Judge Alonso de Zorita, and the Franciscans: A Collaborative Effort for the Spiritual Conquest of the Borderlands." *The Americas* 38 (July 1981): 45–57.

———. "The New Borderlands History: A Critique." *NMHR* 58 (July 1973): 189–208.

Vigneras, L. A. "A Spanish Discovery of North Carolina in 1566." *North Carolina Historical Review* 46 (Oct. 1969): 398–414.

Vigness, David M. "Don Hugo Oconor and New Spain's Northeastern Frontier, 1764–1776." *JW* 6 (Jan. 1967): 27–40.

Vivian, Gordon. *Excavations in a 17th-Century Jumano Pueblo: Gran Quivira*. Archaeological Research Series, no. 8. Washington, D.C.: National Park Service, 1964.

Wagner, Henry R. *The Cartography of the Northwest Coast of America to the Year 1800*. 2 vols. Berkeley: University of California Press, 1937.

_____. "Fr. Marcos de Niza." *NMHR* 9 (Apr. 1934): 184–227.

_____. *Juan Rodríguez Cabrillo, Discoverer of the Coast of California*. San Francisco: California Historical Society, 1941.

_____. *The Spanish Southwest, 1542–1794: An Annotated Bibliography*. 2 vols. Albuquerque: Quivira Society, 1937.

_____. *Spanish Voyages to the Northwest Coast of America in the Sixteenth Century*. San Francisco: California Historical Society, 1929.

Wagstaff, R. M. "Coronado's Route to Quivira: The Greater Weight of the Credible Evidence." *West Texas Historical Association Year Book* 42 (Oct. 1966): 137–66.

Walker, Phillip L., Patricia Lambert, and Michael J. DeNiro. "The Effects of European Contact on the Health of Alta California Indians." In *CC*, vol. 1.

Ware, John D. "St. Augustine, 1784: Decadence and Repairs." *FHQ* 48 (Oct. 1969): 180–87.

Warner, Ted J. "Don Félix Martínez and the Santa Fe Presidio, 1693–1730." *NMHR* 45 (Oct. 1970): 269–310.

Warren, Harris Gaylord. *The Sword Was Their Passport: A History of Filibustering in the Mexican Revolution*. Baton Rouge: Louisiana State University Press, 1943.

Waterbury, Jean Parker, ed. *The Oldest City: St Augustine, Saga of Survival*. St. Augustine: St. Augustine Historical Society, 1983.

Watson, Thomas D. "Strivings for Sovereignty: Alexander McGillivray, Creek Warfare, and Diplomacy, 1783–1790." *FHQ* 58 (Apr. 1980): 400–14.

Webb, Walter Prescott. *The Great Plains*. Boston: Ginn and Co., 1931.

Weber, David J. "Blood of Martyrs, Blood of Indians: Toward a More Balanced View of Spanish Missions in Seventeenth-Century North America." In *CC*, vol. 2.

_____. "Coronado and the Myth of Quivira." *Southwest Review* 70 (Spring 1985): 230–41.

_____. "Here Rests Juan Espinosa: Toward a Clearer Look at the Image of the 'Indolent' Californios." *WHQ* 10 (Jan. 1979): 61–68.

_____. "John Francis Bannon and the Historiography of the Spanish Borderlands: Retrospect and Prospect." *Journal of the Southwest* 29 (Winter 1987): 331–63.

_____. *The Mexican Frontier, 1821–1846: The American Southwest under Mexico*. Albuquerque: University of New Mexico Press, 1982.

_____. *Myth and the History of the Hispanic Southwest: Essays by David J. Weber*. Albuquerque: University of New Mexico Press, 1988.

_____. " 'Scarce More Than Apes': Historical Roots of Anglo-American Stereotypes of Mexicans." In *NS*.

_____. *The Taos Trappers: The Fur Trade in the Far Southwest, 1540–1846*. Norman: University of Oklahoma Press, 1971.

_____. "Turner, the Boltonians, and the Borderlands." *AHR* 91 (Feb. 1986): 66–81.

_____, ed. *Foreigners in Their Native Land: Historical Roots of the Mexican Americans*. Albuquerque: University of New Mexico Press, 1973.

————, ed. *The Idea of the Spanish Borderlands*. New York: Garland Press, 1991.

————, ed. *New Spain's Far Northern Frontier: Essays on Spain in the American West*. Albuquerque: University of New Mexico Press, 1979.

Weckmann, Luis. *La herencia medieval de México*. 2 vols. Mexico City: El Colegio de México, 1984.

Weddle, Robert S. *San Juan Bautista: Gateway to Spanish Texas*. Austin: University of Texas Press, 1968.

————. *The San Sabá Mission: Spanish Pivot in Texas*. Austin: University of Texas Press, 1964.

————. *Spanish Sea: The Gulf of Mexico in North American Discovery, 1500–1685*. College Station: Texas A&M University Press, 1985.

————. "The Talon Interrogations: A Rare Perspective." In *La Salle, the Mississippi, and the Gulf: Three Primary Documents*, ed. by Robert S. Weddle, Mary Christine Morkovsky, and Patricia Galloway. College Station: Texas A&M University Press, 1987.

————. *Wilderness Manhunt: The Spanish Search for La Salle*. Austin: University of Texas Press, 1973.

Wenhold, Lucy L. "Manrique de Rojas' Report on French Settlement in Florida, 1564." *FHQ* 38 (July 1959): 45–62.

Weniger, Del. *The Explorers' Texas: The Lands and Waters*. Austin: Eakin Press, 1984.

————. "Wilderness, Farm, and Ranch." In *San Antonio in the Eighteenth Century*. San Antonio: San Antonio Bicentennial Heritage Committee, 1976.

West, Elizabeth Howard. "The Indian Policy of Bernardo de Gálvez." *Proceedings of the Mississippi Valley Historical Association* 8 (1914–15): 95–101.

West, G. James. "Early Historic Vegetation Change in Alta California: The Fossil Evidence." In *CC*, vol. 1.

Whitaker, Arthur Preston. *The Mississippi Question, 1795–1803: A Study in Trade, Politics, and Diplomacy*. New York: D. Appleton-Century, 1934.

————. "New Light on the Treaty of San Lorenzo: An Essay in Historical Criticism." *JAH* 15 (Mar. 1929): 435–52.

————. *The Spanish-American Frontier, 1783–1795: The Westward Movement and the Spanish Retreat in the Mississippi Valley*. 1927. Lincoln: University of Nebraska Press, 1969.

————. "The Spanish Contribution to American Agriculture." *Agricultural History* 3 (Jan. 1929): 1–14.

White, David Hart. "The Indian Policy of Juan Vicente Folch, Governor of Spanish Mobile, 1787–1792." *Alabama Review* 28 (1975): 261–75.

————. *Vicente Folch, Governor in Spanish Florida, 1787–1811*. Washington, D.C.: University Press of America, 1981.

White, Richard. *The Roots of Dependency: Subsistence, Environment, and Social Change among the Choctaws, Pawnees, and Navajos*. Lincoln: University of Nebraska Press, 1983.

Whitehead, Richard S. "Alta California's Four Fortresses." *SCQ* 65 (Spring 1983): 67–94.

Widmer, Randolph J. *The Evolution of the Calusa: A Nonagricultural Chiefdom on the Southwest Florida Coast*. Tuscaloosa: University of Alabama Press, 1988.

Wiget, Andrew O. "Truth and the Hopi." *Ethnohistory*, 29 (Summer 1982): 181–99.

Wilcox, David R. "Changing Perspectives on the Protohistorical Pueblos, A.D. 1450–1700." In *The Protohistoric Period in the North American Southwest: A.D. 1450–1700*, ed.

by David R. Wilcox and W. Bruce Masse. Tempe: Arizona State University Anthropological Research Papers, 1981.

Wilcox, David R., and W. Bruce Masse, eds. *The Protohistoric Period in the North American Southwest: A.D. 1450–1700.* Tempe: Arizona State University Anthropological Research Papers, 1981.

Wilkie, Everett C., Jr. "New Light on Gálvez's First Attempt to Attack Pensacola." *FHQ* 62 (Oct. 1983): 194–99.

Williams, J. W. "Moscoso's Trail through Texas." *SWHQ* 46 (Oct. 1942): 138–57.

———. "New Evidence on Moscoso's Approach to Texas." In *Old Texas Trails*, ed. by Kenneth F. Neighbors. Burnet, Tex.: Eakin Press, 1979.

Williams, Jack S. "Architecture and Defense on the Military Frontier of Arizona, 1752–1856." Ph.D. diss., University of Arizona, 1991.

———. "Bastion, Baluarte y Torreón: Fortification in Northern New Spain, 1540–1821." Unpublished manuscript, 1986.

———. "Fortress Tucson: Architecture and the Art of War at a Desert Outpost." *Smoke Signal*, nos. 49–50 (Spring and Fall 1988): 170–76.

———. "Pedro de Nava's Instructions for Governing the Apache Establishments of Peace, 1791." Unpublished manuscript, 1975.

———. "The Presidio of Santa Cruz de Terrenate: A Forgotten Fortress of Southern Arizona." *Smoke Signal*, nos. 47–48 (Spring and Fall 1986): 129–48.

———. "San Agustín del Tucson: A Vanished Mission Community of the Pimería Alta." *Smoke Signal*, nos. 47–48 (Spring and Fall 1986): 113–21.

Williams, Jack S., and Robert L. Hoover. *Arms of the Apachería: A Comparison of Apachean and Spanish Fighting Techniques in the Later Eighteenth Century.* Greeley, Colo.: Museum of Anthropology, University of Northern Colorado, 1983.

Williams, Stanley T. *The Spanish Background of American Literature.* 2 vols. New Haven: Yale University Press, 1955.

Wilson, John P. "Before the Pueblo Revolt: Population Trends, Apache Relations and Pueblo Abandonments in Seventeenth Century New Mexico." In *Prehistory and History in the Southwest*, ed. by Nancy Fox. Santa Fe: Ancient City Press for the Archaeological Society of New Mexico, 1985.

———. "The Southern Apaches as Farmers." In *Reflections: Papers on Southwestern Culture History in Honor of Charles H. Lange*, ed. by Anne V. Poore. Santa Fe: Ancient City Press, 1988.

Wilson, Maurine T., and Jack Jackson. *Philip Nolan and Texas: Expeditions to the Unknown Land, 1791–1801.* Waco, Tex.: Texian Press, 1987.

Wilson, Samuel, Jr. "Architecture in Eighteenth-Century West Florida." In *Eighteenth-Century Florida and Its Borderlands*, ed. by Samuel Proctor. Gainesville: University Presses of Florida, 1975.

Winther, Oscar O. *The Story of San José: California's First Pueblo, 1777–1869.* San Francisco: California Historical Society, 1935.

Woldert, Albert. "Expedition of Luis de Moscoso in Texas in 1542." *SWHQ* 46 (Oct. 1942): 158–66.

Wolf, Eric R. *Europe and the People without History.* Berkeley: University of California Press, 1982.

Wolff, Thomas. "The Karankawa Indians: Their Conflict with the White Man in Texas." *Ethnohistory* 16 (Winter 1969): 1–32.

Wood, Peter H. "The Changing Population of the Colonial South: An Overview by Race and Region, 1685–1790." In *PM*.

————. "La Salle: Discovery of a Lost Explorer." *AHR* 89 (Apr. 1984): 294–323.

Wood, Peter H., Gregory A. Waselkov, and M. Thomas Hatley, eds. *Powhatan's Mantle: Indians in the Colonial Southeast.* Lincoln: University of Nebraska Press, 1989.

Wood, Raymund F. "Juan Crespi: The Man Who Named Los Angeles." *SCQ* 53 (Sept. 1971): 191–234.

Woodbury, Richard B. "Zuni Prehistory and History to 1850." In *HNAI*, vol. 9.

Worcester, Donald E. *The Apaches: Eagles of the Southwest.* Norman: University of Oklahoma Press, 1979.

————. "The Significance of the Spanish Borderlands to the United States." *WHQ* 7 (Jan. 1976): 279–93.

————. *The Spanish Mustang: From the Plains of Andalusia to the Prairies of Texas.* El Paso: Texas Western Press, 1986.

————. *The Texas Longhorn: Relic of the Past, Asset for the Future.* College Station: Texas A&M University Press, 1987.

Wright, Irene A. "Spanish Policy toward Virginia, 1606–1612." *AHR* 25 (Apr. 1920): 448–79.

Wright, J. Leitch, Jr.. *Anglo-Spanish Rivalry in North America.* Athens: University of Georgia Press, 1971.

————. "British East Florida: Loyalist Bastion." In *Eighteenth-Century Florida: The Impact of the American Revolution*, ed. by Samuel Proctor. Gainesville: University Presses of Florida, 1978.

————. *Creeks and Seminoles: The Destruction and Regeneration of the Muscolgulge People.* Lincoln: University of Nebraska Press, 1986.

————. *Florida in the American Revolution.* Gainesville: University Presses of Florida, 1975.

————. *The Only Land They Knew: The Tragic Story of the American Indians in the Old South.* New York: Free Press, 1981.

Wroth, William. "The Flowering and Decline of the New Mexican Santero: 1780–1900." 1976. In *NS*.

Yates, Richard. "Locating the Colorado River Mission San Pedro y San Pablo de Bicuñer." *JAZH* 13 (Summer 1972): 123–130.

Yela Utrilla, Juan F. *España ante la independencia de los Estados Unidos.* 2 vols. Lérida: Gráficos Academia Mariana, 1925.

Yoakum, Henderson. *History of Texas . . . .* 2 vols. New York: Redfield, 1855.

Young, Otis E. "The Spanish Tradition in Gold and Silver Mining." *AW* 7 (Winter 1965): 299–314.

Zelinsky, Wilbur. *Cultural Geography of the United States.* Englewood Cliffs, N.J.: Prentice-Hall, 1973.

Zubillaga, Félix. *La Florida: La Misión Jesuítica (1566–1572) y la colonización española.* Rome: Instituto Historicum S. I., 1941.

Index